DS
890
.T57
B8
1969

Butow, Robert Joseph
Charles, 1924-.

Tojo and the coming
of the war

DATE			
OCT 9 '84			

Tojo

AND THE COMING OF THE WAR

Tojo

And the Coming of the War

ROBERT J. C. BUTOW

STANFORD UNIVERSITY PRESS
STANFORD, CALIFORNIA

"It is my earnest hope that pondering upon the past may give guidance in days to come, enable a new generation to repair some of the errors of former years and thus govern, in accordance with the needs and glory of man, the awful unfolding scene of the future."
—WINSTON CHURCHILL in *The Gathering Storm*.

Stanford University Press
Stanford, California
© 1961 by Robert J. C. Butow
Printed in the United States of America
First published in 1961
by Princeton University Press
Reissued in 1969 by Stanford University Press
L.C. 73-93492

Foreword

By a skillful blending of history and biography, of political events and diplomatic issues, this book provides an absorbing account of events in Japanese public affairs leading up to and beyond the war in the Pacific. The career of Hideki Tojo, premier of Japan at the time of Pearl Harbor, provides an excellent background against which to reveal the relentless advance by the military toward full control of Japan and the hardening of the attitudes and fears of the people which made war with the Western nations possible. The capacity for national self-deception that was displayed in this period regarding the motives and aims of other peoples gives a disturbing insight into the paths that can lead to war.

Tojo's career paralleled the growing encroachment of Japan upon Chinese territory and the development of the ambitious conception of the "Greater East Asia Co-prosperity Sphere." Tojo's share of responsibility for what occurred is portrayed here, as well as the dramatic events of his attempted suicide and his trial before the war crimes tribunal. The final part of the book is in the nature of an epilogue—a footnote to those brief but fateful years of power during which Japan dominated the world of Eastern Asia.

This book is part of a continuing program of research into the processes of foreign policy making carried on under the auspices of the Center of International Studies. The Center was established at Princeton University in 1951; its basic purpose is to bring to bear on the elucidation of foreign policy problems the full resources of knowledge and modern methods of analysis. The members of the Center work at all times in close association, but each member is free to formulate his research projects in his own way and each published study represents an individual analysis of a problem.

Frederick S. Dunn
Director

Center of International Studies
Princeton University

A Note to the Reader

WITHIN a few months after the Japanese surrender in 1945 the International Prosecution Section, representing the countries that had been at war with Japan, began preparing for the Far Eastern equivalent of the Nuremberg trial. The Prosecution believed that Japan was an aggressor nation whose civil and military leaders should be brought to the bar of justice to answer for their crimes. Of the defendants subsequently named in the indictment, the most important was General Hideki Tojo, who had stood at the head of the Japanese government on December 7, 1941.

This book deals with the coming of the war between Japan and the United States, with Tojo's responsibility in that regard, and with the consequences—for the man and the nation—of Japan's decision to break the peace of the Pacific. The unifying theme throughout the book is the role of the Japanese army in affairs of state as seen through the career of General Tojo.

I have written about these matters in a single volume because they are interrelated—any one of them without the others would be less meaningful and less interesting—and because a proper appreciation of Tojo and Japan's resort to war requires the broadest possible frame of reference. Part I of the book therefore endeavors to set the stage. Tojo's early years are covered briefly, but beyond that the purpose is more historical than biographical. Although events take precedence over the man in Part I, they are essential to an understanding of the milieu in which Tojo lived and from which he later drew his judgments. In Part II the man gradually emerges into full view as developments at home and abroad move toward an ominous climax. The aspect of Tojo revealed in the heart of the book may occasion some surprise in the light of what has generally been regarded as his role. Part III summarizes the aftermath of the choice made by Tojo and his colleagues in 1941. This third and last section of the book completes the story of the man and his times by bridging the years between Japan's decision for war and the final calling to account, by the victorious powers, of a leader and a nation in defeat.

ROBERT J. C. BUTOW

July 26, 1960

Contents

Illustrations

CARTOONS

PHOTOGRAPHS

Following page 264

I · IN THE SHADOW OF THE SAMURAI

Hana wa sakuragi; hito wa bushi.

The cherry is first among blossoms;
the warrior is first among men.

CHAPTER 1

Tojo's Early Years

In the panorama of Japanese history the year 1868 stands as an enduring landmark. A virtually bloodless imperial "restoration," long in the making and only casually connected with the earlier coming of Commodore Perry, brought the power of the Tokugawa shogun to an end. The more than two-century-old policy of seclusion by which Japan had been insulated from the outside world had already been forsaken. A once-mysterious and forbidding land was thus on the threshold of extraordinary changes.

Some innovations were longer in evolving and in commanding general acceptance than were others, but nothing remained static for long. The government's policy was to adopt the new whenever it was clearly evident that the new was superior to the old, or that the security of the state demanded adherence at least to the form, if not to the essence, of Western practice. The principal sacrificial victim of this approach was the samurai class—the members of the warrior elite who had lived largely as parasites throughout the Tokugawa period, supported in idleness by the toil of the common people. The peasants were to remain the backbone of the state but with greater freedom and opportunity than ever before. The merchants, previously regarded with contempt, were to come at last into their own, their experience in industrial and mercantile procedures giving them a place of growing importance and influence. What a man could do, rather than his station in life, was to count in the future.

The government wasted comparatively little time in bringing this home to the warrior class. In 1871 an imperial proclamation formally abolished the clans—a blow that struck at the roots of the old feudal order. In 1873 a military conscription system open to all classes was inaugurated, thus destroying the professional monopoly that had given the samurai their distinctive position. Three years later, in 1876, the government felt strong enough to force the compulsory commutation of all feudal incomes. The hardest hit by these measures were not the great lords but the lesser samurai. Indeed, by 1876—only eight years after the restoration—the choice was already clear: either the samurai could adapt to the new in the hope of finding an honored place in it, or they could resist the trend of the times and thus risk the danger of sinking into obscurity—into the trough of the masses. Such was the challenge faced by Hideki Tojo's father.

Hidenori Tojo traced his descent to one Hidemasa, the youngest son of the fifth generation of the Hosho line, a family which had devoted its talents to the *Nō* form of drama. Hidemasa had adopted the surname Tojo and in the year 1832 had established a connection with Nanbu, the lord of Morioka, who employed him as a master of *Nō* and awarded him an annual rice stipend of roughly 800 bushels. Lacking a male heir, Hidemasa had brought into his house the son of another of Nanbu's vassals and had married him to his daughter to ensure a continuation of the Tojo line.[1] It was Hidemasa's grandson, Hidenori, who felt the full brunt of Meiji Restoration changes. Even the comparatively humble relationship which his family had held toward the lord of Morioka disappeared with the abolition of the feudal structure, and with it, for all practical purposes, the meager income on which the family had depended. In 1871, the year in which the clans were abolished, the 16-year-old Hidenori set out for Tokyo, traveling by foot so as to conserve the scant means on which he hoped to live in the capital until he could establish himself.[2] Thanks to the training he had received in Morioka, Hidenori gained admittance to a military school designed to produce noncommissioned officers for the new imperial army.[3] After completing the prescribed course of study, Hidenori was sent as a sergeant to the 14th Infantry Regiment stationed in Kyushu. There, in the year 1877 he participated in the suppression of the Satsuma rebellion, the last major challenge to the government.

The rebellion created such a need for fighting-men that the central authorities called for volunteers. Most of those who responded were members of the warrior class. It was assumed that their samurai background would make them far better soldiers than the new conscripts, who lacked any personal military tradition. To everyone's surprise, the event proved the assumption false. The volunteers, samurai though they were, exhibited less bravery and resolution than the conscripts, most

[1] Strictly speaking, the Hōshō line. In becoming a vassal of Nanbu, Hidemasa had been required to change his name back to Hōshō. Tōjō became the family name again under Hidetoshi, Hidemasa's adopted son.

The details on the Hōshō-Tōjō family are from interviews with Mrs. Hideki (Katsuko) Tōjō and from a genealogical record in her possession. Also, Shunichirō Itō, *Shisei, Tetsu no Hito: Tōjō Hideki Den*, 9, and *Who's Who in Japan* (1913).

[2] All ages are given in the Western manner. Thus Hidenori was 16 by Western count, but 17 by Japanese reckoning.

[3] The so-called *rikugun kyōdōdan*.

of whom had by that time undergone several years of regular training and discipline.

The discovery that the former "nameless ones" could out-fight the samurai of old "opened up great hopes for conscription, and imparted self-confidence to the nation at large."[4] It also gave greater opportunity to young men like Hidenori Tojo who could prove themselves worthy not only of their heritage but of occupying positions of leadership in the new military forces. In 1878, at the age of twenty-three, Hidenori was returned to Tokyo and promoted to sub-lieutenant of infantry. Several years later, he was enrolled as a member of the first class of the newly established war college. So much importance was placed on individual performance that young officers of ability and promise obtained rapid promotion and top appointments, to the great encouragement of their group as a whole.[5]

Opportunity beckoned to Hidenori Tojo and he was quick to respond. At the war college he studied under Jacob Meckel, a Prussian major who performed great services for the Japan of his time. Meckel gave instruction in the art of war and the nature of military organization; his methods and approach immediately kindled an eager response. He emphasized the practical application of the principles of warfare and employed map exercises, terrain studies, and field problems in a way that was novel to his Japanese students and colleagues.

Meckel's influence was not limited solely to the war college. Outside the classroom his thinking reached to the army high command. Some said his views even received attention in the cabinet and at the court, despite the suspicion that the Kaiser had secret designs in sending him to Japan. In the end, Meckel proved instrumental in furthering the reorganization of army command and administration that had been put into effect some years before. Meckel believed military progress required a triangular structure, with the general staff (which employs troops), the war ministry (which is the administrative organ), and the inspectorate general of military training (which is concerned with education) standing in equal relationship to each other and working, hand in hand, to carry out their assigned functions under the direct command of the Emperor. This structure, which had its beginnings in 1878, was to last, in theory at least, until 1945.

[4] Yamagata, "The Japanese Army," in Ōkuma (comp.), *Fifty Years of New Japan,* I, 204-5. The rebellion also disclosed a number of defects in the new imperial army—a lesson which Yamagata and other leaders took very much to heart and from which the army profited greatly.

[5] *Ibid.,* I, 207-8.

Whatever its advantages may have been from a military point of view, the system inaugurated under the Emperor Meiji proved to be a curse under his grandson, for it not only interfered with the proper functioning of civil government but also lent itself to the creation, within the Japanese army, of a division of responsibility and an independence of decision which eventually helped to destroy the very army it was supposed to serve. At the time in question, however, and during perhaps the next twenty or thirty years, the system worked extraordinarily well in both a military and a political sense.

Meckel's activity as a teacher produced equally good results. Hidenori Tojo and others who studied under him during his short stay in Japan felt themselves in his debt for the rest of their lives. Hidenori, who had stood at the head of his class during his three years at the war college, and who had won Meckel's special admiration for his outstanding ability and promise as a tactician, rose rapidly in his profession. After three years in Germany as a student, he returned to Japan in 1891, was promoted to major, and assigned to the general staff. He subsequently served in both the Sino-Japanese and the Russo-Japanese war, as a lieutenant colonel in the former and as a major general in the latter. He also wrote a book on the art of war which was highly acclaimed as a work of distinction. Upon entering the reserve in 1908, at the age of 53, he was promoted to the rank of lieutenant general.[6]

Such, in brief, was the career of Hideki Tojo's father. His youth had been spent in a period of transition in which nothing remained unchanged for long, once defects were found or improvements discovered. He was a self-made man, taking advantage of native intelligence and ability to rise from the ranks, step by step, to become at last a general officer.

Along the way, in the year 1878, he had married Chitose Tokunaga, the daughter of the Buddhist priest of the Mantoku-ji at Kokura in Kyushu. Hideki, who was one of ten children (seven boys and three girls), was born in Tokyo on December 30, 1884.[7]

---

[6] On the role of Meckel and the career of Hidenori Tōjō, see *ibid.*, I, 199-210; Shunichirō Itō, 9-18; *Kaikōsha Kiji*, No. 754, 130 and 158-50, No. 759, 12, 24, and 136, No. 783, 146; Mrs. Tōjō, Matsudaira, and Yano intv.; Tōjō interrog., Jan. 14, 1-2; Tanaka, "I Know Everything About Them," 3; Kenryō Satō corresp.; Maxon, *Control of Japanese Foreign Policy*, 19 and 22-24; *Japan Year Book (1943-44)*, 241-42; and *Who's Who in Japan (1913)*. Dr. Ernst L. Presseisen of Stanford, who is preparing a biography of Meckel, was also very helpful.

The title of the elder Tōjō's book was *Senjutsu, Fumoto no Chiri*.

[7] The following account of Hideki Tōjō's boyhood and schooling through the military academy is based on Shunichirō Itō, 9, 11, 19-21, 23-28, 30-35; intv. with Mrs. Tōjō and a genealogical record in her possession (which incorrectly gives July 30 instead of

Many stories have been told about the young Tojo—an inevitable by-product of his later rise to fame—but for the most part they are an uncertain blend of fact and fiction. His childhood and adolescent years were by no means unusual. His father maintained a simple home as befitted a military man of the old samurai class. His mother is remembered as a steady, precise person who secretly took in sewing to keep the family's finances reasonably stable. As the eldest son,[8] Hideki received considerable parental attention as well as the deference due his superior position from his brothers and sisters.

The chief characteristics of his boyhood were a reasonably average distaste for studies and a perhaps more than average tendency to be quarrelsome. He was spirited, competitive, and self-confident, and was not one to give in easily. His schoolmates dubbed him "fighting Tojo"—because if anyone picked a quarrel he would take up the challenge, regardless of the odds, and carry through as best he could on his own resources. He was quick and decisive and was impatient with those who were not—qualities which later produced the nickname *kamisori*, "the razor."

The purpose of Hideki's early education was to prepare him to strike out upon the prescribed path leading to a commission as a second lieutenant. In September 1899, at the age of fifteen, he was enrolled in the Tokyo area military preparatory school. There were six such establishments in Japan at that time—one for each of the so-called six garrisons—with a combined enrollment of about 300 students.[9] The three-year program corresponded roughly to the first or second year of the average middle school, but the education received and the training methods employed were predominantly military. In the beginning, Hideki's academic record was by no means outstanding, but from the second year onward he paid close attention to his studies. Thereafter, throughout his life, he proved to be a hard worker—a trait which his admirers noted with approbation and which his detractors cited as proof of his need to compensate through greater effort for his lack of real ability.

The year following the young Tojo's entry into the Tokyo preparatory school saw the rise and spread of the Boxers in China and their

---

December 30 as Tōjō's date of birth), and also a roster entitled "Meiji Sanjūhachinen Sangatsu Shikan Gakkō Dai-jūshichi-ki Seitō Sotsugyō Jinmei"; Tōjō interrog., Jan. 14, 1-2 and Mar. 27, 2-3; Tōjō aff., S 342:12, T 36171-72; Yano, Umezu, and Stunkard intv.; Bainbridge, "Razor on Horseback," *New Yorker*, Vol. XIX, No. 9 (April 17, 1943), 26; Brines, *Until They Eat Stones*, 310; and Tolischus, *Tokyo Record*, 278.

[8] Hideki's two older brothers had both died as infants.

[9] Tōkyō, Sendai, Nagoya, Ōsaka, Hiroshima, and Kumamoto, each boasting a *chihō yōnen gakkō*.

investment of the legation quarter in Peking. As a result, the program at the school was placed on a wartime footing. The arm of service was decided—Tojo entered the favored infantry. Excitement mounted as target practice with live ammunition and full-scale military exercises were begun. In the spring, the students from the six garrison schools were assembled and trained together—the high point being a "great march" which was far more strenuous than was usual at these annual joint exercises. This was designed, in the seemingly universal phrase, to separate the men from the boys.

In September 1902 Tojo passed on to the central military preparatory school[10] for an additional year and a half of the most rigorous type of conditioning. The normal procedure was to assign those who successfully completed this phase of their military education to six months of duty with the troops, to be followed by enrollment for one year in the military academy. Upon graduation, the cadets would spend six months as probationary officers before finally receiving their commissions as second lieutenants. But in February 1904 war came to the Russians, as it was to come to the Americans many years later, "with dangerous and dramatic suddenness." This led immediately to a streamlining of the program by which Japanese youths were readied for the battlefield.

The six months with the troops and the half-year probationary period were both eliminated. At the military academy the training imparted to Tojo and his classmates assumed an urgency that was heightened by Japan's successive but costly victories. The usual summer vacation was eliminated and even half of every Sunday, normally a rest day, was now devoted to further training for war. The mood of the students was intense. They eagerly awaited the arrival of news from the front and devoured it enthusiastically. The great Russian Bear was being hounded at every turn, and the world's surprise merely added to their own welling consciousness of achievement—a development that at times led to a considerable and not always justifiable conceit. The main concern of the students was that the war might end before they had a chance to participate in it. They therefore threw themselves into their studies with the utmost devotion, even going so far as to spend their half-holiday on Sunday discussing military subjects and singing patriotic songs.

As a result of the changes brought about by the war, Tojo became a second lieutenant of infantry at the age of twenty-one, in less than half the time normally required. As a member of the seventeenth class of

[10] *Rikugun chūō yōnen gakkō*, subsequently renamed *rikugun yoka shikan gakkō*.

the military academy, he was graduated in the early spring of 1905, ranking tenth in a group of 363. The overwhelming majority of his classmates belonged, as he did, to the proud infantry. Cavalry, artillery, the engineer corps, and the army service corps each accounted for less than 10 per cent of the total. The last-named branch was generally avoided, for those engaged in transport and related activities were not regarded as soldiers at all.

Most of the members of the seventeenth class received assignments in Japan, far from the scene of action. They bemoaned their fate and envied the comparatively few "lucky devils" like Tojo who were ordered to pack their gear and ready themselves for departure for the front. By the time Tojo and his companions reached the mainland, however, the war was rapidly drawing to a close. Instead of winning glory on the battlefield as "human bullets," they spent their days and nights to no purpose, fretting over their enforced idleness and unwanted security as members of the garrison forces stationed ingloriously behind the lines.[11]

The extraordinary success of Japan's army and navy in the Russo-Japanese war produced a great impact upon the Japanese nation as a whole and upon its role in the world. It was a far more significant triumph than Japan's victory over China a decade earlier—a victory which had been marred by the intervention of Russia, Germany, and France to force a return to China of part of the spoils of war. Among Japan's military men the reaction to the interference of the powers in 1895 had been especially intense. The belief had quickly taken hold that Japanese foreign policy was obsessed by a fear of Europe and America and that Japan's trouble lay in an abject worship of Western countries. One can therefore easily imagine the eagerness with which these same men greeted Japan's resort to war against Tsarist Russia in 1904—a war, it was said, that would decide the fate of the Empire. In describing the situation to the throne, the Japanese premier reportedly declared, "Things have come to such a pass that our Empire cannot avoid fighting for the sake of the peace of the Orient."[12] Interestingly enough, Hideki Tojo and his colleagues were to use largely the same argument in their reports to the throne prior to the decision for war in 1941.

[11] Shunichirō Itō, 40-45, and Mrs. Tōjō intv. Also, "Meiji Sanjūhachinen Sangatsu Shikan Gakkō Dai-jūshichi-ki Seitō Sotsugyō Jinmei" and Sakurai, *Human Bullets*, 214 and *passim*.
[12] As quoted in Maxon, 234 (n. 112). See also Shunichirō Itō, 34-37, and IPS Doc. 59-B20-3 (papers obtained from the Karuizawa residence of Prince Konoe following his death in Tōkyō).

Just as the Russo-Japanese conflict marks the beginning of Tojo's career as an officer, so, too, does it stand as the great divide in Japanese-American relations. Despite Commodore Perry's "conciliatory but firm" intention to use force if reason did not prevail, all had gone comparatively smoothly once contact had been established and a treaty signed. Americans from the first consul-general onward had played an important part in rendering assistance to Japan not only on the international scene but within the nation itself—helping to impart expert knowledge in education, medicine, science, and other fields.

Although there had been incidents involving American nationals and complaints about Japanese, the years before 1905 had passed without serious conflict. So close did the Japanese government feel to the United States that when the Russo-Japanese war threatened to outlast Japan's resources, the government readily followed the lead of the American minister in Tokyo in securing the good offices of Theodore Roosevelt.[13] The result was the Treaty of Portsmouth. In the United States and the world at large, Roosevelt was acclaimed for his role in restoring peace. But in Japan, where the great victories on land and sea had bred a kind of hysteria of expectation, the terms of the Portsmouth treaty produced a reaction equally intense. The masses knew nothing of the facts. They did not appreciate that Japan, in spite of its seeming military prowess, was in no position to continue the war indefinitely. No one told them that Japan's funds were depleted or that further credit could not be obtained abroad. Nor did the people of Japan appreciate that since their military forces had exhausted the nation's resources in war without securing the enemy's capitulation, the diplomats would now have to save the day as best they could. Not knowing this, the masses regarded the Portsmouth treaty, which provided not a kopeck of indemnity, as thoroughly unsatisfactory. Japanese public opinion placed the blame on Theodore Roosevelt, and the Japanese government—relieved at being provided with a scapegoat—did nothing to set the record straight or apprise the people of the truth. Anti-American riots raged throughout Japan and in Tokyo surged so violently that martial law was proclaimed.[14]

In spite of the popular uproar, Japan walked away from Portsmouth very much the victor—a position on which it had already capitalized earlier in negotiations with Great Britain and the United States.[15] Per-

[13] See Eugene H. Dooman's letter to the editor, *NYT*, March 31, 1958, 26.
[14] See Dulles, *The Imperial Years*, 276-84, and Ike, *Japanese Politics*, 254.
[15] The reference is to the renewal and revision of the Anglo-Japanese Alliance and to the Taft-Katsura Agreement.

haps the alleged "shame" of Portsmouth might not have lingered unduly in Japanese memories had it not been for another event which served to rekindle and intensify public feeling.

For some years American agitation against Chinese immigration had been growing—resulting finally in 1904 in a law which forbade the entry of Chinese laborers into the United States. The Congress wished to extend this discriminatory legislation to the Japanese, but Roosevelt successfully prevented such action. Suddenly, in October 1906, little more than a year after the Portsmouth treaty, the San Francisco School Board took matters into its own hands by ordering all Japanese children to attend the Oriental school in Chinatown. The Japanese government described this order as "an act of discrimination carrying with it a stigma and odium which it is impossible to overlook."[16] The issue was finally settled by Presidential threats to the Board, and through diplomatic negotiations with Japan, but events of later years were to demonstrate that action of the type taken in San Francisco served as a tool ready to the hands of those in Japan who wished to undermine friendly · relations between the two countries.

Although smoldering resentment over the Portsmouth treaty and the flaring anger caused by the San Francisco affair may have been more in the nature of symptoms than causes, the fact is that Japanese-American relations deteriorated so rapidly and completely that there was even talk of war. The press in both countries added jingoistic comment and the Rough Rider in the White House—always alert, if not necessarily spoiling, for a fight—sent secret orders to the commanding general of the Philippines to ready his forces for a possible Japanese attack.[17] Although the emotional pendulum swung to its other extreme with the arrival in Japan of the great "white fleet," this demonstration of American naval might and the warm reception given the American sailors by the Japanese people were but matters of the moment. At any time the pendulum could swing again in the opposite direction.

The Russo-Japanese conflict had been a short war—especially for those officers who had hoped to gain earlier advancement through combat than would be possible under normal conditions. It was therefore with mixed feelings that many of the professionals greeted the end of hostilities. The early years of a career were not easy ones for men in

---

[16] See Bailey, *Theodore Roosevelt and the Japanese-American Crises*, 63-64, and Dennett, *Roosevelt and the Russo-Japanese War*, Ch. 11 and *passim*.

[17] The instructions went out on July 6, 1907. See Bailey, 230-31, and Dulles, 278-84.

the service, particularly in peacetime. In the army there was a saying, *bimbō shōi, yarikuri chūi, yattoko taii*: "penniless second lieutenant, somehow-managing first lieutenant, just-getting-by captain."[18] That was the prospect faced by Hideki Tojo at the war's end and was, in fact, the course of his life for the next decade and a half.

Upon his return from overseas in 1906, Tojo was awarded a minor decoration and given a small sum of money in recognition of his war service. In December 1907, he was promoted to first lieutenant, a rank in which he was to serve for more than seven years—not an ideal position for an army man beginning to raise a family.

Like his father before him, Hideki had decided to marry a girl from the island of Kyushu, Katsu Ito by name. One of a family of eight children, Katsu was the daughter of a landlord, a man of respectable though modest station, who served first as his village headman and later as a prefectural assemblyman for his district. Although personally of a studious bent, he had been unable, as the only son and heir, to follow a scholarly career. This had inclined him toward pampering his daughter at a time when educating a girl beyond the minimum was unusual. After four years in the village school, Katsu went on to six years of advanced education and then asked for more. Although it took some urging, her father agreed to send her to the Japan Women's College in Tokyo for an additional four years of the best training then available. Upon arrival in the capital, she got in touch with the family of General Hidenori Tojo, with whom the Itos enjoyed a distant relationship. Because of the family connection and the fact that the Tojos were serving as her sponsor, she became a fairly frequent visitor at their home. Hidenori and his wife were so impressed with her accomplishments that they set out to find her a good husband. They were actually so engaged, when Hideki, discovering her charms, decided that if she were that excellent a young lady he would like her for himself. The usual go-between procedures were initiated, and in April 1909, when Hideki was twenty-five and Katsu nineteen, the two were married. At least one relative felt that they made an excellent pair—if only by contrast. Hideki tended to be churlish and unyielding; Katsu was cheerful and bright. She was also adaptable and energetic—qualities which were immediately put to the test.

The young Tojos moved in with Hideki's parents, and Katsu, following the traditional but frequently abused custom, took over the manage-

[18] Quoted in Kennedy, *The Military Side of Japanese Life*, 166. I have altered the translation slightly.

ment of the thirteen-member household under the watchful eye of her mother-in-law. At first Katsu hoped to return to college to complete her major in Japanese literature, but time for study, to say nothing of attending school, was hopelessly lost to the constant demands of her new responsibilities. The burden became even greater soon after her marriage, when her father-in-law was forced by illness to move himself and his wife to a town south of Tokyo which had a pleasanter climate and quieter surroundings. Katsu thus fell heir to the task of feeding and clothing Hideki's brothers and sisters and of looking after their general welfare. In the spring of 1911 Katsu gave birth to a son—the first of seven children which she and her husband were to bring into the world, three boys and four girls, the last of whom was born in 1932, when Tojo was a forty-eight-year-old colonel. Thus Mrs. Tojo never did get back to college, but the fact that she had had so much schooling set her apart throughout her life. Even years later, as the premier's wife, she was still something of a curiosity—a circumstance which may explain stories to the effect that she was the driving force behind her husband's career.

As a young officer with growing responsibilities Hideki Tojo devoted a great deal of his free time to his own advanced studies. He was a man of nervous temperament. He liked to keep busy; work was pleasure. He believed in a direct and powerful relationship between effort and achievement. "If only you apply yourself, you will be able to accomplish whatever you set out to do." This was a view ingrained in the military men of his generation and which they, in turn, imparted to those who followed in their footsteps. It seems to have inspired a sublime confidence and optimism in the future and a firm belief that literally nothing was impossible.[19]

At the end of 1912, the year in which the Emperor Meiji died after forty-five years on the throne, Hideki Tojo was admitted to the army war college. Completion of its three-year command-and-general-staff course normally placed a man in a favored position with respect to subsequent assignments and promotions. Entrance requirements were stiff and only those who were particularly well-qualified and showed exceptional promise could make the grade. Together with other select students, including Masaharu Honma of later "Bataan death march"

[19] The text is based on interviews with Mrs. Tōjō; Shunichirō Itō, 46-49, 253-55; Tōjō interrog., Jan. 14, 2; and the cabinet secretariat personnel file for Hideki Tōjō, CF 20, II, 77. Mrs. Tōjō's father's name was Mantarō Itō; her mother's maiden name was Tō (changed after marriage to Terue) Tomokiyo. In writing her given name, Mrs. Tōjō normally used *kana*. Her husband, however, preferred to use the Chinese character, *katsu*, which means "to gain a victory." The ending "ko" was sometimes added to form "Katsuko."

fame, Tojo worked hard to prove his worth. Within a year after his entry into the war college, he saw the passing of his father, whose death was attributed to a heart condition brought on by beriberi contracted during the Russo-Japanese war. Thus, at twenty-nine, Hideki Tojo became the head of the family.

The outbreak of hostilities in Europe less than a year later resulted in a Japanese declaration of war against Germany. By November 1914 Japanese forces had taken the Chinese port of Tsingtao from the Germans and had begun absorbing Shantung. Thereafter, except for patrols at sea, Japan took little part in the war, which was regarded as a European concern. This comparatively disinterested attitude was a far cry from the intensely personal identification with hostilities exhibited a decade earlier. If the European conflict meant anything to Japan, it signified an opportunity to concentrate on Eastern Asia at a time when her leading competitors among the belligerents were engaged in a life-and-death struggle on the Western front. Early in 1915 the Japanese government secretly phrased its recognition of this opportunity in the form of the "twenty-one demands." These were designed to give Tokyo such extraordinary influence over Chinese political and economic affairs that China would probably have been reduced in time to the status of a Japanese province, had Peking accepted the demands in their entirety.

In the spring of 1915 Hideki Tojo was graduated "with honors" as a member of the twenty-seventh class of the war college and promoted to captain. Up to that rank, advancement was possible whether a man had ability or not, but from captain onward preferment was tied more and more to merit, and the competition became severe. Those who had completed the war college course had an enormous advantage over those who had not; the latter, who constituted the majority, generally encountered a narrowing of opportunity which meant early retirement at low rank. But even among the elite—the possessors of the staff officer's badge—many would share the same fate. They could not all become generals; hence, their intense competition.[20]

[20] The text, covering the period 1912-1915, is based on Shunichirō Itō, 18 and 55; Mrs. Tōjō and Yano intv.; Tōjō interrog., Mar. 27, 1; and Kennedy, *The Military Side of Japanese Life*, 166. Although the reference is to a later period, Lory, *Japan's Military Masters*, 103-5, is also applicable.

The most reliable chronological record of Tōjō's career is the cabinet secretariat personnel file cited previously. Other chronologies used here as well as hereinafter (without further reference) include: Shunichirō Itō, 253-57; Tōjō interrog., Jan. 14, 1-4; *Who's Who in Japan* (18th Annual Edition, 1937); *Who's Who in Nippon* (1943-1944); U.S. Office of War Information, "Japanese Personalities in Japanese Propaganda," 1-3; and *Current Biography* (1941).

After the usual assignments and reassignments, including a year as a company commander, another year at the main ordnance depot, duty at the war ministry, and even a short trip to Siberia, Captain Tojo received orders to proceed to Europe—another indication of his superior performance.

Each war college class usually consisted of about fifty men. Following graduation, ten or twelve of the more outstanding would be sent abroad for three years of study and residence. The languages taught at the college level included German, French, Russian, Chinese, and English. Because of the strong Prussian influence upon the Japanese army, the officers who went to Germany were generally the more brilliant, with those going to France running a close second. Only a few students of English were ever sent to the United States. Most were ordered to Britain, where the cost of living was lower and life was more congenial. Even so, the total combined number posted in the two countries remained very small—a fact to which one general later tied Japan's lack of knowledge of the Western democracies.

Generally, the men sent abroad were not given specific military assignments. They were told to develop their proficiency in the language in which they had already specialized for some years, to absorb as much as possible of the history and culture of the country in question, to do their best to understand the conditions of their respective areas, and in some instances—particularly in China and Russia after 1936—to gather whatever information they could legitimately acquire that might serve an operational or intelligence purpose.[21]

In Hideki Tojo's case, the intrusion of World War I and other duties delayed his departure until the autumn of 1919. Leaving his family in Japan, he proceeded first to Switzerland, where he was assigned to the office of the Japanese military attaché in Berne. Also in the Swiss capital at that time, as third secretary of the Japanese legation, was Shigenori Togo—the man who would one day become foreign minister in the Tojo Cabinet.

What Tojo thought of his European duty is lost to history. The many letters he wrote to his wife were all subsequently destroyed. Perhaps in the total picture the gap is not very important, but it does cover his only extended absence from Japan and his only visit abroad with the exception of the countries of Eastern Asia. From Switzerland he went to Germany, but if the hardships of German defeat made an impression

---

[21] On tours of duty abroad: JRD, "Interrogations," I:49157 (Seizō Arisue), 28-29, and Hattori intv.

on him, it was not one which exercised any restraining influence in later years. When he was finally ordered home, Tojo decided to travel via the United States. After visiting the principal cities of the eastern seaboard, he took a train for San Francisco, where he boarded ship for Japan. Since he was not conversant with English, he had little reason to prolong his stay. Growing daily more restless for the sight of his homeland and family, Hideki Tojo—by now a major—passed quickly as a tourist through the land against which, in less than twenty years, he was to lead the Japanese people in war.[22]

The Japan to which Tojo returned in 1922 was on the way to becoming a far different country from the one he had left in 1919—the one he had known throughout his early years. The nation had enjoyed extraordinary wartime prosperity and apparently had confidently expected the good times to go on forever. When they did not, there was trouble.

Among the sons of the peasants who constituted the backbone of the Japanese army, the memory of poverty in the rural areas, of long hours of back-breaking toil only to do without more each year than in the year before, bred a rankling discontent and encouraged many to search for ogres on whom to blame the misery of life. The revolutionary panaceas of a kind of home-brewed ultranationalistic military socialism soon began making an impression.[23] The quest for answers and for new approaches also spread among university students throughout the country. Avant-garde clubs were formed where earnest young men secretly pored over radical literature and where they occasionally became unwilling hosts to the police.[24]

The pattern of the past was changing in other respects as well. Japan was turning from oligarchic monopoly of political life toward apparent democracy. In 1918 the premiership had gone to a commoner—the first ever to hold that office—and thereafter for roughly a decade the post was alternately filled by the respective heads of Japan's two leading political parties. Partly because of this trend toward democracy, the once immensely popular and highly eulogized Japanese army began to fall upon evil days. This added to the discontent of conscripts and

[22] Jusshi Itō, "Tōjō Taii to Yamashita Taii," *Bungei Shunjū*, Vol. XXX, No. 6 (April 1952), 63-65; Shunichirō Itō, 55-56; Tōgō, *Jidai no Ichimen*, 9-10; Tōjō interrog., Jan. 14, 2; and Mrs. Tōjō and Umezu corresp.

[23] See Deverall, "The Imperial Japanese Army: Hideki Tojo's Military Socialism," for one point of view regarding this subject. Also Maxon, 32-33; Brown, *Nationalism in Japan*, 177-78; and Storry, *The Double Patriots*, Chs. 2 and 3.

[24] The clubs were called *shinjin-kai* because their membership was composed of "new (awakened) men."

officers alike, but especially to the chagrin of the professionals, who might be retired prematurely to a drab and restricted civilian life because of economy cutbacks.

Among the causes of this loss of favor was the simple fact that Japan's prosperity owed little if anything to the profession of arms. Since 1905 the nation had maintained a peacetime army at a cost which was hard to justify in view of the continuing absence of any serious military threat. And yet, in spite of exorbitant spending, which added to popular discontent, military men complained that the current standard, which supposedly left much to be desired, was being only barely maintained. The professionals were further shocked when the number of young men seeking careers as officers in the imperial army and navy began declining sharply. Self-appointed military propagandists could vigorously declare: "The national defence should be replenished . . . for the sake of defending the honour and existence of the Empire and . . . for our self-protection," but without a believable threat the sound was hollow.[25]

It was thus with considerable relief and noticeable relish that a number of military men, particularly army officers, greeted the appearance of a new "national crisis." A typical Japanese view was that Japan had learned her lesson from the West "unwillingly but . . . well; but just as she was getting really skilful at the game of the grab, the other Powers, most of whom had all they wanted anyway, suddenly had an access of virtue and called the game off."[26] Foremost among these culprits was the United States, "a selfish meddler, interfering unreasonably with Japan's natural aspirations."[27]

The Japanese of the early 1920's were roughly divided into those who were overwhelmed by American material progress and those who were not. To the latter, the United States was a giant with feet of clay. They acknowledged that Americans could construct buildings that scraped the sky, railroads that crossed and crisscrossed the continent, automobiles and ships and flying machines, guns, tanks, typewriters, and mechanical gadgets galore. But they refused to be daunted by such materialistic achievements. As one army publicist put it, "In point of

[25] On the low estate to which the army was falling, see Kōjirō Satō, *If Japan and America Fight*, 33, 109-10, 152, 162; Kennedy, *The Military Side of Japanese Life*, 308; Lory, 159-60; and Deverall, 30.

[26] Kennedy, *Some Aspects of Japan and her Defence Forces*, 125, quoting an unnamed Japanese delegate to the 1925 meeting of the Institute of Pacific Relations, held in Honolulu.

[27] *Ibid.*, 132 n., citing Nicholas Roosevelt, "The Restless Pacific." See also Kōjirō Satō, 37-38.

mentality, Japanese are rather superior than inferior to Americans."[28] Army optimists blandly ignored the strength and vitality of the nation they cast as their enemy. They denounced those Japanese who were so impressed with American progress that they advised Japan "to take off her helmet." The positive-minded insisted that only a masterful spirit was needed to overcome America. Although this view was most prevalent among military men, it came, in time, to penetrate the thinking of others as well.[29]

Careless, goading, irrational talk of a Japanese-American war was once again heard. It began sometime in 1919 and continued into 1922, when it temporarily ceased, partly as a result of the Washington Conference, partly because of continuing public dissatisfaction in Japan with the schemes of the military—specifically with the Siberian intervention, which was costing enormous sums of money and yet was producing no tangible results. Resentment against the United States in this period flared for various reasons: American opposition to the twenty-one demands and to Japan's continued presence in Shantung—an opposition which had effectively bolstered Chinese resistance, or even created it where there might otherwise have been none or only a negligible amount; American immigration policy, including the alleged American role in "defeating" Japan's efforts to have a "racial-equality" clause written into the Covenant of the League of Nations—another case of mistaken identity and a misunderstanding or confusion of the facts; finally—and interestingly enough in view of popular displeasure in Japan over the same issue—growing American feeling against the imperial army's occupation of Siberia and northern Sakhalin.

As always in such cases, communications media took advantage of the situation to boost sales. Glaring titles appeared to flag the reader's attention.[30] Among these was a book by a retired lieutenant general, Kojiro Sato, called *If Japan and America Fight*. Although the degree of influence exerted by this Russo-Japanese war veteran may be open to question, his views make startling reading not only in the context of his day but also in the light of 1941.

To General Sato, who was advertised to the public as "the Japanese Bernhardi," Japan's troubles could all be laid at America's doorstep. For years the United States had "insolently" been manifesting imperialistic

[28] Kōjirō Satō, 3-5.
[29] See *ibid.*, 16-19 and *passim*.
[30] On talk and threats of a Japanese-American war, see Kōjirō Satō's book and Kennedy, *The Military Side of Japanese Life*, 346-51. Also, Fukuda corresp.

designs, all the while professing a hypocritical concern for the "open door." America's earlier feelings of friendship for Japan had dissolved in jealousy when Japan had acquired a position of power as a result of the Russo-Japanese war. Thereafter, the United States—a society corrupted by "gold poisoning"—had hindered Japan at every turn in her dealings with China and had insulted the Japanese race through anti-immigration agitation. What had saved the Japanese Empire before and what would save it again was the "indomitable will" of the Japanese people.[31]

Although Sato admitted the "enormous achievement" of America in industrial mobilization during World War I, this did not temper his aggressive enthusiasm for a policy and program of action.[32] He even outlined a sort of battle plan in which he advocated sending death-defying bands of several thousand men each against the United States and its possessions, in the manner of the Japanese pirates who had preyed upon the China coast during the Ming dynasty. The interval of four centuries might have suggested a certain inapplicability to some persons, but not to General Sato. His was a boundless faith, an attitude common to Japanese fighting men. It found expression in such old sayings as "Even though we be hard-pressed, we shall find a way out" and "Once you determine to do a thing, nothing will be impossible." Thus courage or cowardice was the decisive factor, strength or weakness only of subsidiary importance. Having such faith, Sato could seriously suggest that if a band of only fifty Japanese pirates could once have overrun ten or more Chinese provinces (according to popular belief), then certainly several thousand Japanese soldiers should be able to do the trick against the more advanced American enemy of 1920, terrorizing, in the process, the entire American people. "My idea," he said, "is that if bands of such death-daring men . . . should be thrown in upon San Francisco it would be very interesting, indeed."[33]

Views similar to General Sato's were found throughout the ranks and were even occasionally expressed to foreigners. Captain Malcolm Kennedy of the Cameronians, who spent several years with the Japanese army, found military opinion returning again and again to the "threat" posed by the United States. During the early months of 1920, for

[31] See Kōjirō Satō, 31, 69-74, and 222. Also Fukuda, Ohmae, and Kennedy corresp. I am indebted to Capt. Kennedy for calling Satō's writings to my attention.
[32] See *ibid.*, 79-81.
[33] *Ibid.*, 42, 81, 83-84, 163-66, and 173. With regard to such "daring movements" as surprise naval attacks, Satō declared (p. 106): "It may not be too much to say that we are peerless in the world."

instance, some Japanese officers referred to the policies of America, Germany, and Britain as the three A's, the three B's, and the three C's. They were not particularly concerned about the Germans linking Berlin, Budapest, and Baghdad or about the British connecting Cairo with Capetown and Calcutta, but they were "strongly opposed" to any attempt by the United States to bind America, Alaska, and Asia by means of a much talked-about tunnel under the Bering Straits. The construction of such a tunnel, they declared, would be as much of a threat as the establishment of American bases on Guam and in the Philippines, since it would bring the American enemy to Japan's very gates.

In writing later of his experiences, Captain Kennedy pointed out the fallacies in the Japanese argument: it was not at all certain that such a tunnel could be constructed; even if it were, years would pass before completion; a tunnel alone would be of no value without railways leading to and from it; any transportation network built on the Asian continent would be in Russian territory and hence not available to American troops unless Russia also declared war on Japan; even if Russia allied herself with the United States, the field of battle would still lie on the Asian mainland unless a fleet were assembled at Vladivostok for an invasion of Japan; such a fleet would be subject to Japanese naval attack unless Japan's task forces had already been destroyed; if they had been, the Americans would not bother with the Bering Straits or Vladivostok but would sail directly across the Pacific and be done with it.[34]

Although the Japanese fear of such a tunnel was patently nonsense, the value of the mental gymnastics in which the imperial army engaged, then and later, clearly lay in keeping its members, and eventually the whole nation, psychologically alert and ready for action by creating imaginary enemies where none actually existed.

The initial result of the Washington Conference of 1921-1922 was to dispel much mutual distrust, but it was not long before the effect wore off. The movement begun in 1921 toward abrogation of the diplomatic arrangements made by Theodore Roosevelt burst the bounds of reason in the spring of 1924, when the Congress overwhelmingly approved an immigration bill denying entry into the United States to aliens ineligible for citizenship. Although this bill was not aimed solely at Japanese, they

[34] Kennedy, *The Military Side of Japanese Life*, 309 and 341-42; Kennedy and Ohmae corresp.; Kōjirō Satō, 217-18. On the general question of the hostile feelings of the Japanese army toward the United States, see Kennedy, pp. 346-51; on the danger of war, see Kennedy, *Some Aspects of Japan and Her Defence Forces*, 133-35.

were among its leading targets. Thus, to the already existing immigration barriers ringing the Pacific—barriers in Canada, Latin America, Australia, and New Zealand—were added the unscalable walls by which America was to be kept "American."[35]

This perversity on the part of the Congress happened to coincide with a further deterioration in the position of the Japanese army. Since the Washington Conference had settled the problem of naval building programs, public attention in Japan had naturally turned to the twenty-one divisions of the Japanese army. The more the movement for reduction grew, the more the army clamored for armaments to hold its own; the more the army did that, the more the movement grew.

When army leaders finally realized that the game would be lost if they persisted, they offered a plan whereby some manpower cuts would be effected but no changes made in the existing organization. One purpose of this plan was to create the impression of complying with the demands of the time while, in fact, doing as little as possible. But it did not work—the agitation in favor of reduction continued. In 1923, after the great earthquake had added further point to the economy question, General Kazushige Ugaki, the war minister, appointed a commission to study and report on the matter. Within the army it was generally assumed that the commission would recommend a change in organization rather than an elimination of units. The army was duly shocked when the commission advised Ugaki to scrap four divisions. When he subsequently acted upon the recommendation, the shock deepened; anger and bitterness ran through the ranks of officers and soldiers alike. The fact that the elimination of four divisions was to be counterbalanced by expanding the air force, by introducing military training in the schools, by adopting and developing modern weapons, by establishing a tank corps nucleus and antiaircraft units, and by promoting research on poison gas made not the slightest difference.[36]

[35] Reactions in Japan were many and varied, ranging from the hurt to the angry, from the reasonable to the extravagant. Although some understanding of certain aspects of American thinking on immigration was expressed, it was only rarely that the general criticism leveled at the United States included indictments of the Empire's own policies with respect to Chinese and Korean laborers. See, for example, *Japan Times & Mail*, October 1, 1924 (special immigration edition).

[36] On the army reduction question: Kennedy, *Some Aspects of Japan and Her Defence Forces*, 106-10 and 115-16; Ugaki, *Ugaki Nikki*, 27-28 and *passim*; *Kaikōsha Kiji*, No. 754, 48-50 and 144-45; Yano intv.; Kennedy, *The Military Side of Japanese Life*, 307, 310-12, 315-16; Maki, *Japanese Militarism*, 219; and Lory, 159-60. An earlier reduction, begun in 1922, had been rendered largely meaningless by 1925 when Ugaki's decision was put into effect. In spite of their research on poison gas, the Japanese desired to have its use outlawed.

Although these were not Hideki Tojo's battles, he was nonetheless
concerned in their outcome. Of all the changes in this period perhaps
the most fateful for Japan, as well as for Tojo, were in the composition
of the army rank and file, in the nature of the army's leadership, and
in the relationship between the two.[37] In essence, the Japanese army was
inducting more and more conscripts from the economically depressed
classes, especially peasant farmers and fishermen, men who had long
and intimate knowledge of poverty and who were thus ready converts
to programs advocating radical change to redress the social and economic balance. The noncommissioned officers and even many of the
younger commissioned officers either came from the same group or
from similarly oriented groups in sympathy with anyone who shared
a common experience. At a time of general social ferment, with a
Korean anarchist laying plans to assassinate the Emperor, the writings
of Karl Marx successfully invading the country, and native propagandists joining in the fray, the army became a natural seedbed for
subversive thought, with the younger officers—lieutenants, captains,
and majors for the most part—suddenly resorting to direct action in
defiance of both civil and military authority. They loudly indulged
their prejudices against the nobility, the wealthy, and the politicians,
whom they indiscriminately accused of degeneracy, lack of patriotism,
failure to contribute to the national defense needs of the state, and
similar vices. Their charges received impetus when political-party government, which was then in the hands of the leading financial interests,
was suddenly exposed as very corrupt. In a country with a longer tradition of democratic processes, or with greater stability, this exposé might
have been taken in stride. In the Japan of the middle and late 1920's,
increasingly plagued by deteriorating economic health, the revelation
of graft in high places gave democracy a bad name and enhanced the
prospects for totalitarianism.

Within the top echelon of the army, the old order was passing and
a new one was gradually taking its place. The death in 1922 of the
army's outstanding elder—Yamagata—had created a power vacuum
which conflicting elements desired to fill. The struggle which ensued
robbed the army of effective leadership at a time when decisiveness was
essential if discipline was to be maintained. It was in this situation that
the "younger officer" group obtained their golden opportunity. Within

[37] The discussion which follows is based on interviews with Matsudaira, Yano, Satō,
Yamanashi, and Ōi; CF 20, I, 55; Craigie, *Behind the Japanese Mask*, 25 and 37; Lory,
17, 99, 106, 171-72, 178; Deverall, 7 and 10; and Maxon, 43-44.

a few years, they inaugurated military ventures abroad that were eventually very nearly to destroy the state. At home, they introduced that extraordinary period of "government by assassination"[38] through which the nation came more and more under the sway of military dictatorship.

Although the early 1920's were marked by a surprising decline in the popularity and influence of the imperial Japanese army, the phenomenon did not last in any significant way beyond the middle years of the decade. The army lost little time in seeking to remedy the situation. It intensified its propaganda activities, especially its counterpropaganda against further disarmament, and turned its attention more fully to the problem of public relations.

Developments in which the army was concerned, and others in which it was not, soon helped to stem the tide of public dissatisfaction. The army's withdrawal from Siberia removed one source of friction. Ugaki's elimination of four divisions served a similar purpose, though it infuriated the military. Even more important was the effect produced by the American immigration legislation of 1924 and by what seemed then to be a growing Communist threat. Fear of the latter sparked a desire throughout the nation to inculcate once again "right-thinking" based upon the old virtues of loyalty, obedience, and sacrifice. The death of the Emperor Meiji's son and the succession of his grandson, formally confirmed in elaborate enthronement ceremonies of ancient origin, created in many Japanese a sense of renewed dedication to service in behalf of the state. Nationalists vied with each other in their "incoherent effusions on the subject of the divine heritage"; military propagandists played upon the theme that Japan was living in a hostile world surrounded by enemies who might swoop in for the attack at any moment.[39]

As early as 1920, General Sato had pointed the way. To perfect Japan's security it would be "absolutely necessary," he had declared, to encourage the veterans' associations and young men's volunteer groups to take a more active part in providing for the national defense. Physical culture, military training in the public schools, and "military spirit education" in general should be encouraged. The annual cost would be

[38] The phrase is borrowed from the well-known book by Hugh Byas.

[39] The text draws on an unpublished study entitled "The Brocade Banner" (p. 18), which was prepared by an intelligence officer of General MacArthur's headquarters in 1946 (see under "United States Army" in Section I of the Bibliography). I am not at liberty to divulge the identity of the author of this valuable document. Personal knowledge pertaining thereto, including the primary nature of the Japanese source materials employed, inspires confidence in its reliability.

about 30,000,000 yen, or 5 per cent of the total expenditure for armaments. "If so small an amount can produce so great a result in the interest of national defense," Sato had written, "I would not be content, were I minister of education, with merely ranking in the cabinet like a camp-follower but would stake my position in my attempt to get that amount of money. . . . But no one will make a minister of education out of me, a safe thing, indeed."[40]

Although Sato was right—he did not become minister of education— the idea which he shared with many others did take hold. Included in the army reorganization plan of 1925, along with the elimination of the four divisions, was a clause establishing a system of military training in middle, upper, and normal schools throughout the Empire, with some 2,000 active army officers providing the instruction. This training was at first optional in some schools and compulsory in others, but in the end it became required throughout the country. In 1926 the program was extended to take care of those who did not go beyond a grammar school education.[41] This was a reasonably good way, under the circumstances, to offset Ugaki's reduction in force and, at the same time, to secure a platform from which "right-thinking" could be inculcated in the youth of the nation. Right-thinking naturally included a proper appreciation of the past services rendered by the Japanese army to the state and unquestioning advocacy of the role the army must play in the future if the nation was to surmount the many obstacles in its path.

As economic difficulties spread across the world in the late 1920's, the Japanese military gave increasing thought to "opening a way to the future" by implementing Japan's historic mission to expand on the continent, to secure the peace of East Asia, and to save its 600,000,000 people from imperialistic "oppression." "A tree must have its roots," General Sato had written; so, too, must a nation. Britain had such roots. They stretched into Africa, India, Australia, and Canada, giving strength and wealth and power to the mother country. The United States had such roots—nurtured in her own vast territory and in the rich soil of Central and South America. Unless Japan were permitted to extend her roots to the Asian continent and thus escape her "potted-plant" existence, she would shrivel up and die. And yet, Sato had declared, the United States, a country two and one-half times as large as Japan

[40] Kōjirō Sato, 168-69.
[41] On military training in the schools, see J, B/IV, 149-51; Kennedy, *Some Aspects of Japan and Her Defence Forces*, 116, 170-73; Ugaki, 28; and Deverall, 25.

proper, with a population density of only 31 per square mile to Japan's 400, was "cruelly" endeavoring to sever Japan's roots in order to pursue more fully her own grandiose designs. The Russian menace prior to 1904 paled by comparison. The American method was perhaps more subtle, but "homicide is homicide, whether committed with a dagger or by administering a narcotic." Why should the United States, Britain, and other powers which had had every opportunity to advance their own vital interests now cry, "Thief!" if Japan even so much as looked at neighboring territory?[42]

This kind of thinking, which was characteristic of the Japanese army, spread gradually among the civilian population. In time the people came inherently to believe that the West was determined to prevent any further development on Japan's part. The powers were chagrined, it was said, that Japan had escaped the fate of China and had thus frustrated their intention to include Japan within their imperialistic orbit. The twenty-one demands of 1915 were described as nothing more than a natural expression of Japan's legitimate fear of further nefarious moves by the West. Japan's leaders had been acting defensively—seeking to strengthen Japan's position in China as a means of preventing the Chinese from "falling an easy prey to Occidental ambition." One veteran Japanese journalist declared, "You may rightly blame these men for their shortsightedness and errors of judgment, but they do not deserve the charges of wanton aggression and land hunger which have been freely hurled at them. They fancied dangers which, as the event proved, were not destined to materialise, but which the whole course of . . . past history as it pertained to the relationship between East and West, certainly did not tend to make incredible."[43]

This argument, which is less far-fetched than most later Japanese attempts at justification, cannot easily be ignored. Perhaps a question will always remain in foreign minds as to whether such fears were sincere images or hypocritical pretexts adopted to gloss over Japan's own aggressive designs. If one assumes that such opinions were sincerely held by a majority of Japanese, it is not difficult to understand how succeeding events would be misinterpreted in the light of these prior misapprehensions and errors of judgment. Men tend to believe what they wish to believe and generally they join the herd. Only the mavericks strike out on their own.

[42] See Kōjirō Satō, 5-6, 37-38, 76, 141-42, 145-46, and Kennedy, *The Military Side of Japanese Life*, 347-49.

[43] Kennedy, *Some Aspects of Japan and Her Defence Forces*, 150-51, quoting Motosada Zumoto.

Hideki Tojo was not a maverick. He was tutored to obedience by his samurai father and by the military training of his early years. In 1895, at the time of the Sino-Japanese war, he was a boy of ten, excited by Japan's victory over the ethnocentric Middle Kingdom which had looked for so long with disdain upon self-conscious, easily antagonized Japan. In 1905, he was a youth of twenty, spoiling to engage in the fight against Russia, crestfallen when it passed him by, angry and resentful, as were millions of his countrymen, when Japan was "robbed" by the peace of Portsmouth of the full measure of the victories won in Manchuria with the blood of the nation. In 1915, at the time of the twenty-one demands, he was a mature thirty, nearing completion of the studies at the war college which would one day help to qualify him for the highest posts available in the army which he served.

The evidence of later years clearly shows that Tojo remained a prisoner of his environment and training.[44] Western opposition to the twenty-one demands, pressure upon Japan to withdraw from Shantung and Siberia, the continuing refusal of the United States and Britain to sanction Japanese naval parity, the tightening of hateful immigration restrictions, the raising of tariffs against Japanese goods, and similar policies came to be regarded by the people of Japan as a Western effort not only to restrict their nation but to do so while adding substantially to the West's own power and influence.

Although this attitude of mind helps explain many subsequent actions of the man and his country, it cannot justify them. At the same time, it does point up the nature and degree of Western responsibility for the further deterioration of relations with Japan. Certainly not enough attention was paid early enough to the possibility of encouraging the Japanese to adopt a more reasonable outlook by initiating diplomatic negotiations with them in the interests of peace, even at a time when it was generally felt in the West that Japan lacked a sound basis for her hostile feelings. In international relations, as in all other enterprises

[44] In this regard, the following glimpse of Tōjō by Maj. Gen. Piggott (sometime His Majesty's military attaché at Tōkyō) is interesting: "The tradition of friendly association with the Higher Command can hardly be said to have been maintained when General Tojo held the post of Vice-Minister of War in 1938; in fact, he was one of the very few army officers with whom I failed to establish any relations other than formal. On the occasion of my first interview it was obvious from his references to the effect on Japan of such matters as the German seizure of Tsing-tao in 1898, the Russian aggression in Manchuria of 1903, the abrogation of the Anglo-Japanese Alliance in 1921, and the American Immigration Act of 1924, that he regarded most foreigners with some suspicion, if not dislike. General Tojo gave me the impression of a strong man badly disillusioned, who intended to pursue his path unhindered by any interest other than Japanese; he never showed any sign of sociability." Piggott, *Broken Thread*, 336.

governed by man, the alleged case, the case that is *believed* to exist, can be as important as the actual case. And at times more important. Nor are there only the extremes of true and false; unlimited subjectivity plays its role. Partly true and partly false, a combination of the two, is often at the heart of the matter.

CHAPTER 2

The Neighbor's Garden

FROM Japan's point of view perhaps the most significant aspect of the foreign scene from about 1927 onward was the dual threat in Northeastern Asia of Chinese nationalism and Russian communism. The Japanese seemed to think that the Asian heritage they shared with China should make their brand of imperialism more acceptable to the Chinese than that of the Western powers; consequently, they never really understood the nature of the resistance against them. They acted with brash assertiveness generally at the worst possible moment—and tried to smother Chinese resistance with Japanese slogans of peace. When they chose to rely finally upon the employment of brute force on an extensive scale, they simply compounded their original error. It was this decision in favor of force, which was first made in the field by subordinate military commands without the knowledge or consent of the government in Tokyo, that started Japan down the path which ultimately led, after many detours, to Pearl Harbor.

By the spring of 1928 Chiang Kai-shek had successfully executed the Northern Expedition, accepting the submission of warlords who let discretion form the better part of valor and attacking those who did not. Chang Tso-lin, the Old Marshal of Manchuria, who had earlier extended his control over North China and set up headquarters in Peking, was the sole remaining obstacle to the reunification of China—a reunification regarded by some Japanese as practically equivalent to the end of the world. Since the Old Marshal had received considerable support from Japan in the past, it occurred to General Baron Giichi Tanaka, the Japanese premier, that Chang Tso-lin ought to be amenable to reason.[1] When it became clear that the Nationalists were moving on a tide of victory which could not be stopped, Tanaka advised the Old Marshal to trade Peking and North China for Manchuria: to withdraw to the northeast, where he would be afforded the protection of Japan's Kwantung army while he regrouped his own shattered forces.

But the Old Marshal, in spite of a recent and major defeat by the Nationalists, was not easily persuaded. For some time he had shown an increasing unwillingness to allow Japan the free hand she felt she

[1] See the testimony of Keisuke Okada and Morito Morishima, S 23:14, T 1817, and S 39:10, T 3014-16.

deserved. Like so many other warlords, he had also remained open to suggestions coming from afar and generally from sources unfriendly to Japan. It was not until the Chinese Nationalists were practically at his doorstep that he finally ordered an evacuation of the Tientsin-Peking area and himself entrained, together with his bodyguard, for Mukden. Early in the morning of June 4, 1928, as his special train passed under a South Manchurian Railway bridge controlled by Japanese forces, a terrific explosion shook his private car, injuring him fatally.

The incident was immediately hushed up in Japan, where reliable news proved singularly lacking. Although a secret investigation eventually turned up the facts, it was not until after the Japanese surrender, seventeen years later, that the people of Japan and the world at large learned the truth. It then developed that the Kwantung army had become dissatisfied with Tanaka's policy of expanding Japan's substantial rights and interests through cooperation and collaboration with Chang Tso-lin. By June 1928 certain members of that army were no longer willing to wait for the process of negotiation to produce results. They wanted direct action—the seizure of Manchuria by force of arms. It was these men, with a staff colonel named Daisaku Kōmoto in the vanguard, who carried out the murder of the Old Marshal. The railroad was carefully mined with dynamite by members of a Japanese engineer regiment. As Chang's car passed over the spot, an imperial army captain personally pushed the plunger. Other soldiers, who had taken up positions around the mined area, opened fire on the survivors as they emerged from the wreckage.

The perpetrators of this crime immediately attempted to secure an order which would have distributed the Kwantung army, confined by treaty to the Liaotung peninsula and the railway zone, throughout Manchuria. With the entire area in the army's hands, a new state would have been proclaimed under the nominal leadership of none other than the Young Marshal, the son of the murdered man. Thus the Manchurian issue would be "solved" and the government in Tokyo would be forced to accept the army's *fait accompli*. This broader conspiracy apparently failed only because the staff officer who was supposed to issue the order misunderstood the true intentions of those who demanded it and hence refused. The frustration of this scheme, however, was to assume peculiar significance some three years later when another explosion on another track in Manchuria did produce the desired results.

The Chang Tso-lin episode was the first overt attempt on the part of the Japanese army—in this case, the Kwantung army—to project itself into the formulation of national policy. By and large it can be said that the army succeeded, for even though the seizure of Manchuria was temporarily postponed, the cabinet of General Tanaka was dealt a crippling blow, and the constitutional process in Japan received the first of the thousand cuts from which it was destined to suffer a slow but certain death.

Tanaka and his cabinet had been caught off guard by the assassination of the Old Marshal. In reporting the matter to the throne, the embarrassed premier had advised in favor of strong disciplinary measures and the Emperor had given his approval. When Tanaka had subsequently reported this to the war and navy ministers, both had expressed their "wholehearted backing." But after the war minister had pursued the matter further, his stern attitude toward the culprits had begun to weaken. Five months had passed before he had finally admitted privately that Japanese army officers were responsible for the Old Marshal's death. By that time, "violent opposition" to the punishment of the guilty had developed within the general staff and elsewhere in the army. The war minister had then reported to Tanaka that this opposition was based on the view that to punish would be to expose to the public *that which the army desired to keep secret.* In the face of this attitude, the premier—general and baron though he was—had had no choice but to resign.[2]

From the murder of Chang Tso-lin onward the Japanese army began more and more to influence the formulation of Japan's Manchurian policy, a task in which it received assistance and inspiration from militaristic-minded groups of fanatical nationalists.[3] Such activity was by no means new in Japan, but its increase at this time, and its utilization of the younger officer group which was now coming to the fore, soon involved the nation in a succession of troubles at home and abroad. Within Japan the economic depression was worsening and the number

[2] On the Chang Tso-lin affair: Takeuchi, *War and Diplomacy in the Japanese Empire,* 247-61, 275-82; S 23:6, T 1752-53; S 23:8, T 1771-72; Okada's testimony, S 23:13-14, T 1810-20; Morishima's testimony, S 39:10, T 3014-16; Okada, *Kaiko-roku,* 35-41; "The Brocade Banner," 15, 19-20; J, B/IV, 86-87 and B/V, 526-29 and 530-31; SCAP "Summary," Nos. 4 and 11; Dull, "The Assassination of Chang Tso-lin," *Far Eastern Quarterly,* Vol. XI, No. 4 (August 1952), 453-63; Yanaga, *Japan Since Perry,* 456-57; and Maxon, 73-75, which notes several versions of Tanaka's role.

The war minister was Yoshinori Shirakawa. The cases of the Kwantung army staff officers involved in the murder of Chang Tso-lin were settled "administratively." Colonel Kōmoto, who was permitted to resign, subsequently had a very successful career in business. Some years later the Japanese government even considered giving him a key appointment in Manchuria.

[3] See S 23:14, T 1820; "The Brocade Banner," 7, 9-14, 20; and Brown, *Nationalism in Japan,* 178-95.

of adherents to communism grew proportionately. The world panic of 1929 struck the island empire with full force, leaving the farming and fishing communities, from which the army drew its best recruits, in dire straits. Abroad, powers like the United States and Great Britain rushed to protect home industry by raising higher and higher tariff barriers, which made it impossible for Japan to sell her goods and recoup her losses, and thus, in turn, contributed further to the already significant anti-Western resentment of her people. At the same time, the clamor in favor of reducing government expenditures, especially with regard to defense, received new impetus with each further relapse in the nation's economic health.

On the continent, the Kuomintang began vigorously pushing Chinese immigration into Manchuria, which in former years had been exclusively reserved for China's Manchu rulers and their people. In encouraging the movement of Chinese into Manchuria, the Nationalists wished not only to emphasize their ownership rights but also to begin economic development of that tremendously rich treasure house, including the initiation of projects implicitly inimical to Japan's extensive interests there.

Manchuria was Chinese, and while that did not give the Nationalists any right to ignore China's treaty obligations toward other powers, neither did geographical propinquity or even special rights and interests confer upon Japan any kind of patent to sever the area from China the moment there was the slightest trouble. Indeed, so far as the Japanese government was concerned, that was not the intention. As problems multiplied at home and abroad, the moderates in Tokyo began thinking in terms of Japan's overcommitment in Manchuria. There was even talk of retrenchment as a means of remedying the situation. As soon as that became known, the extremists in the Kwantung army, aided and abetted by various ultranationalists, began planning action that not only would make retrenchment impossible but also would tend to reverse the still dangerous and seemingly persistent movement toward a reduction of military expenditures.

Following the death of Chang Tso-lin, Sino-Japanese relations went from bad to worse.[4] Whereas the British had previously been the chief

---

[4] On the aftermath of the Chang Tso-lin episode (including the emergence of the Sakura-kai, which follows in the text), J, B/V, 529-33 and B/IX, 1138; Kōjirō Satō, 133-37 (quoting S. Inada on uprooting evils on the continent); "The Brocade Banner," 18-19; IMTFE, "Analyses of Documentary Evidence," Doc. No. 12; Kido intv.; JRD Monograph No. 144, 1-5; Storry, *The Double Patriots*, 54-57 and *passim*; and JRD,

object of the antiforeignism stimulated by China's new nationalistic fervor, the Japanese now suddenly became the focus of Chinese hatred. Goods bearing the mark "Made in Japan" were widely boycotted and Japanese nationals were, on occasion, publicly insulted. The Young Marshal, in whom the Japanese had a misplaced confidence, revealed his basic loyalties by making his peace with Chiang Kai-shek and the Kuomintang. As a result, relations between China and Japan, even in the latter's once privileged preserve in Manchuria, deteriorated further. Between 1928 and 1931 one hundred and twenty cases of infringement of Japanese rights and interests were said to have occurred. The accusations ranged from excessive taxation and unlawful detention of individuals to interference with property rights and oppressive treatment of Koreans, who were supposed to enjoy special protection as members of the Japanese Empire.

The Chinese and Japanese press contributed to the public clamor on the slightest pretext. Military agitators and civilian ultranationalists in Japan eagerly joined in the fray, oversimplifying the issues and blandly discussing Manchuria as if it were a separate entity rather than an integral part of China. The way to settle the matter once and for all, they said, was to occupy the area and thus strike at the roots of the problem. This was not a new idea by any manner of means. Militaristic commentators had long been in the habit of declaring that Japanese history clearly taught that the way to preserve Japan's territorial integrity was to uproot the evils on the continent.

Under such reasoning as this there could be no limit to the requirements of Japanese security, for with each new acquisition of territory the ever-changing problem of defense would demand further advances. But this was the view of many military men, especially of Kwantung army officers, who were prone to exhibit a rather proprietary interest in Manchuria, the seat of their power. Dr. Shumei Okawa, whose name was soon to figure in a number of incidents, returned to Japan from the continent to tour the length and breadth of the country, lecturing and showing pictures. Friends in the army general staff and in the South Manchurian Railway Company, by which he was employed, backed his efforts to arouse the Japanese people against the Chinese. The army general staff, cleverly talking in terms of Japan's lifeline in Manchuria,

---

"Translation," V:29027 (Item 20, Kanemitsu), 2-3. CF 20, I, 55 contains a list (showing rank and assignment) of ninety-seven officers who were among the original members of the Sakura-kai. The "inner group" was composed of field-grade officers in the army general staff. In time the company-grade officers were referred to as the "Little Cherry Society."

began also to concentrate its energy upon plans for possible military action there.

Following the fall of Tanaka in July 1929 and the emergence of the Hamaguchi Cabinet, with the moderate Kijuro Shidehara as foreign minister, the possibility of a peaceful solution briefly returned. The new cabinet adopted a "friendship policy" through which it hoped, in time, to reach a settlement with China. On the mainland, the authorities of the Nationalist government showed a willingness to cooperate toward that end. The boycotts began steadily declining, and there seemed little reason why outstanding issues could not be solved through the exercise of restraint and good will on both sides. But not all parties were so inclined. Civilian ultranationalists and younger officers kept up an unceasing barrage of propaganda. In the forefront of the former group was Dr. Okawa, heading a newly established "research" foundation supported by South Manchurian Railway funds; assuming the lead of the latter were two rising officers, Lieutenant Colonel Kingoro Hashimoto and Colonel Seishiro Itagaki.

Hashimoto had recently returned to Japan from Turkey, where he had been greatly impressed by the achievements of Kemal Pasha. During the voyage home, he had begun drafting plans for the reform of his native land. His subsequent assignment to the army general staff, early in 1930, must have seemed like a signal from heaven. He plunged at once into devising schemes to put his ideas into practice. After some nine months of further thought and planning, he organized the inevitable "research" society composed of dissatisfied company- and field-grade officers, drawn largely from the army general staff and the war ministry. The ultimate aim of these officers was "national reorganization, by armed force if necessary, in order to settle the so-called 'Manchurian Problem' and other pending issues."[5] The group referred to itself as the "Cherry Society" after the flower which has traditionally been associated with the Japanese warrior. The cherry blossom bursts into being and then suddenly, when the time has come, falls in an instant to the ground in clean and beautiful death. It was an appropriate symbol for an organization which has been called the "main force of the plot to seize Manchuria."[6]

At Kwantung army headquarters in Port Arthur, staff officers, including Colonel Itagaki, returned again and again in their conversations to

[5] J, B/V, 533.
[6] This is the judgment of the "Saionji-Harada Memoirs" as recorded in "The Brocade Banner," 19.

the Manchurian question. On one occasion Itagaki allegedly told a fellow officer that the many unsolved issues between Japan and China were so serious that only force, and not diplomacy, could lead to a settlement. He believed that the Young Marshal should be driven out of Manchuria so that a new state—a paradise on earth—could be established. Although Itagaki later denied this conversation, such views, which were central to all that Okawa and Hashimoto were doing, became immensely popular within the Kwantung army.[7]

As in the murder of Chang Tso-lin in 1928, so again in 1931 the work of that army began with an explosion. Night maneuvers were in progress in the vicinity of barracks housing the 7th Chinese Brigade, located near the tracks of the South Manchurian Railway slightly to the north of Mukden. The roughly ten thousand Chinese soldiers belonging to the brigade were confined to quarters on orders from the Young Marshal, who hoped in that way to avoid any further clash with the Japanese. At approximately nine o'clock on the evening of September 18 a Chinese officer at the barracks noticed that a train consisting of several coaches had stopped opposite the brigade compound. An hour or so later a loud explosion ripped the air, followed instantly by rifle fire. A Japanese lieutenant and six men, upon hearing the explosion, rushed to investigate. They found that a small segment of track had been damaged (so small—it later developed—that the regular southbound train due in Mukden at 10:30 p.m. was able to pass over the spot without difficulty). According to the lieutenant, he and his patrol were fired on from the dark fields bordering the track. Not knowing what to make of the situation, he withdrew with his men to report to higher headquarters. There the decision was swift and purposeful. At 11:30 p.m. soldiers of the Kwantung army suddenly opened fire upon the brightly lit barracks of the 7th Brigade. Concurrently, other Kwantung detachments descended upon the walled city of Mukden, capturing it by the following morning with the aid of two heavy guns which had only recently and very secretly been installed for that purpose.[8]

What happened subsequently in Manchuria became public knowledge almost immediately. The Japanese army launched a general attack upon Chinese garrisons throughout the area. Colonel Kenji Doihara, a Japanese expert on China, was installed as mayor of Mukden, a position in which he performed the functions of "over-all advisor and coordinator in the planning, execution and exploitation" of this so-called Manchurian

[7] J, B/V, 533-35; S 25:12, T 1984-87; and S 288:5-6, T 30324-27.
[8] S 25:12-13, T 1987-92.

Incident. Army propagandists informed the government in Tokyo and the world at large of the dastardly attack which the "Chinese" had launched on law-abiding and unsuspecting Japan. The similarity of method between this second bombing and the earlier one in 1928, however, and the manner and speed with which Japan's troops followed up the explosion with well-timed and coordinated attacks, suggested the possibility that the entire affair had been planned by the Kwantung army.

Unlike the earlier case, the government in Tokyo had not been taken completely unawares.[9] Shortly before September 18, Foreign Minister Shidehara had received confidential information to the effect that the Kwantung army was massing troops and bringing up ammunition and other military supplies. He had immediately gone to the war minister and had prevailed upon him to send a high-ranking officer to investigate the situation and to stop any impending action. The man chosen for this mission was Maj. Gen. Yoshitsugu Tatekawa of the general staff— an officer who was privy to the Kwantung army plot and in favor of it. Upon arrival at the scene Tatekawa allowed himself to be "decoyed" by Colonel Itagaki to a Japanese inn where he passed the evening in the company of "geisha girls," listening to the sound of firing in the distance. He eventually retired and slept soundly until called the following morning—the morning of September 19.

Nor was that all. About 10:30 p.m. on the 18th, a local Japanese consular officer named Morito Morishima received a telephone call from the Kwantung army's special service headquarters in Mukden advising him that an explosion had occurred on the South Manchurian tracks. He was instructed to report at once to headquarters. Upon arrival, he found Colonel Itagaki very much in command of the situation. When Morishima tried to advise in favor of a peaceful adjustment through negotiations with the Chinese, Itagaki rebuked him and pointedly asked whether the foreign office authorities in Mukden intended to interfere with the rights of military command. When Morishima persisted, a staff major angrily drew his sword from its scabbard and threatened the consul. Morishima's superior, Consul-General Kyujiro Hayashi, who was in receipt of repeated Chinese assurances of a desire to settle the affair through peaceful means, also talked with Itagaki, but to no avail.

[9] See Shidehara's testimony, S 18:7, T 1324, as amended in S 18:8, T 1333; Morishima's testimony, S 39:10-11, T 3016-20; and J, B/V, 545. Hamaguchi had been replaced as premier in April 1931 by Baron Reijiro Wakatsuki; Shidehara remained in the new cabinet as foreign minister.

The colonel chose to interpret all of Hayashi's suggestions concerning the possibility of a peaceful solution as an unwarranted and improper attempt to interfere with the supreme command prerogative. Hayashi was forced to cable Shidehara that Itagaki had linked the incident to military and national prestige and had declared that the Kwantung army was going to see the matter through to the end.

In the weeks and months which followed, the cabinet in Tokyo was consistently outmaneuvered by the army in the field. As soon as the events of September 18 were reported, the cabinet's initial reaction was to limit the area of the incident and to prevent any expansion of hostilities. The military authorities in Manchuria paid absolutely no attention to this decision. The war minister in Tokyo personally aided the Kwantung army by acting as a buffer between it and the cabinet. He thereby minimized the danger that the cabinet would implement decisions which might be detrimental to the intentions of the Kwantung army. The war minister also appointed the chief of the military affairs bureau of the war ministry to provide liaison between the army general staff and the cabinet—further evidence of the locus of power not only within the army, but also within the government.

Although the war minister played a very important part, the star performers then, as later, came from the executive officer group within the army general staff and within the military affairs bureau of the war ministry. There thus emerged now, in addition to the younger company-grade officers, a second group of somewhat older, higher-ranking career men: the so-called *chūken shōkō*, the mainstay group of officers at the center—in short, the nucleus clique which began by intruding its influence upon affairs of state and ended by dominating the scene. As one observer described it, the trouble in later years was not with the younger element, but with the old men, officers of the rank of colonel and general. The Manchurian Incident marked the first stirrings of this group, soon to be encouraged by the extraordinary activity of their juniors toward an ever-deeper penetration of the decision-making process.[10]

How effective such a purposeful cadre could be was clearly revealed in the use made of the war minister at the time in question. Although a member of the cabinet, he was first and foremost an army officer, a

---

[10] The activities of the *seinen shōkō* are treated in Chapter 3. The question of differentiating between them and the *chūken shōkō* (whose role is discussed in detail in subsequent chapters) came up frequently in interviews (Kido, Yano, Ōi, and Kurihara) as well as in Kido and Ōi corresp.

general on active service and one of the army's so-called Big Three (the war minister, the chief of the army general staff, and the inspector-general of military training). In sparring with the cabinet on the army's behalf, the war minister personally characterized the Japanese role in Manchuria as an act of righteous self-defense. He explained and excused each further advance on "strategic and tactical" grounds, saying that the continued fighting was necessary for "protective" reasons. Actually, the Chinese army, such as it was, was tumbling over itself in its haste to retreat before the onrushing forces of Japan. Daily in Tokyo the war minister pointed to maps on which he indicated a boundary beyond which he said the army would not go, and almost daily that boundary was ignored and further advances made, always with assurances to the premier that the latest move was the final one.[11]

When it was reported that the Emperor had given his approval to the cabinet's localization policy, army leaders grew indignant and suggested, in effect, that the Emperor had been insincerely advised by traitors close to the throne. In time, this charge was to become the standard army response to any imperial action or opinion not in accord with army wishes.[12] And since the Emperor had been carefully trained from boyhood to reign but not to rule, there was little that he or his advisers could do about the situation unless they were prepared to go to the length of a purge—a dangerous business at best. In this particular instance, it was decided that His Majesty should refrain from further remarks about the cabinet's policy and that his closest adviser, the aging elder statesman, Prince Saionji, had better not come to the capital from his country villa lest he intensify the antipathy with which he was already regarded by the army clique.

[11] On developments in the field and in Tōkyō immediately following the outbreak of the Manchurian Incident, see the Shidehara testimony cited above; J, B/IV, 91-96, B/V, 538-64, and *passim*; Wakatsuki, *Kofūan Kaiko-roku*, 375-80; Shidehara Heiwa Zaidan, *Shidehara Kijūrō*, 467ff.; Morishima's testimony, S 39:10-11, T 3014-24; Kenryō Satō, "Dai-Tōa Sensō wo Maneita Shōwa no Dōran," *Kingu*, Vol. XXXII, No. 10 (October 1956), 89-90; Kido SKD; IMTFE, Doc. No. 0001, pertinent items for 1931; SCAP, Summary No. 11; Storry, "The Mukden Incident of September 18-19, 1931," *Far Eastern Affairs: Number One* (St. Antony's Papers, No. 2), 1957, 1-12; and Ferrell, "The Mukden Incident: September 18-19, 1931," *Journal of Modern History*, Vol. XXVII, No. 1 (March 1955), 66-72; Horwitz, "The Tokyo Trial," 509; Storry, *The Double Patriots*, 74-86; Rōyama, *Foreign Policy of Japan: 1914-1939*, 67-68; and "The Brocade Banner," 32-33. The war minister at the time in question was General Jirō Minami.

[12] The "kunsoku no kan" argument was by no means new: ". . . after defeating the Imperial forces in 1221, the leader of the Kamakura forces felt impelled to explain, before one of the Shinto shrines, that he did not resist the Emperor's mandate for selfish reasons but wished merely to punish the evil councilors who had misled the Emperor" (Brown, *Nationalism in Japan*, 23).

THE LIGHT OF ASIA

This comment on Japan's actions in Manchuria appeared in the *Washington Daily News* early in 1932. It subsequently won a Pulitzer prize for editorial cartoonist Harold M. Talburt. (Courtesy of the *Washington Daily News*)

The cabinet in Tokyo was therefore left with the very difficult and thankless task of trying to explain the Manchurian Incident to the world at large. In so doing, both the premier and the foreign minister turned the prestige of their reputations toward the solution of a problem which might have been better solved, or at any rate more strongly highlighted, by their resigning from office in protest against the army's unauthorized action in Manchuria and their own obvious inability to deal with the situation.[13]

Any hope individual cabinet ministers might have entertained of prevailing over the military in the autumn of 1931 soon proved vain. The Kwantung army simply turned its back on Tokyo and continued its penetration of Manchuria. Neither the League's advice to the belligerents to withdraw their troops nor the American resurrection of the nonrecognition formula, first enunciated at the time of the twenty-one demands, had any appreciable effect upon developments in China's northeastern provinces. Indeed, the violence spread from Manchuria to Shanghai, where hostilities continued for more than a month with Japanese forces bombing and strafing the city, and in general conducting what amounted to full-scale war. This extension of the fighting into North China proper brought Japan into more direct conflict with the Western powers because of the existence at Shanghai of the International Settlement. There was thus not only greater likelihood of an unlimited war between Japan and China, but now also the possibility that Japanese violations of the International Settlement and of Western rights and interests there would produce an armed clash with the offended powers.

In view of this new danger, certain highly placed Japanese tried to urge a policy of caution upon the army. It is especially revealing that they carried their appeal, not to the war minister directly, or even to the chief of the army general staff, but rather to the strategically placed and increasingly powerful chief of the military affairs bureau of the war ministry, an office which was to become more and more important as the policy-forming organ for the war ministry and as the liaison link between the chief of staff and the war minister. In this particular case, the appeal seems to have had some effect. It should be noted, however, that those who urged caution on the army at this time were aided by the

---

[13] On the Wakatsuki-Shidehara decision to remain in office, see the views of the British ambassador (1937-1941), Sir Robert Craigie (*Behind the Japanese Mask*, 27), who argues—rightly, I believe—that the ". . . civilian members of the cabinet would have served their country and the cause of world peace better had they resigned the moment they discovered they had lost control of the situation."

fact that the Japanese commander at Shanghai was personally in favor of localizing the incident.[14]

While the fighting was in progress in Shanghai, while China was appealing to the League, and while the United States and other powers were watching and waiting, alert but inactive, the Kwantung army was completing its conquest of Manchuria and establishing there the so-called independent state of Manchukuo. At its head this same army placed, first as chief executive and later as emperor, the last Manchu ruler of China, "Mr. Henry Pu Yi."[15] Thus did the bastard state of Manchukuo achieve a questionable legitimacy.

The League of Nations at length became involved in the issues posed by the Japanese action in Manchuria and sent Lord Lytton to the area with a commission of inquiry. The commission's report went decidedly against Japan—a fact which gave a rising Japanese diplomat named Yosuke Matsuoka the opportunity to lead his nation's delegation out of the League, pleading on Tokyo's behalf that no one understood Japan's real aims or her genuine desire for peace. How often was that refrain to be repeated in the future! And always under circumstances in which it appeared, especially to the British and Americans, that Japan's intentions were perhaps understood all too well.

The League ballot on the report condemning Japan was 42 to 1, with Japan voting in support of herself against the condemnation. By coincidence or design, the very next day after this vote was taken the Kwantung army invaded Jehol province. By this further act of aggression, Japan's legions were brought to the Great Wall of China, where they took possession of all of the strategic gateways providing access to the south. The imperial army thereby secured a springboard from which it could at any moment launch the government in Tokyo, and the Japanese nation it supposedly represented, into an unlimited war against China.[16] Despite these further hostile acts by the Japanese military, the world was being asked to understand Japan's true intentions and sincere motivations. "Sincerity" was a word which was to be used frequently

[14] Kido SKD. The chief of the military affairs bureau was Kuniaki Koiso. Kido states that, in addition to himself, Saionji, Makino, Konoe, and Harada were all concerned about the dangerous possibilities inherent in the Shanghai incident.

[15] P'u-yi, born in 1906, was proclaimed the Emperor Hsüan T'ung in 1908 at the age of two and was deposed in 1912. He was made Emperor of Manchukuo in 1934 under the title K'ang Te. The "Henry" was chosen from a list of English royalty given him by his tutor, Sir Reginald Johnston. The name was intended only for special use on rare occasions, but the "uncouth hybrid," Henry Pu Yi, became standard usage in the Western press (Johnston, *Twilight in the Forbidden City*, 231-32 and 439).

[16] On the League condemnation and the invasion of Jehol, see J, B/VI, 617-22; *Foreign Relations (Diplomatic Papers: 1933)*, III, 205-12 and *passim*; and *NYT*, February 25, 1933, 2.

as time passed, until in the end Japanese newspapers took to reporting that the fighting in China had to continue because the Chinese were refusing to show "sincerity." Ambassador Grew felt that he would hate that word foreverafter because it would always remind him "of the Japanese connotation of it: if I hit you and you hit back, you are obviously insincere."[17]

From the Manchurian crisis onward, Japanese propaganda hammered at the theme that Japan had acted in self-defense and that Manchukuo, far from being a creature of Japan, was the product of a spontaneous and bona fide popular movement in behalf of "independence." Years later, after the Lytton Commission's verdict to the contrary was fully substantiated by testimony presented during the Tokyo trial, the view was still current among Japanese that they had been unjustly censured by the world at the time of the Incident. One army officer turned historian suggested that China, instead of appealing to the League, should have negotiated directly with Japan. As he saw it, the League's "intervention" had further complicated the matter and had made an early settlement extremely difficult. Japan had thought, he said, that the League's commission of inquiry would learn the facts of the case and thus would be able to contribute toward a just solution, but instead the commission had produced a report that was fundamentally antagonistic toward Japan.[18]

It was not until long after 1931 that the full history of the Manchurian Incident came to light. Yet at the time in question, when the event briefly monopolized world attention, Ogden Nash, an American commentator thousands of miles from the scene, scornfully described what was happening in Manchuria in words which proved all too prophetic:[19]

> How courteous is the Japanese;
> He always says, "Excuse it, please."
> He climbs into his neighbor's garden,
> And smiles, and says, "I beg your pardon";
> He bows and grins a friendly grin,
> And calls his hungry family in;
> He grins, and bows a friendly bow;
> "So sorry, this my garden now."

At the beginning of the turbulent decade in which Japan stood at the crossroads of her destiny, Hideki Tojo was still, comparatively speaking, unknown. His friends remember him as a promising officer

[17] Grew, *Turbulent Era*, II, 1205n. See also Redman, "Things I Have Learned in and from Japan," *Japan Society Forum*, Vol. VI, No. 5 (June 15, 1959), *passim*.

[18] See Hattori, I, 30-31.

[19] "The Japanese," by Ogden Nash in *The Face Is Familiar*, 233-34, and Nash corresp.

who was austere when circumstances demanded it, yet basically considerate—especially in dealing with Japanese troops.[20] Like most other officers he seems to have thought of himself as the father of his men and as the elder brother of his junior colleagues.

From the fall of 1925, after a tour of duty as a military science instructor at the war college, until the spring of 1928, Tojo had served with the army affairs section of the military affairs bureau of the war ministry and then, for about a year, as chief of the mobilization section of the bureau of supplies and equipment of the same ministry. In this latter capacity, he had conducted a thoroughgoing investigation with respect to Japan's ability to carry out a general mobilization. He had then become the commander of the 1st Infantry Regiment in Tokyo, a post in which he had remained until March 1931. The name *kamisori Tōjō* dated from this period, because those who came in touch with him found his mind as sharp-edged as a razor. When subordinates made stupid or inept remarks, Tojo was brusque in his retort, but he also revealed on other occasions that he had the interests of the men under him at heart. He placed great importance on military discipline, yet believed that an officer should share the hardships of the troops.

One test of a good officer, especially of a good regimental commander, was the extent to which he would exert himself to help his soldiers find employment in civilian life upon completion of their required service with the regiment. Tojo met this test at times went so far in his efforts as to put a strain on his own limited resources. The assistance he rendered to former subordinates forced his wife to economize to make ends meet and caused her to say, in later years, that her house had always been on a "war footing."[21]

Tojo's assignments—certainly the more important ones—were mostly of an administrative nature. He was, by all accounts, a good executive officer. He got things done and the work ran smoothly. The light in his office burned late. If he left in the early evening, he often took papers with him—looking, some said, like a schoolboy carrying his load of homework. It was not long before his superiors were noting his accomplishments with recommendations for promotion and with assignments of greater responsibility.

A little more than a month before the Kwantung army's "punitive

---

[20] Shunichirō Itō, 49-53 and 57-60, gives a hero-worshiping account of Tōjō's service with the troops. This should not be taken too seriously but it does seem correct in its general implications.

[21] On Tōjō's career from about 1925 to 1931, see Tōjō interrog., Jan. 14, 2-3; cabinet secretariat personnel file for Hideki Tōjō, CF 20, II, 77; and Shunichirō Itō, 56-60.

burst" in Manchuria,[22] Tojo was assigned to the general staff in Tokyo in what appears to have been a major shift in personnel. He was not associated with the inner group or with the "Cherry Society," nor was he in any other way connected with the plot that was already secretly taking shape. Tojo's new post, in fact, was a nonsensitive one—important, but not of great influence. He was thus out of sight of the intrigue in Manchuria, though well within sound of its repercussions in Japan.[23]

Tojo's thoughts on the matter, then and later, were by no means unusual. He followed what might be called the army's party line: Japan had no territorial ambitions in Asia. She neither needed nor wanted more land, but she was concerned about food, oil, and other raw materials essential to her livelihood. Japan had "copper and lead, but not enough . . . food and coal, but not enough." Her population was increasing at the rate of about one million per year; the only way to deal with the problems posed by the increase was either through emigration (but the once-open areas were all fenced in by immigration barriers) or through raising more food at home and producing goods which could be sold abroad for rice and other foodstuffs (but the markets for Japan's products were being closed by the protective tariffs of the other powers). Japanese rights in Manchuria, acquired "at great sacrifice" during the Russo-Japanese war, were being violated; Japanese and Koreans were being molested. "The Japanese both in Manchuria and Japan were very annoyed and angry about it." The attitude throughout the army was that the situation in Manchuria was "very unsatisfactory"—in fact, "intolerable"—and that the economic and political policies of the Japanese government were not good. Tojo, who shared these feelings, reacted unfavorably—as did the rest of the nation—to the report made by the League's commission of inquiry. As he saw it, "The League point of view was unacceptable, so Japan got out of the League."[24]

It is perhaps not without significance that among the central observers of the scene at this time were a number of civil and military figures who were to hold important positions ten years later and whose destinies were thus to be tied to Hideki Tojo's star: Major Akira Muto, in the army general staff; Lt. Col. Teiichi Suzuki, at the military affairs bureau; Marquis Koichi Kido, chief secretary and aide to the lord keeper

[22] The phrase is typical of the euphemisms the army employed (JRD Monograph No. 144, 2).
[23] See p. 505 below.
[24] See Tōjō interrog., Jan. 14, 4-6, 8-15, and cross-examination, S 345:7, T 36550-52.

of the privy seal; Naoki Hoshino and Okinori Kaya, both in the finance ministry; and Shigenori Togo, at the League of Nations.[25]

It is perhaps equally interesting that some two years later, following Japan's angry withdrawal from the League because of its "antagonistic" attitude, Tojo briefly served as chief of the so-called military research bureau of the war ministry, an organization which had grown out of the army's bitter experience with Ugaki's elimination of four divisions in 1925. The bureau was concerned with combating the tendency of the times toward reductions in force and with studying problems relating to national defense and government—a role in which it functioned as one of the elements comprising the war minister's brain trust with respect to political problems. It was also charged with the dissemination of military thought. Having been defeated in the political arena with regard to armaments reduction, the army had decided a promotional organization was needed to provide better public relations in the future by apprising the people of the critical importance of the army to the state.[26]

Shortly after he assumed this post, Tojo—by then a major general—publicly went on record with respect to "the new situation in the Far East."[27] Although he was speaking for the army, there seems little doubt that he personally supported the views he was expressing and that they shaped his future thoughts and actions. The burden of what he had to say amounted to a refrain which had been heard practically from the moment of Japan's emergence from the feudal past into the modern world: Japan was living in a hostile environment surrounded by neighbors who would destroy her if they could. Japan must therefore look to her security and take whatever action opportunity permitted in order to defend the nation.

Despite favorable developments in Manchuria, Tojo warned that Japan's situation would become more critical with the passage of time, with a climax being reached within two or three years. Under certain circumstances an appeal to force might even be necessary to safeguard the national security. The fact that Japan would soon be confronted by a great crisis was being used by other countries to their advantage. Fore-

---

[25] See IMTFE, Doc. No. 0001, 3-4, for a complete list.

[26] Tōjō interrog., Jan. 14, 3; Shunichirō Itō, 61-63; Hattori corresp.; and Yano intv. The *gunji chōsabu* was divided into a *chōsahan*, the parent-body of the later *gunmuka*, and a *shinbunhan*, which was eventually transformed into the war ministry's *hōdōbu*.

[27] See *Tōjō*, "Kyokutō no Shin-jōsei ni Tsuite," in *Gaikō Jihō*, December 15, 1933, 68-78. (The issue in question, which also bears the title, *Revue Diplomatique*, No. 697, is incorrectly dated December 1, 1933.)

most among these, Tojo declared, were China, the Soviet Union, and the United States. China expected to complete its new national defense structure by 1935; the Soviet Union was steadily moving forward with its second five-year plan; the United States was bent upon implanting its influence on the Asian continent.

Thus, as early as 1933, Tojo was already claiming the existence of an international conspiracy against Japan—a charge which was to develop into the ABCD encirclement phobia of 1940-1941. If Tojo's argument is measured against the background of events, however, one must conclude that China's defense efforts at that time constituted nothing more than a belated response to Japanese aggression in Manchuria and a precautionary countermeasure against possible future Japanese aggression in other parts of China. The Soviet five-year plans were not designed primarily to threaten Japan but to provide security against conceivably hostile neighbors including Japan. Rather than working to implant her influence in China, the United States was trying desperately to hold her own against Japanese encroachments upon American rights and interests.

Even if Japan is given the benefit of some doubt on each point, one still cannot ignore the causative effect of her activities during World War I, her occupation of northern Sakhalin and Siberia in the period 1918 to 1925, and her actions in Manchuria from 1931 on. In view of her own record, Japan would have had little reason for complaint even if all that Tojo was saying in 1933 had been true.

Tojo nevertheless set out to support his argument with what he would have called "the facts." He cited innumerable details to underscore the recurring theme that the Empire was being confronted in every quarter by dangers not sufficiently appreciated by the people of Japan. So vividly did he portray the Soviet threat that one might have thought a concentration of Japanese energies to meet that single challenge would be required. The Japanese army, however, was not thinking in terms of appeasing either China or the United States in order to secure greater freedom of action against the Soviet Union. If the latter was in the front rank of Japan's enemies, China and the United States were close behind.

Japan had to decide, Tojo said, whether she would ascend the road to a vast development in the future or be bottled up within her narrow islands. There was only one way for the Japanese people to overcome the difficulties besetting them and that was to rely solely upon themselves. Each and every Japanese must be conscious of the traditions and of the mission of the great Yamato people. A united country and the perfection of Japan's national defense were basic. To break through the pressing international political situation, Japan must also employ diplomatic maneuvers, *but history clearly showed that diplomacy, unless backed by force, would produce no effect whatsoever.*

Such were the views of Major General Hideki Tojo some months after Japan's withdrawal from the League of Nations. They seemed to suggest, as had recent events as well, that in its thinking the Japanese army was never very far from resorting to force to get its way.

To date, the object of the army's direct action had been Manchuria and North China. Just how large the target area might eventually become was graphically illustrated in the summer of 1933 by a motion picture based on a speech made by the then war minister, General Sadao Araki. On the sound track were these words: "Can we expect the waves of the Pacific of tomorrow to be as calm as they are today? It is the holy mission of Japan to establish peace in the Orient. . . . The League of Nations does not respect this mission. . . . The siege of Japan by the whole world under the leadership of the League was revealed by the 'Manchurian Incident.' The day will come when we will make the whole world look up to our national virtues."

The screen at this point portrayed Japan and Manchukuo in the center of a "new order," with China, India, Siberia, and the South Seas forming the outer edges. "Compatriots!" the sound track continued, "let us look at the situation in Asia. Is it to be left unamended forever? Our supreme mission is to make a paradise in Asia. I fervently beseech you to strive onwards united."

On the screen a legend appeared which read: "Light comes from the East!"[28]

Araki's frequent militant utterances, together with other army pronouncements of a similar nature, soon left little doubt that the Japanese people were being encouraged to believe in the gradual encirclement of Japan by a hostile coalition of powers which might pounce upon their victim at any moment. Japan was being besieged by the rest of the world under the leadership of the League of Nations! The duty of each and every Japanese was to rise to the Empire's defense, to break the ring before it closed. Japan's holy mission beckoned: defend the imperial way and build a paradise in Asia!

[28] See J, B/IV, 104-5, and J, B/V, 622-23.

This was the mind of the Japanese army—the nature of the mentality with which moderates in the cabinet and the foreign office would have to deal if they were to provide the only leadership which could preserve Japan from military dictatorship at home and unending embroilment in foreign adventures. One army-line diplomat struck at the heart of the matter in a private letter in which he spoke, with disparaging intent and revealing candor, of those of his colleagues who advocated a policy of conciliation in international affairs. "Have they enough courage," he asked, "to return Manchuria to China, to get reinstated in the League of Nations, and to apologize to the world for the crime?"[29]

History has since answered that question, but at the time it was posed a negative response was not necessarily a foregone conclusion. Despite that fact, the seeds of a new conflict that would be more terrible than any before, of wider scope and of greater intensity, had already been sown.

[29] Toshio Shiratori, in a private letter dated November 1935, as quoted in J, B/V, 620.

CHAPTER 3

Fires of Radicalism

In the early morning of November 14, 1930, some ten months before the outbreak of the Manchurian Incident, Premier Osachi Hamaguchi was walking along the platform of the Tokyo Railway Station when he was suddenly felled by a bullet fired by a young man named Sagoya. Violence had long been a feature of the conduct of government in Japan, but the adoption of democratic and parliamentary procedures in recent years had held some promise that assassinations perpetrated to influence decision-making might give way to more orderly processes.[1] The shooting of Hamaguchi, who was to have joined the Emperor in southern Japan for the army's annual grand maneuvers, served as a reminder that the hand of the past still lay heavily on the present.

The attack was motivated by Hamaguchi's vigorous defense of Japan's acceptance of the inferior ratio in cruisers and other categories established at the London Naval Disarmament Conference. This had produced the very serious charge that the premier was interfering with the prerogatives of the supreme command—with the exclusive right of the general staff to advise the throne on national defense without any reference whatsoever to the wishes of the cabinet.[2] The opposition which developed within Japanese naval and ultranationalistic circles was widespread and rabid. Sagoya, who was a member of a reactionary organization of superpatriots, was chagrined that Japan should be ranked an ignominious third among the naval powers. Emotion suggested that the United States and Britain had formed a conspiratorial majority of two, bestowing parity on each other while at the same time joining forces to push Japan's head under water every time it appeared above the surface. Hamaguchi was not only the "evil genius" behind Japan's acquiescence but also a persistent advocate of further reductions in military expendi-

[1] For more on the role of violence in Japanese politics, see, for instance, Ike, Ch. 13 and p. 284, and Young, *Imperial Japan*, 117-18 and p. 306n.

[2] This attitude concerning cabinet interference with supreme command prerogatives was expressed not only in naval circles but also by the privy council, which was strongly opposed to the treaty (J, B/V, 536). Kido notes that within one section of the navy the charge was made that the lord keeper of the privy seal was similarly interfering (Kido SKD). For more details (especially on the role played by the chief of the naval general staff), see Maxon, 75-78.

tures. He thus became the natural target once Sagoya decided to register his opposition by direct action.

On the morning in question, Sagoya mingled with the crowd on the railway platform. Emerging suddenly as the premier approached, he fired a single shot from a distance of about six feet. Hamaguchi clapped his hand to the wound and dropped to the ground without uttering a sound. Sagoya was immediately hauled off to jail. The premier was taken to the stationmaster's office and given a blood transfusion which was later credited with saving his life virtually at the point of death. Those who were present, however, heard Hamaguchi murmur: "The bullet is in my abdomen. I cannot live." This prediction proved correct. After continuing in uncertain health for many months, Hamaguchi at length succumbed, in late August 1931, to the effects of the assassin's bullet.[3]

The shooting of Hamaguchi in November 1930 was the beginning of a long fuse which soon touched off further explosions of violence within the Japanese homeland, inaugurating what has been called the period of "brainless patriotism."[4] One assassination followed another in a seemingly unending reign of terror. In part, these acts of murder—perpetrated by civilian ultranationalists and army and navy extremists—originated in the social unrest that had marked the decade following World War I. The appeal made by alien ideas and concepts, especially those of Karl Marx, had reached both the universities and the military services. Within the army, in particular, a strong urge toward radical reform had soon become apparent. By 1930 a group of younger officers had begun to advocate political control over affairs of state and the establishment of a new national economy deriving support from the unpropertied classes. The members of this embryonic "control faction" came to the conclusion that a prerequisite for the absorption of Manchuria would be a favorably disposed cabinet in Tokyo. When the attempt on Hama-

[3] On the assassination of Hamaguchi: S 18:7, T 1323 (Shidehara); J, B/IV, 89 and B/V, 535-36; *NYT*, November 14, 1930, 1-2, and November 18, 1930, 8; and Young, *Imperial Japan*, 59-60. Also, an interview with a person who wishes to remain unidentified. Sagoya was sentenced to prison for attempted assassination. In 1956, his name suddenly reappeared in the national press in connection with Japan's then prime minister, Ichirō Hatoyama. As the leader of a new patriotic organization called the "National Defense Corps," Sagoya staged a mock funeral service for Hatoyama at Tōkyō's Shinbashi station. The purpose was to dramatize the Corps' opposition to the way in which the "traitor" Hatoyama proposed to conclude peace with the Russians. See *Japan Times* for September 25, 1956, 1 ("Dietmen Get Invitations to Hatoyama's 'Funeral'") and 8 ("Real or False Alarm?" by Kiyoaki Murata).

[4] Young, *Imperial Japan*, 59. For detailed accounts, see Byas, *Government by Assassination*, and Storry, *The Double Patriots*.

guchi's life did not produce an immediate cabinet resignation, the more impatient of the group established a working-partnership with Dr. Okawa and the equally ubiquitous Colonel Hashimoto of the Cherry Society. Together, they laid plans for a *coup d'état* to take place on March 20, 1931. The scheme called for the staging of a demonstration directed against the political parties and the imperial Diet. The army would bide its time until the inevitable clash with the police provided an opportunity to intervene, to declare martial law, to dissolve the Diet, and to assume control of the government by having War Minister Ugaki declared premier.[5]

The chief of the military affairs bureau, the vice-chief of the army general staff, the chief of the intelligence bureau of the general staff, and other officers called on the war minister to apprise him of their plans and to sound out his intentions.[6] Precisely what was said has never been determined, but the war minister's callers went away feeling that they had won him to their side. Colonel Hashimoto subsequently delivered to Dr. Okawa some three hundred "practice bombs" which were to be used during the planned demonstration to turn natural alarm and confusion into a genuine riot. The bombs were "supposed to give forth as much noise as four artillery guns fired simultaneously and to raise smoke to a height of about seven feet."[7] The idea was to create an effect conducive to success without spilling too much blood—a somewhat unusual feature for such a plot. But as the day approached, so did certain misgivings, and in the end fate intervened in the form of an enthusiastic letter from Okawa to the war minister. It is said by some that only then did Ugaki comprehend the true intentions of the plotters and the nature of the role he himself was expected to play. Others imply that Ugaki was never in doubt, but that at the last minute he lost the heart to carry the matter through.[8] As a result, the plot born

[5] On the *Sangatsu jiken*, see J, B/IV, 89-91, B/V, 536-38; "The Brocade Banner," 28-32, 36-37; IMTFE, "Analysis," Doc. No. 12; CF 20, I, 55; and Ohmae corresp. Dull, 461, notes that Colonel Kōmoto was also involved in the March plot.

Although there was still some feeling against Ugaki because of his elimination of four divisions, he was apparently chosen because the younger officers felt he was the best man available to head a military government.

[6] The chief of the military affairs bureau was Kuniaki Koiso (the same officer to whom a high-level appeal was made in 1932 with reference to the hostilities at Shanghai); the vice-chief of staff was Harushige Ninomiya; the chief of the intelligence bureau was Yoshitsugu Tatekawa (the officer who spent the evening of September 18 with the geisha of Mukden). Tetsuzan Nagata, although an initiator of the purification movement, seems not to have been an active participant in the March plot.

[7] "The Brocade Banner," 30-31.

[8] Within the ruling elite, men frequently spoke to each other with such circum-

in darkness was buried in darkness:[9] the intrigue was suppressed behind the scenes before it ever saw the light of day. Ugaki personally ordered Hashimoto and the chief of the military affairs bureau, who had supplied the bombs, to take all measures necessary to prevent any outbreak.

The fact that such a *coup d'état* had even been planned, however, caused great excitement among well-informed circles. Years later, the Emperor's closest wartime adviser referred to this March fiasco as the initial step in the direction of internal reform by the "driving-force" of the army.[10] The affair was also important in that it constituted the first conspicuous appearance of that factor of insubordination—of domination of superiors by inferiors—which was to plague Japan increasingly and eventually lead her to the miserable circumstances of later years.[11]

The seeming reversal which was dealt to the forces of change by the abandonment of the March plot in no way dampened the spirits of the more aggressive exponents of reformation at home and expansion abroad. Even the sudden spurt of activity in Manchuria in September failed to satisfy Colonel Hashimoto's appetite for intrigue. Having been deserted by Ugaki and other ranking officers, Hashimoto and the Cherry Society now pinned their hopes on the possibility of installing the up-and-coming General Araki as Japan's next premier. Once again the scheming centered among officers in the army general staff. This time the plans called for something more than the "soap-bubbles" of the spring: a thorough purging of the ideological and political atmosphere through the wholesale assassination of the ministers of the cabinet.[12] The deed was to be done while the ministers were gathered together at the premier's official residence. The war ministry and general staff headquarters would be surrounded and all officers not cooperating would be arrested. The naval hero of the Russo-Japanese war, the aging Admiral Togo, would be "prevailed upon" to obtain an audience with the

---

spection that they failed to make themselves understood. The example of the Kwantung army staff officer who refused to issue an order for the occupation of Manchuria apparently because he failed to comprehend the true intentions of the men who demanded it has already been noted. Other examples will be cited, from time to time, in the text. See Butow, *Japan's Decision to Surrender*, 70-72 (and as indexed under *Haragei*), and Ike, 266-67.

[9] An adaptation of Kido's postwar phrase: ". . . Yami kara yami ni hōmurarete. . . ." Kido SKD.

[10] Kido SKD.

[11] *Ibid.* The phrase, in Japanese, for such insubordination is *gekokujō*.

[12] On the *kinki kakumei jiken* of October 1931, which is described below, see "The Brocade Banner," 33-36; CF 20, I, 55; and J, B/IV, 94-95 and B/V, 567-68.

Emperor to plead for a military cabinet headed by Araki.[13] Thus was the political party system to be destroyed and a new military government inaugurated that would bestow its blessings upon the "solution" of the "Manchurian Problem" undertaken by the Kwantung army.

In this new government Colonel Hashimoto would be named home minister (the better to conduct internal purges and reformations) while Dr. Okawa would be posted as finance minister (in order to cut the Gordian knot on military expenditures and thus make the Japanese army the master of Asia). The leader of the assassination gang, after cleansing himself of the blood of his victims, would don the white gloves of the chief of the metropolitan police. The Emperor would then be escorted to a warship anchored in Tokyo Bay. This was ostensibly to guarantee His Majesty's safety but was actually to place him entirely at the mercy of the gang. The chief assassin is said to have declared that the plan must succeed even if it meant threatening the Emperor with a drawn dagger. "Yet the revolt was [supposedly] planned on behalf of and in the name of the Emperor, from whose councils it was proposed to remove all traitors who had violated the Imperial Prerogative!"[14]

This so-called October incident proved as ill-starred as its March predecessor. Once again high-ranking officers in the war ministry and the general staff, upon learning of the plot, decided to prevent its occurrence. On October 17, one week before the scheduled bloodletting, the military police arrested the ringleaders. Despite the evidence against them, some of which was allegedly sold to the authorities by Dr. Okawa, not a single conspirator was punished. The military officers involved were simply given new assignments.[15] Although the plot was reported to the cabinet ministers who were to have been its victims, they permitted the matter to be wrapped in the folds of state secrecy. The war ministry thereafter assumed a censorship function which eventually developed such scope that the few editors who continued to resist found themselves more and more frequently being investigated by the police.

In addition to such obvious repressive measures, the army resorted to more subtle methods. Shortly after the failure of the October incident, a

[13] An appeal to the throne to sanction the *fait accompli* was also planned at the time of the March incident. As "The Brocade Banner" points out (page 29n.) this kind of thing was "pure eyewash to simulate normal procedure."

[14] "The Brocade Banner," 34.

[15] One general later admitted that charges should have been lodged against the officers involved, but explained that this was not done because of the "motives and state of mind of the conspirators" and because such legal action would have hurt the prestige of the army (Maxon, 86, citing a quotation attributed to Tetsuzan Nagata in Kido "Nikki" for March 9, 1932).

whispering campaign "warned" the central authorities in Tokyo that unless they rallied behind what was taking place in Manchuria, the Kwantung army might find it necessary to declare its "independence" and proceed on its own responsibility. As past events had already indicated and as future developments were still further to confirm, rumors could sometimes be as effective as facts in their influence upon decision-makers.

Both the March and October incidents had had an internal reformation and a "solution" of the Manchurian Problem as their ultimate goals. The effect of the two plots was to widen the cleavage already present in the ultranationalistic camp and to sharpen competition within the army between the control faction and a rival clique called the "imperial way."[16] After 1931 the control group became increasingly powerful and never again felt the need to engage in subversion. But this accommodation to the wiser course of penetration from within contained a threat to the power and influence of the aggressive advocates of the imperial way. The latter were thus encouraged to resort to activities which grew more shocking with each further attempt on their part to capture for themselves the power being garnered by their rivals. Although the ultimate aims of the two cliques seem largely to have been the same insofar as control of the state was concerned, their methods after 1931 proved essentially different. Their continental views, as distinct from their ideas about internal reform, were also at variance. Whereas the control faction generally looked to China and the South, the imperial-way clique turned its attention primarily to Russia and the North. Hideki Tojo was eventually to become the nominal leader of the control group, but at the time in question and even much later he regarded the Soviet Union as the power most menacing to Japan. This fact, as well as his own hostile response to the now impending actions of the imperial-way clique, helps to explain the development of his career in a direction which led finally to his elevation to the highest political office in the land.

Although it was not until the latter half of the 1930's that Tojo's career began picking up the momentum that carried him to the premiership, the chain of cause and effect links the occurrences of the early years of the decade to Tojo's later life in a way that is important

---

[16] On the nature of the two factions and the rivalry between them: CF 20, I, 55; "The Brocade Banner," 36-37; Takahiko Kido intv. and Ōi corresp. See also Yanaga, 510-11; Lory, 173-81; Storry, *The Double Patriots*, 135-43, 153-91; and Colegrove, *Militarism in Japan*, 55.

to an understanding of the man and his role in history. Incidents of violence now followed each other in confusing succession. What is perhaps most instructive about these incidents is not the fascinating detail of preparation and execution, but the psychology that prompted them and the manner in which they were viewed by both the Japanese public and the ruling elite.

Toward the end of 1931 the revolutionary fervor which had found expression in the March and October incidents began bubbling to the surface once again. The new activity centered around an ultranationalist named Nissho, who had returned to the capital from a retreat in the country to organize a "blood brotherhood"—a group of direct-actionists composed of students and the sons of farmers and fishermen.[17] Shortly after the new year began, the "brothers" decided to assassinate a number of political and financial leaders who they thought were exercising an evil influence on Japan. The date chosen was a historical one, February 11, the 2,592nd anniversary of the accession of Jinmu, credited in Japan as the first Emperor but regarded in the West as probably a latter-day personification of several early chieftains about whom little is known. Eleven distinguished persons were selected for elimination, but the list was kept flexible to provide for last-minute substitutions. Included were such leading figures as the managing director and the president of the Mitsui Bank, Ltd.; the last of the elder statesmen of the Meiji period; the premier, foreign minister, and finance minister of the preceding cabinet, as well as the premier of the current cabinet; the speaker of the House of Peers; the lord keeper of the privy seal; and a privy councillor with a record of long service to the state.[18] Each of the conspirators was assigned a specific individual as his personal target. When the available weapons were exhausted, one "brother" was told to obtain a pistol wherever he could and then to entrain for the south to perpetrate murder and terror in that region. He was supplied with a list of nine prominent figures from which he could choose at random as the opportunity to shoot presented itself.

[17] On the *ketsumei-dan* affair and the role of Akira Inoue (Nisshō), see "The Brocade Banner," 16-17, 40-43, 142, and 144, which contains many additional details from unimpeachable sources, and Young, *Imperial Japan*, 118-20.

[18] Seihin Ikeda and Baron Takuma Dan, managing director and president, respectively, of the Mitsui Bank, Ltd.; Prince Kinmochi Saionji, the last of the *genrō*; Baron Reijirō Wakatsuki, Baron Kijūrō Shidehara, and Junnosuke Inoue—premier, foreign minister, and finance minister, respectively, of the cabinet which had resigned on December 12, 1931; Tsuyoshi Inukai, Wakatsuki's successor as premier; Prince Iesato Tokugawa, speaker of the House of Peers; Count Nobuaki Makino, lord keeper of the privy seal; Count Miyoji Itō, privy councillor; and any one of nine designated figures (primarily from the *zaibatsu*) who might present a good target.

Unlike the plots of the previous March and October, this one was not nipped in the bud. Early in February 1932 one of the executioners was handed his pistol and ration of ammunition. He went briefly to a deserted beach in the country for target practice and then returned to the capital to fulfill his mission. On February 7, four days prior to the date originally chosen, he pumped three bullets into former Finance Minister Junnosuke Inoue, as the victim stepped from his car in front of an elementary school where he was to make a political speech. The assassin was apprehended on the spot; Inoue died within twenty minutes. Japan was thus deprived of another of the forthright figures of the Hamaguchi line who had earned considerable enmity in various quarters for his tendency to badger the army on budget matters.

Almost a month later, this same method of operation was repeated. The target this time was Baron Takuma Dan, an imposing man of great wealth who was a powerful figure in the Mitsui enterprises, a combine which had many enemies. As Dan alighted from his automobile in downtown Tokyo in the late morning of March 5, a gun was shoved in his back and fired. He died instantly, and his murderer, like the assassin of Inoue, was taken into custody at the scene of the crime. These two assassinations, within less than a month, led eventually to the arrest of the entire blood brotherhood and to the implication of none other than Dr. Okawa, who had obtained arms and ammunition for the group from friends in the navy.

Before any substantial progress could be made in the legal disposition of the case, the volcano of violence erupted once again. This time a more elite company composed of young naval officers, civilian ultranationalists, and army cadets were the source of the trouble. The day chosen—May 15, 1932—was a Sunday. The chief target and principal victim was Japan's 75-year-old premier, Tsuyoshi Inukai, known to some as a "God of the Constitution," but to others as a robot who functioned as directed by the militarists.[19] His relations with the army had worsened considerably after the discovery that he had sent a secret emissary to Generalissimo Chiang Kai-shek to explore the possibilities of a peaceful solution of the Manchurian Incident. Although Inukai's cabinet had subsequently bowed to the military *fait accompli* in Manchuria, the premier had been warned on several occasions that his life might be in danger. On the Sunday in question he was suddenly confronted, while inadequately guarded, by the members of the gang sent to kill him. He tried to talk

[19] On the role and personality of Inukai, see Young, *Imperial Japan*, 116-18, 120; J, B/IV, 96-99; and J, B/V, 578, 594-95, 606-7.

the men into a calmer mood, but they shot him down. The murder, which occurred in the late afternoon at the premier's official residence, was immediately followed by bomb-throwing attacks against the Bank of Japan, the residence of the lord keeper of the privy seal, the head-quarters of one of the two major political parties, the Mitsubishi Bank, a number of power stations throughout the city, and the metropolitan police headquarters. In the course of these crimes, the gang succeeded in killing one policeman, injuring another, and severely wounding a rival ultranationalist who had refused to participate in their conspiracy. Although he had not been in any of the raiding parties, Dr. Okawa had played a prominent role in helping those who had taken an active part.[20]

The trial of the blood brotherhood for the earlier murders of Inoue and Dan, which was by now in progress, soon became a *cause célèbre* throughout Japan. It was a fantastic affair, comparable to a revival meeting, complete with fanatical oratory and emotional pleadings.[21] Through it all ran heartfelt affirmations that the assassins had acted with a sincerity that merited exoneration by the court and deep understanding by the Japanese people. As the trial neared its end, tension mounted. Death sentences were expected, especially for the men who had done the actual killing. Their relatives even brought the family ancestral tablets to the courtroom the day judgment was passed, but three sentences of life imprisonment were the severest imposition and, after that, fifteen years at hard labor. In pronouncing sentence, the presiding judge enjoined the defendants to take care of their health while in prison. The evidence against Dr. Okawa was deemed insufficient and he was released.[22]

In the case of the "May 15" trials, the basic "sincerity" behind the deeds was again dinned into the public mind. In the end, the nation showed an enormous concern for the men on trial and practically none at all for those who had been their victims. The officials connected with the "May 15" trials received thousands upon thousands of petitions for clemency. Some letters were signed, or even written entirely, in blood, and the popular war minister, Araki, was the recipient of a grisly package of severed little-fingers from nine men who wished to

---

[20] On the *go-ichigo jiken*, see "The Brocade Banner," 43-46; J, B/IV, 98-99 and B/V, 606-7; IPS Doc. No. 59-B20-3; Young, *Imperial Japan*, 116-21; Maxon, 90-92; Maki, 214-16; and Byas, Ch. 1. The rival ultranationalist was Chikara Nishida.

[21] "The Brocade Banner," 43.

[22] *Ibid.*, 54. The fourteen sentences that were prescribed were all later reduced as a result of annual amnesties, with those subject to life imprisonment going free in 1940.

take the place of those who it was then feared might be put to death.[23]

Punishment was eventually meted out to forty defendants, the most severe being a single sentence of hard labor for life. Dr. Okawa, the "brains" of the incident, whose luck had finally run out, drew fifteen years. As time passed, all of the sentences were reduced by appeal or by amnesty.[24] Murder, when committed out of sincere motives, was apparently not murder at all, just as the taking of Manchuria had not been aggression because the motives of the Kwantung army had been pure.

Although the incidents of 1932 did not result in changes in the top army positions, the widening breach between the control group and the imperial-way faction became "openly abusive." "Acrimonious pamphlets emanated from all directions. . . . The mud-slinging was worthy of six-year-old boys."[25] In the months that followed, the hatching of one minor plot after another continued, resulting in further arrests and trials. Typical of this activity and of the response in the courts was the two-year suspension of a sentence of eighteen months at hard labor given to one of Okawa's friends, a medical doctor who had been caught in the act of plotting the murder of Premier Inukai's successor.[26]

Among the assassins of this period were some who hunted their quarry, not with pistols, but with allegations based on innuendo, insinuation, and quotation out of context—in short, "fundamentalist scholars who seemed suddenly to have awakened to the necessity of purging the country of free thought, who in frenzied words and maniacal phrases, in snatches of sentences from the writings of their enemies, proceeded to make violent attacks on men of liberal reputation."[27] One of the most notorious of these was an instructor at a school specializing in judo and Japanese fencing who took it upon himself to accuse several Imperial University professors of ranking the throne below the constitution. In the fall of 1932 this self-appointed crusader began campaigning against what he called "the red judges and the scarlet professors." This resulted, the following spring, in an effort to oust a Kyoto University professor who advocated the theory of constitutional monarchy that so enraged the fanatics. The movement against this professor had not only the full backing of the education minister but also the apparent approval of the

[23] *Ibid.*, 47. Brown, *Nationalism in Japan*, 193, also mentions the package received by Araki.

[24] On the "May 15" sentences and Ōkawa's role, see "The Brocade Banner," 38-39, 47-48, 55-56, and CF 20, II, 82.

[25] "The Brocade Banner," 48.

[26] See *ibid.*, 48-49.

[27] *Ibid.*, 57.

whole cabinet. The courageous president of the university refused to bow to pressure which he regarded as at least improper, if not actually illegal. When the education minister ordered the professor's dismissal, the president and the entire law faculty of the university resigned in protest. Just where the minister stood in the matter had been publicly announced even before his order. In a revealing statement to a reporter he had declared, "Let all of the professors resign if that is how they feel. We do not mind closing the universities altogether."[28]

Concurrently with these developments, which also coincided with Matsuoka's exit· from the League, a new resort to violence was being planned for July 11, 1933. The name chosen by the conspirators was *shinpeitai*, "soldiers of the gods." What they had in mind is clear from their manifesto—almost a standard feature of all such activity:

1. The Soldiers of the Gods are ready with Celestial swords to accomplish the Restoration of Showa as their life mission for the glory of the Empire.

2. The Soldiers of the Gods denounce all institutions and activities which are based on liberalism and socialism, and aim to establish a government, an economic policy and a culture which shall be based upon the position of the Emperor.

3. The Soldiers of the Gods aim at the annihilation of the leaders of the financial groups, the leaders of the political parties, the villains of the Imperial Entourage and their watchdogs who are obstructing the progress of the Empire. They shall thereby establish the Imperial Restoration and proclaim the Imperial Rule throughout the world.

In addition to the celestial swords mentioned in the manifesto, the *shinpeitai* arranged to have on hand such down-to-earth weapons as firearms and bombs. They were also equipped with a quantity of white cotton cloth (for head, arm, and belly bands) and a number of seven-foot streamers with such legends as "Establishment of Government by the Emperor!"; "Imperial Restoration, Banzai!"; "Extermination of the Communists!"; "Annihilation of Politicians and Plutocrats!"; and "Perfection of the National Defense!"[29]

At the last moment, however, the gods apparently deserted their self-appointed instruments. At dawn on the day chosen for the revelation of

---

[28] See *ibid.*, 57-60, for additional particulars. The *jūdō* expert was Muneyoshi Minoda. The other principals were Professor Yukitoki Takigawa and President Shigenao Konishi of Kyōto Imperial University and Education Minister Ichirō Hatoyama.

[29] *Ibid.*, 49-53. Samurai used head bands (*hachimaki*) to keep perspiration out of their eyes during combat. In recent years, similar bands have been worn at sports events, in sword practice, and during labor union strikes. Belly bands have been used at times to keep the mind composed; as the seat of the emotions, the "mind" is said to rest in the region of the stomach.

the divine will, the police sprang a trap which they had readied for the occasion. Had this police action not taken place, the premier's residence, which attracted conspirators like a magnet draws iron, would once again have been attacked. The plan called for bombing from the air, to be followed by an on-the-spot assault. Any cabinet ministers found on the premises would have been killed and the building burned to the ground. The headquarters of the two major political parties were also to have been attacked and put to the torch. A nerve-center, to be established in the Industrial Bank of Japan, would have coordinated the activities of two assassination levies dispatched to murder various public figures, including a long-retired, eighty-one-year-old admiral who had served as premier in 1913 and again in 1923.[30] Martial law was to have been declared and an imperial rescript sought designating the formation of a new cabinet under an imperial prince. According to rumors current at the time, one army faction wanted to replace the Emperor with his brother, Prince Chichibu; the prince slated for the premiership was Higashikuni, an imperial relative whose name was to arise again just before General Tojo received the mandate in 1941 and once more, and successfully, at the time of Japan's surrender.

As in the case of the blood brotherhood and "May 15" incidents, the trial which resulted from the arrest of the *shinpeitai* dragged on for many months, exposing the people of Japan not to an exhibition of justice at work but to clever propaganda designed to mislead as many of them as possible. In spite of the most incriminating evidence, including confessions from members of the group, "the court condoned the conspiracy because of its 'patriotic' motive" and, in the end, dismissed the charges "because the plot had been discovered before any damage had been done."

Long before this travesty of justice was enacted to the full, other events and issues were crowding in upon the public consciousness. The question of the Emperor's relationship to the constitution and to the state was revived once again, with accusations emanating from various nationalistic societies. In this new movement designed to "clarify" the national polity, a leading Tokyo university professor named Tatsukichi Minobe, an advocate of the constitutional monarchy theory, was called upon to resign from the House of Peers and to commit

[30] The reference is to Admiral Count Gonnohyōe (Gonbei) Yamamoto, whose first cabinet resigned following the disclosure of a naval scandal and whose second bowed out after an attempt was made on the life of the crown prince.

suicide.[31] The furor among the nationalists reached such a high pitch that the government felt compelled to reaffirm publicly the divine origin of the Emperor and of the nation. And when the government tried to defend the president of the privy council and the director of the cabinet bureau of legislation, who were under attack for their alleged sympathy with the Minobe viewpoint, the imperial reservists' association passed a resolution strongly criticizing the government.[32] Over a three-month period in the fall of 1935, Professor Minobe was denounced to the public procurator on three separate occasions. In mid-October the government was finally forced, by the fury of the nationalists, into issuing a proclamation attacking as disrespectful any view which held that the Emperor was merely an organ of the state. Later that same month a 21-year-old youth, who had been disporting himself in one of Tokyo's licensed quarters, looked up Minobe's address in a telephone book and then set out for the professor's house with the object of killing him. Fortunately, the police intervened in time. but four months later Minobe was wounded by another zealot with murderous intent.

Although there were some individuals in Japan who deplored developments such as these, very few made any public protest. When force pushes on, reason proverbially draws back.[33] Since the imperial house was involved, defense of men like Minobe might make the defender liable to charges of *lèse-majesté*. If he were a man of any prominence, his name might also appear on the next assassination list.

In addition to the Minobe affair, the period which coincided with the trial of the "soldiers of the gods" was marked by arrests made in connection with five other murder plots in which the names of "privileged individuals" figured prominently as targets. Arrests were also made in a burglary and in a counterfeiting, both of which had been planned to procure funds for the nationalistic movement. Factional strife among the ultranationalists and within the imperial army also continued—with the role that Japan should play on the continent becoming a bone of contention. The imperial-way faction favored limiting Japan's activity to Manchuria (at least initially), presumably because it feared that any wider commitment might weaken Japan vis-à-vis the Soviet Union. This view was unpopular with those who believed that the maintenance of Japanese

---

[31] On the "clarification" movement of 1935 and related activities, see "The Brocade Banner," 59-64, 142, and 146.

[32] The privy council president was Kitokurō Ikki; the director of the cabinet bureau of legislation was Tokujirō Kanamori. The events described occurred during the Okada Cabinet.

[33] *Muri ga tōreba, dōri hikkomu.*

military activity abroad on a wider basis was essential to the welfare of the state. The rivalry of this period was such that one knowledgeable court official later likened the imperial army of the 1930's to an *o-mikoshi*, a portable Japanese shrine carried first in one direction and then another, sometimes with different groups of men alternately taking charge. The bearers of such shrines generally run in short bursts of energy, frequently stopping dead in their tracks. They jostle the shrine upward and downward and from side to side in a frenzy of movement, while they and the onlookers provide vigorous vocal accompaniment to the rhythmic beat of drums. Just where the shrine will go or how far it will travel at any given moment is usually impossible to predict.[34]

Although Araki had been succeeded as war minister by an officer who was regarded as neutral, the possibility of trouble continued to exist. In the forefront were two rival generals, Jinsaburo Mazaki of the imperial-way clique and Tetsuzan Nagata of the control faction. The former was serving as inspector-general of military training; the latter as chief of the military affairs bureau of the war ministry. Suddenly, in November 1934, a number of army officers and cadets were arrested for allegedly conspiring to assassinate men in high places. A secret court martial was held and the following spring an announcement was made to the effect that the case had been dropped.

Although it was not widely known at the time, this "November plot" was closely tied to the growing factional strife within the army. The dropping of the case represented a victory for Mazaki and the imperial-way group but, as the event turned out, a short-lived one. Within three months the supposedly neutral war minister asked for Mazaki's resignation as a step toward the unification of army policy. When Mazaki refused, the war minister obtained imperial sanction for the appointment of a successor. In relinquishing his post, Mazaki expressed his indignation to a number of younger officers who were advocates of the imperial-way faction. Two of them immediately wrote and distributed a pamphlet entitled "Some Opinions on Cleaning up the Army." A copy of this tract came into the hands of a lieutenant colonel named Aizawa on August 10, 1935. Two days later Aizawa burst into the office of General Nagata, brandishing a sword. Nagata rose from his chair and moved toward a military police colonel who had been delivering an oral report. Aizawa brought his sword down across Nagata's back. The general

[34] I have enlarged upon an analogy made by the late Yasumasa Matsudaira during an interview in Tōkyō.

turned toward an exit, but as he did so Aizawa plunged the sword "through his back and pinned him to the door." Nagata fell to the floor and Aizawa slashed him across the head. The police colonel, who had vainly tried to check the attack, received a wound in the left arm. The next day the war minister publicly announced that Lt. Col. Aizawa had murdered General Nagata in a fit of rage induced by false rumors.

That was by no means the whole truth. Aizawa had been connected with a prominent ultranationalist since 1929. He had been among those who frequented Mazaki's home. He had already received orders transferring him to Formosa, a punishment for having demanded an explanation of Mazaki's dismissal from the authorities. His choice of target indicated that he personally placed the blame on the chief of the military affairs bureau rather than on the war minister.

At his trial Aizawa revealed that "after stabbing His Excellency" he had gone to the office of the general whom Nagata had replaced as chief of the military affairs bureau. This officer bound up Aizawa's left wrist, which was bleeding badly, and asked what his intentions were. Aizawa replied that he had some shopping to do at the army club and that he would then leave for his post on Formosa![35]

The Aizawa incident introduced a new factor into the pattern of political assassination. Earlier victims had been highly placed civilians, not army officers on active duty at what was called "the center." Although the origin of the blood brotherhood, "May 15," and *shinpeitai* affairs could all be traced to the imperial-way faction or to outside groups in sympathy with it, these earlier incidents had primarily been expressions of a desire to renovate the state along extremist lines and hence had not necessarily been a direct or immediate threat to the rival faction. But the murder of Nagata was a different matter. The real issue in his death was control of the army and maintenance of military discipline. Unless that was settled once and for all, the army—divided against itself—would hardly be in a position to direct the nation's destiny.

In retrospect, it is easy to detect the danger signals of future trouble. Between December 1934 and Nagata's murder the following August the police bureau of the home ministry had found in circulation a considerable number of seditious pamphlets and other ephemeral pieces collectively classified as "reprehensible literature." The tract which had

[35] On the further development of factional strife, including the *Aizawa jiken*: "The Brocade Banner," 65-71; CF 20, I, 55; Ōi and Ohmae corresp.; J, B/IV, 113-14; Maxon, 101; and Yanaga, 511.

goaded Aizawa into action belonged to that category. Immediately following Nagata's death, such writings increased in number, with further inflammatory effect.[36] Nationalistic societies rushed to Aizawa's defense and the stage was set once again for an appeal to the nation based on the noble motives and pure intentions of the man on trial.

At the same time, the people began to manifest a distrust of extreme rightists, very few of whom were voted into office in the prefectural elections of 1935. This drift away from the ultranationalists and imperialists was also marked in the national Diet elections of February 20, 1936, a fact which alarmed the direct actionists. By that time, too, Aizawa's court martial had been in session several weeks, reaching a climax on February 25 with the testimony of General Mazaki. Excitement was thus at fever pitch when orders transferring the 1st Division from Tokyo to Manchukuo suddenly produced the most extraordinary episode of this entire period: a full-scale army mutiny.[37]

Included in the 1st Division, which had not seen overseas duty since 1905, were a large number of extremist younger officers of the imperial-way orientation who interpreted the new orders as an effort by the control group to eradicate their influence by sending them as far from the center as possible—"a thousand long miles beyond the sea." Gone now was the discipline of the Japanese army of earlier years, when even the reading material of a common soldier had been censored by his officers lest he become a prey to dangerous political ideas.[38] In place of the discipline of old was a determination to rise in defiance of authority so as to open the way for a Showa restoration which would permit the august virtues of His Majesty to shine forth in untrammeled brilliance.[39]

Here once again were the social revolutionary tenets of the 1920's, preached now by the younger officers to their men in terms which vacillated between communism and nationalism. Marked for elimination because of their alleged responsibility for the "miserable" condition

[36] For further details regarding the *kai-bunsho* and other signs of the time, including alignments within the various factions, see "The Brocade Banner," 37, 40, 64, and 69-72.

[37] On the *ni-niroku* mutiny, which is discussed below, see *ibid.*, Ch. 7, from which the details and quotations are taken unless otherwise specified; Tōjō interrog., Jan. 15, 1-3; Maki, 216-19; Ōi corresp.; IPS, Doc. No. 59-B20-3; J, B/IV, 114-17 and B/V, 666-67; and Kase, *Mizuri-gō e no Dōtei*, 62-65. Allowances must be made for quotations for which the original Japanese was unavailable.

[38] See Kennedy, *Some Aspects of Japan and Her Defence Forces*, 153 and 156. The breakdown of discipline in the Japanese homeland was naturally reflected in the actions of the Japanese army overseas. See, for instance, Grew, II, 1205.

[39] Jusshi Itō, 68, briefly notes a series of conversations he had, as early as 1932, with some of the men who later became leaders of the February 26 incident. He concluded then that they would go as far as revolution if they got the chance.

of the nation at home and abroad were such prominent "traitors" as the senior statesmen, top army and navy officers, the heads of the political parties, the leading financiers, and other members of the privileged classes. In a manifesto explaining their "Great Purpose," the leaders of the mutiny declared, "With due reverence, we consider that the basis of the divinity of our country lies in the fact that the nation is destined to expand under the Imperial Rule until it embraces all the world." Attributing "the majesty and superiority" of the Japanese nation to the establishment of the country by the Sun Goddess and the Emperor Jinmu, the ringleaders of the mutiny asserted that the time had come "to expand and develop in all directions." Recently, however, "self-seeking refractory men" had encroached upon the imperial prerogatives. The people of Japan, whose "true growth" was thus obstructed, had been driven to despair and the nation had been made "an object of contempt" in the eyes of the world.

"It is clearer than light that our country is on the verge of war with Russia, China, Britain and America, who wish to crush our ancestral land. Unless we now rise and annihilate the unrighteous and disloyal creatures who surround the Imperial Throne and obstruct the course of true reform, the Imperial Prestige will fall to the ground. . . . We are persuaded that it is our duty to remove the villains who surround the Throne.

"We, the children of our dear land of the gods, act with pure sincerity of heart.

"May the spirit of our Imperial Ancestors assist us in our endeavors."

Thus spoke the leaders of the insurrection on the eve of the event. To perpetrate murder and mutiny was to carry out their "ultimate duty" as "loyal subjects" of His Majesty. What hope could there be for a land and a leadership which had permitted such a definition of loyalty and duty to come into being and to flourish? What hope for a nation where, in regard to such essential ingredients of government as power and responsibility, the seeming reality was mere pretense, facts were fiction, and the sum of the parts was never equal to the whole?

Had the central authorities learned beforehand of the intended action of the younger officers of the 1st Division, they might have forestalled the conspiracy. But they were not informed. Once again, as in the case of the London disarmament treaty, the fanatics raised the issue of supreme-command prerogatives. It was in this light that they portrayed Mazaki's removal and on this basis of alleged violation of constitutionality that they prepared to "restore order" by resorting to violence. The wife of an ultranationalist (Ikki Kita) who belonged to an early "apostle" group which had included Okawa and Nissho served as the medium between the conspirators of this world and the divine voice of revelation coming from outer space. From the sanctum of her home, this "sibyl of the revolution" passed along the instructions she supposedly was receiving. In one trance she murmured, "Since your relationship to the Emperor is true and clear, the rest is trivial." And on another occasion: "Light shines in the Palace grounds. There is no dark cloud."

Although primarily an army plot, many like-minded civilians attached themselves to the conspiracy. An anticipated spontaneous uprising of troops throughout the country did not materialize, but the final and official count of those who participated actively at the center reached an impressive total of nearly fifteen hundred men, including twenty-four commissioned and ninety-one noncommissioned officers. Although the units involved were predominantly from the 1st Division, the 3rd Infantry Regiment of the Imperial Guards, which had its share of fanatics, also participated.

The "incident" began at 5:00 a.m. on February 26, 1936, with the dispatch of six select groups of men on missions of calculated importance. The first group seized the official residence of the war minister, where they presented a list of demands which called for the immediate arrest of the leaders of the control faction and the discharge of their associates, the naming of General Araki as commander of the Kwantung army "for the purpose of coercing Red Russia," and the distribution of key positions to members of the imperial-way party so that a reform government could be installed. To underscore their demands, this first group proceeded to occupy the war ministry and the offices of the army general staff.

The second group seized the metropolitan police headquarters, opposite the Sakurada gate of the imperial palace, and set up machine guns at key points.

The third group, composed of about two hundred men, descended upon the home of the Emperor's grand chamberlain, Admiral Baron Kantaro Suzuki, whom they shot down in his bedroom. The leader of the band knelt to feel the victim's pulse. He was about to inflict the *coup de grâce* with a dagger when the admiral's wife intervened. If a death stab were necessary, she said, she should be allowed to inflict it herself. The man stared at her for a second and then rushed from the room. The life of the critically wounded admiral was thus saved by the courage of a woman whose only weapon was the presence of mind to say exactly the right thing at exactly the right time. Nine years later, as Japan's last wartime premier, Suzuki helped bring to an end the madness of which this attack in 1936 was symptomatic.

The fourth group of about three hundred men invested Premier Okada's official residence, where they killed four policemen and Okada's brother-in-law, whom they mistook for the premier because his features resembled those in a photograph of their intended victim. Okada hid in a closet for two days and only managed to escape when he surreptitiously joined the mourners who had gathered to escort his remains from the house to the cemetery. In that way he was able to pass safely through a guard of rebels which still had the residence under surveillance.

The fifth group, containing over one hundred men, attacked the home of an outspoken proponent of the now otherwise defunct Hamaguchi line, Finance Minister Korekiyo Takahashi. The scene which followed was later vividly described by one of the three lieutenants who led the attack: "It was I who found my way to Takahashi's room. I pulled off the bedclothes and yelled, 'Tenchū!' (Punishment of Heaven!).[40] When Takahashi opened his eyes, I gave it to him three times with my revolver. At the same time Nakajima [another of the lieutenants] slashed him twice with his sword, once in the right arm and once in the belly. I think Takahashi died instantly."

The sixth group of two hundred men led by four lieutenants surrounded the home of the lord keeper of the privy seal and former premier, Admiral Viscount Makoto Saito. Here, too, a room of quiet slumber was converted in a matter of moments into a bloody bier. The admiral's wife courageously endeavored to protect her husband, but she was pushed away by the assassins, who began pumping bullets into the defenseless man. As he fell to the floor, Mrs. Saito threw herself on her husband's body. What ensued was described later in court by one of the principals: "Since we had no intention of injuring anyone but her husband, we had to shove her aside and thrust our weapons under her body. We fired again and again until we were sure that there was no more life left in the old man. When a soldier entered and asked that he be allowed to fire too, we let him have several shots. We wanted to cut Saito's throat to make sure of him, but we gave up the idea because the woman refused to leave the body. Afterward, we all gathered at the front gate and gave three 'Banzai' for the Emperor."

[40] This same phrase was employed by extremists during the Meiji Restoration period.

When the body of the lord keeper of the privy seal was later examined, *forty-seven* bullet wounds were found. Mrs. Saito, in her heroic effort to save her husband, had been shot in both arms and in her right shoulder.

Thus did the "children" of the land of the gods "act with pure sincerity of heart."

By sunrise on February 26 seven men lay dead and one other severely wounded. They had fallen in the first wave of the attack. The second wave began with the destruction of the facilities of a leading Tokyo newspaper and with further armed sorties against two more highly placed individuals. One was General Jotaro Watanabe, the officer who had succeeded Mazaki as inspector-general of military training and who only a month before had been the target of another and smaller group of would-be assassins.[41] The other was Count Nobuaki Makino, a former lord privy seal and a close adviser of the Emperor. The attack upon Watanabe followed the classic pattern: a quick descent upon the house, a rapid search of the premises, the pushing aside of the wife who sought to protect her husband, and then the execution, with the *coup de grâce* being administered this time by a sword applied to the general's throat. In the mountains south of Tokyo where Count Makino was staying, another band killed the ninth man, a police officer, and then set fire to the building in which the count had been sleeping but from which he had already made good his escape with the aid of his granddaughter.

In the aftermath of this blood bath, prolonged negotiations took place between the insurgents and the authorities. Instead of being vilified as traitors, the rebels were considerately described by the war ministry on the night of this terrible day as "a party which rose to uphold and clarify the national constitution." Two days later they were "timidly called 'rioters.' The term 'insurgent army' was not applied until 29 February, when the Emperor himself was rumored to have coined the phrase."

During all this time no really decisive action was taken by the authorities against the rebels. Their fortified positions were merely cordoned off by regular police, military police, and loyal troops. An order to disband was issued but had no effect. When the authorities finally suggested to the ringleaders that the only honorable way out was suicide and that, if they obliged, the enlisted men under them would not be punished, the officers showed some willingness to comply but wanted a guarantee that the Emperor would be advised of their deaths. The argument they offered was that "even airplane accidents are customarily reported to

[41] See "The Brocade Banner," 63-64.

the Throne." When this *pourparler* failed, the authorities decided to approach the enlisted men directly. Radio appeals, advertising balloons, and exhortatory handbills were all employed. The general in charge of the Tokyo defense district personally broadcast a message which said: "I speak to the soldiers. The Emperor himself has ordered you to return to your regiments. It is not yet too late. Cease your resistance and go home in order that your sins may be forgiven. Your fathers, your mothers and the whole nation are praying for you. Return! Return!"

The men responded to this campaign and slowly began drifting away. By two o'clock in the afternoon, only the officers remained. All subsequently surrendered except one army captain, who killed himself in the war ministry building, leaving behind a final statement which ended with these words:

Our Division has not been in action for more than thirty years since the Russo-Japanese War, while the officers and men of other divisions have shed their blood for the Emperor. In recent years the sins of the traitors at home have been redeemed by the blood of our comrades in Manchuria and Shanghai. What answer can I give to the souls of these men if I spend the rest of my days in vain here in the Capital?

Am I insane or am I a fool? There is but one road for me to take.

In the plaintive "Our Division has not been in action for more than thirty years..." one may perhaps detect a dangerous note for the future. Japan's minor action against Shantung in 1914 had not appeased the army's appetite for combat. The later fighting in Manchuria had provided a wider opportunity but not for very long or for very many. There is no doubt that a hunger for glory gnawed at the younger professionals. Once, when a trusted teacher asked some of them why they wanted war, one man patted his chest and said, *Koko ga sabishii*: "It's bare and lonely here"—a reference to the absence of medals or the rows of ribbons which betoken medals. These younger officers wanted to bedeck themselves with visible proof of their exploits, with what is called in military slang *monohoshizao*, after the bamboo poles that serve as clotheslines throughout Japan. The older officers may not have personally thirsted for combat, but some of them no doubt worried about the effects of prolonged inactivity on the men under them. As the central authorities had learned in the 1920's, when a pressing reason does not exist for the maintenance of lavish military forces, civilians soon tire of the expense. Such thoughts may be typical of all military establishments, but in Japan the army was in a unique position to translate those thoughts into action.

The legal farces which had followed in the wake of the earlier incidents were not now repeated. The army was severely shaken by the insurrection. The control faction, which had always placed great emphasis on discipline, came to the fore. The trials, which were generally short and to the point, resulted in sentences for some 103 men. Although the death penalty had not been expected, this time it was imposed. Fifteen men (with bull's eyes marked on their foreheads) were subsequently executed in three groups of five. As they were being bound to racks and blindfolded, one of them—the chief assassin of Viscount Saito and General Watanabe—first sang a little song and then declared, "Indeed, indeed, I hope the privileged classes will reflect upon their conduct and be more prudent." Another cried out, "The people trust the Army. Let them not be betrayed. Don't let the Russians beat us!" A third then led the group in three rousing banzais for His Majesty and the Empire.

Among the more fantastic footnotes to this mutiny is the fact that the general who broadcast to the troops on the morning of February 29 was later court-martialed for *lèse-majesté*! In declaring, "The Emperor himself has ordered you to return to your regiments. *It is not yet too late,*" he had committed the crime of suggesting "that obedience to the Emperor could be delayed." In the end, however, he was acquitted.[42]

Mazaki, Araki, and a number of other senior officers who had been at the center during these events were put on the reserve list. This left vacancies at the top and thus created something of an opportunity for junior generals like Hideki Tojo to move into positions which might otherwise have remained closed to them for a longer period of time. All officers, regardless of rank, were once again publicly enjoined not to mix in politics or to establish connections with civilian nationalists. A few moderates were emboldened by this turn of affairs to go forth once again to do battle, and the electorate, when its next opportunity

---

[42] See "The Brocade Banner," 87-93 and 95-101. Although the verdicts against the men involved in the February 26 affair were severe by comparison with those imposed as a result of the earlier incidents, it should be noted that a stay of execution was granted on many sentences. Others subsequently had their sentences reduced by amnesties, and some—a rather large number, in fact—had their civil rights restored. Details pertaining to the trial of Lt. Col. Aizawa, who was sentenced to death and executed, are briefly covered in *ibid.*, 71-72. Also, Ōi corresp. and Lory, 195-96, in which the "purge" which followed the February 26 incident is described as having "proved to be less drastic than first appeared. The radicals were too strong to be held down long."

occurred, once more endorsed the parliamentarian as against the nationalist parties. But there were many others, it seems, and some in high places, who decided in favor of being "more prudent."

The compromise with naked force that had begun after the assassinations of 1932, when an admiral rather than a civilian political leader was given preference for the premiership, was now extended—despite the fact that the circumstances of the time were certainly not unfavorable for a reassertion of civilian authority.[43] In the light of public opinion and the damage done to army prestige by the mutiny, those close to the throne could have used the many incidents of this period as justification for constitutional or other reforms aimed at stripping the military of their growing control over affairs of state. Opposition within the military services could have been overcome by marshaling the Emperor's influence and prestige in such a way as to ensure a minimum of further trouble. His Majesty's advisers and ministers did not like implicating the Emperor so directly in matters that were actually their responsibility, but they could bring themselves to do so in moments of national crisis and, surely, this was such a moment.

The civilian members of the ruling elite, however, chose to fight fire with fire and so threw their support behind the faction whose very name, "control," with its connotation of discipline, created a confidence-inspiring, if somewhat nebulous, vision of future law and order. They gave that faction virtual carte blanche to suppress the imperial-way clique. Perhaps this decision was first formed merely as a hasty expedient. Perhaps it was more than that—a conscious capitulation by the civilians to a faction of the army which in effect said: "The government stands at the crossroads. If it wants peace and order at home, it must give us its support, for only we can deal with the fanatics. But in dealing with them—in suppressing their social-revolutionary, extremist tendencies—we must have a free hand overseas. If we are to bottle up such energies at home, we must be allowed to uncork them abroad. Only thus can His Majesty's mind be put at ease. Only thus can the holy mission of our nation be assured and the livelihood of our people safeguarded. This is the price that must be paid to restore order at home and open a way to the future."

[43] Konoe was especially harsh, in later years, in his judgment of Saionji's recommendation of Admiral Saitō to succeed the assassinated Inukai (IPS Doc. No. 59-B20-3). In general, the point seems well-taken despite the fact that Saitō was himself a moderate. On this question, see also J, B/IV, 99 and B/V, 607.

If this was not said in so many words, it was part of the rationale which governed all subsequent events, all later decisions, and all future leaders. While some Japanese may simply have given opportunistic support to a policy of peace at home and war abroad, others actively sought, in one way or another, to give substance to such a program, and thus contributed to the catastrophe which followed. Machine guns in the hands of younger officers had already proved more powerful than the samurai swords worn by generals.[44] After 1936 more and more members of the ruling elite succumbed without protest to an ever more aggressive encroachment by the Japanese army upon affairs of state

Slowly but surely the national crisis which had been predicted for so long actually came into being. As the crisis deepened, many civilians found it easy to rationalize their capitulation to the militarists by endorsing the view that the men of the imperial army and navy, by virtue of their profession of arms and responsibility for national defense, must indeed have—as they frequently claimed—*all* of the answers. In the land of the blind, the one-eyed became king.[45] After 1936 both civilians and militarists alike began talking in terms of the inexorable forces of history. Thereafter, that convenient though meaningless concept was to be cited again and again in support of decisions at home and actions abroad which need never have transpired.

It was a strange and fateful time indeed—a time requiring men of vision and experience, modern embodiments of Meiji Restoration prototypes, leaders who could master the unprecedented problems of this period rather than be overwhelmed by them. Hideki Tojo was not such a man, but in comparison with possible rivals he had much to recommend him. He was difficult to type, and perhaps for that reason he came to be regarded favorably by groups and interests not necessarily sharing a common purpose. While still chief of the military research bureau of the war ministry, Tojo had clearly indicated that he would not allow political censure to interfere with the prestige of the army which he served. During the course of an election campaign, a number of politicians had begun criticizing the way in which the military were emerging as a new political force. Some even went so far as to talk against the Manchurian Incident. Tojo carefully checked all such speeches and

[44] An adaptation of a view expressed in similar terms early in 1946 by several members of the Central Liaison Office (CF 20, II, 82). On the trend toward "compromises" after the assassinations, see J, B/IV, 114-17; IPS Doc. No. 59-B20-3; and Maxon, 1.

[45] *Tori naki sato no kōmori.*

then suddenly struck back with charges that the politicians were endeavoring to drive a wedge between the fighting services and the people. The phrase he employed, *gunmin rikan*, reverberated throughout the country with such effect that the politicians abruptly ceased their attack.[46]

After subsequently serving briefly as the second in command at the military academy in Tokyo, where he supervised the corps of instructors, Tojo spent a year in Kyushu as a brigade commander. His next assignment, while carrying him still farther from the center in point of distance, actually placed him in an extremely important position—one from which his contemporaries date his rise to power. In October 1935, shortly after the murder of General Nagata, with whom he had been on intimate terms, Tojo was appointed commander of the military police of the Kwantung army in Manchuria. Before his death, Nagata had said on more than one occasion, "Tojo is a man who will someday stand at the head of the army." The Manchurian appointment was the first of several which brought Tojo to precisely that position.[47]

It was in Manchuria that Tojo became friendly with a number of men who were later to be closely associated with him in Japan. One of these, Naoki Hoshino, who had previously been "completely unaware" of the general's existence, subsequently recalled the impact made by the new chief of the military police. Although technically called Manchukuo, and allegedly independent, the fledgling state was in reality under the control of Japanese army officers, who "held the final power of decision in all matters."[48] As a result, the military police group in Manchuria was far more powerful in this period than its sister organization in Japan proper.

Although the mission originally given to these *kenpei*, as they were called, was merely to inspect and superintend military personnel and civilians in the employ of the military services, the military police interpreted the scope of their mission in Manchuria (as later in Japan) in rather broad fashion. They not only devoted themselves to ensuring the safety of the army in all parts of Manchukuo and to preserving law and order there, but also went so far as to intrude upon the lives and activities of the general public in a way which soon earned them a Gestapo-like reputation. What was needed in such an organization was a strong figure at the head, a man capable of controlling his subordinates. Tojo's

[46] Shunichirō Itō, 61-63.   [47] *Ibid.*, 63-64, and Tōjō interrog., Jan. 14, 3.
[48] Hoshino, "Kenpei Shireikan Tōjō Hideki," in *Bungei Shunjū*, Vol. XXXIII, No. 12 (June 1955), 142. See also Morishima's testimony, S 39:11, T 3023-24.

immediate predecessors had not filled that need. They had been military bureaucrats who were either ignored by their vigorous young staff subordinates or ordered about by them. Tojo changed all that by establishing his personal right to command and by grasping firmly, in his own hands, the reins of control.

Then in his early fifties, Tojo was a bespectacled man of small stature (five feet, four inches) who seemed older than he was. His penetrating eyes and firmly set lips suggested a determination that his actions soon confirmed. His organization was "completely a one-man set-up." The authority of the *kenpeitai* was thoroughly enforced. No interference was allowed, not even from the "driving-force" of the Kwantung army—the younger staff officers who had caused so much trouble in the early 1930's in Manchuria and whose colleagues were now running wild in Japan.[49]

Tojo made it clear that he would not brook any questioning of his approach to problems or of his jurisdiction. Since he did not himself exceed the legal limits, he expected his subordinates to follow his example. He stressed experience and ability in his selection of men for assignment to various posts. He proved eminently successful in the preservation of law and order and equally successful in the implementation of a decision to unify the *kenpei* and several conflicting and empire-building civilian police forces, a policy decision which sharply divided Japanese with a voice in Manchurian affairs into two opposing camps. Although he was not personally responsible for this policy, Tojo's ability to carry the matter through without a hitch made a favorable impression on those who had expected trouble.

A further indication of Tojo's capacity for dealing with difficult situations occurred at the time of the February mutiny in Tokyo. To many who were then in Manchuria, but by no means to all, the news of the insurrection was totally unexpected. Exactly what was happening in Tokyo or who was in control was difficult to determine. Military communiqués were emanating from the capital but no one knew whether they came from the insurgents or from the loyal troops. In this extraordinary situation, Tojo acquitted himself well. Acting on orders from the commander of the Kwantung army, Tojo proclaimed a state of emergency and imposed censorship upon communications passing into and out of Changchun and other important centers. He immediately launched a thorough investigation of military and civilian personnel suspected of complicity in the Tokyo mutiny. The results

[49] Hoshino, 142-43.

showed that there were many who either had some connection with what was happening in the capital or at least sympathized with the insurrection. In fact, the number of those who sent letters of encouragement and who indicated a desire to participate in the incident or to start a similar uprising in Manchuria was surprisingly large. With this information in hand, Tojo ordered a police roundup of all who were thus implicated. As a consequence, peace and order were maintained in Manchuria at a time when trouble there would have been of great aid and comfort to the mutineers in Tokyo.[50]

Tojo's actions clearly revealed that he took a simple, legalistic view of the matter. The military services were under the command of His Majesty the Emperor. Anyone who resorted to action or who issued orders without imperial sanction was a rebel. This attitude on the part of Tojo was to have great influence upon the further development of his career. Although he certainly did not become war minister or premier because of it, his legalistic outlook which condemned the mutinous activities of the younger officers as "absolutely unpardonable," his rigid countermeasures to maintain law and order in Manchuria, his known association with members of the control group which led some to regard him as Nagata's successor, his staunch obedience to the will of the Emperor—in the rare and true sense of that term—as well as his growing experience as an administrator, all eventually made him appear to be a wiser choice for those posts than many other officers would have been.

Toward the end of 1936, perhaps as a reward for his loyal service at the time of the February incident, Tojo was promoted to lieutenant general. Some three months later he became chief of staff of the Kwantung army, replacing Lt. Gen. Seishiro Itagaki, who had played a prominent part in the taking of Manchuria in 1931. In the fourteen months during which Tojo held this new post, he continued the policies for which he had already become known: the preservation of law and order and the maintenance of obedience and discipline. He tended to concentrate his attention strictly upon army business, including the strengthening of the military power Japan would need in the event of operations against the Soviet Union. He continued his close association

[50] On Tōjō as *kenpeitai shireikan*, see Hoshino, 143-47; Tōjō aff., S 344:15-16, T 36481-82; Shunichirō Itō, 64-65; CF 20, I, 55; Ōi corresp.; Kido intv.; and Tōjō interrog., Jan. 14, 3-4, and Jan. 15, 1, in which Tōjō described the February 26 "uprising" as "absolutely unpardonable."

with Naoki Hoshino, who was in charge of economic affairs in Manchuria under the authority of the Kwantung army.[51]

Tojo also became friendly with another strategically placed individual, Yosuke Matsuoka, then serving as president of the South Manchurian Railway. As various problems arose, Matsuoka—a law graduate of the University of Oregon—discussed with Tojo what later became known as Japan's new order in East Asia.[52] Also included in Tojo's circle of friends were Nobusuke Kishi, vice-chief of the economic section of the Manchukuo government, and Yoshisuke Aikawa, president of the Manchurian Heavy Industries Development Corporation, which stood in the vanguard of Japan's mobilization of Manchuria's economy.

Together, these five men—Tojo, Hoshino, Matsuoka, Kishi, and Aikawa—became known in certain quarters as the *ni-ki san-suke*: "the two *ki* and the three *suke*"—a reference to the fact that the first names of Tojo and Hoshino ended in the syllable "ki," while those of the other three ended with "suke." When he was pressed, after the Pacific war, for the origin and significance of this phrase, Tojo finally volunteered that it had probably arisen because "the five of us knew the ropes pretty well in Manchuria" and were the ones who "could get things done." He said that he had heard about this "disagreeable" expression "by hearsay" and that it was "contrary to the facts ... and a nuisance," since his actions in Manchuria, as well as those of Hoshino, were taken in response to orders from Tokyo and were not the result of any "individual notions." So far as he was concerned, "the expression was a kind of propaganda" to which he had paid "very little attention."[53]

[51] See J, B/IV, 108-9; J, B/V, 629-30, 632, 643-44; and Iwakuro interrog., May 29, 6-9.

[52] Yōsuke (Frank) Matsuoka came to the United States at the age of thirteen, enrolled in the public schools of Portland, and later entered the University of Oregon, from which he received an LL.B. on June 14, 1900. He briefly visited his alma mater in the spring of 1933, following his now-famous exit from the League. Dull and Kuroda corresp. See also the *Eugene Register-Guard*, Vol. LXXXIV, No. 97 (April 7, 1933), 184; *Old Oregon*, Vol. XIV, No. 10 (April 1933), 3, and Vol. XVII, No. 10 (June-July 1937), 11; and the *Oregon Daily Emerald*, April 7, 1933, 2 (editorial by Richard L. Neuberger) and April 8, 1933, *passim*.

[53] On Tōjō in Manchuria, see Shunichirō Itō, 65-67; Hoshino, 147-48; Tōjō interrog., Jan. 14, 1-2, Jan. 24, 2-4, Jan. 25, 1, and Feb. 5, 3; CF 20, III, 253 and 255; S 346:4, T 36575-77, and S 349:4, T 36832; J, B/V, 642-43 and C/X, 1206; and Kubota intv. Tōjō apparently also made some enemies in Manchuria, including Ryūkichi Tanaka and Kanji Ishiwara (usually appears in *rōma-ji* as "Ishihara," but according to the family "Ishiwara" is correct. Ōi and Hattori corresp.).

Tōjō's remarks about the *ni-ki san-suke* phrase are from his interrogations. Postwar testimony regarding prewar matters must naturally be handled with care, but a study of the entire transcript of the Tōjō interrogations makes it clear that Tōjō was not seeking to avoid responsibility or to escape any penalties the Tribunal might decide to impose (see Ch. 15).

The fact that Japanese army officers who could work harmoniously with civilians in getting things done were a rarity in those days suggests that Tojo made an increasingly favorable impression on people in high places. Japanese who traveled between Japan and the continent at the time in question were gratified by what they saw in Manchuria; among them, Tojo's name was not infrequently mentioned in connection with achievements there.

It is sometimes said that a man's fate hangs by a single thread. In Tojo's case the thread had its beginning in his service in Manchuria—more particularly, in his becoming chief of staff of the Kwantung army. It was from that time onward that his participation in the alleged Japanese conspiracy to commit aggression was subsequently dated. In settling upon 1937 as the year of Tojo's initiation as a conspirator, the prosecutor at Tojo's postwar trial acted partly on the assumption that no one in such an important post could be entirely innocent and partly on what he regarded as clear and certain proof of Tojo's guilt.

For Japan, 1937 was also to prove a fateful year. With the outbreak of the China Incident, which was now impending, the nation was plunged into a crisis which eventually assumed unprecedented proportions. The optimism prompted by Japan's initial victories, which were so easily won, was not long sustained. As the prospect of conquering China diminished, Japanese militarists spoke more and more of spirit and sacrifice, and of the encirclement of Japan being carried out by her hostile neighbors. It was in these bleak and distorted circumstances that Tojo's career took a turn which was to carry him ultimately to the official residence of Japan's premiers.

CHAPTER 4

The Dawn of a Renaissance

THE months immediately following the outbreak of the Manchurian Incident had been devoted by the Japanese army to a consolidation of its military position and to a sustained effort to force a reluctant Japanese government into accepting the *fait accompli*. Hamaguchi's successor, Baron Reijiro Wakatsuki, had resigned in December 1931 after his inability to bring the army to heel had been more than amply illustrated by events on the continent. By the spring of 1932 the new cabinet headed by the ill-fated Inukai, who was to fall victim to assassination in the May 15 incident, had reconciled itself to the situation in Manchuria and had bowed to the will of the Kwantung army. While the murder-and-revolution societies were at work within Japan, the army strengthened its position in Manchuria in preparation for an infiltration of Inner Mongolia and North China that was designed to detach those areas from the sovereignty of the Republic of China. This naturally led to new clashes with the Chinese and to a further deterioration in Japan's relations with the Western powers. At the same time, Japanese army opinion kept stressing the inevitability of war with the Soviet Union and the consequent need for all-out military preparedness.

The success of the Kwantung army in Manchuria, together with the government's subsequent decision to isolate Japan from the international community by withdrawing from the League, gave naval planners in Tokyo an excellent opportunity to revive national dissatisfaction with the current limitation on naval armaments. Their campaign proved so effective that at the end of 1934 Japan served notice of her intention to abrogate the naval treaty to which she had become a party at the Washington Conference of 1921-1922. In December 1935 Japan further revealed the direction in which she was moving by her actions at the naval conference which was then meeting in London. Japan's principal delegate, Admiral Osami Nagano, who was to serve as chief of the naval general staff in 1941, vigorously pressed for a common upper limit. The United States delegation argued that "parity" would actually give Japan overwhelming superiority in the Pacific, whereas the system then in existence provided equality of security to all participating nations. If the Japanese delegation persisted in its demands, competitive naval construction would once again prevail. The Japanese "made no substantial attempt to answer these objections, saying merely that, in their country's view, while the United States Navy was superior in strength, it menaced Japan's very existence."[1] When Japanese arguments failed to produce support for a common upper limit, Nagano simply walked out, as Matsuoka had done two years earlier in Geneva. Long before the London conference had convened, the vice-chief of the naval general staff had forecast this development. "We are going to the Conference in 1935," he had said, "with a demand for parity. If our demand is rejected, we shall return home." Once home, Nagano and others in the navy immediately started drafting plans for the creation of a Japanese force strong enough to take command of the Western Pacific. These plans became established national policy in August 1936.[2]

In this same period, statements issued by the Japanese government began to reflect, in a rather ominous way, thoughts which previously had been expressed almost exclusively by figures like General Araki. Despite repeated Japanese assurances to the contrary, it soon became apparent that Japan was prepared to ignore the "open door" provisions of the Nine-Power Pact signed at Washington in 1922. Whenever protests were lodged against Japanese treaty violations in Manchuria, the Japanese government disclaimed responsibility by asserting that Manchukuo was an independent state for which Japan could not be held responsible. In point of fact, Manchuria was completely under the control of the Kwantung army, with the commander of that army serving concurrently as the Japanese ambassador to Manchukuo. Precisely where matters stood was revealed years later by General Jiro Minami, who served in that dual capacity in the mid-1930's. In a postwar interrogation Minami admitted that as ambassador to Manchukuo he had offered advice on a variety of matters. When it was suggested that this so-called advice constituted "a direction" to the Manchukuo government, Minami replied, "You might say so—Yes."[3]

By the summer of 1935, the Japanese military had obtained control of a number of local regimes in both Inner Mongolia and North China. Such Manchurian adventurers as Itagaki and Doihara were busily trying to organize "autonomous" governments in those regions of China. The establishment of such governments would permit Japan to obtain control over all of North China and Inner Mongolia without leaving

---

[1] See J, B/IV, 130-42.

[2] *Ibid.* See J, B/IV, 228-31 for a brief summary of the situation after 1936. The action taken by Japan prompted the United States to begin extensive naval construction.

[3] J, B/V, 630. See also Iwakuro interrog., May 29, 10 ("It was just like nursing a baby").

the telltale traces of complicity revealed at the time of the Manchurian Incident. The Western powers might suspect the truth, but they would have greater difficulty proving it.

By early 1936 the power of the Japanese army on the continent had been enhanced by a reconciliation between the war ministry and the foreign office in Tokyo—a development which led to the coordination of foreign policy with military planning. The Japanese army, which had numbered a quarter of a million men at the beginning of 1930, had grown to a standing strength of 400,000. News media were being subjected more and more to a censorship which allowed only a parroting of the distortions and fictions supplied by military and governmental propaganda agencies. Civilian and military extremists like Dr. Okawa and Colonel Hashimoto continued to provide ideological justification for the territorial aggrandizement which had already taken place and for the further expansion then being contemplated.[4] In so doing, they delved back into the mythical past to 660 B.C., when the "first" Emperor, Jinmu, allegedly issued an imperial rescript in which two expressions, *kōdō* and *hakkō-ichiu*, were used. The original meaning of each was innocuous enough. *Kōdō*, "the way of the Emperor," was part of a longer phrase signifying "the oneness of the Imperial Way"; *hakkō-ichiu* meant "the eight corners of the world under one roof," in the moral sense of universal brotherhood. *Kōdō* and *hakkō-ichiu*, being vague, could be interpreted broadly; hence their great utility. As employed by the ultranationalists, the two expressions were gradually transformed into symbols of a determination to create, through military force, a world dominated by Japan.[5]

From the evidence at hand, the conclusion is inescapable that the Japanese people were slowly but surely being prepared against the day when an all-out war might become necessary to sustain the current trend of Japanese foreign policy. It was thus with considerable point, as developments were shortly to confirm, that Ambassador Grew informed the Department of State, early in 1936, of his rather dismal outlook: "We should not lose sight of the fact, deplorable but true, that no practical and effective code of international morality upon which the world can rely has yet been discovered, and that the standards of morality of one nation in certain given circumstances have little or no relation to the standards of another nation in other circumstances, and

[4] On the developments between 1931 and 1936 summarized in the text, see J, B/IV, 93-117, 142-46, 151-53, and B/V, 577-78, 594-95, 601-4, 607-13, and 648-66.
[5] On *kōdō* and *hakkō-ichiu*, see J, B/IV, 85-86, 148-49, 153-54; Tōjō interrog., Jan. 14, 6-9 and 11-12, Jan. 24, 1-6, and Jan. 28, 1 and 4; and Tōjō aff., S 342:13, T 36184.

little or no relation to the standards of the individuals of the nations in question. To shape our foreign policy on the unsound theory that other nations are guided and bound by our present standards of international ethics would be to court sure disaster."[6]

Just as 1936 marked the culmination of the period of internal violence, so was it the year of decision with respect to the further expansion of Japan on the Asian continent and in the regions to the south. A principal result of the February incident, unsuccessful though it had been, was the emergence of a new cabinet headed by Koki Hirota, who had been serving as foreign minister for the past two and one-half years.[7] By 1936 the nature of the Japanese political process was such that the very ability of a man to form a cabinet was a gauge of his willingness to compromise with the situation which had caused the fall of the preceding cabinet. Although this factor was to become more pronounced later on, it had been present from at least 1932, when Inukai had led his cabinet in accepting what his predecessor had avoided by resigning. The fact that Admiral Nagano, who had headed the Japanese delegation to the London naval conference, became navy minister in the Hirota Cabinet was clear proof that there would be no second thoughts on Japan's withdrawal from that conference.

Another measure of Hirota's readiness to accommodate the military was his acceptance of their demand that thenceforth only officers on the active service list with the respective rank of at least lieutenant general and vice-admiral be eligible for the war and navy portfolios. The effect of this return to a system that had prevailed prior to 1912 was to guarantee that the service ministers would be able to control cabinet policy by threatening to resign whenever cabinet colleagues showed any hesitancy about adopting the military program.[8] If the army found a cabinet not to its liking, the war minister would consult with the other members of the Big Three—the chief of the army general staff and the inspector-general of military training. If they agreed that a more favorable attitude was unlikely to develop in the cabinet, the war minister would submit his resignation. Since no cabinet could legally exist without a war minister and since the Big Three would

[6] *Foreign Relations (Diplomatic Papers: 1936)*, IV, 48-49 (Cable No. 1665, February 7, 1936).

[7] See J, B/IV, 117-18.

[8] See IPS Doc. No. 59-B20-3; Konoe, *Ushinawareshi Seiji*, 3-5; *Kaikōsha Kiji*, No. 754, 43 and 148; T 441-42; Yano intv.; Storry, *The Double Patriots*, 196, n.4; and J, B/IV, 118-19 and B/V 667-68. The new ordinance also provided that vice-ministers were to be active duty officers with a rank not lower than major general and rear admiral.

obviously refuse to supply a new one, the resignation of the war minister meant the end of that particular cabinet.

Under such circumstances, the successor to the outgoing premier, unable to draw on retired officers who might possibly hold views at variance with those of younger men on active duty, would be forced to ask the army to recommend a general or lieutenant general on active service. Such an officer would not only be subject to army orders but would also be indebted to those who had nominated him and hence amenable to their wishes. The Big Three, who were responsible for such matters, would name a likely candidate for war minister only if they were satisfied that the cabinet being formed would do what the army wanted. If it appeared that the new cabinet might follow in the footsteps of the old, the premier-designate would find that the Big Three "regretfully" could not agree on a war minister candidate or that the man they "recommended" would decline to enter the new cabinet for "personal" reasons. In either case, the premier-designate would have to notify the throne of his inability to carry out the imperial mandate. In accepting the reinauguration of this system in 1936, the Hirota Cabinet voluntarily relinquished one of the last vestiges of civilian control over state affairs—an abdication of power and responsibility to the military services which accelerated the advance of the army to a position of domination over all phases of national life.

Illustrative of the role already being played by the army was a meeting which took place, in the summer of 1936, at a restaurant called the Takara-tei in the Kojimachi ward of Tokyo. It was attended by section and bureau chiefs and key staff members of both the war ministry and the army general staff—in short, by those army officers who were concerned, in one way or another, with the most important affairs of state—or, at least, who felt they ought to be. The purpose of the meeting was a frank exchange of opinions with respect to future national policy and what thenceforth was rather broadly termed the "national defense." According to Major Kenryo Sato, who acted as secretary, agreement was reached on the need to launch an epoch-making expansion of productive power so as to put Japan in a position to cope with the progress being made by Soviet heavy industry. It was also decided that the administrative machinery of the state should be reformed and parliamentary politics renovated.[9] This constituted the army's position with respect to the Hirota Cabinet.

[9] See Kenryō Satō, "Dai-Tōa Sensō wo Maneita Shōwa no Dōran," 90-91. At the time in question, Satō headed the *naiseihan* which was established shortly after the February 26 incident as part of the military affairs section of the military affairs bureau, war ministry.

An important aspect of the Takara-tei meeting was the convenient way in which the concept of national defense was distorted. The real or alleged threat posed by other nations was not the key factor. Rather, "national defense" came to mean the *offensive* striking power needed by the army to carry out the national policies it planned to inaugurate.[10] The army intended to push its program through essentially civilian cabinets which could serve as scapegoats if anything went wrong. But if civilian cooperation should ever flag, the army might deem it necessary or desirable to form a cabinet of its own and so accept in name the responsibility that it already possessed in fact by virtue of its direct access to the throne and its control over the very existence of each and every cabinet.

Another meeting, which also occurred in the summer of 1936, further reveals the role played by the military services in relation to the Hirota Cabinet. This was a conference on June 30 between the war and navy ministers, at which the two officers agreed on a draft-proposal for a basic national policy for Japan—a policy which was no doubt prepared by the same officers who had met at the Takara-tei and by their naval counterparts.[11] The service ministers subsequently submitted their draft to Premier Hirota and to the ministers for finance and foreign affairs, none of whom expressed any dissatisfaction with the document or any censure of the fact that the draft had originated within the war and navy ministries and the army and navy general staffs.[12]

As a result, this inner cabinet of five men decided that the *army and navy* should work the draft-proposal into a concrete plan. The month of July was spent in that pursuit, with the navy apparently playing a more active role than the army. This was a reflection of the new mission now to be assigned to the guardian of the sea approaches to Japan. Between 1931 and 1936 Japanese expansion abroad had required comparatively little naval activity, a fact which had produced dissatisfaction among younger naval firebrands. After 1936, the navy's assignment in the further expansion of Japan was to become increasingly important. This made the navy a stronger advocate of overseas "development" than has generally been realized.

[10] See J, B/V, 669.

[11] The two meetings were perhaps related, though the evidence is insufficient to establish a connection. Policies of the type discussed in the text were drafted, as a matter of course, by the section and bureau chiefs (and their respective staffs) of the war ministry and the general staff.

[12] See J, B/IV, 124-25, 130, and B/V, 668-69. The ministers were Hirota (premier), Terauchi (war), Nagano (navy), Arita (foreign affairs), and Baba (finance).

Interservice rivalry and jealousy—the navy view that the army had been monopolizing for too long the center of the stage—also explain the growing naval desire to share in the glory accruing to the army as a result of victories on the continent. The fact that a few senior admirals later urged caution when their army colleagues favored throwing it to the winds is noteworthy but not of any real significance. In the navy, as in the army, the locus of power rested far below the level of those who nominally held the rank and authority which should have placed them in the decision-making category. At any rate, when Premier Hirota and his four most important ministers again met on August 7, the plan as finally evolved by the services received their approval. Four days later Hirota and his colleagues affixed their signatures and seals to an official statement validating a basic national policy which subsequently "proved to be the corner-stone in the whole edifice of Japanese preparations for war."[13]

On August 15, 1936, this new national policy was informally reported to the throne. His Majesty was advised that his government would thenceforth work toward the acquisition of a secure position on the Asian continent so as to make Japan a "stabilizing power" in East Asia and thus permit her to contribute toward the maintenance of peace in that area and ultimately toward the peace and welfare of all mankind. Japan was also to undertake a gradual advance toward the South Seas for the purpose of developing Japanese influence there. She would attempt to achieve unity in Eastern Asia by destroying the aggressive policy of the great powers. (How this would be done was not specified.) The Soviet menace would be eliminated by diplomatic measures as well as through assistance to Manchukuo and a strengthening of Japan-Manchukuo defenses. Japan would also undertake preparations against the United States and Britain and strive for close cooperation with Manchukuo and China.

In carrying out these policies, the Japanese government proposed to forsake a "self-effacing attitude" in favor of a "positive" one. At the same time Tokyo would take care to maintain friendly relations with other powers. Within Japan, priority would be given to the completion of the "defense" preparations required to implement this basic national policy. All adjustments necessary for that purpose would be carried out. Army strength would be developed to the point where Japan could deal with Soviet forces in the Far East. Naval armament would be increased so as to give the navy the power to obtain command of the

[13] *Ibid.*

Western Pacific despite the existence of the American fleet. The determination of the Japanese people to overcome the crisis facing them would be enhanced "by guiding and unifying public opinion." Japan would adopt "a dignified attitude and just measures" toward China, and would devote herself, in view of the Soviet menace, to the creation in North China of a special "anti-communist, pro-Japanese and pro-Manchukuo area."

Since the adoption of such a policy could lead to difficulties with the United States that might interfere, in turn, with the execution of Japan's Soviet policy, the report to the throne advised His Majesty that steps would be taken to secure the understanding of the United States. Japan would also assume the initiative in improving relations with Great Britain so as to obtain British support for Japan in her dealings with the Soviet Union. Friendly relations with Germany would be pursued and measures would be adopted to establish German-Japanese collaboration as occasion demanded. If called upon to do so, Japan would be prepared to guarantee the neutrality of the Philippines. "Appropriate measures" would be taken to allay the misgivings of the people of the Netherlands East Indies and to convert them to a pro-Japanese attitude. "Proper guidance and assistance" would be extended to Thailand and other underdeveloped countries on the basis of Japan's principle of co-existence and co-prosperity. Foreign trade, indispensable to Japan's economic well-being, would be "expanded to the utmost."[14]

Although this may not have been a plan for the conquest of the world or even the Far Eastern part of it,[15] the basic national policy of August 1936 clearly indicated the directions in which Japan would develop and also—though perhaps less clearly—the means she would employ. Despite the verbal emphasis upon peace and friendship, it should have been obvious to the men who formulated this policy that any attempt by Japan to carry it out would inevitably jeopardize her relations not only with the Soviet Union but also with the United States and Great Britain. If the five ministers did not understand that, they were incredibly naïve. If they did understand it, they were using euphemisms to cloak their real intentions. It is possible that these men had been encouraged by the success of the Manchurian Incident to believe that there were practically no limits to the expansion of Japan, so long as they contrived to advance Japanese interests with a semblance

[14] See Gaimushō, *Nihon Gaikō Nenpyō narabi ni Shuyō Bunsho*, II, 344-47. JRD Monograph No. 144, Appendix 1; J, B/IV, 119-22 and B/V, 668-69; and S 37:7, T 2727-28.
[15] The view offered in J, B/IV, 123-24 is perhaps too sweeping, but it contains much that is correct. For a dissenting judgment, see IMTFE, "Roling Opinion," 73-81, 93-95.

of respect for the *status quo*—at least until Japan had acquired a position sufficiently strong to allow her to challenge the powers openly if she so desired. They may thus have adopted this basic national policy in order to test the theory that Japan need only exhibit a positive attitude to obtain further gains on the continent and in the regions to the south. Presumably, if their theory was wrong, they could always desist.

For those who might be chary of accepting the August 1936 policy statement as the basis for a condemnation of the Hirota Cabinet, the record provides a wealth of specific detail.[16] It was during the Hirota Cabinet that an "information" bureau was established to coordinate and reconcile propaganda emanating from all government ministries. It was under Hirota that "steps were . . . taken to develop a new war-supporting economy in Japan." The nation thus "embarked upon a series of financial measures emphasizing state control of the national economy for political purposes." Government subsidies and tax exemptions were bestowed on such activities as the building of automobiles—an economically unsound venture that could be justified only on the grounds of its potential contribution to the "national defense." Subsidies were also directed toward the encouragement of ship-building, with such success that by the end of 1936 Japan possessed "the most modern merchant fleet, in proportion to size, of any nation in the world." It was the Hirota Cabinet, also, that was responsible for a new naval building program that made the increase in Japanese naval tonnage in 1937 the greatest on record for the critical period 1931-1945.

It was under the Hirota Cabinet, moreover, that the process of creating a political satellite out of the nominally independent Manchukuo was completed. As a concomitant, Hirota and his colleagues approved a policy designed to establish an anti-Communist regime in North China, divorced from Nationalist control but subject to such direction as Japan saw fit to provide. Finally, it was during the Hirota Cabinet that the earlier efforts of the Japanese military attaché in Berlin to secure formal German-Japanese cooperation were brought to fruition in negotiations between the Japanese ambassador and von Ribbentrop that produced, in November 1936, the Anti-Comintern Pact.[17]

[16] The text which follows draws on J, B/IV, 126-29, 141-42, 153, and IPS Doc. No. 59-B20-3. On Hirota's later role, see also J, B/IV, 224-32, in which the following "majority" opinion occurs: "It was a cardinal principle of his policy to have Japan's preparations for war completed behind the façade of friendly foreign relations." For the findings against Hirota on the counts of the indictment, see J, C/X, 1158-61 and 1215. For a dissenting view, see IMTFE, "Roling Opinion," 191-210.

[17] On the Anti-Comintern Pact (including a secret protocol which established a limited alliance against the USSR), see J, B/IV 226, 270, 276, 278-80, 312, 319-20; J, B/VI, 785-89; IMTFE, "Roling Opinion," 85-89; *Documents on International Affairs,*

Certainly such a cabinet can hardly be regarded as an unwilling tool of the imperial army and navy. It must instead be seen as the first of the civilian collaborationist cabinets which, from then on, proved of such immense assistance in the rise of military dictatorship in Japan.

Despite the extraordinary extent to which the military services penetrated the policy-making process in the few short months following the February 1936 mutiny, they did not immediately secure without further strenuous effort the unchallengeable position that was soon to render military participation in politics a subject which even men of high station found it healthier to ignore. The fact that key war ministry and army general staff personnel had gathered at the Takara-tei in the summer had not gone unnoticed. Some time after the meeting, rumors to the effect that the officers concerned were in favor of reforming the administrative and parliamentary organs of the state became current. Newspapermen began hounding Major Sato in an effort to learn the contents of the military program. Toward the latter part of October a skillful reporter, piecing together various remarks made by Sato, obtained what he called "The Military's Plan for the Reform of the Parliamentary System." This scoop, which was carried widely in the Japanese press, produced a sensation. It also served as the spark which eventually ignited an explosion in the Diet that helped bring about the downfall of the Hirota Cabinet.

The fact that the army was suspected of harboring a reform plan of the type published in the press created an opening for a general attack upon the cabinet by those who were either seeking power themselves or who sincerely took issue with the government's plans for internal "reform" and for overseas expansion. The uproar had temporarily subsided by the end of the year, but when the Diet reconvened in January 1937 a new crisis occurred in the form of a direct challenge by the Seiyukai party. On January 20, a mass meeting of members of the party issued a declaration criticizing the policies of the Hirota Cabinet and calling for a return to and strengthening of parliamentary procedures. The militarists were openly attacked for their attitude of self-complacency and superiority and for their efforts to involve themselves in all phases of government. The next day this initial thrust was pushed further in a speech delivered in the Diet by a leading Seiyukai member

---

1936, 297-99; *Documents on German Foreign Policy, 1918-1945*, Series D, Vol. I, 734; CF 20, III, 270; and Hattori, I, 33. The Pact was renewed for an additional five years in November 1941 (J, B/VI, 822).

and former president of the House named Kunimatsu Hamada. War Minister Hisaichi Terauchi took exception to Hamada's speech, for he regarded certain remarks as amounting to an insult directed at the army. Hamada angrily demanded that Terauchi indicate in the record precisely where the insults had occurred: "If any words of mine have insulted the army," he said, "I shall apologize to you by committing suicide. If there are no such insults, then *you* should commit suicide."

This "hara-kiri exchange" pitched Hamada's fellow Seiyukai members into such wild cheering and clapping that pandemonium broke loose. Terauchi, infuriated by this open revolt on the part of the politicians, insisted that the Diet be temporarily adjourned. The army also immediately counterattacked with a statement bristling with *kōdō* and *hakkō-ichiu*. The political parties were advised to reflect upon their own shortcomings before criticizing others. The army implied that only its policy could satisfy the Japanese people, since the alternative was to deny the nation an opportunity to develop outside the home islands, thus making it impossible for Japan to contribute to the stabilization of East Asia. The army therefore proposed to abolish the Diet as currently constituted, so as to permit the inauguration of a form of government capable of "clarifying" the national polity and contributing to the "national defense."

Actually, the army had no intention of entering into a public debate with either the Seiyukai, Mr. Hamada, or anyone else. The "hara-kiri" episode had occurred on January 21; the next day War Minister Terauchi announced that he was resigning. In explanation he declared that it would be impossible for him to continue in a cabinet in which the views of some members were in basic disagreement with those held by the army. Under such circumstances he could not be responsible for the maintenance of military discipline, the completion of the national defense, and the perfection of the administrative reforms to which he had been devoting his efforts. Terauchi's remark about military discipline sounded rather like a threat that unless the army got its way, the extremists within it might once again take the law into their own hands.

The specter of a resumption of personal attacks of the type current during the first half of the decade was never far from the minds of those most likely to be selected as targets. Although Terauchi did not say so, the Big Three apparently felt that the army could accomplish more by creating a governmental crisis through the resignation of the war minister than by trying to bolster a cabinet which had now outlived its usefulness. "So passed the Hirota Cabinet," remarked one foreign observer, "brought in by military insubordination and thrust out by military arrogance."[18]

Just how insubordinate and arrogant the army could be was immediately revealed in another demonstration of its power to bend each and every cabinet to its will through manipulations centering around the figure of the war minister. The circumstances leading to the fall of the Hirota Cabinet suggested the unlikelihood of the army being satisfied with anything less than a cabinet headed by a general. Prince Saionji, who advised the Emperor on such matters, therefore recommended that the mandate be bestowed upon General Ugaki, whom he regarded as the most eligible and least objectionable of the senior officers whose reputations and accomplishments made them possible candidates. The designation of Ugaki as the successor to Hirota apparently took the army completely by surprise, thus forcing it into a drastic response. Ugaki, who was no longer on active service, was unpopular because of the role he had played in the 1920's in carrying out reductions in force. The alleged connection between him and the March incident of 1931 also gave rise to hostile feelings against him in certain army circles. From the army point of view, therefore, he was definitely not the man to succeed Hirota. The fact that the imperial mandate was about to be issued, however, made the situation rather delicate, but not so delicate that the army would refrain from interfering.

Shortly after the word was received that Saionji had recommended Ugaki, several key officers converged on the war minister's official residence and there "lit the signal fire of opposition" to a cabinet headed by the general. According to Major Sato, who was one of those present, the group included the chief of the military affairs bureau of the war ministry, the chief of the operations section of the army general staff, and the commander of the military police.[19] Sato felt that preventing the formation of a cabinet by an army elder might be rather awkward, but he believed the problem could be solved by briefing Ugaki on the situation prevailing in the army and then asking him "to use his discretion"—a polite way of suggesting that he "voluntarily" decline to accept

---

[18] On the Takara-tei aftermath, the *harakiri mondō*, and the fall of the Hirota Cabinet: Kenryō Satō, "Dai-Tōa Sensō wo Maneita Shōwa no Dōran," 91-92; "The Brocade Banner," 93; J, B/IV, 154-56 and B/V, 676; Yanaga, 527; and Young, *Imperial Japan*, 290-92 (from which the sentence in quotes is taken).

[19] Isogai, Ishiwara, and Nakajima, respectively. For the details which follow, see Kenryō Satō, "Dai-Tōa Sensō wo Maneita Shōwa no Dōran," 92-93; Ugaki, 270; and Watanabe, *Ugaki Issei no Ayunda Michi*, 120-21. All agree in essence, although there is some variation on specific points. All quoted remarks are from Satō's account.

the imperial mandate. When the others readily agreed, Sato asked, "Who shall go and tie the bell to the cat's tail?"—a question to which he provided his own answer: Nakajima, the military police commander. The choice was dictated by the fact that the group wished to intercept Ugaki before he reached the palace, where he was scheduled to arrive about midnight. To do so would require stopping his car somewhere between Yokohama and Tokyo. Since the *kenpei* were stationed along the route Ugaki would follow, Nakajima was obviously the man for the job.

Precisely what Ugaki thought when Nakajima suddenly appeared and requested permission to enter the general's car is not known. According to Nakajima's later report, Ugaki proved annoyingly dense. Nakajima warned Ugaki that revolutionary and subversive symptoms were still present in the army and that it would be advisable for him to decline the mandate, since maintenance of discipline might otherwise be difficult. Ugaki showed neither anger nor surprise. He simply asked whether there was danger of another uprising of the type which had occurred the previous year and Nakajima replied in the negative. Ugaki then calmly changed the subject by saying, "You and I were once at the same field maneuvers, weren't we?" With that the matter was closed. Nakajima left the car near the famous Sengaku temple (the gravesite of the Lord Asano and of the warriors who avenged his death, early in the eighteenth century, in a celebrated act of "loyal" defiance of authority). Ugaki drove on to the palace, where he proceeded to accept the mandate despite Nakajima's far from subtle warning.

If Ugaki thought that the imperial mandate would act as a magic charm, he was soon rudely returned to reality. Since the Sato coterie had tried and failed, it was now General Terauchi's turn. As outgoing war minister, Terauchi was a member of the Big Three who controlled the selection of the army's representative in the cabinet—in this case, the nomination of a war minister to succeed himself. When Ugaki called upon the Big Three to recommend a replacement for Terauchi, the triumvirate proved reluctant to comply, citing once again the unrest within the services and the difficulty of maintaining discipline. Since Ugaki refused to be dissuaded, Terauchi informed him that three generals had been asked to serve but that they had all refused. When the lord keeper of the privy seal declined to involve the Emperor in a direct order to the Big Three to supply a war minister, Ugaki had no choice but to report to the throne that he was unable to form a cabinet and hence must respectfully withdraw.[20]

Had it not been for the ordinance specifying that the war minister must be an officer on active service, Ugaki might have triumphed—at least momentarily—by assuming concurrently the post of war minister. But even if that had been possible, it seems likely that he would not long have survived as Japan's premier. The significance of this political miscarriage clearly lay in the further revelation of the extent to which the army would go to obtain a cabinet amenable to its wishes.

The abortive efforts of General Ugaki added yet another ingredient of importance to the psychological outlook of those civilians who still concerned themselves with matters of state. Whereas the events of the period of "brainless patriotism" had prompted fear of their repetition, the Ugaki episode produced a fatalistic lethargy which helped encourage the belief that the army was riding a wave of the future which could not be stopped or turned back. One could watch its progress from a safe distance, ride with it, or be drowned by it. To more and more Japanese, resistance seemed more and more pointless. It was this psychology, and the memory of all that had gone before, that was to influence the selection of Hideki Tojo as premier in 1941. That Tojo had not been a party to or participant in the tumultuous events of the 1930's naturally constituted a further recommendation.

Having absolutely refused to accept Ugaki, imperial mandate or no imperial mandate, the army now gave its assent to the formation of a cabinet by General Senjuro Hayashi, who had figured in the enforced resignation of Mazaki in 1935. The difficulties Hayashi encountered were reflected in the fact that he and several other ministers had to hold more than one portfolio in order to construct a working cabinet. Even then the new combination managed to last only a bare four months. Major Sato later referred to it as "the eat-and-run cabinet"— by which he presumably meant a cabinet that had bilked those who had made it possible.[21]

One of the factors in the fall of the Hayashi Cabinet was its inability to win support in the Diet. In the general elections which followed the

[20] On Ugaki's inability to obtain a war minister, see Ugaki, 277-80; J, B/IV, 156-58 and B/V, 676-77; IPS Doc. No. 59-B20-3; Young, *Imperial Japan*, 291-92; and Yanaga, 527-28.

[21] See J, B/IV, 158, and Kenryō Satō, "Dai-Tōa Sensō wo Maneita Shōwa no Dōran," 93-94 (in which the phrase, "kuinige naikaku," is used). See also J, B/V, 677-78, and Shunichirō Itō, 71-73. Despite frequent cabinet changes, continuity was maintained by the retention of key personnel (J, B/IV, 159).

dissolution of that body, the nation once again favored the two major parliamentary parties. The nationalists, who had seventy-two candidates up for election, obtained only fifteen seats. Whether this development might eventually have made a return to parliamentary practices possible remains a matter of speculation. In the Chinese quarter of the Japanese horizon, storm clouds were already gathering. The new cabinet formed by Prince Fumimaro Konoe in June 1937 (with Hirota as foreign minister) was almost immediately plunged into a crisis which made a return to normal procedures more difficult than ever.[22] The 1936 election had been followed by the February mutiny; the 1937 election was followed by the eruption of fighting on the continent.

With the outbreak of the China Incident, General Hideki Tojo again became identified with the progression of events that led to the parting of the ways in 1941. The connection was in the form of a top-secret and urgent telegram dated June 9, 1937, which Tojo, in his capacity as chief of staff of the Kwantung army, sent to the vice-chief of the general staff and the vice-minister of war in Tokyo.[23] The telegram related to the current situation in China as viewed from the standpoint of operational preparations against the Soviet Union. Military power permitting, Tojo cabled, the best policy would be to deliver a blow against the Nanking "regime" so as to eliminate the Chinese "menace" that would otherwise threaten Japan's rear.

In a later attempt to justify this advice, which preceded the China Incident by only one month, Tojo referred to the anti-Japanese sentiments which were then rampant throughout China. In the north, Chinese Communist armies had publicly proclaimed their hostile attitude. In the Peking-Tientsin area, Japanese residents were exposed to dangers that might lead to a clash at any moment. Tojo argued that the Kwantung army, which had the responsibility of defending Manchukuo against a Soviet attack, could not tolerate such conditions at its rear. It therefore desired an immediate stabilization of North China.

To put the matter more bluntly: the Kwantung army, which should have been merely an instrument in the implementation of policy laid

---

[22] On the general election of 1937 and the emergence of the Konoe Cabinet: J, B/IV, 158-59; "The Brocade Banner," 94; IPS Doc. No. 59-B20-3; Young, *Imperial Japan*, 292-94; and Shunichirō Itō, 73-79.

[23] On the Tōjō telegram, which is discussed below, see S 85:21, T 7336-37; T 16951 and IMTFE, IPS Doc. No. 0003, 104; Tōjō aff., S 342:12, T 36173-76; J, B/IV, 169-70, 184-85; J, B/V, 678-79; and IMTFE Exh. No. 672 (the Japanese text of the telegram). The "tai-Bei" at the beginning of the second paragraph of the telegram would appear to be a mistake for "tai-Shi."

down by the government in Tokyo, was once again arrogating to itself policy-making functions—or at least was tending in that direction. If the authorities in the capital did not see the situation in the same way as the army in the field, one could expect that army to take matters into its own hands by attacking the Nanking government in order to "ameliorate" the conditions prevailing in China. At least, that would seem a valid expectation in the light of the murder of Chang Tso-lin in 1928 and the absorption of Manchuria in 1931—actions in which the initiative had been taken by prominent staff members of the Kwantung army.

According to Tojo, Japan recognized the necessity of adjusting her relations with China, but prerequisite to such a settlement was the abandonment on China's part of her anti-Japan policy. It apparently did not occur to Tojo that Japan could reasonably expect China to abandon her anti-Japanese attitude only when Japan renounced her own aggressive approach toward China. He was therefore advocating, in effect, that China turn the other cheek at a time when the hand of the Japanese army on the continent was already raised to strike that cheek. Again and again in the years after 1937, Japanese voiced their complaint against Chinese "insincerity" and cited Chinese "hostility" toward Japan as an excuse for Japanese military efforts to conquer China. And always this was done in utter disregard of the fact that Japan had played an enormous part in creating the very hostility which Tokyo subsequently endeavored to use as justification for further Japanese aggression.

If a peaceful settlement with China was Japan's aim, Tojo was proposing a rather extraordinary way of achieving it. What he really seems to have been saying was that so long as the Generalissimo's government continued to exist, a peaceful settlement was impossible. So long as a peaceful settlement was impossible, Japan would be menaced by the threat of hostile Chinese action at a time when Japan might be fully engaged against Soviet forces. Therefore, the thing to do was to deliver a blow against the Nanking "regime" and then reach some kind of settlement with whatever government succeeded the Generalissimo. If it were one favorable to or dominated by Japan, as seemed likely, so much the better. Security in the rear would be all the greater and Japan would be free to concentrate on the "problem" to the north.

In linking a peaceful settlement with China to an abandonment by the Chinese of their anti-Japanese attitude, Tojo later qualified his recommendation about delivering a blow at Nanking by specifying in his postwar testimony that such action was to be inaugurated only in the event of provocation. Japan might also have exerted pressure on the Chinese, he said, by building up and perfecting her "national defense" preparations. To humor the Chinese or to pay court to them would have served no useful purpose. The Chinese would merely have become more presumptuous.[24]

It was Tojo's further contention that the central authorities had not acted on his advice and that the incident which launched the war in China on July 7 had absolutely nothing to do with the recommendations contained in his telegram of June 9. The only evidence he could cite in support of his claim was the entirely "passive attitude" which the central authorities in Tokyo assumed toward the affair from the very beginning.

Despite the weakness of his argument, the truth of the matter seems to be that Tojo actually had no part in the outbreak of hostilities in China. The June 9 telegram remains damaging, nevertheless, because it reveals that Tojo—speaking for the Kwantung army—fully supported such action as the best way in which to eliminate the "menace" at Japan's rear. The episode is thus significant as an early example of Tojo's implicit belief in the legitimacy of resorting to arms to overcome obstacles—or, euphemistically, to "clarify" situations which did not readily lend themselves to successful solution by less drastic means.

[24] The prosecution introduced only the first sentence of Tōjō's telegram: "Genka Shina no jōsei wo tai-So sakusen junbi no kenchi yori kansatsu seba waga buryoku kore wo yurusaba mazu Nankin seiken ni tai shi ichigeki wo kuwae waga haigo no kyōi wo jokyo suru wo motte mottomo saku wo etaru mono to shinzu."

In the second sentence of the telegram, Tōjō specified that if Japan's military power were not sufficient to permit delivering a blow to Nanking, Japan should adopt a watchful attitude pending the completion of her defense preparations lest the Chinese attempt to interfere with Japan's current undertakings in China.

In the third sentence, Tōjō described Nanking as having no intention of adjusting relations with Japan and therefore advised against adopting the initiative in that respect. An attempt by Japan to restore friendly relations with Nanking would, in his view, merely enhance the disdain which that government was already exhibiting toward Japan.

With reference to the practice of submitting excerpts of documents, the question was repeatedly raised as to whether the entire document or only the excerpt read before the Tribunal constituted "evidence" in the eyes of the court. According to Ben Bruce Blakeney, a leading defense counsel at the trial, "The Tribunal as repeatedly ruled that all documents in their entirety were part of the 'record' as distinguished from the 'transcript.' This meant, nominally, that all judges might (and, I believe, there were statements that they would) read all exhibits in their entirety. . . ." That any of them did so, with perhaps one or two exceptions, ". . . no one for a moment believed. I think that as a practical matter you must assume that the judges knew, except perhaps in rare cases, nothing of the exhibits beyond what was read into the 'transcript' (what an American lawyer knows as 'reading into the record'). That was one of our continual complaints—that we never knew the extent of the case which we had to meet." (Blakeney corresp.)

Justification always lay in the allegedly hostile mood and threatening posture of Japan's neighbors. The influence exerted on China, the Soviet Union, Great Britain, and the United States by such earlier manifestations of Japan's own attitude as the exploitation of the Manchurian Incident was never given sustained or serious consideration. It was this narrow outlook, this refusal to face the facts, this adoption of the propaganda line, that made Japanese leadership in the period from 1937 onward so incapable of dealing effectively with succeeding crises which were largely of Japan's own making. That this was indeed the case became even more apparent when the "China Incident" was suddenly expanded, after four long and costly years of fighting, into the incomparably greater gamble of the equally misnamed "War for Greater East Asia."

Although there was much in Sino-Japanese relations in 1937 to warrant concern, the final break which occurred in July of that year came as suddenly and unexpectedly as the incident at Mukden in 1931.[25] Behind the new affair lay a history stretching back to the turn of the century. Japan had been one of the powers which had taken part in the international relief expedition necessitated by the Boxer uprising. By the terms of the protocol that was subsequently negotiated, the powers represented at Peking had obtained the right to station soldiers in the Chinese capital and along the railway which provided communication with the sea. The purpose was to prevent a recurrence of the siege of the legations which had so nearly ended in disaster. A supplementary agreement had also given the foreign troops the right to engage in field exercises, including rifle practice, "without informing the Chinese authorities except in the case of *feux de guerre*." Although more than thirty years had passed, the powers still kept legation guards in the former capital and maintained other troops between the city and the coast. But whereas the British had a handful more than a thousand men, and the French somewhere between 1,700 and 2,000, the Japanese supported a force of at least 7,000 soldiers (and possibly as many as 15,000)—a number far in excess of that needed for the purposes envisaged in the Boxer Protocol.

Beginning in June 1937 these Japanese troops engaged in night maneuvers in the vicinity of the Marco Polo Bridge on the outskirts of Peking. The area was both sensitive and strategic. The Japanese had

[25] The brief summary which follows is based on material contained in J, B/IV, 183-89 and B/V, 658-63, 682-88.

earlier tried in vain to secure a firmer footing there and had thus invited Chinese suspicion and hostility. Having had considerable experience since 1931 with Japanese encroachment upon their territory and sovereignty, the Chinese had taken the precaution of requesting that notice be given whenever such night maneuvers were planned so that the Chinese inhabitants of the area could be kept out of harm's way. Although the Japanese had hitherto acceded to this request, the maneuvers held on the night of July 7 were conducted without prior notice. About ten o'clock that evening the Chinese were informed by the Japanese that Chinese garrison troops at Wanping had opened fire upon the Japanese forces on maneuver and that one Japanese soldier was missing. The Japanese demanded the right to enter Wanping to conduct a search. The Chinese general to whom this was relayed refused to sanction Japanese entry into the town. He took the view that the maneuvers then in progress were illegal and that consequently the Chinese could not be held responsible for the missing soldier. He did offer, however, to order a Chinese search of Wanping.

After further negotiation, the Chinese consented to a joint investigation. While this was in progress during the course of the night, the Japanese brought their troops into position and opened fire on the town. On the afternoon of July 8 the Chinese garrison commander was notified that the Japanese forces would begin a general bombardment unless he surrendered by seven o'clock that evening. In the fighting that resulted from the Chinese refusal to bow to this ultimatum, the Japanese suffered a substantial number of casualties. On the very next day, July 9, they suddenly informed the Chinese that the missing soldier had been found! They also suggested terms for an immediate truce, which the Chinese accepted.

The affair would presumably have been settled without further difficulty had it not been for another inexplicable development. In the general withdrawal of troops on both sides which was part of the truce arrangement, a Japanese detachment of about one hundred men remained behind. At midnight on July 9, these soldiers began firing, once again, into the town of Wanping. As a result, Japanese troops poured back into the area in such numbers that within three days the total reached 20,000 men, with air cover and support provided by one hundred planes. Now present on the scene for the first time were large units of the Kwantung army. The danger of an expansion of this new incident was thus greatly increased.

Word of the trouble at Wanping had reached Tokyo on July 8. The following day, at an extraordinary meeting of the Konoe Cabinet, a decision was made to limit the scope of the incident so as to achieve a speedy local settlement. Within twenty-four hours of that decision, the army general staff proposed action which could only result in making fulfillment of the cabinet's announced policy immensely difficult, if not absolutely impossible. Specifically, the army advocated *reinforcing* Japan's troops in North China with two brigades from the Kwantung army, one division from Korea, and three divisions from Japan. The cabinet gave its approval on July 11. When the authorities in Tokyo were subsequently informed that the Chinese had agreed to new Japanese terms, the planned reinforcement—except for the units from the Kwantung army—was held in abeyance pending further developments.

Negotiations conducted at Nanking on instructions from Tokyo revealed that when Japan spoke of "local settlement" she meant the acceptance of her demands by regional officials in North China without the consent or confirmation of the Chinese government. This was in line with the entire trend of post-1931 Japanese policy and was the only means, short of full-scale war, by which Japan could destroy the power of Chiang Kai-shek. It was as if Mexico, in an altercation involving Texas, asserted the right to impose a settlement upon the local authorities at Austin without any reference whatsoever to the federal government in Washington. In the Chinese case, the result would have been the loss of all of North China to Japanese control.

There were undoubtedly good reasons for a policy of localization. The Japanese army and navy had never really agreed on the identity of Japan's primary enemy. The army looked to the north and the Soviet Union; the navy to the east and the United States. Since Japan could not afford to prepare against both simultaneously, the two services competed vigorously for the appropriations which were the key to preparedness. Allowing the Marco Polo Bridge affair to expand into full-scale war throughout China would complicate the army's problem of maintaining adequate forces in Manchuria against a possible Soviet attack. It would also mean delaying—perhaps indefinitely postponing—any army plans for launching an attack in that area. From the navy point of view, war in China would require commitment of forces along the China coast as well as consumption—primarily by the army—of the economic resources which might otherwise flow into navy coffers for the expansion of the fleet. Protracted war on the continent could thus seriously impair the navy's effectiveness vis-à-vis the American "enemy." Financial circles, realizing far more clearly than the services that Japan lacked the means for such full-scale involvement, also urged a policy of caution.[26]

How then can the alleged attitude of the cabinet in favor of "localization" be reconciled with its observed response in favor of expansion? The task is not easy. Even today, after so much elaborate and patient investigation by so many, the truth remains embedded in conflicting versions of events and in the continuing mysteries of motivation. To have voted one day for localization and two days later for reinforcement suggests a variety of possibilities: the Konoe Cabinet may have been confused, irresponsible, or inept; it may have been an accessory before the fact; or it may have set such narrow limits to its policy of localization as inadvertently to render that policy a practical impossibility. In this sense, without even considering the consequences of what it proposed, the cabinet may actually have been willing to be reasonable so long as the other side gave in completely, apologized for current and past wrongs, and accepted—in advance of the event—full responsibility for any future occurrences. If this was the case, then it is certain that the Konoe Cabinet, like the army, was prepared and determined to use force if the other side refused to act in the manner suggested.[27]

A postwar Japanese view of the China Incident, prepared for the Military History Section of U.S. Army headquarters in Tokyo, provides much basis for speculation in a few words: "Although both the Japanese and Chinese Governments tried to avoid full-scale clashes in the hope of realizing an early peace, they missed the opportunity of entering formal negotiations. . . . This was due in part to the effort of the Chinese Nationalist Government to save face both domestically and internationally by discrediting Japan's real intentions and in part to the lack of unity within the Japanese Army caused mainly by the *unyielding attitude of radical elements.*"[28]

Konoe himself later attributed the blame to the passive resistance of those in the army who ostensibly agreed with the nonexpansion policy while actually working behind the scenes to undermine that policy. At least, that was what the chief of the operations bureau of the army general staff had told the prince when asked for an explanation. The culprits were said to be officers in the war ministry and in the field. Such an explanation fits well with the fact that the machinations of

[26] See JRD Monograph No. 144, 10 and 13.
[27] See, for instance, the policy reported to the Emperor on July 11, 1937, in *ibid.,* Appendix 5.
[28] *Ibid.,* 20. Italics mine.

certain strategically placed officers had indeed made the government dance to a military tune on other occasions, but the probable prejudice of Konoe's source of information and the existence of evidence showing greater civilian collaboration with the military in 1937 than in 1931 impair the plausibility of that interpretation as representing the whole truth.[29]

On July 20, 1937, the Konoe Cabinet authorized the mobilization of three divisions after all. A week later the commander of Japan's garrison forces informed Tokyo that he had exhausted every means at his disposal to achieve a peaceful settlement of the issue. He therefore requested permission to use force. This request was approved by the central military authorities in Tokyo without any recorded objection or even questioning on the part of the cabinet. In fact, the mobilization orders were extended, with one division being earmarked for Shanghai and another for Tsingtao, ostensibly to guarantee the safety of Japanese nationals residing in those cities and to protect Japanese property. This concern with lives and property has frequently been cited as justification for the sending of additional forces to China.[30] Yet it does not seem far-fetched to suggest that a government sincerely desirous of limiting the scope of hostilities could at least have protected its nationals, and possibly its property as well, by means other than those employed. Or, if reinforcement had proved necessary after all, Japan's long-term good intentions could have been demonstrated by a prompt withdawal of troops once their specific mission of saving lives had been accomplished. Unfortunately, the nation that walked out of Geneva in 1933 because it had been judged responsible for the Manchurian Incident was unlikely, in 1937, to adopt a policy of reasonableness when involved in a similar affair south of the Great Wall.

Sporadic fighting and further clashes occurred as the situation in North China continued to deteriorate. Nanking offered to submit the matter to negotiation, and the United States tendered its good offices, but Japan remained aloof. On July 26, 1937, a new Japanese ultimatum demanded the withdrawal from the Peking area, within twenty-four hours, of China's 27th Division. The failure of the Chinese to comply resulted in the outbreak of hostilities at Peking. The next day, in Tokyo, Premier Konoe told the Diet that his government was determined to

---

[29] See Konoe, 22-23. In postwar interrogations, Tōjō laid the failure of the localization policy to the independence of the supreme command. "Premier Konoye," he said, "had a terrible time." See Tōjō interrog., Mar. 13, 5-6.

[30] See, for instance, CF 20, III, 270. The views of General Matsui (J, B/V, 707) add an interesting dimension.

achieve a "new order" in East Asia. Japan, he said, did not want Chinese territory, but she did seek mutual cooperation and assistance. A local settlement of outstanding issues was no longer sufficient. Something more was needed now: specifically, a basic adjustment of Sino-Japanese relations. Thus was Japan "irrevocably committed to the conquest of China."[31]

By the end of July the Peking-Tientsin area was under heavy attack by Japan's North China expeditionary forces, commanded by Shozo Kawabe, who had been with Tojo in Switzerland years before. When Peking was captured on August 8, Kawabe paraded his troops on the streets of the city, posted proclamations designating himself military governor, and threatened death to any Chinese who disobeyed his orders. Such was the Japanese concentration of military strength in the area that by early September neutral observers estimated that Japan had 160,000 men fighting in North China.[32]

In the meantime hostilities had spread to the great port city of Shanghai. Although the evidence later presented on the origins of the fighting there proved contradictory, this expansion of hostilities marked Tokyo's complete abandonment of the localization policy.[33] Japan dispatched further reinforcements to the area and began employing aircraft to supplement action on the ground. Japanese planes did not confine their activities to the immediate area of attack but ranged far afield—bombing the Nationalist capital at Nanking and other key cities in the interior. At the same time the Japanese navy began tightening its blockade along the China coast. Major harbors were subjected to aerial attack.

While this pounding was in progress, Japan's vice-minister for foreign affairs, in a broadcast to the United States, described what was taking place as resulting from the anti-Japanese acts of the Chinese. Reaffirming his nation's peaceful intentions and speaking in a vein which had by now become characteristic of official pronouncements, he blandly declared that the ultimate purpose of the current hostilities in North China and Shanghai was to create a situation which would permit the realization of genuine cooperation between Japan and China.[34] An imperial edict issued several days later emphasized that Japan was seeking, through her military action, "to urge grave self-reflection upon China and to establish peace in the Far East without delay."[35]

[31] J, B/IV, 185-89 and B/V, 688-92.
[32] J, B/V, 693-94.
[33] See *ibid.*, 693-702.
[34] *Ibid.*, 698-99.
[35] *Ibid.*, 700-1.

In order to ensure that such developments would be forthcoming, the Japanese supreme command dispatched additional troops. It also expanded the area of hostilities and established, for the more effective consummation of its purposes, the Central China expeditionary forces. Thus the fighting spread south and north and west from Shanghai, with Nanking on the Yangtze River becoming the new focus of concentration. If the Japanese could annihilate the Nationalist armies and capture the capital, it was believed that the Chinese house of cards would collapse and the immediate goal—an autonomous region in North China dominated by Japan—would be achieved.

By early December Nanking was ripe for the plucking. On the 13th Japan's expeditionary forces entered the city without encountering any effective or sustained resistance. Despite the fact that the Chinese military had evacuated Nanking and were in full flight, the members of the ever-victorious Japanese army perpetrated in the former Nationalist capital an orgy of murder, rape, and pillage which is almost beyond power of belief.[36] The soldiers of Japan were "let loose like a barbarian horde to desecrate the city." Individuals and small groups of two or three roamed at will "murdering, raping, looting and burning. There was no discipline whatever. Many soldiers were drunk." They "went through the streets indiscriminately killing Chinese men, women and children without apparent provocation or excuse until in places the streets and alleys were littered with the bodies of their victims." Chinese were "hunted like rabbits, everyone seen to move was shot. At least 12,000 noncombatant Chinese men, women and children met their deaths in these indiscriminate killings during the first two or three days of the Japanese occupation of the city. . . . Approximately 20,000 cases of rape occurred . . . during the first month [with many of the women being killed afterwards and their bodies mutilated]. . . .

[36] The details which follow, and all quotations referring to the Rape of Nanking, are from J, B/VIII, 1011-19 and 1023-24. See also J, B/V, 707-8, and IMTFE, "Roling Opinion," 204-9. At the time of these events, the German representative in China informed Berlin of the "atrocities and criminal acts" being committed by the Japanese army, which he described as a "bestial machinery."

The Japan Year Book, 1946-48 (p. 177) describes what happened at Nanking as follows: "By December 7, the outer defenses of Nanking were under attack, and a week later Japanese anger at the stubborn Chinese defense of Shanghai [which had slowed the Japanese advance and had caused heavy casualties] burst upon Nanking in an appalling reign of terror. . . . For four weeks the streets of Nanking were splattered with blood and littered with mutilated bodies, while Japanese soldiers ran amok, causing untold suffering among the civil population."

With reference to Japanese claims that the laws of war did not apply to the fighting in China, see J, B/VIII, 1003-4 and 1008-10.

Japanese soldiers took from the people everything they desired." They would stop unarmed civilians and search them for valuables. If none were found, the soldiers would take their revenge by shooting whoever had thus deprived them of their due. Stores and warehouses and private homes were looted of their contents and put to the torch. "Such burning appeared to follow a prescribed pattern after a few days and continued for six weeks. Approximately one-third of the city was thus destroyed."

"Organized and wholesale murder of male civilians was conducted with the apparent sanction of the commanders on the pretense that Chinese soldiers had removed their uniforms and were mingling with the population. Groups of Chinese civilians were formed, bound with their hands behind their backs, and marched outside the walls of the city where they were killed ... by machine gun fire and with bayonets. More than 20,000 Chinese men of military age are known to have died in this fashion."

Similar atrocities were committed against Chinese outside the city to a distance of more than sixty miles. Some 57,000 civilian refugees were captured and interned, only to be starved and tortured in captivity and, upon occasion, machine-gunned and bayoneted to death. Chinese soldiers who had surrendered outside Nanking were subsequently killed en masse along the Yangtze River by the machine-gun fire of their captors. "Estimates made at a later date indicate that the total number of civilians and prisoners of war murdered in Nanking and its vicinity during the first six weeks of the Japanese occupation was over 200,000."

Japanese embassy officials who entered Nanking with advance army units admitted to an International Committee for the Nanking Safety Zone that the army intended "to make it bad for Nanking." When complaints to the army by foreigners present in the city failed to produce any results, these same embassy officials advised the foreigners to "try and get publicity in Japan, so that the Japanese Government would be forced by public opinion to curb the Army." Such was the nature of the situation confronting the Committee that its secretary found it necessary to file, with the Japanese authorities, two protests per day for the first six weeks following the army's entry into the former Nationalist capital.

It was not until much much later that open boasting about their misdeeds by Japanese officers and men returning to Japan from China gave the central military authorities cause for reflection. Top-secret orders were issued in February 1939, not against the commission of such atrocities, but *against revelations concerning them* within the home islands. It was feared that "improper talk" would give rise to rumors, undermine the confidence of the people in the army, and thus possibly endanger the objectives of Japan's "Holy War."

Midway between the outbreak of the "Incident" in July and the terrible events of December, Yosuke Matsuoka, who was to become foreign minister in a later Konoe Cabinet, explained to the Associated Press what was happening on the continent: "China and Japan are two brothers who have inherited a great mansion called Eastern Asia. Adversity sent them both down to the depth of poverty. The ne'er-do-well elder brother turned a dope fiend and a rogue, but the younger, lean, but rugged and ambitious, ever dreamed of bringing back past glories to the old House. He sold newspapers at a street corner and worked hard to support the house. The elder flimflammed the younger out of his meagre savings and sold him out to their common enemy. The younger in a towering rage beat up the elder—trying to beat into him some sense of shame and awaken some pride in the noble traditions of the great house. After many scraps, the younger finally made up his mind to stage a show-down fight. And that is the fight now raging along the North China and Shanghai fronts."[37]

Equally revealing were the words of General Iwane Matsui, who had also once represented Japan at Geneva but who was now commander of the Japanese army which was wreaking such terrible and senseless vengeance upon Nanking. Matsui, who had remained in a rear area, entered the city in triumph on December 17. In a statement issued the next day he said, in part: "Now the flag of the Rising Sun is floating over Nanking, and the Imperial Way is shining forth in the area south of the Yangtze. The dawn of the renaissance of Eastern Asia is about to take place. On this occasion, it is my earnest hope that the 400 million people of China will reconsider."[38]

This was a favorite Japanese theme of those years. Regardless of the

[37] Recorded in the *Japan Weekly Chronicle* for October 21, 1937, 548-49 (also quoted, in part, in Quigley, *Far Eastern War, 1937-1941*, 59-60). See also Tōjō interrog., Feb. 4, 4: "There was real fighting to be sure, but it was considered to be a family quarrel, in which the younger [*sic*] brother, China, was being made to reconsider its various illegal acts typified by such anti-Japanese phrases as kōnichi (oppose the Japs) and hainichi (expel the Japs). The basic purpose was always the fostering of good neighborliness and friendship and for that reason the thing was never called a war nor was there a declaration of war."

[38] S 44:13, T 3509-13, and J, B/VIII, 1016-17. The sentences quoted have been retranslated from the original. A brief résumé of Matsui's career (he was delegate plenipotentiary to the Geneva General Disarmament Conference during 1932) is found in T 735-37. Matsui was sentenced to death by hanging in 1948 by the IMTFE (see J, C/X, 1180-82 and 1216).

injustice done them, the Chinese were supposed to "reconsider" once they had been beaten nearly to death. But they did not. The Generalissimo, driven from Nanking, established his headquarters at Hankow, from which he subsequently retired still farther to the west and south to the city of Chungking. By October 1938 both Hankow and Canton were in Japanese hands, and the opportunity for a solution seemed less and less likely to materialize. Despite the advisability of avoiding a deterioration of relations with the West, which had been clearly recognized in the basic policy decision adopted by the Hirota Cabinet in 1936, the Japanese had succeeded through their military action in condemning themselves in the eyes of the United States and Great Britain. Yet in Japan this simple fact never seemed to penetrate the national consciousness.

For Hideki Tojo, who was still serving in Manchuria as chief of staff of the Kwantung army, the China Incident brought a sudden and unexpected break in his routine administrative duties. It gave him, too, his only opportunity in a long career of soldiering to lead men into combat. Shortly after the trouble began, the Kwantung army was ordered by Tokyo to send troops to Tientsin to reinforce Japan's North China expeditionary forces. Although these orders were instantly obeyed, the situation soon developed to a point where the commander-in-chief of the Kwantung army personally decided that further reinforcement, from a different direction, was necessary. According to Tojo's postwar account, Japanese troops in the Peking area were being hard-pressed by Chinese forces approaching the ancient capital from the north and northwest. He was therefore ordered by the commander-in-chief to lead two Kwantung army brigades in a flanking movement which would bring them in behind the Chinese—a sortie of at least several hundred miles and possibly a good deal more. Although Tojo made light of the matter, at the time of the event he was credited with having carried out an extremely successful lightning operation—a *blitzkrieg* which launched the pick of the Kwantung army into Chahar province with a force likened to that of surging waves on an angry sea.

One triumph followed another until the whole of Inner Mongolia came under the control of Hideki Tojo. The "Tojo corps" set up supply bases and took command of a line of communications to the rear which stretched across the great Mongolian desert. Tojo then flew back to Manchuria to launch preparations for operations against the Soviet Union, which was still considered the real enemy and likely to attack at any moment. Included among these preparations were plans calling for the establishment of meteorological stations at various points in Inner Mongolia, the extension of the enlistment of Japanese soldiers serving in Manchukuo, and the construction of fortifications.[39]

While Tojo confined his own activities largely to military matters, others turned their attention to an economic and industrial development of Manchukuo and North China that would permit those areas to contribute effectively toward preparations for what the commander-in-chief of the Kwantung army called "the fast-approaching war with Soviet Russia."[40] Following Germany's recognition of Manchukuo in February 1938, Tojo informed the army general staff in Tokyo that the Kwantung army felt that Manchukuo should become a party, as soon as possible, to the Anti-Comintern Pact. The vice-minister of war "replied that the Japanese Cabinet would offer no objection, but desired to preserve the fiction of Manchukuoan independence. It was thought best that the Manchukuoan government should take the first step, acting as if of its own volition, and requesting Japanese assistance."[41]

Tojo's combat experiences in Chahar, brief though they were, gave him a firm appreciation of the importance of mechanized warfare. The reputation he gained from his successful exploits at the beginning of the China Incident saved him from embarrassment later on when he headed Japan's war effort against the Western powers. For Japan to have had a war minister and premier who had never been any closer to battle than a rear area in 1905, and whose only fighting assignment had been "bandit" suppression in Manchuria after 1931, would no doubt have been regarded with some consternation. It is a rather startling fact that Tojo was actually a 53-year-old lieutenant general before he had his first real taste of war and that the enemy he faced then was frequently ill-trained, underfed, poorly equipped, inadequately led, and generally disorganized.

Although Tojo later readily admitted that his troops had been engaged in offensive military operations in Chahar, he drew attention to the cabinet's policy of localization and declared, ". . . in the overall picture, Japan was on the defensive. . . . The Chinese had more men, the weather was very bad so that Japanese planes could not fly, a number of railroads

---

[39] See Shunichirō Itō, 67-71; Tōjō interrog., Jan. 14, 14, Feb. 5, 1-5, and March 8, 1-2; Lory, 130; and J, B/IV, 203-4 and 219-22.

[40] J, B/IV, 220. On Japan's economic domination of Manchuria and other parts of China, see J, B/IV, 161-65 and B/V, 761-75.

[41] J, B/IV, 221-22. The vice-minister of war (Umezu) was presumably acting for the army general staff.

were washed out because of heavy rains, and it was impossible to dispatch sufficient troops from Japan proper."[42]

To Tojo, the whole China Incident was a matter of self-defense. In his words, it "burst out suddenly and just developed," but "the underlying cause was the illegal actions of the Chinese." There is no doubt that Tojo supported the policy of the Japanese army and of the government in Tokyo. His own telegram of a month earlier, even if read in the most favorable light, suggests that had he been at the scene in China or at the center in Tokyo he would certainly have followed a similar course. In fact, he might have acted with even more dispatch than that which turned the Marco Polo Bridge affair from a minor clash into a full-scale war. As Tojo saw it, the Japanese troops sent into the area of conflict were never numerous enough to settle the Incident. "For that reason, losses were great and the fighting dragged on. My own opinion at that time," he later said, "was that it would have been better to send a great many more troops and get the thing over with."[43]

From a purely military standpoint that would no doubt have been best. From a purely military standpoint, also, there was probably good reason to believe that the Chinese, if confronted with superior force, would be unable to offer any more effective resistance than they had in 1931 in Manchuria. But Japan had yet to learn in China the lesson of the French in Russia—the lesson that Chiang Kai-shek was to turn to profit now by trading space for time. "China?" Napoleon had once said. "There lies a sleeping giant. Let him sleep! For when he wakes he will move the world."

Had the Japanese realized in 1937 that they were dealing with a waking giant, the war which they were then waging in China under the pretext of settling an incident might never have spread to the Pacific. But, once committed to chastising the Chinese for the insolence and insincerity of wanting to be masters in their own house, the Japanese chose to think of their enemy in such derogatory terms that the only explanation they could find for their failure to achieve a thorough victory was the machinations of the Communists, on the one hand, and of the great powers, on the other. It was this search for a scapegoat—this quest for any way out other than the only way out—that was to lead them to the vast Armageddon of the Pacific and to the greatest and costliest gamble in their entire history.

[42] Tōjō interrog., March 8, 1-2.
[43] Ibid.

CHAPTER 5

Toward a New Order in East Asia

WITH the outbreak of the China Incident in 1937 the leaders of Japan assumed an inexorable position. They felt compelled either to dictate terms of peace to China or to continue fighting even though there was little prospect of success. Each new military thrust by Japan resulted in further gains but did not bring the war any closer to an end. And yet, despite this inability to secure a Chinese capitulation, Japan remained rigid and unrelenting in her demands upon China, thus rendering the possibility of a diplomatic settlement ever more remote.

Once again China appealed to the League. Japan was invited to join in its deliberations, but Tokyo refused. This unwillingness to give support to international efforts designed to secure a peaceful settlement of the dispute did not inspire confidence in the sincerity of Tokyo's intentions. After studying the situation in China, the League announced that Japanese military operations were in excess of any need imposed by the incident which had triggered the hostilities. The League further charged that Japan's action in China was in direct and open violation of Japan's obligations under the Nine-Power Pact of 1922 and the Kellogg-Briand Treaty signed at Paris in 1928. A resolution was passed which stated that League members should avoid doing anything which might undermine China's position vis-à-vis Japan. The resolution also called upon each member to give consideration to rendering positive assistance to China.[1] This relatively mild action by the League was bitterly denounced in Japan.

According to Yosuke Matsuoka, who qualified as a Japanese "expert" on League affairs, there was no doubt that Japan had been "exceedingly annoying" to China. "Japan is expanding," he declared. "And what

[1] See J, B/IV, 193, 324-26, and B/V 702-3, in which the League's findings of October 6, 1937, are summarized. The United States, although not a member, concurred in the findings the very same day. In November 1938 Japan gave notice that the cooperative relations she had maintained with the League despite her withdrawal in 1933 could no longer be sustained in the light of the League's condemnation of Japan (see J, B/IV, 331-34 and B/V, 732-33).

country in its expansion era has ever failed to be trying to its neighbours? Ask the American Indian or the Mexican how excruciatingly trying the young United States used to be once upon a time."

"But Japan's expansion, like that of the United States, is as natural as the growth of a child. Only one thing stops a child from growing:—death.

"Geneva has been trying to pass this death sentence on Japan since the Manchurian incident, masking it with tinsel phrases of pious hypocrisy. But Nippon does not seem amicable enough to die even for the sweet sake of Geneva-made peace."[2]

And so the fighting in China continued, and the authorities in Tokyo kept insisting that Japan's actions there were legal and natural.[3] Independent Japanese efforts to secure a settlement by timing diplomatic overtures to take advantage of victories on the field of battle invariably failed to produce results. What Japan wanted (such as Chinese recognition of the *fait accompli* in Manchuria and the establishment of a demilitarized zone in North China) was always more than China could reasonably have been expected to offer.[4] At the same time, Japan seemed determined to reject arbitration by a third power. When the foreign minister on one occasion accepted a British proffer of good offices, the matter had subsequently to be deferred because of the opposition which developed within the Japanese army with respect to utilizing the British in even that minor role.[5]

In this same period Japan received two invitations from the Belgian government to attend a multipower conference at Brussels composed of the signatories of the Nine-Power Pact. Although the conference was being organized in accordance with the provisions of that treaty in order to study ways and means of securing an amicable solution, the Konoe Cabinet declined to participate on the grounds that "frank and full discussion to bring about a just solution of the conflict could not be expected." Despite this rebuff, the conference met at Brussels. It accomplished nothing concrete with respect either to aiding China or to staying Japan's hand, but it did produce a further resolution declaring

[2] *Japan Weekly Chronicle*, October 21, 1937, 548.

[3] Japanese propaganda efforts to convince the world of the lawfulness of Japan's activities in China can be traced to a Kwantung army plan of December 1935. See J, B/IV, 191 and B/V, 658-63.

[4] See, for instance, the so-called "August Plan" (J, B/V, 708-10), the decision made by the Japanese government on October 1, 1937 (J, B/V, 703-4), and the developments of January 11 and 16, 1938 (J, B/V, 710-13).

[5] J, B/V, 704-5.

Japan the aggressor. To all such pronouncements, the Japanese government officially remained indifferent. Tokyo continued adamantly to insist that Japan's military operations in China constituted defense against Chinese acts of provocation and that such operations did not therefore fall within the scope of Japan's treaty obligations. Unofficially, each new condemnation of Japanese aggressive action in China was pounced upon as further proof that Japan was being victimized by a hostile combination of powers.[6]

Censure of Japan was not confined to Geneva and Brussels; disapproval emanated even from Berlin. The German foreign office was afraid that hostilities in China would interfere not only with Germany's rights and interests there but also with Hitler's general anti-Soviet policy—a policy in which the Chinese Nationalists, weak though they were, could still play a part. The Wilhelmstrasse was thus extremely annoyed at the actions of Hitler's Anti-Comintern Pact partner and lost no time in making its views known. As seen in Tokyo, this was once again a case of the other party failing to understand Japan's true intentions: the anti-Communist nature of Japanese activity in China and the "benefit" to Germany of this implementation of Japan's treaty "obligations." Berlin remained unconvinced; Reichminister Weizsäcker even went so far as to remind the Japanese ambassador that the pact had not been designed to encourage attacks upon communism in territories not belonging to the signatories. He also declared that the German government looked with disfavor upon Japanese radio propaganda in Germany aimed at convincing the German people that Japan was fighting a war against communism in China.[7]

This was certainly pointed enough, but it failed to produce any modification of the Japanese position. Although the German ambassador to China subsequently acted as a go-between in Sino-Japanese peace negotiations, the effort came to naught. The conditions forwarded to him from Tokyo left no doubt as to the heavy price Japan was placing on its willingness to negotiate. The ambassador became annoyed with the Japanese approach and subsequently informed Berlin that Germany

[6] On the Brussels conference and Japan's attitude toward her treaty obligations, see J, B/IV, 193-96; J, B/V, 705-6; and Hattori, I, 41, in which the conference is described as an effort to check Japan and to interfere in the Sino-Japanese "dispute" (*funsō*).

[7] J, B/V, 692-93. See also Schorske, "Two German Ambassadors: Dirksen and Schulenburg," in Craig and Gilbert (eds.), *The Diplomats, 1919-1939*, 479-81, and von Dirksen, *Moscow, Tokyo, London*, 188-91 (". . . responsibility for the Marco Polo Bridge incident is a minor issue. The paramount fact is that Japan must be held responsible for the outbreak of the war with China for the reason that she pursued a continuous policy of aggression.").

was "losing face" with the Chinese. Soon thereafter the matter was abruptly taken out of his hands when the "Konoe declaration" of January 16, 1938, slammed the door to negotiations which thus far had been kept just barely ajar. Behind this episode lies the interesting fact that, for once, the civilian cart was before the military horse.

The Japanese army had been extremely optimistic during the opening days of the fighting on the continent. It had boasted that it would be able to take care of China in three months. But by the end of the year the general staff had grown more cautious. Its members were becoming concerned lest the incident develop into a protracted war which not only would consume valuable resources (that Japan could ill afford to squander) but would also result in a progressively deteriorating military position with respect to the Soviet Union, Great Britain, and the United States. The members of the "main current" felt that Japan should offer more specific and conciliatory terms than those sent to the German ambassador. Foreign Minister Hirota, on the other hand, argued that it was China who was beaten and not Japan, that the Chinese were lacking in good faith, and that they would simply take advantage of any conciliatory moves initiated by the Japanese government. Hirota apparently also feared that China might attempt to secure great-power intervention, or that the powers themselves might arbitrarily endeavor to impose mediation upon the belligerents.

In view of Hirota's stand, the vice-chief of staff (who was representing the army's viewpoint to the cabinet) decided to leave the matter to the cabinet's discretion. Several days later, despite continuing objections from members of the "main current" of the army general staff, Prince Konoe publicly declared that Japan would thenceforth refuse to have any dealings with the Nationalist government of China.[8] This attitude committed Japan, in the short run at least, to a do-or-die attempt to impose its will by force. It led inevitably to the formation of various Japanese-dominated local regimes in the occupied areas—a preparatory step toward the creation of a new puppet government in China.[9] It also

[8] On the German role as go-between and the divergence of views between the Konoe Cabinet and the army general staff, see J, B/IV, 214-19, 294-96, B/V, 708-13; Hattori, I, 37-38 and 246; JRD Monograph No. 144, Appendix 11; and Kido SKD. In late January 1938 the German ambassador in Tōkyō advised Berlin to throw its support behind the Japanese *fait accompli* in China. Hitler did so a month later.

The translation of Konoe's declaration, as given in the "Judgment," requires considerable revision. In a small book published posthumously, Konoe admitted that his declaration had been a mistake (Konoe, 17-18). See also Wakatsuki, 414-15.

[9] On the creation of Japanese-dominated local regimes and plans for the establishment of a new "central government," see J, B/IV, 222-24 and B/V, 714-21, 724-32. The financing of such local regimes was met in part by the development of an extensive

led to perhaps the most serious development of all: the complete mobilization of the Japanese nation for war—a move which necessitated fundamental changes in Japan's internal political structure.

The beginning of Japanese industrial and economic planning for war had actually preceded the outbreak of hostilities in China by several months. The plans which were drafted in the spring of 1937 embodied the principles which had been laid down in the basic national policy decision of August 1936. The general purpose was to secure national self-sufficiency in important resources by 1941. With the onset of war in China, these plans assumed a special urgency. Emphasis was placed upon the manufacture of synthetic petroleum, the production of iron and steel, and the expansion and control of all transportation facilities. This activity naturally included Manchukuo and the areas of China proper that were then under Japanese occupation. As a necessary concomitant of these developments, measures were adopted to establish a controlled economy.[10]

Every conceivable step was taken to mold the nation to the requirements of the new situation created by the China Incident. This meant securing enthusiastic and self-sacrificing devotion to the military cause and to the army's will. An immediate intensification of existing censorship procedures was inaugurated, with the ministry for home affairs assuming a key role in the suppression of public criticism. The drive for uniformity of thought and the glorification of death on the battlefield were carried into the schools and pursued with a vengeance. The bureau which had been established in 1936 to coordinate the control and dissemination of information and propaganda emanating from government ministries was reorganized as a cabinet information bureau. A cabinet advisory council was established, composed of ten leading public figures representing the military services, the political parties, financial

---

drug traffic carried out under the guise of "opium suppression" (see J, B/V, 771-75). "Throughout both Manchukuo and China, drugs were openly advertised and sold. . . . In China in 1939 the Japanese military estimated that the annual revenue from the narcotization policy was $300,000,000" (Horwitz, 511-12).

[10] On Japanese industrial and economic planning for war prior to the China Incident, see J, B/IV, 163-68 and 176-83; on developments after July 1937, J, B/IV, 196-207, 210, and 222-24. While the government was encouraging the development of strategic industries through special legislation, tax exemptions, and subsidization, it was also lavishing funds upon the military services through disbursements from a newly established "War Expenditure Account." In the case of the army, total expenditures rose from more than 500 million yen in 1936 to nearly 2,750 million yen in 1937. In the same period, the army's fighting strength jumped from 450,000 men to 950,000.

interests, and diplomatic circles.[11] These "men of stature" were to advise and assist the government in the formulation of important national policies relating to China. Included among its members were Mr. Matsu-oka and General Araki. There can be little doubt that while serving on the council both exercised their considerable vocal talents in behalf of the very decided opinions which each, from time to time, had already placed on public record.

In a statement to the press, Matsuoka declared that Japan was at last in for "the final . . . knockout decision; a once-for-all house cleaning of all tortuous tangles in . . . Sino-Japanese relations" that had been "plaguing the East for ages." In 1904 Japan had "staked her national existence in a fight against Russia . . . to beat back a nightmare avalanche from without." That had been an affair revolving around Japan's "outer fences." Now, however, in China, Japan was "dealing with a festering sore deep down within the bosom of Eastern Asia threatening . . . all Asian races with sure and inescapable death." The situation called for "heroic surgery." Japan had "taken up her scalpel" and would "permit no foreign interference whatsoever." The current crisis on the continent was "infinitely bigger and more significant than the Russian war" of 1904-1905. "The destiny of Asia" could be worked out only through "constant and hearty co-operation between the peoples of Japan and of China." No one appreciated this more than Japan. "She knows also," Matsuoka declared, "that the two things poisoning the atmosphere between the two peoples are the drunken orgy of China's own war lords and politicians, and . . . red Communism eating into the heart of China from without. Japan is out today to put a potter's field wooden cross over these common enemies of the Chinese people and of the lasting peace of Eastern Asia. . . . Japan has no quarrel whatever with the people of China."[12]

[11] On the further development of thought control and the creation of the cabinet advisory council (on October 15, 1937), see J, B/IV, 208-14 (in which reference is made to the fact that the defendants, Kido and Kaya, served as education and as finance minister, respectively, during the period in question); J, B/V, 702; *Tōkyō Asahi Shinbun*, October 15, 1937, *yūkan*, 3H and October 20, 1937, *yūkan*, 1; and *Japan Weekly Chronicle*, October 21, 1937, 543.

[12] *Japan Weekly Chronicle*, October 21, 1937, 548. Matsuoka also said that it was thanks to Japan that Manchuria existed at all (a reference to Japan's victory over Russia in 1904-1905): "There would have been no Manchuria, for which the Chinese patriots froth at the mouth or the League of Nations denounce Japan as an international robber. And in place of the proud Republic of China, one would have seen a crazy quilt of European colonies after the fond fancies of the author of the 'Break-up of China' [Lord Charles Beresford]. For some mystic reason our Chinese friends in Nanking find it so convenient to forget this little fact."

For a nation which had no quarrel whatever with the Chinese people, Japan was acting in a rather curious manner. In November 1937, the cabinet capped its earlier moves toward strengthening Japan's internal structure by giving its blessings to the establishment of "imperial headquarters"—an organization which normally came into existence only in time of war.[13] Concurrently, a cabinet crisis was narrowly averted when the then education minister, Marquis Koichi Kido, managed to talk Prince Konoe out of his declared intention to resign. Konoe's desire to withdraw was linked to his inability to cope with the many problems that pressed for solution as the area of fighting continued to expand. Perhaps for the first time since July, Konoe truly understood the magnitude of the task Japan had undertaken, as well as the degree of his own responsibility. Kido advised the prince that the repercussions of a resignation might be extremely serious. The national economy, already laboring under considerable difficulties, would be subjected to greater strain, the internal political situation would be thrown into confusion, the fighting in China would be adversely affected, and the unfriendly attitude of the powers, as revealed at Geneva and Brussels, would be enhanced. Because of these arguments, Konoe decided to remain in office a while longer.[14]

Shortly after this show of "determination" on the premier's part, the Japanese army again proved itself to be the real master of the situation. Trouble arose over Diet opposition to legislation proposed by the cabinet with regard to industrial expansion. In this emergency the army rushed into the breach with a proposal for a national mobilization law which would deprive the Diet of the remaining vestiges of its control over government measures pertaining to war. The Konoe Cabinet and the army, working hand in hand, were so successful in balancing or eliminating the forces of opposition that the Diet proved willing to vote for its own capitulation.

Contributing to the government's victory was the same Kenryo Sato who had been involved in the "Ugaki miscarriage" and in the decisions reached at the Takara-tei. During a committee meeting on the proposed

[13] On imperial headquarters, see Tōjō interrog., Mar. 14, 1-7 and Attachment; Tōjō aff., S 344:4, T 36386-88 (which corrects a statement in the preceding interrog.); Hattori, I, 243-44; J, B/IV, 208-10 and B/V, 706; JRD, "Statements," II:50724 (Takushirō Hattori and Katsuhei Nakamura), 653-54; and Ohmae corresp. Despite the establishment of imperial headquarters, Japan was careful to maintain the fiction that the war in China was merely an "incident." On this question, see J, B/VIII, 1003-4 and B/V, 723-24; Tōjō interrog., Feb. 4, 4 and Feb. 5, 1-3 and 5; Tōjō cross-examination, S 346:3, T 36566; and Hattori, I, 41.

[14] The cabinet crisis of November 1937 is summarized in J, B/IV, 214-16.

law, a Diet member demanded an explanation of the bill from someone who really understood it. He declared that the law had probably been drafted by young bureaucrats and army officers and that consequently the responsible cabinet ministers would not know what it was all about and would be unable to discuss it, even if they were asked to do so. Sato, who was then a lieutenant colonel and very much at the center of things, was serving as a *setsumei-in*: a person authorized by a cabinet minister to offer explanations in the Diet on certain specified matters. "Explainers" were not supposed to stand up and volunteer their own views, but the Diet member who wanted an expert opinion declared that anyone would do so long as he was thoroughly conversant with the bill. Sato therefore took it upon himself to respond. After speaking for about thirty minutes, he was interrupted by a representative named Miyawaki who objected to Sato being permitted to continue. The chairman of the committee, acting with the concurrence of a majority of the members, told Sato to resume his explanations. When Sato endeavored to do so, Miyawaki angrily stood up and again interfered. Losing his temper, Sato shouted, "Shut up!" Needless to say, this breach of etiquette made a bad impression and led to charges that the army was bringing pressure to bear on the Diet and was attempting to force a decline in its influence.[15]

Despite his rudeness to Representative Miyawaki, Sato rendered yeoman service to the army and the cabinet in helping to secure passage of the bill. The national reorganization which had been a key topic at the Takara-tei in 1936 was thus brought to the threshold of reality. The provisions of the national general mobilization law emphasized "the many-sidedness and all-embracing nature of Japanese preparations for war. It was not merely a matter of military or naval or economic preparedness. Every aspect of national life was to be so ordered as to produce the maximum pitch of warlike efficiency. The entire strength of the Japanese nation was to be harnessed and developed with this single end in view. The National General Mobilization Law provided the instrument through which that goal might be achieved."[16]

In explaining the law to the Japanese people, the army again repeated

[15] On the national general mobilization law, see J, B/IV, 183, 242-53, and B/V 723; Kenryō Sato, "Dai-Tōa Sensō wo Maneita Shōwa no Dōran," 102 (from which the account of the *damare jiken* is taken); and JRD Monograph No. 45, 16-17. At the time in question, Sato was secretary of the cabinet planning board and a member of the military affairs bureau. In his 1956 article cited above, Sato declared that the *damare jiken* had simply been a mistake due to his youth; he had not been acting under orders; if the Diet was so weak that its influence would decline as a result of a single "shot" by one *setsumei-in*, then it would probably have collapsed of its own accord if it had simply been left alone.
[16] J, B/IV, 248.

the refrain which the nation had already learned by rote and which it seemed incapable of questioning: Japan was a small country living in a hostile environment; Japan had too few resources to provide for her many people; she was surrounded by those who would do her harm if they could—the Chinese, the Russians, the Americans, and the British; opening a way to the future would require the full development of the nation's strength; the national general mobilization law would accomplish that purpose.[17]

The people were also told that the fighting in China, no matter how long it continued, must not be allowed to stand in the way of the basic objectives of Japan's national policy. The army portrayed Japan, Manchukuo, and the areas of China under Japanese control as a special sphere which must be protected not only against China's "anti-Japanese" forces but also against the hostile schemes of the Soviet Union, Great Britain, and the United States. The acquisition of a war potential equal to this enormous task constituted the army's principal purpose.[18]

Working behind the "smoke screen of the China emergency," the army secured the passage of economic- and thought-control measures that the British ambassador later described as "the precursors of the movement which was gradually to place Japan on a fully totalitarian footing." "Looked at in retrospect," he wrote, "these earlier measures may not appear more draconian than those which we ourselves were later obliged to take in order to equip the country for total war against Germany. But there is one great difference between the two cases. In Britain we temporarily handed over some of our liberties to a Government ready and anxious to restore them when the emergency had passed. In Japan each successive measure of repression added to the political power of the Army, to which the very name of liberty was anathema. For behind the Civil Government stood the Army—in those days still an *eminence grise*, but soon to emerge as the undisputed ruler of Japan. Liberties lost to the Japanese Army were lost for good."[19]

The national general mobilization law, which had been enacted in late March 1938, was invoked early in May in an atmosphere of deepen-

[17] See *ibid.*, 249-53.

[18] *Ibid.*, 257. See also Hattori, I, 312-13, in which the expansion of the army's preparations for war after the "accidental" outbreak of the China Incident in 1937 is explained in terms of the necessity of effecting a speedy solution of the Incident and of maintaining "a feeling of security" with respect to the Soviet Union, which is described as being engaged in greatly expanding its own military preparations.

[19] Craigie, 59.

ing economic crisis caused by the war in China.[20] During that same month, with Prince Konoe again uncertain as to whether to continue in office, a less drastic solution was attempted in the form of a cabinet reorganization, carried out in the hope that a stronger government would emerge. Lt. Gen. Itagaki of Manchurian Incident fame became war minister, and General Araki—seemingly a man of many talents— assumed direction of the education ministry.[21]

Accompanying these and other changes in the cabinet were shifts in personnel in the war ministry and the army general staff. Lt. Gen. Kenji Doihara, the "Lawrence of Manchuria" who had recently been in command of a division actively engaged in the fighting in China, was assigned to duty with the general staff in Tokyo. Lt. Gen. Hideki Tojo was recalled from his service in the field to become vice-minister of war under Itagaki, the man he had earlier replaced as chief of staff of the Kwantung army.

The reasons offered for Tojo's appointment to this new post vary considerably. Some observers lay it entirely to favoritism or to personal maneuvering made possible by an accretion of influence resulting from his tenure as *kenpeitai* commander in Manchuria. Just how this worked in practice, if indeed it ever did, remains obscure. Others point out that Tojo became vice-minister because of his record as an administrator and a man of action. As an officer of considerable executive experience, of determined character, and of quick decision, he was the one best qualified to assume the post at that critical moment. Still another explanation stems from an idea which seems to have been in Konoe's mind for some time: the advisability of balancing the growing power of the control group by a reintroduction of men oriented toward the imperial-

[20] The national general mobilization law was passed in late March 1938. On May 5, 1938, some of its provisions, though not all, were invoked by the Konoe Cabinet. (See, for instance, J, B/IV, 245-47 and 258; Kenryō Satō, "Dai-Tōa Sensō wo Maneita Shōwa no Dōran," 102; and *NYT*, November 29, 1938, 11.) Despite this fact, the first mention of the law in the *Japan Year Book*, for instance, occurs in the volume for 1941-1942, in which it is stated (p. 234) that the law became effective as of May 5, *1939*. Presumably this is an editorial or printer's error for 1938. All separate and subsequent printings, based on this source, naturally repeat the same date. The fact remains that the Konoe Cabinet invoked certain articles of the law on May 5, 1938.

[21] Kido relinquished the education post but remained in the cabinet as welfare minister. Hirota was briefly succeeded (May-September) as foreign minister by Ugaki. Kaya was replaced as finance minister by Seihin Ikeda, who served concurrently as minister of commerce and industry. See Kido SKD (in which reference is made to Araki, Ikeda, and Ugaki as *iwayuru ōmono*: "the so-called big shots"); Konoe, 20-22 (in which the cabinet reorganization is ascribed to an intention to alter Japan's China policy—the so-called *Shōkaiseki wo aite to sezu* declaration of January having been recognized, in the meantime, as a mistake); Shunichirō Itō, 80-83; and J, B/IV, 256-60 and B/V, 723-24.

way faction, which had lost its earlier influence as a result of the February 1936 mutiny. Since the control group was all-powerful, however, it would permit the appointment of a man like Itagaki only if the No. 2 spot were filled by an officer from its own ranks. Hence the selection of Hideki Tojo.

The mere fact that Tojo had thus been promoted to one of the more important posts at the center did not actually indicate very much with respect to his future. The vice-ministership was not necessarily the gateway to the army portfolio in the cabinet, but it did involve its occupant in a very close association with the day-to-day business of the ministry. At the time in question, this meant an intimate connection with the mobilization of the Japanese nation for war.

Although Itagaki and Tojo were firm friends, they were men of rather different character. Itagaki, who graduated from the military academy a year ahead of Tojo, stood at the bottom of his class—"the first from the end." According to General Ryukichi Tanaka, an early associate, Itagaki enjoyed *sake*, horseback riding, and Japanese fencing. He was "a man of spotless integrity" who never indulged in "lewdness." He was "very fond of reading books" but, since his "head" was "not good," he soon forgot what he read. Like the great Saigo who led the Satsuma rebellion, Itagaki was a man of easy-going personality—"very strong in battles . . . but tactless" in other encounters. He was "magnanimous" to his subordinates and was always willing to listen to what they had to say. Consequently, the success or failure of his undertakings depended on the quality of the men under him.

When Itagaki and Tojo were both instructors at the war college, the students found it difficult to comprehend Itagaki's nature. If a student yawned while Tojo was talking, Tojo would interrupt his lecture and scold the offender. If the same thing happened in Itagaki's classes, he would continue to the end of the hour without apparently paying any attention. At first the students were contemptuous of Itagaki, but soon they began to feel that he was making fools of them instead. This difference in character later gave rise to the opinion that as war minister and vice-minister, respectively, Itagaki and Tojo would complement each other and thus make an effective team.[22]

[22] On Tōjō as vice-minister of war: Shunichirō Itō, 80-90 (the source of the account of the differences in character between Tōjō and Itagaki); Tōjō cross-examination, S 346:4, T 36574-75; Tōjō cabinet secretariat personnel file, CF 20, II, 77; Hattori and Umezu intv.; Hattori corresp.; Tanaka, "I Know Everything About Them," 6; Konoe, 21-22; Harada, *Saionji Kō to Seikyoku*, VI, 304-5; IMTFE, Def. Doc. No. 2122; J, B/IV, 265A-267; and Stunkard intv.

People also remarked on the fact that the war and navy ministers, the vice-minister of war, and the vice-chief of the army general staff all came from the old Nanbu clan in northern Japan—the present-day Iwate prefecture. This common clan origin—which was stretched somewhat in Tojo's case since he had actually been born in Tokyo—did not prevent the development of differences of opinion, especially between Tojo and Tada, the army's vice-chief of staff. In the most neutral terms, the question was whether Japan could maintain her security in the northern reaches of the Asian continent while fighting south of the Great Wall, or whether the China Incident would undermine Japan's defense capability with respect to a Soviet attack across the Manchukuo border. In less neutral terms: could Japan fight the Chinese and the Russians at the same time, or would the China Incident force a postponement of army plans to attack Soviet forces in the north when the time was ripe?

Tojo believed it would be possible to wage a two-front war. As vice-minister under Itagaki, he began calling for the material and spiritual preparations that would permit Japan to fight China and the Soviet Union concurrently. As the months passed, this approach came more and more into conflict with the advice being tendered to Itagaki and others by members of the army general staff—especially by Vice-Chief Tada. As Tojo's counterpart on the supreme-command side of the army fence, Tada favored the original nonexpansion policy and felt that all energies should be devoted to bringing the war in China to a successful conclusion.

In late November 1938 Tojo publicly detailed the views then current within the war ministry—especially among the members of the powerful military affairs bureau. Speaking to an audience drawn from Japan's munitions industry, Tojo emphasized that in the past Japan had merely attempted to keep abreast of the Soviet Union's increasing military strength and that China had occupied a secondary place in Japan's thinking. Now, however, whether Japan liked it or not, she must acquire an armaments position that would permit her to conduct simultaneous operations on two fronts—against the Soviet Union and against China. It was the Soviet intention, he said, to keep Japan engaged in China so as to exhaust Japan's war strength and then to join with the Chinese in fighting Japan. The Soviets were not only building up their forces for an eventual collision with Japan but were also plotting the communization of China. The Japanese army must therefore be capable of settling the China Incident and of facing a Sino-Soviet combination as well.

Even if the Nationalists surrendered, Tojo declared, pro-Communist, anti-Japanese guerrillas would fight on, and aid from Britain, France, and Russia would continue to bolster China's "stubborn resistance." The British were afraid, he said, that if Japan's continental policy succeeded, their position in China would be threatened and Singapore, India, and Australia would be endangered. Japan must bear in mind that the roots of Britain's policy of aiding China ran deep. The occasional assumption by Britain of the part of the "coquette" with respect to Japan should be regarded as nothing more than a "stratagem" designed to protect the rights and interests in China that the British were already losing. Although the United States government was currently following a policy of neutrality, it was insisting—despite the changes taking place in the Far Eastern situation—that Japan observe treaties concluded in the past. Since there was no indication that the United States would recognize the new state of affairs, Japan must remain on her guard. She must become a nation-in-arms capable of fighting a two-front war.

In advocating such a program, Tojo by no means stood alone. He was expressing views held by a large segment of the army. But he was also flatly contradicting the advice of General Tada. In the Japanese context, the only alternative to a concession by either Tojo or Tada was a resignation by both. In this case, Tojo and Tada stepped out—Tojo to become inspector-general of the army air force and Tada to take over an undisclosed command on the China front.[23]

The adverse effect upon the stock market caused by Tojo's speech of late November 1938 was followed, early in the new year, by a slight flurry in the imperial Diet. When asked to explain Tojo's remarks, War Minister Itagaki suggested that his vice-minister had merely been attempting to encourage the manufacturers of munitions by establishing a goal toward which they should strive. It was well known, he declared, that certain European countries, including the Soviet Union, were

---

[23] On the Tōjō speech of November 28, 1938, delivered at the *Gunjin Kaikan*, and his quarrel with Tada: Shunichirō Itō, 90-96; Hugh Byas, "Gen. Tojo Predicts War with Soviet," *NYT*, November 29, 1938, 11; Hattori corresp.; Tanaka, *Hai-in wo Tsuku*, 20-22; CF 20, I, 16 and III, 298; J, B/IV, 287-98; and *Who's Who in Nippon (1943-44)*. Tanaka refers to a similar speech at a reservists' meeting in September 1938 and Yanaga (*Japan Since Perry*, 598-99) to one in August 1939, also to reservists. It is not clear whether these were other public presentations of the November 28 address or whether the Tanaka and Yanaga references are actually to the *Gunjin Kaikan* speech.

Tōjō's difficulties at this time stemmed, in part, from the "limitation of dividends" affair in which Kenryō Satō played the leading role (see his *Tōjō Hideki to Taiheiyō Sensō*, 104-10).

capable of waging a two-front war and it was felt that Japan should be in a state of comparable preparedness. When he was asked whether finishing the China Incident or preparing against Russia was more important, Itagaki replied that for the present Japan was concentrating on settling the China Incident, but that in the long run that task could not really be separated from the problem of providing for war against two enemies at the same time. Itagaki gave assurances that the army would not adopt a provocative attitude, although it would be ready to destroy Soviet forces should they move against Japanese troops. He succeeded in convincing the Diet that Tojo's speech had been in the nature of propaganda designed merely to spur the production of armaments, and that the army, fully occupied in China, was not planning to launch a preventive war against the Soviet Union.[24]

In addition to these stirrings within the imperial army, the months of November and December 1938 witnessed important developments in other quarters, notably in naval circles and within the Konoe Cabinet. Two days before Tojo achieved his first international press by advocating preparations for a two-front war, the American ambassador in Tokyo was told "in strictest secrecy . . . that the Japanese Navy had definitely decided to declare war [on Britain], presumably in the near future, as the first step toward war with Soviet Russia." Mr. Grew's informant, who was "a prominent member of the Italian Embassy," emphasized that he personally "wouldn't give a nickel for Hong Kong."[25]

The long-standing rivalry between the military services was once again threatening the harmony which was always stressed in public but which was so rarely in evidence behind the scenes. The younger and more impatient naval officers felt that they had been "a beast of burden for the Army" long enough and that they should now have an opportunity to share in the glory which had been going almost entirely to the army since 1931. They believed that the time for naval action was ripe.

[24] Itagaki's responses in the Diet were prompted by questions put to him by Representative Kōjirō Tsutsumi on January 25, 1939. See Hugh Byas, "Japan Denies Plan to Attack Russia," *NYT*, January 26, 1939, 8. By that time Tōjō had already resigned his post and the Konoe Cabinet had been replaced by one headed by Hiranuma (see pp. 134-36 below). Itagaki continued as war minister in the Hiranuma Cabinet.

[25] Grew, *Ten Years in Japan*, 262-63, and Grew corresp. (in which Mr. Grew states, ". . . it was undoubtedly war against England and the United States by Japan that my Italian colleague had in mind. There was also, however, the thought that war against Great Britain and the United States by Soviet Russia would eventually break out.").

Mr. Grew reported that his informant might be "prone to exaggeration," but he did have access to information unavailable to others and thus might accurately be reflecting the "wishful thinking of the younger naval officers."[26] At the time in question, their thinking was wishful, but it was also an early and positive indication of the trend of naval opinion—a frequently forgotten element of growing importance in the complex equation of factors affecting Japanese decision-making. Increasing restlessness within the imperial navy and its deepening inferiority complex with regard to the army could hardly contribute to the stabilization of the situation facing Japan at home and abroad.

That this situation required greater effort toward solution became more apparent with each passing month. Within Japan the provisions of the national general mobilization law were being put into effect as a measure of response to some of the major problems besetting the nation. On the foreign policy front during this same period, there was a locking of the door which had so vigorously been slammed in the Generalissimo's face at the beginning of the year. In a proclamation issued on November 3, the authorities in Tokyo announced that the Nationalist government of China had been reduced to a local regime and that it was now Japan's intention to create a new order in East Asia that would ensure the permanent stabilization of that area. Mutual cooperation and assistance through a "good-neighborly union" on the part of Japan, Manchukuo, and China in political, economic, cultural, and other spheres were to be the foundation upon which this new order would rest. Among its declared purposes were the securing of "international justice," joint defense against communism, the creation of a new East Asian "culture," and the realization of economic union among the countries of that region. Japan expressed confidence— misplaced though it was—that the powers would "correctly appreciate her aims and policy and adapt their attitude to the new conditions prevailing in East Asia. . . ." In the official double-talk characteristic of that time, this unilateral fiat was described as a "moderation" of Japan's earlier stand.[27]

When the Konoe Cabinet spoke of a "good-neighborly union," it did not mean one embracing free, independent, and sovereign states but rather one in which a dominant and all-powerful Japan would direct the performance of the puppets which her military aggression had established in a vast area of China, extending from the Amur River in

[26] *Ibid.*

[27] See the sources cited in footnote 30 below.

the north to the Yangtze in the south, and inland for hundreds of miles from the sea. It was on the basis of such an extraordinary power-position that Japan expected not only the West but also millions upon millions of subject-Chinese to "appreciate" her aims and policy and to comply with Japan's demands, whatever they might be. This was revealed in Japan's formal response to an American representation prompted by the proclamation of the new order. As it had done before and was to do again and again until December 1941, the American government urged Japan to honor her treaty commitments, to uphold the principles of the open door and of equal opportunity in China, and to respect American interests there. In answering this, the Japanese foreign office provocatively asserted that in the face of the new situation in Asia, an attempt to apply pre-China Incident ideas and principles to either present or future issues would contribute nothing to the solution of current problems or the establishment of permanent peace in the East.[28]

What General Tojo personally thought of all this at the time did not come to light until years later.[29] As he explained it in the immediate postwar period, the creation of Japan's new order had been "a matter of fundamental importance." A need for close ties between Japan and China had existed "from very early times." The building of a new order had become government policy following the outbreak of the China Incident. As time passed, the concept had gradually grown "more and more explicit," but the idea that a new order was necessary stretched back at least to the Manchurian Incident.

China was "the focus of forces." She possessed an abundance of natural resources, a great population with a large capacity to buy and to consume, and a well-developed culture different from that of Europe and America. Trade with China was of vital importance to Japan, especially with respect to food and "other necessities of life." In view of her geographic position, Japan was influenced to a greater extent by internal conditions in China than were the other powers. "Disorder and instability in China could spread quickly to Japan. By contrast, England

[28] Hattori, I, 42.
[29] The views which follow represent a reconstruction based on material in Tōjō interrog., Jan. 15, 3-6, Jan. 16, 1-5, Jan. 17, 1-6, Jan. 18, 1-2, Jan. 23, 2-5, and Jan. 25, 2-4. The text also draws, in part, on CF 20, III, 253; S 342:15, T 36195; S 344:9, T 36430; S 345:4-5, T 36537-38; S 345:5-7, T 36544-50; and S 348:13, T 36807.
On later developments concerning the new order and the establishment of the so-called Greater East Asia co-prosperity sphere, see Tōjō aff., S 344:9-10, T 36426-34; Tōjō interrog., Jan. 28, 1-5, Mar. 5, 2-6, Mar. 6, 1-5, Mar. 11, 1-4, Mar. 19, 4; JRD, "Interrogations," I:49157 (Seizō Arisue), 47-48; and IMTFE, "Roling Opinion," 99-102, 128-35.

and America were more remote from China and were not seriously affected by chaotic conditions there." Consequently, for those two nations "the problem was much less serious."

As the "central power" in East Asia, Japan wished "to insure the stability of the Far East." This did not mean that other nations would either be under Japan or become her dependencies, but only that Japan, "by reason of her greater strength, would have the initiative." Japan did not intend to "push aside" the Far Eastern interests of the European powers and of the United States. The sole purpose was "to effect lawful adjustments."

According to Tojo, an enlightened approach had characterized Japan's thinking about the new order from the very beginning. He insisted that such a selfish thought as greater wealth for Japan had not existed. "The basic intention was that the raw materials which China possessed in abundance would be contributed by China and the technique, capital and skilled personnel [would] be contributed by Japan for the mutual benefit of both countries. Manchuria would come into the picture similarly. . . . The idea of profit or loss did not enter in. The idea of mutual benefit was the main one. It had a moral basis."

The true nature of things was revealed with the passage of time. In December 1938 a new Konoe declaration enunciated three fundamental principles as the key to a solution of Sino-Japanese difficulties: "good neighborly" friendship, joint defense, and economic cooperation and affiliation. This was designed to bring home to the Chinese and to the world at large Japan's "true intentions" and "good faith" with respect to settling the Incident, but Tokyo's expectation that the Nationalists would utilize the Konoe declaration to make peace with Japan proved ill-founded.[30] There was still too great a gap between

[30] On the *Tōa Shin-chitsujo* proclamation of November 3, 1938, and the so-called *Konoe Seimei* of December 22, which grew out of decisions reached at an imperial conference on November 30, see Hattori, I, 38-39 and 42 (in which the purpose of clarifying Japan's true intentions is specifically expressed); Konoe, 17-22; Grew aff., T 10106-7; Grew, *Turbulent Era*, II, 1206-7; J, B/IV, 328, 336-37, and B/V, 733-36, 740-41; and "The Brocade Banner," 105, in which it is stated that the Konoe declaration of December 1938 encouraged Wang Ching-wei to desert Chungking "even though the principal promise that Konoye had privately tendered was missing from the official statements. The promise to withdraw all Japanese troops from China was omitted at the last moment because of Army pressure. Thus the one concrete evidence of good faith was absent. Konoye has frankly admitted his weakness and his guilt in yielding to the Army at this crucial point."

The IMTFE judgment to the effect that Konoe's declaration expressed "Japan's resolution to exterminate the Chinese National Government" was based on the view that an acceptance by the Nationalist government of Japan's proposal would have resulted in a self-elimination of that government as a factor determining the future fate of China.

the general principles upon which a settlement might be achieved and the concrete stipulations proposed by Japan as a means toward that end. There was also the growing hostility of the United States and Britain and their marked inclination to help the Chinese help themselves.[31]

As the fighting in China had progressed, Western rights and interests had more and more frequently been violated by Japan's military forces.[32] At times it had even appeared as if hotheaded elements in the field were trying to instigate a war with the United States and Great Britain. Among the many provocative incidents of the period were repeated attacks upon foreign school, business, and church properties; the machine-gunning by a Japanese plane of five Americans who were horseback riding within the limits of the International Settlement at Shanghai; the wounding of the British ambassador, Sir Hughe Montgomery Knatchbull-Hugessen; the bombing and destruction of an American church at Chungking after eight previous bombings, each of which had been made the subject of a separate protest; the sinking of the American gunboat *Panay* on the Yangtze River with a loss of two American lives; and—on the very same day—the bombing of two British gunboats, a merchantman, and some junks.[33]

Although such incidents were likely to happen in a situation of the kind then prevailing in China, they were soon occurring rather too frequently and in too similar a manner to be accepted as simple errors. The powers recognized that Japanese forces were operating under peculiar difficulties in the Shanghai and Nanking areas and attempted at times to assist them in the prevention of abuses which might cause trouble, such as the illegal use of foreign flags. On one occasion, British authorities gave the Japanese military command a map on which every point entitled to fly the Union Jack was clearly

---

[31] That Japan intended to strip the other great powers of their rights and interests in Asia had by then become unmistakably clear. See, for instance, Grew aff., T 10091-95, 10097-10105, and J, B/IV, 196-98, B/V, 724, 736, and 748.

[32] Konoe himself later noted that by the summer of 1938 his government had already received more than three hundred protests in connection with Japanese infringements upon American and British rights and interests in China (Konoe, 16-17). See also Grew aff., T 10094-97 and 10107-8 (which briefly notes "a few of the more flagrant examples"), and J, B/IV, 226-28 and 321-29. Mr. Grew testified that by the end of 1938 he had personally filed "over 400 separate protests," that Japanese outrages against American lives and property were "steadily increasing," and that they continued to increase until the end of his term as ambassador on December 7, 1941.

[33] In addition to the sources in the preceding footnote, see *NYT*, August 27-30, 1937, and *passim* thereafter; *Japan Weekly Chronicle*, December 23, 1937, 816-17; and JRD Monograph No. 144, 32-33. Implicated in the *Panay* affair was Colonel Kingorō Hashimoto of ultranationalistic fame.

marked. "Armed with this information, Japanese planes immediately bombed certain Chinese buildings which were flying the British flag . . . ," thus rendering it doubtful that any Chinese in the future would regard the Union Jack as offering much protection.[34]

It was as if the bombings and strafings and other "mistakes" were following a set pattern and purpose: as if the Japanese forces in China thought themselves capable of creating a situation in which the foreign powers would "remove all their ships, deport all their nationals, and let their property go hang." In the case of the *Panay* and the two British gunboats, the nature of the attacks caused those on board the vessels to conclude that the Japanese had acted deliberately, with full knowledge of what they were doing. As one British newspaper published in Japan dryly remarked: "It was 2:30 in the afternoon, presumably daylight, and it need scarcely be added that all foreign vessels on the Yangtze, gunboats and merchantmen, are decorated conspicuously with their national flags."[35]

As Japan continued to press the war in China, the violations increased and the protests mounted. Even the British government, which had initially adopted a hands-off policy, began to stiffen its resistance. The efforts of Washington and London to bring Japan back to a policy of reason through moral suasion had absolutely no effect. Late in 1938 the Japanese foreign minister again repeated to Ambassador Grew the formula which was rapidly becoming Japan's standard response: a new situation had developed in East Asia in which the ideas and principles of the past were no longer applicable; Japan's security and defense required control over certain natural resources and economic opportunities in China; those resources and opportunities would no longer be available to foreigners.

Thus did the Japanese government admit finally that it did not intend to honor its treaty obligations. In citing the changes which had occurred in the Far Eastern situation as justification, the government blandly chose to ignore the fact that Japanese military aggression was responsible for those very changes.[36]

In the face of such an attitude, the West soon found that it had to choose either capitulation, resistance, or negotiation. From 1938 onward,

[34] See "The Yangtze Bombing" in *Japan Weekly Chronicle*, December 23, 1937, 816-17.
[35] *Ibid.* See also *NYT*, December 13-21, 1937. Upon being asked when the imperial navy's report on the bombing of the *Panay* could be expected, a Japanese foreign office spokesman "jokingly" replied: "That is indefinite . . . maybe in one hundred years."
[36] See Grew, *Turbulent Era*, II, 1206-7; J, B/IV, 327-29, 333, and B/V, 733-36.

Anglo-American support of the Generalissimo increased steadily. Many Westerners who had dismissed the original sin of the Manchurian Incident, or who had given the matter very little thought, began to find it difficult to adopt a similar nonchalance toward the continuing rape of China. The requirements of Western security demanded that Japan be prevented from achieving victory there. And so transfusions of supplies and money were given to the Generalissimo to strengthen the resistance of China's five hundred million people and to aid them in holding the line against an Asia dominated by the Japanese army and a Pacific menaced by the Japanese fleet. When moral embargoes against Japan and economic aid to China did not bring results, a more serious measure was adopted. In July 1939 the United States gave notification that the treaty of commerce and navigation concluded with Japan in 1911 would not be renewed when it expired early in 1940. In the postwar view of a Japanese admiral, this was "the first step in the alienation of the two countries."[37]

Everything the United States and Great Britain did to assist China and to strengthen their own security was denounced in Japan in terms which ignored Japanese aggression in China. The powers were repeatedly accused of seeking to deny Japan her rightful place in the world. The continual irritation which this produced in Japan's relations with America and Britain after 1938 created the situation for which Hideki Tojo ultimately became responsible. If this cancer of animosity could not be healed by the medication of diplomacy, then it would have to be cut away by the surgery of war. In two short years, this thought became the underlying principle of Japan's foreign policy—the irrefutable logic of those who sought to diagnose the nation's illness so as to prescribe a cure.

Nor was it only with the British and the Americans that relations worsened. In 1938 and again in 1939 the two-front war which was so prominent in Tojo's thoughts seemed on the verge of becoming a reality. An attitude of mutual suspicion had colored the views of Russians and Japanese from their very first contact with each other in the inhospitable seas and islands north of Japan proper. Once the seizure of Manchuria had placed Japan in the position of sharing a long and poorly defined frontier with Russia, the opportunity for friction was greatly increased. Within Japan, military opinion focused on the fre-

[37] Admiral Sadatoshi Tomioka (JRD Monograph No. 144, 53-55).

quently repeated prediction that a war with the Soviet Union was inevitable.[38]

Suddenly, in July 1938, a specific issue was raised with respect to the Changkufeng-Lake Khassan area in the southeastern quarter of Manchuria, close to the point where the Manchukuoan frontier joins those of Korea and of the USSR.[39] The problem was control of a "height of land . . . of considerable strategic importance overlooking . . . the Tumen-Ula River, the railway running North and South and the roads communicating with the Soviet Maritime Province and the city of Vladivostok." The Soviets maintained that the boundary ran along the crest of the hills between the river on the west and the lake on the east, but the Japanese insisted that the frontier lay beyond the crest and that, in fact, it coincided with the western shore of Lake Khassan.

Early in July Japan initiated diplomatic negotiations in Moscow to obtain the withdrawal of Soviet border guards to the eastern shore of the lake—a withdrawal which would have given Japan control of the area in dispute. At the same time, Japan's own patrols were reinforced with field troops from Korea. Moscow based its claims upon the Hunch'un Protocol of 1886, which included a map indicating a boundary running along the watershed. When advised of this, the Japanese negotiator, Mamoru Shigemitsu, is said to have replied: "To my mind, at this critical moment to speak of some map is unreasonable. This will only complicate matters."

Shigemitsu later demanded the withdrawal of Soviet troops and warned that Japan would feel obliged to use force if the Soviet Union did not evacuate the area voluntarily. Fighting broke out on July 29 and continued on a growing scale until August 11. By that time, the Soviet Union had a preponderance of strength on the ground and in the air. In these circumstances, the Japanese government agreed to a termina-

[38] The Tribunal (J, B/VI, 803) was "of the opinion that a war of aggression against the USSR was contemplated and planned throughout the period under consideration [in this instance, approximately 1931-1943], that it was one of the principal elements of Japan's national policy and that its object was the seizure of territories of the USSR in the Far East." For the Tribunal's findings in this regard, except for the Tripartite Pact phase, which is discussed in Chapter 6, see J, B/IV, 203-4, 219-22, 268-80, 336-37, and B/VI, 776-842. For a dissenting view, see IMTFE, "Roling Opinion," 70-73, 114-18.

[39] The facts pertaining to the Changkufeng-Lake Khassan affair remain in dispute. For a summary of the "Japanese Guilt" approach, see J, B/IV, 273-76 and B/VI, 827-34, 840-41 (the source of the quotations in the text). For the other side of the story, see Blumenson, "The Soviet Power Play at Changkufeng," *World Politics*, Vol. XII, No. 2 (January 1960), 249-63. See also IMTFE, "Roling Opinion," 90-92, and Shigemitsu, *Shōwa no Dōran*, I, 199-205 (in which mention is made of the presence on the scene of *chūken shōkō* who had earlier been "shooed" away from Tōkyō and of an infantry regimental commander affiliated with the Cherry Society).

tion of hostilities and to a restoration of the boundary along the watershed between the river and the lake.

The continuing drain of the China Incident upon Japan's resources and the precarious position of her economy were already matters of considerable concern. The failure to impose its will at Lake Khassan now forced the Japanese army into fundamental reappraisals and belated second thoughts. The revised army view, as subsequently stated by Kenryo Sato (newly promoted to full colonel) was that preparations for a war with the Soviet Union would continue as a matter of course, but that Japan would not enter into such a war until her armaments and other necessary war potential had been expanded—in other words, presumably not until after 1942.

Despite the unfavorable impression made upon both the field commanders and the authorities in Tokyo by the fiasco at Lake Khassan, the lesson was apparently not sufficiently clear to prevent a repetition of the experience some ten months later, when the Japanese and the Russians again came to blows. The scene this time was far to the northwest, in the vicinity of Nomonhan and the Khalkhin-Gol on the border between Manchuria and Outer Mongolia—or, in the terminology of the day, between Manchukuo and the Mongolian People's Republic.[40] The existence of this Soviet satellite extending across the top of China from Manchuria in the east to Sinkiang in the west was a matter of concern to many Japanese. As early as 1933 General Araki had publicly described Outer Mongolia as an "ambiguous area" which should be occupied by Japan. Several years later, General Itagaki had privately indicated the Kwantung army's goal of extending the power and influence of Japan and Manchukuo into that area by every available means.

From the point of view of possible operations against the Soviet Union, Outer Mongolia was of great strategic importance. If Japan won control there, her armies would be in a position to seize the Lake Baikal region and the entire Far Eastern portion of the Trans-Siberian Railway. Because of the area's role in Soviet security, Russian soldiers were stationed in Outer Mongolia under the terms of a mutual assistance pact. Early in May 1939 a segment of the Kwantung army suddenly took action which immediately led to clashes with Mongolian border guards in the Nomonhan sector. Fighting continued throughout the

[40] On the Nomonhan-Khalkhin-Gol incident, see J, B/IV, 391, B/VI, 827 and 834-42; IMTFE, "Roling Opinion," 92-93; Shigemitsu, *Shōwa no Dōran*, I, 242-45; and JRD Monograph No. 144, 47-49 (in which the Japanese military authors still maintain that Japan was the victim rather than the perpetrator of aggression in the 1938 and 1939 border clashes with the Soviet Union).

month, with the Japanese taking the offensive through small-scale attacks which were repeatedly repulsed. Reinforcements were called up by both the Japanese and the Russians. On May 28 the hostilities assumed major proportions with the employment of aircraft, artillery, and tanks. In the words of one Japanese general, the army was thus "cast into a whirlpool of irregular war on the frontier between Manchuria and Mongolia." The fighting continued into September, with operations being conducted along a front some fifty to sixty kilometers in length and twenty to twenty-five kilometers in depth. Japanese casualties exceeded 50,000—including those killed, wounded, or taken prisoner. The Mongolian and Russian losses amounted to more than 9,000. The repeated failure of Japanese arms to overwhelm the enemy finally resulted in a cessation of hostilities and an eventual settlement through diplomacy. The Japanese army learned from the experience that all was not well with its armored units and its tactics. In the months which followed, "strenuous efforts" were made to set matters right. Priority of attention was given to the remodeling of equipment and the building-up of tanks and fire power.

These armed clashes with the Soviet Union, together with the rapid deterioration of Japan's relations with the United States and Great Britain, served to isolate Japan still more and to leave her with very few friends outside the Axis bloc of nations. Meanwhile, the fighting in China continued. Not even the establishment of a collaborationist puppet regime at Nanking, headed by Wang Ching-wei, brought any immediate prospect of capitulation by the remainder of the country.[41]

Within Japan, the temporary lull in ultranationalistic activity which had followed the 1936 mutiny had come to an end. Irresponsible zealots conducted "soap-box rallies," distributed pamphlets and handbills, organized protests to the government, and promoted "inspection trips" to China. Nationalistic societies were formed in rapid succession—many of them by men connected with the assassinations of the first half of the decade. As a consequence, new murders were planned.[42] In July 1939 there was a plot to kill the lord keeper of the privy seal and the vice-minister of the navy because they were said to be pro-British. Other

[41] On the establishment of the Wang regime in March 1940, see J, B/V, 743-47, 751-53, and JRD Monograph No. 144, 51-53 and Appendix 13. It is interesting to note that on July 29, 1937, Wang Ching-wei had issued a statement in which, even by Japanese admission, he had spoken of Japan's *aggressive attitude* toward China since 1931 (JRD Monograph No. 144, 18).

[42] On the activities of the nationalists after the outbreak of the China Incident, see "The Brocade Banner," 108-10, 120-22; Kido "Nikki," S 75:13, T 6240-41; Kido SKD; Harada, VIII, 154, 281; and Maxon, 140.

extremists were scheming to murder the imperial household minister and to attack the British embassy. In October 1939 shots were fired at a leader of one of Japan's two major political parties, but the aim was poor and the intended victim escaped unhurt.[43] Early in January 1940 another plot was uncovered. The participants had planned to blow up the American and British embassies, kill the ambassadors, and assassinate highly-placed Japanese who were regarded as responsible for Japan's "nanjaku gaikō"—her weak-kneed diplomacy.

The culmination of these episodes came on July 5, 1940, when a group of *shinpeitai* men who had gone scot-free seven years before were suddenly arrested, along with some newly recruited cohorts, on the very morning that they were to "eliminate" a number of alleged friends of America and Britain. The list included the premier and his predecessor, two retired lord keepers of the privy seal, the imperial household minister, a leading financier, the president of one of Japan's two major political parties, the secretary-aide to Prince Saionji, and a noted novelist.[44] In making the arrests, the police netted nine pistols, two hand grenades, thirty Japanese swords, thirty beer bottles filled with benzine, and—inevitably—many copies of a statement explaining the motives of the "patriots." Twenty-nine sentences were subsequently handed down as a result of this "July 5" incident. The severest was five years' imprisonment. Eighteen of the twenty-nine convicted men were granted stays of execution amounting to two or three years each.

If wishing could have made it so, Japanese victory in China would have been achieved in the declining years of the turbulent 1930's. But neither the efforts of the Japanese army in the field nor the incantations of the nationalists at home produced any effective means for dealing with the situation. In the postwar analysis of Kenryo Sato, the China Incident had become a "quagmire."[45]

Perhaps there were some who rethought the matter from the beginning, yet none was successful in devising a program offering enough

[43] The men marked for assassination in the July and October plots were Kurahei Yuasa (lord keeper of the privy seal), Isoroku Yamamoto (vice-minister of the navy), Tsuneo Matsudaira (imperial household minister), and Chikuhei Nakajima (a leader of the Seiyūkai).

[44] Mitsumasa Yonai (premier) and Keisuke Okada (ex-premier), Kurahei Yuasa and Nobuaki (Shinken) Makino (ex-lord keepers of the privy seal), Tsuneo Matsudaira (the imperial household minister), Seihin Ikeda (the financier), Chūji Machida (president of the Minseitō), Kumao Harada (the chronicler of Saionji's thoughts), and Kan Kikuchi (the novelist). Hisashi Asō (chief secretary of the Shakai Taishūtō), and Baron Kitokurō Ikki (ex-president of the privy council and before that minister of the imperial household) were also marked for assassination.

[45] Kenryō Satō, "Dai-Tōa Sensō wo Maneita Shōwa no Dōran," 101.

advantages to balance out its disadvantages. Despite their well-founded reputation for expert knowledge of continental affairs, Japan's military extremists had indeed miscalculated. They thus faced a situation which had been appreciated nearly one hundred and fifty years before by Lord Macartney, sent by George III as a special envoy to the Middle Kingdom.[46] Although he saw but a very small part of China and remained there only briefly, Macartney accurately forecast in 1793 the probable consequences of any endeavor to conquer the Chinese: "The circumstance of greatest embarrassment to an invader would be their immense numbers, not on account of the mischief they could do to him, but that he would find no end of doing mischief to them. The slaughter of millions would scarcely be perceived and, unless the people themselves soon voluntarily submitted, the victor might indeed reap the vanity of destruction, but not the glory or use of dominion."

[46] The Macartney prediction which follows in the text is quoted in Collis, *The Great Within*, 296.

II · MAKING THE IMPOSSIBLE POSSIBLE

I no naka no kawazu taikai wo shirazu.
The frog in the well knows nothing of the ocean.

CHAPTER 6

The Crystallization of National Policy

For years preceding the outbreak of the China Incident the general trend of Japanese opinion, especially among the military, had been that Japan must guard against encirclement by a hostile combination of powers. Through those years, also, self-conscious emphasis had been placed on the impression Japan was making on others. "The eyes of the world are upon us" was a frequently recurring thought.[1] After 1937, however, the government in Tokyo as well as individual Japanese found it more and more difficult to convince other nations that Japan's military activities on the continent could be justified on the grounds of self-defense. As the China Incident wore on, the increasingly critical response of the United States and Great Britain added to Japanese annoyance at the repeated inability or unwillingness of those powers to understand Japan's "true intentions." Of the many attempts at explanation and clarification which resulted, perhaps none is more revealing than that of Yosuke Matsuoka, soon to become Japan's foreign minister—or, in Tojo's phrase, "the mouthpiece for the national will as debated and decided upon by the cabinet":

Japan is fighting for loot and profit! That is the refrain of all anti-Japanese propaganda the world over. It is an insult to plain arithmetic. Japan has already spent billions of yen in the present crisis. The Imperial Diet a few weeks ago voted for more than two billion yen just to tide over a few months. The final total may reach fifty billions or more, who knows? Can a financial optimist anywhere conceive of Japan getting back even two, three billion yen a year from China? And that amount would be meagre annual interest charges on the Japanese outlay for this present crisis. Absurd even to a primary school arithmetic class, all this fight-for-loot theory.[2]

Why then was Japan at war? According to Matsuoka, she was

---

[1] See Reischauer, *The United States and Japan*, 108-12.
[2] The Tōjō phrase is from interrog., Jan. 24, 2. Matsuoka's remarks are found in the *Japan Weekly Chronicle*, October 21, 1937, 549.

fighting "simply for her conception of her Mission in Asia." She was fighting to prevent Asia from becoming a second Africa and to preserve China from the "death grip" of the Comintern. The billions of yen she was pouring into the effort, the thousands of lives of her young men, were all "offerings on the altar of her own conviction and aspirations." She was paying the price that the leadership of the races of Asia demanded:

No treasure trove is in her eyes—only sacrifices upon sacrifices. No one realizes this more than she does. But her very life depends on it as do those of her neighbours as well.

The all-absorbing question before Japan today . . . is:—Can she bear the cross?[3]

Matsuoka left the matter there, but clearly his implied answer was that Japan could. And that became the uncompromising answer of the Japanese government as well, despite periodic changes within the ruling elite group.

Premier Konoe, who had come close to resigning on several earlier occasions, finally decided definitely on that step. The prince was one of the very few leaders of Japan in whom the Emperor seems personally to have had great confidence. Konoe's urbane presence masked the uncertainties of thought—the misgivings about action—which constituted the stamp of his character. Foreign experts of his day generally considered him a liberal (or at least a moderate) struggling against the rising military tide and therefore deserving of consideration and support. Post-1945 judgments were to be much harsher. The period of Konoe's premiership was then described as having been marked "by recurrent political crises, which had on several occasions prompted him to threaten to resign. Each threat had served only as a stimulus to the military faction, which had prevailed upon him to remain in office. On each occasion opposition to the development of the Army's plans had been overridden. While Konoye was Premier those plans had come to fruition. Japan had founded her 'new order' on the Asiatic continent, and the national general mobilisation for war had been undertaken whole-heartedly."[4]

Despite these achievements, dissension had developed not only within the cabinet but also on the outside. The government was being criticized for its indulgence toward the rightists, the intelligentsia were powerless, the question of unemployment was being widely

[3] *Japan Weekly Chronicle*, October 21, 1937, 549.
[4] J, B/IV, 338.

discussed, middle and small commercial and industrial enterprises were in a wretched condition, and the policy of not dealing with Chiang Kai-shek was becoming a serious issue. There was also the beginning of a realization that the bearing of the cross would be easier if Japan were supported in her progress by her Anti-Comintern Pact partners, Germany and Italy.

Konoe first mentioned his desire to resign in the latter part of November 1938, but he did not actually carry out his intention until January 4, 1939. Among those who tendered advice to him in the interim were Welfare Minister Kido, War Minister Itagaki, and Finance Minister Ikeda. Baron Hiranuma, who was destined to relinquish the presidency of the privy council to become Konoe's successor, urged the prince to remain in office because of the situation then existing in China. Maj. Gen. Teiichi Suzuki, who was slowly rising to prominence, seconded Hiranuma's views, but Konoe did not change his mind. The significant consideration at all times was the effect a resignation would have upon the army, which had already sent some 1,600,000 fighting men overseas. When confidence developed that the army would remain calm, Konoe was permitted to resign and the mandate was bestowed upon Hiranuma, a long-standing and powerful leader of the ideological right. In the cabinet which he formed, General Araki, Admiral Yonai, and Mr. Arita continued as education, navy, and foreign minister respectively; Marquis Kido relinquished the welfare portfolio to assume direction of home affairs; and General Itagaki stayed on in the war ministry. The emphasis upon continuity was further illustrated not only by Konoe's assumption of the privy council presidency vacated by Hiranuma but also by his entry into the baron's cabinet as a minister of state without portfolio.[5]

The army's willingness to give Hiranuma its backing was tied to a number of specific requirements conveyed to the premier-designate by the war minister. Itagaki revealed that the cabinet would be expected to carry out the aims of Japan's "Holy War" in China in accordance with fixed national policies. There must be an expansion of armaments that would render Japan capable of coping with the new situation in Asia. Relations with Germany and Italy were to be strengthened and the nation's general mobilization reinforced. The cabinet must also

[5] On the fall of the Konoe Cabinet and the emergence of Hiranuma: Kido SKD; J, B/IV, 337-41 (which also contains a résumé of Hiranuma's earlier activities and views); and J, B/V, 741-42, 745-46. Two other Konoe ministers retained their portfolios in the Hiranuma Cabinet: Suehiko Shiono (justice) and Yoshiaki Hatta (overseas affairs).

increase productivity, stimulate the people's morale, and promote foreign trade. The general target date was 1941; the goal—to provide for an "epochal development" of Japan's destiny.[6]

Within a few weeks after these demands were made, and accepted, Premier Hiranuma affirmed in the Diet that his cabinet was pledged to the China policy of his predecessor. There was no alternative except to exterminate those who failed to understand this policy and who persisted in their opposition to Japan.[7]

Foremost among the problems facing the new cabinet was the question of aligning Japan with Germany and Italy. The idea of joining the Rome-Berlin axis appealed to the army general staff in Tokyo and to its spokesman in Berlin, Lt. Gen. Hiroshi Oshima, who held the post of military attaché. Just where Oshima stood in relation to his nominal superior, Ambassador Shigenori Togo, was later revealed by Togo himself: "Already at that time the Japanese military had established the deplorable custom of having its military attachés assigned to Embassies in certain countries make direct contacts with the government of the country to which they were accredited on matters of high policy."[8]

Togo's opposition to an alliance with Germany soon resulted in his transfer to Moscow. The erstwhile military attaché then became the new ambassador. The replacement of Togo by Oshima "set the seal of the Cabinet's approval upon negotiations for a military alliance made in contemplation of war with the Soviet Union. It placed a soldier, who enjoyed the complete confidence of the Army, in a position until then occupied by a professional diplomat. It was a triumph for the Army in the field of Japanese foreign policy, and a step forward in the Army's preparations for war."[9]

Following his appointment, Oshima redoubled his efforts in behalf of an alliance with Hitler.[10] Throughout the ensuing negotiations he was ably seconded by his colleague in Rome, a career diplomat named Shiratori who consistently took the army's part against the foreign office.

---

[6] See J, B/V, 741-42. [7] Ibid.

[8] CF 20, III, 269. Military and naval attachés were under the control of the army and navy chiefs of staff (Ohmae corresp.).

[9] This is the judgment of the Tribunal: J, B/IV, 315. Ōshima was named military attaché on March 5, 1934, and envoy extraordinary and ambassador plenipotentiary on October 8, 1938. He held that post until December 27, 1939, and again from December 29, 1940 until 1945 (T 766-68, S 12:6).

[10] The following summary of the emergence of the Tripartite Pact is based on material in Kido SKD; J, B/IV, 269-70, 276-78, 281-87, 311-24, 362-478, and B/VI 785-92; "The Brocade Banner," 108 and 111; Hattori, I, 44-45; Kido aff., S 292:23-24, T 30855-56; CF 20, III, 269; JRD Monograph No. 144, 16, and No. 146, 16-19; IMTFE, "Roling Opinion," 102-14; and Feis, The Road to Pearl Harbor, 19-20, 25-37, and 117.

Together, these two men conducted a personal diplomatic campaign of their own, the distinguishing feature of which was the number of times they disregarded the restrictive instructions sent them from Tokyo. On at least one occasion, the instructions disdainfully ignored by Oshima fully reflected the thinking of the army general staff, which he represented.

In spite of Oshima's eagerness, the negotiations did not progress. The creation of an alliance was snagged by the different aims of the two sides: the Germans wanted an all-embracing pact directed against any potential enemy; the Japanese, with the exception of Oshima and Shiratori, were thinking only in terms of the traditional "Russian menace." Some members of the foreign ministry and the naval general staff even had misgivings about concluding an alliance aimed at the Soviet Union. They wanted greater security in the north, but not necessarily at the cost of full-fledged commitment to Berlin. The problem of resolving differences in this regard constituted the most important political task confronting Hiranuma.

The matter was discussed endlessly by the five key cabinet officers: the premier, the war and navy ministers, and the foreign and finance ministers.[11] Because of its desire to sign a military pact with Hitler, the army gradually accepted the German idea of a broad alliance rather than one limited to the Soviet enemy. The army's views in this respect were repeatedly made clear by War Minister Itagaki at Big Five meetings during the first half of 1939. And just as repeatedly these views encountered the opposition of Foreign Minister Arita and Navy Minister Yonai.

In the eight months he held office, Hiranuma met with his colleagues more than seventy times without being able to bring them to agreement on the alliance question, despite the pressure exerted in its favor by the army and by civilian ultranationalists. In the forefront once again was Colonel Kingoro Hashimoto, who seemed to reappear on the national scene—whenever a crisis threatened—like a jack-in-the-box when the lid is released. On this occasion, Hashimoto produced a number of newspaper articles which reflected the subtle change which had been taking place in military thinking—a change which stemmed, in part, from the reappraisal of strategy caused by the recent Japanese defeat by the Russians at Changkufeng-Lake Khassan. Hashimoto maintained that Japan's future lay in the South, but that Britain stood in the way—as she did in China. He called for war against the British and for the

[11] Hiranuma, Itagaki and Yonai, Arita and Ishiwata.

creation of a common front against democracy and communism through the conclusion of an alliance with the European Axis. The Hiranuma Cabinet, Hashimoto declared, should be replaced by one capable of acting in the manner desired.[12]

Such writings helped to produce dissatisfaction in the minds of people who did not have the vaguest notion of what was basically involved. As the spring turned to summer, the pressure increased, frequently taking the form of popular demonstrations. According to police records of the period, the growing agitation against the British and in favor of an alliance with the Germans reached a climax during July 1939, when some 850,000 Japanese participated in roughly four hundred anti-British mass meetings.[13] The fact that the Soviet Union was popularly regarded as another of the intended targets of a German-Japanese alliance added to the public fervor. There was consequently a national gasp of astonishment in late August 1939 when the Nazi-Soviet Non-Aggression Pact was signed. Even the government seemed at a loss to explain this "breach of faith," though it had been warned more than once that Berlin might turn to Moscow unless the Hiranuma Cabinet made a speedy decision. The thunderstruck premier, who was already sorely beset by the split in his cabinet, had no choice but to resign.[14]

Hiranuma's successor, General Nobuyuki Abe, eked out a mere four and one-half months as premier. In that short time his cabinet so contrived its affairs that it lost the support of the army, the Diet, and the people.[15] Abe was succeeded, in turn, by Admiral Mitsumasa Yonai, who was to last only six months. Secretary Hull interpreted the emergence of the admiral's cabinet, with Arita serving again as foreign minister, as a sign that the State Department's stiffening attitude toward Japan was producing a wholesome effect. Several months later, however, the conduct of the cabinet was regarded "as showing a wish for peace without resolve or power to achieve it."[16]

The failure of the Yonai-Arita combination to reshape the course of Japan's policy was a measure of the already extensive power and influence of the militarists and ultranationalists. It was also an indication, as postwar evidence was to prove, that the cabinet was not nearly as prepared to adopt a new approach as some Americans believed.[17]

[12] J, B/IV, 384-85.   [13] "The Brocade Banner," 108.
[14] "Breach of faith" (*haishin kōi*) is from Hattori, I, 45.
[15] *Ibid.* On the Abe Cabinet, see also J, B/IV, 398-402, 409-10, 454, and B/V, 745-46.
[16] Feis, 46 and 51. Hull seems not to have appreciated Arita's personal connection with policies that did not meet the approval of the United States government. In this regard, see J, B/IV, 411-15.
[17] See J, B/IV, 410-78.

Yonai and his colleagues wanted to stabilize Japan's international position by obtaining the "understanding" of Great Britain, France, and the United States without offering any concessions whatsoever. These powers were told that the way to be friends with Japan was for them to stop helping Chiang Kai-shek. If they would only do that, Japan would be able to end the fighting in China and the world would be a better place for all (but especially for Japan).

On June 1, 1940, Marquis Koichi Kido assumed the key post of lord keeper of the privy seal. During the next six weeks the spectacular successes achieved by the Germans in the European war, which they had launched in September 1939, greatly stimulated both the army and the rightists. The Yonai Cabinet came more and more under attack as a *status quo* government friendly toward the United States and Britain. Three days after the abortive July 5 assassination plot, Kido received a visit from the vice-minister of war, Lt. Gen. Korechika Anami. The gist of Anami's remarks was that a shift in the political situation might occur within four or five days. The army was doing everything in its power, he said, to cope with the rapid changes taking place in the world, but the character of the Yonai Cabinet rendered talks with Germany and Italy extremely "inconvenient." The army feared that a propitious moment might be lost and consequently felt that a cabinet change was necessary. The army unanimously desired the reemergence of Prince Konoe.

Anami also informed Kido that War Minister Shunroku Hata would meet with Konoe on July 10 when the latter returned to Tokyo. "Important advice" would then be given to Premier Yonai—in other words, Yonai would be told to resign. Kido subsequently learned that the officers who formed the backbone of the army general staff (*chūken shōkō*) had reported to their superiors (*shunōbu*) that the Yonai Cabinet was incapable of dealing with the world situation.[18] As a conse-

---

[18] The terms *chūken shōkō* and *shunōbu* generally appear without explanation in Japanese material. Both are extremely loose and vague, thus making it difficult but not impossible to determine who is meant. In the present passage, the terms are used in reference only to the army general staff. Usually, however, they also embrace officers in the war ministry. In this broader sense, *shunōbu* would refer to the chief and vice-chief of the army general staff and to the minister and vice-minister of war.

The term *chūken shōkō* would generally include (1) in the army general staff: the members of the first and second bureaus (*daiichibu* and *dainibu*: operations and intelligence, respectively) and key section personnel, especially the members of the second section (*dainika*: operations) of the first bureau; and (2) in the war ministry: the members of the military affairs bureau (*gunmukyoku*) and key section personnel, especially the members of the military affairs section (*gunmuka*) of the military affairs bureau. The bureau (*bu* and *kyoku*) chiefs form an important link between the *shunōbu* and the *chūken shōkō* as a whole (*bu, kyoku,* and *ka* personnel) and may thus be

quence, the chief of staff had talked with War Minister Hata. The next move was up to the cabinet. Depending on what it decided to do, the war minister might feel called upon to "manifest his firm determination."[19] In less quaint idiom: Hata would resign if the premier did not voluntarily adopt that course himself. Following the war minister's resignation, the army would find it impossible to recommend a successor, and so Admiral Yonai—like it or not—would be forced to bow out, together with all of his cabinet colleagues.

That indeed was how the Yonai Cabinet came to the end of the road. When Marquis Kido arrived at his office in the late morning of July 16, he learned that a political crisis was imminent. War Minister Hata had decided to withdraw from the cabinet. The Big Three had concluded that the selection of a suitable replacement would be "difficult." The upshot was that Admiral Yonai tendered his cabinet's resignation to the Emperor.[20]

The following afternoon, Japan's former premiers—known collectively as the *jūshin*, or senior statesmen—and the then president of the privy council, Dr. Hara, met with Marquis Kido at the imperial palace to discuss the question of a successor to Admiral Yonai.[21] Baron Wakatsuki, who had been Japan's premier at the time of the Manchurian Incident, volunteered the opinion that there was no suitable candidate other than Prince Konoe.[22] Hara, Hiranuma, Hayashi, and Okada im-

---

regarded as having a foot in each camp. When applied to the navy, the terms *shunōbu* and *chūken shōkō* designate officers holding equivalent positions.

[19] The text is based on the account in Kido SKD. See also Kido "Nikki," S 75:13-14, T 6242-44, and Harada, VIII, 282-89. The role of General Hata in the downfall of the Yonai Cabinet is a complicated subject requiring detailed study (see, for instance, S 276:14-15, T 29006-19; J, B/IV, 455 and 474; IMTFE, "Roling Opinion," 184-85, 187; and Maxon, 143-48). The important fact here is that Yonai was forced out as a result of army machinations.

On the impression made in Japan by the German victories in Europe, see also JRD Monograph No. 146, 10-11, 14, and JRD, "Interrogations," I:49157 (Seizō Arisue), 38.

[20] Kido SKD; Kido "Nikki," S 75:14, T 6244-48; and Kido corresp. On events connected with the fall of the Yonai Cabinet, see also J, B/IV, 456 and 459-78. The lord privy seal's "office," mentioned in the text, was at the imperial villa (*goyō-tei*) in Hayama, where the Emperor was in residence. Kido returned to the capital the next day to meet with the senior statesmen.

[21] The ex-premiers present at the palace meeting in Tōkyō were Hayashi, Hiranuma, Hirota, Konoe, Okada, and Wakatsuki. Abe was in China, serving as Japan's ambassador to the Nanking government of Wang Ching-wei. The outgoing premier (in this case, Yonai) never attended a senior statesmen's conference called to recommend his own successor. For more on *jūshin kaigi*, see the references under "Senior statesmen" in Butow, *Japan's Decision to Surrender*. The Tribunal's view that Kido and Konoe intended to use such conferences "as a means of eliminating Saionji's influence in political affairs" seems questionable (see J, B/IV, 476-78).

[22] Kido had earlier learned, on July 7, that this was also Hiranuma's view. Excerpt from Kido "Nikki," S 75:13, T 6242.

mediately seconded this view, but Konoe demurred. He felt that a man was needed who was thoroughly familiar with the situation within the army and who fully understood that situation. He did not regard himself as so qualified. Kido replied that the leaders of the army unanimously desired Prince Konoe to assume the office and that the army's action at this time was based on the belief that the prince would come forward. After Hiranuma and Hirota had added further encouragement, Kido concluded that the consensus was in favor of Konoe. The meeting then adjourned; the entire matter had taken only a half-hour. In the early evening of that same day, Prince Konoe, for the second time, received the imperial mandate to form a cabinet.[23]

Kido later admitted that he had felt somewhat uneasy about recommending Konoe because of the danger that the army might take advantage of his "overwhelming popularity" to advance its own policies. Yet Kido had also felt that if he failed to recommend Konoe, there would be no alternative but to hand Japan's politics over to the army completely.

On the evening Konoe received the mandate, he told Kido that he planned to go at once to the Peer's Club for an exchange of views with the outgoing war and navy ministers. He hoped to obtain the appointment of successors capable of cooperating with each other and of thus bringing about army-navy harmony. He would wait until the two service posts had been filled before choosing anyone for the foreign affairs portfolio. He would then meet with the three ministers for a full discussion of such matters as national defense, foreign policy, army-navy cooperation, and relations with the supreme command. Only when agreement had been reached on these basic questions would he undertake to complete the formation of his cabinet.[24]

As the event turned out, the foreign minister's mantle fell on the shoulders of Yosuke Matsuoka, aptly described by one Japanese general as "voluble and unconventional by nature"—attributes not usually regarded as an asset in Japan.[25] A prominent admiral felt that Matsuoka had "the good point of coming up with splendid ideas, but . . . the fault

---

[23] Kido "Nikki," S 75:14-15, T 6245-46, 6249-54; Kido SKD; and Kido corresp. In the Tribunal's view, Konoe's second cabinet "was resolved to complete the military domination of Japan" (J, B/IV, 482). On the general policy of the cabinet, see J, B/IV, 479-520.

[24] Kido SKD; Kido "Nikki," S 75:15, T 6255-56. This kind of approach to the problem of forming a cabinet had been discussed by Prince Konoe, Marquis Kido, and Count Arima at a private dinner-meeting at a restaurant called the "Kinsui" in Kioi-chō on May 26, 1940. It was anticipated then that Konoe might soon be recalled to the premiership and that a new political party, embracing all of the existing parties, would be established.

[25] JRD, "Interrogations," I:49157 (Seizō Arisue), 45.

of recklessly advancing in the wrong direction." It was bad enough that he did not judge matters objectively, but even worse that he should be blinded by the notion that his subjective opinions were "absolutely correct." Hence, he was "dangerous."[26]

The decisive cabinet portfolio for war went to Lt. Gen. Hideki Tojo, who was then touring Manchuria in his capacity as inspector-general of the army air force. On July 17 Tojo suddenly received orders from War Minister Hata in Tokyo instructing him to report to the capital immediately. He boarded an airplane at Mukden that same day and arrived at Tachikawa airfield near Tokyo the following evening. Tojo went at once to the official residence of the war minister, where he was briefed on the fall of the Yonai Cabinet. It was only then that he learned that he was to succeed Hata in a cabinet headed by Prince Konoe.

The following afternoon Tojo attended a meeting at Konoe's Teki-gaiso residence in the Ogikubo section of Tokyo at which no secretaries were present and no minutes were taken.[27] The purpose of this private session, which was also attended by Navy Minister Zengo Yoshida (a holdover from the Yonai Cabinet) and by Matsuoka, was to reach an agreement of views on national defense, foreign affairs, domestic policies, and similar matters.[28] According to Tojo, settlement of the China

[26] JRD Doc. No. 55773 (Takagi Notes: Admiral Yonai), 8. Tōjō once described Matsuoka as a man who did "a lot of talking" (Tōjō interrog., Jan. 24, 2). For other characterizations, see Feis, 80-81, 87, 115, 120, and 161.

One of Matsuoka's first official acts was a shake-up of Japanese diplomatic personnel. This "Matsuoka cyclone" was designed to rid the diplomatic service of "conventionalism." Key men who had been in the main stream of the foreign office up to that time were asked to retire from their posts voluntarily. To fill the vacancies thus created, Matsuoka gave ambassadorial appointments to men like Lt. Gen. Tatekawa, who had spent the night of September 18, 1931, with the geisha of Mukden, and to Lt. Gen. Hiroshi Ōshima, whose long-continued efforts on behalf of an alliance with the Axis were soon to be crowned with success. See Kido SKD and Kido corresp. See also Moore, *With Japan's Leaders*, 116-19 ("The Army had long held the foreign service in contempt, its leaders saying that what the fighting men gained for the nation the weak-kneed diplomats gave away. . . . Matsuoka was making an exhibition of his contempt for the 'weaklings.' ").

[27] "Tekigaisō" signifies "a residence (on a cliff) just outside Ogikubo." *Teki* refers to Ogikubo (*Ogi* is also pronounced *Teki*); *gai*, which means "outside," can also mean "cliff" when written with another character; *sō* means "villa" or "residence." Ushiba corresp.

On the July 19 conference, see Tōjō aff., S 342:12-13, T 36176-79; Tōjō cross-examination, S 346:4, T 36572-74; S 346:8 and 9, T 36600 and 36605; S 347:3, T 36655-56; and S 347:4-5, T 36662-64. See also J, B/IV, 456, 459-81, 493; IMTFE, "Roling Opinion," 82-83, 106; Harada, VIII, 292, 299-300; Gaimushō, II, 435-36; and Yabe, *Konoe Fumimaro*, II, 116-22.

[28] Four-minister conferences of this type (which were sometimes broadened to include the finance minister or the home minister) had occupied an important place in the decision-making process during Hirota's premiership. Following the outbreak of the China Incident, four- and five-minister conferences served as the channel by which

Incident was foremost in Konoe's mind. Better coordination between the supreme command and the cabinet and closer harmony between the two military services were essential. The others present expressed complete agreement with Konoe's suggestions and promised to do their best in the desired direction. There was also unanimity of opinion regarding the need to establish "a high-degree defense state"—a nation fully armed.[29]

The selection of suitable persons for the remaining cabinet vacancies was left entirely to the discretion of Prince Konoe. The premier completed this task in due course, with the result that the imperial investiture ceremony took place at 8:00 p.m. on July 22. Thus was the second Konoe Cabinet formed and thus did General Tojo achieve, at the age of fifty-six, a position of political responsibility.

Tojo's emergence as war minister in mid-1940 was the result of orthodox administrative procedures. The primary responsibility rested with a major general named Kengo Noda, who was then the chief of the personnel bureau of the war ministry.[30] In recalling the appointment years later, Noda stressed that he had given the utmost care and attention to recommending a successor to General Hata. He had taken into full account the views prevailing within the war ministry and the general staff. He had also consulted closely with Vice-Minister of War Anami. The feeling in army circles was that no one except Tojo would do. After further study, Noda had decided that Tojo was indeed an appropriate man for the job and consequently had recommended him to General Hata. There were others who could have been chosen, but they were already in important positions from which a speedy transfer

the entire cabinet was quite arbitrarily committed to policies which frequently originated in the army general staff. See T 679-80; Hattori, I, 44 and 246; Tōjō interrog., Mar. 18, 6, Mar. 19, 1-2; J, B/IV, 308-9; and the Araki interrog. cited in Maxon, 15.

[29] Tōjō's specific denial of the prosecution charge that "an authoritative foreign policy program" was formulated (i.e., a program covering such matters as relations with the Axis, the attitude to be adopted toward the United States, and policy toward the Soviet Union) is not supported by his general testimony or by other evidence. His denial seems to represent a semantic problem, although he may have been troubled somewhat by this example of the differences between theory and practice with regard to decision-making. On this question, see also S 75:15-16, T 6261-64; Hattori, I, 48-51; and CF 20, III, 298.

Feis, 84, notes that Konoe later told Harada that at the July 19 conference Matsuoka had spoken out as if he advocated war with the United States and that this had alarmed Navy Minister Yoshida, who was placated only when Matsuoka toned down his remarks in the course of explaining what he had meant. " 'To say something out of line and scaring others,' Konoye explained, 'is one of Matsuoka's weak points.' " See also Yabe, II, 122.

[30] See S 280:1-2, T 29394-96, 29398-401 (Noda testimony). Also, Kido and Umezu intv.

would have been difficult.[31] That was not the case with Tojo, who had the further advantage of having previously held various administrative assignments, including the post of vice-minister of war in the first Konoe Cabinet.[32] Acting upon Noda's recommendation, General Hata had submitted Tojo's name at a meeting of the Big Three held on July 18. The result had been a unanimous endorsement of Tojo.[33] Noda insisted that the nomination had followed standard operating procedure and that neither he nor War Minister Hata had ever had any close personal relations with General Tojo.

The implication of Noda's entire testimony was that there had been nothing extraordinary about Tojo's becoming war minister in July 1940, and that, indeed, seems to be the case. One knowledgeable officer later ascribed Tojo's selection to the "paucity of suitable candidates at the time." The "dignity" Tojo had displayed while serving as chief of staff of the Kwantung army, as vice-minister of war, and as inspector-general of army aviation, his proven efficiency and—above all—his executive ability, made him a "logical choice." Neither partisan backing nor political leanings were involved. As inspector-general for air, Tojo was a key man at the center and thus comparatively well-informed on political as well as military matters. It was expedient to utilize such an officer, who ranked next to the army's Big Three in importance, to fill the post of war minister during a time of unexpected political upheaval.[34]

In one respect, however, Tojo's nomination was unusual. In the early afternoon of July 18, outgoing War Minister Hata had privately reported to the Emperor that Tojo was being recommended as the next

[31] Among the more important officers who had seniority over Tōjō, in addition to Hata, were Terauchi (supreme war councilor), Sugiyama (who became chief of staff in October 1940), Umezu (commander of the Kwantung army), and Yamada (inspector-general of military training). JRD, "Interrogations," I:49157 (Seizō Arisue), 29-30.

[32] Tōjō was never vice-minister of war in the Hiranuma Cabinet, as stated in Noda's testimony. The witness was also in error in declaring that Tōjō was in Tōkyō at the time of the cabinet change. The fact that Tōjō was touring Manchuria does not necessarily undermine Noda's contention that it was easier to transfer Tōjō than some of the other likely candidates. The "Transcript" incorrectly states that Tōjō "had formerly been Chief of the Military Affairs Bureau and of the Maintenance Bureau."

[33] The Big Three were War Minister Hata, Chief of the Army General Staff Prince Kan-in (the then vice-chief was Lt. Gen. Shigeru Sawada), and Inspector-General of Military Training Yamada.

[34] JRD, "Interrogations," I:49157 (Seizō Arisue), 29-30. In postwar testimony Tōjō declared that he had been both "surprised and not surprised" by his appointment as war minister. Prior to the event, he had not heard any rumors that he would get the job. The Yonai Cabinet had fallen not because of army general staff intrigue—"a petty idea"—but because the cabinet lacked political power and had become alienated from the public. See Tōjō cross-examination, S 346:4, T 36572-74; S 346:4-5, T 36577-83; S 346:6, T 36587; S 346:8, T 36598-602; S 346:12, T 36623-25; and redirect, S 349:4-5, T 36833-35. Also, motion picture footage (sound) of Tōjō on the witness stand.

war minister and that Lt. Gen. Yamashita was slated to take over as inspector-general of army aviation.

The customary procedure at the time of a cabinet change was for the Big Three to make their recommendation directly to the premier-designate. Once the candidate proffered by the army had been accepted, the outgoing war minister would informally advise the throne. In this particular case, Prince Konoe was still in the process of forming his cabinet. The Emperor therefore concluded that Konoe had probably not as yet acted on the Big Three's recommendation. He mentioned this to Hata and indicated that he thought the war minister's advance disclosure somewhat strange.

The most likely explanation of Hata's action is that he made an honest mistake in prematurely informing the throne or that, on the basis of his meeting with Konoe the previous evening, he saw no reason to delay advising the Emperor that Tojo had been recommended for the war portfolio. Although mistakes in protocol involving the Emperor were rare, the event seems to have had no special significance. At Tojo's postwar trial, however, the prosecution tried to capitalize on the incident by charging that Tojo had "secretly" been recommended to the Emperor by General Hata. It was suggested, in effect, that Tojo was somehow at the bottom of a plot aimed at improperly influencing the throne in his behalf. Tojo denied any knowledge of the affair. He pointed out that on the afternoon in question he had been en route by air from Mukden to Tokyo. He estimated that he must have been flying over Taegu or the Korean straits at approximately the time when Hata was in audience with the Emperor.

When the chief prosecutor continued to hammer at the matter, Tojo suggested that a mistake was being made in the translation of a character-compound in the account by Marquis Kido on which the prosecution was basing its contention. According to the prosecution's version, the Emperor had told Kido that Hata had "secretly recommended" Tojo. The word in question was *naisō*, normally used to convey the idea of an informal or private report to the throne. When Tojo objected to the prosecution's rendition of the word, the language arbiter in the courtroom advised that "informal recommendation" might be a better translation. Tojo replied that that was not exactly correct either, but at least it was better than "secretly recommended."[35]

[35] On Hata's audience and the *naisō* question, see Kido "Nikki," S 75:16, T 6266-67; Tōjō cross-examination, S 346:8-12, T 36602-25; Noda cross-examination, S 280:2, T 29401; IMTFE, "Roling Opinion," 186-87; and Kido corresp. The use of the term

As Japan's new war minister, Tojo soon let it be known that he was determined to do what he could to bring about a settlement of the China Incident. He expected to wield more disciplinary control over the army than had been evidenced in the past and felt that an adjustment between the supreme command and military administration was necessary. He planned to encourage better army-navy relations and closer coordination between the supreme command and the cabinet. He said he would also work for unity between political and military strategy and would seek to correct the practice of the premier's being a mere robot. When Kido was personally advised by Tojo of his outlook, the lord privy seal felt encouraged. He got the impression that at last a new departure might indeed be made and that "politics resembling politics" might be carried out.[36]

Tojo's avowed program touched upon several key problems that had interfered with the proper and efficient functioning of the Japanese government for some years and that were to hinder its operation even more seriously in the immediate future. The all-absorbing question of the moment, however, was not the solution of these problems, but rather the charting of a course to guide Japan both at home and abroad. The course itself and the consequences it produced reflected the continued existence of interservice rivalry and of a serious dichotomy in the government between the supreme command and the cabinet. It was the tragedy of modern Japan that in any test of strength on policy matters the narrow military view—the Bering Straits tunnel psychology—generally prevailed. It was the tragedy of Hideki Tojo that he subscribed to that view wholeheartedly. When given a position of political power and responsibility as the army's advocate within the cabinet, he vigorously advanced that view with all the energy and decisiveness at his command.

Tojo was not so much an initiator of policies as a promoter of them and propagandist for them. He controlled the army with respect to disciplinary matters, but not on policy matters. It was the chief of staff and his subordinates—particularly the latter—who determined army attitudes and who foisted them, through the war minister and the chief

---

naisō to convey the idea of an informal or private report to the throne is indirectly confirmed by the way in which it is employed in Konoe, 120, and Hattori, I, 182, in reference to a Konoe audience with the Emperor on September 5, 1941. The term also appears in Tōjō's affidavit (S 344:8, T 36420) with reference to a report to the throne that resulted in the commutation of five of the eight death sentences originally meted out to the Doolittle fliers. It is obvious that the prosecution was incorrect in assigning a sinister meaning to the word.

[36] See Tōjō aff., S 342:13, T 36180, and Kido SKD. With the exception of the "robot" remark, which is found only in Kido, the two accounts are in general agreement.

of the military affairs bureau, upon the members of the cabinet.[37] At the same time, Tojo would never have become war minister if he had not shared the views that prevailed within the general staff in 1940. The particular advantage to the army's decision-makers of having him in the second Konoe Cabinet was that Tojo believed implicitly in the program then being advocated and hence was a powerful persuader whose sincerity lent effectiveness to his presentation of the army's plans for the future.

The two principal items then on the agenda were the conclusion of an alliance with the Axis, and the establishment within Japan of a "one nation, one party" system. From the army's point of view, it was the war minister's job to help guide the cabinet in the desired direction. Tojo did so with considerable facility. It was not *his* program; it was the army's. But Tojo helped to make it possible. That the task was by no means difficult—that there was no necessity to browbeat unwilling or uncooperative civilian colleagues—is revealed, in the first instance, by the agreement of views reached at the Ogikubo conference on July 19, and, in the second instance, by the formal confirmation of that agreement which came on July 26-27. Midway between those dates, the shape of the future was succinctly suggested by Premier Konoe in a radio address to the Japanese people: ". . . no nation has ever become powerful by devoting itself to luxury and pleasure."[38]

It was this quest for power that dominated the minds of the men responsible for Japan's destiny in 1940 and 1941. The fact that Konoe's ministerial roster included three of the *ni-ki san-suke* from Manchuria—Hideki Tojo, Naoki Hoshino, and Yosuke Matsuoka—was in itself indicative of the unity of viewpoint which might be achieved. In his talks with the outgoing war and navy ministers of the Yonai Cabinet, Konoe had apparently shown such a willingness to cooperate that the services had not felt it necessary to resort to the usual procedure of imposing conditions on the formation of his cabinet.[39] This was demon-

[37] The role of the army general staff (especially of the *chūken shōkō*) in the decision-making process will be covered in greater detail in subsequent chapters. The background of the decision of July 27, shortly to be discussed, illustrates one aspect of that role.

[38] From Konoe's radio address to the nation on July 23, 1940 (Hattori, I, 50). I have adjusted Konoe's words to accord with English idiom. The sentence in Japanese reads: "Oyoso shashi itsuraku wo koto to shite kōryū seru kokka wa imada katsute kore wo minai." This calls to mind a statement by Justice Roling: "The path for the militarists was cleared by those who set the goal." IMTFE, "Roling Opinion," 82.

[39] Tōjō testified that no conditions were imposed. As has been suggested in the text, the circumstances surrounding the formation of the cabinet, including the agreement of views reached at the Ogikubo conference on July 19, would seem to have made the usual procedure of imposing conditions unnecessary.

strated by the results of the Ogikubo conference and by the formalization of those results, in specific terms, on July 26 and 27.

On the former date, cabinet approval was given to a document entitled "The Main Principles of Japan's Basic National Policy."[40] This had been drafted by the cabinet planning board, headed by Naoki Hoshino, along lines suggested by Prince Konoe. In the mumbo-jumbo of that time, the world was described as approaching "a momentous historical turning point," with Japan herself facing "a great ordeal without precedent in her past." A new form of government, economy, and culture were in the process of creation. It was urgently necessary "to seize the inevitable trends of these historical world developments," to institute speedily fundamental innovations throughout the government, and to advance toward the perfection of a national defense state by overcoming all obstacles.

The basic aim of this policy was allegedly the establishment of world peace. As a first step in that direction, Japan would build a new order in Greater East Asia based upon a strong union of Japan, Manchukuo, and China, with Japan serving as the nucleus. The government would devote its efforts to achieving an armaments position that would enable Japan to carry out her national policies. On the foreign affairs front, emphasis would be placed on bringing the China Incident to a successful conclusion. On the home front a complete reform of Japan's internal administration would be carried out. Education would be made to reflect the fundamental principles of the national polity. Devotion to the state and the elimination of all "selfish thoughts" would be stressed. A scientific spirit would also be promoted. A strong new political structure would be established, and Diet reforms would be inaugurated so as to bring that body into conformity with this structure.

On the economic front, Japan would drive for self-sufficiency within her new order. A planned economy would be established with a unitary control structure. Other specific measures would be adopted in various fields of economic activity so as to enhance Japan's economic power and permit her to cope with the world situation.

The nation's human resources would also receive attention. Japan's population would be increased and the mental faculties and physical stamina of her "one hundred million people" would be enhanced. Inequalities in individual sacrifices would be rectified and a standard of living maintained which would permit the nation to face and overcome the decade of hardships lying ahead.

[40] *Kihon Kokusaku Yōkō*. See footnote 45 below.

Such was the basic national policy sanctioned by the full Konoe Cabinet on July 26—one week after the preparatory Ogikubo conference and only four days after the formal investiture ceremony. On the next day, July 27, a far more detailed decision, relating specifically to foreign affairs, was adopted at a liaison conference composed of members of the cabinet and of the supreme command—the latter acting in their capacity as officers of the general staff holding key posts in imperial headquarters. The nature and scope of this second decision were such that the army and navy general staffs were intimately concerned with its formulation and implementation.

Membership in liaison conferences varied according to circumstances but always included the army and navy chiefs of staff and the four principal ministers of the cabinet (the premier and the war, navy, and foreign ministers). Of these six constituent members, no more than two could ever be civilians. When either the premier or the foreign minister was a military man, this minority was reduced to one. Even the *ad hoc* inclusion of other cabinet officers, such as the finance or home minister, did not seriously affect the balance of power within the liaison conference. Although the war and navy ministers attended as members of the cabinet, for the most part they joined forces with the chiefs of staff in acting as spokesmen for the army and the navy. The vice-chiefs of staff were generally on hand to assist in the presentation of supreme-command matters. The chief cabinet secretary and the heads of the military and naval affairs bureaus of the service ministries acted as secretaries. They or their subordinates drafted the agenda and took care of all other matters pertaining to the functioning of the conference. Not infrequently it was this small "second string," or even the "third string" composed of the men under them, who not only drew up the policies but actually made the decisions.[41] The vice-chiefs of staff and the heads of the military and naval affairs bureaus were subject to the influence of the nucleus group within the army and navy. The *chūken shōkō* were therefore able to infiltrate even that phase of the decision-making process which took place within the highest councils of the state.

Subjects for discussion at liaison conferences could be raised either

[41] The "third string" or "assistant secretary" group (*kanji hosa*) was composed of one man of section-staff rank from each of the following: cabinet, war ministry, navy ministry, army general staff, and navy general staff.

This is a twentieth-century example of what Sir George Sansom calls, in another context, the "descent of authority down the stairs of rank." Although there are parallels in other countries, the practice was carried "to extreme lengths" in Japan (Sansom, *The Western World and Japan*, 183).

by the cabinet or by imperial headquarters. In the latter case, a prior agreement of views on the part of the army and navy divisions of that headquarters and the approval of the war and navy ministers were required. Because of this arrangement, a civilian cabinet minister harboring unorthodox ideas would find it impossible to play the army and navy off against each other. The differences of opinion and the quarrels which did exist within or between the services were generally confined to the military family circle. Such an open break as that which had occurred in late 1938 between General Tada, representing the army general staff, and General Tojo, speaking for the war ministry, was quite unusual. Even more extraordinary was the "victory" won by Konoe at the beginning of 1938 when he had prevailed upon the army general staff, during the course of one of the early liaison conferences, to give its reluctant consent to his policy of refusing to have anything further to do with Chiang Kai-shek. Thus, the convocation of a liaison conference on July 27, 1940—the first in more than two years—actually represented a reconciliation between the cabinet and the supreme command.[42] It also attested to the changes in direction which were now contemplated and to the importance of the decisions being made.

The draft policy which came before the July 27 conference bore the rather cumbersome title, "The Main Principles of Japan's Policy for Coping with the Situation in Accordance with World Developments."[43]

[42] I have expanded upon certain basic facts pertaining to liaison conferences presented in Hattori, I, 87 and 245-47; Tōjō interrog., Mar. 14, 4-5, Mar. 15, 1-3 ("Discussions were continued until there was unanimous agreement"); Oikawa aff., S 316:2, T 33337-39; Tōgō aff., S 337:4, T 35677-79; Mutō redirect, S 315:6, T 33270-71; and JRD, "Statements," II:50724 (Takushiro Hattori and Katsuhei Nakamura), 654-55.

During Konoe's second premiership, Minister of State Hiranuma participated in liaison conferences because he was serving, in effect, as deputy premier. The chief of the joint planning board was eventually added (the date is not specified) as a "secretary." Except for the April 1941-October 1943 period, the cabinet planning board was headed by a civilian. It should be recalled that the vice-chiefs of staff played an especially active role at this time by virtue of the fact that until October 1940, in the case of the army, and April 1941, in the case of the navy, the chiefs of staff were imperial princes. Hattori notes that between November 1940 and July 1941 a less formal type of conference, called *daihon'ei-seifu renraku kondankai*, was held regularly at least once a week at the premier's official residence. This "liaison round-table conference" procedure was adopted on November 26, 1940, at the suggestion of War Minister Tōjō. Even though the service ministers spoke for the supreme command at four- and five-minister conferences, such conferences had proved less than satisfactory, especially with regard to matters relating to war guidance. The *kondankai* proposed by Tōjō was designed to solve this difficulty by bringing the supreme command directly into the discussion of policy questions on a regular basis. The liaison conference procedure discussed in the text refers to the original and more formal type of liaison conference, which met inside the palace whenever matters of grave national importance were being decided.

[43] *Sekai Jōsei no Suii ni Tomonau Jikyoku Shori Yōkō.* See footnote 45 below.

This document was not a product of the foreign ministry, as might have been supposed, nor was it even the work of Hoshino's cabinet planning board. In its final form it was purely and simply the creation of the army and navy divisions of imperial headquarters and hence primarily the brain-child of the nucleus group (*chūken shōkō*) within the supreme command. Thus it was the military and not the civilians who were prescribing the course of Japan's foreign policy.[44]

Their prescription leaves no doubt as to their intentions. They desired not only to expedite a settlement of the China Incident but also to turn, when a favorable opportunity presented itself, to solving the "problems" confronting Japan in the South. Every means would be employed to force the Generalissimo to submit—including the eradication of third-power aid to his "regime." Political solidarity with Germany and Italy would be strengthened at once and a bold adjustment of diplomatic relations with the Soviet Union would be attempted. Japan would maintain her "just claims" and a "stern attitude" toward the United States. Since the pursuit of Japan's policies would result in an unavoidable deterioration of relations with America, constant vigilance would be required. At the same time, Japan would also endeavor to avoid antagonizing the United States further. Relations with the French and the British would be geared to the basic problem of bringing the China Incident to an end.

The recommendations made with regard to French Indo-China accurately forecast developments there over the next few months: Japan would endeavor to get the French to halt supplies to the Generalissimo, to sanction the passage of Japanese troops through Indo-China, to allow Japan the use of airfields, and to provide the natural resources demanded by Tokyo.

The crux of the matter, the basic philosophy underlying this foreign policy statement of July 27, was candidly explained in Article 3, "The Employment of Force." In the event that the China Incident had

[44] A draft policy was adopted at a conference of the key men in the army general staff and the war ministry on July 3, 1940 (a so-called *shunō kaigi*). The next day this draft was submitted to the naval general staff. Between July 4 and July 22 a number of army-navy conferences were held to discuss the draft and to decide upon the explanations which would be offered when the proposal was presented for final adoption. Immediately following the fall of the Yonai Cabinet, the draft was shown to Konoe and Matsuoka. The agreement of views reached at the Ogikubo conference on July 19 with respect to the general features of this draft served as the prerequisite for the formation of the cabinet. On July 22, the day on which Konoe and his colleagues were formally invested, the draft was finally adopted as a joint proposal of the army and navy divisions of imperial headquarters. Five days later (July 27) it came before the liaison conference.

generally been settled and the situation at home and abroad permitted, Japan would seize a favorable opportunity to resort to arms in the South. Should the China Incident remain unsettled, Japan would endeavor by and large to avoid hostilities with third powers in the southern regions. But if the domestic and foreign situation developed in a particularly favorable way, force would be employed in the South even though Japan remained committed in China. The decision as to how, when, and where force would be used would depend upon future conditions. If Japan went to war in the South, she would attempt to confine her military moves to action against the British, but since a war with the United States might become inevitable in such circumstances, thorough preparations would be carried out to provide for that contingency.

Within Japan, emphasis would be placed upon expediting the formation of a national defense state. "High-powered government" would be inaugurated, the national general mobilization law would be more widely invoked, a wartime economic structure would be established, war materials would be stockpiled, and Japan's shipping tonnage would be expanded. Although it was recognized that the implementation of some features of this program might require a longer time than others, the end of August 1940 was proposed as the target date for the completion of the preparations needed to accomplish Japan's primary objectives.[45]

Thus did the army and navy divisions of imperial headquarters—the

[45] On the *Kihon Kokusaku Yōkō* of July 26, 1940, and the *Sekai Jōsei no Suii ni Tomonau Jikyoku Shori Yōkō* of July 27, 1940 (including the explanations offered at the liaison conference by the officers representing imperial headquarters), see Hattori, I, 48 and 51-59 (which includes the full texts of both policies and correctly describes their adoption as a major turning point in the development of the China Incident into the Greater East Asia War—a conclusion emphasized at the end of this chapter without further citation); Gaimushō, II, 436-38 (texts); S 75:17, T 6271-76; S 123:18, T 11713-16; and S 124:7-8, T 11794-95; Tōjō aff., S 342:13-14, T 36180-88; Tōjō cross-examination, S 346:6-8, T 36584-98; S 346:12-14, T 36625-40; S 347:3-7, T 36655-83; S 347:8-9, T 36688-94; and S 348:12, T 36798-99; JRD Monograph No. 146, 10-16 (in which the significance of the July 27 policy with regard to the outbreak of the Pacific war is also noted) and Appendixes 2 and 3; JRD, "Interrogations," I:49157 (Seizō Arisue), 38-40; JRD, "Translation," II:51903 (Item 18), 1; J, B/IV, 481-84, 494-97; IMTFE, "Roling Opinion," 83-84; and CF 20, III, 298 and 20, IV, 397 (Japanese text). See also Feis, 84-87, in which the "lack of full texts and authoritative translations" (as of 1950) is noted.

The July 27 policy also stipulated a reliance, for the time being, upon diplomatic measures designed to secure the vital resources of the Netherlands East Indies. Japan was to endeavor, through friendly means, to induce other countries in the South (principally Thailand) to act in concert with her.

The prosecution missed the significance of the July 27 policy because it had in its possession only a brief "gist" of that policy (presented in court in inadequate translation, T 11794-95).

decision-makers within the supreme command—kindle the imaginations of the men of the war ministry and of the civilians within the cabinet. Such was the power of this particular brand of positive thinking that no voice questioned the vision of a Japan taking advantage of the war in Europe to gobble an empire in Asia. Perhaps some of Japan's leaders deluded themselves with justifications of self-defense or allowed themselves to believe that the noble end (an Asia freed from the Western yoke) vindicated the questionable means (aggressive military action by Japan). Others may have thought that diplomacy would indeed be able to serve Japan's purposes and that the implications of the recurring phrase, *buryoku kōshi*, "the use of force," need not occasion concern. Although not stated in so many words, it was well understood that Japan could not keep fighting in China without obtaining the resources of the South—especially with the Generalissimo receiving aid from powers which were daily becoming more hostile as they began more fully to comprehend the threat to their own security posed by Japan's drive for hegemony over Asia.[46]

With its acceptance of these principles of policy drafted by the army and navy divisions of imperial headquarters, the second Konoe Cabinet committed Japan not only to a continuation of the fighting in China but also to a possible broadening of hostilities to include the southern area. Since an attack upon British possessions in that region might prompt an American entry, Konoe also pledged himself and his cabinet to undertake preparations for war against the United States. The readiness with which the government assumed responsibilities of such magnitude suggests that the people of Japan were in danger of being plunged into total war, at almost any time, by leaders who were over-eager to seize what the supreme command described as a golden opportunity.[47] Despite a general implication that diplomacy would take precedence, the essence of the entire proposal was that *if Japan could not get what she wanted through negotiation, she would take what she wanted by force.*

This, then, was the beginning of a trend in official thinking within Japan that was to lead the nation, in less than a year and a half, beyond the point of no return. The decisions of July 26 and 27, 1940, constituted a pivotal stage in the metamorphosis of the China Incident into the Greater East Asia War.

[46] See, for instance, Tōjō aff., S 342:14, T 36187-88.
[47] Although Hattori (I, 57) finds it remarkable that such an important national policy was so speedily decided at a single liaison conference without extensive argument, he does not pursue the point.

CHAPTER 7

Tightening Japan's Helmet Strings

ALTHOUGH War Minister Tojo had not personally been active in the formulation of the national policies of late July 1940, there is no doubt that he fully supported them and steadily adhered to their provisions as more and more matters posing the problem of diplomacy versus force pressed for decision. Years later, when the war had ended and Tojo was a prisoner in the dock, he consistently maintained that he had not harbored thoughts of aggression or plans of conquest and that, so far as he knew, neither had any of his cabinet colleagues.[1] He called the prosecution's contention in that regard "nonsense." Japan, he said, was acting in self-defense against the mounting pressure of the powers. It was necessary to free the Japanese people from the international isolation in which they had been living and to place them once again in a secure position. That was the purpose behind the strengthening of political connections with Germany and Italy and the adjustment of relations with the Soviet Union.

From the Emperor on down, Tojo declared, everyone desired to see an improvement of relations with the United States and Great Britain. Within the cabinet, it was felt that a solution of the China Incident required that Japan remain on good terms with the Americans and the British. Matsuoka had strongly advocated taking a bold stand, but at the same time he had also argued that a war with the United States would result in the destruction of the world. Since such a war must be avoided at all costs, it was necessary to improve relations, and the only way to do that, according to Matsuoka, was to adopt a firm attitude.

Despite the specific references to the possible use of force in the liaison conference decision of July 27, Tojo categorically stated that at the time in question there had not been the slightest thought of instigating a war with Britain and the United States. It was feared, however, that whether Japan wanted it or not, war might be forced upon her through military action directed by those powers against Japan.[2] Adopt-

[1] See Tōjō aff., S 342:13-14, T 36180-83.   [2] *Ibid.*

ing a "firm attitude" toward the United States meant advocating what was right and not resorting to servility. When it was suggested to Tojo that Japan had really intended to have her own way, he replied that Japan's purpose had not been so narrow-minded, that diplomatic negotiations always involved more than one party, and that no one could force his own point of view upon another. Japan, he said, had been prepared to concede where concession was possible. He denied that he had made up his mind to advocate war against the United States unless that country ceased aiding the Generalissimo and the Chinese Nationalists.[3]

Although the tendency during the trial was not to take such statements very seriously, Tojo was being quite candid. He and his colleagues seem frequently to have made decisions without fully exploring their possible consequences. They took things as they came and preferred to pass from one imminent problem to another. Matters not requiring immediate attention were left to the future with the thought that each bridge would be crossed when they came to it. As a result, they were unprepared at times for the responses which their own actions engendered.

Whether Tojo's memory was somewhat hazy or whether his testimony represented his honest interpretation of the meaning of the July 27 policy statement is not known. The prosecution introduced only a very brief and inadequate "gist" of that statement. There was no mention of Japan's determination to resort to force if diplomacy failed to produce the desired effect. In fact, the prosecution's "gist" rather indicated a Japanese intention to avoid war.[4] Had the full scope of the government's program been appreciated, Tojo's assertions would probably have been interpreted as the efforts of a man vainly trying to squirm out of a decisively incriminating position. Given Tojo's personality, however, as well as his entire approach to the trial, that would have been the least satisfactory explanation.

Perhaps some of the Tokyo trial defendants testified with design,

---

[3] See Tōjō cross-examination, S 347:8-9, T 36688-94. The majority view of the Tribunal was that Matsuoka's "get tough" line represented a reversal of the government's earlier belief that Tōkyō could not take a firm stand against the United States because of Japan's great reliance upon that country as a source of vital raw materials. Early in March 1940, however, a policy was formulated to establish industrial self-sufficiency and to eliminate economic dependence upon the United States. "It was intended that as a result . . . Japan would be enabled to adopt a firm attitude towards the United States; and it was expected that that country, confronted by the threat of war and under the pressure of the public opinion of its own people, would acquiesce in Japanese actions and remove embargoes upon the supply of raw materials." See J, B/IV, 421-26.

[4] See T 11794-95.

calculating the effect their words would have upon the outcome of their cases, but Tojo spoke with conviction regardless of the consequences. He was a simple man, and he thought in simple terms. The attitude which colored his views in the years when he held positions of power and responsibility was that force was a legitimate instrument of national policy. At times Tojo may have realized that Japan could not seriously claim the existence of an unprovoked threat to the nation, but it seems more likely that he was actually incapable of thinking the problem through to the cause-and-effect relationship which constitutes the only meaningful measure of which came first: Japanese aggression prompting Western hostility or Western hostility prompting Japanese aggression.

The chief prosecutor, Joseph B. Keenan, did not see Tojo in this light. To him the defendant was a man brimming with purposeful deceit. One of their more interesting exchanges occurred when Keenan attempted to delve into the cabinet decision of July 26, by which the main principles of Japan's basic national policy had been established:

Q.: Now you, Mr. Tojo, helped to make that cabinet decision, did you not?

A.: Yes, very much.

Q.: And you did that about four days after you took office as War Minister, didn't you?

A.: Well, four wouldn't be quite enough. I think there was (sic) about nine days.

Q.: Oh, was it? Well, let us say within ten days of the time. That would be safe, wouldn't it?

A.: No, then you won't be mistaken.

Q.: The point I am making is that you got to work pretty quick.

A.: No, not one second of idleness was permitted.

The awkward wording of this exchange was typical of a frequently encountered language problem. In the process of on-the-spot interpretation, meaning was often blurred or even lost entirely. Sometimes the difference between the English and the Japanese would be rather slight; at other times, the gap would be very wide. On this particular occasion Keenan's implication that Tojo had not let any grass grow under *his* feet did not emerge, with comparable caustic effect, in the Japanese equivalent which Tojo heard. Thus, Tojo's statement that no time was wasted was not so much an answer to Keenan's actual question as a response to the interpreter's rendition of what Keenan had said.[5] It was the English and not the Japanese, however, that got through to the court.

When Keenan suggested that the new cabinet had only desired to reform the Diet so as to make that body subservient to the wishes of the military, Tojo vigorously denied the prosecutor's contention.[6] Keenan was equally unsuccessful in his effort to get Tojo to admit that the July 26 policy statement describing the world as being on the threshold of a momentous historical turning point was a reference to the anticipated emergence of a European dictatorship under Hitler. When Keenan sarcastically asked whether Tojo wanted him to believe that the turning-point statement referred to events in the Duchy of Liechtenstein, the taunt was lost through the interpreter's inability to get Keenan's meaning across and through Tojo's failure not only to understand the interpretation as a whole but also to comprehend the meaning of *Rihitenshutain*—the Japanese phonetic equivalent of "Liechtenstein."[7]

The two protagonists also came to verbal blows over the true meaning and purpose of the liaison conference decision of July 27. Tojo took particular exception to the introduction by the prosecution of an excerpt from the "Saionji-Harada Memoirs" purporting to be an account of what had happened on that day. It was Tojo's contention that Harada either had manufactured certain items out of whole cloth or was referring to an attitude which might have existed at a later date. Since neither Prince Saionji nor Baron Harada had been present at the liaison conference, Tojo's point was not without merit. The prosecution, which frequently quoted from the "Memoirs," placed exceptional confidence in Harada's personal record of the many years he had spent in the shadow of the great Saionji, who had often been very near if not always at the center of major events. Tojo, who had never met either man, respected the prince, but regarded the baron with contempt. He referred to him as a "high-class information broker" and described the excerpt introduced by Keenan as a typical example of the kind of thing such an information peddler would produce. The chief prosecutor was understandably annoyed and tried to pierce Tojo's armor by suggesting that he was only saying such things about Harada because he knew the

---

[5] See T 36586, S 346:6. Keenan's question was interpreted as follows: "Watakushi ga iwan to shite iru yōten wa, sōtō hayai tokoro shigoto wo hajimeta to iu koto desu." Tōjō replied, "Sono tōri, ikkoku mo yurusanakatta no desu."

[6] T 36633, S 346:13: "Tondemo nai hanashi desu."

[7] See S 346:6, T 36587-88. Tōjō also disclaimed any intention on the government's part to institute in Japan a form of government patterned after the Nazi model (S 346:12, T 36628-29).

baron was dead and could not reply. But Tojo parried the thrust with one of his own. He was not such a petty person as that, he declared. Whether Harada was alive or dead was beside the point. He would say the same thing about him in either case. After further wrangling on the subject, Tojo suggested that the prosecutor refer to the gist of the July 27 decision which had already been introduced into evidence and that any further questions to him concerning that decision be based on that gist, which he regarded as accurate, and not on the material recorded by Harada. Keenan angrily shot back: "I will pursue my questions to you, Mr. Tojo, in accordance with my own desire. I am doing the questioning and you are doing the answering. Do you understand?" Tojo momentarily let the matter drop with a simple *Ē, wakarimashita*: "Yes, I do," but a few seconds later he let it be known that nothing Keenan had said had changed his mind in the least.[8]

Despite Keenan's general lack of success in eliciting admissions from Tojo, much is clear from the actual record of events. Once Japan's basic policies with respect to problems at home and abroad had been decided within the first week after Konoe's reemergence as premier, the obstacles which had earlier stood in the way of preparing the nation for possible further armed encounters were rapidly removed. Foremost among the new cabinet's achievements were the conclusion of an alliance with the Axis and the establishment, within Japan, of the Imperial Rule Assistance Association.

The IRAA concept was by no means new, but the rapid progress now made toward the close-order drilling of internal political forces was noteworthy.[9] The idea was to "strengthen politics" through the establishment of a one-nation, one-party system capable of conveying the will of the government to the people and the will of the people to the government. Konoe's aim was supposedly the creation of a powerful organization designed to keep the army out of politics and to marshal the national effort toward a settlement of the China Incident. Just how army meddling could be eliminated when the military were already so deeply involved in politics that there was little opportunity for the parties to function seems not to have received very much attention.

---

[8] See Tōjō cross-examination, S 347:3-5, T 36655-68. Tōjō's term for Harada was "kōtō naru jōhō burōkā."

[9] On the emergence of the IRAA (*Taisei Yokusankai*), which is discussed briefly in the text which follows, see "The Brocade Banner," 5-6, 102-3, 106-8, 110-15; Kido SKD and corresp.; Tōjō interrog., Mar. 20, 3-6, Mar. 21, 1-7; Tōjō aff., S 342:13, T 36183; Hattori, I, 46-47, 49, 88-90; J, B/IV, 292-94, 338, 459-61, 471-72, 482-84, 486-87; J, B/VII, 852-54; *Japan Year Book, 1941-42*, 175-82; *Japan Year Book, 1943-44*, 178; Kido aff., S 292:25, T 30868; Maxon, 76-78 and 119; and Young, *Imperial Japan*, 265-66.

It has been said of Konoe that he "could sit at his private table with a communist at his left and a nationalist at his right, and keep the conversation on an idealistic plane which indicated sympathy for each tint and shade of social thought."[10] This aspect of his character was well illustrated by his personal involvement in the new structure effort. His activity in that regard became more pronounced in the spring of 1940, while he was still serving as president of the privy council.[11] He was later described by a semiofficial publication as having exhibited then "a positive zeal and enthusiasm" in favor of a new national structure.[12]

The fall of Yonai in July and Konoe's assumption of the premiership lent impetus to the movement. The culmination came in mid-October 1940 with the inauguration of the IRAA to take the place of Japan's political parties, which had by then voluntarily and patriotically dissolved themselves. The new organization, with headquarters in Tokyo and local branch offices in every prefecture, was to serve as a "pivotal body" in guiding "the nation's march toward the completion of the domestic structure and the construction of a high-tensioned defense State through the cooperation of all strata."[13] In short, the IRAA was an effort to mobilize totally the political, economic, ideological, cultural, and spiritual resources of the nation so as to permit the government to do what it wished at home and abroad. Under such a system anyone who failed to agree, who showed signs of doubt, who dared to question would be subject to arrest and prosecution.

And yet, there was opposition. The nationalistic societies were dissatisfied because the organization was not Fascist enough; the constitutionalists were dissatisfied because it was too totalitarian. It was not surprising, however, that the moderates soon lost out and that the IRAA was reorganized along ultranationalistic lines, ensuring that the nation would march, "one hundred million strong," in whatever direction the government chose.

[10] "The Brocade Banner," 103.

[11] Konoe discussed the new structure movement in detail with Marquis Kido and Count Yoriyasu Arima. He also received advice from the diverse elements represented in a research society (*Shōwa Kenkyūkai*) he had been sponsoring since 1938. Whether he realized it or not, he was being exposed to bureaucratic nationalism, progressive individualism, idealistic socialism, and even communism. He seems to have listened to everyone and everything and to have enjoyed doing so. Such figures as Colonel Hashimoto, General Matsui, and Lt. Gen. Tatekawa all offered their advice, as did other younger and more fanatical members of the ultranationalist community. Konoe's personal notebooks indicate that over an extended period his home was frequently visited by men who had been tried and convicted for participation in the blood brotherhood, "May 15," and *shinpeitai* incidents.

[12] *Japan Year Book, 1943-44*, 178.

[13] *Ibid.*

The creation of a new internal structure was paced by vigorous action in behalf of an alliance with the European Axis. Unlike War Minister Itagaki, who had been in the forefront of the movement in the Hiranuma Cabinet, Lt. Gen. Tojo proved to be a minor member of the cast— a supporting player overshadowed in every respect by the foreign minister, on the one hand, and by the chief of staff speaking for the nucleus group within the army, on the other. The pattern of decision-making remained the same: key section members of the army general staff exceeded their legitimate duties in regard to policy formulation, with the result that the locus of power and the locus of responsibility were far removed from each other. In this instance, however, the army's efforts were enormously enhanced by the purposeful actions of Matsuoka at stage center, while Oshima and Shiratori, who had both returned from Europe to lend assistance where it was needed most, busily flitted around behind the scenes.

Formal activity again began with a four-minister conference held at the premier's official residence on September 4. The participants were the same as on July 19, with the exception of the member representing the navy. Admiral Yoshida, who had fallen ill, was shortly to be replaced as navy minister by Admiral Koshiro Oikawa. In the interim, all responsibilities normally requiring the minister's attention were undertaken instead by the vice-minister.[14] From both army and navy testimony it would appear that even if Yoshida's physical condition had not forced his retirement, he might well have preferred to relinquish office rather than share responsibility for what now ensued. Tojo himself later remarked that illness could not be regarded as the only factor in Yoshida's resignation. A former chief of the first section of the naval affairs bureau attributed the deterioration in Yoshida's health to "anxiety and tension caused by the political situation."[15]

In agreeing to the July 27 policy statement calling for a strengthening of ties with Germany and Italy, Yoshida presumably had not realized that an actual alliance was being contemplated. He apparently thought, as did some other high-ranking naval officers, that political collaboration

---

[14] Vice-Admiral Tokutarō Sumiyama, who was replaced (as of September 6) by Vice-Admiral Teijirō Toyoda. Yoshida resigned on September 3; Oikawa took over on September 5. (IPS charts; Hattori, I, 61, and IV, *Fuzu Dai-san*; and JRD Monograph No. 146, 19 and Appendix 5.)

[15] On Yoshida's resignation: Tōjō aff., S 342:14, T 36189; Hattori, I, 61; and JRD Monograph No. 146, 13, 19, and Appendix 5 (which contains the views of Admiral Toshitane Takata, former chief of the first section [*gunbi*] of the naval affairs bureau). Hattori states that Yoshida had a heart attack; Takata says "a severe nervous breakdown."

could be strengthened without going to the extreme of an Axis pact—especially one directed against the United States and Britain. The army general staff felt otherwise, as did Foreign Minister Matsuoka. The Soviet Union was now bound to Germany by a nonaggression treaty. The war in Europe was going very much against Great Britain; France and the Netherlands were no longer in the fight. In view of the situation in Europe and the need to settle the China Incident, the South was assuming more and more importance in Japanese political, diplomatic, and strategic planning. What better way to solve the problems confronting Japan than to form an alliance with Germany and Italy? Perhaps Japan might even be able to achieve security in the North (and consequently greater freedom of action elsewhere) by enticing the Soviet Union into the arrangement. If that proved impossible, Japan, Germany, and Italy as allies would be in a far better position than any one of them alone to curb the ambitions of the Kremlin. So ran the argument at the time.

At the four-minister conference on September 4, without prior arrangement or consultation, Matsuoka suddenly raised the question of strengthening the Japan-Germany-Italy axis. He suggested that the three powers cooperate in the establishment of a new order in Europe and in Asia and that they confer on the best method of doing so. Among the matters defined in his proposals were the area to be covered by Japan's new order, the nature of future tripartite economic cooperation, the attitude to be assumed toward the Soviet Union, and Japan's approach to the problem of employing force against Britain and the United States.

The Matsuoka plan, which was readily accepted by the other ministers, left little to the imagination. His conception of the *Lebensraum* needed by Japan for the establishment of a new order in Greater East Asia embraced—in addition to Manchukuo and China—French Indo-China, Thailand, Burma, British Malaya, British Borneo, the Netherlands Indies, the former German mandated islands, French insular possessions in the Pacific, and India.[16] In his negotiations with the Germans, however, Matsuoka intended to be somewhat less precise. He would speak of the "southern area" and would define it, rather vaguely, as the region lying east of Burma and north of the Netherlands East Indies and New Caledonia. Although Japan ultimately wished to see the Indies and French Indo-China become "independent," for the time being Tokyo

---

[16] At the Tōkyō trial the prosecution added Australia and New Zealand to what was called in Japanese "Dai-Tōa shin-chitsujo kensetsu no tame no seizonken."

would press only for a predominant political and economic position. If the Soviet Union joined the tripartite alliance, Matsuoka said, the original members should attempt to restrain the new partner from the west, east, and south and thus divert an expansion of Soviet influence into areas where it would have little direct effect upon Axis interests. The Persian Gulf was regarded in Tokyo as one such area. Depending on the circumstances, India might be another.

Matsuoka's plan was equally clear-cut concerning the United States. In his negotiations with the Germans, the foreign minister was to stress that peaceful measures would be employed as far as possible in dealing with the Americans. In order to obtain her foreign policy objectives, however, Japan would strive for an economic and political coalition of Europe and Asia that would permit her to exert pressure on the United States should the need arise. A decision to use force against the United States and Britain would be made independently by Japan in accordance with the conditions prevailing at any given moment.

What Matsuoka here proposed, and what the others accepted, was a policy guide on the employment of force which restated the basic premise formulated earlier: Japan would endeavor to secure acceptance of her demands without fighting for them; if she could not, she would resort to force whenever circumstances permitted her to do so.

This decision was in some respects even more extraordinary than that which had already emerged during the course of July, since it specified that in certain eventualities Japan would use force *regardless of whether or not her preparations had been completed.*[17]

A week after this decision was made at the four-minister conference, Prince Konoe called at the palace to talk to Marquis Kido. Konoe told the lord privy seal that the special German envoy, Stahmer, had already had three meetings with Matsuoka and that his proposals included the signing of a military pact by Japan, Germany, and Italy.[18] The army was in favor of such a tie, but the navy had expressed a desire to study the matter further. As a result, a liaison conference would be held within a few days. This time, Konoe said, it would be impossible to

[17] On the four-minister conference of September 4 (which was followed by several similar meetings soon thereafter), see Hattori, I, 60-63; Tōjō aff., S 342:14, T 36188-90; Tōjō interrog., March 19, 4-6; S 76:4-5, T 6307-21; Kido SKD; J, B/IV, 504-8; IPS Doc. No. 0004, 238; and Hattori corresp.

[18] Kido SKD. Kido notes that the negotiations with Stahmer were conducted personally by Matsuoka at his private residence. Except for his advisers, Shiratori and Saitō, no one at the foreign office—not even the bureau chiefs—knew anything about the matter until a concrete plan had been evolved.

hold one meeting after another, so a prompt decision would have to be made.[19]

Kido was surprised that so much progress had been made. He was also concerned about the direction in which the government was moving. Both he and Konoe were among the so-called disciples of Prince Saionji. For a number of years Kido had been in the habit of visiting the aging prince about once a month at his residence in Okitsu to listen to his views on various matters. Saionji had repeatedly stressed that Japan should base her foreign policy on the principle of acting in concert with Britain and the United States. Kido apparently shared this view and believed that an alliance with Germany would inevitably result in a Japanese-American war. He discussed this with Konoe and Matsuoka, but they declared that the alliance was designed to *prevent* America from going to war. They also said that if Japan did not join with Germany, and subsequently became isolated in the Pacific, there would be no telling when she might be attacked by the United States. This interesting response was to become, during the next two weeks, the standard approach of those who favored the alliance toward those who were troubled by misgivings or doubts.

The day after Konoe's visit to Kido, Foreign Minister Matsuoka was received in audience by the Emperor to report on his talks with Stahmer. Presumably he repeated what he and Konoe had already told the Emperor's chief adviser. The next evening, September 14, Kido attended a wake at the residence of Prince Kitashirakawa. There he met General Tojo, who informed him confidentially that *the army and navy had just reached an agreement of views with respect to the question of Japan's relations with Germany and Italy.* Sometime after 9:00 p.m. Kido received a phone call from Prince Konoe. The premier told the privy seal that Matsuoka had proposed including the senior statesmen in the imperial conference at which the now emerging decision in favor of an Axis alliance would be formalized in the presence of the Emperor. Konoe wanted Kido's opinion. Since both War Minister Tojo and the vice-minister of the navy were at the wake, Kido immediately consulted them. Both men were opposed. A separate senior statesmen's conference would be all right, they said, but they did not think the ex-premiers should participate in the conference in the presence of the Emperor.[20]

[19] Konoe's remark was in reference to the more than seventy meetings held by the five most important ministers during Hiranuma's tenure as premier. In the case of liaison conferences, decisions were usually made at a single session or after two or three meetings at the most. Holding many meetings was very rare. (Kido corresp.)

[20] Kido SKD.

Although this response is open to more than one interpretation, it would seem that the army's interest lay in avoiding the possibly embarrassing questions of certain senior statesmen. Included among the ex-premiers were Wakatsuki, Okada, and Yonai—all of comparatively moderate views. Yonai had only recently been forced out of the premiership by the army because of his opposition to the type of Axis alliance which was now being drafted. To have invited his participation, along with that of Wakatsuki, whom the army had flouted in its expansion of the Manchurian Incident in 1931, and of Okada, who had only narrowly escaped a band of army assassins during the mutiny of 1936, would have been to run the risk of something going wrong. The only way to minimize that danger was not to consult the senior statesmen at all or to do so in a setting where opposition on their part could more easily be handled. Since the senior statesmen had not previously been consulted about matters of high policy, there was no particular reason for starting now.

After returning home from the wake, Marquis Kido informed Konoe of the views expressed by the service representatives. From the premier's remarks, Kido gathered that a separate conference would probably be held. Around midnight, however, Konoe telephoned again to advise Kido that Matsuoka was withdrawing his proposal and that the ex-premiers would not be consulted.[21]

The army-navy agreement of views confidentially reported to Kido by Tojo on the night of September 14, 1940, represented a major breakthrough for the decision-makers within the general staff. Army success was all the more surprising in view of the strong opposition to an alliance which had long characterized naval thinking. Since the chances of victory could not be estimated, the naval general staff had argued in the past that "war with the United States must be avoided." To achieve, once again, successes like those obtained against the Russians in 1905 would be difficult. Even if Japan did win, heavy losses would certainly be incurred in the process.[22]

In the light of such thinking, why did the imperial navy suddenly reverse itself and consent to an alliance about which it had previously had misgivings? There is no simple answer, but in general certain facts

[21] *Ibid.*

[22] These views were expressed to the Emperor by the chief of the naval general staff, Imperial Prince Fushimi, and the vice-chief, Nobutake Kondō (JRD Monograph No. 146, 25).

emerge.[23] The army and navy each interpreted the July 27 policy decision in its own way. A typical vagueness in the language of that decision made this possible. The army took a phrase about speedily strengthening political solidarity with Germany and Italy to mean that the conclusion of the long-awaited military alliance with Hitler could go forward without further opposition. The navy, on the other hand, apparently did not seriously consider that the phrase in question meant the negotiation of such a pact. When it became clear to the navy what was in store, it had to face the fact that the army dominated the government and hence was in a position, especially in view of the navy's concurrence in the July 27 decision, to develop the nation's policies along any lines it desired, even to the extent of practically disregarding the views of the imperial navy.

The army was not above resorting to extreme measures to win endorsement for its program. Within the army there were those who looked upon the navy as "Public Enemy No. 1." A little more than a year before, it had been rumored that an army unit would attempt to occupy the navy ministry so as to force the navy to reconsider its opposition to a pact with Germany. When word of this had reached the ministry, countermeasures had immediately been taken. An armed "escort" had been assigned to the minister and vice-minister. A battalion of marines had been alerted, machine guns had been set up within the navy building, and both pistols and swords had been issued to the guards. The naval authorities had remained in this state of readiness for four months, until the fall of the army-dominated Hiranuma Cabinet had relieved the tension and had eliminated the need for such drastic precautions. Who could guarantee that something similar would not happen again?

Naval opposition to an alliance with Germany was based primarily on the belief that such an arrangement would require Japan's automatic entry into the war in certain circumstances. The text of the pact which was under consideration in September 1940 envisaged a pledge by the signatories "to assist one another with all political, economic and military means" at their disposal if one of the contracting parties was *attacked* "by a power at present not involved in the European War or in the Sino-Japanese Conflict." In his frequent statements on the matter,

[23] The discussion which follows draws on views presented at a series of round-table conferences held in 1946, in which twenty-six top naval leaders of the prewar period participated, including the former navy minister, vice-minister, and vice-chief of staff. For the opinions and remarks quoted in the text, see JRD Monograph No. 146, 10-19, 25-29, and Appendix 5.

Matsuoka insisted that the question of peace or war would be decided independently by Japan and that the Germans understood this. As it was presented to the navy, a tripartite pact would allow Japan to concentrate her attention on settling the China Incident and on expanding to the South. With Germany as her ally, Japan for the first time would be free of the danger of being isolated in the Pacific and of the threat of hostile military action by the United States. The Germans, it was said, wanted particularly to keep the Americans from joining in the war. Matsuoka urged that "the conclusion of a tripartite alliance would force the United States to act more prudently in carrying out her plans against Japan" and thus, in the long run, would constitute the "best method" of preventing a Japanese-American war.

The navy "did not necessarily agree" completely with Matsuoka, but it felt that it "had to respect the opinion of a responsible diplomatic specialist." The navy apparently held this view even though Matsuoka's predecessor (presumably as much of a specialist and equally responsible) had strongly opposed the conclusion of a close military alliance. Equally ironic is the fact that Japan's naval leaders seem to have overlooked in 1940 what they belatedly recognized in 1946: ". . . if Japan took an aggressive attitude toward the United States, the United States would be compelled to resort to equally aggressive measures, thus aggravating relations between the two countries to a degree where compromise would be impossible."

The danger that such a situation would develop was by no means slight. The army wanted to advance southward, by force if necessary— even if that meant fighting the United States and Britain. The navy also wanted to push to the South, but by peaceful means. The army was annoyed by this attitude, and perhaps even confused. Army leaders wanted a clear-cut statement from the navy as to whether or not it believed it could wage a successful war against the United States and Britain. Frankness of speech, in the sense of openly taking categorical stands, did not fit the pattern of Japanese life. In this instance, the navy felt there was a "distinct difference" between saying it could not wage such a war successfully, and saying that it would be inadvisable to wage such a war. Since the navy would admit only to the latter view, the army was in a position to say: "Well, then, we all agree; there is no problem."

The navy was also motivated by another and related thought. Since July 1937 the army had enjoyed, by virtue of its larger and more direct share in the China Incident, a priority of allocation with respect to budget appropriations, matériel, and personnel. It thus occurred to the admirals that the navy would continue to suffer in these respects unless they adopted a broader view, including the possibility of involvement in war in the South under certain circumstances. The army was already saying that if the navy were so opposed to war with Britain and the United States, it would not need either money or matériel.

Finally, there was the demoralizing effect not only of army pressure but of public opinion. Resentment against the Western democracies, long seeded in the soil of Japan, was being nurtured now by men who said that America and Britain were responsible for China's continuing resistance. The Anglo-American bloc was adding to Japan's casualties and sacrifices while helping to postpone the long-awaited day of final, glorious victory. German successes in Europe provided an opportunity for army and government propagandists to strengthen the public demand for a firm attitude toward the United States. "Feeling ran so high that the Navy found it impossible to withstand pressure to ratify the pact." It was felt that the continuation of naval opposition (which was by now not only unpopular but unpatriotic as well) would seriously undermine Japan's preparations to meet any emergency. An adamant naval stand against the alliance might have prevented the deterioration of relations with the United States, but the naval leaders convinced themselves that this was doubtful. Japan had to obtain the resources of the South. The navy recognized that need and let itself be persuaded that linking arms with Hitler and Mussolini would prevent the United States from interfering with Japan militarily and would also strengthen Japan's bargaining power in the South.

According to postwar naval testimony, these were the principal reasons why the Japanese navy suddenly cast off earlier restraints and began to clear its decks for action. But they were not the only reasons. Some further revealing glimpses have been provided by the highest naval authorities. In 1940 top naval leaders were by and large hostile to the conclusion of an alliance, but *even in the navy* there were those who felt otherwise, especially when it was pointed out that Japan was not obliged to join Germany automatically if the United States should enter the European war. This admission suggests that some naval leaders were perhaps not really so deeply opposed to the alliance as later testimony insisted, and that the locus of power in the navy, as in the army, rested with the nucleus group of officers serving in the key sections of both the general staff and the naval ministry rather than with their nominal superiors.

There is also a question as to the willingness of the senior officers to maintain their convictions in the face of majority pressure. The then vice-chief of the naval general staff later frankly stated: ". . . the Navy leaders of the time lacked the courage to maintain firmly their opposition to the alliance. This is borne out by the fact that the Commander in Chief of the Combined Fleet Yamamoto, upon hearing of the approval of the alliance by the leaders of the Naval General Staff and the Ministry of Navy, said: 'Their line of thinking is far too political.' "[24]

Thus, within a few critical weeks in September 1940, the entire complexion of Japanese-American relations was altered. At an audience with the Emperor on September 15, Kido was deeply impressed when His Majesty remarked that he would be in an awkward position if Konoe again "ran away." The Emperor said he would be distressed unless Konoe truly shared his joys and sorrows (that is, stayed at the Emperor's side to face whatever was in store).[25] The next day His Majesty spoke in the same vein directly to Konoe. The prince afterwards told Kido that he had referred, in reply, to the example of Marquis Ito at the time of the Russo-Japanese war and had assured the Emperor that he was equally determined to serve the throne.[26]

Three days later, on the morning of September 19, the liaison conference which Konoe had earlier mentioned to Kido finally convened. The discussion revolved around four points.[27] The first was whether the strengthening of relations among the three powers should be expressed in the form of a treaty or merely covered by a joint declaration of an agreement of principles. Matsuoka, who was opposed to limiting Japan's cooperation with Germany and Italy to such a declaration, spoke strongly in favor of concluding a treaty.

The second point, and a very critical one, was the effect a closer alignment of the three powers would have upon Japanese-American relations. This was answered by Matsuoka in much the same terms as before: since Germany did not want Japan and the United States to come to blows, the conclusion of the proposed pact would decrease the likelihood of such a collision.

[24] See the reference cited in footnote 23 above. Also Kurihara, *Tennō: Shōwa-shi Oboegaki*, 156-57.

[25] "Konoe kō ni tsuite wa Konoe wa sukoshi mendō ni naru to mata nige-dasu yō na koto ga atte wa komaru ne [.] Kō nattara Konoe wa shin-ni watakushi to ku-raku wo tomo ni shite kurenakute wa komaru to no ōse ari [.] Shin-ni kyōku no itari nari [.]" Kido SKD and corresp.

The Emperor's statement about the possibility of Konoe's running away again referred to the prince's resignation as premier in January 1939.

[26] Itō had promised the Emperor Meiji that if the war developed unfavorably, he would personally shoulder a rifle and fight to the bitter end, even as a common soldier.

[27] See Tōjō aff., S 342:14, T 36190-91.

The third point concerned the military position of Japan in the event the United States entered the European war. In this regard Matsuoka made the extraordinary statement that the influence in the United States of Americans of German and Italian ancestry was considerable and that they were in a position to exert pressure upon public opinion. Had General Kojiro Sato been present, he would undoubtedly have nodded in vigorous agreement. As early as 1920-1921, he had described America's World War I population as including 12,500,000 German-Americans and 15,000,000 "colored people (including mixtures)" who "had not necessarily been truly patriotic."[28] Twenty years later, Matsuoka was advancing a similar argument, advising his colleagues that German- and Italian-Americans, out of loyalty to the lands of their birth, might conspire to prevent an American entry into the war.[29]

The fourth and final point discussed at the liaison conference concerned the chances of an alignment with the Soviet Union. Matsuoka maintained that Germany also desired such an arrangement and would exert herself to the utmost to bring it about.

As a result of these confident assertions, all present at the conference accepted Matsuoka's views. The key role played by the foreign minister at this time was a reflection of the extent to which he had assumed control over the final stages of the negotiations with Germany which had been inaugurated so long before by the army general staff.

Since the earlier divergence of views on an alliance with the Axis had been eliminated before September 19, the liaison conference served merely as a final dress rehearsal for the performance which immediately followed. At 3:00 o'clock in the afternoon, a specially convened imperial conference began deliberations that were to culminate in formal approval of the decision in favor of a German alliance.

The practice of holding such conferences in the presence of the Emperor extended back to the reign of Meiji. Prior to World War I, imperial conferences had apparently formed an important part of the actual, as distinct from the purely ceremonial, decision-making process.

[28] Kōjirō Satō, 78.
[29] John Huizenga, in a chapter on Matsuoka in Craig and Gilbert (eds.), *The Diplomats*, notes (p. 629) that Ribbentrop sometimes referred to the twenty million Americans of German descent "to discount the American danger." Huizenga suggests that Matsuoka "could hardly have been ignorant" of the falsity of this argument. This is a matter of opinion; my own is that Matsuoka actually hoped to exploit those Americans whose ancestry made them, in his eyes, potential subversives.
Matsuoka also advised his colleagues that he intended to reserve full freedom of action with regard to rendering assistance to Germany in case the United States joined in the European conflict.

Opinions were exchanged freely, and unanimity was by no means inevitable. When there was agreement, the conclusions reached were not later regarded as irrevocable.[30] After 1915, however, imperial conferences gradually lost their free and open character and by 1940 and 1941 had assumed the aspect of puppet performances.[31] Although the Emperor attended them, he never presided. Strictly speaking, imperial conferences did not have a regularly constituted or permanent "chairman," in the usual sense. The standard procedure, however, was for the premier to conduct the proceedings after receiving the Emperor's permission to do so. Each time such a conference was held, the permission had to be granted anew. The reason behind this *ad hoc* arrangement seems to have been a desire not to alienate the chiefs of the army and navy general staffs or detract from their dignity and importance. These officers, possessing the right of direct access to the throne and exercising the supreme-command prerogatives of the Emperor, held positions constitutionally on a par with that of the premier. In point of power, they had already proved to be his superiors, but so long as appearances were maintained they were willing to defer to the premier with regard to the "chairmanship," especially since policies brought before imperial conferences, while generally originating in their offices, would nevertheless require full cabinet approval.

Imperial conferences were convened whenever the cabinet or the supreme command deemed them necessary by the simple procedure of petitioning the throne. Membership varied with the occasion but almost always included (in addition to the Emperor) the premier, the two chiefs of staff, the service ministers, the vice-chiefs of staff, the foreign and finance ministers, the president of the privy council, and the president of the cabinet planning board. Other cabinet ministers or supreme-

[30] For a brief summary of the more important imperial conferences of the earlier period and the changing nature of that organ, see Maxon, 63-69. Maxon describes the later conferences as being arranged so that the Emperor's presence could be exploited "in order to subvert or circumscribe the normal processes of government." This point is perhaps debatable.

[31] In the following discussion of the role of the Emperor and the nature of imperial conferences (*gozen kaigi*) in 1940-1941, I have expanded at length—by way of interpretation—upon factual material (generally presented without comment) in the following: Hattori, I, 247-50; Kido SKD; Mutō redirect, S 315:6, T 33269-70; Tōjō aff., S 343:18, T 36336-37 and S 344:3, T 36379-83; Tōjō interrog., Feb. 6, 3-5; Tōjō cross-examination, T 36621, S 346:11; Kido intv. and corresp.; Konoe, 142-43; *PHA*, Part 20, 4014-15; Kenryō Satō and Ohmae corresp.; CF 20, IV, 358; T 681-83 and 36160-61; Horwitz, 505-6; and Butow, *Japan's Decision to Surrender*, 99-100, 101 (n. 75), and 102 (n. 76). A statement by Tōjō to the effect that the purpose of imperial conferences was to ensure coordination between the cabinet and the supreme command is really more applicable to liaison conferences.

command representatives were invited if their presence was considered advisable. The chief cabinet secretary and the heads of the military and naval affairs bureaus of the war and navy ministries usually attended, serving both as "secretaries" (*kanji*) and as *setsumei-in*—"explainers" who could offer the detailed information which the "responsible members" (the cabinet ministers and the supreme-command representatives) did not have at their finger-tips. The chief of the military affairs bureau was especially important since the drafts of the decisions presented at imperial conferences were frequently prepared, in the first instance, by the majors and lieutenant colonels (the *chūken shōkō*) of the key sections of the war ministry and the army general staff. It was almost as if this nucleus group wound up the senior officer robots, pointed them in the direction of a cabinet meeting, liaison session, or imperial conference, and then pushed them slightly to start them on their way. Occasionally there would be a breakdown or a momentary loss of control, but that did not happen very often and generally little damage resulted. The junior master-minds were all-powerful and would soon set their superiors straight once again.

The Emperor was escorted to imperial conferences by his chief aide-de-camp.[32] The lord keeper of the privy seal never attended, but he advised the Emperor beforehand as to what might be expected at the conference. If His Majesty was troubled about anything, the president of the privy council would be requested to ask questions touching upon those matters which were causing imperial concern.[33] How little opportunity even this practice provided for a reconsideration of national policy, let alone a reversal, is seen from the fact that not a single imperial conference ever failed to endorse a proposal placed before it.

As a general rule, such conferences opened with a statement of the policy being presented, a detailing of its essential features, an accounting of the reasons for the proposal, and an explanation of the meaning of each separate item of the policy. This was followed by a closely prescribed question-and-answer period. The primary purpose of an imperial conference was to complete action on a major national policy by officially informing the Emperor how matters stood with regard to a decision

[32] The chief aide-de-camp did not participate in imperial conference proceedings. Maxon, 54-55, describes the *jijū bukanchō* as sometimes more in the employ of the general staff than in the service of the Emperor.

[33] Hattori, I, 248, suggests that the privy council president may also have served as a representative of the *jūshin* (senior statesmen), but he does not develop the point. The practice of having the privy council president attend imperial conferences began in the days of Prince Itō.

already made by the government, so that imperial "approval" could be obtained. Those who attended were regarded as having responsibility not as participants in the conference as such, but as cabinet ministers or as members of the supreme command. The Emperor, of course, was entirely exempted.

The proceedings were very strait-laced. Once the Emperor had taken his seat in front of a gold screen mounted on a dais at the superior end of the chamber, the others would sit down at two long, brocade-covered tables which faced each other and were at right angles to the Emperor's throne-like sanctuary. There they would maintain a stern posture, sitting at attention with hands placed on their knees, all looking very proper and yet somehow unreal, as if they belonged in a display at Madame Tussaud's waxworks. In turn, each speaker arose, bowed carefully in the direction of the Emperor, and then declaimed, almost by rote, the words that were expected of him. It was not just the agenda that was prearranged, but everything else as well, including the explanations that were to be offered, the questions that were to be asked, and the answers that were to be given. This careful ordering of the proceedings was generally fixed at a liaison conference of the type held on the morning of September 19. Once this had been done, nothing could be altered during the imperial conference itself. Other than the Emperor, the only person present not involved in the official "dry run" which preceded all imperial conferences was the president of the privy council. But even his part in the performance was not entirely spontaneous. He always came prepared to inquire about certain points. Knowing this, those who would have to respond to his questions took special pains to anticipate the line he would take so that they could reply correctly.

It was the custom for the Emperor to sit quietly throughout the conference, no matter how long it lasted, without uttering a single word. In addition to lending an indisputable dignity to the occasion, his presence served to clear the way for what was generally but rather erroneously called imperial "sanction." This sanction, which was more of a ceremonial function than an exercise of political power, was not actually bestowed during the conference, but was given later when the cabinet and the supreme command had each again officially endorsed the decision already recapitulated in the presence of the Emperor.[34] This

---

[34] The Emperor sometimes attended imperial headquarters conferences which dealt exclusively with operations, as distinct from broader questions of national policy. When he did so, these were also called "imperial conferences." The type of "imperial conference" described in the text, however, always involved representatives from both the cabinet and the supreme command. Decisions reached at such conferences required the

post partum processing of imperial conference "decisions" had to be completed before imperial "sanction" could be obtained. So long as the above procedures were followed, that sanction could not be withheld. In short, the Emperor could neither grant nor refrain from granting that which he did not, in fact, possess.[35] Imperial sanction was something unanimously authorized by the government (the cabinet and/or the supreme command, depending on the nature of the matter for which such sanction was intended). As soon as such an authorization had been made, the Emperor would automatically affix his signature and the office of the lord keeper of the privy seal would apply the device by which authenticity was ensured.[36]

Herein lay the great difference between the *actual* and the *theoretical* force of the throne. Such power as was imputed to the Emperor in the Meiji Constitution was to be exercised in accordance with the advice of his ministers, who were thus made responsible for affairs of state. It was recognized that the Emperor could not be all-knowing and that decisions of state must reflect the combined wisdom of those whose specialized training gave them collectively a competence which no individual could command.

While theoretically possessing the right to do many things, the Emperor was actually allowed, for the good of the state and for the

---

equal though separate approval, *afterwards*, of both the cabinet and the supreme command.

[35] A statement by Prince Itō (*Commentaries*, 10-11) to the effect, "If the power of sanction belongs to Him, it is scarcely necessary to remark that, as a consequence, He also possesses the power to refuse His sanction," must be read in the context in which it was made: the process of legislation in the Meiji period. It may be presumed that the sanction would only be given, or withheld, on the advice of His Majesty's responsible ministers.

For other discussions of the Emperor and his role, see, for instance, Maki, 91-122; IMTFE, "Roling Opinion," 213-17; IMTFE, "Separate Opinion of the President, Sir William Webb," 12-13; and Maxon, 1-16, 48-71, and *passim*. Even Maxon, who writes in terms of a role he believes the Emperor might have played as a coordinating instrument, notes various limitations, such as the time and circumstances, the personalities involved, the growing formalization of court procedures, the restrictive effect of the advice given the Emperor by persons close to the throne, and the demands made upon him by routine functions (*ibid.*, 4, 8-12, 25, and 224, n. 23).

[36] After an imperial conference had approved a policy, the document in question was taken to the cabinet secretariat, where a clean copy was made on official stationery. When the premier and army and navy chiefs of staff had affixed their signatures, the document was delivered by a secretary of the cabinet to the board of chamberlains. A member of the board would hand-carry it to the Emperor for his signature. The document would subsequently be taken by a chamberlain to the office of the lord keeper of the privy seal, where the imperial seal would be affixed by a confidential secretary. The document would then be returned to the board of chamberlains. Upon receiving notice from the board that imperial sanction had been bestowed, the cabinet would send a secretary to retrieve the document. (Kido corresp.)

sake of the imperial institution, to do very little. He was permitted only a limited discretionary power—nothing approaching a right to veto. In all things, the practices which had prevailed since the days of his grandfather, the Emperor Meiji, served as his guide. When cabinet decisions concerning general policy or personnel matters were reported to the throne by the premier, the Emperor could express his views, if he so wished. He might caution the premier or even ask him to have the cabinet reconsider the question, but he could do no more than that. Even after such an imperial request, if the cabinet still felt that the proposal was correct, it would resubmit the matter to the Emperor through the premier. In such an event, time-honored practice dictated that the Emperor accept the situation. He could not impose a veto.

Even the Emperor Meiji, who is frequently described as having played a much more active role in affairs of state than either his son or grandson, seems to have employed an indirectness not consonant with absolute power. When he did not wish to approve a state document, he kept putting it at the bottom of the pile of "in-papers" which were daily placed on his desk. If he did this repeatedly over a period of several days, those close to him concluded that the matter would have to be restudied before His Majesty would pass it along. Although this can be regarded as showing the existence of some kind of imperial "power," the way in which it was exercised reveals its limitations.

With regard to high policy, as distinct from normal administrative affairs, the requirements of the Emperor's position were equally clear. Only on the very rare occasions when there was a definite contradiction between reports tendered to the throne by the cabinet and those submitted by the supreme command could the Emperor temporarily withhold his sanction. Indeed, in such a circumstance he was not supposed to act until the contradiction had been eliminated. In all things, the Emperor was to remain above practical politics. He must not involve himself in the business of government, and certainly not in quarrels either between individuals or between separate organs of the state. But when the contradiction had been eliminated, or when unanimity existed from the first—as was usual with issues coming to his attention—he was not supposed to interfere no matter what his personal views might be.

The Emperor's youth had been spent in rigid training for the throne and in acquiring the self-discipline which his role would demand. From the age of six months he had been the pawn of a separate household of his own composed of advisers, tutors, and factotums of every description whose special task was to see that His Highness grew up properly. Although of a pedigree exalted beyond all others, this Emperor-to-be was nevertheless the son of a land in which every aspect of life—from the serving of tea to the contracting of marriages—was carefully prescribed. In all relationships, reciprocal action in accord with prior arrangements was expected. Refusal was not only uncouth; it was unthinkable.

The prince who was known in the world as Hirohito was never allowed to forget that one day he would be the 124th Emperor of Japan, the descendant of an imperial line "unbroken for ages eternal." The restraints which were imposed upon the boy, and which he eventually recognized as the inescapable burden of one in his extraordinary station, came naturally to the man and were readily accepted. The system may not have been designed to make a puppet of the Emperor so that willful men could dominate the scene from behind the throne, but it was certainly designed to perpetuate the imperial institution. The fundamental requirement was to keep the Emperor out of politics. The more complex matters became, the more necessary it was to insulate the throne. The Emperor saw only with the eyes of his advisers, heard only with their ears, and spoke only with their lips.

Included in the court circle were the lord keeper of the privy seal, the imperial household minister, the grand chamberlain, and the chief aide-de-camp. The first of the four served as the Emperor's counselor on civil affairs; the last—indirectly and unofficially—as a source of information on supreme-command matters. At times the Emperor also conferred with the board of field marshals and fleet admirals, but as Tojo himself once pointed out, "This body was not very active, since most of the members were of advanced years. Therefore, in practice, the Emperor was in a difficult position. He had no one on his staff to help him on High Command matters." The chief aide-de-camp, although a full general, had "actually no authority" to conduct direct liaison between the throne and the army and navy general staffs.[37] The imperial household minister and the grand chamberlain possessed a variety of duties and responsibilities, but none of these had any close connection with vital civil or military affairs. Since court officials were conservative by nature and convinced that the system as it then existed was the best, they did not seek to alter the functions which traditionally pertained to their offices.[38]

[37] See Tōjō interrog., Mar. 13, 5-6 and supplement. Also, footnote 32 above.
[38] The Tribunal took a more hostile view, charging, for instance, that imperial consent to the Tripartite Pact had been secured through the connivance of the lord keeper of the privy seal (see J, B/IV, 513-14).

For the Emperor successfully to have intervened in such a way as to direct state affairs along lines more in accord with his personal conscience would have required him to be a man of less retiring personality, with a very practical grasp of political affairs. Moreover, he would have needed the support of an enforcement machinery capable of coping with powerful dissidents, and the encouragement of advisers who believed a more active, personal participation by His Majesty to be necessary and desirable.

Although he did lack power, the Emperor was in a position to influence and to inspire those around him. The capacity for doing so effectively altered with circumstances beyond imperial control and depended upon the line taken by his advisers, but the essence of this somewhat intangible factor was always the gravitational pull of the throne. As one strategically placed colonel later expressed it, imperial influence ranged between a "passive and indirect leadership" manifested in the course of audiences granted to cabinet ministers and to the chiefs of the army and navy general staffs. Sometimes His Majesty clearly expressed strong likes and dislikes. But that was not usually the case. In fact, as a general rule, those reporting to the throne had to infer what the Emperor had in mind from the content of his questions, which tended to be vague or cryptic, and from his demeanor. The attitude of the Emperor during the course of an audience was a matter of grave concern to those who had thus been honored; they would later rack their brains for a clue that would permit them to act in accordance with His Majesty's wishes.[39]

The whole truth behind the Emperor's thoughts and actions inevitably remains something of a mystery, but this much is clear: the imperial conference held on the afternoon of September 19, 1940, did not depart from the standard pattern. Although many questions were asked and answered, the entire procedure was nothing more than a formal ritual. There was little likelihood of a serious challenge and even less chance of a last-minute reversal.

When the chief of the army general staff posed the problem of the effect the Axis alliance would have upon Japan's ability to deal with the China Incident, he was raising a rhetorical question. He certainly was

[39] To cite but one example, Admiral Ōnishi (the "father" of the *kamikaze* corps of the war in the Pacific) once reported to his men: "When told of the special attack, His Majesty said, 'Was it necessary to go to this extreme? They certainly did a magnificent job.' His Majesty's words suggest that His Majesty is greatly concerned. We must redouble our efforts to relieve His Majesty of this concern. . . ." Inoguchi *et al.*, *The Divine Wind*, 64.

not motivated by any desire for enlightenment or by any wish to probe further into issues already thoroughly discussed. His purpose was merely to give someone else—in this instance, the foreign minister—an opportunity to recite the prearranged reply, thus setting His Majesty's mind at rest on that particular aspect of the problem. The fact that the Emperor would sit quietly throughout such proceedings, without ever participating, serves as the ultimate focus for an understanding of the nature of a conference which in protocol, if not in power, ranked above all others in the Japanese scheme of things.

When the discussion on September 19 had at last exhausted itself, Prince Konoe called for a final expression of opinion by way of summation. This proved to be the signal for the two chiefs of staff and for the president of the privy council to endorse the "cabinet's proposal"-to strengthen relations with the Axis. The chief of the army general staff earnestly called for greater effort toward the adjustment of Japanese-Soviet relations. The navy chief of staff again spoke of the navy's wish to avoid a war with the United States and to skirt unnecessary friction with third powers by relying upon a peaceful penetration of the South. He also asked for stricter control over public expressions of hostility toward Britain and America and for earnest cooperation by the government in completing naval preparations for war. The president of the privy council expressed his approval of the proposed pact as an "unavoidable measure" made necessary by Japan's involvement in China and by current developments in the world situation. He noted that many difficulties would arise in the future, including the very real possibility of an American embargo against Japan. Although a Japanese-American clash might eventually prove inevitable, he strongly urged the government to take every precaution to see that such a collision did not occur in the immediate future.

And with that, the imperial conference adjourned.[40]

The tying of the knot that bound Japan to the Axis was now quickly completed, but not without some further interesting developments. The diary of Marquis Kido reveals that even prior to the imperial conference of September 19 the question had been raised as to whether the Tripartite Pact should be submitted to the privy council for its approval. Matsuoka—anxious to avoid further delays and perhaps afraid that

---

[40] For a summary of the main features of the discussion at the imperial conference of September 19, to the extent that reconstruction is possible in the absence of precise records or minutes, see Hattori, I, 63-71. See also Matsuoka's draft explanation, S 76:7-9, T 6329-44; Tōjō aff., S 342:14, T 36191; and Tōjō cross-examination, S 348:12, T 36799.

opposition would arise—wanted to bypass the council entirely and so advised the Emperor. Although it was generally standard procedure to consult the privy council in matters of such importance, its members had not been called into session at the time of the Anglo-Japanese alliance in 1902 or when Korea was annexed by Japan in 1910. These exceptions provided the precedent which Matsuoka cited to support his argument. In discussing this later with Kido, the Emperor indicated that he personally favored consulting the privy council. If there were any need for haste, he said, the councilors could deliberate through the night as they had done at the time of the February 26 incident, when the question of imposing martial law had been under consideration. Kido immediately consulted the premier and foreign minister and found that Prince Konoe was also inclined to submit the proposed pact to the privy council. Matsuoka then withdrew his original suggestion, saying that if His Majesty wanted it handled in that way, he himself would naturally offer no objection.

In comparatively minor matters, or where the ultimate goal of the state ministers would not be placed in serious jeopardy, the Emperor could generally win acceptance for a point of view that bore the stamp of approval of those close to the throne and also reflected the attitude of either the premier or of someone of similar rank within the supreme command. That Matsuoka's willingness to oblige did not really endanger the desired outcome is seen from the fact that the Emperor also told Marquis Kido that the cabinet could always file a counterpetition with the throne in the event that the privy council rejected the alliance.[41]

The Emperor's thoughts on the matter were further revealed in a conversation with Kido on September 24. He then told the lord privy seal that he had consulted the imperial household minister and had learned that apparently no action had been taken by the court when the Anglo-Japanese alliance was signed in 1902. This time, however, it was not a simple case of rejoicing, as it had been then. There was a possibility that the alliance with Germany might lead Japan into a crisis. He therefore wished not only to report to the gods at the *Kashiko-dokoro* (a palace sanctuary) but also to pray for their divine protection.[42]

[41] According to Kido, the Emperor was simply stating the facts of the case; he was not trying to suggest a way around possible privy council disapproval. If the council voted against the pact, the premier would be expected to resign. Although the Emperor was worried about the conclusion of such a pact, he did not want to lose Konoe as premier. The imperial remark to Kido was meant as a reminder that in such circumstances a counterpetition (*hantai jōsō*) could be lodged with the throne. (Kido corresp.)

[42] Kido replied that the imperial household minister would be consulted and that everything would be arranged to His Majesty's satisfaction. In his devotions on October

Two days later, on September 26, the pact which was to put the Axis nations into each other's uncertain trust was submitted to the privy council for approval.[43] As was usual in the case of all such high-level conferences, no precise minutes were taken. The secretaries simply recorded the gist of what was said. Although the major points of the presentation presumably did not escape their attention, no certainty is possible with regard to exact phrasing. Such records as do exist, however, reveal that several privy councilors expressed themselves with a candor rarely encountered elsewhere in the decision-making process—a fact which may help to explain the eclipse which soon overtook this advisory organ, which could function only upon the request of the Emperor and, hence, only when his ministers so recommended.

On this occasion the deliberations lasted throughout the day and into the evening.[44] At times there was an almost hostile line of questioning. There seems to have been a general understanding that Japan was getting involved in a situation in which she might suddenly find herself face to face with the "worst eventuality"—a war with the United States. There was concern not only about what Japan would do in that case but also about how well prepared she was to do it. It seems

17, 1940, the Emperor gave special attention to the conclusion of the alliance with Germany and Italy and prayed for the divine protection of the gods. Kido SKD.

[43] Strictly speaking, to the council's "investigation committee" (variously referred to as the *shinsa iin-kai* and *chōsa iin-kai*) and then to the council itself. It should be noted that Dr. Hara, the president of the privy council, had already given his personal approval to the decision to conclude an alliance with Germany at the imperial conference held on September 19. The issue on September 26 was the pact itself. Councilors Araki, Matsui, Minami, Ōshima, and Suzuki should not be confused with postwar "Class A" defendants of the same name.

[44] On the privy council meetings of September 26, see S 76:9-13, T 6350-90; S 91:17, T 7925-28; S 106:17-19, T 9755-67; Tōjō aff., S 342:14-15, T 36192-94; Tōjō cross-examination, S 347:2, T 36645-47; Tōjō interrog., Mar. 13, 1-4 and supplement; IPS Doc. No. 0004, 111-24; J, B/IV, 510-12, B/VI, 790-92, B/VII, 902; JRD Monograph No. 146, 20-25; and JRD, "Translation," II: 51903 (Item 18), 1-2. See also Feis, 110-21. The role of the Konoe Cabinet in the emergence of the Tripartite Pact is summarized in J, B/IV, 487-520.

The evidence submitted by the prosecution with reference to a privy council meeting and an imperial conference which allegedly took place on September 16 may relate instead to the imperial conference of September 19 and the privy council meetings of September 26. See S 76:9, T 6345-49; IPS Doc. No. 0004, 109-10; and Tōjō aff., S 342:14, T 36190-91. The matter is further confused by a statement in the "Judgment" (B/IV, 510) to the effect that "an Imperial Conference which took the form of a meeting of the Privy Council in the Emperor's presence" was held on September 16. This statement is presumably based on the evidence already cited. Hattori, I, 63, notes that a special cabinet meeting was held on September 16. Explanations were also offered at a regular meeting of the privy council on September 25.

An assertion by the prosecution that a remark by Tōjō on September 26 constituted evidence of aggressive intent is not borne out by the facts (see S 342:15, T 36193-94; S 76:10, T 6353-54; and S 106:17, T 9756).

generally to have been assumed that every effort would be made to avoid placing Japan in a position in which she would have no choice but to fight America and Britain, and yet maximum preparations for such a war and against the possibility of a worsening of relations with the Soviet Union were to be undertaken. There were very definite warnings that Hitler would be an unreliable ally.

Ministerial replies to questions put by individual councilors tended to be optimistic generalities that ranged from the obscure to the vacuous. The basic theme was that if Japan did not join Germany now, the Germans and the British might conclude peace with each other, establish a new situation in Europe, and endeavor to deal with the South Seas and other areas to suit themselves. It was therefore necessary to "manifest the Empire's determination" without delay. In plain language, this meant that an extraordinary opportunity existed to take advantage of the situation in Europe in order to enhance Japan's position in Asia. If that opportunity was ignored, there might never be another chance.

In the end, the privy councilors gave their unanimous endorsement to the conclusion of the Tripartite Pact—the hope being expressed to the governmental authorities that efforts would be made to minimize the American and British antagonism which might result, that harmonious relations with the Soviet Union would be established, and that there would be no neglect of the preparations needed to cope with the worst eventuality should it develop after all.

The cabinet's triumph was rather spoiled, however, by a final warning voiced by Viscount Kikujiro Ishii, who had gained fame as a diplomat during World War I. Modern alliances, Ishii said, were not like those of old in which the relationship between the participants had been especially close. Alliances now resulted in one country trying to profit at the expense of the other. It was an outstanding fact that not a single nation which had joined with Germany or Prussia had ever benefited. Some had even incurred unforeseen disasters and in the end had lost their sovereignty. Bismarck had once said that the requirement in international alliances was for one horseman and one donkey and that Germany must always be the horseman. The experiences of Austria-Hungary and of Turkey during World War I bore this out. Some might believe that Nazi Germany would not necessarily follow in the footsteps of imperial Germany, but so far as he was concerned, Ishii declared, Hitler was dangerous. Machiavelli was said to be his model and a copy of *The Prince* was reportedly always at his side. Hitler had publicly spoken of alliances as nothing more than temporary expedients. The conclusion by Germany, in August 1939, of a pact with the Soviet Union that was clearly inconsistent with the earlier German-Japanese Anti-Comintern Pact should not have occasioned any surprise.

According to Ishii, Hitler had long ago made a study of the Far East and had decided that Japan should not be allowed to become a great power. No matter how the matter was viewed, it was impossible to think that Nazi Germany under Hitler would remain a loyal friend to Japan indefinitely. Italy was not any better. In short, neither of Japan's allies could be trusted very much. Japan must be on guard lest the Germans boast of being the horseman. He was agreeing to the alliance, Ishii said, because it provided an opportunity for Japan, but in the light of past history he could not help but express the wish that the government would take such care as to leave no room for future regrets.[45]

The leaders of Japan subsequently did prove cautious in dealing with Hitler's efforts to have them participate in the European war at a time and place of his choosing, but they never rethought the alliance problem through from the beginning—not even after events had occurred which might have justified them in so doing. Thus, they failed in that very aspect of the problem about which Ishii had been most concerned.

The next day, September 27, 1940, the fateful Tripartite Pact was signed in Berlin amid the usual fanfare; in Tokyo a rescript was issued in the Emperor's name which noted that His Majesty was ardently anxious to see an end brought to disorder in the world, that he earnestly desired peace, and that he was deeply gratified at the conclusion of an alliance with two countries sharing identical aims with his Empire. Thus were joined, at last, what Secretary Hull dubbed the "bandit nations."[46]

Years later it was learned that the negotiations leading to the conclusion of this pact had been conducted on the basis of an English text. It was easier for the parties concerned to agree on such a text than to correlate German and Italian idiom with the Japanese. Problems of interpretation and construction could more readily be solved and the danger of further postponement arising out of demands for a minute comparison of German, Italian, and Japanese texts could be avoided. The student of history is thereby treated to the interesting spectacle of democracy's arch-antagonists concluding a military alliance aimed primarily

---

[45] See the references cited in the preceding footnote.

[46] J, B/VI, 787. For the texts of the various pertinent documents, see S 76:13-14, T 6391-95; Hattori, I, 71-73; *Foreign Relations (Japan: 1931-1941)*, II, 165-66. See also *NYT*, September 28, 1940, *passim*.

at the United States of America, and doing so by means of a treaty couched in the language of the enemy.[47]

Although War Minister Tojo had had very little to do with the conclusion of the Tripartite Pact, he had no misgivings about it.[48] He realized that the alliance rendered a war with the West conceivable in certain eventualities, but in view of the circumstances existing at the time he remained in favor of the pact. He felt that Japan should not be reluctant to join the Axis simply because the danger of war with the West existed. Japan was in a difficult position and the alliance offered a way out.

When it was suggested to Tojo in late 1947 that his memory for details might be fading as a result of feelings of shame concerning the alliance, he indignantly replied, *Watakushi wa sonna hikyō na kangae wa mochimasen*: "I do not have any such cowardly thoughts."

Tojo's memory was not very sound, but neither was the implication that he recalled only what he wanted to and conveniently forgot the rest. Throughout his life, he jotted down items in a little book for later reference. After the war, such material as did remain was generally unavailable to him and he frequently declared that he might be able to give better answers if he had access to documents and other data that would refresh his memory.[49]

In Tojo's case the problem of accurately recalling the past was compounded by the fact that from the middle of 1940 on he had carried an extremely heavy work-load. Six or seven years later it was very difficult for him—at times impossible—to be precise about dates. He did remember that during the weeks preceding the conclusion of the pact with Germany and Italy "periodic reports on the military situation in Europe and the Balkans" had been received and that there had also been

[47] Although the negotiations had been based on an English text, the Germans specified that German, Italian, and Japanese texts should be secretly substituted for the English text about two weeks after the original signing and that these new texts should be duly endorsed with the appropriate signatures. Presumably this was never made known to the privy council. See S 267:14, T 28015, and S 267:11, T 27991.

[48] The following presentation of Tōjō's views regarding the alliance with Germany is based on Tōjō interrog., Jan. 28, 1-5, Jan. 29, 1-3, Jan. 30, 1-4, Feb. 1, 1-7 (as corrected in Feb. 4, 4), Mar. 12, 1-2, Mar. 19, 4-6; Tōjō aff., S 342:15, T 36194-95; and Tōjō cross-examination, S 345:5-7, T 36542-50; S 346:5, T 36580-81; S 346:5-8, T 36583-98; and S 347:1-3, T 36642-55.

[49] During an interrogation on February 7, 1946, Tōjō complained, as he frequently did, of the lack of documents or records with which to refresh his memory. In reply, the interrogator stated, "If there are any documents we can get to assist you, we will be glad to do so, but we want only your best recollections." See Tōjō interrog., Feb. 7, 6.

political reports. He was sure that he had seen some of these, but without reference materials of any kind he had "nothing to go on" but his memory. He did not recall any specific reports on the national policies of Germany and Italy. Matsuoka, as the responsible minister, might have studied such matters, but Tojo had not, nor did he think there had been any investigation by the cabinet as a whole. It seemed likely, he said, that the cabinet had simply assumed that the winning of the war constituted the principal national policy of Germany and Italy at the time. Prior to the signing of the pact there had been "general intelligence reports" on the military and political situation in Europe but no specific information concerning the national policies of Japan's proposed allies. Nor could he recollect any "deep discussion" of the matter. In fact, the cabinet had not been greatly concerned with German or Italian policies in Europe. Japan, Germany, and Italy "could contribute to world peace by the alliance. The approval or disapproval of specific policies was not a matter of very much moment in Japan."

Both in interrogations preceding his postwar trial and in cross-examination during it, Tojo exhibited an appalling lack of knowledge about what had been going on in Europe—about Hitler's treatment of neutrals, for instance, and about his grandiose plans for a Nazi-enslaved new order. When asked what he thought had been the basic cause of the outbreak of the European war in 1939, Tojo replied: "I don't clearly remember, but as I recall it, Germany and Italy were dissatisfied with the situation then existing. The settlement of World War I was . . . a basic cause of this dissatisfaction." He later spelled this out in terms of territorial issues (East Prussia, Alsace-Lorraine, the Ruhr), the limiting of the German army to 100,000 men, and the instability existing in the Balkans and the Baltic.

Beyond that, Tojo was much less precise. He had heard of the "Munich Agreement," but he denied any knowledge of what it was about. When the chief prosecutor, Mr. Keenan, lashed out at this in disbelief, Tojo replied that whether he was speaking before a court of law or in the presence of the gods, he was not accustomed to telling lies. The prosecution regarded this as merely another self-serving attempt on the part of the witness. Such a reaction was both natural and too simple. Tojo's statements reflected not so much guile as a limited knowledge of men and deeds outside Asia and a peculiarly restricted understanding of the responsibilities of leadership. He had been surprised when the European war had broken out. After that he had given the matter very little thought except as regards the probable outcome and how

Japan might profit from the situation in general. The need for her to profit was fundamental. The way to do so was to join the winning side. The detailed policies and procedures of the Germans or the Italians and their philosophy of life were simply regarded as irrelevant to the requirements of Japanese decision-making and policy formulation.

The nature of Tojo's candor is perhaps best revealed in a matter which was decisive in the emergence of the Tripartite Pact. On one occasion he flatly denied the existence of a pro-Axis "faction" in the Japanese army. He invariably objected to the use of that term and to the variant "clique," probably because he associated both words with an implied lack of discipline within the army and with disrespect for the throne. But when "faction" was dropped, he readily admitted that "a majority of officer opinion was pro-Axis for a variety of reasons." He explained that following the Franco-Prussian war of 1870-1871 Japan had turned to Prussia as a model for her military system. Even though Germany had been defeated during the First World War, the Japanese army had still looked upon German strategy and tactics as "excellent." Another reason for the pro-Axis sentiment was Japan's desire to escape the "diplomatic isolation" in which she found herself. A third reason was the comparatively favorable manner in which the military situation had developed for the Axis countries. Thus, Tojo emphasized, while "there was such a pro-Axis atmosphere in [the] Army, there was no faction or clique.... You must remember that the military set-up in Japan is very different from that in America. The Chief of Staff is independent of the War Department [i.e., War Ministry] in matters of command, and also from the point of view of organization. He is not subordinate to the War Minister but is equal to him. Hence, this atmosphere which permeated the Army was ... communicated to the War Minister by the Chief of Staff and communicated to the Cabinet deliberations by the War Minister. However, I repeat again that this was not a clique or a faction."

In these words Tojo not only described the essence of the power of the army but accurately and honestly revealed the part he personally had played. The tenor of his replies during interrogation was always such as to lead one to believe that had he indeed occupied a more active leadership position he would undoubtedly have admitted it. He never endeavored to place the burden elsewhere or to shy away from questions of political responsibility during the period of his cabinet service.

Tojo correctly pointed out that all matters of command passed formally from the throne through the chiefs of staff to the commanders-in-chief on land and sea, and that all matters of military administration

flowed from the throne through the service ministers.[50] At the time the
Tripartite Pact was signed, the China Incident had been in progress for
several years and therefore "a great many decisions" passed through the
hands of the chief of the army general staff, who was thus "an exceedingly important individual." Although he did not attend cabinet meetings, "his feelings on a multitude of matters relating to strategy" were
conveyed to the cabinet through the war minister. The chief of staff
also kept the premier and foreign minister "similarly informed." Foreign policy matters of "secondary importance" were transmitted to the
minister or vice-minister of foreign affairs by the vice-chief of staff. In
this way the pro-Axis feelings within the army were made known to the
cabinet ministers. Tojo admitted that he personally had introduced such
feelings into the discussions of the second Konoe Cabinet and that they
had exerted an influence upon subsequent decisions. In fact, it was usual
for army views on domestic as well as foreign policy to reach the cabinet
through the war minister, so long as he agreed with those views. Although Tojo did not elaborate, the implication would seem to be that
if a man did not agree with the thinking in the army as a whole, he had
no business being war minister. Either he must accept the prevailing
views, attempt to change them within the framework of decision-
making peculiar to the army, or resign. There could be no thought of
his sabotaging the army by siding with the cabinet. Being a minister of
state was secondary to being a general.

When Tojo was asked about the new order to be established in Europe
and Asia under the aegis of the Tripartite Pact, he proved rather vague,
but he acknowledged that the sphere of the new order in Europe was to
be expanded as new lands were conquered.

Q.: Then both in Europe and in Asia the sphere to be included in the
new order decreased or increased with the military situation?

A.: That was about the long and short of it (*kekka teki ni ieba sō
deshita*).[51]

Q.: Was all of this then in accordance with the spirit of Hakko Ichiu?

A.: Yes. It is a concept of virtue, not a territorial concept.

[50] When Tōjō talked of matters of military command and administration passing
from the throne, he was speaking loosely of the formal chain of command. He was not
suggesting that the matters which were so handled originated with the Emperor
personally.

Maxon, 22-28 and 34-44, also discusses the superior power of the supreme command.

[51] It is only rarely in interrogations that the original Japanese is indicated as in the
example: *kekka teki ni ieba sō deshita*, which could be rendered, somewhat less freely,
as "In the final analysis, yes," or "In terms of the result, yes."

Q.: Was the same concept of virtue to be a part of the sphere to be controlled by Germany and Italy in Europe?

A.: Japan's interpretation was that it was to be similar, with no exploitation or special interests. In fact, in the Three-Power Treaty, it is expressly stated that each country is to have its own place and that there is to be co-existence and co-prosperity in both the East Asiatic and European spheres.

Q.: What reason was there to believe that Germany and Italy would have this virtuous understanding of the new order in Europe?

A.: (Laughter by the witness.) I believe that Germany and Italy, both of whom had been exploited as a result of defeat in World War I, had found it necessary in order to exist to set up a sphere within which the various countries could minister to each other's needs. This was a concept within the meaning of the word "virtue."

Q.: But this ministration was to be done under the supervision of Germany and Italy?

A.: It was not supervision but leadership. Germany and Italy were to have the initiative in bringing about a new order of co-existence and co-prosperity of all the countries concerned.

This represented the approach of Japan, Tojo said. She was not seeking to exploit others or merely to fill her own coffers. "That was absolutely not the spirit of the Greater East Asia new order at all. . . . The new order was based on mutual benefit." No one in Japan had dreamed of partitioning the world or of dominating it. The alliance with Germany and Italy was a defensive measure against the "have nations"—a means of opening a way to survival for Japan. The phrase "position of leadership," as used in the Tripartite Pact, referred to the role of "a pioneer"—of "one who would lead the way." The idea was initiative and guidance, not subjugation and subordination. The new order was to be based on mutual existence and prosperity and upon the autonomy and independence of all concerned.

At the time of the signing of the Tripartite Pact, Japan naturally hoped that her new allies would win. According to Tojo's testimony, "the Government thought the comparative probability was that Germany and Italy would be victorious." And yet he argued that this had not been the primary cause of Japan's decision to join the Axis. That lay rather in the international isolation in which Japan found herself "after the lapse of the Anglo-Japanese Alliance and Japan's withdrawal from the League of Nations." Even Japan's desire to create a new order in East Asia "was not," he said, "a direct cause at all." That policy constituted "a fundamental Japanese aim which would have been continued regardless of whether the Three-Power Pact had been signed or not. However, Japan did desire that the new order in East Asia be recognized in the Pact itself."

When he was asked whether he had ever been the leader of the army officers who were pro-German, he replied: "As I explained to you before, I hate very much this idea of pro-German or pro-English. Of course, when I lived in Germany and because of the language and all, there was some connection, but I am not pro-German or pro-English or pro-American. I go by the national standard. If I have to be 'pro' anything, I am pro-Japanese."

For Tojo, the signing of the pact came as a relief because it seemed to mark the end of Japan's isolation in the world. As was soon to be apparent, however, the Axis alliance led Japan and the United States to assume positions of greater watchfulness and of greater hostility toward each other. It also encouraged Tokyo to undertake a further advance in the South. This was accomplished through the acquiescence of regimes whose choice was made under a double threat of duress: that imposed by Hitler in Europe and that contrived locally by Japan. The result was an American reaction the intensity of which was wholly unexpected by Japan's leaders. In their failure to meet this new crisis in their relations with the West, the fate of the Japanese nation was sealed.

CHAPTER 8

$\mathcal{ABCD}$ Encirclement

WHILE the government in Tokyo had been concentrating its attention on a new structure designed to enhance the nation's military preparedness, much had been happening in the world that touched upon the developing crisis in Japan's relations with the Western powers. Since the outbreak of the war in China, those relations had steadily deteriorated. Although it was the Chinese who had borne the brunt of Japanese aggression, the rights and interests of the United States and Great Britain had not escaped the effects of Japanese plans for a new order. Incidents involving British and American citizens and property had increased as the scope of hostilities had broadened. The failure of diplomatic protests to secure protection against repeated Japanese "mistakes" had given rise to a determination in Washington to implement a policy of resistance even though it was recognized that the Administration was not in a position to act very decisively.

The first measure by which the United States government had sought to impose some restraint upon the fighting in China had been a rather belated request to American manufacturers and exporters, in June 1938, to cease shipments of aircraft and related products to areas where they might be used against civilian targets. Although obviously limited in nature, this "moral embargo" had proved effective.[1] As new developments had occurred in Europe and Asia, other appropriate responses had followed. In February 1939 the Japanese had occupied Hainan Island—a strategic position midway between the southeastern coast of China and the northeastern littoral of French Indo-China. The next month Japan had proclaimed its annexation of the Spratly Islands, which lie below the Philippines, some 650 miles southeast of Hainan and roughly halfway between Indo-China and British North Borneo.[2] Soon thereafter the American government, reacting to concern in London and Paris, had ordered the United States fleet (which had been in the Atlantic

[1] Feis, 19, n. 3.
[2] See J, B/IV, 330-31 and 359-61; *Foreign Relations (Japan: 1931-1941)*, II, 277-81; Hull, *Memoirs*, I, 628-29; and Morison, *The Rising Sun in the Pacific*, 37-38. The area annexed by Japan was actually the Shinnan Guntō, composed of a number of coral reefs (including Spratly Island). Most English-language records, however, refer to the area as either the "Spratly" or the "Sinnan" Islands. Both Hainan and the Spratlys had previously been claimed by France.

since January) back to the Pacific.[3] This had been followed several months later by an indication that the United States was moving toward the abrogation of a treaty of commerce and navigation signed with Japan in 1911.

With the outbreak of war in Europe in September 1939, the United States had inevitably found it necessary to take a closer look at its own defenses. This had resulted in a new request from President Roosevelt aimed at restricting the export of certain raw materials that were deemed vital to American security. Although Tokyo had previously imposed similar controls, the President's action had given rise to private and public grumbling in Japan to the effect that the United States was trying to strangle the Empire. It was at that time, too, according to expert opinion, that there had developed, in Washington, ". . . a state of mind, becoming more confirmed, which forbade compromise with Japan."[4]

In December 1939 Roosevelt had urged that the moral embargo be extended to cover a wider range of war supplies. Despite such promptings from the Executive, the Congress had refrained from enacting bills which would have limited the quantity of iron- and steel-scrap that American business was so regularly funneling into the maw of Japan's war industries. It was not until July 1940, when Japan's basic national policies were secretly being decided in Tokyo in a form which gave special emphasis to the use of force, that the President was able to begin to prohibit the exportation of such products as oil, copper, scrap iron, and steel. He could do so then only because the progress of events in Europe had resulted in the passage of the National Defense Act. It is one of the ironies of this period that the prohibition thus imposed did not actually stop the flow of strategic materials to Japan until a full year later—little more than four months before the attack on Pearl Harbor.

By the spring of 1940 it had become increasingly difficult to isolate events in the Far East from those in Europe. Earlier in the year the Japanese government had begun a major diplomatic offensive to secure a preferential position for Japan in the Netherlands East Indies. Two months later, in April, Washington had ordered the fleet based at San Diego to proceed to Pearl Harbor.[5] It was hoped that this might restrain Japan from seizing the Dutch East Indies in the event the

[3] See Hull, I, 630. Ambassador Bullitt's cable from Paris advised, " 'Twere well it were done quickly."
[4] Feis, 41. The action-reaction state of affairs being summarized in the text is discussed in greater detail in Feis, *passim.* See also J, B/IV, 421-24.
[5] See Morison, 42-43.

Germans invaded Holland. As Secretary Hull later described it, posting the fleet in Hawaii was like keeping a "double-barreled shotgun" in the house while "talking to a desperado."[6] To General Tojo, however, it looked as if the United States might be moving toward entry into the European conflict. He regarded the American fleet standing by in Hawaii ("with very sanguine expectations") as equivalent to an American military threat aimed at Japan.[7] Many of his countrymen shared that view. And yet in May 1940, despite the heightened crisis in Europe and the fear that Japan might play Pied Piper to French, Dutch, and even British possessions in Eastern Asia, the President and the State Department had refused to make any commitments which might entangle the United States more deeply with Japan. On May 27, the chief of naval operations had written to the commander-in-chief of the American Pacific fleet: "Suppose the Japs do go into the East Indies? What are we going to do about it? My answer to that is, I don't know and I think there is nobody on God's green earth who can tell you."[8]

Less than three weeks later, Japan had concluded a treaty of "friendship" with Thailand. Half a world away, in Washington, despite the urgings of Secretary Morgenthau of the Treasury, the President and Mr. Hull had remained unwilling to invoke the new National Defense Act in a way that would deny Japan what she needed most: scrap iron and oil. At the end of June—only one month before Japan's course was set toward the South—the joint planning committee of the United States army and navy had recommended that American policy in the Pacific be defensive only.[9] This had come at a time when the Japanese government was demanding that Petain's France permit a Japanese military mission to operate in French Indo-China, that the Netherlands East Indies guarantee to continue supplying Japan with needed raw materials, and that Britain remove her troops from Shanghai, seal the frontier between Hong Kong and China, and close the Burma Road. The French, the Dutch, and the British were in an unenviable position. Japan had the force to compel them and threatened to use it.[10]

[6] *PHA*, Part 2, 556-57 (Hull testimony).
[7] See Tōjō cross-examination, S 346:5, T 36579 and S 347:2-3, T 36648-55. Tōjō's "Amerika no dai-kantai wa sude ni Hawai ni ketsu wo shite, hijō naru ikigomi wo agete taiki shite otta . . ." was interpreted as ". . . a large United States fleet was concentrated in Hawaii, its smokestacks exuding black smoke, its personnel active and on the alert. . . ," but this was immediately altered by the deletion of the colorful "black smoke" phrase which, of course, does not appear in Tōjō's comment.
[8] Stark to Richardson, May 27, 1940, as quoted in Feis, 57, n. 3, citing *PHA*, Part 14, 943-44.
[9] Feis, 62-63 and Chapter 9: "The American Government Forbears."
[10] See *ibid.*, 66-68, 71 and 91. See also *NYT*, June 25, 1940, 1, and July 18, 1940, 15.

What was a low-water mark for the United States was a high-water mark for Japan, but the tide was turning. By July 1940 concern was being expressed in Washington about the continuing flow of scrap iron and oil to Japanese stockpiles. Consular reports were suggesting a probable Japanese intention to accumulate oil on Hainan Island in preparation for a move southward. The President was informed that the Japanese were making such enormous purchases of aviation gasoline that the American army and navy faced the prospect of a shortage. Secretary Morgenthau again argued for export control of *all kinds* of oil and scrap metal. Sumner Welles, acting for Secretary Hull who was absent from Washington, advised in favor of the more cautious policy of controlling only aviation gasoline and lubricants and only top-grade scrap iron and steel. The State Department feared that a show of strength of the type advocated by Morgenthau would push Tokyo into Hitler's camp and that Japan would then not only wage war against England but decide to take the Dutch East Indies as well. In the end, the State Department view prevailed, even though Roosevelt himself had earlier seemed to prefer the sterner alternative. With diplomatic tongue in cheek, the United States rather anxiously disclaimed any intention of discriminating against any country.

The Japanese government dispatched a protest reserving the right to take action in the future as it saw fit. The State Department deftly replied that the matter was not open to discussion, since it touched upon the national defense of the United States. To this was added a pointed reminder concerning the many restrictions and restraints imposed by Japan upon American nationals in China.

The issue passed and others came to the fore, but behind this less than perfect control of the export of the means of war lay a new element in the President's thinking: the belief that Japan would more likely be deterred "by a firm, though not crushing, show of our will than by any sign of fear."[11] Thus, the approach of Tokyo and of Washington in July 1940 was one and the same: nothing could be accomplished by a weak-kneed policy; an attitude of strength must be shown; that was the way to success.

The emphasis given in the Japanese policy decision of July 27, 1940, to settling the China Incident and solving the "problems" of the South soon took concrete form. Indeed, Japanese civil and military attention,

[11] The words here are those of Dr. Feis, whose discussion (pp. 88-94) of the Morgenthau-Welles approach to FDR in July 1940 forms the basis for the comments in the text.

for the next twelve months, was directed predominantly toward those twin objectives. With each new success, Japan obtained a more favorable strategic position from which to launch a military offensive in the South should an opportunity arise.

The full record of how Japan accomplished this is long and involved, but the salient facts are simple.[12] The first achievement concerned French Indo-China. On September 22, 1940, five days before the signing of the Tripartite Pact in Berlin, a convention was concluded at Hanoi which gave Japan the right to establish garrisoned air bases in northern French Indo-China and to use that area as a corridor for the passage of Japanese troops and matériel into China. In return, the Japanese government guaranteed the territorial integrity of Indo-China and French sovereignty there. The details of the negotiations which led to this development leave no doubt that the authorities at Vichy, burdened by France's recent defeat and by mounting Japanese pressure, could not in fact refuse Tokyo's demands. As Paul Baudouin, the Vichy foreign minister, analyzed the situation at the time, it was a matter of choice. "If we refuse to let the Japanese through," he wrote in his diary, "they will launch an attack, preceded by bombing, and we shall certainly lose the whole of Indo-China. On the other hand if we try to come to an agreement with Japan, this will begin by recognizing our complete sovereignty over Indo-China, and we shall only partly lose the colony. It is true that the Japanese troops might remain in the country and annex it, but they might also respect French sovereignty, and withdraw once the fight against Chiang Kai-shek is at an end. Between two evils one must choose the lesser, and I choose an understanding with Japan."[13]

Admiral Decoux, who was in charge of the negotiations at Hanoi, advised in favor of defending Indo-China. According to the foreign minister, however, "the Admiral made no secret of the fact that he possessed only eleven modern planes, that his anti-aircraft defences were non-existent, that his munitions were very limited in quantity, and that his principal weapon consisted of twenty old tanks dating from the previous war."[14] Despite this uninspiring picture, Decoux asked that airplanes, arms, and munitions be sent across Russia and China as soon as possible. Even if France risked losing Indo-China, he cabled, it would

[12] Individual items are documented separately. For general information on Japan's policy of advancing southward, see, for instance, Hattori, I, 58-59; JRD Monograph No. 45, 28; and J, B/IV, 330-31, 341-43, 359-61, 399-401, 408-9, 414-16, 424-28, 430, 449-53, 455-56, and 464-69.
[13] Baudouin, *The Private Diaries* . . . , 203.
[14] *Ibid.*, 227.

be better to have it lost in defense than in betrayal. Needless to say, the view of the foreign minister prevailed.

Arguments to the effect that the Japanese action at this time was justifiable as a defensive necessity cannot seriously be entertained. Japan's purpose was to secure a position of strength that would permit her to coordinate an offensive against Chungking from the south with further military pressure from the east in an all-out effort to eliminate the Generalissimo's "regime." Since Japan already had quite enough fighting on her hands in China proper, the government in Tokyo naturally desired to obtain French "cooperation" by peaceful means. To secure such a position of strength not only would make the Nationalist task of defending what remained of Free China more difficult but would also clear the way for Japan to exert control over the economy and politics of Indo-China. The military authorities in Tokyo actually believed that if they sent a brigade of soldiers into one corner of that country, the French colonial administration would do whatever it was told.[15] They also felt that the presence of Japanese troops in the north would be advantageous in the event that the occupation of the southern half of Indo-China should later prove necessary or desirable.

Despite evidence of an effort to avoid hostilities, the dispatch of Japanese troops to Indo-China was not accomplished without incident. Early in September 1940, while the negotiations were still in progress, a sector of the Indo-Chinese frontier had been violated by a battalion of Japanese troops apparently engaged in "reconnaissance." Later that same month, during the authorized movement of Japan's forces into Indo-China, an "error in signals" between a unit commander and his subordinates had resulted in some bombs being dropped, by mistake, on the outskirts of Haiphong. Farther to the north, along the frontier where rugged terrain made communications difficult, Japanese and French troops had exchanged fire.

The two border incidents had an unusual sequel in Tokyo when War Minister Tojo proceeded to court-martial the battalion and regimental commanders who were implicated in each affair, together with some of their subordinates. Tojo also relieved the commanding general of the South China expeditionary force, and either dismissed, transferred, or otherwise penalized a number of other officers, including staff members of the army division of imperial headquarters.[16] He took this action

[15] Kenryō Satō, "Dai-Tōa Sensō wo Maneita Shōwa no Dōran," 117. Satō notes that this view proved overly optimistic.

[16] Among those affected by Tōjō's disciplinary action were Lt. Gen. Rikichi Andō,

because the Emperor had enjoined him to be especially diligent in controlling the army, and because the maintenance of discipline represented his own consistent policy as war minister.

Information received in Vichy from that government's ambassador in Tokyo revealed that the Japanese army in the field had been up to its old tricks once again. General Nishihara, who was Admiral Decoux's counterpart in Hanoi, seemed to be subject more to the orders of the South China expeditionary force, with headquarters at Canton, than to those of the government in Tokyo whom he supposedly represented. The vice-chief of staff of the "Canton army," who was none other than Colonel Kenryo Sato, had been serving concurrently as a member of the Nishihara group and as the channel through which the "Canton army" made its wishes known and its influence felt. The authorities in Tokyo who were aware of what was happening either saw no reason to object or were powerless to interfere. The armed clash between Japanese and French soldiers, however, greatly embarrassed the government and so steps were finally taken to bring the situation under control by transmitting a cease-fire order in the name of the Emperor.[17]

The success which marked Japan's acquisition of special facilities in northern French Indo-China was followed shortly by a decision to offer Chiang Kai-shek one more chance to capitulate ("to make peace," in the idiom of the day).[18] Had the Generalissimo accepted Tokyo's terms, all of China would have become a vast appendage of Japan. But "Mr. Chiang," as Tojo later explained it, "without the slightest recon-

---

commanding general of the South China area army, and Maj. Gen. Kyōji Tominaga, chief of the first bureau (operations) of the army general staff and thus a member of the army division of imperial headquarters (*daihon'ei rikugunbu*). In March 1943 Tominaga became vice-minister of war under Tōjō.

[17] On Japan's activities in (and regarding) northern French Indo-China, see Tōjō aff., S 343:1-2, T 36197-205; Hattori, I, 75-78; Kenryō Satō, "Dai-Tōa Sensō wo Maneita Shōwa no Dōran," 106-11 and 117; Baudouin, *passim* (the role of the "Canton army" is noted on pages 188, 230, 240, 248, 251-52); Kido SKD; Tōjō cross-examination, S 347:11-13, T 36708-721 (in which Tōjō, while admitting his participation in the decision, correctly notes that the dispatch of troops to northern French Indo-China was carried out in response to the demands of the supreme command) and S 349:2, T 36821-23; J, B/IV, 330-31, 399-401, 414-16, 443-49, 457-59, B/V, 746, 750, and B/VII, 882-85; Hull, I, 903-7; Feis, 66-68, 96, 98, 103-4, 189, and 234 (ns. 16 and 17); Satō corresp.; and *PHA*, Part 12, 2-3.

[18] For the trend of Japan's policy toward China in 1939 and 1940, see, for instance, J, B/IV, 308-9, 411-15, 418-24, 432-35, 441-42, 464-66, and B/V, 750-55. It was the majority view of the IMTFE that only Japan's dependence upon foreign sources of raw materials prevented her from openly repudiating the Nine-Power Pact, which had been repeatedly violated by Japan's actions in China. See also Hattori, I, 78-88; Tōjō aff., S 343:2-3, T 36206-12; Tōjō cross-examination, S 347:6, T 36672; and JRD, "Translation," II:51903 (Item 18), 2-3.

sideration, despite Japan's sincere efforts, continued fighting with the backing of America and Britain. . . ."[19] When Japan's maneuver failed, a basic treaty was signed with Wang Ching-wei, who earlier had defected from Chungking and subsequently had established (in March 1940) a puppet government of China with its capital at Nanking. By means of this basic treaty of November 30, 1940, "Japan secured the right to a voice in China's diplomatic activities, to maintain military and naval forces in China, to use China for strategic purposes, and to use Chinese natural resources for [Japan's] 'national defense.'"[20] Diplomatic protestations to the contrary notwithstanding, "China was to become at the best a province or satrapy of Japan, and at the worst a country to be exploited to satisfy Japan's military and economic needs."[21] This meant, significantly, that Japan was forsaking any further attempt to arrange peace with Chungking and was digging in for a long war against the "insincere" Nationalists.

Scarcely had the negotiations with Wang Ching-wei been settled than Japan became involved, with questionable purpose, in a border dispute between French Indo-China and Thailand.[22] The trouble arose at such a convenient time that a certain suspicion still lingers in regard to its spontaneity. The dispute began when Thailand suddenly demanded the return of territory that France had added to her Indo-Chinese empire roughly half a century earlier. When the French authorities did not capitulate, Thai troops began invading the area in question. The Japanese offered to mediate the dispute but the two sides proved hesitant. British efforts in the same direction also were fruitless. Being closer to the scene and having a good deal at stake, Japan resolved not to be dissuaded by any reluctance on the part of the disputants to avail themselves of her good offices. In late December 1940 a liaison conference decided in favor of such pressure as would induce French Indo-China and Thailand to accept Japan's mediation.[23] When the fighting showed

---

[19] "Shikaru-ni waga hō no shinshi naru doryoku ni mo kakawarazu Shōkaiseki-shi wa sukoshimo hansei sezu Bei-Ei no shien ni yori sentō wo zokkō shi jijitsu-jō no sensō kōi ga shinkō shi-tsutsu arimashita" (Tōjō aff., S 343:3).
[20] J, B/V, 753.   [21] *Ibid.*
[22] The following factual material (concerning Japan's role in the Thailand-French Indo-China border dispute) comes primarily from the account in Hattori, I, 93-104 (Colonel Hattori was the "senior staff officer" of the operations section of the army general staff from October 1940 to July 1941, and chief thereof from July 1941 to December 1942 and from October 1943 to February 1945) and Hattori corresp. See also Tōjō aff., S 343:5-6, T 36231-35; Tōjō cross-examination, S 347:12, T 36714-15, and S 348:6-7, T 36761-68; Kido SKD; JRD, "Interrogations," I:49157 (Seizō Arisue), 38-39 and 43; Gaimushō, II, 479-80; and Feis, 151-52 and 181, n. 5.
[23] "Tai oyobi Futsu-In ni tai shi torubeki Teikoku no Sochi," December 27, 1940.

signs of going against the Thai forces, another liaison conference hurriedly adopted "emergency measures" specifying that Japan would employ her good offices whether the participants wanted her to or not.[24] As a result of this decision, mediation talks were begun in Tokyo early in February 1941. A treaty of peace was concluded in May and a new boundary, favorable to Thailand, was established. In the process, Japan secured protocols of guarantee and understanding with both Thailand and French Indo-China by which Tokyo was assured that neither would conclude hostile political or military agreements with third powers directed against Japan.

Behind these substantial achievements, which were public knowledge, lay secret developments that were vastly more significant. At a liaison conference held on December 12, 1940, Foreign Minister Matsuoka had referred to a "let's get tough" cable from a special Japanese envoy, then engaged in negotiations in French Indo-China, who urged the dispatch of Japanese troops to the southern part of that country.[25] The interest of imperial headquarters was immediately stimulated. The prevailing view was that the Dutch and the British were firm allies and could be expected to act in concert. An attack by Japan on the Netherlands East Indies would result in war by Britain against Japan. Such action, in turn, would require a Japanese strike against Malaya. For that, Japan would need military bases in southern Indo-China and, if possible, in Thailand. Even if Japan were not to become involved in war in the South, her goal of self-sufficiency demanded that she obtain as full a share as possible of the strategic resources of Thailand and of Indo-China. A general concurrence developed among members of the government that those areas had to come under Japan's wing. It was realized that there would be numerous difficulties, including aggravation of Japan's relations with the West, especially if more troops were dispatched. But no one in either the cabinet or the supreme command touched very deeply upon the basic problem of whether the will and determination existed for a war with Britain and the United States.

The repeated failure of Japan's leaders to come to grips with such key factors in the decision-making process as the risks involved in implementing a particular policy frequently resulted in their finding themselves confronted by a reaction which they had not expected and which consequently confounded them all the more. In this particular case, the failure seems to have stemmed from a belief that so long as Japan

[24] "Tai, Futsu-In Funsō Chōtei ni kan suru Kinkyū Shori Yōkō," January 19, 1941.
[25] Matsuoka was referring to a cable from Ambassador Matsumiya.

limited her southward expansion to French Indo-China and Thailand, war with Britain and the United States would probably not occur.

The army and navy divisions of imperial headquarters both wanted military bases in Thailand and southern Indo-China. They still believed that the German offensive in the spring of 1941 might be directed against Britain and they wanted to be in a position in southern Asia by about March or April that would permit them to take advantage of developments in Europe (euphemistically: to cope with developments there). What imperial headquarters desired, therefore, was the conclusion of a military pact with Thailand providing for the establishment of Japanese air bases in that country. Since it was assumed that Thailand would negotiate such a military pact more readily if the border dispute were settled in her favor, Japanese mediatory efforts were directed toward that end. Tokyo's objective was the establishment of "a close and inseparable military, political and economic union" on the part of Japan, French Indo-China, and Thailand.[26] "Pressure" would be applied first; if that did not produce the desired results, Japan would employ military measures. This held true not only for French Indo-China, but also for Thailand, with whom Japan clearly desired to be on the best of terms. Despite the new treaty of friendship, which might have suggested the propriety of restraint, Japan was determined to achieve her goals one way or another.

Once again it was imperial headquarters—the army and navy general staffs—that originated this foreign policy and argued for its acceptance. War Minister Tojo and Navy Minister Oikawa had reservations about using force against French Indo-China. In fact, they were fairly reluctant to do so. The basis of Tojo's objections lay in his recollection of the armed clashes of the previous September and in his concern lest the policy now being proposed give rise to similar occurrences. Foreign Minister Matsuoka was also lukewarm, but whether because he thought the matter could be settled through diplomacy, or because he was piqued by the tendency of the supreme command to interfere in questions of foreign policy, poses an interesting problem.

In the liaison conferences of this period, Prince Konoe is said to have taken little active part. He spoke but seldom, and rarely gave an indication of his views. The supreme-command representatives of imperial headquarters were not aware of what he thought, but since he raised no

[26] Japan's policy was spelled out in the "Tai Futsu-In-Tai Shisaku Yōkō" of January 30, 1941.

objections to their proposals, they concluded that he agreed with them and they acted accordingly.

The decisions which had been reached concerning French Indo-China and Thailand were reported to the throne in due course. The Emperor approved the proposed military pact after cautioning the chiefs of staff to give careful consideration to the time of implementation so as to avoid stimulating American and British hostility. The chief aide-de-camp to the Emperor told Kido that the navy was thinking of using Camranh Bay and air bases in the vicinity of Saigon. Since the navy could not come right out and say that, however, it talked in terms of "protection of commerce and communications" and "guarantees for the prevention of conflicts" between French Indo-China and Thailand.

Formal reports to the throne were generally stiff and vague. Informal conversations with Kido were freer and more satisfactory, so far as content was concerned. That a great deal of what Kido learned at this time also reached the Emperor is clear from an unusual remark made by His Majesty to the privy seal early in February. The Emperor said that personally he did not like the idea of Japan's playing the thief at a fire— of taking advantage of the weakness of the other side by making demands upon it. But if Japan were to cope with the tremendous changes occurring in the world, a policy of mistaken benevolence (i.e., of uncalled-for leniency) would not do. For that reason, he had approved the measure. In the implementation of that policy, however, prudence would be necessary.[27]

By the early spring of 1941 much had been accomplished with respect

[27] Seven years later, during the course of the Tōkyō trial, Tōjō was confronted with the Emperor's "kajiba dorobō" remark. General Sugiyama, who had been chief of the army general staff in 1941, was dead, and the prosecution apparently felt that Tōjō, having been war minister at the time, might find the Emperor's words difficult to explain. To some extent, Tōjō did. He declared that he thought the fault lay with Kido and with the very strange language he had used to record what purported to be a statement by the Emperor. Kido, Tōjō said, must be mistaken; the Emperor would not have used such a low-class, vulgar expression as "a thief at a fire." In Kido's own account, however, the Emperor's words of February 1941 are matched by a much earlier expression of imperial concern. After an audience with the Emperor on June 20, 1940, Kido had recorded in his diary that His Majesty had touched upon the question of French Indo-China. The Emperor had then said that he did not want to see Japan acting like Frederick the Great or Napoleon—or, to put it in an extreme way, doing Machiavellian-like things. He told Kido that he wanted the real spirit of *hakkō-ichiu*, the policy handed down from the age of the gods, not to be forgotten. Kido SKD; Tōjō cross-examination, S 347:12, T 36714-15; and Kido corresp. See also Higashikuni, *Ichi Kōzoku no Sensō Nikki*, 71-72, 79-80 (diary entries for August 5 and September 7, 1941).

to the program outlined the previous July in "The Main Principles of Japan's Policy for Coping with the Situation in Accordance with World Developments."[28] Solidarity with Germany and Italy had been achieved and vigorous steps had been taken in southern Asia aimed at the strangulation of the Chinese Nationalists. What remained primarily was the completion of a diplomatic effort to secure the vital resources of the Netherlands East Indies and the consummation of a contemplated "bold adjustment" of Japan's relations with the Soviet Union. The decision as to how, when, and where to resort again to force was also left pending. That the government would rely on military might if less drastic measures failed was axiomatic. The only limitation was the state of Japan's preparedness and the nature of the situation abroad. In the spring of 1941 it did not seem likely that either would serve as a restraint. What was disturbing to Tokyo, however, was that Japan's negotiations with the Netherlands East Indies ground on week after week without any basic issues being resolved.

The effort to secure a predominant economic position in that region had begun indirectly more than a year before with a rather ominous notification by Japan, in January 1940, that a treaty with the Netherlands providing for the peaceful settlement of disputes would expire later that year.[29] The following month Japan had given a hint of its desires in regard to the East Indies: ". . . a lowering of trade restrictions; greater facilities for Japanese enterprise . . . ; easier entry for Japanese merchants, employees, and workers; mutual control of the press."[30] Three months later the demands had been increased, with the Japanese consul-general conveying "condolences, requests, and veiled threats almost in the same breath."[31] Among the items sought by Japan had been an amount of bauxite equal to the annual production of the Indies and approximately equivalent to Japan's total requirements. Tokyo had also asked that her previous imports of oil be doubled. Had the Dutch agreed, the Japanese would have obtained one-seventh of the oil produced annually in the Indies and about one-fifth of what Tokyo felt it needed.

[28] See pp. 150-53 above.
[29] The Treaty of Judicial Settlement, Arbitration, and Conciliation of August 1935 (J, B/VII, 885-86).
On Japan's negotiations with the Netherlands East Indies, the text follows the more detailed account presented in Feis, 51-53, 58-59, 96-105, 131-32, 150-51, and 206-7. See also JRD, "Interrogations," I:49157 (Seizō Arisue), 38-40; JRD, "Translation," II:51903 (Item 18), 4; JRD Monograph No. 45, 28; J, B/IV, 408-9, 414-16, 435-43, and B/VII, 885-902. The Dutch side of the story is told in van Mook, *The Netherlands East Indies and Japan*.
[30] Feis, 52.
[31] *Ibid.*, 58.

By September 1940 this figure had grown significantly. The supply of oil wanted then was approximately five times the quantity Japan had previously obtained from the Indies and about three-fifths of Japan's normal total supply from all sources—in other words, "enough to let her struggle along even if American shipments ended."[32]

Despite growing pressure from Tokyo, the authorities in Batavia had decided to continue to play a waiting game. In mid-January 1941 Japan had again launched a diplomatic offensive to capture control of the economic life of the Netherlands East Indies, but the Dutch had talked the Japanese negotiators down and had forced them to reduce their vigorous demands. This particular failure had had two interesting by-products. In Washington the previously held view that "Japan would pause longer before points of real resistance" was confirmed.[33] In Tokyo a cable arrived from Japan's chief negotiator in Batavia which was reminiscent of the content of the "let's get tough" cable sent by that gentleman's counterpart in French Indo-China some six weeks before. Matsuoka had then been advised by a member of the *diplomatic corps* to settle the Indo-China question immediately by the dispatch of Japanese troops to the southern part of that country. Now he was being told by another of his ambassadors that "without momentous determination and maneuvering on Japan's part," progress in the negotiations with the Dutch would be "most difficult."[34] The fact that this telegram also went to the vice-minister of war and to the vice-chief of the army general staff suggests that the phrase *jūdai ketsui*, "momentous determination," may have been a circumlocution for "a decision in favor of force."

The telegram from Batavia pointed an accusing finger at America and Britain, the real culprits on whom the Dutch were said to be relying more and more. In large measure that was true, but not quite the way Japan saw it. Just as earlier manifestations of the direction in which Japan was moving had prompted defensive responses, these further developments now resulted in additional precautions on the part of those powers whose interests and security were being increasingly jeopardized as the figure of Japan loomed larger and larger on the horizon. There would have been no purpose to tightening controls in the

[32] *Ibid.*, 104.   [33] *Ibid.*, 151.

[34] The cable in question was sent on January 27, 1941, by Ambassador Yoshizawa. The sentence referred to reads as follows in Japanese: "Yotte teikoku ni shite jūdai ketsui naishi kōsaku wo nasu ni arazareba Nichi-Ran kaishō no shinchoku wa motoyori Nichi-Ran kankei no dakai wa shi-nan nari to kansatsu seraru" (S 124:15). "Momentous determination and maneuvering" was inadequately rendered at the IMTFE as "determined resolutions or measures" (T 11857).

United States on the supply of strategic materials if Japan were to be allowed to flank those restrictions by bearing in the direction of the oil-rich Indies.

The American intention was to discourage Japan through various trade prohibitions without challenging her by total economic blockade. But even this comparatively pacific approach failed. American curbs on strategic materials were termed an "unfriendly act." Japan warned that future relations would be "unpredictable" if the United States pushed such policies further. Washington officially contented itself with pointing out the defensive necessity of such restrictions in the light of international circumstances not of the American government's making. Hull told the Japanese ambassador that "it was astonishing that a government with a record such as that of the Japanese should complain about discrimination, or feel entitled to call our defense measures unfriendly. Certainly, he asserted, the United States was not called upon to provide the means for Japanese acts of force and aggression."[35]

Hull disliked this "policy of pinpricks," but he agreed to it and saw to its implementation. And it was well that he did, for behind Japan's protests a more active response was taking shape. The supreme command was beginning to study plans for operations against the United States, Great Britain, and the Netherlands. The Japanese army was starting to train divisions for tropical combat. Reconnaissance flights were being sent over Malaya and the Philippines. Military currency for use in the southern area was being run off the presses. In Mexico City an office was opened for the purpose of gathering data on U. S. fleet movements in the Atlantic.[36]

Japanese naval intelligence activity of this type was by no means new. Specially trained agents had long paid particular attention not only to maximum code dispatches but also to simple cipher and straight messages, especially to personal ones sent by crew members of the Pacific

[35] On the American response to developments concerning the Netherlands East Indies, see Feis, 95-109 and 129 (the source of the Hull paraphrase quoted in the text).

[36] Earnest study of the problem of operations against the Western powers began in late 1940. For material on Japan's war planning, see Hattori, I, 104-7, 250ff., 298ff.; the testimony of an "expert" witness for the prosecution, T 8245ff., and documents submitted in evidence, T 8450-70; JRD, "Interrogations," II:35901 (Shinichi Tanaka), 417, 437-43; JRD, "Translation," V (Item 34, Shinichi Tanaka); JRD, "Interrogations," I:49157 (Seizō Arisue), 44 and 52; JRD, "Statements," IV:50609, 352, and IV:50460, 339-42 (both Sadatoshi Tomioka); Tōjō aff., S 343:12-13, T 36283-89; JRD Monograph No. 150, 1-3 and 6-13; J, B/VII, 877-82; Morton, "The Japanese Decision for War," *United States Naval Institute Proceedings*, Vol. LXXX, No. 12 (December 1954), 1326; and JRD, "Translation," VI:64718 (Item 14), which concerns Japanese naval intelligence activities.

fleet. The stationing of the American force at Pearl Harbor had resulted in a spate of messages dealing with the availability of housing and calling for wives and children to come to Hawaii. The Japanese agents who monitored these cables thought it comical when an irate wife wired her husband's commanding officer that she was not receiving her subsistence allowance. They concluded that there was "no difference in human feeling, East or West." As the fleet stayed on in Hawaiian waters, Japanese naval intelligence was advised that homesickness was spreading among the crew. Japan's agents felt that they had detected clear signs of this in a St. Valentine's message sent by a sailor to his girl in Seattle: "Blue Hawaii would not be so blue if you would be my Valentine."[37]

More significant, and less likely of misinterpretation, were data gathered on the technical side. The weekly training schedule of the fleet was easily learned, as was the berthing pattern. Regularly, on Fridays, the paymaster of each ship would requisition a certain amount of fresh meat and vegetables and would order delivery to a specific pier. By calculating how many men could be served by the rations, the Japanese were generally able to estimate what ships were where. That such attention to detail ultimately proved immensely valuable is well known. What is perhaps more interesting is that the basic intelligence needed for an attack upon Pearl Harbor was already in Japanese hands more than eighteen months before the blow was dealt. The opening of the Mexico City branch of the Japanese "Naval Secret Chamber," together with other offices in Peking, Shanghai, and Canton, bespoke the worsening of Japanese-American relations and the growing importance of intelligence with respect to the American navy.[38]

In Washington and London the coming of 1941 had inaugurated what an American authority has called a "winter period of alarm" resulting from British fears that Japan was about to attack Singapore and perhaps the Netherlands East Indies as well.[39] The United States was moving toward the formation of a united front against Japan, but still "without admitting it or promising to maintain it by force."[40] In spite of apprehension concerning Japan's next move, Far Eastern experts at the State Department remained convinced that Japan would decide on war "only as an unhappy last resort."[41]

[37] JRD, "Translation," VI:64718 (Item 14), 11-12 (the February 1940 date assigned to the Valentine message quoted in the text seems to be a mistake for February 1941).
[38] See *ibid.*   [39] Feis, 160.
[40] *Ibid.*, 134. On American retaliatory moves in this period, see Feis, 139-44 and 156-60.
[41] *Ibid.*, 155.

This was only partially correct. Japan would indeed feel unhappy about engaging the United States in war because of the uncertainty of success, but employment of force was always considered as the next step to be taken as soon as it became clear that Japan could not get what she wanted by less drastic methods. The imperial navy, for example, wanted to achieve results in the South by peaceful means if possible, but it did not rule out the use of force.

Military action, for the navy, was tied to four specific instances in which Japan would find it necessary to go to war "for her very existence." An all-out American embargo, supported by third powers, would constitute one such instance. Another would be Anglo-American co-operation against Japan, with the United States using British strategic bases such as Singapore. Still another would be the adoption by either Britain or the United States of measures posing a "direct threat to the existence of Japan," such as a large reinforcement of United States military strength in the Philippines or of Great Britain's strength in East Asia. The fourth and final instance, and by far the most revealing, would be a conclusion on the part of the navy that "Great Britain could be defeated, that America would not open hostilities against Japan and that Great Britain and America were completely separated."[42]

There is no doubt that the army shared these views. Matsuoka and other members of the diplomatic corps also appreciated the use to which force could be put in certain circumstances. What the members of the Japanese government did thereafter, perhaps more inadvertently than by design, was to create the very conditions in the Far East which the army and navy had already said would require Japan to go to war. And in so doing, the leaders in Tokyo endangered the security of American and British possessions in that area and thus unintentionally provided, *by virtue of their own reasoning*, a clear justification for hostile action against themselves.

The occupation of Hainan, the annexation of the Spratlys, the dispatch of troops to northern French Indo-China, the conclusion of the Tripartite Pact, the creation of a puppet government at Nanking, the role played in the border dispute between Thailand and French Indo-China, and the continuing pressure for an ever-larger share in the economic opportunities of the Netherlands East Indies—separately and together—demanded an Anglo-American response of the type envisaged in the first three instances specified by the Japanese navy.

[42] See JRD Monograph No. 146, 11-12 and 14-16.

Discussions between the army and navy divisions of imperial headquarters frequently returned to the problems posed by Japan's desire to expand to the South. If Japan endeavored to take the Netherlands East Indies by armed force, Manila and Singapore would stand in the way. The imperial navy adamantly asserted that it was absolutely impossible to think of Britain and the United States as separate entities; consequently an attack upon the Philippines would be the prerequisite for a successful advance to the South.

The army more or less agreed that the two Western powers were probably inseparable politically, but nevertheless believed that a wedge could be driven between them strategically. To do so, the army said, Japan would have to avoid attacking the Philippines.

The navy would not budge. It argued forcefully for its point of view, which it supported with practical arguments based upon operational requirements. In the end, the army concurred, and so by the spring of 1941 agreement existed between the army and navy general staffs that the use of force in the South was equivalent to undertaking war against the United States.[43]

By the time these developments had taken place, the peripatetic

[43] On April 17, 1941, just as the Hull-Nomura conversations in Washington were about to produce Nomura's first important cable to Tōkyō, the army and navy divisions of imperial headquarters reached a general agreement ("Tai Nanpō Shisaku Yōkō") on what amounted to a further development of the January 30 liaison conference decision in favor of establishing "a close and inseparable military, political, and economic union" with French Indo-China and Thailand (see the text corresponding to footnote 26 above). Close economic relations with the Netherlands East Indies and the maintenance of normal commercial contacts with other countries in the southern area were also specified. This was to be accomplished fundamentally by diplomatic means, but force was to be employed for Japan's "self-existence and self-defense" in case an American-British-Dutch embargo threatened Japan's existence, or in case the United States, Britain, the Netherlands, and China intensified their "encirclement" of Japan to the point where Japan judged the situation unbearable in terms of maintaining the national defense.

This prescription for the malady afflicting Japan, and the unwholesome effects it produced, may be more readily understood if it is realized that Japan actually lacked an over-all defense plan based upon a thorough and interrelated study of political, economic, and strategic factors.

On the "Tai Nanpō Shisaku Yōkō" of April 17, 1941, see Hattori, I, 107-8; S 123:22, T 11751-52; Tōjō aff., S 343:8-9, T 36254; Gaimushō, II, 495-96; and JRD, "Interrogations," I:49157 (Seizō Arisue), 38-40. There are textual differences between the Hattori and IMTFE versions. The former is also more complete than the latter. Hattori specifies the use of force by Japan if the encirclement is intensified by the United States acting either alone or in concert with the other powers.

In view of the fact that the Japanese-American negotiations were about to begin, the "Tai Nanpō Shisaku Yōkō" did not come before either a liaison or an imperial conference, but on June 6, 1941, the army and the navy formally adopted this program as a joint decision of the army and navy divisions of imperial headquarters.

Mr. Matsuoka was on the point of returning to Japan, in self-considered triumph, from his European "good-will tour." His had been an ambitious if somewhat unrealistic program. Before his departure, he had told Marquis Kido that in Germany, in March, he would ask Hitler, Ribbentrop, and others about the real situation with respect to their operations against England and would thoroughly discuss matters with them. At the same time, he would arrange an adjustment of Japan's relations with the Soviet Union. In April, he hoped to bring about a general peace with China, and after that he planned to devote his entire energies to the southern area. Without a solution of the problems in the South there could be no settlement of the China Incident in the true sense of the word. He stressed that the southern area constituted a major policy issue affecting the fate of the entire Japanese nation.[44]

Two days after this conversation with Kido, Matsuoka had met with his civil and military colleagues in a liaison conference called for the purpose of discussing a plan of action that would serve as a guide in his forthcoming negotiations. War Minister Tojo, who was present, later revealed some of the opinions held by the conference members. Japan's purpose was still to bring about harmony between the Axis powers and the Soviet Union (preferably in the form of a quadripartite pact).[45] It was felt that if this could be achieved, Japan would be able to improve relations with the United States (presumably because of the greater threat the new alliance would represent) and get the Soviets to agree to stop aiding the Chinese Nationalists.

As Tojo recalled it, four main problems were aired at the conference. The first was whether the Soviet Union could be prevailed upon to act in concert with the Tripartite Pact powers. An affirmative conclusion was drawn on the basis of the existing Nazi-Soviet Non-Aggression Pact and other evidence, such as earlier German expressions of a desire for Soviet participation in the Tripartite Pact, and explanations offered by von Ribbentrop's special envoy, Stahmer.

The second problem, which was related to the first, dealt with possible German reactions to Soviet-Japanese cooperation. Again, be-

---

[44] Kido SKD. Matsuoka had revealed all this to Kido on February 1, 1941.

[45] On the liaison conference of February 3, 1941, see Tōjō aff., S 343:3-4, T 36213-18; Tōjō cross-examination, S 348:7-8, T 36768; Hattori, I, 111-16 (which includes material on Matsuoka and Moscow); Gaimushō, II, 480-82 (text of "Tai Doku-I-So Kōshōan Yōkō; note the discrepancy between this source and Hattori on the amount of oil to be supplied); Hattori corresp.; JRD, "Interrogations," I: 49157 (Seizō Arisue), 37 and 45; JRD, "Translation," V (Item 24); and Feis, 145-49 and 180-85. The Japanese records make it clear that Tōkyō was not aware of the strained relations between Berlin and Moscow prior to Matsuoka's trip.

cause of the already existing Nazi-Soviet Pact, this question largely answered itself. There was also a feeling that the Germans would probably be prone to think in terms of utilizing Japan and the Soviet Union in the war against Britain and so would welcome cooperation between Moscow and Tokyo.

The third problem concerned the cost of purchasing Soviet assistance. Depending on the circumstances, the *quid pro quo* might include a restoration of fishing privileges reserved to Japan by treaty as well as the abandonment of certain rights and interests in the oil fields of northern Sakhalin. Although Tojo did not mention it in his testimony, this was to be done only in return for a Soviet engagement to supply Japan with 1,500,000 tons of oil during the next five years. An attempt to purchase northern Sakhalin through the good offices of Germany, which would have suited Tokyo best, was described by Tojo as more of an opening move in the negotiations than anything else. The Japanese navy, which was worried about the supply of oil from that region, wanted the foreign minister to exert himself in that regard.

The fourth problem was Matsuoka himself. The army and navy chiefs of staff were very much concerned lest the foreign minister commit Japan on matters that would involve the supreme command in responsibilities it was not then prepared to meet. Matsuoka was therefore forbidden to make any binding promises about possible Japanese participation in the European war.

The supreme command's distrust of Japan's foreign minister stemmed not only from his "voluble and unconventional nature" but also from his interest in launching a surprise attack on Singapore—a move which was then being urged upon Tokyo by Berlin.[46] The chiefs of the army and navy general staffs appreciated the many tactical and strategic problems connected with such an attack to an extent that Matsuoka apparently did not. This created an extraordinary situation: a foreign minister calling for a *banzai* effort against the naval base of a Western power and the army and navy chiefs of staff forcibly sheathing his sword instead of eagerly drawing their own. They were undoubtedly correct in doing so and the only regret is that they did not exercise similar wisdom and restraint during the months remaining in 1941.

The plan of action which Matsuoka took with him on his journey reveals how poorly informed Japan really was. Even Tojo later remarked that upon Matsuoka's arrival in Europe the foreign minister discovered that the actual situation bore little resemblance to the view of it then

---

[46] On the Singapore question, see J, B/VII, 877-82 and JRD Monograph No. 150, 6-8.

prevailing in Tokyo. Matsuoka found that German-Soviet relations were so strained that there was no possibility of Moscow acting in concert with the Rome-Berlin-Tokyo Axis. Consequently, the only concrete result of Matsuoka's various courtesy calls was the Neutrality Pact which was rather unexpectedly bestowed upon him in Moscow on his way home. In his anxiety to avoid coming back empty-handed, he apparently gave no thought to the implications of Stalin's sudden change of mind. On April 12, 1941, Matsuoka had so despaired of securing a treaty that he had even sent a cable to Tokyo to that effect. The next day, April 13, the Neutrality Pact was signed.[47]

To the Japanese, the importance of this diplomatic undertaking was in the short-term security it provided with respect to the frontier between Manchukuo and the Soviet Far East. Because of weather and related factors, it was believed that an invasion could be launched in that area only from May to September. If that season could be got through safely by means of a neutrality pact, the Japanese need not concern themselves about any Russian threat until the spring of 1942. By that time, the southern regions would presumably be under Japanese control and Japan would thus be in a position to defend herself against a Soviet attack in the North. If necessary or desirable, Japan would even be able to launch hostilities there on her own initiative. The same weather factor would also work to the advantage of the Russians. If the Neutrality Pact could contain the Japanese through September 1941, the Kremlin need not fear a Japanese attack upon the Soviet Far East until the following spring. Thus, a great deal depended on the short-term intentions of each contracting power with respect to honoring the "scrap of paper" that served as the only tangible memento of Matsuoka's European tour.

As the event turned out, the Russians were in far greater danger than the Japanese. And in the forefront of those who were hostile to the Soviet Union and anxious to invade her territory was Mr. Matsuoka, the man whom Stalin had personally seen off at the Moscow station and over whom he had made such an uncharacteristic public display of friendship.

---

[47] For material relating to the neutrality pact and its implications, see, for instance, Tōjō aff., S 343:4, T 36217-18; Hattori, I, 115-16; J, B/VI, 810-12 and 818-26; Feis, 184-87; and U. S. State Dept. *Bulletin*, XII, No. 305 (April 29, 1945), 812. Both Tōjō and Hattori minimize the value of the pact with regard to providing security in the North. Tōjō also denies that there is any connection between the pact and Japan's policy toward the South. A different interpretation is offered in the text in terms of the military strategy that was contemplated.

Some idea of the muddle which surrounded Japanese decision-making at this time is revealed by the state of Matsuoka's mind soon after his return to Japan. At a liaison conference held on May 22, 1941, the foreign minister proposed breaking off the negotiations with the Netherlands East Indies that had been in progress for months. "If we do not make up our minds now," Matsuoka said, "will not Germany, Great Britain, the United States, and the Soviet Union in the end join forces to oppress Japan? There is also a possibility that Germany and the Soviet Union will unite against Japan and that the United States will join in the war. I would like to hear the views of the supreme command with reference to these possibilities."[48]

One can only marvel at the foreign minister's omission of the planet Mars. Could it be said to be truly friendly toward Japan?

General Sugiyama, the army chief of staff, pointed out that it was not just a matter of "making up one's mind." French Indo-China and Thailand were the prerequisite to any move southward. Why had the foreign minister done nothing about that? Matsuoka answered that what was needed, first of all, was determination on Japan's part with reference to the United States and Britain (by which he meant a willingness to go to war with those powers, if necessary, to gain Japan's ends). Without such determination on the government's part, he could not conduct negotiations for military bases. If there was such determination, Matsuoka declared, he would go ahead. With a bluntness unusual in Japan even in jest, Navy Minister Oikawa turned to his colleagues and observed, "The foreign minister is crazy, isn't he?"[49]

Crazy or not, Matsuoka was actually anticipating the next move. Early in June, Tokyo received the first official confirmation of rumors which had been coming in from various quarters since the latter part of April. A cable arrived on June 6 from Lt. Gen. Oshima, whom Matsuoka had reappointed to his former ambassadorial post in Berlin,

[48] See Hattori, I, 133-34.

[49] *Ibid.* Oikawa's comment ("Gaishō wa atama ga hen de wa nai ka?") recalls a remark attributed to the elder statesman, Prince Saionji. The prince had as his aide and personal "Boswell," Baron Kumao Harada, sarcastically described in a rabid ultranationalistic publication as "that comic little baron"—"Saionji's boy." When Harada told the prince that some people were saying that Matsuoka must be demented, the prince replied that it would be an improvement if Matsuoka were to become insane. "The Brocade Banner," 70, 141, and Feis, 120.

In this connection it is interesting to note that some three months earlier Mr. Roosevelt had been moved to comment on the state of Matsuoka's mind after reading the instructions which the foreign minister had purportedly sent to Ambassador Nomura. "These instructions," the President wrote Sumner Welles, "seem to me to be the product of a mind which is deeply disturbed and unable to think quietly or logically." *PHA*, Part 20, 4296.

reporting that Hitler seemed to be thinking of waging war against the Soviet Union. Hitler had not said so openly, but Oshima had got the impression that Germany desired to have Japan participate in such a conflict. A liaison conference was called immediately to discuss the Oshima cable, but the current estimates of the supreme command and the reports Matsuoka had made upon his return from Europe argued against the likelihood of a German-Soviet conflict. Japan's leaders simply refused to believe that a war would break out between Germany and Russia. They did not comprehend that relations between those powers had deteriorated to such an extent. This view was supported by information sent from Moscow by Ambassador Tatekawa. It also fitted well with Japan's preconceptions and desires. Wishful thinking carried the day in the form of a conclusion that the whole thing was nothing more than a German maneuver designed to camouflage an intention to invade England. No concrete policy was formulated other than a perfunctory decision to pay close attention to developments.

An earlier softening of the Soviet approach toward Japan had not gone unnoticed in Tokyo, but Moscow's change of heart had nevertheless failed to cue Japan's leaders to what was coming. The improvement in relations was attributed to the conclusion of the Neutrality Pact. No one gave any serious thought to the possibility that the thaw in the Soviet attitude might suggest the outbreak of a German-Soviet war.[50]

A similar inability to evaluate facts on an objective basis was revealed a few days later when the government again turned its attention to the "problems" of the South. The army and navy divisions of imperial headquarters had by then lost patience. It was decided that no further delay could be countenanced with respect to the conclusion of a military agreement permitting Japan to station troops in *southern* French Indo-China. The question was whether Matsuoka would go along with the

---

[50] See Tōjō aff., S 343:9, T 36255-57, and JRD, "Interrogations," I:49157 (Seizō Arisue), 44. In addition to the Ōshima cable of June 6 (also noted in Hattori, I, 134 and 145), cables had arrived on April 21 from Nomura (in Washington) and Ōshima (in Berlin) stating that a German-Soviet war might start soon (Hattori, I, 122). On May 14 a report was received from Japan's military attaché in Berlin quoting the chief of intelligence of the German general staff to the effect that an outbreak of war between Germany and the Soviet Union was inevitable (Hattori, I, 130). That Matsuoka should have had a better appreciation of the German-Soviet situation than he did is clear from evidence in German records. See, for example, the discussion in Feis, 183-87, and J, B/VI, 819-22. See also Hattori, I, 74-75, 104, 116, and 144, in which emphasis is placed on Japan's lack of prior knowledge of Hitler's intentions. The validity of this point depends on the degree of reliability assigned to the indirect information received by Tōkyō.

idea or not. The day before the Oshima cable had arrived, the chiefs of the military and naval affairs bureaus of the war and navy ministries had discussed the matter with him, but he had again spoken of the necessity of first having a plan to capture Singapore. This had led imperial headquarters to declare that if America and Britain tried to obstruct Japan's policy toward the South, the army and navy were ready to fight. Actually, neither the army, the navy, nor Premier Konoe believed that America and Britain would resort to force in response to a Japanese advance into southern French Indo-China. Although Matsuoka warned of the danger of a collision with Britain, there was no serious examination of the possibility of a total embargo being imposed upon Japan by the Americans, the British, and the Dutch. In fact, everyone was overly optimistic on that score.

The result was the formulation by imperial headquarters on June 11, 1941, of still another policy statement outlining the steps by which Japan's advance toward the South would now be accelerated.[51] Japan would recall her ambassador from the Netherlands East Indies and would effect an arrangement with French Indo-China providing for the military occupation of the southern part of that country by Japan. The use of force was precisely stipulated: if French Indo-China resisted, Japan would resort to arms; if America, Britain, and the Netherlands attempted to interfere, and if no other solution were possible, Japan would "not avoid risking" an all-out war.

Liaison conferences were held on June 11, 12, and 16 to discuss this new policy. On the 11th, the conference turned exclusively on the views expressed by the foreign minister and the supreme command. Navy Chief of Staff Nagano, who had a tendency at times to sweep his colleagues off their feet "by making abrupt statements," took this occasion to state that the establishment of military bases in southern French Indo-China and Thailand was necessary and that Japan should deal decisively with anyone who tried to stand in her way. "If and when it is necessary to strike," he declared, "we will strike." Since this

[51] On developments between June 11 and 16, 1941, the text relies on the detailed presentation in Hattori, I, 134-42. Although some of the material postdates the events under discussion, the following were also useful: Tōjō aff., S 343:6-9, T 36232 and 36235-54 (a loose translation, T 36232, makes it appear that Tōjō is contradicting himself with reference to T 36236 when, in fact, he is not) and S 343:10, T 36267-69; Kenryō Satō, "Dai-Tōa Sensō wo Maneita Shōwa no Dōran," 106-11 and 117; S 123:22, T 11753-54; Tōjō interrog., Feb. 13, 3-7, 9-10, 12-13, Feb. 15, 1-4, Feb. 18, 1, and Mar. 8, 2-3. Tōjō's contention that the sending of troops into southern French Indo-China was not prompted by the outbreak of the German-Soviet war deserves more credence than might at first appear.

did not jibe with earlier naval attitudes on the question of war or peace, the army chief of staff is said to have doubted inwardly that this remark represented the true intentions of the leaders of the navy.

At the meeting on June 16 Matsuoka continued to raise objections to the plan being advocated by the supreme command, even going so far as to point out that what the military proposed doing would adversely affect Japan's international reputation, since the world would look upon an enforced occupation of southern French Indo-China as an act of bad faith. He said that he would be unable to avoid reporting in that vein to the Emperor. He also taunted the supreme command by declaring that the current situation had resulted from the failure of the army and navy to attack Singapore as he had urged them to do the year before. The meeting ended with Matsuoka requesting a few days to think things over.

Even though the foreign policy under consideration was the product of the decision-makers within the army and navy general staffs, Matsuoka, as foreign minister, would have the primary responsibility vis-à-vis the throne. Matsuoka's colleagues were uncertain whether his negative attitude was a reflection of basic opposition on his part to an occupation of southern French Indo-China or a manifestation of lack of confidence in his ability to secure imperial acquiescence. On June 21 and 22 the chiefs of the military and naval affairs bureaus[52] again called on the foreign minister to discuss the question with him. After some revisions were made in the text of the original draft, Matsuoka finally yielded, at 11:00 p.m. on June 22, to the majority view. The magical unanimity thus achieved was formalized at a liaison conference three days later. Following immediate cabinet approval, Premier Konoe, Army Chief of Staff Sugiyama, and Navy Chief of Staff Nagano jointly reported to the throne and obtained His Majesty's sanction.[53]

The day on which Matsuoka let himself be persuaded by the two service ministry bureau chiefs, acting on behalf of imperial head-

[52] Major General Akira Mutō and Rear Admiral Takasumi Oka.

[53] The joint report to the throne was a comparatively new procedure which had been employed for the first time (in this period at least) following a liaison conference held on January 30, 1941 (see S 123:21, T 11744).

Although the policy, as finally approved, no longer contained the statement about Japan's willingness to risk war with Britain and the United States, that thought was by no means suppressed (as the imperial conference proceedings of July 2 were shortly to reveal). And, of course, the decision to use force to carry out the planned occupation of southern French Indo-China, in the event French authorities refused to comply with Japan's demands, was retained.

quarters, was the very day on which Hitler threw his armies against Germany's Non-Aggression Pact partner, the Soviet Union. And it was only then, on June 22, 1941, that the Japanese government learned definitely, through a cable from Oshima, that the Nazis had broadened the European conflict into a two-front war. In the words of one Japanese colonel, the outbreak of German-Soviet hostilities, despite the existence of the Non-Aggression Pact of 1939, "deeply impressed us with the fact that the vicissitudes of history are beyond man's power to surmise."[54]

The real purpose behind Matsuoka's objections to the establishment of military bases in southern French Indo-China at the risk of war with Britain and the United States was now suddenly revealed. His opposition had not been prompted by any fear of such a war or by any concern for Japan's international reputation. It had arisen solely because acquiescence in that policy would have made very difficult and perhaps impossible another project that he had been harboring in his mind. *Regardless of the Neutrality Pact, Matsuoka wanted Japan to join Germany in a war against the Soviet Union.* On June 16, the day on which Matsuoka had requested time to think things over, Oshima had cabled that a German-Soviet war would break out during the coming week. The June 22 cable announcing the fulfillment of that prediction arrived in Tokyo sometime prior to four o'clock in the afternoon. At that precise hour Matsuoka telephoned the news to Kido and asked for an audience with the Emperor. The lord privy seal checked with the chamberlain then on duty to determine when it would be convenient for the Emperor to see the foreign minister. As a result, an audience was scheduled for 5:30 p.m. On the strength of impressions obtained the previous evening during an informal talk with Premier Konoe and Baron Hiranuma, Kido requested permission to speak with the Emperor prior to Matsuoka's arrival. Upon being received, Kido explained that Matsuoka's views on the attitude Japan should adopt and the policy she should follow did not appear to be necessarily in accord with those of the premier. Since the decision now required of Japan would affect the nation's rise or fall, Kido advised the Emperor to ask Matsuoka whether he had discussed the matter with Prince Konoe. Kido also suggested that the Emperor command Matsuoka to cooperate closely with the premier and that His Majesty impress upon the foreign minister that Konoe should be the focus of any decision made at this

[54] See Tōjō aff., S 343:9, T 36257, and Hattori, I, 148 (the source of the quoted remark).

time. Kido felt that he was being very forward in offering this line of advice, but he believed the situation warranted it.

Exactly what Matsuoka said to the Emperor late that afternoon will probably never be known. It is clear, however, that Matsuoka was acting entirely on his own initiative without having consulted Konoe or other members of the cabinet. It is also clear that he advocated the inauguration of a "positive" policy in the form of an immediate attack by Japan upon the Soviet Union. Refraining from any action in the South would consequently be the best procedure for the time being, but sooner or later it would be necessary to fight in the South as well. In the end, Japan would find herself simultaneously at war with the Soviet Union, Britain, and the United States.

As soon as Matsuoka had bowed himself out of the Emperor's presence, His Majesty called Kido in for further consultation. As a result, Prince Konoe was informed by Kido of what had transpired at the palace. About 10:00 p.m. that evening Matsuoka called on Konoe at the latter's Ogikubo residence. Konoe did not find the remarks of his foreign minister very explicit, but he nevertheless concluded that Matsuoka's report to the throne had represented merely personal views with regard to what would be required in the worst eventuality. At 12:30 a.m., June 23, Konoe so informed Kido by telephone, adding that Matsuoka's advice to the Emperor had not been meant to suggest that such measures must be carried out immediately.[55]

All this helps explain why Matsuoka finally gave his consent, at 11:00 p.m. on the 22nd, to the demands of the supreme command for an acceleration of Japan's policy toward the South. In the light of the stand taken by the foreign minister during the very hectic ten days that followed, however, it would appear that either Konoe misunderstood the explanation Matsuoka gave him or the foreign minister subsequently decided to revert to his originial idea of having Japan attack the Soviet Union at once.

Although the Japanese government had not been taken entirely unawares, the new hostilities in Europe were in the nature of a distasteful reality for which Japan's leaders were not prepared. For the second

[55] Hattori, I, 137-38 and 148, notes the arrival of the June 16 cable; and Kido SKD states that Matsuoka telephoned him at 4:00 p.m. on June 22, advising him of the receipt of the Ōshima cable announcing the outbreak of war. The details of the Kido and Matsuoka audiences and of the Matsuoka-Konoe meeting are from Kido SKD; Konoe, 83-84; and PHA, Part 20, 3993. It is not entirely clear whether Matsuoka's acceptance of the supreme command's program at 11:00 p.m. on June 22 occurred while he was with Konoe or not. The significant consideration is that the events coincided in the manner described.

time in slightly less than two years, the Japanese government had been drawn up short by the Nazi habit of springing unpleasant surprises on friend and foe alike. In each instance, Japan's leaders had, in some measure, helped to create the troubles in which they found themselves. In 1939 Hiranuma had been unable to herd his colleagues fast enough into an alliance, and so the Germans had extended a hand to Stalin. In late 1940 and early 1941, despite the conclusion of the Tripartite Pact, Tokyo had refused to enter into the kind of partnership Berlin wanted. The question now facing Japan was how to deal with the new situation created by Hitler. For all practical purposes, that foreign policy question was answered almost exclusively by the armed services. It was largely the nucleus group within the army and navy who specified the program to be followed in the immediate future and who led the fight for its acceptance by the nonmilitary members of the government, who had still to give their consent even though they were otherwise powerless. As had been true earlier, initially there was not the unanimity which always emerged, in one fashion or another, at the end.

Even before June 22, a conflict of opinion had arisen over the significance, for Japan, of a possible Soviet-German war. One view was that such a war would finally free Japan of Soviet pressure in the North and so permit her to establish a structure of self-sufficiency by advancing southward. The other view was that the weakening of Russian strength in the Soviet Far East would create an opportunity for Japan to rid herself of concern about that region by advancing northward. Opinion within the army was split between these views, but the lines of cleavage were by no means clear-cut. In general, the key officers in the war ministry were not disposed to give serious consideration to an attack in the North until after southern French Indo-China had been occupied and closer military ties with Thailand had been established. Within the army general staff, opinion in favor of a northward advance was much stronger, but in the end a decision was made to postpone such a move until a favorable opportunity presented itself.

There was also disagreement between the army and the navy. The latter felt that for the moment Japan should concentrate on completing her military preparations and should only decide later, in accordance with circumstances, on the direction in which to move. The army wanted a determination of the direction first, followed by all-out preparations to attain the selected objective. The resolution of these differences of opinion was achieved through meetings between key bureau and section personnel in the army general staff and the war ministry and through consultations between the army and navy divisions of imperial headquarters. The final agreement was reached on June 24 in the form of a joint proposal rather loosely entitled, "The Main Principles of the Empire's Policy for Dealing with Changes in the Situation."[56]

Two days later, on June 26, the matter came up for discussion at a liaison conference. Foreign Minister Matsuoka exhibited concern about an apparent unwillingness on the part of the army and the navy to consult Germany and Italy on various matters, especially Japan's intentions with respect to entering the German-Soviet war. The vice-chief of the army general staff expressed the opinion that consultations with Germany on supreme-command questions would result in Japan's being dragged in the direction the Germans wanted her to go. In order to avoid that, Japan would have to make her decisions independently. He did not know about political affairs, he said, but there was no need for consultation on strategy. Moreover, the requirements of secrecy and speed of action rendered consultation impossible. Both War Minister Tojo and Chief of Staff Sugiyama seconded this view, the former drawing attention to the fact that the Germans had thus far been doing what they wanted without talking it over with Japan.

Further discussion also revealed that the supreme command felt that a decision by Japan in favor of war against the Russians should be made solely on the basis of self-interest. If a given situation was judged very promising by Germany but not by Japan, Tokyo would refrain from fighting. If a given situation was regarded as advantageous by Japan, she would participate in the war even if the Germans did not concur.

It is hardly unusual for nations to think in selfish terms. Privy Councilor Ishii had pointed to the German tendency to do so during the discussions which had preceded the council's approval of the Tripartite Pact and had suggested, almost in the same breath, that Japan seek to protect herself by taking advantage of German strong points in science and technology. By June 1941 the leaders in Tokyo had perhaps an added incentive to think only of the profit to Japan in deciding for or against certain actions. As Tojo had pointed out, the Germans had not taken Japan into *their* confidence.

[56] "Jōsei no Suii ni Tomonau Teikoku Kokusaku Yōkō," June 24, 1941. The text of this document, in its original form, can be found in Hattori, I, 149 (see pages 154-55 for revisions made on June 28).

There are several English versions of the document as it was adopted at the imperial conference on July 2, 1941, but the only reliable basis for judgment is the Japanese original as given in S 77:21; Gaimushō, II, 531-32; or Tōgō, *Jidai no Ichimen*, 168-69.

Nevertheless, the reasoning in Tokyo was fallacious. It represented an emotional reaction to a very practical problem which could be solved, if at all, only on a rational basis. The view expressed reveals that Japan's decision-makers did not understand the nature of modern warfare. Successful strategic cooperation between the European Axis and Japan would have been difficult under the best of circumstances. They were separated from each other by the vast land mass of the Soviet Union. Communication by sea during wartime would mean traversing more than 15,000 miles of ocean. Such contact would almost inevitably be confined to submarine voyages. Yet here was the Far Eastern "partner" in this world alliance of aggressive forces deciding that Japan should act on her own initiative, in accordance with her own desires and purposes, without any concern for the views of her allies.

The discussion of the new policy-draft presented by imperial head-quarters spilled over from June 26 to the 27th. Matsuoka continued to press his view that Japan should decide immediately on participating in the German-Soviet war, that she should advance northward first and then to the South, and that in the interim she should attempt to settle the China Incident! Although his proposal was fantastic in terms of strategic requirements, the foreign minister was not easily dissuaded. He offered the argument that the United States did not like the USSR and in all probability would not go to her aid by joining in the war. To watch the situation develop before deciding to act, as suggested by the supreme command, would result in Japan's being surrounded by Britain, the United States, and the Soviet Union. Therefore, attack first to the North, Matsuoka said, and then to the South. Unless one took certain risks, one could not obtain any rewards.

When Tojo asked Matsuoka how his proposals related to the China Incident, the foreign minister replied that until the end of 1940 he had believed in the reverse of what he was now advocating. He had thought that an advance to the South should be made first, because such an advance would aid in settling the China Incident. But now that strategy would not work. If Japanese troops drove as far as Irkutsk on the northwestern shore of Lake Baikal, or even half that distance, Chiang Kai-shek would feel the effect and a general peace might be possible.

And on top of this, with extraordinary disregard for the logic of the situation, Matsuoka blandly declared, *Wagahai wa dōgi gaikō wo shuchō suru*: "I insist upon diplomacy based on moral principles." Japan could not abrogate the Tripartite Pact, he said. (*That would be immoral.*) It would have been better if Japan had not concluded a Neutrality Pact with the Soviet Union in the first place. (*Yet, only two months before, that had been his great achievement.*) Japan should not think in terms of advantages and disadvantages, but should strike now while Germany's war situation was still unclear. (*And so, by breaking a Neutrality Pact with the Soviet Union, demonstrate Japan's moral diplomacy to the world.*)

The effect this had on the gathering as a whole is not recorded, but ex-premier Hiranuma—who was then serving as home minister in Konoe's cabinet—was apparently so astounded by Matsuoka's advocacy of an all-out, immediate war against the Soviet Union that he could not quite believe what he had heard. "Mr. Matsuoka," he exclaimed, "I ask you to give careful thought to the problem confronting us. Are you saying that we should strike the Soviet Union immediately? Are you telling us that as a matter of national policy we should go to war with the Soviet Union at once?" Without the slightest hesitation Matsuoka replied, "Yes, I am."

Hiranuma then asked if preparations were not the prerequisite of action, but Matsuoka hedged by saying that what he wanted was a decision in favor of going North and the right to report that decision to Germany. (*And thus reaffirm Japan's adherence to an alliance with Hitler, aimed at the United States, by attacking the Soviet Union in violation of Japan's solemn pledge to remain neutral.*)

The last word was spoken by Chief of the Army General Staff Sugiyama. "There is no argument with moral diplomacy," he said, "but so long as we are employing a vast army in China at present, we cannot do what you suggest. The supreme command will carry out the preparations, but whether we will strike northward or not cannot now be decided. . . ."[57]

---

[57] For factual material relating to the outbreak of the German-Soviet war, and Japanese attitudes pertaining thereto as revealed in the various top-level conferences mentioned in the text, see Hattori, I, 73-75, 104, 116, 144-58; Tōjō aff., S 343:9, T 36254-57; Kido SKD; Konoe, 83-84; Kenryō Sato, "Dai-Tōa Sensō wo Maneita Shōwa no Dōran," 114-17 (in which it is noted that while the advocates of a positive policy were afraid of missing an opportunity, others argued in behalf of letting the persimmon ripen on the tree—i.e., favored a wait-and-see policy); J, B/VI, 792-803, 810-12, 818-23, and J, B/VII, 926 (in which Tōjō is described as having favored a wait-and-see policy and as having said, on one occasion, "Japan would gain great prestige by attacking the U.S.S.R. at a time when it is ready to fall to the ground like a ripe persimmon"); JRD, "Interrogations," I:49157 (Seizō Arisue), 34-36, 41-45; JRD, "Translation," II: 51903 (Item 18), 6-7; and Feis, 183-87, 209-12, and 219-20.

The Matsuoka, Hiranuma, and Sugiyama quotations are translated from statements attributed to them in Hattori, I, 153-54 and 158.

Konoe (p. 84) notes the holding of *renraku kaigi* (what Hattori describes as *renraku kondankai*) on June 25, 26, 27, 28, 30, and July 1. Konoe also indicates that he

The conference subsequently adjourned with a statement from Matsuoka that he was in basic agreement with the policy submitted by imperial headquarters, and with a promise from Sugiyama that an effort would be made to include Matsuoka's views on "diplomacy" in the draft policy. As a consequence of this promise, Major General Muto, the chief of the military affairs bureau of the war ministry, and Rear Admiral Oka, his naval counterpart, met together that same evening (June 27) to resolve the matter in a manner acceptable to all. This was standard procedure. In cases where members of the cabinet and the supreme command differed, the heads of the military and naval affairs bureaus frequently served as the go-betweens.

On this occasion, General Muto favored revising a key phrase in the imperial headquarters draft in such a way as to make it reflect Matsuoka's view in behalf of a war with the Soviet Union, while preserving at the same time the supreme command's insistence upon the undesirability as well as impossibility of launching an immediate attack. The opposition of Admiral Oka and of the chief of the first bureau (operations) of the army general staff proved sufficient to block the Muto revision. The following day, however, at still another liaison discussion, certain changes were made as a gesture toward bringing the proposed policy into line with the foreign minister's very firm views. In its revised form, the imperial headquarters policy was approved by the Konoe Cabinet on July 1 and by an imperial conference on July 2.[58] Thus it was finally and firmly decided that Japan would adhere to her program of "attempting to contribute to the establishment of world peace through the construction of a Greater East Asia co-prosperity sphere," regardless of the changes that might take place in the world situation.

Japan would endeavor to conclude the China Incident. She would advance to the South to establish a basis of "self-existence and self-defense."[59] She would settle the northern problem in accordance with

---

conferred with the war and navy ministers as a step in determining the government's attitude.

[58] See footnotes 56 and 57 above. On the imperial conference of July 2, the following were also consulted: Tōjō aff., S 343:9-10, T 36258-65 (Tōjō's correction of a statement made during an interrogation on February 13, 1946—an extract from which was introduced by the prosecution, T 10181—accords with other evidence); Tōjō cross-examination, S 348:13, T 36807-8; Tōjō interrog., Feb. 13, 1-13; Kido SKD; Kido interrog., March 11, 705-15; CF 20, IV, 358; IPS Doc. No. 0004, 10-12; JRD, "Translation," II:51903 (Item 18), 6-7; J, B/VI, 812-13, 815; and Feis, 209-18.

[59] Although rather awkward in English, this phrase (*jison jiei*) was a standard one in Japanese documents and speeches of the period.

developments there. To accomplish this program, Japan would eliminate any and all obstacles in her path.

That the United States and Great Britain might prove to be in the "obstacle" category was clearly understood. The preparations necessary for fighting those powers were to be carried out. "In order to achieve her objectives" in the South, the policy literally read, "Japan will not decline a war with England and the United States."

Teikoku wa . . . mokuteki tassei no tame Ei-Bei sen wo jisezu.

Jisezu—"will not decline"—a carefully chosen word which expressed negatively a thought oriented toward the positive: Japan would be ready to use force against anyone who cut across the bow of her driving ambition.

For the time being, Japan would not enter the German-Soviet war. Instead, she would secretly carry out military preparations against the Soviet Union. Although the "spirit" of the Tripartite Pact would constitute the basis of her action, she would nevertheless make her own decisions. In the meantime, she would cautiously engage in diplomatic negotiations. If the German-Soviet war progressed "in a manner favorable for Japan," she would employ force in the North and thus establish "stability" in that region.[60]

In implementing this northern policy, every care would be taken to interfere as little as possible with the maintenance of the basic structure needed for a war against Britain and the United States. In accordance with established policy, however, all-out efforts would be made, "through diplomacy and every other means," to keep the United States from going to war. If the Americans did enter the European conflict, Japan would then join Germany in accordance with the provisions of the Tripartite Pact. The time of attack, and the method, would be decided independently by Japan. Emphasis would be placed on the thorough

[60] Originally, the policy drafted by imperial headquarters had read, ". . . if the German-Soviet war progresses in a manner very favorable for Japan . . . ," but Matsuoka had pounced upon even that limited restriction. On June 27, he had said, "I dislike the word, 'very,' in the phrase 'very favorable.'" In the policy approved on July 2 that distasteful qualifier was not in evidence. The circumstances no longer had to be *very* favorable. Now, if they were simply propitious, Japan would attack her Neutrality Pact neighbor, the Soviet Union.

The president of the privy council, Dr. Hara, noted on July 2 that the existence of the pact might lead to charges of "betrayal" if Japan struck at Russia, but he had an answer: ". . . the Soviet Union is a habitual devotee of faithless conduct. No one will call Japan treacherous if she strikes the Soviet Union. I am fervently praying for the advent of a favorable opportunity to attack." See Hattori, I, 149, 154-55, and 158. On the question of Japan's intentions with respect to war with the Soviet Union, see J, B/IV, 203-4, 219-22, and J, B/VI, 776-842.

strengthening of a wartime structure throughout the country. Special efforts would be devoted to enhancing and consolidating the defense of the homeland.

This was the proposal that Premier Konoe placed before the imperial conference of July 2, 1941. This was the means he offered to achieve Japan's national policy: to contribute to world peace through the establishment of a co-prosperity sphere in Greater East Asia—a policy that was to remain immutable *regardless of changes in the world situation.* No one seems to have understood that changes might occur that would render a rigid adherence to Japan's policy the equivalent of inviting national catastrophe.

Such fear as may have existed in court and other circles that the Kwantung army might react unfavorably to the decision to postpone action in the North was quelled by an assurance given to Marquis Kido by War Minister Tojo that the attitude of the army in Manchuria was one of "calmness and prudence."[61] In line with the imperial conference decision of July 2, however, immediate steps were taken to strengthen Japanese military forces against the possibility of a war with the Soviet Union. In fact, the mobilization and concentration of ground and air units at that time were the greatest in the history of the Japanese army. The Kwantung force alone doubled its personnel strength. Such vast amounts of war matériel were gathered in Korea and Manchuria that, despite later inroads, about 50 per cent remained in the area when the Pacific war ended in 1945.[62]

The order to attack the Soviet Union was not given. Instead, attention shifted first to southern French Indo-China and then, as 1941 waned, toward the last chance for success that many saw, or thought they saw, in the Japanese-American conversations taking place in Washington. As Japan became more involved with the United States and as the German offensive against the Soviet Union began encountering serious difficulties, the possibility of a Japanese drive into the Soviet Far East faded. The desire to strike in the North still existed, but the capability and the opportunity did not.[63]

[61] Kido SKD; extract from "Kido Nikki" for June 28, 1941, S 108:9, T 10036-37 (subject to revision); and Kido corresp.

[62] Hattori, I, 158-59, and J, B/VI, 815-16.

[63] On further Japanese plans, after July 2, for war with the Soviet Union, including some which envisaged creating an excuse to abrogate the Neutrality Pact by making such far-reaching demands upon Moscow that the Kremlin would be obliged to refuse, see J, B/VI, 795-803. The idea of going North in 1941 was abandoned by the army

The July 2 imperial conference decision was both a defeat and a victory for Matsuoka. His failure to secure approval for an immediate attack northward was counterbalanced by the declaration that Japan was ready to fight Britain and the United States to attain the Empire's objectives in the South. According to the testimony of a well-informed general, this statement of Japan's determination to forge ahead regardless of the consequences was made rather lightly. Neither the army nor the navy believed that occupying southern French Indo-China would involve Japan in war with the Western powers.[64] According to the general, Japan's admirals had no intention of fighting Britain and the United States, but they wanted a greater share of the budget and a larger allocation of war matériel. By insisting upon the inclusion of positively worded phrases in the July 2 policy, they automatically created a situation in which their demands for money and matériel became more meaningful and more imperative. The army agreed to the insertions even though it, too, had no intention of fighting such a war and was unprepared to do so.

Testimony of this type is obviously difficult to evaluate—credibility must be weighed against the source. Such testimony nevertheless reveals once again an aspect of the decision-making process, and of the approach of Japan's leaders to the problems confronting them, that was to involve the Japanese nation repeatedly in crises which the government had not foreseen and for which it proved hopelessly unprepared. When that happened, a new and cautious attitude, a backtracking or a change of direction, did not emerge in any real or fundamental sense. Temporary adjustments might be made to tide the nation over the moment, but nothing more than that. Thus each new crisis simply lured Japan's nominal leaders into taking another fateful step in line with the do-or-die psychology by which they gradually entrapped themselves. Nowhere is this clearer, perhaps, than in the circumstances under which Japan and the United States now came into open confrontation.

This final forming of the ranks happened very quickly. On June 17, 1941, Japan broke off her negotiations with the Netherlands East Indies. Soon thereafter, very much in the manner of the previous September,

---

division of imperial headquarters on August 9, 1941 (Hattori, I, 162). The final top-level decision to postpone any military action against the USSR until at least the spring of 1942 was made by early September 1941. The Tribunal also found that, despite the existence of the Neutrality Pact, Japan rendered aid to Germany in the war against Russia (see J, B/VI, 792, 810-16, and 818-26).

[64] JRD, "Interrogations," I:49157 (Seizō Arisue), 44-45.

the government in Tokyo began lodging demands with the French for a Japanese occupation of southern Indo-China. By mid-July, the situation had progressed to the point where Vichy had to choose between an occupation accomplished by force and one concluded through "diplomatic negotiation" and "mutual consent." The United States was aware of what was in store through "Magic"—the interception and deciphering, despite the cover of code, of Japanese diplomatic messages exchanged between the foreign office in Tokyo and Japan's representatives abroad.[65] But Washington was powerless to forestall a Japanese inroad in that region by the use of counterforce, and last-minute American efforts to invite Japan to participate in a multilateral guarantee of the neutralization of Indo-China proved unavailing. A so-called protocol of mutual defense was duly concluded by Vichy with the Empire of Japan, whereby the French agreed, under duress, to permit the "peaceful" entry of Japanese military forces into southern French Indo-China.[66]

[65] The United States intercepted a two-part circular (No. 1390) sent from Tōkyō on July 2, 1941, giving the gist but not the full text of the decision reached at the imperial conference on that day. Nothing was said, in the circular, about Japan being ready to fight Britain and the United States to achieve her objectives in the South, but the following statement was included: "Although every means available shall be resorted to in order to prevent the United States from joining the war, if need be, Japan shall act in accordance with the Three-Power Pact and shall decide when and how force will be employed." *PHA*, Part 12, 1-2. According to Feis, 219, the text of this circular "was available to the heads of the American government by July 8 at the latest." See also the "Canton to Tokyo" intercept in *PHA*, Part 14, 1399. Hattori, I, 158, states that the imperial conference decision of July 2 became known to the Kremlin through the Soviet spies, Richard Sorge and Hidemi Ozaki. Although Hattori does not say so, Ozaki presumably learned of the decision from Prince Konoe (to whom he had access) or from a member of Konoe's staff, and then passed it on to Sorge.

"Magic" was the name given to "the cryptocomputer that simulated the code apparatus used by the Japanese for key messages out of Tokyo" (*Newsweek*, May 14, 1956, 119). See *PHA*, Part 3, 1124-39, 1146-47; Ballantine cross-examination, T 10922-24 and 10951; and Theobald, *The Final Secret of Pearl Harbor*, 32-39.

[66] See the Tōjō references in footnote 51 above; J, B/VII, 930-33; JRD Monograph No. 150, 8-9; Suzuki aff., S 333:9, T 35198-99; JRD, "Interrogations," I:49157 (Seizō Arisue), 46-47; Konoe, 117 (in which the prince declares that the "leaders of the government" were able to beat down the demand for an immediate war against the Soviet Union but were forced to agree to the occupation of southern Indo-China as "a sort of consolation prize"); and Feis, 198-99, 206-7, 210, 212, 213, 219, 224, 226-41, 246-50 (on information available to the United States concerning Japanese intentions and on the American attitude with regard thereto).

The Germans apparently did not cooperate very readily with Japan's repeated requests for German assistance in persuading Pétain to consent to Japan's demands. The thanks subsequently extended by Tōkyō to Berlin for its cooperation need not necessarily be regarded as a contradiction of Tōjō's claim that the Germans did not help Japan in the matter. Tōjō also denied that there was a connection between Japan's advance into southern French Indo-China and the outbreak of the German-Soviet war. He further scoffed at the idea that the occupation of that area was prompted by the desire to establish bases there for an aggressive attack aimed at the southern regions. See Tōjō

The forbearance which had previously been shown in Washington toward Japan's trick-or-treat policy in Asia now came abruptly to an end on July 26, 1941, with the freezing of Japanese assets in the United States. When Britain, the Dominions, and the Netherlands East Indies followed suit, Japan suddenly faced the prospect of a total economic blockade. At long last Washington had decided that such a drastic policy represented the only remaining means, short of war, by which the decision-makers in Tokyo could be shocked into realizing that the United States would not permit Japan further to endanger America's security by continual nibbling at the outposts of American and Allied defense in the Far East. It was hoped that such a shock might awaken Japan to reality and encourage her to adopt a policy of conciliation. The freezing order was explained to the Japanese government in precisely the same terms which that government subsequently used to defend the action that had prompted the order: under the prevailing circumstances the measure was unavoidable, but it need not necessarily be permanent.

The American move was an appropriate response not only to the Japanese occupation of southern French Indo-China but to the entire trend of Japanese activity on the international scene. It was appropriate, and long overdue, but in the end it failed. In Japan, it did cause shock, and dismay, but these reactions did not produce the anticipated awakening. Had the structure of decision-making been different, had the supreme command—especially the army general staff—held a less preeminent position in affairs of state, the economic-blockade approach might have worked. In 1941, however, this new American measure of restraint was regarded as the final, major link in a chain of encirclement which Tokyo accused the Americans, the British, the Chinese, and the Dutch—the ABCD powers—of drawing around the island Empire. As seen in Tokyo, the encirclement was without cause, and represented the culmination of years of effort on the part of those powers to deny Japan her rightful place in the world by destroying her only available means of self-existence and self-defense.[67]

aff., S 343:6, T 36235; S 343:8-9, T 36252-54; S 343:9 and 10, T 36260 and 36265. An explanation may lie in a statement by Kenryō Satō, who was then chief of the military affairs section, to the effect that he slept in the same bed with imperial headquarters but did not have the same dream (*dōshō imu*): IGHQ was interested in southern French Indo-China as a base for war in the South but Satō and other officers in the war ministry were only concerned with settling the China Incident and securing self-sufficiency in "Lesser East Asia" (the French Indo-China-Thailand area). See Kenryō Satō, "Dai-Tōa Sensō wo Maneita Shōwa no Dōran," 106-11 and 117.

[67] From his postwar affidavit it would appear that the lord keeper of the privy seal, Marquis Kido, personally took this development in stride, although he recognized the

The views of General Tojo are a case in point.[68] In interrogations at Sugamo Prison in February 1946, Tojo attempted to explain his avowed belief that in ultimately going to war against the Western powers, Japan had been "exercising the right of justifiable self-defense in the face of challenge." He began by referring to an article which had appeared in the *Japan Advertiser* in August 1921. It had been argued then that Japan was "absolutely dependent on the continent for food-stuffs and raw materials"—so much so that she could not permit "even temporary interference" with her access to that source of supply. So long as peaceful trade was maintained, no problem would arise. But if the flow of products from the continent were suspended for even so brief a period as a month, "great suffering and calamity" would result. Conse-quently, Japan's demands on her neighbors in Asia, aimed at maintain-ing the regular flow of goods so vital to the economic life of the Empire, were "certainly not unreasonable." Nor were they contrary to interna-tional practice. In fact, Japan's approach was "not unlike relations between the United States and Mexico." The issue involved was actually "a matter of life or death to Japan."

Both in interrogations and in his later testimony in court, Tojo tended to emphasize the growing sense of frustration that had prompted Japan, in the end, to resort to drastic measures. "Although Japan was not prepared," he said, "she had been challenged and had to fight, no matter what the state of her preparedness was." American and British aid to Chiang Kai-shek prolonged Chinese resistance and hampered Japa-nese efforts to secure a settlement on the continent. As the various restrictions imposed by the American government cut off the flow of necessary goods and matériel, Japan turned to the South to obtain the raw materials she needed. In Thailand and Indo-China she found her efforts to secure the rice and rubber that were vital to her existence blocked by America and Britain. In the Netherlands East Indies the "hostile attitude" of the Dutch left Japan no choice but to break off negotiations. And then, late in July 1941, the United States froze Japan's

---

effect it was having on others. Those not versed in diplomatic affairs, he later wrote, regarded the freezing order as America's first step toward war (S 293:10, T 30939).

[68] For Tōjō's views on the "ABCD encirclement," some of which are summarized here, see Tōjō interrog., Feb. 18, 4, Feb. 26, 1-5, and Feb. 27, 1-4; Tōjō aff., S 343:7-8, T 36241-51; S 343:11, T 36272-78; S 343:9-10, T 36262-63 (the difference between the Japanese and the English here is probably the result of a revision, perhaps made by one of Tōjō's lawyers, which did not find its way into the Japanese text); S 343:19, T 36338-44; S 343:20-21, T 36352-55; and Tōjō cross-examination, S 347:2-3, T 36648-55.

assets, placing the Empire "in extreme danger." This was an "unjust" and "hostile" action, comparing "not . . . unfavorably with war itself."

Although Anglo-American assistance to China was of major concern, there were other pressures as well. The stationing of the "main strength" of the American fleet in the Pacific, Tojo said, "seemed to the Japanese like having the fleet placed right under their very nose . . . a great fleet like that, so concentrated, could be moved by a single order at any time. . . ." There was "the boastful talk of the American admiral who said that if a Japanese-American war were to break out, the Japanese fleet would be sunk in a matter of weeks." There was also the statement of the British prime minister that in case of war between Japan and the United States, a British declaration would follow "within the hour." According to Tojo, it was thus clear that "Japan was being coerced by a circle of force directed against her by America, Britain, China, and the Dutch."

Tojo did not limit himself to such "obvious" threats as the aid to China and the presence of the fleet at Pearl Harbor. He also cited Roosevelt's "arsenal of democracy" speech; the reported expenditure between July 1940 and May 1941 of more than thirty-three billion dollars for military expansion; the establishment of a new base of operations in the 13th naval district in Alaska; the construction of a two-ocean fleet; the strengthening of the American air force; the State Department's insistence upon upholding the *status quo* in French Indo-China; the recommended evacuation of American women and children from eastern Asia (an attempt to intimidate Japan by implication); the granting of approval to Pan-American World Airways to establish an air route linking Manila and Singapore (a charge rendered rather ironical by the fact that, in 1939, Tojo had served briefly as a member of a group concerned with establishing the Great Japan Aviation Company, Inc.);[69] the presidential proclamation, on May 27, 1941, of a state of unlimited national emergency; and the declaration made earlier that same month by the Dutch foreign minister to the effect that the Netherlands East Indies were prepared to respond to a challenge at any time. (According to Tojo, Japan "had to fight" when challenged, but the same argument apparently did not extend to the Dutch.)

Even the Far Eastern itineraries of American and British officials

[69] Tōjō's connection with the establishment of the *Dai Nippon Kōkū Kabushiki-kaisha* is noted in his cabinet secretariat personnel file.

assumed a menacing significance in Japan. An innocuous statement by King George VI, at the opening of Parliament in November 1941, to the effect that the British government was concerned about the situation in East Asia was duly noted in Tokyo, as was the laying of mines in the immediate vicinity of Manila and Singapore.[70]

The King's remarks to Parliament could hardly be called provocative. The mines at Manila and Singapore were not laid to sink vessels plying a peaceful trade. They would be entirely harmless to those who came with harmless intent. Undoubtedly Japanese waters were similarly protected.

Even such measures as might legitimately be regarded as offensive in nature could be described as a "threat to Japan" only if one automatically agreed, for some inexplicable reason, that 1941 had no relation whatever to the decade of violence and aggression which had begun in 1931.

How many of Tojo's colleagues in the cabinet and the supreme command saw the developments of 1940-1941 in perspective, and how many in acute distortion, will never accurately be known. The vantage point afforded by the passage of time, a willingness to allow the benefit of the doubt, and a reading of the entire record suggest that a number of Japan's leaders, and Tojo in particular, suffered from greater occupational astigmatism than is normally found in men charged with formulating national responses to international problems.

The relationship of cause and effect may have been understood in the narrow sense, but that understanding was never applied broadly to the confrontation of Japan and the ABCD powers. Tojo seems never to have recognized that many of the developments he found so irritating were designed to provide for America's own defense and hence were aimed at Japan only to the extent that Japan threatened the United States. Nor did he permit himself this dangerous thought: American justification for measures specifically directed against Japan lay in the prior acts of aggression committed by His Majesty's Empire. Thus, the problem of 1941 is carried back and back, to 1937 and to 1931, to the murder of Chang Tso-lin and to the twenty-one demands, and indeed even to 1905, when the fear, the jealousy, and the misunderstanding all seem

[70] See the citations in footnote 68 above. For more on the encirclement issue, see also JRD, "Translation," II:51903 (Item 18), 8 and 20-29; Hattori, I, 41-43, 58, 78, 88, 122, 132-33, 173-74 (in which various measures are noted, although not necessarily described as "encirclement" in so many words); JRD, "Interrogations," I:48484 (Higashikuni), 133; and J, B/VII, 864-65, 903-12, and 990-1000.

to have begun. In the final analysis, the Empire of Japan inexorably encircled itself.[71]

[71] In a conversation with the Japanese ambassador on August 8, 1941, Secretary of State Hull remarked that "today he had told press correspondents that there is no occasion for any nation in the world that is law-abiding and peaceful to become encircled by anybody except itself. [This is a judgment, in the case of Japan, which the record fully justifies.] The Secretary [also] said that while in Japan the press was being officially inspired in ways calculated to inflame public opinion this Government was not treating Japan in any such way but was doing all that it could to deprecate agitation. . . . The Ambassador replied that he thought that the efforts being made to inspire the press in Japan were motivated purely by a desire to invigorate the Japanese people and were not inconsistent with a sincere desire on the part of the Japanese Government to improve relations with the United States." *Foreign Relations (Japan: 1931-1941)*, II, 551.

CHAPTER 9

The Quest for Peace

By the time President Roosevelt had signed the executive order freezing Japanese assets in the United States, the government in Tokyo had undergone another of the frequent changes characteristic of the political scene of that day. In terms of what the man-in-the-street could see, this latest shift did not appear especially drastic. The second Konoe Cabinet resigned en masse, to be succeeded by the third Konoe Cabinet—the only noteworthy difference being the absence of Mr. Matsuoka from the revised line-up. The problems faced by the new cabinet were essentially the same as those which had troubled the old, except that with each passing day the need for a solution of those problems grew more imperative. For the comparative few who constituted the ruling elite, however, the removal of Matsuoka signified high-level recognition of the fact that so long as he remained foreign minister a diplomatic settlement with the United States was not very likely. This was by no means the only element in Matsuoka's fall from favor, but it was at least a factor.

Dissatisfaction with the handling of Japan's foreign affairs—with Matsuoka's bull-in-a-chinashop approach to many fragile issues—had been growing for some time, especially within the supreme command. After the conclusion of the Tripartite Pact Matsuoka had proved a disappointment, and—as time passed—more and more of a problem. He seemed to think that because he was foreign minister he should make foreign policy. And to do that, he involved himself in matters within the prerogative of the supreme command, a holy of holies that had never successfully been challenged. By the beginning of 1941 Matsuoka had already gone far toward antagonizing the decision-making cadre in imperial headquarters by frequently urging an attack upon Singapore. His failure to appreciate problems of military tactics and strategy and his pro-German myopia had led his colleagues to fetter the initiative that he so clearly had wanted to exercise on his trip to Europe. It was not that the supreme command was necessarily opposed to Matsuoka's views, but merely that the army and navy were not prepared to do what he was suggesting at that particular time. The general staffs were jealous of their own decision-making powers, which had grown enormously in every sphere since 1937. They were not disposed toward letting a civilian foreign minister, no matter how chauvinistic, intrude upon policy-oriented functions that they now regarded as primarily their own.

Ill-will between Matsuoka and the supreme command deepened over political strategy toward French Indo-China and Thailand and again over the question of Japan's proper response to the German-Soviet war. In both cases, Matsuoka made a nuisance of himself, stepping on supreme-command toes in the process. He was also blocking the only avenue down which the Japanese government could travel that did not lead directly to war. Ensuring through an alliance with Germany that Japan would not be isolated diplomatically was one thing, but ignoring an opportunity to talk the United States into a "reasonable" frame of mind, simply out of a misplaced concern for that alliance, was quite another.

From the moment of his return from Europe, Matsuoka had adopted a hostile attitude toward the Hull-Nomura conversations, which had grown out of the private endeavors of two Maryknoll missionaries, Bishop James E. Walsh and Father James M. Drought. For three whole weeks Matsuoka had managed to ignore the desire of his colleagues to respond quickly and favorably to what they regarded as the "American" initiative exhibited in a proposal that had arrived in Tokyo on April 18, 1941. Although no one knew it at the time, this "draft understanding" had actually been written by an imperial army colonel on temporary duty at the Japanese embassy in Washington.[1]

Before departing for the American capital, Admiral Nomura had traveled on the Asian continent, visiting key Japanese generals and their staffs in Korea, Manchuria, and China to discuss his new assignment with them, to pick up ideas, and to obtain the "understanding" of the armies in the field (a revealing indication of the role of field commanders in the formulation of Japan's foreign policy in the period in question).[2] Upon his return to Tokyo, Nomura had also spoken with the chief of the army general staff and the vice-minister of war.[3] He had expressed the hope that he would receive the cooperation of the authorities at the center. He had also specifically requested that an army officer

[1] Colonel Hideo Iwakuro, who had been the chief of the army affairs section (*gunjika*) of the military affairs bureau (*gunmukyoku*) before going to Washington. See Butow, "The Hull-Nomura Conversations: A Fundamental Misconception," *American Historical Review*, Vol. LXV, No. 4 (July 1960), 822-26.

[2] Nomura visited Generals Minami, Umezu, and Nishio (respectively: governor-general of Korea, commander of the Kwantung army, and commander-in-chief of the Japanese forces in China).

[3] Sugiyama and Anami.

with a thorough knowledge of the China Incident, and of problems pertaining thereto, be sent to Washington to assist him. Since the army at that time had reason to share Nomura's desire for success, the admiral's request had received prompt consideration. On the recommendation of Maj. Gen. Muto, who headed the military affairs bureau, War Minister Tojo had ordered the chief of the army affairs section of that bureau to proceed to Washington to help Nomura in his difficult mission.[4]

When Matsuoka had first heard about the "draft understanding," he had immediately assumed that his recent suggestion to the American ambassador in Moscow to the effect that President Roosevelt should *gamble* on Japan's sincerity had borne fruit. But when he had subsequently been told that the proposal was connected with the efforts of Walsh and Drought, his buoyant mood had suddenly changed, and he had become sulky and uncooperative. On May 8, during an audience with the Emperor, Matsuoka had even threatened to resign if Japan's handling of the American problem resulted in a policy running counter to her obligations toward Germany and Italy. This had prompted Premier Konoe to extend a secret invitation to War Minister Tojo and Navy Minister Oikawa to discuss ways and means of coping effectively with the foreign minister's attitude. The three men had met at Konoe's Ogikubo residence on the evening of May 9 and had decided that close liaison should be maintained in the future, not only with regard to Matsuoka but also on matters pertaining to Japan's relations with the United States.

For a time thereafter, the immediate attention of all concerned had been directed toward reaching a decision on policy for the South and then, briefly, on the even more fundamental issue raised by the outbreak of the German-Soviet war. With the solution of these problems on July 2, the question of what to do about Matsuoka had reentered Konoe's mind. After the imperial conference adjourned on that day, Konoe had privately told Kido that he was finding it difficult to grasp Matsuoka's true intentions. From that moment on, relations between the premier and foreign minister had gone from bad to worse, with Konoe frequently complaining to the lord privy seal that he could not fathom what Matsuoka had in mind.

The arrival of a so-called oral statement from Secretary Hull, together with a proposed basis for negotiations, precipitated a crisis.

[4] Butow, "The Hull-Nomura Conversations," 822-24.

Although Hull's phraseology was suitably diplomatic, his statement was interpreted as meaning that the American government could not trust Japan's foreign minister. Matsuoka was furious. He called the Hull message a national humiliation—a page from the book of the Kaiser whose rantings had forced the French foreign minister, Delcassé, out of office in 1905 at the time of the first Moroccan crisis. At a liaison conference held on July 10, Matsuoka vigorously attacked the desire of his colleagues to negotiate with the United States. He demanded that the oral statement be returned to Washington immediately and that the negotiations be broken off. The only question, he declared, was when and how this should be done.

That evening Prince Konoe secretly discussed the foreign minister's disturbing attitude with the war, navy, and home ministers. Two days later, at another liaison conference, the army and navy jointly presented views which indicated a desire to continue the negotiations with the United States—at least until Japan's pending occupation of southern French Indo-China was completed. Matsuoka finally gave his consent to the preparation of a counterproposal to the United States based on the views of the army and navy. After the liaison conference adjourned, a meeting on what might be called the "secretary level" drafted Japan's "final plan." This was the work of Maj. Gen. Muto; his naval counterpart, Rear Admiral Oka; Mr. Terasaki, the head of the American bureau of the foreign office; Chief Cabinet Secretary Tomita; and Mr. Saito, a foreign office adviser who was a confidant of Matsuoka's.[5] Despite the prominent role of the military in all these proceedings and their desire to respond to the United States as soon as possible, Matsuoka continued his delaying tactics. While using illness as an excuse not to look at the final plan drafted by the secretary group, Matsuoka nevertheless felt well enough to meet with various individuals—including the German ambassador, to whom he presumably revealed all that he knew, as was his custom. This further incensed the army and navy.

On July 14, Matsuoka belatedly condescended to let Saito explain the draft to him, with the result that Japan's final plan, incorporating revisions by the foreign minister, was at last ready to be cabled to Washington. But even then Matsuoka conducted a rear-guard action. Everyone else was anxious to send it off at once, but not the foreign minister. He wanted to reject Hull's oral statement and then, after several more days had elapsed, dispatch Japan's counterproposal. The

[5] The head of the American bureau of the foreign office was Tarō Terasaki; a younger brother, Hidenari, was first secretary at the Japanese embassy in Washington.

rejection would indicate Japan's inability to continue the negotiations unless the American government withdrew its oral statement. Konoe and the army and navy favored sending both items together so as not to create more obstacles and risk a rupture of the negotiations. Late that night, ignoring the wishes of his colleagues and the efforts of Prince Konoe to obtain his cooperation through the mediation of Saito, Matsuoka arbitrarily cabled the rejection to Washington without the counter-proposal. The next day, July 15, adding insult to injury, he directed one of his subordinates to inform the Germans confidentially of the contents of the final plan, which had not even been sent as yet to the United States.

Again Konoe consulted the war, navy, and home ministers. Tojo assumed the initiative by declaring that he had done his best to work with the foreign minister but that cooperation with Matsuoka was no longer possible. Either the foreign minister would have to go or the cabinet would have to resign. The other three were in absolute agreement with this—the only problem being the best procedure to follow. If Matsuoka alone were forced out, he and others of similar orientation would have an opportunity to create more trouble by claiming that the Japanese government was giving in to American pressure and was accepting foreign interference in its internal affairs. A final decision was briefly postponed to allow time for further thought and consultation. Konoe journeyed to the imperial villa at Hayama to inform the Emperor of the cabinet crisis. He also apprised Marquis Kido of the facts pertaining to the affair and suggested that Home Minister Hiranuma would be a good choice to succeed him as premier. Without indicating agreement or disagreement, Kido advised Konoe to take prompt action one way or another.

The following day, July 16, Konoe met privately with those cabinet officers who regularly participated in liaison conferences: War Minister Tojo, Navy Minister Oikawa, Home Minister Hiranuma, and Lt. Gen. Teiichi Suzuki, the president of the cabinet planning board—an organization of growing importance in the decision-making scheme of things. Matsuoka, who would normally have attended, was not present. The assembled ministers not only favored a general resignation of the cabinet but agreed that it should be carried out that same evening. At 6:30 p.m. an extraordinary cabinet session was held at which the concurrence of the other ministers was obtained. Matsuoka, who was ill in bed, had no choice but to accede. Prince Konoe submitted the cabinet resignation to the Emperor at Hayama at approximately 9:00 p.m. and then returned to the capital to tender a late evening report to his colleagues.[6]

The cabinet's resignation was followed by the usual gathering of the senior statesmen at the palace.[7] In view of the negotiations with the United States, the ex-premiers decided that Konoe was the only suitable person available for the premiership. His past experience would stand him in good stead, and the continuity provided by redesignating him premier would permit the negotiations to progress without serious interruption. As a result, shortly after 5:00 p.m. on July 17 the prince again received the imperial mandate to form a cabinet.[8] He completed the task within twenty-four hours, a record made possible by the comparatively few changes in cabinet assignments. Tojo and Oikawa remained as war and navy ministers. Hiranuma relinquished his old home ministry post but joined the new cabinet as minister without portfolio. Matsuoka's reluctantly discarded mantle fell to Vice-Admiral Teijiro Toyoda, who had been minister of commerce and industry in the second Konoe Cabinet. The importance of both the army and navy in affairs of state was emphasized by the fact that seven of the fourteen ministers comprising the new line-up were military men—four generals and three admirals.[9]

At 7:00 p.m. on July 18, Konoe reported the names of the cabinet officers to the throne. At 8:50 the investiture took place within the palace. At 9:45 the cabinet held its first meeting. Later, in a statement

[6] On Matsuoka's adverse attitude, the desire of the military to follow through on the Hull-Nomura conversations, and the resignation of the second Konoe Cabinet, see Kido SKD; Kido "Nikki" and aff., S 293:9-10, T 30933-37; S 109:6, T 10155-56 (revised, 10666); S 109:7, T 10161-65 (revised, 10666-67); Konoe, 62-78, 89-97; Tōjō aff., S 343:4-5, T 36218-31; and S 343:10, T 36266-67; Tōjō cross-examination, S 347:8, T 36691; Kenryō Satō, "Dai-Tōa Sensō wo Maneita Shōwa no Dōran," 111-14; Hattori, I, 121-23, 125-26, 128-29, and 167-72; Mitarai direct examination, S 173:6, T 17796-97; Foreign Relations (Japan: 1931-1941), II, 485-86 (the text of Hull's oral statement of June 21, 1941); JRD, "Interrogations," I:49157 (Seizō Arisue), 40-41; PHA, Part 20, 3986-89, 3991, 3995-97; CF 20, III, 253; IMTFE, "Roling Opinion," 117-18; Feis, 193-95, 219-26; Yabe, II, 307-20; and Kenryō Satō, Tōjō Hideki to Taiheiyō Sensō, 170-81.

[7] The jūshin kaigi began at 1:00 p.m. on July 17 and adjourned an hour later. In addition to Kido and Vice-Grand Chamberlain Kanroji (who conveyed the imperial wishes to the gathering), the following were present: Abe, Hara, Hayashi, Hirota, Okada, Wakatsuki, and Yonai.

[8] On the formation of the third Konoe Cabinet, see Kido SKD; Kido "Nikki" and aff., S 109:7-8, T 10166-68 (revised 11138-39); and S 293:10, T 30937-39; Konoe, 96-97; PHA, Part 20, 3997; Hattori, I, 172; IPS chart on cabinets; Facts on File: 1941, 300J; Japan Year Book, 1941-42, 131-32; Tolischus, 167-68; and Feis, 229-31.

[9] The seven military members of the fourteen-minister cabinet were Lt. Gen. Hideki Tōjō (war minister), Admiral Koshirō Oikawa (navy minister), Admiral Teijirō Toyoda (foreign minister and concurrently overseas affairs minister), Lt. Gen. Teiichi Suzuki (president of the cabinet planning board and minister of state without portfolio), Vice-Admiral Seizō Sakonji (commerce and industry minister), Surgeon Lt. Gen. Chikahiko Koizumi (welfare minister), and Lt. Gen. Heisuke Yanagawa (minister of state without portfolio).

to the nation, the prince declared: "The policy of the country has already been fixed . . . it now remains for us to put it into practice with decision and speed."[10] The attitude expressed in that single sentence summed up the program of the third Konoe Cabinet: the policy formalized at the imperial conference of July 2 would remain unchanged.

More revealing than any public pronouncement, however, was information obtained through "Magic" and other sources. Within three days after Konoe's third cabinet was formed, the United States government secretly learned, through an intercepted message sent by Japan's new foreign minister, that the Tripartite Pact still served as "the keystone of Japanese national policy" and that there would be "no departure" from that principle.[11]

The new cabinet was scarcely in office before it became apparent that American feeling was turning more and more against Japan. The Emperor became extremely concerned, raising the question with Marquis Kido practically every time the lord privy seal was received in audience. This concern, which deepened after the freezing of Japanese assets on July 26, was expressed in specific terms on July 31. On that day the Emperor received Admiral Nagano, the chief of the naval general staff, to whom he put various questions. After Nagano departed, the Emperor told Kido that the naval chief had said that he wanted to avoid war with the United States, if at all possible. The admiral seemed to be strongly opposed to the Tripartite Pact and to feel that no adjustment could be made with the United States so long as Japan adhered to that treaty. If Japan lost her sources of oil through a failure to reach a settlement with the United States, she would be left with only a two-year stockpile—a quantity which would actually be consumed in eighteen months in the event of war. In such a situation, Nagano had said, Japan would have no other choice but to sally forth![12]

Upon being asked by the Emperor about the prospects for a great naval victory if Japan and America fought, the admiral had replied that it was doubtful whether or not Japan could even win, to say nothing of achieving a decisive victory of the type gained at the time of the Russo-Japanese war. Thus, the Emperor had arrived at the conclusion—and so

[10] Tolischus, 167-68.
[11] Feis, 229-30.
[12] On the Emperor's growing concern, the Nagano audience of July 31, and the Kido-Konoe conversations of August 2 and 7 (which follow in the text), see Kido SKD; Kido aff. and "Nikki," S 293:10-11, T 30939-47; Kido "Nikki" for August 2 and 7, 1941, S 109: 11-12, T 10196-201 and 10667-68 (even as corrected, the translation requires revision); and Kido corresp.

informed Kido—that it would be extremely dangerous for Japan to wage a war of desperation. Kido tried to reassure His Majesty by advising him that the admiral's views were on the "simple" side. The existence of the Tripartite Pact was already recognized by the United States. How would it look, from the standpoint of respect for treaties, if Japan were now to abrogate the alliance? The situation, Kido said, was not yet beyond solution. There should still be various ways of bringing about an adjustment of relations with the United States. Persistent and constructive efforts should be made toward that end. The premier would be asked to give careful consideration to the matter.[13]

Two days later, on August 2, Konoe told Kido of his uneasiness over the problem of cabinet cooperation with the supreme command, pointing out that even within naval circles the argument in favor of using force against the United States was gradually coming to the fore. Here was a new element in the situation. Until at least June 1941 the navy had wanted to avoid taking on both Britain and the United States in a war in which its responsibility for victory or defeat would be very large. In theory, it still wanted to avoid such a conflict, but not at the price of being denied access to the fuel that was the lifeblood of its fleet. If negotiations with the United States were not concluded soon, Japan would reach the point of diminishing returns. Rather than be put in that position, the navy would seek a decision at sea. That was why Konoe found the argument in favor of force becoming prominent within the very group that had earlier acted, at times, as a restraining influence upon army colleagues who did not always appreciate the nature of naval

[13] The privy seal's outlook was very optimistic, especially in the light of the freezing order of July 26 and Hull's apparent intention, conveyed to Ambassador Nomura on July 23, not to continue negotiations for which there now seemed so little basis. Except for Matsuoka, the belief that Japan could and should reach a settlement with the United States, while maintaining the alliance with Germany, was by no means uncommon among Japan's top leaders. The prevailing view was that conflicts of interest could be reconciled. The desire for success in the Washington negotiations was real enough, but it was fettered from beginning to end by a determination not to abrogate the Tripartite Pact ("not to break faith with Germany") and not to agree to any program incompatible with the envisaged construction by Japan of a new order in East Asia. That had been the essence of an agreement of views on the part of Konoe and Kido on April 19, the day after the arrival of the Nomura cable containing the "draft understanding." That was still the sentiment in late July, and it was to prevail from then through each successive crisis in the subsequent negotiations. When Japan had originally concluded the pact with Germany, there had been some concern about the effect the new alliance would have on Japanese-American relations. Notwithstanding that concern, the government had decided to go ahead anyway. Then, in the spring of 1941, the same government had elected to open negotiations with the United States despite the anticipated "chill" such negotiations would produce in Japan's relations with Germany and Italy. Many of the difficulties the government encountered were thus of its own making.

warfare. Kido advised Konoe to talk in detail with the war and navy ministers about Japan's basic national policies. If Konoe could not reach an agreement of views with the service ministers, a resignation by the prince might be unavoidable. In that event, Kido said, there would be no alternative but to make the army and navy accept the responsibility for controlling the situation.

Coming only two weeks after the investiture of the cabinet, Kido's advice seems to have surprised Konoe somewhat, perhaps because Kido had generally tried to dissuade the prince from rushing headlong toward resignation whenever a crisis threatened. The prince found the advice gratifying, since he had expected Kido to say that a resignation would be embarrassing. The fact that the lord privy seal himself envisaged such a course in certain circumstances was reassuring.[14]

Three days later, on August 5, Konoe informed Kido that he had decided to seek a personal meeting with President Roosevelt in order to discuss Japanese-American differences. On August 7, the day on which this proposal was transmitted to Washington, Konoe again called at Kido's office in the palace. On this occasion, the lord privy seal revealed his thoughts to the premier in great detail.[15] Prefacing his remarks by saying that the current situation was truly grave, Kido told Konoe that the matter could not be put off from day to day. A policy decision must be reached promptly by means of thorough discussion between the cabinet and the supreme command.

According to the information he had acquired to date, Kido said, it appeared that concurrent operations against the United States and the Soviet Union would be very difficult. In a sense, the whole problem facing Japan had been reduced to a very simple factor, and that was *oil*. The navy maintained that there was only enough for eighteen months

---

[14] The particular importance of Marquis Kido in this period lay not only in his position as *naidaijin*—literally, "the inside-minister"—in daily contact with the Emperor, but also in the fact that because of that position many persons looked to him for advice. Although the lord privy seal was rarely present at audiences granted to officials of state (and, indeed, could be present only if specifically invited by the Emperor), he invariably discussed the details of such audiences with the Emperor before and after they took place. He also frequently met with whoever was involved: the premier, the foreign minister, the service ministers, or the chiefs of staff (though the military were perhaps somewhat less habitual callers at his office than were the civilians). Such meetings usually took place immediately after the imperial audience concerned, but they could take place beforehand. Kido was also available for consultation even when no audience was involved. Those who regularly called on the lord privy seal frequently crossed the line between the mere reporting of what was happening and the more significant discussing of what should be done, thus giving Marquis Kido an opportunity to air his views if he was so inclined.

[15] On the Kido-Konoe conversations of August 2 and 7, 1941, see the references cited in footnote 12 above.

of war. The army's supply would last for roughly a year. If these estimates were correct, the conclusion was inescapable that Japan could not possibly fight a war of certain victory against the United States.

There were only two sources of oil close to Japan—the Netherlands East Indies and northern Sakhalin. It would be hard to invade the Indies without first conquering Singapore, the Philippines, and other vital points. During such operations, the oil fields would be destroyed, thus making it very arduous for Japan to acquire what she needed within the eighteen months of grace provided by her current reserves. If Japan moved against the Netherlands East Indies, the United States would go to war against Japan. In that event, even assuming that oil would be forthcoming from the wells of the Indies, there would still be the problem of transporting it to Japan. The danger of doing so under the threat of Anglo-American submarine and air attacks would be very great. In fact, it was extremely doubtful that Japan would be able to succeed. If there had been any miscalculation either about the oil on hand or about how long it would last, a grave situation would inevitably arise and Japan would be forced to give in simply because of a lack of oil. In short, *Japan could not do what she wanted because she did not have the strength.*

As Kido saw it, there seemed to be no other course for Japan than to manifest the determination shown at the time of the triple intervention following the Sino-Japanese war of 1894-1895. That is, everyone would have to accept the fact that it would be necessary to undergo great hardships for the next ten years.[16] For the present, Kido said, Japan must adjust her relations with the United States and thus secure the resources vital to her existence. At home, a program of careful national planning must be inaugurated. Japan must build up her heavy and machine-tool industries and devote herself to the establishment of synthetic petroleum plants. A great expansion of ocean-going tonnage must be carried out. If all this were done, Japan would in the end be able to achieve her

[16] In speaking of undergoing great hardships for a period of ten years, Kido used an interesting phrase, *gashin-shōtan*—literally: "to lie down on faggots and lick gall," and hence "to go through unspeakable hardships and privations." The term, borrowed from the Chinese (*wo hsin ch'ang tan*), can also convey the sense of "struggling against difficulties for the sake of vengeance." In Japan, in the latter half of 1941, it seems to have been employed fairly commonly to describe "the alternative to going to war" (Konoe used it in his letter of resignation to the Emperor: see p. 278, footnote 15). Kido states that he was absolutely opposed to the use of force and that he believed an eventual expansion southward through peaceful means would be possible. He had to fit his actual words, however, to the problem posed by the military, since their compliance would be necessary to put his plan into effect.

objective of expanding in the South. War at the present time, however, must be avoided.

Thus did Kido speak to Prince Konoe on August 7, 1941. The crux of the problem, however, lay not in what either man thought but in what the supreme command would accept. "To save herself from disaster Japan needed a young Saionji, but she got a middle-aged Konoe."[17] Although the prince did what he could, he proved unequal to the task. His proposal for a summit conference was a good one, but it was to founder on the same shore that threatened each and every phase of the negotiations and on which, in fact, the entire effort subsequently broke up. In the circumstances of 1941, both sides wanted positive, tangible results as a down-payment on the ultimate purchase of peace. Since neither was prepared to agree to the price demanded by the other, the only hope for success lay in the possibility that while the talks proceeded, circumstances on one side or the other might alter so radically that a breach in the no-compromise stand could be made.

This situation of stalemate, reflecting an American reluctance to bend and a Japanese refusal to bow, had existed since the summer of 1940. From that time onward there had been little room for a settlement and little chance that one would prevail. On the American side of the Pacific, the thought had begun taking hold that sterner measures would be required to bolster American security in the face of the continuing threat emanating from the Asian quarter. On the Japanese side, the program adopted in mid-1940 had revealed a certain fear that Japan might miss the opportunity of a century unless she was ready to act decisively at a moment's notice. What happened thereafter showed that the army general staff in Tokyo and its commanders in the field were always *willing* to resort to force but were not always prepared to do so. There was also Matsuoka's view, which permeated the thinking of his colleagues and remained in their minds even after he had departed, that the only way to deal with the United States was to take a strong stand. Reasonableness in the form of concession would be interpreted as weakness—the antithesis of firmness, which was regarded as of fundamental importance.

Putting up a bold front, being resolute, taking a strong stand had worked against Japan's weaker Asian neighbors but it failed against the more distant and powerful United States, which drew added strength—at least of conviction—by relying upon moral principles as a standard of measure in a world in which those principles were daily being flouted.

[17] "The Brocade Banner," 102.

In adhering to such a position, the United States helped create a situation in which Japan would ultimately be required, all other factors remaining equal, either to fight or to back down. Compromise on the American side would be possible, but only if it did not impair the moral principles involved. On the practical plane, China could not be written off, the once open door could not be left closed and bolted, and Japan could not be allowed to combine with Germany to destroy Britain and conquer Russia. A Japanese-American compromise restricted by such requirements, without an extensive *quid pro quo*, would almost inevitably be regarded in Japan as a demand for capitulation and, hence, as a justification for war.

A recognition of the dangers involved in becoming too rigid had led Hull to refrain from the all-out measures advocated by some members of the President's official family, especially by Mr. Morgenthau. It was believed that such restraint would bolster the position of the moderate group which was still thought to exist within Japan and to be capable, if given such assistance, of overcoming the die-hards. By the spring of 1941, however, patience and optimism in that regard had begun to wear rather thin. Prior to Admiral Nomura's arrival in Washington, Mr. Hull had reviewed with the President, in great detail, the whole of American relations with Japan and the prospects for success in the forthcoming negotiations. "I estimated right at the outset," Hull later wrote, "that there was not one chance of success in twenty or one in fifty or even one in a hundred. Japan's past and present record, her unconcealed ambitions, the opportunity for aggrandizement lying before her while embroiled Europe demanded a large part of our attention, and the basic divergence between our outlooks on international relations, were all against the possibility of such an accord. The President and I agreed that the existing treaties relating to the Far East were sufficient, provided the signatories, meaning especially Japan, lived up to them. There was no real need for new agreements—but if new agreements would contribute to peace in the Pacific, we believed we should not throw the chance away, however microscopic it was."[18]

There was full realization of a host of factors which touched in some way, and in varying degree, upon the problems confronting the United

[18] Hull, II, 985-86, and Ballantine aff., T 10750-51 (which notes that Hull "on numerous occasions at which I was present emphasized to the Japanese Ambassador that this Government was aware of the difficult internal situation which the Japanese Government faced and was prepared to be patient and to give the Japanese Government ample time to bring Japanese public opinion into line in support of a liberal broad-gauge program, such as the Secretary of State and the Japanese Ambassador had been discussing in their conversations").

States in her relations with Japan, including the advice repeatedly given by the highest military officers of the United States that time was needed to prepare defenses vital to American security. There were also statements by the British, the Australians, and the Dutch that "they were dangerously vulnerable in the Far East." Thus, "the far-reaching consequences to the whole world that would follow the outbreak of war in the Pacific" were foreseen. In Hull's own words: ". . . the President and I agreed that we would do whatever we could to bring about a peaceful, fair, and stabilizing settlement of the whole Pacific question. We knew we would have to be patient, because the Japanese government could not, even if it wished, abruptly put into reverse Japan's march of aggression. Implementation of promises Japan might make in any peaceful agreement would demand much time. But we also agreed that, while carrying no chip on our shoulders in our negotiations with Japan, we could not sacrifice basic principles without which peace would be illusory."[19]

In Washington, decisions were made by political leaders who turned to the military for advice on purely military matters. The supremacy of the civilian over the soldier was a fundamental tenet of American life. In Japan, the reverse was true. By 1941 the decision-making functions which the Meiji Constitution had divided between the cabinet and the supreme command were held almost exclusively by little-known general staff officers serving in the army and navy divisions of imperial headquarters. While lacking a basic understanding of political and diplomatic affairs, these virtually "nameless ones" nevertheless possessed a confidence in their ability and in their program that was the more sublime because it was so misfounded. They proceeded, again and again, to draft policies to meet problems that were completely over their heads and for which their narrow military approach was wholly inadequate. And those were the very policies which were not only accepted by the senior officers, who were equally restricted in their outlook, but also by the civilian cabinet ministers. Some of the latter were perhaps incapable

[19] *Ibid.* A November 1945 presentation by Mr. Hull before the joint congressional committee on the investigation of the Pearl Harbor attack (*PHA*, Part 2, 417-18), detailing views similar to those noted in the text, has since been picked up in Japan, where emphasis is placed on the "not one chance of success . . . in a hundred" and "time was needed to build up American strength" aspects. Even where Hull's remarks are not misunderstood, misquoted, or cited out of context, the implication is that there was a great difference between the attitude of American leaders toward the negotiations and that of their Japanese counterparts. In short, some Japanese are now saying, "Little did we know then that the United States was not sincere in undertaking the negotiations." The fact that this does not follow from Hull's remarks is clear from the quotations in the text.

of doing anything about the situation even when they felt something should be done. The sanity occasionally achieved by virtue of an individual's fuller knowledge of the world had always to contend with the madness by which it was surrounded. There was also fear of the reprisals which might be meted out to those who still thought clearly, and hence dangerously. Other civilian ministers seem to have regarded what was happening with equanimity. The fact of a military monopoly of decision-making powers that properly belonged elsewhere was not questioned. Still others favored the military program and eagerly gave it their support. Thus, the nature of the policy-making process in Tokyo was hardly conducive to a solution of the issues being posed in the Japanese-American conversations in Washington.

Among the factors touching upon the endeavor to negotiate a settlement were the growing rigidity of the positions taken by each side and the mounting tension between them as the weeks of talk passed into months. Much room for misunderstanding lay in the erroneous conception of the American negotiating position that had inevitably resulted from the assignment of a false value to the "draft understanding" of April 18 by the decision-makers in Tokyo. From April onward, Japanese cabinet and supreme command leaders had regularly used that document as a yardstick against which to measure the various proposals which emanated from the United States government. From incorrectly assuming in the spring of 1941 that the American attitude was more favorable than it was, Japan's leaders moved toward the belief, some two months later, that the American mood was stiffening and that the terms then being offered by Washington were far harsher than those "originally proposed."[20]

This alleged "change in the American attitude" proved more and more disappointing as time passed. The initial Japanese hope of being able to retain the essence by compromising on the form (*na wo sutete, jitsu wo toru*) gradually waned and, as it did so, Japan's own bearing in the negotiations stiffened. Those who had been suspicious of Washington's motives from the outset, or who were opposed to even the slightest diplomatic concession, began finding it easier to interfere. A typical method was to attack the sincerity of the United States by pointing to the marked differences between the "American" offer of mid-April (that is, the "draft understanding" written by the colonel who was sent by Tojo to help Nomura) and a "second" proposal of June 21

---

[20] For the details, see Butow, "The Hull-Nomura Conversations," 822-36.

(actually the *first American statement* of a basis on which conversations might be conducted).[21]

By the late summer of 1941, the atmosphere in which decisions were being made in the Japanese capital had become highly charged with emotion.[22] The freezing of Japan's assets had produced feelings similar to those that grip a man when a noose is placed around his neck. The fact that the placing of the noose follows the commission of an act for which death is the prescribed punishment does not lessen the surging fear and desperation that overwhelm him at the end. With the Japanese nation already standing on the scaffold awaiting the reprieve it was hoped that diplomacy would provide, apparently no one within the government was capable of entertaining the thought, let alone of suggesting, that the American response might be the final cause-and-effect result of Japan's own actions in the past.

Even at that late date, however, the leaders in Tokyo—including the military men—were still desirous of reaching a settlement with the United States through diplomacy. Bringing the talks in Washington to a successful conclusion was regarded as a matter of life or death for Japan.[23] The government was not using the negotiations as a blind behind which to complete preparations for an infamous attack, secretly planned as the last phase in a decade-old conspiracy to commit aggression in the Pacific. Tokyo was hard-headed enough to realize that a victory achieved through Japanese diplomacy would be as satisfactory, in terms of results, as one garnered through war. It would also be far less costly and would allow greater freedom of action in regard to other problems, such as the Soviet "menace" in the North. The decision-makers from the armed forces recognized this and therefore supported the negotiations. The trouble lay in the nature of the settlement envisaged by the Japanese military and in their great haste to achieve what they had in mind. As it gradually became apparent that Nomura's display of diplomatic charm, like Japan's earlier demonstration of military might, was failing to prompt an American capitulation, the

[21] *Ibid.* Copies of all in-coming and out-going cables relating to the Hull-Nomura conversations went, as a matter of course, to the war and navy ministers and to the army and navy general staffs. Copies of important messages were also sent to the lord privy seal. The foreign ministry, on the other hand, did not receive copies of army-navy cables—not even those from the military and naval attachés in embassies abroad (Tōgō, 151). See also Yamamoto aff., S 251:3, T 25908.

[22] There is much evidence on the reaction in Japan to the freezing order and on the significance it had for the Japanese nation. See, for example, Tōjō aff., S 343:12, T 36277-83; Hattori, I, 173-74; Kido aff., S 293:10, T 30939; and JRD, "Interrogations," II:35901 (Shinichi Tanaka), 461.

[23] Tōjō aff., S 343:5, T 36231.

Japanese army and navy general staffs grew less interested in continuing the negotiations and more interested in attempting a solution through force *before it was too late*. Thus, the old argument was again heard: Japan should stop wasting time; she should resort to positive measures.

Military men, whose training emphasizes the value of decisive action, seem by nature to become impatient when confronted by the slowness which frequently characterizes the progress of diplomatic and political affairs. In the circumstances of the late summer and early autumn of 1941, the time factor, from a military point of view, was becoming ever more compelling. Each day of additional delay meant an expenditure of another 12,000 tons of oil.[24] In an attempt to meet the growing military argument that further procrastination would merely result in a greater drain upon oil and other items vitally needed in the event of war, Konoe turned toward the possibility of avoiding a "gradual impoverishment of military supplies and resources" through an expansion of domestic facilities and an increase of production.[25] His reasoning was that the cost of such an effort, no matter how great, would still be preferable to the sacrifices entailed in a war with America and Britain. The president of the cabinet planning board, whose advice Konoe sought, readily agreed but he also added a friendly warning: no matter what the premier did, the question of opening hostilities would remain "a matter of domestic politics."[26] Presumably this meant that unless a program of expanding production could clearly be shown to be capable of meeting the full demands of the military services, the premier would be forced to resign.

The inevitable consequence of the "now or never" psychology that was gaining headway was an effort on the part of the army and navy divisions of imperial headquarters to devise an escape from the miserable situation to which their earlier decisions had brought the Empire of Japan. Their activity took two forms: a willingness, on the one hand, to support Konoe's proposal for a meeting with Roosevelt, and a determination, on the other, to begin laying plans to obtain a solution by military means.

Whereas the navy gave Konoe its complete endorsement, the army sent a more equivocal reply and imposed certain conditions on the holding of a summit conference.[27] Even so, the army's answer, as relayed by

---

[24] Hattori, I, 174 (an approximate calculation).   [25] See *PHA*, Part 20, 4012-13.
[26] *Ibid*. The president of the cabinet planning board was Lt. Gen. Teiichi Suzuki.
[27] When Konoe first broached such a meeting to the war and navy ministers, neither was able to give an immediate reply. This is understandable in the light of the fact that the service ministers were primarily spokesmen, in the cabinet, for the decision-making group centered in the supreme command. For the most part, the army's attitude on

Tojo, clearly recognized that Japan was in the midst of a crisis. Konoe was told that he could go ahead with his plan but that, in doing so, he must stick to the position already taken in the negotiations being conducted by Ambassador Nomura in Washington.[28] The army would not object to a Konoe-Roosevelt meeting so long as the premier was firmly resolved to go to war with the United States in the event that the American President "did not interpret correctly the Empire's true intentions" (i.e., in the event that Roosevelt continued to adhere to the policy which had prevailed up to that time). If the meeting was to be held, it must be with the President and not just with Secretary Hull or someone else on a lower level. The prince must also bear in mind that a failure to achieve success could not be used as an excuse for resignation. Rather, he should go to such a meeting with the firm determination, in case of failure, to return to Japan in order to lead the nation in war against the United States.[29]

This army bill of particulars, as well as other evidence, strongly suggests that the proposed meeting in the Pacific could have succeeded only if the United States had at last indicated its understanding of Japan's "true intentions" by agreeing to step out of the China picture, by saying no more about the Axis alliance, and by restoring normal eco-

---

foreign policy questions was formulated by members of the army general staff. Such liaison as seemed necessary or desirable (with either the service ministries or the foreign office) was processed through the chiefs of the military and naval affairs bureaus of the war and navy ministries. It was actually these subordinates rather than the war and navy ministers themselves who had a direct connection with matters pertaining to the Japanese-American negotiations (a Japanese term; Hull always used the word "conversations"). Issues of substance were naturally cleared with the service ministers, but routine delegations of authority provided a rather large area for freedom of action. Mutō, who was chief of the military affairs bureau from late 1939 through early 1942, later testified that War Minister Tōjō had never remonstrated with him about concessions he had made at his own discretion with respect to the policy to be followed in the Japanese-American negotiations, but that the army general staff had frequently demanded explanations from him. See Mutō aff., S 313:10, T 33102-3, and Iwakuro aff., S 312:13-14, T 32994.

[28] Konoe's Japanese text (p. 106) clears up a point which has been in doubt ever since the prince's so-called memoirs were printed, in English translation, as part of the Congressional proceedings relating to the Pearl Harbor attack. The translation (*PHA*, Part 20, 4000) reads: ". . . with determination to firmly support the basic principles embodied in the Empire's Revised Plan to the 'N'-Plan. . . ." Konoe's text reveals that " 'N'-Plan" is a mistranslation of *N kōsaku*—a convenient term used to describe the diplomatic efforts being made by Ambassador Nomura in Washington. Hattori, I, 180, also notes that *N kōsaku* stands for *Nichi-Bei kōsaku*.

[29] Accounts which emphasize that this was Tōjō speaking, rather than the army, seem to me to be in error, though Tōjō presumably was in agreement with what he presented. Tōjō also expressed the prevailing army view that the meeting would in all probability end in failure. See Konoe, 102-6, 124; Tōjō aff., S 343:10, T 36269-70; Hattori, I, 176; Grew, *Ten Years in Japan*, 426-27; and Oikawa aff., S 316:2, T 33341.

nomic relations. Seen in that light, the subsequent American refusal to consent to such a meeting unless a concurrence was first reached on fundamental principles reflects the extent to which Washington realized that the Konoe proposal in no way represented a new departure.[30]

While Prince Konoe waited hopefully for a favorable American response, the military services turned their attention to other measures for dealing with the situation. The feeling had grown that Japan was like a fish in a pond from which the water was gradually being drained away.[31] It was therefore natural for the supreme command, which always scanned foreign policy questions from the strategical-tactical point of view, to become concerned over the military implications of the freezing of Japanese assets abroad. In the past, the army had generally taken the initiative in drafting the basic national and foreign policies, which were later accepted by first the navy and then by the civilian members of the government. In the circumstances of August 1941, however, the army decided that any major decision involving the United States should emanate initially from naval quarters. One reason for this was that the army had been trying, without success, to come up with a plan of its own that inspired confidence. Another reason may have been a desire to force the hitherto vacillating navy to take a definite

[30] The United States did not hurriedly or lightly reject Konoe's proposal but in the end decided that the holding of such a meeting should be made contingent upon a prior agreement, at a lower level, upon basic principles. It should not be forgotten that the promises Konoe might have made to Roosevelt would have been only as good as the army's willingness to honor them. In this regard, an immediate postwar statement by Konoe is interesting: The Japanese government was "unable to control the Japanese militarists in the field, or often didn't know what the militarists were doing. It was that way when I was trying to see Roosevelt. . . . The government was considered a liar, because no matter what we promised regarding China, final decision on the removal of our troops from China depended upon the military. That was one reason why the meeting was never held." *NYHT*, September 14, 1945 (late city lift), 8. See also *NYT*, September 12, 1945, 3, in which Konoe is quoted as saying, "I don't blame Roosevelt, in view of our past performance, for his suspicions."

Konoe was to have been accompanied by a number of army representatives, including Lt. Gen. Osamu Tsukada (vice-chief of the army general staff), Maj. Gen. Akira Mutō (chief of the war ministry's military affairs bureau), Colonel Yadoru Arisue (chief of the army general staff's "Group 20," which was charged with matters pertaining to war guidance)—all of whom were very much "at the center."

[31] The "fish in a pond" figure of speech is adapted from a remark in Kenryō Satō, "Dai-Tōa Sensō wo Maneita Shōwa no Dōran," 118. Where this feeling might lead was carefully noted by Ambassador Grew in a cable dated August 27, 1941: "While in Japan there are groups who are entirely cognizant of the perilous possibilities inherent in the present positions and who are ready to make far-reaching efforts in an endeavor to avoid an armed clash with the United States, the possibility that the constructive statesmen of Japan will be able to counteract the increasing psychology of desperation is at present diminishing daily. Traditionally in this country *a national psychology of desperation develops into a determination to risk all . . .*" (Grew, *Turbulent Era*, II, 1285).

stand, once and for all, and to assume responsibility for a program in the execution of which it would have so large a role.

On August 9, just two days after the Konoe suggestion for a top-level meeting was communicated to Washington, the army division of imperial headquarters at length decided to drop any thought of pushing northward during 1941 and to concentrate, instead, upon the South. Sixteen divisions would be maintained in Korea and Manchuria to keep watch on the Soviet Union, the current operations in China would be continued, and war preparations against the United States and Great Britain would be accelerated, with the end of November as the target date for their completion. This latter decision was made with specific reference to the southern area.[32]

The determination shown by the army general staff on August 9, together with the pressure of events, left the navy no choice but to come firmly to grips with a problem with which it had been toying for some time. At a joint army-navy conference at the bureau chief level, held exactly one week after the army's operational decision, the navy suggested the course to be followed thenceforth in carrying out the Empire's policies. The essence of this plan of August 16, 1941, was a recommendation that diplomatic efforts go hand in hand with war preparations, with the latter part of October serving as the terminal date for those preparations. If diplomacy failed to bring about a settlement by the middle of October, the navy said, the use of force would be unavoidable.[33]

In this way, the navy not only committed itself to a specific course of action but also advanced the time for decision by an entire month—from the end of November to the end of October. In thus going on record in favor of the use of force in the event diplomacy failed, the navy was boldly assuming the initiative regarding a war with America and Britain. Since the navy had offered a concrete basis for decision,

[32] On the army decision of August 9, "Teikoku Rikugun Sakusen Yōkō," see Hattori, I, 162.

[33] The joint army-navy conference held on August 16, at which the navy submitted its "Teikoku Kokusaku Suikō Hōshin" (which became the "Teikoku Kokusaku Suikō Yōryō" of September 3 and September 6, as explained in the text which follows), was a so-called *kyokubu-chō kaigi* comprising the heads (Mutō and Oka) of the military and naval affairs bureaus (*gunmukyoku*) of the service ministries, the chief (Shinichi Tanaka) of the operations bureau (*daiichibu*) of the army general staff, and other officers belonging to the decision-making cadre (*chūken shōkō*), such as Colonel Kenryō Satō, who was then chief of the military affairs section (*gunmuka*). See Hattori, I, 177-78, and Kenryō Satō, "Dai-Tōa Sensō wo Maneita Shōwa no Dōran," 120. Konoe, 118, notes that from about August on [i.e., after the freezing of Japan's assets] the army general staff, even including the *shunōbu*, began to advocate war on the grounds that further negotiation was useless.

subsequent discussions all revolved around *the navy's program*, which was precisely what the army wanted in this particular instance.

This is not to say that there were no differences of opinion or that the army let the navy do very much more than step on the starter. The navy plan envisaged a decision in favor of war but implied that such a decision was to be deferred until October. The army, on the other hand, insisted that war preparations could not be carried out properly unless they were based, from the very beginning, on a determination to go to war. This view arose partly from the character and requirements of hostilities on land as compared with warfare at sea and partly from a suspicion that, in the final analysis, the navy might back down on a decision to use force.

This issue, which was a very serious one, came up for discussion at army-navy bureau chief conferences held on August 27 and 28.[34] Rear Admiral Oka, the head of the naval affairs bureau, made it plain that he did not share the army's view. He argued that a decision to launch hostilities should not be made until the European situation and other factors had been taken into consideration. The army thereupon suggested a compromise on wording that led to a resolution of all remaining differences.[35] The plan, as finally endorsed by the army and navy divisions of imperial headquarters, went a significant step beyond the earlier policy formulations that had culminated in the imperial conference of July 2, 1941. War preparations, which were to be completed by roughly the latter part of October, were to be made "on the basis of a determination not to run away from a war" with the United States, Britain, and the Netherlands. At the same time, Japan was to try to obtain satisfaction of her demands by utilizing all diplomatic measures. If those demands were not met by the early part of October, however, she would decide immediately to open hostilities against the Americans, the British, and the Dutch.

Tokyo's minimum demands, and the promises the government would be prepared to make if those demands were accepted, were reserved for an annex. They revealed not the slightest change in Japan's basic

[34] Except for some personal interpretations regarding the army's motives, the discussion which follows (for the period, August 27-September 3) is based on Hattori (who was then chief of the operations section of the operations bureau of the army general staff, and hence a member of the army division of imperial headquarters), I, 178-82.

[35] The army suggested replacing the positive phraseology "are determined to wage war" with the somewhat less direct "acting with a determination in favor of war," but Oka refused to accept this. On August 29, however, he informed the army that the navy would not object if the phrase in question were revised to read, "acting with a determination not to run away from war." Once this concession had been made, all remaining matters were easily resolved.

position. In fact they emphasized, instead, how much Japan was still driven by ambition.

With war a distinct possibility, the general staffs of the two services were in mutual agreement that very careful consideration must be given to the time element. This was true not simply because of the decline of Japan's oil reserves and the increase in American air and naval strength, but because the type of operation being planned imposed certain limitations on the attacker's freedom of action. Landing operations in areas like Malaya and the Philippines, for instance, could not be carried out at will. Such factors as the monsoon season, the rise of the tide, and the phase of the moon had to be taken into account. Studies already made by the supreme command pointed to early November as the best period for a successful landing operation in the South. An amphibious attack in that region in December would be disadvantageous but not impossible; any postponement beyond that month, however, was practically out of the question—as was a naval strike against Pearl Harbor, once winter in the North Pacific had really set in. If hostilities were not launched in the November-December period, Japan would be forced to wait until the following spring, but by that time the oil situation would be critical and the power of the American enemy would be greatly enhanced.[36]

Thus, in late August 1941 it was already clear that a determination with respect to war or peace would have to be made very soon. Launching hostilities in the South would require appropriate military dispositions, including the stationing of air units in southern French Indo-China and the assembling of a fleet of transports in the South China Sea. It would be difficult even to begin such preparations—let alone complete them—so long as diplomatic negotiations were in progress and a decision to go to war had not been made. The army general staff, in particular, wanted at least a month in which to prime itself for the intended blow. As a result of these considerations, and because of the insistent demands of the army general staff, the two services had finally agreed on the *early part of October* as the time to judge whether or not Japan

---

[36] In addition to material in Hattori (as cited in footnote 34 above, and I, 263-64) the text also draws on Satō corresp.; Tōjō aff., S 343:12, T 36280-83; JRD Monograph No. 45, 37-38; and JRD, "Statements," I:50135 (Takushirō Hattori), 340-41, and I:50606 (Takushirō Hattori and Sadatoshi Tomioka), 349-50; JRD, "Translation," II: 51903 (Item 18, Reference No. 4), 34-35; J, B/VII, 939-42; and Morton, 1333.

The English translation of Tōjō's affidavit describes landing operations in January as being "quite impossible of performance" from the supreme command's point of view. This accords with standard Japanese military opinion but is not what the affidavit says in Japanese: ". . . jōriku sakusen no tsugō wa . . . ichigatsu ikō wa shinan. . . ."

was to go to war and, if so, when. Prior to that decision, an effort would be made to avoid carrying out preparations which might cause trouble with respect to the negotiations in Washington. After that decision, and in the event that it was an affirmative one, "preparations in earnest" would be inaugurated at once. In that way, Japan was expected to derive the maximum benefit by going to war under optimum conditions.

By September 2 these crucial matters had been settled apparently to the mutual satisfaction of the army and navy divisions of imperial head-quarters. The foreign ministry was then consulted with regard to the terms of the diplomatic negotiations through which it was thought a solution might yet be found. On September 3 the top cabinet ministers and the leaders of the supreme command met with each other, in the inevitable liaison conference, to discuss what had already been formu-lated within imperial headquarters.[37]

At this conference, the navy attempted to modify its earlier agree-ment with the army concerning the time for decision regarding the commencement of hostilities. The effort in that direction was initiated by Navy Minister Oikawa, who proposed revising Clause No. 3: "If, by the early part of October, we are still unable to attain our demands, we shall immediately decide to open hostilities against the United States, Great Britain, and the Netherlands."[38]

Oikawa suggested changing this to read, "If, by the early part of October, there is still no prospect of being able to attain our demands, we shall carry out final measures for our self-existence and self-defense." Various opinions were expressed on this revision, but in the end it was rejected because it lacked clarity. Rear Admiral Oka, the chief of the naval affairs bureau, then proposed a sort of mélange designed to secure

[37] See Hattori, I, 178-82. The policy under discussion was entitled "Teikoku Kokusaku Suikō Yōryō" [occasionally printed as "Yōkō"]. The "besshi" portion of the text as given in Hattori differs somewhat from that found in Gaimushō, II, 544-45.
 The liaison conference met at 11:00 a.m. and adjourned at 6:00 p.m. Since the navy had originally initiated the policy on the agenda, the primary explanation was given by the chief of the naval general staff, Admiral Nagano. Neither Premier Konoe nor Foreign Minister Toyoda (himself an admiral) raised any serious objections to what was being proposed. This was not because they agreed with the supreme-command view but because they placed a different emphasis than some of their colleagues on the com-ponent parts of the policy. There is no indication that War Minister Tōjō played anything but a comparatively unimportant role either in these proceedings or in the conferences which had taken place during August.
[38] A more literal though cumbersome rendition of the original would be as follows: "If, by [as late as] approximately the early part of October [i.e., October 10], we are still unable to attain [satisfaction on] our demands [through diplomacy], we shall immediately decide in favor of the commencement of hostilities against the United States (Great Britain and the Netherlands)."

the support of all by linking the phrases on which they agreed with the ones to which they objected: "If, by the early part of October, there is still no prospect of being able to attain our demands, we shall carry out final measures by immediately deciding to open hostilities against the United States, Great Britain, and the Netherlands." But this also failed of acceptance, and so finally—and perhaps in some confusion of mind—the conferees agreed upon a rather simple and seemingly insubstantial substitution of phrases whereby the "if . . . we are still unable to attain" of the original became "if . . . there is still no prospect of being able to attain."

In other words, the liaison conference at length decided to adopt the first but not the second half of Navy Minister Oikawa's original suggestion. Thus Clause No. 3, as finally approved, read essentially as follows: "If, by the early part of October, there is still no prospect of being able to attain our demands, we shall immediately decide to open hostilities against the United States, Great Britain, and the Netherlands."[39]

In this way, the key factor of "prospect" was eased into an issue which was to grow in importance as the weeks passed.[40]

On the same day that this decision was made by the liaison conference, the President of the United States sent a message to Premier Konoe

[39] The original phrasing of Clause No. 3 was "[Zengō gaikō kōshō ni yori] jūgatsu jōjun goro ni itaru mo nao waga yōkyū wo kantetsu shi ezaru baai ni oite wa tadachi ni tai-Bei (Ei, Ran) kaisen wo ketsui su." The Oikawa revision read ". . . jūgatsu jōjun goro ni itaru mo nao waga yōkyū wo kantetsu shi uru mokuto naki baai wa jison jiei no tame saigo teki hōsaku wo suikō su." Oka's compromise proposal read ". . . jūgatsu jōjun goro ni itaru mo nao waga yōkyū wo kantetsu shi uru mokuto naki baai wa tadachi ni tai-Bei (Ei, Ran) kaisen wo ketsui shi saigo teki hōsaku wo suikō su." The form in which Clause No. 3 was finally approved was "[Zengō gaikō kōshō ni yori] jūgatsu jōjun goro ni itaru mo nao waga yōkyū wo kantetsu shi uru mokuto naki baai ni oite wa tadachi ni tai-Bei (Ei, Ran) kaisen wo ketsui su." See Hattori, I, 179 and 181-82.

Such English translations as do exist are almost invariably unsatisfactory. For example, the translation of Clause No. 3 above, as given in *PHA*, Part 20, 4022, reveals (as italicized) how wrong an impression can be conveyed by too imaginative a translation: "If by the early part of October there is no *reasonable hope* of having our demands agreed to in the diplomatic negotiations mentioned above, we will immediately make up our minds *to get ready for war* against America (and England and Holland)."

[40] Colonel Hattori's interpretation of the revision of Clause No. 3 is that the change in wording, although simple, emasculated the policy by deferring to a later date a decision on the basic question of war or peace. Hattori also lays stress on the great importance of the policy approved by the liaison conference on September 3. He notes that, whereas a number of such conferences were held before the national policy with respect to the German-Soviet war was finally decided, the issue in question on September 3, on which the fate of the nation would hinge, was settled in the course of a single day. The effectiveness of this point is rather impaired when it is realized that the real decision-making in this regard was done at the army-navy bureau chief conferences held on August 16 and between August 27 and 29.

advising him of the American desire to have an agreement of views on basic principles prior to a summit meeting of the type the prince had proposed. Twenty-four hours later, on September 4, the third Konoe Cabinet gave its rubber-stamp approval to the liaison conference decision, and forty-eight hours after that, on September 6, the matter was placed before an imperial conference.

Since the army-navy bureau chief conferences, where the real power lay, had already firmly fixed the basic national policy prior to the arrival of the Roosevelt message, it is clear that the President's unwelcome response was in no way responsible for the proceedings on either September 4 or 6. The most that the presidential message did was to confirm the army in its opinion that the chances of getting the United States to accept Japan's demands were not very good. Whatever this might have meant earlier, in the circumstances of August-September 1941 it simply reinforced the army's determination that a failure of the current diplomatic negotiations must automatically result in the inauguration of war by Japan. From about the latter part of July, a similar view had been gaining ground in the generally more cautious, less chauvinistic navy. The two services had thus come to an estimate of the situation which pictured Japan as slowly being forced to the wall. Unless a way could be found over it or around it, they would stand and fight, backs to the wall, regardless of the odds.

In arriving at such a view, the armed services were conscious of the growing unrest within ultranationalistic quarters. The ever-zealous exponents of imperial expansion were particularly incensed by the freezing of Japanese assets and by the failure of their government to act with dispatch. As the Konoe maneuver regarding a meeting with Roosevelt became publicly known, a number of ultranationalistic societies set up a hue and cry for immediate war against the United States. "The cross-currents of enmity were such that almost no man of consequence was safe." The police bureau of the home ministry found a parallel between the conditions then existing and "the uneasy days" of the blood brotherhood, the May 15 incident, and the February 26 mutiny.[41]

In mid-August a young Shinto priest who was a member of a society pledged to undying devotion to the imperial cause had shot at 75-year-old Minister of State Hiranuma, wounding him in the neck and jaw.

[41] On the ultranationalistic propensity to resort again to violence, see "The Brocade Banner," 116-18 (from which the "cross-currents" sentence is quoted); Kido aff., S 293:11, T 30947-48; and Tolischus, 224-30.

The attempted murder had apparently been motivated by anger over the baron's failure to terminate his connection with the Konoe Cabinet at the time of Matsuoka's ouster. Police investigation revealed that the pistol employed by the priest was one which a leading ultranationalist had lent, years before, to a friend in Shanghai who had planned to use it in the *shinpeitai* plot of 1933.[42]

It was subsequently discovered that Hiranuma's name had also figured on a list compiled by another group of fanatics hailing from the traditional seat of trouble, Ibaragi prefecture. The motive for the assassination, which was to have taken place in August, was a desire to manifest the group's unswerving admiration for the recently deposed Matsuoka.[43] Only the vigilance of the police had prevented this attack and other similar, premeditated crimes from taking place. Such was the renewed risk for members of the ruling elite that the police doubled the guard that had been continuously assigned to Marquis Kido and his family since the assassination of General Nagata in August 1935. Had the police been less diligent, Premier Konoe himself would very likely have fallen a victim to assassination. Fortunately, the police learned in time that he had been marked for death by a band of four men who called themselves "the squad of heavenly punishment." It was their intention to kill Konoe on September 18, 1941, the tenth anniversary of the Manchurian Incident.[44]

Continuing arrests during this unsettled period also thwarted ultra-nationalistic plans to attack the American embassy, the home ministry, the metropolitan police headquarters, and other key points. Although all of these schemes were prevented by police action, the threat remained that one day an assassination attempt, or even something on the order of a *coup d'état*, might escape police surveillance and succeed. The mood

[42] See "The Brocade Banner," 117. The Shintō priest (Naoshi Nishiyama) belonged to the *Kinnō Makoto Musubi-kai*. Kodama, *I Was Defeated*, 97, reveals that the weapon was a pistol he had lent to a friend years before. Kodama also notes that a large number of ultranationalistic societies cooperated with each other to form the *Hachigatsu-kai* for the purpose of *studying* the Japanese-American question. The group was forced to disband as a result of the attempt on Hiranuma's life.

[43] Five men were involved—known collectively as the *Mito-gaku Kenkyū-kai*. They also planned to kill Seihin Ikeda. See "The Brocade Banner," 117.

[44] The *Tenchū-gumi* attempt to assassinate Konoe remains shrouded in mystery. On the basis of present evidence, there is no doubt that Konoe was marked for death but there is a question regarding how far the plot progressed before the participants were arrested. Grew, *Turbulent Era*, II, 1332, and Feis, 282, describe an actual attack upon Konoe's automobile as the prince was leaving his residence to go to his office. A reference in "The Brocade Banner" (p. 118), which is based on police records, is very brief; Kido and Ushiba were unable to provide any details (Kido and Ushiba corresp.).

of the ultranationalists was consequently a factor which could not be ignored by members of the ruling elite.

On September 5, after the cabinet had already unanimously endorsed the liaison conference proceedings of September 3, Prince Konoe went to the palace to lay the new national policy before the Emperor. As usual, the premier also called on Marquis Kido, who later recorded his surprise at the suddenness with which Konoe thus revealed a matter of such enormous importance. According to the privy seal, Konoe had not previously discussed the new policy with him. He therefore reproached the premier on the grounds that the abruptness with which this momentous proposal was being brought to the Emperor's attention would embarrass His Majesty, because he would scarcely have time to give the matter thought before the imperial conference convened the following day. Noting the emphasis placed on "early October," Kido also remarked that he felt it was very dangerous to set a specific time limit of that kind. But when he pressed the point and questioned the wisdom of adopting such a policy at all, Konoe replied that to modify or suspend it would be difficult in view of the liaison conference decision in its favor. All he could do, the prince said, was to exert himself to the utmost in the Japanese-American negotiations and thus obviate any need to invoke those provisions which pertained to war.[45]

Prince Konoe also encountered difficulties during his audience with the Emperor. His Majesty observed that the item dealing with war preparations came before the one relating to diplomatic negotiations. This suggested, he said, that war was being given precedence over diplomacy. He would want to question the two chiefs of staff on that point at the conference the following day. Konoe replied that the order in which the items were listed in the policy was not meant to indicate their relative importance. The cabinet intended to work "until the very end" to obtain a settlement through diplomacy. Only if diplomatic efforts proved hopeless would the government begin preparations for war.

The fact that this directly contradicted the text of the policy, which clearly specified that war preparations would go hand-in-hand with diplomatic efforts, seems not to have been discussed. Such records as are available with respect to the decision-making process reveal that the responses of members of the Japanese government did not always really answer the queries put to them, nor did the conclusions reached in a presentation inevitably correspond with the facts which were offered along the way. One would expect that when such disparities

[45] Kido SKD.

occurred, further questions would be raised to clarify the point in doubt. But apparently that did not necessarily happen—perhaps because putting anyone on the spot was considered a rather drastic thing to do and was commonly avoided.

In this particular case, the Emperor simply took Konoe's statement at face value. He then referred to other matters, including some which related to military operations. Since Konoe could not answer such questions, and since he would have infringed upon the prerogatives of the supreme command if he had tried, he suggested summoning the two chiefs of staff. He also advised the Emperor that it might be more appropriate to ask the chiefs at the same time about the issue which had come up at the beginning of the audience, rather than to do so at the imperial conference the next day. The Emperor reacted favorably to this suggestion and Konoe briefly withdrew to inform Kido of the imperial wishes and to await the arrival of General Sugiyama and Admiral Nagano. When they appeared, the premier and the two chiefs went before the Emperor together. His Majesty again asked about the order in which war and diplomacy were mentioned in the policy, and both Sugiyama and Nagano replied in the same vein as Konoe had previously. The Emperor then turned to various military problems, including the army's estimate of the time required "to dispose of the matter" in the event of a war between Japan and the United States. Sugiyama apparently intended to give a detailed reply, but he got no further than a first sentence to the effect that the initial phase of operations in the South would take about three months. The Emperor broke in at once, tersely observing that as war minister in 1937 Sugiyama had said the China Incident would be over in about a month. That had been four years ago and the fighting was still in progress.[46]

Sugiyama tried to explain that there was a difference between the two situations. China was a continent with a vast hinterland. That fact had prevented the army's original expectations from being realized. The southern area, however, was composed of islands and consequently the

[46] On the two audiences of September 5 (the first of which occurred sometime between 4:30 and 5:00 p.m. and the second between 6:00 and 7:00 p.m.), see Konoe, 120-22; Kido SKD and corresp.; Kido aff. and "Nikki," S 293:11-12, T 30948-52; Hattori, I, 182-83 (in which Sugiyama's estimate with regard to the initial phase of operations in the South is put at five months rather than at three, as per Konoe); and *PHA*, Part 20, 4004-5. The Emperor had instructed Konoe to be present at the second audience. A Konoe request for imperial sanction (noted in Kido) was presumably a preliminary request contingent upon the completion of the procedures normally followed after an imperial conference. In other words, the sanction Konoe requested on September 5 would not be given until after the imperial conference on September 6.

problem was not the same. But this only aroused the Emperor more. "If you call the Chinese hinterland vast, would you not describe the Pacific as even more immense? With what confidence do you say 'three months'?"[47]

Sugiyama hung his head, unable to reply, but Nagano quickly came to the rescue. The supreme command, he said, was speaking from "a broad point of view." The current relations between Japan and the United States might be compared to an illness in which a decision was necessary on whether to perform an operation. Avoiding surgery would contain the threat of a gradual wasting-away of the patient. Great danger would attend an operation, but it could not be said that surgery offered no hope of saving the patient's life. The supreme command was anxious to obtain a solution through diplomacy, but should that fail, an operation would be necessary. The policy being submitted to the throne had been approved with such thoughts in mind.

When Nagano had finished, the Emperor said he interpreted what he had heard thus far as signifying that the supreme command was emphasizing diplomacy as the way to solve the issues at stake between the United States and Japan. Was that correct? Sugiyama and Nagano together replied that it was.[48]

In the Japanese context, the Emperor's remarks as a whole were taken to mean that His Majesty doubted very much whether success would crown Japan's efforts in the event the nation became involved in war. The two chiefs of staff had been unable to do more than nip at the fringes of that basic problem. They had actually advised the Emperor that they could not say Japan would certainly win. All they could do was to argue that in the worst eventuality Japan would have to attempt a breakthrough by force, while she still had some striking power left.

From September 5 on, every debate which was held on the question of war or peace inexorably ended on that same note. Thus, for all practical purposes, the decision in favor of expanding hostilities into the Pacific was actually made by army and navy staff officers between August 16 and September 5, 1941. Thereafter, war was inevitable unless the United States accepted Japan's terms or the monopoly of decision-making held by the supreme command was broken. Without a develop-

[47] "Shina no okuchi ga hiroi to iu nara, Taiheiyō wa nao hiroi de wa nai ka. Ikanaru kakushin atte sankagetsu to mōsu ka." Konoe, 121.

[48] As soon as the audience was over, Prince Konoe, who had been more of a spectator than a participant, stopped by Kido's office to inform the privy seal of what had transpired. See the sources cited in footnote 46 above and Kurihara, 164-69 (especially Nagano's version of the audience, as told by him to members of his staff).

ment in the latter direction, it is doubtful whether any leader, political or military, would have been able to change the policies of the nation so as to bring about a solution through peaceful means.

The supreme-command view, which by now was decisive, was that either the government would have to entice the United States into accepting Japan's program, or Japan would have to fight. In this sense, the policy being proposed was consistent with all earlier ones; it bore an especially close relationship to the agreement reached between the army and navy general staffs in the spring of 1941 and to the imperial conference policy of July 2, both of which had stressed the possible "necessity" of using force and the willingness to do so. These policies, in turn, were an outgrowth of the decisions made on July 26 and 27, 1940. And from there, one can trace the connection back to the basic national policy of August 1936. Throughout that period generally, and in the autumn of 1941 in particular, the supreme command was either unwilling or unable to give any consideration to changing the course of events by reviewing the policies of the past as a first step away from an emphasis upon force. Certainly the results of Japanese reliance upon military measures, particularly in China, scarcely warranted a blind faith in their efficacy. And yet it was precisely such a faith that underlay the program being advocated by the supreme command, with the time for action already set, and the clock of decision ticking toward the pre-arranged hour.

Insofar as this program was concerned, the imperial conference held on September 6, like all such gatherings, was an anticlimax. In another respect, however, it was unprecedented.[49] Kido had learned enough from Konoe to assume that the Emperor might not be satisfied with the explanations tendered by the chiefs of staff and might desire further clarification during the imperial conference itself. Early in the morning of September 6, therefore, Kido suggested to Dr. Hara, the president of the privy council, that he utilize the opportunity provided by the

[49] On the imperial conference of September 6: Kido aff., S 109:13-14, T 10215-16; S 159:14, T 16199-204; and S 293:12, T 30952-54; Kido SKD and corresp.; Konoe, 122-23; Tōjō aff., S 343:10-14, T 36271-72, 36277-83, 36295-96; Tōjō cross-examination, S 343:20, T 36512-13; Tōjō interrog., Feb. 6, 4, Feb. 7, 1, Feb. 23, 5, Feb. 25, 3-6; Oikawa cross-examination, S 327:13-15, 17-18, T 34575-84, 34600-2 (a statement at the beginning of S 327:15, mistakenly attributed to Keenan, was actually made by Oikawa); PHA, Part 20, 4005; Hattori, I, 183-89 and 248; Kenryō Satō, "Dai-Tōa Sensō wo Maneita Shōwa no Dōran," 118-20; IPS Doc. No. 0004, 13-17; JRD, "Statements," I:50135 (Hattori), 340-41; JRD, "Translation," II:51903 (Item 18), 8-9 and references; JRD, "Interrogations," II:35901 (Shinichi Tanaka), 442; CF 20, IV, 358; J, B/VII, 939-42; Feis, 264-67; and Higashikuni, Ichi Kōzoku no Sensō Nikki, 75-82.

conference to ask questions designed to commit the participants to stressing diplomatic negotiations rather than war preparations. When the Emperor subsequently revealed that he wished to query the conferees along the lines mentioned, Kido informed the throne of his conversation with Dr. Hara. The privy seal suggested the desirability, however, of having His Majesty make a brief statement at the end of the conference, noting the tremendous importance of the decision and directing the supreme command to extend its wholehearted cooperation so that an amicable settlement could be achieved through diplomacy.

Five minutes after this advice was given, the imperial conference convened in Room No. 1, East, of the palace.[50] Since the policy under consideration had evolved from the navy plan of August 16, Chief of the Naval General Staff Nagano was the first to offer a detailed explanation. He was followed by Chief of the Army General Staff Sugiyama and President of the Cabinet Planning Board Suzuki. These three men dominated the conference—the first two because the policy being advocated might lead directly to military operations, and the third, Lt. Gen. Suzuki (Retired), because the question of war or peace was intimately connected with various economic factors being studied by the cabinet planning board.

The explanations offered by these men revealed an attitude that was to pervade the innumerable liaison conferences which followed—an attitude of basic optimism which enabled the leaders of Japan to disregard apparent shortcomings whenever someone in the group advised that *countermeasures* were under consideration. When that magic word was uttered, the atmosphere of decision-making was purged of all worrisome thoughts and haunting images, and the men who had briefly been forced to dwell on a particular problem could pass, with greater confidence, to another issue.

As soon as Suzuki completed his presentation, Dr. Hara performed according to plan. Navy Minister Oikawa arose at once and replied to the effect that the order of the items in the policy was insignificant and that the president of the privy council was correct in interpreting the policy to mean that every effort would be made to obtain a solution through diplomacy and that Japan would resort to war only if those

---

[50] Kido met with the Emperor from 9:40 to 9:55 a.m. The imperial conference convened at 10:00 a.m. and adjourned sometime prior to 1:10 p.m., at which time Kido again spoke with the Emperor.

The palace consisted of two parts: the outer palace (*omote kyūden*), which was used for official business, and the inner quarters (*naitei*), where the Emperor lived. It was in the *omote kyūden* that the imperial conference convened. Kido corresp.

efforts failed. No sooner had this been said than the Emperor unexpectedly broke the silence which he traditionally maintained throughout such conferences. Referring to Dr. Hara's remarks, His Majesty expressed his regret that the representatives of the supreme command (Sugiyama and Nagano) had not personally responded. He drew a slip of paper from his pocket and proceeded to read from it a poem composed by his grandfather, the Emperor Meiji:

> *Yomo no umi mina harakara to omou yo ni*
> *Nado namikaze no tachisawaguramu*[51]

> All the seas, in every quarter,
>   are as brothers to one another.
> Why, then, do the winds and waves of strife
>   rage so turbulently throughout the world?

Observing that the poem was a favorite of his, the Emperor declared that his efforts were being directed at introducing in his own time the spirit of his late grandfather's love for peace. His Majesty then lapsed once again into silence.[52]

The effect of this upon the gathering was so overwhelming that everyone appeared to have been struck dumb. Admiral Nagano was the first to recover. He humbly acknowledged the imperial censure of the supreme command. He had not replied to Dr. Hara, he said, because it had been his impression that Admiral Oikawa was speaking for both

[51] The wording of the Emperor Meiji's poem as given in the *Sokki-roku* is incorrect; the correct version is as given in the text.

[52] On October 25, 1941, Ambassador Grew reported: "A reliable Japanese informant [possibly Toshikazu Kase, chief of the first section of the American bureau of the foreign office and concurrently secretary to the foreign minister] tells me that just prior to the fall of the Konoye cabinet a conference of the leading members of the Privy Council and of the Japanese armed forces had been summoned by the Emperor, who inquired if they were prepared to pursue a policy which would guarantee that there would be no war with the United States. The representatives of the Army and Navy who attended this conference did not reply to the Emperor's question, whereupon the latter, with a reference to the progressive policy pursued by the Emperor Meiji, his grandfather, in an unprecedented action ordered the armed forces to obey his wishes..." Grew, *Ten Years in Japan*, 462, and U.S. Dept. of State, *Foreign Relations (Japan: 1931-1941)*, II, 697-99. The informant's report is obviously a somewhat garbled and misleading reference to the imperial conference of September 6 described in the text above. In this connection, the following extract (Tōjō interrog., Mar. 13, 1), containing an even more garbled version, is especially interesting: Question: "The official Pearl Harbor Report states that Ambassador Grew reported, on 25 October 1941, that 'the Emperor ordered the Privy Council before him and asked them if they intended war. When they refused to answer, he instructed them that there should be no war with the United States.' Was this the case?" Answer: "I deny it. It isn't likely that there was any such talk around that time. Especially due to the character of the Privy Council, it is very unlikely that the Emperor would have asked them such a question."

the cabinet and the supreme command. He wished now to affirm that the army and navy general staffs fully endorsed Admiral Oikawa's response; diplomacy would be stressed; war would be chosen only as an unavoidable, last resort.[53]

With that declaration, the imperial conference of September 6 adjourned. Whether the Emperor's remarks had sprung from a sudden and disturbing realization on his part of how dangerously close to war Japan really was, or whether they were motivated by a desire on the part of those close to the throne to place the Emperor on record in favor of peace so that he would be in the clear in case war came, is a historical problem of a type which has a perverse tendency to stay some distance ahead of the pursuer. The arguments for and against seem equally good, with the possibility existing that this extraordinary imperial pronouncement was the product of the two extremes, and therefore represented a compromise between them. Whatever the origin of the Emperor's unusual action, in the end those who had been present, and those who had heard about the imperial admonition afterwards, could only express their profound regret at having been unable subsequently to comply with the imperial will.

On the very evening of the day on which this momentous imperial conference was held, Premier Konoe secretly met with Ambassador Grew to discuss, over dinner, various matters of mutual concern to their countries.[54] From Grew's account, it would appear that the prince's purpose was to emphasize his desire to see the Japanese-American conversations end in success and to reiterate his hope that a settlement of outstanding issues could be achieved through a personal meeting with President Roosevelt. Konoe did not reveal to the ambassador that an imperial conference had been held that day, but his remarks repeatedly

---

[53] There is a difference of opinion as to whether Nagano and Sugiyama intended to remain silent with regard to Hara's questions, or simply had the words taken out of their mouths by Admiral Oikawa. It is difficult to see what they would have gained by silence on September 6 in the light of their assurances to the Emperor on the fifth, although an imperial conference was less private than an imperial audience. According to Oikawa's testimony, he regarded himself as representing, on this occasion, not only the navy ministry but Nagano and the naval general staff as well. Thus, when he spoke up in answer to Hara, he was doing so on behalf of the entire navy; that was why Nagano said nothing.

[54] See Grew, *Ten Years in Japan*, 425-28 and 436-42; Grew, *Turbulent Era*, II, 1324-32; *PHA*, Part 2, 663-69, Part 12, 54-56, 58-60 and Part 20, 4002, 4005-6; *Foreign Relations (Japan: 1931-1941)*, II, 604-6 and 645-50; and Konoe, 113, 123-26. The Japanese communication of August 28, mentioned in the Konoe account, would seem to be a reference to the statement which appears on pp. 573-75 of the *Foreign Relations* volume cited herein. On the American attitude at this time, see Feis, 255-60.

reflected the fact that time was of the essence. It was Grew's impression, also, that the premier, "and consequently the Government of Japan," agreed "conclusively and wholeheartedly" with the four principles that Hull had stipulated as the basis for successful negotiations.[55]

Konoe's own account of this same meeting, however, suggests that Japan's position was not nearly so definite. All of the evidence indicates that the military members of the government were fundamentally opposed to the Hull formula. When Konoe told Grew, therefore, that Hull's four principles were "splendid," he was letting his desire for a peaceful settlement run away with him. Opposition to those principles within the Japanese army and even in the foreign office had not abated in the least. The insurmountable problem which this posed caused the prince endless worry. And so he decided it would be best to tell the American ambassador that the Hull position was "splendid as a matter of principle." When it came to actual application, a number of problems would arise. To solve those problems, a meeting with Roosevelt was necessary.[56]

More important perhaps than even this aspect of the Konoe-Grew dinner on the evening of September 6 was the fact that the premier's invitation had been extended to the ambassador in the utmost secrecy so as to prevent extremists from learning of the affair. The two men were driven to the home of a mutual friend in automobiles from which the usual diplomatic tags and official paraphernalia had been removed.[57] Throughout dinner, and afterwards, the prince and the

[55] The four principles were "(1) respect for the territorial integrity and the sovereignty of each and all nations; (2) support of the principle of non-interference in the internal affairs of other countries; (3) support of the principle of equality, including equality of commercial opportunity; (4) non-disturbance of the *status quo* in the Pacific except as the *status quo* may be altered by peaceful means." *Foreign Relations (Japan: 1931-1941)*, II, 407. In this connection, see also Butow, "The Hull-Nomura Conversations," 827-31.

[56] Konoe's recollection of what had been said was as follows: "Gurū taishi wa, Haru no yon-gensoku ni tai suru yo no iken wo tadashi, yo wa 'Gensoku-teki ni wa kekkō de aru ga, jissai tekiyō no dan to naru to shuju mondai ga shōji, sono mondai wo kaiketsu suru tame ni koso [daitōryō to no] kaiken ga hitsuyō ni naru no da.' " Grew's report (as *paraphrased* by the Department of State) reads, "Prince Konoye, and consequently the Government of Japan, conclusively and wholeheartedly agree with the four principles enunciated by the Secretary of State as a basis for the rehabilitation of relations between the United States and Japan."

[57] Sir Robert Craigie, British Ambassador to Japan (1937-1941), notes a similar experience with "a certain Prime Minister": ". . . it was suggested [apparently by the premier's 'cautious secretary'] that, using my smaller car, I should go in by a side entrance, an ordinary number plate being substituted for the official Embassy one." Sir Robert's chauffeur, desiring to cooperate fully, doffed his usual attire for a "tattered coat, tweed cap and a battered pair of sand-shoes." Craigie, 122-23.

ambassador were attended only by the daughter of the house. All the servants had been sent away on one pretext or another, so that they would be unable to tell the secret police what had transpired.[58]

Aside from the question of the Hull formula, the essence of what Prince Konoe told Ambassador Grew was that his cabinet, including the war and navy ministers, was completely unified in its desire to see the negotiations brought to a successful conclusion, and that if the present opportunity were not grasped, another chance might not arise again in their lifetime. This, indeed, proved to be the case, but in the light of the precautions taken to avoid detection on the evening of September 6 one must wonder how a premier who felt it necessary to resort to such tactics could possibly have hoped to carry his nation with him on any settlement other than one based on American concessions and compromises far in excess of any reasonable program of "constructive conciliation." In the measures of masquerade employed by Prince Konoe on the evening of September 6, 1941, lay further evidence of the nature of the times, and of the atmosphere in which the government of Japan would now be called upon to make a fateful decision.

[58] The dinner in question took place at Baron Itō's. Grew was accompanied by Dooman, and Konoe by Ushiba. The invitation had been extended by Konoe with the full knowledge and understanding of the war, navy, and foreign ministers.

CHAPTER 10

Wiping the Slate Clean

THE month of grace provided by the policy confirmed at the imperial conference of September 6 passed quickly and without any noticeable improvement in the chances for a Japanese diplomatic success. What was fully appreciated later by those who had hoped to avoid a military showdown with the United States apparently received little consideration at the time—the difficulty of maintaining a distinction between a decision for war and a decision to carry out *war preparations*. As the latter progressed, and as the talks in Washington failed to produce the anticipated American capitulation to Japan's terms, military opposition to a continuation of the negotiations grew proportionately.

On September 18 the chiefs of the army and navy general staffs called for an immediate determination of Japan's final position with respect to a Japanese-American understanding—a matter which had been under discussion, in one form or another, for some five months. The purpose behind this maneuver was to establish a suspense date beyond which Japan would shift from "phase one" of military preparations to "phase two": the final troop movements and fleet dispositions necessary for the launching of hostilities. The method chosen by the supreme command was to require the government to formulate Japan's final proposal and transmit this at once to the United States. If the Americans accepted it, all would be well. If not, then the supreme command would immediately insist upon a decision in favor of war.[1]

Two days later, on September 20, the supreme-command program was accepted by Premier Konoe at the usual liaison conference. Five days after that, at still another liaison session, the supreme command carried its new political offensive one step further by declaring that the decision for war or peace must be made *by October 15 at the latest*. Again operational considerations were the determining factor; again

[1] On developments after September 6, see Hattori, I, 190-94. On the views of the army, especially the general staff, see also JRD, "Interrogations," I:49157 (Seizō Arisue), 49 and 59-61.

The fact of supreme-command independence and the manner in which the army general staff, in particular, kept pressing for a decision hardly need documentation, but the following are pertinent: Hattori, I, 242-43; PHA, Part 20, 4004, 4006, 4012, 4014-16; Konoe, 117, 125, 142-44; Tōjō interrog., Feb. 7, 3-5, and Mar. 19, 1-4; JRD, "Statements," II:50724 (Takushirō Hattori and Katsuhei Nakamura), 653-55; Kido intv.; Kido and Satō corresp.

national policy of an extraordinarily complex nature was being shaped by staff officers in imperial headquarters solely on the basis of a narrow military viewpoint.[2]

Konoe was apparently shocked by this new demand, although it was a logical outgrowth of the September 6 decision to which he had given his official consent. As soon as the conference was over, Konoe turned his back on the luncheon which had been prepared for the occasion and returned at once to his official residence. At his request, the other cabinet ministers who had been present accompanied him. A short discussion followed during which Konoe endeavored to get the reactions of his cabinet colleagues. In response to a question from the premier as to whether or not the supreme-command statement was a strong demand, Tojo volunteered the opinion that it was. He noted, however, that "demand" was perhaps not the proper word, since the chiefs of staff had really done nothing more than advocate strict adherence to the early October deadline set several weeks before. Konoe apparently said nothing further, but he gave the impression of being perplexed. The next day, September 26, he informed Marquis Kido that if the army intended to go ahead in such a fashion, a resignation might be the only way out. The premier's words struck Kido as irresponsible. Konoe had been a party to the decision confirmed at the imperial conference on September 6. Rather than resign from lack of confidence, Konoe should take the initiative by advocating a reconsideration of the entire question. Kido spoke to the prince in this vein and urged him to give the matter careful thought.

On September 27 Konoe left the capital for nearby Kamakura, where he remained "resting" until October 1. This was regarded by some observers as an indication that all was not well on the political front. It was commonly said that whenever a crisis threatened, Konoe took to his bed. On this occasion, however, the prince did not remain entirely idle. Even though his position was like that of a man in a dream who feels that he is falling and yet is powerless to do anything about it, Konoe

[2] On developments after September 20 (which are discussed in detail below), see Hattori, I, 194-96 and 281-82; Konoe, 126-27; *PHA*, Part 20, 4006-8; Kido "Nikki" for September 26, 1941, S 109:15, T 10230; and for October 7, 1941, S 109:15-16, T 10232-33 (requires revision); Kido "Nikki" and aff., S 109:15-16, T 10232-33 (see also 10668-70) and S 293:12-13, T 30955-59; Kido interrog., Mar. 11, 715-29; Kido SKD and corresp.; Kido, "Dai-sanji Konoe Naikaku Sōjishoku no Zengo no Jijō," 1-2; Tōjō aff., S 343:13-14, T 36289-98; JRD Monograph No. 147, 57 and No. 150, 15-20; JRD, "Interrogations," I:49157 (Seizō Arisue), 49 and 59-61; JRD, "Translation," II: 51903 (Item 18, Reference No. 3), 30-31; *Foreign Relations (Japan: 1931-1941)*, II, 656-61 (oral statement handed by Hull to Nomura on October 2); and Hattori corresp.

grasped in the only direction from which help could conceivably come. He privately conferred with Navy Minister Oikawa about the "atmosphere in naval circles." Konoe presumably believed that the army might be held in check if the admirals still had doubts about the wisdom of going to war, and if they were confident of being able to control their subordinates should the need arise. Precisely where such a thought would lead was shortly to be revealed.

The premier's return to the capital from Kamakura coincided with the arrival of a message from the United States which dashed whatever hope Konoe still entertained with respect to an immediate meeting with President Roosevelt. The communication did not reject such a meeting but rather reiterated the earlier American view that a conference between the two leaders could serve no useful purpose without the prior establishment of a common ground of agreement. The door was left ajar, but it was clear that it would not be opened further unless Japan proved willing to forsake the policy of aggressive military adventures with which her very name had by then become synonymous. Although the American position was entirely justifiable in the light of Japan's record and of Tokyo's recent proposals to the United States, the arrival of the American message served as an opportunity for the direct-actionists to say, in effect: "We told you so."

On the evening of October 5, Konoe advised War Minister Tojo that he would endeavor to continue the negotiations to the very end. The next day, the army's "top men" held a conference to determine the army's policy. This was brief and to the point. The army judged that there was no prospect of reaching a settlement in the Japanese-American negotiations; consequently, the outbreak of war could not be avoided; the army would not change its views on the stationing of troops on the continent; if those responsible for foreign affairs believed a prospect of settlement existed, they were free to continue their efforts until October 15.[3]

Within the imperial navy, opinions were not quite so unanimous. Navy Minister Oikawa wanted the negotiations continued, but Chief of the Naval General Staff Nagano largely echoed the army's demand for

---

[3] The original estimate of the time required to complete the war preparations which were to be carried out during "phase two" had been three weeks. This was later revised to a minimum of two weeks. Hence the emphasis on a decision by October 15 so that Japan could go to war early in November, which was considered the best time to attack. JRD, "Statements," I:50135 (Takushiro Hattori), 340-41.

The so-called *shunō-kaidan* of October 6 may simply have been a meeting between Tōjō and Sugiyama. If so, presumably the policy decided at that time was completely in accord with the views and recommendations of the *chūken shōkō*.

Premier Hamaguchi being carried from the platform of Tokyo Station shortly after
he was shot by an ultranationalist, November 14, 1930

This photograph appeared in a
936 issue of *Fortune* Magazine de-
oted to Japan. The caption read
s follows: "Koki Hirota: Premier
f Japan . . . and anonymous
iend. The friend is the more
mportant of the two. His bayonet,
dge outward against the world,
oint inward against the ministerial
osom, symbolizes with extraordi-
ary felicity the position of the Jap-
nese army in the government of
pan. Between the civil govern-
ent and the army it is the position
f the point that counts; between
pan and the rest of humanity the
osition of the blade. . . ."

Stalin and Matsuoka just after the signing of the Soviet-Japanese
Neutrality Pact, April 13, 1941

The Emperor

Fumimaro Konoe

Koichi Kido

Gen Sugiyama

Shigenori Togo

Osami Nagano

General Hideki Tojo, Premier of Japan, 1941-1944

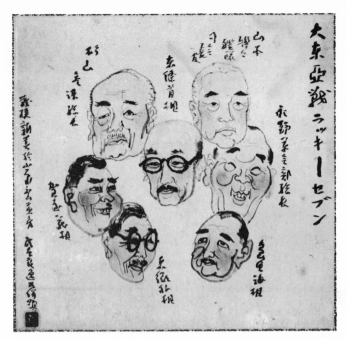

From a 1942 scroll (*kakemono*) featuring "The Lucky Seven of the Greater East Asia War." Premier Tojo is in the center; from the right top, clockwise: Commander in Chief of the Combined Fleet Yamamoto, Chief of the Naval General Staff Nagano, Navy Minister Shimada, Foreign Minister Togo, Finance Minister Kaya, and Chief of the Army General Staff Sugiyama

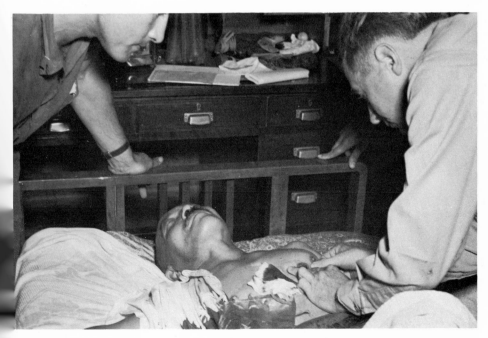

Tojo about two hours after he shot himself, September 11, 1945. He is being examined by Dr. James B. Johnson, Jr., the first U.S. Army medical officer to arrive at the scene

Tojo at the Omori prison camp, about November 1945

Tojo on the stand, December 26, 1947

Former Premier Tojo during the course of
the Tokyo trial, August 1947

The International Military Tribunal for the Far East in session.
Tojo is in the witness box at the center

General Tojo hearing his sentence pronounced, November 12, 1948

a vigorous policy.[4] Nagano personally emphasized that operational requirements prohibited an indefinite prolongation of diplomatic efforts. Konoe and Toyoda could make another attempt, but only if they had such faith in success that they could guarantee that the talks would result in an American acceptance of Japan's proposals. If such conviction were lacking, this was not the time for diplomatic "test-firing." Konoe, feeling frustrated and perhaps even confused by what was happening around him, ruefully remarked to a cabinet colleague that he would like to retire from politics and become a Buddhist monk.

The pessimistic view which Admiral Nagano shared with the army general staff concerning the prospect of success in the Japanese-American negotiations was actually far sounder than the optimistic estimate to which Konoe still gave lip service. An American acceptance of Japan's terms in October 1941 would have cleared the way for Japan to conquer all that remained of China, to establish Japanese hegemony over Asia, and to develop closer and more effective ties with the European Axis. By early October 1941 it was obvious that the United States had no intention of performing in the manner required. Thus, from a *military* point of view, the Japanese supreme command was entirely justified in insisting upon a decision for war or peace by October 15. Konoe's alternative simply called for a continuation of the negotiations in the hope that something might happen that Japan could turn to advantage. His one thought seems to have been that by conceding on the form, Japan might be able to keep the essence—yet that had already been tried without success. The Konoe program might have been acceptable to his military colleagues if Japan's national security could have been maintained indefinitely at the current level. Since it could not be, Konoe's suggestion was unrealistic.

The only meaningful Japanese policy that might have been adopted as an alternative to war would have required a conciliatory approach embracing enough concrete concessions to encourage a lifting of the economic blockade which was then in effect, and the negotiation of a settlement with China that would take into account the great advantages which would accrue to both belligerents if they but worked together. This would have required, in turn, a willingness on the part of

---

[4] On October 7, Chief of the Army General Staff Sugiyama conferred with his naval counterpart, Admiral Nagano, and reached what the army has since described as a complete agreement of views. Concern was still felt, however, over the words and actions of Navy Minister Oikawa, who seemed to have certain reservations about the procedure now jointly being advocated by the army and navy divisions of imperial headquarters.

the Japanese army and navy general staffs to slow the trotting horse of their ambition to a walk. Instead, they decided to spur it to a gallop, choosing the calculated risk in a policy of force based on a purely military judgment of the situation, in preference to a policy of reason based on an appreciation of the political, economic, diplomatic, social, and military factors which together comprise the raw materials for decision-making in the modern world. It is in that regard that they bear a burden of responsibility toward the Japanese people in proportion to the lives which that policy cost, the general misery it engendered, and the dangers of immeasurable duration to which it exposed the nation.

Since it was the military rather than the civilians who were plotting the nation's course, it is not surprising that Konoe found himself losing ground as the days passed. Anxiety and suspicion went hand in hand with impatience and intransigence. The negotiations were plagued by the hoary problem of who would give in to whom. Each side wanted the other to look at the issues from a broad point of view. Within the United States, the argument gained favor that since it was Japan whose hands were stained with blood, Japan must be the one to wash them clean. On the opposite side of the Pacific, the feeling grew that since Tokyo had been going out of its way to be "reasonable" in the negotiations, the time had come for Washington to reciprocate. "It's America's turn to say something" was the way the Japanese military put it. From there it was but a short step to the charge that the United States was attempting to drag the negotiations out as long as possible, that the United States was "insincere," and that it was to Japan's interest not to delay any longer.

Needless to say, such charges did not make the premier's life any easier. In casting about for advice, Konoe talked individually with Oikawa and Toyoda, the two ministers whose views were closest to his own. He also conferred with Kido, who again proposed a policy similar to that which he had already outlined on August 7: avoidance of war with the United States—at least in the immediate future; concentration upon "settling" the China Incident (if necessary, by invoking rights of belligerency); and emphasis upon tightening the belt at home during the next decade so as to establish a maximum defense state and enhance Japan's national power. Again, as on September 26, Kido suggested the advisability of reconsidering the imperial conference decision of September 6, which he described as having been made rather abruptly and without a complete airing of views.

Konoe also talked with War Minister Tojo and from him received more than an inkling of the army's attitude. Seeing Japan as the victim of a hostile combination of powers slowly but surely completing their encirclement of the island Empire, Tojo was convinced that the demands of the supreme command had to be met if he and the other cabinet ministers were to fulfill their responsibilities toward the Emperor and the nation. The requirement was clear—the government must decide for or against war during early October. Those who had participated in the imperial conference of September 6 would be flagrantly remiss in their duty if they failed now to make that decision. Japan was in an unenviable position, but the position would not be improved by having the government assume a do-nothing, wait-and-see attitude.[5]

At one of their meetings, Tojo told Konoe that at some point during a man's lifetime he might find it necessary to jump, with his eyes closed, from the veranda of Kiyomizu-dera into the ravine below.[6] That was Tojo's way of saying that he and others in the army believed that there were occasions when success or failure depended on the risks one was prepared to take, and that, for Japan, such an occasion had now arrived. The remark was striking both for its simplicity of outlook and as a portent for the future. It was a pronouncement in the tradition of the samurai, whose willingness to take up any challenge, regardless of the odds, was legendary. The words had a stirring ring, if one did not linger over their meaning. Konoe merely replied that the idea of jumping from Kiyomizu-dera might occur to an individual once or twice in his lifetime but that as the premier of Japan, responsible for a 2,600-year-old national polity and a nation of 100,000,000 people, he could not adopt such an approach to the Empire's problems.[7]

[5] On Konoe's casting about for advice, see Kido "Nikki" for October 9, 1941, S 109:16-17, T 10241-42 (revised, T 11139); Kido aff., S 293:13, T 30959-62 (in which Kido states that his remarks about all-out war in China were prompted by the knowledge that the army would not have listened, at that time, to a plan advocating a total cessation of hostilities; he had to say what he did because only thus could a collision with the United States be avoided); Kido interrog., Mar. 11, 721-23; Kido SKD; Konoe, 127 and 131-32; *PHA*, Part 20, 4008-9, and 4013; and Yano intv.

Dates present something of a problem, since the various accounts do not always agree. For the most part such differences are more annoying than significant and stem largely from faulty memory.

[6] A Buddhist temple located on one of the heights of Kyōto.

[7] The Kiyomizu-dera exchange, as given by Konoe (p. 131), is as follows: Tōjō: "Ningen, tama ni wa Kiyomizu no butai kara me wo tsubutte tobioriru koto mo hitsuyō da." Konoe: "Kojin to shite wa sō yū baai mo isshō ni ichido ya nido wa aru kamo shirenai ga, nisen roppyaku nen no kokutai to, ichioku no kokumin no koto wo kangaeru naraba sekinin no chii ni aru mono to shite dekiru koto de wa nai."

Later, Konoe reflected that there were others who used expressions like "gambling the fate of the nation" and "all or nothing." Matsuoka was one of them. Such statements gave Konoe an uncomfortable feeling. He felt that "safety first" was the best policy. Unless one were certain of victory, one should avoid getting into war.

By the morning of October 12, Konoe's fiftieth birthday, the premier had practically exhausted whatever opportunity existed for devising a solution through consultations with his key ministers. The activity of the go-betweens was exciting attention, especially the comings and goings of Lt. Gen. Suzuki, whose services were in demand by several of the principals. The procedure of communicating with a second man through a third suited the Japanese way of life. Thoughts could be conveyed subtly through the medium which the source might find it difficult to utter directly. The advantage was that the middleman could always be repudiated if necessary; the disadvantage was that the use of a third party could compound existing complications and thus lead to even greater confusion. The practice was considered indispensable by those who were afraid that their telephone conversations might be overheard and that too much activity on their part might make them the target of fanatics. Thus frequent use was made of Lt. Gen. Suzuki (president of the cabinet planning board), of Mr. Tomita (Konoe's chief cabinet secretary), and of Maj. Gen. Muto and Rear Admiral Oka (the heads of the military and naval affairs bureaus of the service ministries).[8]

On October 12, however, Konoe suddenly decided to meet personally with his key cabinet colleagues at least once more, in the hope of achieving the unanimity he would need in order to tackle the supreme-command side of the table. Navy Minister Oikawa had again informed him, through Rear Admiral Oka, that there were those in the ministry who desired to avoid a war with the United States if at all possible, and who consequently did not want a rupture to occur in the diplomatic negotiations. Since Oikawa did not feel he could come right out and say that openly, Oka reported that the navy minister planned to recommend leaving the decision for war or peace *entirely to the premier*.[9]

This cryptic message is open to a number of interpretations. Oikawa—"by nature a man of few words"—may have planned it as a friendly warning to Prince Konoe not to expect the navy minister to take the initiative in stopping the army's sweep toward war. Without the backing of the naval general staff, such an effort would be doomed to failure. Even with general-staff backing, there would be the old army-navy

[8] See Konoe, 127; *PHA*, Part 20, 4009; and Suzuki aff., S 333:7, T 35185-87.

Although the term *san-chōkan* is usually employed in reference to the "Big Three" of the army (the chief of staff, war minister, and inspector general of military training), as used by Konoe (p. 127) the phrase apparently refers, instead, to the president of the cabinet planning board (Suzuki), the chief cabinet secretary (Tomita), and the director of the cabinet bureau of legislation (Murase).

[9] See footnote 12 below.

rivalry to consider and the question of the people's morale. A hesitant navy would soon be charged with cowardice by army propagandists and would thus incur the disfavor of the public. A navy which did not have the confidence to attack the United States and Britain would also be a navy that would not fare well on budget allocations.

On the other hand, the brief message relayed by Oka may have been designed as a friendly inducement to the premier to declare himself frankly against war so as to obtain Oikawa's personal backing and support. If that was the purpose, the statement must have been predicated on a belief that the naval general staff would not be unwilling to forsake a policy of force so long as the responsibility lay with the premier. Admiral Oikawa may have thought that a Japanese concession on the stationing of troops on the continent would lead to a settlement with the United States, but if he were to say so, an open clash with the army would result. In the light of the war in Europe and the threat of its extension to the Far East, it was incumbent upon the services to avoid any situation that could lead to mutual recrimination. The problem facing the nation covered a whole range of issues. It involved something far bigger than just the position of the navy. It was a political problem which required solution by a man like the premier, who could view it from the broadest possible standpoint. According to this interpretation, the navy minister intended to entrust the whole matter to the premier, it being understood that the navy would abide by whatever Prince Konoe decided. Thus war would be avoided, and relations between the army and navy would be preserved from further deterioration.

A third interpretation, and by far the simplest, is that Admiral Oikawa personally did not like the idea of going to war but knew that the naval general staff favored adopting that course. He thus faced a dilemma. In order to avoid responsibility, he decided to act in a way that was essentially irresponsible. He decided to throw the problem into the premier's lap. Perhaps Konoe would be able to think of a solution. If not, the part of the navy which Oikawa represented would always be able to say, "We were ready to follow the premier's lead, but he remained silent. The decision for war or peace was a political matter which had to be settled between the army and Konoe. We were not in a position to interfere."

Although there has been a certain tendency on the part of civilians and naval officers alike to emphasize the second of these three alternative interpretations, the facts actually point in the direction of both the first and the third. There is no evidence that what Oka said, at Oikawa's direction, represented anything but the point of view of a few ranking officers within the navy ministry. Even if Konoe had taken a firm stand, and even if he had been backed up by Oikawa, the army could have been restrained only if the naval general staff had thrown its support to the navy minister rather than to the army general staff. Actually, however, the army and navy elements of the supreme command were in complete harmony in insisting upon a decision for war or peace by October 15. If Oikawa had not formally subscribed to that development, he was at least cognizant of it and largely committed to it by virtue of the superior importance of the command group vis-à-vis the administrative circle.[10] In the light of the "no prospect of success" conclusion shared by the army and navy general staffs, insistence upon October 15 as the deadline was equivalent to a demand that war against the United States now be made the national policy.

When War Minister Tojo was informed of Oikawa's attitude by Konoe's chief cabinet secretary, he took the view that a decision for war or peace should not be left to the premier alone. If the navy lacked confidence with regard to war, Oikawa should frankly say so. In that case, the army would control the war advocates within its ranks. Although Tojo's opinion was conveyed to Oikawa, the navy minister's attitude remained unchanged.[11]

It was thus apparent to Konoe on October 12 that the situation was extremely critical. The conference which he convened at his home in the hope of resolving differences was a five-minister meeting. In addition to the premier, it comprised the war, navy, and foreign ministers and the president of the cabinet planning board, Lt. Gen. Suzuki. As Konoe himself later described it, this conference was "practically the last" that he held "relative to the question of war or peace." It was certainly the most significant.[12]

[10] On October 9, Oikawa had tried to restrain Nagano from making a strong statement during the course of a liaison conference. He had momentarily succeeded, but as the meeting adjourned Nagano had handed his statement to the foreign minister anyway. Toyoda thus learned that the naval general staff would not support further negotiations unless success could be guaranteed, since any prolongation of the talks in Washington would have an adverse effect upon the military operations with which Japan intended to open hostilities (and would further drain Japan's stock of precious oil, the lifeblood of the navy).

After the change of cabinets, which occurred a week later, the new foreign minister was amazed to find that the navy's attitude was practically as strong and rigid as that of the army. Tōgō aff., S 337:6, T 35689.

[11] The channel of communication on this occasion was as follows: Tomita to Mutō to Tōjō to Mutō to Tomita to Oka to Oikawa to Oka to Tomita to Mutō to Tōjō. Konoe, in turn, was briefed by Tomita as the occasion required.

[12] There are many different versions of what was said at the Ogikubo conference of

The ministers gathered at the premier's Ogikubo residence at 2:00 p.m. and did not depart until after six. Only the gist of what was said during that long afternoon is known. Oikawa set the tone of the meeting with a statement to the effect that the time had come to decide on war or peace; if it were to be peace, it must be peace all the way; to continue the negotiations now, and then suspend them several months later, would place the navy in a quandary; if the decision were to be for war, it must be made at once; now was the occasion—the last opportunity for such a choice; if the decision were to be against war, the negotiations must be conducted to the very end "on the basis of achieving success." Within that context, Oikawa favored leaving the matter to the premier.

In other words, the navy minister believed that a half-hearted approach to the negotiations could not be tolerated. If an American capitulation to Japan's terms could not be guaranteed, the talks would have to be suspended and an immediate decision made in favor of war. This was

October 12, 1941. An attempt is made in the text to reconcile the various accounts and to offer a personal interpretation. For material pertaining to the conference (including Oikawa's cryptic message which was conveyed by Oka to Tomita on the morning of October 12, and by Tomita, in turn, to Konoe), see Konoe, 128-29; Konoe, "Dai-sanji Naikaku Sō-jishoku no Tenmatsu," S 109:17-19, T 10249-57 (in which, among other things, Konoe's residence is incorrectly rendered as "Ogigaiso"); *PHA*, Part 20, 4009; Tomita aff., S 315:10, T 33299-302; Tōjō aff., S 343:13-14, T 36289-304; Tōjō interrog., Feb. 11, 3-5, Feb. 15, 4-5, Feb. 23, 5-6, and Feb. 25, 1-3; Oikawa aff., S 316:2, T 33341-43; Oikawa cross-examination, S 316:4, T 33354½-55 and S 327:16, T 34593 (in which Oikawa denies that Konoe ever said to him that the navy should be ashamed of not speaking up); Suzuki aff., S 333:10, T 35205-6; Oka aff., S 316:9, T 33390-95; Mutō aff., S 313:10-11, T 33104-6; Kido "Nikki" for October 12, 1941, S 109:17, T 10246-48 (revised, 11139-40); Kido aff., S 293:13-14, T 30962-68; Kido, "Dai-sanji Konoe Naikaku Kōtetsu no Tenmatsu," S 159:14, T 16198-204; Kido, "Dai-sanji Konoe Naikaku Sō-jishoku no Zengo no Jijō," 1-2; Kido SKD and corresp.; Kido interrog., Mar. 11, 724-29; Kido aff., S 293:17-19, T 30991-31004 (quoting in full a letter from Konoe, describing the circumstances surrounding the resignation of his cabinet, which Kido read at the senior statesmen's conference held on October 17. The English text requires revision, as does another translation which appears in *PHA*, Part 20, 4026-29, under the misleading and erroneous title "The Details of the Cabinet Resignation and the Progress of Japan-American Diplomatic Negotiations Under the Direction of the Council of Senior Statesmen Following the Resignation of the Third Konoye Cabinet"); Ushiba corresp.; Kenryō Satō, "Dai-Tōa Sensō wo Maneita Shōwa no Dōran," 120-22 and corresp.; Hattori, I, 196-98; JRD Monograph No. 147, 57-60 and Appendix 6; JRD, "Interrogations," I:49157 (Seizō Arisue), 49; JRD, "Translation," II:51903 (Item 18, Reference No. 3), 31-33; CF 20, I, 16; Yabe, II, 379-81; and Kenryō Satō, *Tōjō Hideki to Taiheiyō Sensō*, 208-16.

Since Tomita was not present, his so-called minutes were written up later on the basis of information supplied by Konoe. Konoe's several accounts disagree in comparatively unimportant details. Suzuki testified that Konoe asked him to be present to record what was said, but no minutes were produced at the trial. As noted earlier, word-for-word transcripts were practically unknown. Tomita called on Kido at 9:00 p.m. on October 12 to inform him of what had occurred.

precisely the point of view of both the army and navy general staffs. Their approval of a continuation of the negotiations could have been obtained only through unconditional assurances from both Konoe and Foreign Minister Toyoda that *success itself was actually within grasp.*

If Oikawa's desire to let the premier decide was meant to encourage a positive statement from the Konoe-Toyoda quarter, it fell far short of the purpose. To say—as Konoe did—that there was still a *prospect* of success, and that if it were an either-or proposition he personally would favor continuing the negotiations, was meaningless insofar as the army and navy general staffs were concerned. Tojo pointed out that if the supreme-command view were to be changed, it would have to be done through an expression of firm conviction on the part of the premier, the foreign minister, and their cabinet colleagues. Nebulous statements would not do. When Tojo said that, Oikawa voiced his complete agreement.

To a large extent Tojo merely reiterated, with greater emphasis, what the navy minister had already said. The presentations of the two men differed not so much in the purpose as in the cast of their remarks and in the extent of their commitment. Oikawa apparently had some misgivings about the wisdom of adopting what amounted to a supreme-command demand for war; Tojo did not. Where Oikawa hedged or spoke in riddles, Tojo went straight to the point and left nothing in doubt. This was not only a reflection of the war minister's character but also of his personal judgment of the situation. Believing that the negotiations would not result in success for Japan, Tojo argued that a continuation of diplomatic efforts would place the nation at the mercy of an American policy of planned delay. As the talks continued, America's strength would increase while Japan's power declined. Then, if war came anyway, Japan would find that the time spent in further negotiations had cost her the freedom she now possessed with respect to launching military operations. If the foreign minister were firmly convinced, however, that Japan could win acceptance for her position, then he, Tojo, would reconsider the matter. He was not partial to war, he said, but there must be guarantees that Japan would not be led into the kind of situation he had described. Since the supreme command had a vital interest in a decision for war or peace, that matter was not one which could properly be left to the premier alone. Each and every minister bore the responsibility of tendering his advice, and of assisting the throne. A decision in favor of further diplomatic efforts could be effective only if it were also supported by the supreme command. He would like, Tojo said, to hear the foreign minister's views on the outlook for the negotiations.

Although Toyoda proved more specific than Konoe, the foreign minister's approach lacked the quality of assurance which both Oikawa and Tojo had described as being essential to a continuation of negotiations. On the question of outlook, Toyoda noted that since two parties were involved, he could not state that such-and-such a thing would happen. Consequently, he could not guarantee anything or declare that he was confident of success. Much would depend on the conditions Japan was prepared to offer or accept. There were a number of problems in the negotiations, but the most difficult one was the stationing of troops in China. If the army refused to budge even an inch from its earlier position in that regard, then there was no prospect of success. But if the army were prepared to make some concession on the troop issue, no matter how small, then it could not be said that there was absolutely no prospect of terminating the negotiations successfully.

Tojo tackled this with vigor. From the beginning of the negotiations, he asserted, Japan had recognized the general principle of withdrawing all troops from China. The conditions Japan was offering for a restoration of peace between herself and China were "very generous: no annexations and no indemnities." The talks with the United States had been conducted on the basis of Japan's forces being where they were in accordance with the provisions of a treaty duly signed with the Nanking government. The American aim, however, had gradually become clear. The United States was demanding an unconditional and immediate withdrawal of all troops, in fact as well as in name. The stationing of soldiers in China was a matter of supreme importance to the army and consequently was one on which the army could not possibly make concessions. It should be remembered, he said, that the fighting was still in progress and that the army had in the neighborhood of a million men in China. The Incident had broken out "because of the illegal acts of the Chinese." Japan's purpose was "to force China to reflect." Without guarantees against the resumption of illegal acts, no withdrawal would be possible. The interior of China was beset by Communists and other lawless elements seeking to overthrow peace and order. The stationing of Japanese troops in designated areas was essential for the well-being of both China and Japan and for their successful economic development. Troops not needed for that purpose could be withdrawn once the Incident had been settled. But to pull out before the aims of the war were achieved "would not be in keeping with the dignity [*ishin*] of the Army." The entire general staff "as well as the troops abroad [*desaki no gun*] were absolutely opposed" to such a course.

Tojo's remarks prompted Konoe to suggest exchanging the name for the reality—that is, giving in to the United States on the form (by agreeing to withdraw Japan's troops in principle) but preserving the essence (through an arrangement with China that would permit either the retention of some Japanese troops or the subsequent dispatch of others). But Tojo proved immovable on this point, apparently because he believed that what Konoe was advocating was easier said than done. He argued that if Japan were "to swallow the American demand in one piece" (at his postwar trial, he used the term *unomi*—literally, "to gulp in the manner of a cormorant") and withdraw all of her troops from China, Japanese efforts and sacrifices of more than four years would come to nought and Chinese contempt for Japan would grow and grow. The Communists would intensify their all-out activities against Japan, with the result that Japanese relations with China would worsen. In the end, there would inevitably be a repetition of the kind of trouble Japan had encountered in China in the past and thus the outbreak of China Incident II and China Incident III. Since a cession of Chinese territory had been ruled out by the Konoe declaration of December 1938, the army could not be expected to withdraw entirely from China. The loss of Japanese prestige that would accompany such a withdrawal at the command of the United States would not be confined to China alone but would spread to Manchuria and Korea as well. Nor was the troop question the only stumbling-block in the Japanese-American negotiations. There were, in addition, Hull's four principles, Japan's interpretation of the Tripartite Pact, nondiscrimination in trade, and other matters. Thus, the chances for a favorable settlement could hardly be said to be promising.

How often the talk circled the same issues is not known, but such records as do exist convey a sense of redundancy and hopelessness. At one point, Konoe was moved to say that if the army was insisting upon war, he would not be able to take the responsibility. Tojo quickly replied that the premier's statement was incomprehensible in light of the fact that he had participated in the imperial conference of September 6 and had already accepted responsibility for the decision of that date. Action tantamount to changing a decision made in the presence of the Emperor could not be tolerated. It had been established, at that time, that Japan would continue the negotiations while preparing for war and that the government would resolve upon the use of force if, by early

October, there was no prospect of achieving success through diplomacy. The time to choose between war and peace had now come.

Although Konoe knew this to be true, he nevertheless suggested a broader interpretation of the clause in the imperial conference decision to which Tojo referred. That clause, Konoe said, would be applicable only if achieving success in the negotiations was judged to be *absolutely* hopeless.

By the time all these views had been expressed, it was clear that the five-minister conference had failed to clear the atmosphere. Opinions at the end were as divided as at the beginning. At Tojo's suggestion, however, a kind of compromise was arranged and accepted. It was agreed that Japan would not give in on the stationing of troops in China or change the various policies centering thereon. It was also agreed that Japan would do nothing to jeopardize the gains attained to date in the China Incident. With those points constituting the preconditions of any further effort, the Japanese government would strive for a diplomatic success. Confidence on that score must be expressed by the time desired by the supreme command (that is, by October 15 or later, depending on the willingness of imperial headquarters to postpone the launching of operations beyond the beginning of November). While proceeding thus, Japan would halt operational preparations. The foreign minister would study whether or not success was possible on the basis of the above conditions.

All present approved this proposition, and Tojo—responding to a question from Suzuki—promised that the army would be agreeable. The meeting then adjourned without any fundamental reconciliation of views having been reached at all.

Nor is it surprising that this should have happened. It was not within the power of these five ministers, including Tojo and Oikawa, to go against the will of the supreme command. If these five men were divided on the policy demanded by the army and navy general staffs, they could only break up and go home, skirting a final confrontation for the moment through a stopgap proposal of the type offered by Tojo. Theoretically they might have tried to recast the national policy along the lines suggested by Toyoda and Konoe, but in practice such a departure from standard operating procedure could have been attempted only if the five ministers were in absolute agreement with each other. In fact, they were split, and although Tojo may appear to have been in the minority in a strictly Western sense, he was actually speaking from a position of great strength. Despite the somewhat fuzzy wording of

Oikawa's statement, its purport had placed the admiral at Tojo's side rather than at Konoe's. Even if Oikawa had really backed Konoe and Toyoda, the three together would still have been in a comparatively weak position, for Tojo was a representative of the determining element in the decision-making equation and thus spoke not only as war minister but on behalf of the nucleus group within the army general staff, the true driving-force behind all policy formulation.

The failure of the Ogikubo conference of October 12 to alter the balance in any way whatsoever inevitably meant that Konoe either would have to lead the nation into war or make room for someone who would accept that responsibility if called upon to do so.

Frustration resulting from the impasse in the Japanese-American negotiations as well as the relentless pressure imposed by Japan's military timetable now rapidly combined to produce yet another cabinet crisis. The intra-elite consultations grew in number and intensity—a sign that a storm was about to break. The whole of Monday, October 13, was spent in a flurry of talk and movement.[13] War Minister Tojo met with Chief of the Army General Staff Sugiyama to brief him on the gist of what had occurred at Konoe's residence the day before. As it turned out, the agreement to suspend operational preparations while diplomatic negotiations were continued did not sit well with the supreme command, but in the end the general staff acquiesced.

Premier Konoe spent part of the day at the palace, giving the Emperor a detailed report on the crisis confronting the cabinet and—as usual—conferring with Marquis Kido. During an audience with the Emperor, the lord privy seal found His Majesty extremely worried. The situation prevailing since early October had been unprecedented. By October 13 the Emperor seemed to be afraid that war might break out at any moment. He had regarded the cabinet change of July (the dropping of Matsuoka) as a maneuver aimed at avoiding war, at least for the time being. Now it was apparent that the hope of reaching a successful conclusion in the Japanese-American negotiations was on the wane and that anything might happen. The Emperor therefore spoke to Kido about certain matters which would require attention in case the worst occurred. If war came, a clear outlook with respect to the conclusion of the conflict

[13] With reference to the various consultations which took place on October 13, see Tōjō aff., S 343:14, T 36304; Konoe, 129; Kido SKD and corresp.; Konoe, "Dai-sanji Naikaku Sō-jishoku no Tenmatsu," S 109:19, T 10257-58; Suzuki aff., S 333:10, T 35205-8; Kido "Nikki" for October 13, 1941, S 109:20, T 10274-75; and Kido aff., S 293:14-15, T 30969-71.

would be necessary. The preparation and promulgation of an imperial rescript would also be mandatory. At the time of Japan's withdrawal from the League of Nations, the Emperor said, he had emphasized the concept of *bunbu kakujun*: an admonition that civil and military officials should individually perform their proper functions and should refrain from coveting each other's duties or transgressing upon them. Unfortunately, it appeared that his point had somehow been neglected. Nor was that the only case. The rescript issued at the time of the Tripartite Pact had emphasized that the alliance was being concluded for the sake of peace. Consequently, it was "especially unsatisfactory" that that alliance should now be regarded by the people as being directed against America and Britain. From these past experiences it was clear that greater care was necessary in the future. Should war now occur, His Majesty declared, he would like Konoe and Kido to join with him, he would desire to express his wishes carefully, and he would want those wishes incorporated into the rescript which the cabinet would present for his approval.

The Emperor also told Kido that the government must have a clear understanding of the situation in Europe, particularly with regard to the question of peace between Britain and Germany, or between Germany and the Soviet Union. Negotiations would have to be undertaken to obtain German cooperation in the Japanese war effort and to guard against a separate German peace. It would be essential, also, to study thoroughly—from the very beginning—measures designed to bring the war to an end. In that regard, a policy of friendly relations with the Vatican should be adopted, including an exchange of envoys.

By comparison with other statements attributed to the Emperor from time to time, these remarks to Kido on October 13 are rather surprisingly specific. They accurately reveal how far matters had progressed and how tense the situation had become. The army and navy general staffs wanted a decision for war. The two service ministers wanted either a decision for war or a decision for peace. The latter, however, would be acceptable only if made with the conviction, and accompanied by firm guarantees, that a continuation of negotiations (i.e., a decision for peace) would lead to a Japanese diplomatic victory. The premier argued that there was still a prospect of success and that negotiations should be continued. The foreign minister advised that no one could guarantee a diplomatic victory because no one could say with certainty how the other side would respond to a proposal or what it would offer on its own initiative. He thought, however, that a Japanese concession on the stationing of troops in China would open the way to a settlement with the United States. Privately Toyoda told Konoe that such a concession was the only way to a settlement.

There was, however, one other thought on how to handle the crisis. Kido had already advised the premier to take the initiative with respect to a reconsideration of the imperial conference decision of September 6. This idea now reappeared in the form of a suggestion made by Suzuki to Konoe following the Ogikubo conference. On Konoe's urging, Suzuki sounded out Tojo on October 13. The war minister's reaction was not encouraging. A decision made at an imperial conference was supposed to represent the "last word" on a subject. It was not something that could easily or lightly be changed, and especially not by those who had been responsible for it in the first place—and barely a month before. Tojo therefore said that he would find it difficult to agree to such a course. Only through a change in leadership could such a thing be done. When Suzuki reported this to Konoe, the prince replied that he would talk with Tojo about the matter the following day.[14]

The next morning, October 14, Konoe requested War Minister Tojo to stop by to see him prior to the cabinet meeting scheduled for 10:00 a.m.[15] Referring at the outset to the key issue, the stationing of

[14] *Ibid.* Suzuki and Kido also talked together on the evening of October 13. Suzuki's affidavit indicates that he urged the necessity of obtaining imperial permission to wipe the slate clean so as to be able to continue the negotiations (the gist of his advice to Konoe). Kido's diary does not specifically state what Suzuki said. See also Tōjō aff., S 343:15, T 36307.

[15] On the Konoe-Tōjō exchange of views, which is recapitulated in the text which follows, see Konoe, 129-30 and 133; *PHA*, Part 20, 4009-10 and 4013; Yabe, II, 383-84; Konoe, "Dai-sanji Naikaku Sō-jishoku no Tenmatsu," S 109:19, T 10258-62; and Tōjō aff., S 343:13, T 36294, and S 343:15, T 36304-5 (in which Tōjō noted that, although somewhat embellished, Konoe's account of their conversation on the morning of October 14 was generally in accord with what had occurred); and Tōjō interrog., Feb. 25, 3.

See also Konoe's letter of resignation presented to the throne on October 16, 1941, S 110:3. According to a memorandum of July 8, 1946, attached to the original document (No. 1468) presented as an exhibit (No. 1152), the Japanese text of Konoe's letter of resignation (S 110:3) was "compared with the original located in the Emperor's Archives and found to be word for word the same." The English translation as given in T 10284-88, however, requires correction. In the light of the above memorandum, the texts given in Konoe, 137-39 and 145-47 (containing variations), should be disregarded, as should the English translation in *PHA*, Part 20, 4025-26. A hand-written note, in English, attached to the original file of the several versions of this letter of resignation in the possession of the International Prosecution Section, is quoted here as an item of historical interest: "Major General Tanaka, Ryūkichi, who is now in this building as a witness in the trial, is of the opinion that none of these papers was actually presented to the Throne, because none of them is written on hōsho paper (very fine, thick, white Japanese paper), as is the case with any petition presented to the Throne. But the Major General is sure that a petition in similar wording (written on hōsho

Japanese troops in China, Konoe reiterated his belief that a concession by Japan in that regard would make possible a settlement with the United States. The China Incident, for which he felt grave personal responsibility, was still unsettled after four years. He consequently questioned the wisdom of becoming further involved by extending the Empire's dominion to the South. It might be one thing to do so if only a year or two were required to complete the task, but expert opinion was practically unanimous that no one could predict exactly how long it would take "once the arrow had been shot from the bow." It might take five years; it might take ten.

Having said that much, Konoe did what many of his contemporaries were fond of doing—he turned back to the great days of the Russo-Japanese war to cite a parallel and to quote a precedent. He recalled that on February 4, 1904, prior to the imperial conference at which war or peace was to be decided, the Emperor Meiji had summoned Marquis Ito to ask that trusted adviser whether there was a prospect of victory in the event of a war with Russia. Ito replied that there was not, but that Japan would be able to prevent the Russian army from invading Korea for a year or a year and a half. During that time, he said, Japan must request the mediation of a third nation to bring the war to an end. Since the other major powers had taken sides, the logical choice was the United States. Measures to secure the eventual services of that country would be adopted at once. This answer relieved the Emperor's mind and as a consequence the decision for war was made at the conference. That night Ito called in a Harvard-trained member of the House of Peers on friendly terms with Theodore Roosevelt and asked him to depart immediately for the United States to prepare the way.[16]

According to Konoe, this story revealed the prudence exercised by the elders of that day. War with the United States, the prince said, would become a global conflict, leaving no one to come forth in the role of intermediary. The world situation was entirely different from what it

---

paper) was presented to the Throne, these papers being its copies. The translator humbly communicates the Major General's opinion for what it is worth."

[16] Konoe may have referred to this story (and another analogous tale concerning Ōyama and Kodama) earlier in October (as suggested in *PHA*, Part 20, 4013), but Konoe's "Dai-sanji Naikaku Sō-jishoku no Tenmatsu" (S 109:19) specifies October 14 as the date (which seems more likely).

The Kaneko mission to the United States is also noted briefly in Yanaga, 312, in which it is revealed that Kaneko and Theodore Roosevelt had known each other at Harvard, a factor which obviously influenced the government in its selection of a "publicity agent," just as the Nomura-FDR acquaintanceship of World War I played a part in the choice of the admiral as ambassador in 1941.

had been in 1904. Germany, Japan's ally, might be powerful in Europe but in the Far East she was not. Japan would have to assume the initiative and attack the Philippines. The "down with Hitler" attitude which had been prevalent in the United States would be replaced by a surge of feeling against Japan. Lindbergh's arguments against American participation in the war would be meaningless, since his opposition, which was based on a belief in the invincibility of Germany, would be inapplicable if Japan attacked the Philippines.

Konoe also reminded Tojo that Britain's ability to continue to stand up to the Germans depended greatly on American assistance. In the event of a Japanese-American conflict, that assistance might decline, thus giving rise to a movement for peace within the British Isles. The matter would not be serious if Japan could persuade Germany to launch an invasion of Britain at that opportune moment, but a cross-Channel attack required naval power. Germany's strength was being depleted by the Nazi-Soviet war and so a feeling in favor of peace might become pronounced in Germany as well. It was therefore possible that hostilities in the Pacific would hasten the restoration of peace in Europe. In other words—and here the argument was reminiscent of Matsuoka—Britain, the United States, Germany, and the Soviet Union might settle their differences at the expense of the Far East. Instead of further fighting, Konoe said, it would be better to put an end to the China Incident so that Japan, backed by a navy that was fully intact, would be able to make its influence felt at the peace conference that would follow the end of the war in Europe.

Tojo listened to all that Konoe had to say, but his mind remained unchanged. His purpose was to bring the Konoe Cabinet to a decision in accordance with the policy of September 6 and in accordance, also, with the demands of the supreme command. If the cabinet did not act, he would call for a resignation en masse as the only other means by which the ministers of state could absolve themselves of their responsibility toward the throne. And so when Konoe had finished speaking, Tojo again replied as before. In the light of the many sacrifices made to date, he could not agree to a withdrawal of troops in principle. He could not concede that point even at the risk of his position. Giving in on the form while retaining the essence was easily said, but the morale of the army could not be maintained through such a course. The real purpose of the United States was the domination of the Far East. Consequently, to yield on one matter would be to encourage other demands, until there would be no end to the concessions required of Japan. The difficulty, Tojo said, was that the premier was too aware of the weaknesses within Japan. Since America "must have weaknesses of her own," the premier's opinion was "overly pessimistic."[17] Seeing the uselessness of further discussion, the prince asked the war minister to repeat his views at the cabinet meeting that was to follow. Tojo took his leave with the words, "I guess all this is a matter of the difference in our personalities." When Konoe later recorded this remark, he noted that Tojo had spoken with feeling.[18]

The emotion which Tojo displayed at the cabinet meeting was even more intense than his manner on leaving the premier. No sooner had the proceedings begun than he excitedly and emphatically stated the reasons why the Japanese-American negotiations should no longer be continued. His presentation was a repetition of everything he had said before, but his patience seemed exhausted. Tojo was a man of quick temper by nature, known for his decisiveness of action. The time already spent in trailing the same problem without being able to close in upon it had undoubtedly been exasperating to him. He seems to have entertained a strong suspicion that the navy was trying to avoid the responsibility that would go with urging a decision in favor of war. Since it would be a grave matter to launch hostilities if the navy were not fully confident, Tojo felt Oikawa should declare his views frankly and openly. When Oikawa did not, Tojo became angry. Since the navy would have to play such a large role in any war in the Pacific, the responsibility of the navy minister was very great. Although operational matters fell primarily within the jurisdiction of the army and navy general staffs, certain aspects of any operational question, such as organization and mobilization, involved the service ministers as well. Thus, the issue facing Japan was no longer one which the navy minister could casually assign to the premier.

There had been talk of relying upon the synthetic production of oil as a way out of Japan's difficulties, but the army was of the opinion that such production would fall far short of the quantity needed and consequently could not provide a solution at all. If Konoe decided against war, a clash would result between the cabinet and the supreme command.

[17] Yanaga, 598, states that among the weaknesses mentioned by Tōjō were "the large number of Americans of German extraction and the possibility of labor troubles."

[18] Tōjō's final words, which I have translated somewhat freely, were "Kore wa seikaku no sōi desu naa." Konoe, 133. Higashikuni, *Watakushi no Kiroku*, 62-66, records a discussion he once had with Tōjō about settling the China Incident. When pressed, Tōjō remained adamant, declaring finally: "Kenkai no sōi da!" ("That's a matter of opinion!"). For another conversation which ended on the same note, see Higashikuni, *Ichi Kōzoku no Sensō Nikki*, 79-82.

Along with others in the army, Tojo felt that the admirals, who had long been clamoring about the Anglo-American desire to reduce the Japanese fleet to the level of the Italian navy, should not now be backing down. Entwined with that view was the knowledge that without the navy the imperial army would be landlocked within the Japanese islands, cut off from the continent and the South. Tojo's ire was also aroused by the belief that the navy would probably be only too ready to approve a troop withdrawal from China, since its commitment of forces there was very small in comparison with that of the army.

Despite these opinions, Tojo had somehow managed to keep his temper in check during the Ogikubo conference on Sunday, October 12. By the following Tuesday morning, however, the effort at restraint had become too great. It may have seemed to him that Konoe and others wished to talk the problem to death, and that the only way to get a decision was to force the issue. The meeting at which his "explosion" occurred represented the first time the problem of the Japanese-American negotiations had come before the full cabinet.[19] The arguments he presented as to why the negotiations should not be continued unless there was absolute confidence in their ultimate success were the same that he had used on the earlier occasions when the problem had been discussed within a smaller circle. The only difference was perhaps a greater bluntness on his part and less willingness to continue the debate, as witnessed by the open clash which developed between him and Admiral Toyoda, the foreign minister. The influence of operational considerations was overwhelmingly apparent in all that Tojo said. In one exchange with Toyoda, Tojo asserted that rather than interfering with diplomacy, military and naval affairs were being obstructed by diplomacy. A return to the *status quo ante*, to the "small Japan" of the days before the Incident, was absolutely out of the question. To put into effect a policy of stationing troops in China under the guise of a withdrawal in principle, as was being advocated in some quarters, was manifestly a "practical impossibility." To give in by withdrawing Japan's troops would be equivalent to surrender.

[19] On Tōjō's "explosion," see Konoe, 130 and 134; Konoe, "Dai-sanji Naikaku Sō-jishoku no Tenmatsu," S 109:19, T 10262-63; Tōjō aff., S 343:13, T 36294, and S 343:15, T 36305 and 36307; Tōjō interrog., Feb. 25, 2-3; Suzuki aff., S 333:10, T 35208; Mutō aff., S 313:10, T 33104; Yamamoto aff., S 251:3-5, T 25908-18 (on Toyoda's attitude); Kenryō Satō, "Dai-Tōa Sensō wo Maneita Shōwa no Dōran," 121-22 and corresp. (in which Mutō is said to have been surprised and exasperated by what Tōjō had done); Hattori, I, 198-200; JRD Monograph No. 147, 60-61; and JRD, "Translation," II:51903 (Item 18, Reference No. 3), 31-33; Yabe, II, 384-85; and Kenryō Satō, *Tōjō Hideki to Taiheiyō Sensō*, 218-19.

As Konoe himself later described it, Tojo literally put on a "one-man show." Those cabinet ministers who had not been privy to the debates which had preceded this event were bewildered. They froze in their seats in embarrassed confusion, saying not a single word. Of the ministers who had some reason to expect an outburst from General Tojo, only Toyoda took up the challenge. The rest remained as silent as stone, as if they could treat what was alien to the proprieties as though it had not been heard, and so, by ignoring it, pretend that it had never been said.

For the moment, that was what they did. After Tojo and Toyoda had each had their say, other matters were discussed, without the point at issue being raised again. But, in reality, the clash between the two ministers in front of all of their colleagues meant that the game was up. And yet, still another effort was made to bring the opposing forces into balance before the breach which Tojo had opened with Toyoda engulfed the entire cabinet.

Maj. Gen. Muto, the chief of the military affairs bureau, who occupied in relation to Tojo the same position held by Oka with respect to Oikawa, assumed the familiar role of go-between. Muto hurriedly got in touch with the key officers of the army general staff to discuss the situation. He interpreted the attitude being manifested by Oikawa as an indication that the navy wished, by changing the imperial conference decision of September 6, to avoid going to the point where it would have to decide in favor of beginning a war. In the light of that attitude, he asked the army general staff whether it might not be necessary for the army to change its views as well. But the officers with whom he talked replied that the naval general staff was *not* thinking of modifying the earlier decision, and consequently the army general staff would not shift its position either.

Here was the ultimate result of the rivalry and friction which had been building up over the years between the two services. In a situation in which each had an enormous responsibility, neither would take the initiative in assuming the full measure of that responsibility.

The general staffs of both services were intent upon obtaining an immediate American diplomatic capitulation or an immediate governmental decision in favor of war against the United States. A more cautious element within the navy ministry, being somewhat less committed than the command group, realized that the decision for war that was demanded by the general staffs might be in excess of Japan's capabilities. Instead of assuming this burden squarely, the navy ministry, under Oikawa, endeavored to shift the responsibility to an already tottering premier. Part of the reason for doing so was the knowledge that the naval general staff shared the army general staff's desire to resort to force in the near future so as to take advantage of that brief period, beginning early in November, during which conditions for launching operations would be at their optimum. The war ministry, under Tojo, was determined that the navy ministry should not thus be permitted to shirk its duties. Realizing the great role that Japan's battle fleet would have in hostilities against the United States and Great Britain, Tojo, Muto, and others in their circle began to fear the consequences of towing a possibly reluctant and divided navy into the deep water of a war which it apparently did not want and for which, conceivably, it might not be prepared. But Tojo and his subordinates avoided facing up to that issue. Instead of going directly to the navy and thrashing the matter out secretly until mutual agreement had been reached, the war ministry group demanded an open declaration by the navy of whatever doubts were entertained. Actually, such a semi-public confession was not possible, because the group charged with naval operations did not reciprocate the navy minister's lack of confidence. But even if the admirals of the naval general staff had shared Oikawa's misgivings, it is extremely doubtful that they would have revealed them. Since they did not trust the army, they would not voluntarily have placed in its hands an obvious means of giving the navy a "bad press." The army, for its part, was equally reluctant to adopt any procedures which might be utilized by the navy in a similar fashion.

After his fruitless meeting with the army general staff, Muto proceeded to call upon Chief Cabinet Secretary Tomita to solicit his good offices in obtaining a clear-cut naval statement. No matter how insistent the army might be, Muto said, war could not be carried out without the approval of the navy. If the navy felt it could not conduct a war of the type which now loomed before Japan, or if it did not want such a war, the navy should come right out and say so. If such a pronouncement were forthcoming, ways could be found to dissuade the army from the course now being followed and to control any dissident elements. Such control would be impossible if the navy insisted upon leaving the matter solely to the premier. But this further effort by Muto also failed. When his message was relayed by Tomita to Rear Admiral Oka, the latter replied that the navy could not oblige. The most that it could do was to repeat its earlier stand about entrusting the matter to the premier and abiding by whatever he might decide. Thus was the deadlock of the morning confirmed.[20]

While Muto had been conferring with the army general staff and with Tomita, Prince Konoe had been laying his own plans for dealing with the situation which now confronted him. Late in the afternoon of October 14 the premier summoned the president of the cabinet planning board, Lt. Gen. Suzuki, and asked him to call on War Minister Tojo. Because of the latter's attitude, Konoe said, negotiations with the United States were no longer possible; consequently, the cabinet must resign. Since recourse to such action was unavoidable in view of the war minister's stand, Konoe wanted to learn General Tojo's ideas on controlling the political situation after the fall of the cabinet. He needed the information, the prince said, because he would have to report to the Emperor on the outlook ahead.

Upon leaving the premier, Suzuki dutifully went to the war minister's official residence to deliver the message with which he had been entrusted. Tojo replied that he did not normally like to discuss privately matters relating to the imperial prerogatives, but that in view of the request made by General Suzuki on Prince Konoe's behalf he would state his views. He then launched into a recapitulation of the highlights of the situation. From what he said, it was clear that he blamed the navy for the current state of affairs. It appeared as if the navy did not want war, Tojo said, but he could not understand why the navy minister would not come to him and say so outright. If the navy minister would do that, the war minister would have to reconsider. It was truly regrettable that the navy kept insisting upon placing the entire burden of responsibility on the shoulders of the premier. Such an approach could only perpetuate the impasse. The failure of the navy to come to grips with the problem was equivalent to a complete upsetting of the imperial conference decision of September 6. All who had had a part in that conference should resign, for it was obvious that they had failed to meet their responsibility with respect to advising and assisting the throne. Such a resignation would permit the incoming government to start over

[20] The factual details of the Mutō effort on the afternoon of October 14 are from Mutō aff., S 313:10-11, T 33104-6; Oka aff., S 316:9-10, T 33393-97; Konoe, 134-35; Konoe, "Dai-sanji Naikaku Sō-jishoku no Tenmatsu," S 109:19, T 10263-64; *PHA*, Part 20, 4010; Oikawa aff., S 316:2, T 33343; and Tōjō aff., S 343:15, T 36306-7. See also Kenryō Satō, "Dai-Tōa Sensō wo Maneita Shōwa no Dōran," 122. It should be noted that some elements, especially on the supreme-command side, would have preferred avoiding, through the retention of Konoe, the political vacuum which might result from a change in cabinets. See, for example, Hattori, I, 200.

from the beginning by taking a fresh look at the situation and by devising a new plan to meet it. Two requirements were essential for Konoe's successor: he must be able to understand the imperial wishes without difficulty and he must be capable of unifying the army and the navy. Since there was no one so qualified among His Majesty's subjects, there was no other way but to request the emergence of an imperial prince to head the new cabinet.[21] It was his opinion that Prince Higashikuni was the most suitable man for the post. So far as he himself was concerned, Tojo added, it was very difficult to ask Konoe to resign, but there was really no alternative. He therefore hoped that Konoe would exert his efforts toward requesting the Emperor to bestow the mandate upon His Imperial Highness, Prince Higashikuni.

By the time Suzuki had taken leave of Tojo and crossed the city to Konoe's Ogikubo residence, it was already 10:30 p.m. The premier was extremely pleased by what Suzuki told him, for he believed that Higashikuni was opposed to war and would therefore carry on the negotiations with the United States. Apparently Konoe also thought that the presence of an imperial prince on the scene would serve to restrain those who might otherwise be inclined to cause trouble. He consequently decided that he would recommend Higashikuni to the Emperor. As Tojo had done, the premier requested Suzuki to inform Marquis Kido of these developments. It was 12:30 a.m. when the two men finally parted for the night.[22]

The following day, Wednesday, October 15, was spent much in the manner of the preceding Monday, with Lt. Gen. Suzuki constantly on the move, calling first upon one and then upon another of the principals, with Marquis Kido serving as a focal point. The gulf between Konoe and Tojo had widened so much that the premier felt his position was virtually impossible. Tojo had even suggested that it would be better if they refrained from meeting personally because he was afraid that he might get excited and lose his temper.

[21] Konoe, although a prince (*kōshaku*), was not a member of a family of the blood and consequently was not an imperial prince (*miya-sama*).

[22] With regard to developments from the late afternoon of October 14 through midnight, see Konoe, 135-36; Konoe, "Dai-sanji Sō-jishoku no Tenmatsu," S 109:19, T 10265-66; *PHA*, Part 20, 4010; Tōjō aff., S 343:15, T 36306-7 and 36310-11; Suzuki aff., S 333:10, T 35208-9; Kido SKD and corresp.; and Kenryō Satō, "Dai-Tōa Sensō wo Maneita Shōwa no Dōran," 122. The two Konoe accounts differ somewhat on details but are in general agreement on all key points.

The records are silent on the question of whether Tōjō, in suggesting that Konoe resign, acted purely on his own initiative because of his knowledge of the army general staff's point of view, or whether he formally consulted the chief of the army general staff and the inspector-general of military training, which was the usual procedure.

As the hours passed, it became apparent that notwithstanding the joint recommendation of Tojo and Konoe, the lord privy seal did not look with favor upon the emergence of Higashikuni or, for that matter, any other imperial prince. When Suzuki had reported to Kido early that morning, the Emperor's closest adviser had proved noncommittal, saying only that the matter would require very careful thought because of its unprecedented nature and because of the possible danger that some members of the army might be thinking of marching to war behind the figure of the prince. Later, however, Kido had asked Suzuki to inquire of Tojo whether he would be able to control the advocates of war within the army in the event a cabinet headed by Prince Higashikuni should decide against launching hostilities. Tojo's reply proved as honest as it was unsatisfactory. If the army could not be controlled in such an eventuality, he said, under whom, then, could it be controlled? But from a practical point of view, Tojo added, he could not state unequivocally whether the army could actually be restrained. In answer to another question with respect to the precise purpose of having Higashikuni become premier, Tojo replied that he hoped the prince would be able to bring about harmony between the army and navy.

In the course of the day and on into the evening, Kido spoke also with the Emperor, with Premier Konoe, and with the imperial household minister. He found the latter not only surprised by the Tojo-Konoe suggestion but also strongly opposed to it. The Emperor himself, while not absolutely adverse to bestowing the mandate upon Prince Higashikuni, nevertheless indicated that such a move would be suitable only if there were no danger of the prince being used to lead the nation into war. When Konoe was received in audience late in the afternoon, the Emperor spoke to him in a similar vein. Konoe interpreted the Emperor's remarks as constituting a tacit acceptance of the idea that the third Konoe Cabinet would resign. Whether or not Higashikuni would be named premier remained an open question. A long consultation between Konoe and Kido followed. During the evening the premier informed the privy seal by telephone that he was planning to visit Higashikuni to broach the idea to him informally. Kido replied that he felt it would be premature to consult Higashikuni. If the matter was carried out on the government's responsibility, however, the premier was free to do as he wished. At midnight Konoe telephoned again to say that His Imperial Highness had asked for time to think things over.

And so another day of political maneuvering ended with the Konoe Cabinet one step closer to a resignation.[23]

The reasoning behind Kido's objection to an imperial prince being nominated premier was unquestionably sound. As lord privy seal, he bore a heavy responsibility for overseeing the continued maintenance of an imperial institution unblemished in any way. It was against that duty that every proposal affecting the throne was weighed. He felt it unwise to risk having the selection of a member of the imperial family construed as indicating that no suitable or capable men could be found among His Majesty's subjects. Thus, Higashikuni could become premier only if the army and navy argued that an imperial prince was needed to help secure an orderly transition from a war policy to a peace policy—in other words, only if a *volte-face* was contemplated. In the absence of such an army-navy commitment, bestowal of the mandate upon any imperial prince would be manifestly unwise.

Tojo and Konoe were not the only ones who were talking in terms of Higashikuni. His emergence was also being advocated within civilian rightist circles, notably by several figures who had been involved in the *shinpeitai* incident of July 1933. It was thus clear that the name of His Imperial Highness appealed to quarters which did not share similar motives. Konoe believed that an "imperial cabinet" (i.e., one headed by an imperial prince) could be used to restrain the army and avert war. Tojo, while not necessarily committing himself on the question of war or peace, emphasized that in the event of trouble only a cabinet led by an imperial prince might stand a chance of overcoming the difficulty. If one took Tojo's argument as being candid, it made a great deal of sense—rather more sense, perhaps, than what Konoe was saying—but there nevertheless remained the nucleus group within the army. There

[23] On the events of October 15, see Konoe, 136-37; Konoe, "Dai-sanji Naikaku Sō-jishoku no Tenmatsu," S 109:19-20, T 10266-69; *PHA*, Part 20, 4010-11 (Higashikuni was not "Chief of the General Staff" as stated therein); Kido "Nikki" for October 15, 1941, S 109:20-21, T 10275-79 (revised 11140-41, but further revision is necessary; Kido had an audience with the Emperor from 5:35 to 5:50 p.m., not a.m., as stated); Kido aff., S 293:15-16, T 30972-80; Kido, "Dai-sanji Konoe Naikaku Kōtetsu no Tenmatsu," S 159:14, T 16204-6; Kido SKD and corresp.; Suzuki aff., S 333:10-11, T 35209-11; and Tōjō aff., S 343:15, T 36309-11. See also Kido "Nikki" for October 16, 1941, S 110:2-3, T 10282 (corrected 11141); Kenryō Satō, "Dai-Tōa Sensō wo Maneita Shōwa no Dōran," 123; and Higashikuni, *Ichi Kōzoku no Sensō Nikki*, 88-91.

Higashikuni was also visited by Vice-Minister of War Heitarō Kimura, who was sent by Tōjō to encourage the prince to accept the mandate if it were bestowed upon him. Higashikuni seems to have given both Konoe and Kimura the impression that he might indeed be willing to assume the premiership, but Kido later heard directly from Higashikuni that he was not inclined to accept.

was considerable room for doubt as to whether the members of that group would prove as reasonable as some of their superiors. Tojo himself had been unable to guarantee that discipline could be maintained in any eventuality. Within the rightist camp there was a desire for war that might crystallize into an effort to use a cabinet headed by Higashikuni to push the nation over the brink. Included in this group was a former military aide to Prince Higashikuni who had once stood trial for his part in the *shinpeitai* affair. If the prince were now given the mandate, it would be practically impossible to eliminate such persons from the scene. Somehow or other they might be able to influence policy.

Finally, whatever his accomplishments might be, Higashikuni had had absolutely no training or experience in politics. In fact, his life had been spent in the imperial army, in which he held the rank of general. He might consequently find it impossible to get the current situation, in which one complication was piled upon another, firmly enough in his grasp to devise countermeasures. At the very least, he would find the premiership a most difficult post. He might become a mere ornament or figurehead, "a puppet of the positivists within the army," with the real power resting in the hands of the deputy premier—probably the war minister. Thus, even with a cabinet headed by an imperial prince, the chance of avoiding war seemed exceedingly slight. In case the worst did happen, the responsibility for war would inevitably devolve directly upon the imperial family simply because one of its members held the premiership. If the war went poorly, the imperial family might become an object of hatred on the part of the people and, in the end, the national polity itself might be affected. In view of all these factors, Kido decided to oppose the emergence of Prince Higashikuni as a successor to Konoe.[24]

Thursday, October 16, 1941 proved to be a day of decisions.[25] Early in

[24] The text draws heavily on the writings and testimony of the former lord privy seal as cited in the preceding footnote. See also Kido, "Dai-sanji Konoe Naikaku Sō-jishoku no Zengo no Jijō," 2-4, and "The Brocade Banner," 51, n.3, and 140. The rightists who were involved in the *shinpeitai* incident of 1933 (Kido's 1934 date is incorrect) were Tatsuo Amano and Tetsunosuke Yasuda (a retired lieutenant colonel who had once served as an aide to Higashikuni). There was a rumor at that time to the effect that Higashikuni was slated for the premiership.

The prosecution view of Kido's role was that the lord privy seal, "well aware that a Tojo Government meant war, deliberately chose to make Tojo prime minister" (Horwitz, 524). See also CF 20, I, 16 and II, 81.

[25] See Kido "Nikki" for October 16, 1941, S 110:2-3, T 10281-84 (revised, 11141-42); Kido aff., S 293:16-17, T 30982-90; Kido, "Dai-sanji Konoe Naikaku Kōtetsu no Tenmatsu," S 159:14-15, T 16206-7; Kido, "Dai-sanji Konoe Naikaku Sō-jishoku no Zengo no Jijō," 4-8; Kido SKD and corresp.; Konoe, 137; Konoe, "Dai-sanji Naikaku Sō-

the morning, Lt. Gen. Suzuki called on Higashikuni, at Konoe's request, to report on matters relating to Japan's national strength. From the prince's residence Suzuki went directly to Marquis Kido, by whom he in turn was briefed on some of the reasons why the emergence of a cabinet headed by an imperial prince was considered undesirable. Despite the tenor of Kido's remarks, Suzuki went away with the feeling that the lord privy seal had not actually said that he was opposed to the formation of such a cabinet. Whatever doubts may have existed on that point were cleared up during the afternoon. At three o'clock War Minister Tojo called on Marquis Kido to discuss the situation. According to Kido's account, Tojo frankly admitted that Higashikuni's mission, if he became premier, would be to decide upon the policy to be followed thenceforth. Kido said that under such circumstances he would be unable to agree to the prince as Konoe's successor. He repeated the reasons he had already outlined to Suzuki, adding also that it had become apparent that the imperial conference decision of September 6 contained some "careless points" which required reexamination.[26] A decision resulting from a conference in the Emperor's presence, Kido said, was an extremely important matter. It should be respected at all times and faithfully executed, but if such a decision was not entirely perfect, was it not equally mandatory that it be corrected? Real unity between the army and the navy was imperative. Such unity constituted the nation's "minimum demand." Without it, the growth and expansion of the state would be impossible. Unless a policy of peace had definitely been decided upon, it would not be proper to have a cabinet headed by an imperial prince.

Tojo remained quiet for a while, mulling over what Kido had said. Suddenly he broke the silence with a question that was soon to be on many lips: "Then what will become of Japan?"[27]

From this comment and other remarks, Kido took hope that a way out might yet be found. He realized that Tojo felt there was very little room for breaking through the Japanese-American deadlock by further negotiations, but he judged that Tojo did not think such a breakthrough

---

jishoku no Tenmatsu," S 109:20, T 10269-71; *PHA*, Part 20, 4011; and Suzuki aff., S 333:11, T 35210-12.

[26] Kido's reference to "careless points" ("fu-yōi naru ten") was in relation to the haste with which the decision of September 6 had been processed (i.e., the proposal had been submitted to the throne only a half-day before the imperial conference was held).

[27] "Sore de wa Nihon wa ittai dō naru no ka." Kido states that he replied that Japan would become a third- or fourth-rate power if the program Tōjō was promoting were followed.

entirely impossible. Tojo himself had said that the imperial conference decision of September 6 was "a cancer" and that, without firm conviction and determination on the part of the navy, war could not be undertaken. Kido therefore decided to discuss the matter with Prince Konoe at once. If the premier were to make another effort, a road to a settlement with the United States might yet be found, without a change of cabinets.

But it was too late. When Kido talked with Konoe over the telephone at four o'clock that afternoon, the lord privy seal learned that the prince had already begun collecting the letters of resignation of the members of his cabinet.[28]

Of the reams that might be written on the significance of Konoe's political demise, it is doubtful that anything could be as suggestive of what lay ahead as the lyrics of a new patriotic song which appeared that same day, in rather quaint translation, in Tokyo's leading English-language newspaper:

> Siren, siren, air raid, air raid!
> What is that to us?
> Preparations are well done,
> Neighborhood associations are solid,
> Determination for defense is firm.
> Enemy planes are only mosquitoes or dragon-flies.
> We will win, we must win.
> What of air raid?
> We know no defeat.
> Come to this land to be shot down.[29]

The resignation of the third Konoe Cabinet created a crisis at home equal to the one already being faced by the nation abroad. The political void needed filling immediately; the question was, "By whom?" Should it be Higashikuni or Ugaki, Tojo or Oikawa? Those seemed to be the choices, and although they were few in number, the issues touching upon the selection of a suitable successor were many.

On the evening of October 16, immediately following the cabinet

---

[28] See footnote 25 above. Kido immediately reported to the Emperor. His Majesty received Prince Konoe at 5:00 p.m. When Konoe retired from the imperial chamber a half-hour later, the resignation of his third and last cabinet was an accomplished fact.

[29] *Japan Times & Advertiser*, October 16, 1941; I have added some punctuation. The song in question had been broadcast over station JOAK; it was one of a variety of patriotic numbers then current in Japan.

resignation, Marquis Kido had a long discussion with the outgoing premier during which the lord privy seal reviewed the situation existing at the moment. The prospect was by no means encouraging.[30]

The army, the navy, and the rightists, Kido said, were endeavoring to induce a mass psychology for war by means of propaganda emphasizing the growing pressure of ABCD encirclement. At the same time, the Germans were continuing their advance into Russia. News items from abroad concerning the landing of British and Australian forces at Singapore, the mobilization of troops in the Philippines, and the concentration of the American fleet at Hawaii were also having an effect upon the nerves of the people.[31]

More significant than public opinion as a factor in the selection of a new premier was the state of mind of the nucleus group (*chūken shōkō*) within the army and the navy. Among that group, and especially on the part of those connected with operations, the demand for adherence to the program established at the imperial conference of September 6 was especially strong. A decision on war or peace was to be made by early October; it was now the middle of October—where was the decision?

Because of that attitude, Kido believed that a clear change of the September 6 policy, "at a single stroke," might be practically impossible. Whoever received the mandate, in addition to conforming to the will of the Emperor, must be capable of assuming control over the military—especially the army—and of bringing about cooperation and harmony between the services. A man was required who was thoroughly familiar with the background of events leading to the current crisis. A person brought in from the outside would probably be unable to form a cabinet even if he received the mandate to do so. The army would not provide a war minister, and Japan and the world would be treated to a repetition of the "Ugaki miscarriage" of 1937. Even if such a person were some-

---

[30] On Kido's review of the situation, which is summarized below, see Kido, "Dai-sanji Konoe Naikaku Kōtetsu no Tenmatsu," S 159:15, T 16207-211; Kido, "Dai-sanji Konoe Naikaku Sō-jishoku no Zengo no Jijō," 6-8; Kido statement (IPS Doc. No. 3368; IMT 627) dated March 20, 1946; Kido SKD and corresp.; Kido aff., S 293:16-17, T 30980-90 (English requires revision); Konoe, 139-41; Konoe, "Dai-sanji Naikaku Sō-jishoku no Tenmatsu," S 109:20, T 10269-72; *PHA*, Part 20, 4011; and Suzuki aff., S 333:11, T 35212-13. In this connection, see also Grew, *Ten Years in Japan*, 456-58; *Foreign Relations (Japan: 1931-1941)*, II, 689-92; and Kenryō Satō, *Tōjō Hideki to Taiheiyō Sensō*, 219-23.

[31] One news item in particular rankled in the minds of the Japanese—a statement attributed to Admiral Kimmel to the effect that the battle preparations of the fleet at Pearl Harbor had been completed. In Japan the admiral was quoted as saying, "In the event of war, we shall annihilate the Japanese navy within four weeks."

how able to get a cabinet together, he would probably fail to comprehend fully the nature of the crisis which had led to Konoe's downfall and so, in the end, would find himself dutifully marching behind the nucleus group. Consequently, full knowledge of the developments to date and an ability to control the army constituted the *sine qua non* insofar as qualifications were concerned.

If the actual process of forming a cabinet became drawn out, or if the premier-designate did not measure up to the requirements of the situation then prevailing, internal disorder on a major scale might result. In that event, there would be no telling what the army overseas might do. Thus, the choice of a successor to Prince Konoe was really limited to either War Minister Tojo or Navy Minister Oikawa, since both were thoroughly familiar with what had been taking place behind the scenes. If the mandate went to Oikawa, Kido said, the navy should assume the responsibility of leading the nation by establishing a policy enjoying naval confidence. If Tojo were named, he should use his power of control to prevent any unforeseen incidents from occurring abroad. In either case, it would be necessary to have the Emperor command the premier-designate to disregard the imperial conference decision of September 6 and to reexamine the entire situation. The only question was which of the two men should be chosen.

Since the war minister had precipitated the cabinet crisis by clashing head-on with the premier and foreign minister, bestowal of the mandate upon him might be interpreted as capitulation to the army's demands. It might therefore be better—Kido argued—to entrust the premiership to the navy minister, especially since he had already intimated that he had certain doubts about the wisdom of going to war. On the other hand, it was the *army* that constituted the real problem. If the responsibility for forming a cabinet went to the navy, the army might become all the more defiant and offer greater resistance than before. To avoid such a development, Kido thought it might be preferable to place the responsibility, from the very beginning, squarely on the shoulders of the stronger of the two. The United States was already suspicious of the Japanese army. Among foreigners residing in Japan, and even among some Japanese, it was sarcastically being said that it would be a waste of time to ask either the foreign minister or the premier about Japan's foreign policy; the place to go was the army general staff. With such criticisms being spread about, Americans would interpret Konoe's fall as increasing the likelihood of war. They would be all the more convinced upon seeing the war minister named as his successor. But if, contrary to their expectations, a cabinet headed by Tojo continued the negotiations, they would feel reassured and good results might follow. Regardless of how it looked to the uninformed, a bestowal of the mandate upon General Tojo might consequently be the best, or at least the only, solution.

In essence, this was the view presented by Marquis Kido to Prince Konoe on the evening of October 16. It was a view that made sense to Konoe, and one in which he subsequently concurred, stipulating that he thought Tojo would be a better choice than Oikawa as long as the war minister was instructed by the Emperor to scrap the September 6 decision and to work for peace and for army-navy cooperation. Both Kido and Konoe believed that Tojo was not absolutely or necessarily committed to plunging immediately into war. Indeed, his thoughts appeared rather unsettled. It was not likely that he would advocate hostilities against the United States if the navy were opposed to such a policy. Tojo had a reputation for decisiveness, but that was a trait which could prove of advantage in more than one direction. He was a man who would respect implicitly the wishes of the Emperor. His particularly strong feelings of obedience toward the throne had constituted the underlying cause of his insistence that the Konoe Cabinet either faithfully carry out the policy of the imperial conference of September 6 or resign. Consequently, if the Emperor ordered Tojo—as the new premier —to set that policy aside in order to restudy the entire problem from the beginning, there was no doubt that Tojo would obey.[32]

While Kido and Konoe were thus conferring at the palace, the man on whom their thoughts converged was also giving his attention to the problem of a successor to the outgoing premier. In fact, Tojo had already entrusted his vice-minister of war, who was on friendly terms with Higashikuni, with the task of urging the prince to come forth. Although Higashikuni had given a noncommittal answer, the vice-minister believed that he had the will to emerge.[33] After receiving this report, Tojo summoned Kenryo Sato, chief of the military affairs section of the

[32] See especially the Kido citations in footnote 30 above. Also, JRD, "Interrogations," II:48366 (Sadamu Shimomura), 240; Hattori intv.; and IMTFE, "Roling Opinion," 64-69, 211-27.

Kido's role in the emergence of Tōjō as premier is variously interpreted. Some Japanese believe that he acted on the old principle of combating poison with poison. Others criticize him for having "paid too much for Tōjō"—by which it is meant that the lord privy seal overestimated the capabilities of the war minister and his power to bring about a change.

[33] See the concluding paragraph of footnote 23 above.

military affairs bureau, and ordered him to visit Generals Abe and Hayashi at once. Since both men were former premiers, Tojo knew that they would attend the usual senior statesmen's conference which followed every cabinet resignation. Having already recommended Higashi-kuni to Konoe and Kido, Tojo thought it would be proper to inform Abe and Hayashi of that fact, and he instructed Sato to do so.

Since Sato had had considerable experience with the press over the years, he decided to change into civilian clothes before going on his errand. He realized that if he were seen calling on Abe and Hayashi the night before a senior statesmen's conference, he would be suspected of complicity in some scheme or other, such as the recommendation of a cabinet headed by the war minister. He therefore not only donned mufti but also alighted from his army vehicle some distance from General Abe's house, where he arrived about midnight on October 16. Despite his precautions, however, he was promptly spotted by some alert reporters who were watching the ex-premier's residence. Chagrined and confused, Sato walked into the vestibule and called out in a loud voice for the benefit of the reporters: "Although it is late, I have come to inform you of my promotion to major general." The words were scarcely out of his mouth before Sato realized that despite the truth of his statement it was a clumsy thing to say, since no one in his right mind would be paying his respects at that time of the night.

It was perhaps inevitable, in the circumstances, that Sato's visit to Abe and Hayashi should subsequently have been interpreted as an effort to ensure the emergence of Tojo as Konoe's successor, and that the new major general should have been suspected of having advised the two ex-premiers that unless the mandate went to the war minister, it might be impossible to "control" the army. According to this interpretation, Abe and Hayashi were instructed by Sato to let the other senior statesmen know that unless the army got its way, "internal disorder" (assassinations and the like) could be expected.

At the Tokyo trial, the prosecution favored this interpretation. The picture of such a scheme fitted well with the general theory of conspiracy under which the prosecution proceeded. And certainly it could have happened that way. Anyone recalling Sato's previous appearances, especially his role in the "Ugaki miscarriage" of 1937, could easily imagine a performance of comparable significance in mid-October 1941. But to believe the worst, one must assume that Tojo's earlier advocacy of Higashikuni was pure sham, that he knew an imperial prince would never be given the mandate, and that he was merely using

Higashikuni as a shield for his own ambitions. This is certainly a rather large assumption.[34]

Against such a view is Tojo's character: blunt and decisive, forthright and assertive, naïve and aggressive. Even his worst enemy later described him as a "simple man" (*tanjun na hito*).[35] The ruse attributed to him seems hardly to fit the facts of his personality. Thus, if any conspiracy existed, it would more likely have been one in which both the war minister and the imperial prince were the pawns of the nucleus group within the war ministry and the army general staff.

If the Sato episode lacked the significance later attributed to it, the same cannot be said of the concurrence of views reached by Kido and Konoe regarding Tojo's qualifications for the premiership. Shortly after one o'clock in the afternoon on Friday, October 17, the senior statesmen gathered in the "West" antechamber of the imperial palace to assist in the selection of Konoe's successor.[36] Among the seven ex-premiers who attended were four military men (Generals Abe and Hayashi, Admirals Okada and Yonai) and three civilians (Hirota, Kiyoura, and Wakatsuki).[37] As was customary on such occasions, the president of the privy council, Dr. Hara, although not a former premier, also participated. The importance of this particular meeting was highlighted by the presence of Count Kiyoura, who was then ninety-one

[34] On Sato's visit to Abe and Hayashi, see Kenryō Satō, "Dai-Tōa Sensō wo Maneita Shōwa no Dōran," 123 and corresp.; Tōjō aff., S 343:15, T 36309-10; Ryūkichi Tanaka, direct examination, S 157:3, T 15872-73; Abe aff., S 326:6-8, T 34396-411; Kenryō Satō, *Tōjō Hideki to Taiheiyō Sensō*, 223-24; and CF 20, I, 16. The other principal, General Hayashi, died during the war. Tanaka was the source of many prosecution charges against a number of the defendants, and especially Tōjō. The "Tanaka question" is discussed in Chapter 15 below.

The Sato promotion took place on October 15. On the same day, his immediate superior, Akira Mutō (the chief of the military affairs bureau), was promoted to lieutenant general (T 770 and 745).

[35] Tanaka intv.

[36] On the *jūshin kaigi* of October 17, 1941, which is summarized below, see Kido "Nikki" for that date, S 110:3-4, T 10291-92 (revised, 11142-43); Kido, "Dai-sanji Konoe Naikaku Kōtetsu no Tenmatsu," S 159:15, T 16209; Kido aff., S 293:16, T 30980, and S 293:17-20, T 30990-31018 (requires revision); Kido, "Dai-sanji Konoe Naikaku Sō-jishoku no Zengo no Jijō," 9; Kido SKD and corresp.; Abe aff., S 326:8, T 34406-9; *PHA*, Part 20, 4011; Okada, "Tōjō Seiken to jūshin-tachi," *Dai Nippon Teikoku Shimatsu-ki*, Dai-isshū, Saron Rinji Zōkangō, Tsūkan 38 (December 15, 1949), 88-89; Wakatsuki, 417-18; Ogata, *Ichi Gunjin no Shōgai*, 101-8; and Shigemitsu, *Sugamo Nikki*, 57-59 (containing some interesting Hiranuma comments, including a rumor that members of the Chōshū clique had been at work behind the scenes and had held a meeting at the home of Yoshisuke Aikawa of *ni-ki san-suke* fame).

[37] Hiranuma was not present because he was still recovering from the wounds he received in August (see pp. 251-52 above). Kido corresp.

years of age and in rather weak physical condition. Although he had not attended such gatherings for some time, the old count had decided that his infirmities should not prevent him from performing a last service for the throne. He had therefore arrived at the palace attended by a doctor and a nurse.[38]

The conference began with the imperial wishes being conveyed by the grand chamberlain. The lord privy seal, who acted as a kind of "cabinet midwife" on such occasions, then extended his personal greetings.[39] He told the senior statesmen that he had obtained special imperial permission for the outgoing premier to attend the meeting to explain the circumstances surrounding the fall of his cabinet. Prince Konoe had agreed to do so, but unfortunately he had begun feeling ill the evening before and was now unable to be present because of a fever. However, he had sent a written explanation covering the facts of the case.

After further introductory remarks, Kido proceeded to read Konoe's message, which was a fairly detailed summary of the various developments and points of view which had led to the cabinet's fall. In the discussion which followed, the former premiers contented themselves with talking around the issue, touching here and there upon key points (oil, the possible length of a Japanese-American war, the prospect of victory, the fact of continuing hostilities in China) but never linking the separate parts into any kind of conclusive whole. The first specific recommendation for a successor to Konoe came from General Hayashi, who offered the view that an imperial prince in the naval service might be most suitable.[40] Kido responded with the reasons he had already formulated against the idea of a cabinet headed by a prince of the blood. When Wakatsuki asked him for his own opinion, the privy seal proposed Tojo, explaining in some detail why he thought the outgoing war minister might be best. If Tojo were chosen, Kido said, he would be commanded by the Emperor to bring about true cooperation between the services and to reexamine from the beginning the imperial conference decision of September 6. Kido's statement caused a mild fluttering of opinions, with diverse ideas falling here and there like leaves in autumn which must await the dying of the wind to be raked together.

[38] The importance attached to the October 17 meeting of the *jūshin* is also revealed by the fact that Kido personally took notes during the discussion. These were later written up for deposit in the imperial archives. Kido's affidavit (as cited previously) includes numerous selections therefrom.

[39] The "cabinet midwife" phrase (*naikaku sanba-yaku*) is from Kenryō Satō, "Dai-Tōa Sensō wo Maneita Shōwa no Dōran," 123.

[40] Hayashi was probably thinking of Prince Fushimi, but he did not mention anyone by name, nor was he asked to specify whom he had in mind.

Kiyoura revealed that Higashikuni's name had been mentioned to him but that he personally thought a regular military man might be preferable. This constituted, in effect, an indirect and tentative endorsement of Kido's recommendation.

Wakatsuki, while admitting that there was sense in the lord privy seal's opinion, suggested Ugaki as a possible alternative, noting in the same breath, however, that it would be embarrassing and difficult if the army again stood in the way. Kido spoke against the idea of Ugaki's nomination, but Wakatsuki persisted to the point of asking for the opinions of some of the military men present. General Abe then replied in a way that supported Kido's negative view.[41] Admiral Okada questioned the propriety of naming Tojo because of the army's responsibility for the fall of the Konoe Cabinet. But Kido disagreed. He said the circumstances were not the same as when the Yonai Cabinet collapsed in 1940. This time it could not be said that the army alone was to blame for Konoe's resignation. Kido thus obliquely referred to the navy's role in the cabinet crisis and to Konoe's own attitude. Okada countered by remarking on the army's generally tough, uncompromising views: "In the past . . . the army has been described as shooting from behind with a rifle. Let's hope it doesn't become a cannon."[42] Kido admitted that he was worried about that possibility, but who else could control the situation? Could the navy?

Again the discussion veered momentarily, as it frequently did throughout the session. Sometimes the talk came back to the point of departure, at other times it did not. What Kido had earlier implied, Admiral Yonai now put into words. He wanted to know whether the Konoe Cabinet had fallen because of the navy. Kido, while avoiding a direct answer, left the impression that the navy was not without its share of responsibility. If there were doubts about the wisdom of choosing the war minister as premier, he said, then certainly Navy Minister Oikawa, who was an advocate of prudence, represented an alternative. But Admiral Okada immediately interposed an objection: "I believe it would definitely not do to have the navy come forth at this time."[43] Yonai expressed his agreement and then Okada reintroduced the name

[41] At the Tōkyō trial, the prosecution charged Kido with rejecting Ugaki—the only man (according to the prosecution) who might have averted war. Kido interpreted this to mean that the prosecution agreed that the selection of an army general to succeed Konoe was the right thing to do in the circumstances. The only point at issue was which one. Kido aff., S 293:21, T 30121-22.

[42] "Nai-daijin wa, jūrai rikugun ga ushiro kara teppō wo utsu to iwareru ga, sore ga taihō to naranakereba yoi ga. . . ."

[43] "Kaigun ga kono sai deru koto wa zettai ni ikenai to omou."

of Ugaki. It was almost as if the generals and the admirals in the group had come to the conference determined to pin the tail on the others' donkey.

Unlike liaison and imperial conferences, a senior statesmen's gathering did not operate under the stiff requirement of unanimity, but in accordance with what might be called an unchallenged consensus. In some respects, this made the task easier; in others, more difficult. On this occasion, the groping of the members must have been rather trying to Marquis Kido, who had somehow or other to end up with a recommendation to the throne. As the talk continued, the hands of the clock ticked on toward 3:00 p.m. and then toward 4:00. Finally Dr. Hara remarked that if it were going to be Tojo, the imperial mandate should indicate clearly the policy to be followed. When Kido expressed his agreement, Hirota asked whether Kido's plan called for Tojo to serve concurrently as war minister. Kido said "Yes," and Mr. Hirota replied, "In that case, fine."[44] General Abe then voiced his approval. Thus, it was a civilian whose name had been closely linked in 1936 with the launching of a new national policy contemplating the use of force who took the first real step in the direction suggested by Kido.

As soon as Hirota and Abe had committed themselves, the lord privy seal decided to probe for concurrence or objection. Remarking that Wakatsuki favored Ugaki, Kido asked whether Okada also wanted Ugaki. The admiral did not—at least, not necessarily. It was just that he was somewhat worried about what Kido had proposed. Dr. Hara then stated succinctly the real facts of the case: the lord privy seal's plan could not be described as very satisfactory, but in the absence of any other specific proposal there was no choice but to give it a try.[45]

When no one else said anything to the contrary, Kido announced to the assemblage that, in general, he had understood their intentions. He would report fully to the throne and obtain His Majesty's sanction.

---

[44] "Sore nara kekkō de aru." Even so simple a statement illustrates the problem of translation, since *kekkō* is a word which can be rendered in innumerable ways. To translate it as "excellent" or "splendid," rather than as "fine," might be to err as much as to select such an obviously inappropriate alternative as "toothsome." It should be noted, however, that Mr. Hirota, more than any of the military men present, seemed anxious to ensure that the wishes of imperial headquarters would be met. At the *jūshin kaigi* of July 17, 1941, at which Konoe was nominated for the premiership for the third time, Hirota had also expressed a more positive view than any of his colleagues. He had advocated a strengthening of imperial headquarters and had suggested a "military administration-type cabinet" (*gunsei-teki naikaku*). See Kido "Nikki" for July 17, 1941, S 109:8, T 10168 (revised, 11138).

[45] "Nai-daijin no an wa, amari manzoku to mo ienai ga, betsudan-an ga nai kara mazu sono an de yuku hoka arumai."

It was 3:45 p.m. when the meeting finally adjourned. The name of Prince Higashikuni had hardly been mentioned at all. The cabinet crisis which had caused Kido many "sleepless nights of worry" was now practically at an end. For the first time in Japan's constitutional history, a general closely connected with such a crisis not only would retain his position as war minister but would also succeed to the premiership and would hold, as well, the cabinet portfolio for home affairs.[46]

While the senior statesmen's conference had been in session, War Minister Tojo had been busying himself about the premises of his official residence, packing his personal possessions to make room for his successor. In the latter part of the afternoon he was suddenly informed by the grand chamberlain that the Emperor desired to see him at once.[47] Tojo assumed that he would be asked questions about the cabinet

[46] In this connection, it should be noted that the Tribunal (J, B/IV, 398-99) accepted an argument concerning the formation of the Abe Cabinet (August 1939-January 1940) that it rejected with regard to Tōjō—namely, that in order to reverse the prevailing policy the premier-designate must exercise discretion in selecting ministers for the key portfolios (war, home affairs, justice), and that a war minister was needed "who enjoyed the confidence of and was able to control the Army. . . ."

Tōjō's concurrent and unprecedented retention of the war ministry portfolio required special imperial approval, which was obtained through Kido. This departure had the support of Chief of the Army General Staff Sugiyama, Inspector-General of Military Training Otozo Yamada, and Imperial Prince Kan'in, former chief of the army general staff. See Kido "Nikki" for October 18, 1941, S 110:4, T 10293; Kido aff., S 293:21-22, T 31026-27; Tōjō aff., S 343:15, T 36312 (note the use of *naisō*, which is incorrectly rendered in the English record as "confidential representation"; see p. 145 above, footnote 35, and the text pertaining thereto); Hattori, I, 201 (in which it is noted that General Sugiyama, although agreeing to the move, questioned the wisdom of Tōjō's holding the war portfolio and the premiership for an extended period of time; it was on Sugiyama's special motion that an exception was made to the five-year rule that would have required Tōjō to serve another month before becoming eligible for promotion to full general); and Mrs. Tōjō and Yano intv.

[47] On the events from mid-afternoon, October 17, through the afternoon of October 18, which are discussed in the text which follows, see Kido "Nikki" for October 17, 1941, S 110:3-4, T 10291-92 (revised, 11142-43, but requires further revision); Kido, "Dai-sanji Konoe Naikaku Kōtetsu no Tenmatsu," S 159:15, T 16209-11; Kido aff., S 293:17 and 20-22, T 30990 and 31018-28; Kido, "Dai-sanji Konoe Naikaku Sō-jishoku no Zengo no Jijō," 9-10; Kido SKD, intv., and corresp.; Tōjō aff., S 343:15-16, T 36307-16 (revised, 36683, but requires further revision); Tōjō direct examination, S 344:18, T 36498-500 and 36503; Tōjō cross-examination, S 344:19, T 36504-8; Tōjō interrog., Mar. 12, 1-3; Mrs. Tōjō corresp.; Konoe, 143; Kenryō Satō, "Dai-Tōa Senso wo Maneita Shōwa no Dōran," 123-25; Kaya, "Nippon no Unmei wa Kōshite Kakerareta," *Kingu*, Vol. XXXII, No. 5 (May 1956), 192-93; Tōgō, 147-50; Oka aff., S 316:10, T 33397-400; Inada aff., S 278:8, T 29196-99 and cross-examination, S 278:9, T 29202-3; Hoshino interrogation extract, S 278:9, T 29204; Suzuki aff., S 333:11, T 35212-15; Kase, 55-56; Kobayashi aff., S 291:8, T 30603; Oikawa direct examination, S 316:2-3, T 33344-50; Oikawa aff., S 327:13, T 34569-74 and cross examination, S 327:13-17, T 34575-600; Kaya aff., S 291:13-14, T 30648-50; Shimada aff. S 328:7-8, T 34648-55; Tōgō aff., S 337:3-4, T 35665-74; Hattori, I, 200-1 (the October 16 date assigned to the *jūshin kaigi* is incorrect); Ōi intv.;

resignation of the day before, and so he quickly gathered together various papers which might be of use to him in making his replies. It was past four o'clock when he arrived at the palace, where he was immediately conducted to the Emperor's presence. He was taken completely by surprise when His Majesty declared: "We direct you to form a cabinet and to abide by the provisions of the Constitution. We believe that an exceedingly grave situation confronts the nation. Bear in mind, at this time, that cooperation between the army and the navy should be closer than ever before. It is Our intention to summon, also, the navy minister and to speak to him in this same vein."[48]

Tojo asked for a short time to consider and then withdrew from the imperial chamber.[49] While he was mulling over the matter in the adjacent waiting room, Admiral Oikawa was received by the Emperor and similarly advised of the need for the closest possible cooperation between the services in the crisis confronting Japan. Shortly after the navy minister's audience, the lord privy seal entered the waiting room and addressed himself to both Tojo and Oikawa, saying that in addition to army-navy cooperation the Emperor considered it necessary for the new cabinet, in determining the fundamental policies which would guide the state thenceforth, to deliberate very carefully and to undertake a thoroughgoing study of the situation at home and abroad *without being bound by the imperial conference decision of September 6.*[50]

This further and unprecedented imperial command, which was conveyed directly by Kido, became known as the Emperor's "clean

---

Stunkard intv. (in which Tōjō was quoted as having said, after the war, that if he had known that he would become Konoe's successor, he would not have broken up the Konoe Cabinet); JRD, "Interrogations," I:49157 (Seizō Arisue), 30; and Kenryō Satō, *Tōjō Hideki to Taiheiyō Sensō*, 224-30.

[48] The Japanese text of the imperial mandate to Tōjō, as recorded by Kido, reads as follows: "Kei ni naikaku soshiki wo meizu. Kenpō no jōki wo junshu yō. Jikyoku wa kiwamete jūdai naru jitai ni chokumen seru mono to omou. Kono sai riku-kaigun wa sono kyōryoku wo issō mitsu ni suru koto ni ryūi seyo. Nao gokoku kaigun daijin wo meshi kono mune wo hanasu tsumori da." S 159:15. Adjustments were made to achieve smoothness in translation.

[49] Tōjō's request for time to consider was "normal procedure." Kido corresp.

[50] There are some slight variations in wording in the several available texts of the imperial message conveyed to Tōjō and Oikawa by Kido. See the references cited in footnote 47 above. It should be noted that the Emperor did not instruct the navy *to cooperate with* the army in the sense of doing what the army wanted. An implication to that effect in Tōjō's affidavit was subsequently corrected. The idea was that the two services should cooperate fully and freely with each other. Mr. Tōgō drew special attention, in his affidavit, to the important role of the military services in foreign policy formulation and cited, as an example, the fact that the (outgoing) foreign minister was not included in the special instructions issued by the lord privy seal to the service ministers on the afternoon of October 17.

slate" message.[51] Tojo himself subsequently maintained that he might not have been able to accept the mandate to form a cabinet, had it not been for this injunction. There was a question of propriety, he said, in his entering the new cabinet even as war minister, let alone in his assuming the premiership. After all, it was *he* who had called for the resignation of the third Konoe Cabinet. In addition, he had participated in the imperial conference of September 6 and consequently also possessed responsibility for what had been decided there. His taking over as Konoe's successor, instead of settling anything, might easily lead to greater difficulties. Since he personally believed, however, that matters had progressed to a point where starting with a blank sheet of paper was essential, and since he was determined to do precisely that, he respectfully accepted the responsibility conferred upon him by the throne.[52]

Having thus undertaken to form a cabinet, Tojo immediately turned his attention to the problem of filling the major portfolios. He understandably felt excited by the turn events had taken. Being rather uncertain as to how to proceed, he decided to seek guidance outside himself by relying upon the will of the gods. From the palace he hastened to pay his respects at the great shrine of the Emperor Meiji, to make an offering at the memorial dedicated to the Russo-Japanese war hero, Admiral Togo, and to bow in prayer in the presence of the loyal and the brave of Yasukuni, where enrollment ceremonies for more than fifteen thousand warrior dead were currently in progress. While he was so engaged, the matter clarified itself in his mind, and he hit upon a plan of action: he must exert himself to the utmost in forming a cabinet; the task must be accomplished quickly—delay would be inexcusable; appointments would be made on the basis of individual merit, experience, and capability; the ministers should be men possessing the drive needed to enforce the policies of the cabinet; the selection of a navy

---

[51] "Hakushi kangen no go-jō." An imperial mandate was not supposed to lay down conditions concerning the formation of a cabinet. For that reason, the "clean slate" command was not included in the Emperor's remarks to Tōjō when the latter was received in audience, but was conveyed to the premier-designate afterwards by the lord privy seal. Kido corresp.

[52] A statement in the English translation of Tōjō's affidavit to the effect that Tōjō accepted the mandate ". . . as any loyal subject would have done . . ." (T 36172) is so freely rendered as to be misleading, as is indicated by the original Japanese: ". . . watakushi wa sokaku no taimei wo kōmuri, tsutsushinde kore wo haiju shi . . ." (S 342:12). This embellishment of the English text (perhaps by a well-meaning translator) accounts for an apparent contradiction with a later statement (S 343:15, T 36311) indicating that Tōjō might not have accepted the mandate had it not been for the "clean slate" command.

minister would be left to the navy; the influence of the political parties and of the *zaibatsu* (the great financial combines) would neither be embraced nor shunned.

Although there were later to be many opinions about the exact nature of the end-product, ranging from "a strong but conservative national cabinet" to "the unpredictable Manchurian gang," there was no quarrel with the dispatch with which Tojo formed his ranks.[53] From the three shrines he had visited, he drove directly to the official residence where he had been doing his packing, arriving there at about 6:30 in the evening. The news of the mandate had already preceded him and Generals Muto and Sato, together with other military affairs bureau personnel, were excitedly exchanging views. They had even drafted a list of persons who might serve as cabinet ministers. When Muto handed the list to Tojo, however, the premier-designate turned and walked into his private office, complaining that they were all "meddling too much."

In tackling the problem of selecting men to serve under him, Tojo decided that his first concern should be the post of chief cabinet secretary, since he needed someone to assist him with the many details that required attention.[54] His choice fell on Naoki Hoshino, with whom he had become acquainted in Manchuria some years before and with whom he had more recently served in the second Konoe Cabinet. Tojo considered Hoshino to be the right man for the job because of his ability and his career experience to date. Following a phone conversation with the premier-designate early that same evening, Hoshino arrived on the scene to tender his acceptance and to begin his new duties.

Telephone calls were then made to the various individuals whose services Tojo had decided to seek. Of these, six signified their willingness to join the cabinet at once. Four others also accepted that same evening, but not until they had called at the residence to talk with Tojo in person.[55] Of the latter group, Okinori Kaya, who was slated for the

---

[53] See footnote 47 above. On reactions to the new Tōjō Cabinet, see pp. 305-7 and 312-13 below.

[54] A poor defense translation accounted for some confusion concerning Tōjō's choice of Hoshino. The original Japanese (Tōjō aff., S 343:16), ". . . joshu ga iru kara, mazu naikaku shokikan-chō no sentei wo hitsuyō to shimashita," was rendered as "In the first place, the Secretary General of the Cabinet was to be chosen as my right-hand man" (T 36314). Aside from other aspects, the point is that "right-hand man" carries connotations which *joshu* ("assistant") does not. The matter was taken up and clarified by counsel for Hoshino, T 36498-500, and an official correction was subsequently noted, T 36683.

[55] The six individuals who accepted Tōjō's telephoned request to join his cabinet were Hashida (education), Ino (agriculture), Iwamura (justice), Koizumi (welfare), Suzuki

finance ministry, and Shigenori Togo, whom Tojo wanted as his foreign minister, indicated that they wished "to make doubly sure" that he would do his best to solve existing problems by diplomatic means. Kaya also asked for Tojo's views on supreme command-cabinet relationships and on the ideological and revolutionary tendencies observed in the past. Although Tojo's exact responses cannot be determined with certainty, it is clear that he referred to the "clean slate" message he had received from the Emperor and that he proved sufficiently encouraging about his willingness to avoid war for Togo and Kaya to agree to join the cabinet.

By midnight on October 17, Tojo's ministerial selection was practically completed, thanks to his technique of requiring each candidate literally to make up his mind on the spot. The only important post not yet filled was that of navy minister. In the light of the circumstances which had led to the collapse of the previous cabinet, it would have been rather surprising had Admiral Oikawa retained the naval portfolio. Although the records are silent on the point, Tojo presumably desired a change. Oikawa had personally decided against staying on even before Tojo had been named as Konoe's successor. By the time the premier-designate had asked the navy to nominate a minister, Oikawa had tentatively selected Admiral Shigetaro Shimada. Although the least senior of those eligible to head the navy ministry, Shimada struck Oikawa as the best man both on his own merits and because of compelling reasons why other likely candidates could not, in fact, be nominated (e.g., already holding key posts, or slated to retire). Despite a prosecution charge which linked Tojo and Shimada in a conspiratorial way, Oikawa stressed in postwar testimony that Tojo had not had anything to do with the Shimada appointment. Oikawa's nominee was himself rather reluctant to serve as requested, but was finally persuaded to do so by his naval colleagues.

Thus, by Saturday morning, October 18, Tojo had created a working cabinet. In addition to the premier, the line-up included two other members of the *ni-ki san-suke* group: Naoki Hoshino (chief cabinet secretary) and Nobusuke Kishi (in charge of commerce and industry).

(planning board)—all holdovers from the third Konoe Cabinet—and Kishi (commerce and industry). In addition to Kaya and Tōgō, Terashima (communications and railways) and Yuzawa (to serve as vice-minister for home affairs directly under Tōjō as home minister) accepted Tōjō's invitation after talking with him in person. Tōjō wanted a man of ministerial caliber to serve under him at the home ministry since he did not intend holding that portfolio any longer than necessary. According to Mrs. Tōjō, Kaya was selected because of his qualifications as a financier; Tōgō, because of his record in the negotiations with the Soviet Union for the purchase of the Chinese Eastern Railway.

The new ministerial ranks also contained five military men, two less than in the preceding cabinet. Six men had bridged the gap caused by Konoe's fall, the most prominent after Tojo being Lt. Gen. Suzuki, who retained his position as president of the cabinet planning board and minister of state without portfolio. The military and the bureaucracy were well represented; big business was noticeably absent.

The formal investiture ceremony took place that same afternoon. The 57-year-old premier, whose promotion to full general had also been announced as of that day, subsequently made a very brief radio address in which he spoke of optimism and determination, unity and conviction, trust and cooperation. A successful settlement of the China Incident and the establishment of the Greater East Asia co-prosperity sphere were again described as achievements which would permit Japan to contribute toward world peace.

Shortly thereafter, Tojo left for the grand imperial shrine at Ise where, traditionally, all public figures report on their assumption of office and other matters of moment. The next day, the premier returned to Tokyo by air—an innovation "hailed as an indication of the speed which the new Government would put behind the execution of its policies." One newspaper, the *Yomiuri*, saw in Tojo's already apparent decisiveness an inducement to the nation "to rise to the occasion and administer a great shock to the anti-Axis powers."[56]

Soon there were other words and deeds attributed to Tojo that left distinct impressions. Those close to the scene generally seemed more inclined to view his emergence with equanimity than those at a greater distance. The Tokyo correspondent for the *New York Times* felt that the appointment had come as "something of a surprise. Tojo was no reckless fanatic, but a disciplinarian, and therein lay a certain saving grace which possibly could be of advantage." Ambassador Grew remembered the important fact that Tojo had been "one of the original five members of the Konoye cabinet" who had supported "the opening of conversations with the United States in the face of the opposition of Matsuoka." *Life* magazine, on the other hand, painted a sinister picture under an editorial lead entitled "Japanese 'Itch' ":

[56] For these and other reactions to Tōjō's emergence as premier, the text draws on material in Tolischus, 270-74, 281-82; Tolischus dispatches in *NYT* for October 18-20, 1941; *NYT*, October 18, 1941, 5, and October 30, 1941, 3; Grew, *Ten Years in Japan*, 458-61 and 463-64; *Foreign Relations (Diplomatic Papers: 1941)*, IV, 541-44; *Newsweek*, October 27, 1941, 26-28; *Life*, October 27, 1941, 34; *PM*, October 19, 1941, 5; CF 20, III, 298; JRD, "Nomura Diary," entry for September 2, 1941; Bainbridge, 26-27; and Kido, Matsudaira, Umezu, and Ushiba intv.

More deadly than the Japanese beetle is the Japanese itch, a chauvinistic attitude that makes some Japanese think they can lick their weight in American wildcats. Mindful that the one-ocean U.S. Navy faces the prospect of a two-ocean war, Captain Hideo Hiraide of the Japanese Navy boastfully expressed the attitude last week: "The Imperial Navy is prepared for the worst.... In fact the Imperial Navy is itching for action."

It was *Life's* opinion that the appointment of Tojo, "a friend of the Axis," constituted "a victory for the Nazis." The new cabinet, *Life* asserted, "smelled of powder."

Tojo himself is an itcher from way back. In 1937 he declared: "Japan must be prepared to fight China and Russia simultaneously." She was already

TAKING OVER TWO-MAN JOB

From the *Japan Times & Advertiser*, October 20, 1941. (Courtesy of the *Japan Times*)

fighting China and with the rumored presence of 25 Japanese divisions on the Soviet frontiers it looked as though Japan were about to take on Russia.

Tojo, however, has never said anything about fighting China, Russia, America, Britain and the Netherland Indies all at once. That was his worry last week.[57]

It was the worry of some others as well. Even before Tojo's emergence as premier, Secretary Hull had advised Admiral Nomura that the Chinese believed a military cabinet would soon take over. The ambassador had replied to the effect that the Chinese were the spoiled brats of America and therefore said whatever they pleased. Now Chungking was saying much more. It was warning that the selection of Tojo meant that Japan intended to attack Russia at once and was willing to risk war with the United States. The only good the Nationalists saw in Tojo's appointment was the acceptance of responsibility where it belonged—in the hands of the military. Elsewhere in the Allied world, reports indicated an attitude of watchful waiting.

Within the Hitler camp, something of a reverse reaction prevailed. While Berlin expressed full confidence that the new cabinet would adhere to the Tripartite Pact, Germans living in Japan were not nearly so enthusiastic. They had been hoping for an interventionist slate; Tojo and his colleagues were a disappointment. Local German feelings were estranged further by the arrest of two Reich citizens immediately following the cabinet's assumption of power.

Among the Japanese themselves, Tojo soon attracted public attention.[58] Like the powerful thirteenth-century regent who had secretly toured the country as a Buddhist priest, seeing much and remembering all,[59] Tojo was reputed to be conducting inspections of his own in a *kamisori*-like manner. On one occasion, when he asked why there were no fish in the market, the answer was "No gasoline." "Gasoline!" he scoffed, "Why not get up earlier and work harder?"

Although this story may have come from an overzealous, public relations-minded source, it did express Tojo's basic attitude toward life— indeed, the attitude of many of his countrymen, who believed that compensation for Nature's denial of certain gifts could be obtained by exercising greater determination. This thought was soon to acquire an ever more prominent place in the national outlook under the stimulus of a new and greater war effort.

[57] *Life*, October 27, 1941, 34. See also Langer and Gleason, *The Undeclared War*, 730.
[58] See the citations in footnote 56 above.
[59] The reference is to the Hōjō regent, Tokiyori.

The Japan of which General Hideki Tojo became premier was operated by remote control. It was a country in which puppet politics had reached a high state of development, to the detriment of the national welfare. The ranking members of the military services were the robots of their subordinates—the so-called *chūken shōkō*, the nucleus group, which was active "at the center" and which was composed largely of field-grade officers. They, in turn, were influenced by younger elements within the services at large and by ultranationalists outside military ranks. The civilian members of the cabinet were the robots of the military—especially of the nucleus group, working through the service ministers and the chiefs of the army and navy general staffs. The Emperor himself, through no fault of his own, was the robot of the government—of the cabinet and the supreme command, a prisoner of the circumstances into which he was born—an unfortunate individual who wanted very much to be free to pursue the life of a man, yet who knew that he must instead act like a god and so remain an unapproachable mystery to one and all. Finally, the nation—the one hundred million dedicated souls, the sum and substance of Japan, from whom the blood and toil and tears and sweat of Churchill's phrase were wrung—the nation was the robot of the throne.

When that is understood, the question inevitably arises: who else, if not Tojo? He seemed to possess a power of control greater than that of his colleagues. That power may have been a myth, but—if so—it was a comforting one, inviting confidence. Tojo believed in and stood for discipline. He was honest. His feelings of respect for the throne were especially strong. There was no civilian of sufficient eminence, courage, or experience to undertake the task at which Konoe had failed. Consequently, the prince's successor had to be a military man. In the circumstances of the time, Tojo was the logical choice.

The Emperor himself seemed quite satisfied with the outcome.[60] He had been kept fully informed of developments by the lord privy seal, upon whom he was largely dependent for knowledge of occurrences which might affect the fate of the nation. When Kido submitted a concluding report on the emergence of the new Tojo Cabinet, His Majesty listened with interest and understanding. He even expressed his

[60] See Kido SKD, and Kido "Nikki" for October 20, 1941, S 110:4, T 10294-96. The original of the remark with which the chapter ends is as follows: "Iwayuru koketsu ni irazunba koji wo ezu to iu koto da ne." This saying (the equivalent of "Nothing ventured; nothing gained") seems to have been on many lips in 1941. Matsuoka used it in a different sense, during the policy discussions of late June (paraphrased on p. 216 above as "Unless one took certain risks, one could not obtain any rewards").

appreciation for the part the marquis had played throughout the trying period which was now at an end. And then, as the privy seal was taking his leave, the Emperor captured the essence of the situation in a few words:

"There is a saying, isn't there? 'You cannot obtain a tiger's cub unless you brave the tiger's den. . . .' "

CHAPTER 11

The Decision for War

WHILE the political crisis in Tokyo had been deepening, to be resolved finally in the elevation of General Tojo to the premiership, a little-known and rather unorthodox effort to preserve peace had quietly been taking place behind the scenes. The protagonists again included the two Maryknoll missionaries, Bishop James E. Walsh and Father James M. Drought, who had been active earlier in the year in encouraging talks at the official level between Japan and the United States. Soon after the inauguration of the Hull-Nomura conversations in the spring of 1941, Bishop Walsh had returned to Japan to resume his "interrupted visitation of the Maryknoll missioners there and elsewhere in the Far East."[1] Toward the end of the summer, he had suddenly been sought out by a Mr. Tadao Ikawa, who was known to him as "a friend and unofficial representative" of Prince Konoe. Ikawa revealed that "the peace proposals had encountered difficulties, but that there was still some hope of a successful termination." He therefore asked Walsh if he would again lend his assistance, "particularly in the matter of helping to get messages to and from the State Department in Washington and to and from the American Embassy in Tokyo." Before giving a final answer, Walsh consulted the counselor of embassy, who in turn checked with Ambassador Grew. The bishop was told that his cooperation "might prove useful." In fact, he got the impression that he was being "more or less encouraged to perform this little function of helping to transmit information when need arose." During the next two months (mid-August through mid-October), Walsh joined Ikawa in facilitating the exchange of many messages between the two governments. All of the communications intended for the State Department were cabled by Bishop Walsh over his own name and "in plain English, but concealed under missionary phraseology," to Father Drought at Maryknoll, New York, to be transmitted to Departmental officials in Washington. Messages for the embassy in Tokyo were conveyed by Walsh personally to the counselor of embassy "by word of mouth."

During the period that this rather extraordinary method of communi-

[1] See Walsh aff., T 32985-91 and *Foreign Relations* (*Diplomatic Papers: 1941*), IV, 527-39.

cation was being used, the bishop, sometimes accompanied by Mr. Ikawa, lived first at the Fujiya, a mountain-resort hotel several hours south of Tokyo by rail, and then at the Beach Hotel in Kamakura, about an hour's trip from the capital. One morning at the Fujiya, Ikawa awakened Walsh at a very early hour and suggested an immediate change of residence. According to Ikawa, Maj. Gen. Muto, the chief of the military affairs bureau, was protecting their activities and "would continue to do so to the best of his ability," but providing against every conceivable eventuality was impossible. If they remained where they were, Ikawa explained, some of the extremists might cause trouble.

Under the circumstances, the bishop decided to leave the Fujiya at once and take up residence at the Beach Hotel instead. There, on October 14, he was unexpectedly asked if he would personally deliver a message from Premier Konoe to President Roosevelt. Again Walsh checked with the American embassy and again he was advised to accede to the Japanese request. Walsh then called upon the premier, from whom he received a *viva voce* communication which was "rendered into English . . . on the spot" by the president of the board of information. The message was a short one, reaffirming the desire of the Japanese government to conclude a peace agreement. "Its real intent," as explained to Walsh by the bureau chief and by Ikawa, "was to intimate that the pressure of events on the Japanese Government was such that it would not be able to negotiate much longer, but would have to reach an agreement very soon or not at all."[2] Ikawa gave the bishop a ticket, obtained by General Muto, which entitled the bearer to a seat on a Japanese plane scheduled to leave for Canton the following day. Ikawa also gave Walsh "a safe-conduct letter," written in Japanese, and signed by Muto.[3] It was arranged that thereafter all references to the general, in messages passing between Walsh and Ikawa, would be disguised by use of the code name, *hana*: "flowers."

The next day, October 15, Walsh departed as scheduled. When his plane arrived at Fukuoka in southern Japan, the officials there seemed bent on making him turn back. But when he produced the letter from Muto, the way was cleared. The same thing happened a few days later

[2] *Ibid.* There are some slight discrepancies in the two accounts.

[3] The text of the Mutō letter is as follows: "Irai-sho. Honjō shoji-sha Beikokujin Uorushiyu shi wa tokubetsu no yōmu wo motte Kanton ni ryokō seraruru mono nari. Yotte dōshi ni tai shi jūbun bengi kyōyo ainaritaku irai su. Shōwa jūrokunen, jūgatsu, jūyokka. Rikugunshō gunmukyoku-chō, Mutō Akira. Kankeigun kanken-dono." S 312:13, and a photostatic copy of the original at Maryknoll. Note the absence of any reference to "Mr." Walsh's connection with or status in the Catholic Church.

when Walsh was on the point of leaving Canton to go to Macao and thence to Hong Kong. Again the Muto letter proved its value. While still in Canton, Walsh cabled Ikawa to ask whether Konoe's resignation, the news of which had just reached him, would result in "any change in policy or attitude that would affect the validity of the message" he was carrying. Upon his arrival in Manila, he found a reply awaiting him: "Bon voyage with flowers [stop] no substantial change [stop] urgently require speedy response to avoid worst." Walsh took this to mean that the new Tojo Cabinet was "maintaining the same essential position in regard to the negotiations," and that it was "deferring any other incompatible plans" it might have, "in the hope of yet obtaining an agreement" that would "establish peace" in the Pacific. He consequently proceeded to Washington, where he delivered the Konoe message, together with an explanatory memorandum of his own, to Secretary Hull on November 15, 1941.[4]

By that late date other estimates of the meaning of the political change in Japan had long since reached key figures in the American government. Writing on October 17, the day on which Tojo received the imperial mandate, Captain R. E. Schuirmann, a member of Admiral Stark's staff, noted that current reports indicated that the new cabinet would be "no better and no worse" than the old one. "Japan may attack Russia, or may move southward, but in the final analysis this will be determined by the military on the basis of opportunity, and what they can get away with, not by what cabinet is in power."[5]

In the American War Department the view prevailed that no abrupt change in Japanese foreign policy appeared imminent, even though tension between Japan and the United States still remained. A message to that effect, emphasizing the "no abrupt change" interpretation, was sent to Hawaii and the Philippines on October 20. On that same day in Tokyo, an important American military officer, citing the press as his source ("Reliability: Good") wrote that Konoe's resignation and the elevation of Tojo to the premiership were ". . . not regarded as necessarily indicating any radical change in Japanese policy"—at least not in the immediate future. The composition of the cabinet appeared "essentially conservative in character." The new premier was known to be "in

---

[4] See Walsh aff., T 32985-91 and *Foreign Relations* (*Diplomatic Papers: 1941*), IV, 527-39 (Dr. Hornbeck's comments on the Walsh memorandum should be noted).

[5] Sherwood, *Roosevelt and Hopkins*, 419 and *PHA*, Part 16, 2215-16. Another memorandum for the chief of naval operations, dated October 21, 1941, advised that the political situation was such that "the intimation is clear that positive action detrimental to the United States' interests may be expected" (*PHA*, Part 15, 1845).

sympathy with many of the ideas entertained by his predecessor." Other members of the third Konoe Cabinet "who were likewise thought to have been sympathetic toward its leader" had continued in office. Foreign concern over the accession to the premiership of an army officer on the active list was not necessarily justified: "General Tojo is a known conservative, and while he is first of all a thoroughgoing Japanese, and as such has the national welfare and the national ambitions as an inherent part of his makeup, he is considered as having a breadth of vision which would appear to preclude any action of the more radical or extreme type."[6]

Ambassador Grew himself did not see the sudden change of cabinets as inevitably forecasting the beginning of the end. Writing also on October 20, the ambassador observed that ". . . indications of a willingness on the part of the Tojo Government to proceed with the [Hull-Nomura] conversations . . . would imply that it is premature to stigmatize the Tojo Government as a military dictatorship committed to the furtherance of policies which might be expected to bring about armed conflict with the United States." Tojo's becoming premier as a full general on active service meant that the army had "for the first time . . . openly assumed responsibility for the policies and conduct of government in Japan, which it had previously steadfastly declined to accept. It would be logical, therefore, to expect that General Tojo, in retaining his active rank in the Army . . . [would] be in a position to exercise a large degree of control over Army extremist groups."[7]

The Pearl Harbor attack, which occurred less than two months later,

[6] The War Department view is noted in Millis, *This Is Pearl!*, 185-86; the October 20 memorandum of "an important American military officer" in Tōkyō (whose identity is known but cannot here be revealed) can be found in the National Archives, Doc. No. 14601, OSS. In this connection, see Sherwood, 419.

A November 1 report of the Office of Naval Intelligence gave a contrary view of the new premier. Tōjō was described as "jingoistic and anti-foreign, particularly anti-Russian"—a man with "strong pro-Axis leanings." *PHA*, Part 15, 1815. See also Part 14, 1359-60, for a similar G-2 view (October 17) based on a United Press dispatch.

In a memorandum left with Secretary Hull on November 15, Bishop Walsh wrote: "General Tōjō . . . has long borne the reputation of being a conservative with little if any tinge of the firebrand." *Foreign Relations (Diplomatic Papers: 1941)*, IV, 529.

[7] Grew, *Ten Years in Japan*, 459-61. For Grew's cable to Washington, in which these views were recapitulated and other pertinent factors were noted, see *Foreign Relations (Diplomatic Papers: 1941)*, IV, 541-43.

The morning after Konoe had handed in his resignation, Mr. Ushiba, the prince's confidential aide and secretary, had told Mr. Dooman, the counselor of the American embassy, that thanks to the "intensive and miraculous labors" of Prince Konoe the new cabinet would "not be a military dictatorship bound to the most militaristic and drastic policy." See *Foreign Relations (Japan: 1931-1941)*, II, 689-92 and Grew, *Ten Years in Japan*, 456-61.

was to make some of these remarks appear woefully misleading. Except for the "breadth of vision" attributed to Tojo, however, there was nothing essentially wrong with any of the estimates made at the time. Although perhaps not always based on the best or the most reliable of sources, they did represent the truth to a large extent.

Tojo did not become premier in order to lead Japan into war. He became premier in order to break the deadlock of indecision which had threatened to prevail indefinitely under Konoe. Unlike his predecessor, Tojo was fully prepared *to assume the leadership of the nation in war* should a resort to force be reaffirmed as national policy toward the United States and Great Britain. The extremist group which had done so much damage during the first half of the 1930's was still a factor to be considered, but far more important than any hotheads of that sort were the little-known but ever-meddling members of the nucleus group within the army and navy general staffs. Such was the nature of their infiltration of the decision-making process that Tojo would not have been able to curtail their power even if he had felt inclined to do so.

Mindful of the imperial command to start with a "clean slate," Tojo plunged with his habitual energy and dispatch into what he later described as "the gravest crisis ever encountered in the history of Japan."[8] The remainder of October was largely given over to almost daily liaison conferences between the key cabinet ministers and the leaders of the supreme command. As before, the real power of initiative and of decision lay with the latter (especially with the staff officers in the "nucleus group" category). The army and navy chiefs of staff, acting as spokesmen for the all-mighty supreme command, "requested" that the national policy review be carried out promptly and that a conclusion be quickly reached. Admiral Nagano graphically emphasized the need for speed by pointing out that the navy alone was expending four hundred tons of oil per hour.

From the records available, it is clear that this time-oil factor hovered over the conference table like a demon and that a decision for war was considered the most readily available means of exorcising it. The discussions, which began on October 23, continued off and on until November 2. During that ten-day period, the same old issues cropped up so repeatedly that they tended at times to benumb the participants and

[8] Tōjō aff., S 344:3, T 36383 (which incorrectly renders the Japanese original, ". . . waga kokushi jō kūzen no jūdai kiki . . . ," as "the most perplexing period in the history of the Japanese Empire").

paralyze the proceedings.[9] The holdovers from the third Konoe Cabinet exerted greater influence than the newcomers; they were also more imprisoned in their thinking by what had gone before. Despite their enormous personal responsibility for the welfare of their countrymen, these leaders of Japan, old and new alike, never once asked themselves *why* they were confronted by such a critical choice. They did not look at the record or otherwise seek in past policies an explanation for present difficulties. Their decision-making was cut to the pattern set by tradition: conformity, not independence; acquiescence, not protest; obedience, not questioning. What the mind thought was kept within the confines of the mind.

Conclusions seem to have been based more on intuition than on reason. When agreement was fairly unanimous, it was easier to join the group than to cause trouble by insisting upon further analysis of all pertinent factors. Had anyone attempted to probe deeply, he would very likely have been told not to quibble—not to raise frivolous objections. He might even have been thought a coward. Hence, as a general rule, no one said anything even when assailed by doubts. And because no one said anything, Japan was eventually brought to the verge of ruin.[10]

It is against this psychological background that the "clean slate" proceedings at the liaison conference level—indeed, the whole decision-making process—must be viewed. In all, eleven specific questions were studied and three alternative plans were considered. The answers to the

[9] Except as separately noted, the discussion which follows, relating to the "clean slate" proceedings undertaken at the liaison-conference level between October 23 and November 2, 1941, draws on material in the following: Tōjō aff., S 343:16-17, T 36316-27, S 343:19, T 36338-44, and S 343:20, T 36346-49; Tōjō direct examination, S 344:18, T 36501-2; Tōjō cross-examination, S 347:9-11, T 36694-708 (note the confusion in dates in both the Japanese and English versions), S 348:1-3, T 36729-40, and S 348:14, T 36814-15; Tōgō aff., S 337:4-7, T 35675-703; Tōgō interrog., March 13, 7-9; Shimada aff., S 328:8-9, T 34654-62; Kaya aff., S 291:14-15, T 30650-55; Suzuki aff., S 333:9 and 11-12, T 35200-1 and 35213-21; Yamamoto aff., S 251:5-9 and 11, T 25919-52 and 25973-74; Kido aff., S 293:22, T 31028-31; Kido SKD; Kaya, 193-96; JRD Monograph No. 147, 61-66 and Appendix 7; JRD Monograph No. 150, 21-24 and Appendix 2; JRD Monograph No. 152, 1-2; JRD, "Translation," II:51903 (Item 18), 10-11 and Reference No. 5, and V (Item 31, Kenryō Satō interrogation); JRD, "Interrogation," I:49157 (Seizō Arisue), 34-36, 49 and 52, and I:48484 (Prince Higashikuni), 133-34; Hattori, I, 202-15, 256-61, 266, and 269-80; J, B/VII, 957-62 and 966-74; *Foreign Relations (Japan: 1931-1941)*, II, 709-19 and 753-56; CF 20, III, 269; and Feis, 293, 295, and 309-11.

A statement by Tōjō (S 344:18, T 364-98) to the effect that he did not allow the so-called secretaries (Hoshino, Mutō, Oka, and Satō) to participate in either the discussion or the decision-making phases of liaison conferences should not be interpreted to mean that they were without influence with regard to the outcome of such conferences.

[10] Based on an interview with a very knowledgeable Japanese friend who must remain nameless.

former provided the basis on which the latter were judged. A tone of optimism and confidence was maintained throughout, despite the fact that firm conclusions could rarely be offered because of the presence of certain key "ifs."

On the question of the outlook of the war in Europe, for instance, a sort of neither-nor answer emerged from both the foreign ministry and the supreme command: An imminent peace between Germany and Britain or Germany and the Soviet Union seemed less likely than a protracted war, but an early peace between those powers was not impossible; much would depend on how the war situation developed and on the attitude of Britain and Russia.

With reference to the operations that Japan intended launching in the South, "considerable difficulty" was anticipated during the initial phases, yet despite that fact the army general staff expressed itself as being "fully confident of success." So long as the navy did its part by maintaining surface traffic, the army would accomplish its mission. The naval general staff avowed that it, too, was confident of victory in the early stages. The admirals warned, however, that Japan must be prepared for a long war and that the ultimate outcome would be determined by Japan's ability to keep abreast of the anticipated expansion of American strength.

On the question of what the Soviet Union would do if Japan attacked in the South, the semicomforting answer was given that immediate war in the North was unlikely. How long an uneasy peace would prevail in that region, however, would depend upon subsequent developments. It was even thought possible that the United States might forcibly seize Soviet Far Eastern territory for use against Japan.

What conclusions, if any, were reached concerning ships to be requisitioned and losses to be sustained during the first three years of the war remains largely a riddle. No one seems to remember whether a verbal estimate was made by the supreme command or whether a written report was submitted and later destroyed. It has even been suggested that this matter may not have been studied at all, or that the investigation, although undertaken, may not have been completed in time to be of any use!

On the maintenance of transports for civilian needs and the supply and demand of staple goods, a typical answer was provided by Lt. Gen. Suzuki, the president of the cabinet planning board. If a minimum of 3,000,000 tons of shipping could be assured for civilian use, it would generally be possible, with the exception of some items, to guarantee the supply of goods envisaged in the plans already drawn up for the mobilization of commodities. If the annual loss of shipping were from 800,000 to 1,000,000 gross tons, and if Japan's yearly construction were 600,000 tons for the next three years, it would be possible to maintain the above-mentioned 3,000,000 tons. The obvious and embarrassing question of what would happen if circumstances conspired to produce a higher mortality and a lower construction rate seems not even to have been asked. Suzuki, who was the responsible party in this case, had spoken. The matter was left at that.

Some of the consequences of such an approach to decision-making were revealed in a postwar statement by the chief of staff of Japan's combined fleet: "The figures estimated by the Japanese Navy for total shipping losses were 1,000,000 tons in the first year of the war and 800,000 tons in each succeeding year. In actual fact, however, the losses were as follows: First year, 1,250,000 tons; second year, 2,560,000 tons; third year, 3,480,000 tons, i.e., more than four times the estimated amount."[11]

On Japan's financial ability to support a war of the proportions then contemplated, the civilian bureaucrats in the finance ministry offered a similarly meaningless conclusion: Japan's financial strength was such that she would be able to hold out in a war against the United States, Great Britain, and the Netherlands so long as the supply of materials required for the pursuit of military action and the maintenance of national life proved adequate.

Had anyone delved into the problem of what constituted an adequate supply, or into the probability of its being assured, the officials concerned would no doubt have replied that "countermeasures" were being studied—a favorite way out for all those who might otherwise have been forced to admit their inability to answer the question satisfactorily.

Regarding assistance from Germany and Italy, it was said that an Axis declaration of war and a "no separate peace" agreement could be arranged, but that little more could be expected, except perhaps for commerce destruction in the Pacific and Indian Oceans and some co-ordination between German operations in the Near East and Japan's offensive in the southern regions.

On the key issue of whether Japan could attack the Netherlands alone, or Great Britain and the Netherlands, without having to take on the United States as well, the answer was a very definite "No." The explanation offered was as plain and as simple as the facts themselves—the

[11] See Hashimoto, *Sunk*, 241.

United States had too much at stake to stand idly by while Japan annexed British and Dutch possessions in the Far East. There was the American role in the southwest Pacific, the American need for raw materials such as rubber and tin, the security and independence of the Philippines which would be menaced by the Japanese advance southward, the fate of China, and—last but not least—the pressure of American public opinion. Even if these factors had not existed, operational considerations alone would have led the Japanese supreme command to attack the Pacific possessions of the United States.

Similar considerations also provided an answer with regard to the advantages and disadvantages of postponing hostilities to early March 1942. The conclusion was correctly drawn that the passage of time would work greatly against Japan. In fact, it was said that any delay beyond December would render the commencement of war against the ABD powers "absolutely impossible." Consequently, hostilities had to be undertaken in early December at the latest.

In this connection, further thought was given to an idea which had earlier appealed to Prince Konoe: the retrieving of the national fortunes through reliance upon the synthetic production of oil in preference to the seizure of petroleum by military force. The fact of the matter, however, was that synthetic production simply could not supply enough oil to satisfy Japan's demands. Even in the event of a decision for war, the outlook with respect to oil was going to be far from satisfactory. Japan would have to occupy the Dutch fields within the first four or five months in order to secure a sufficient quantity to continue fighting. Even so, a time would come when the supply would be "dangerously low." An alternative proposal by Finance Minister Kaya, calling for the buying of oil from Northern Sakhalin or for the outright purchase of Northern Sakhalin itself, was dismissed as being impossible of realization.[12]

With respect to the Hull-Nomura conversations, the war, navy, and foreign ministries, together with imperial headquarters, jointly concluded that there was absolutely no prospect of Japan's being able to attain her current "minimum" demands. New proposals would have to be submitted if any hope was still to be placed in a continuation of the negotiations in Washington.

[12] On the oil question in particular (Kaya called it the "last key"—*saigo no kagi*), see Kaya, 193-94; JRD, "Translation," II:51021 (Item 21), 1-34; JRD, "Statements," III:50418, 126-27, and III:61688, 133-36; Kenryō Satō, "Dai-Tōa Sensō wo Maneita Shōwa no Dōran," 121; JRD, "Interrogations," I:49157 (Seizō Arisue), 52, and II:35901 (Shinichi Tanaka), 442; and JRD, "Translation," V (Item 34, Shinichi Tanaka interrogation).

Finally, with reference again to the Asian continent, it was estimated that a war against the ABD powers would initially enhance the determination of the Chinese Nationalists to continue their resistance against Japan, but that Japanese military action, such as the capture of Hong Kong and Singapore and the interdiction of traffic along the Burma Road, would subsequently result in a weakening of Nationalist morale and in increased defections to the Nanking government of Wang Ching-wei.

It was October 30 by the time these conclusions had been reached by one or more of the responsible organs: the supreme command; the war, navy, foreign, and finance ministries; and the cabinet planning board. During the actual liaison conferences, Premier Tojo refrained from expressing his personal opinions, but he did seek and obtain the continued indulgence of the two chiefs of staff, who nevertheless remained openly impatient. With the "clean slate" proceedings drawing to a close, attention shifted to the three "alternatives": (I) a policy of caution even at the expense of great hardships at home; (II) an immediate launching of hostilities; and (III) further diplomatic efforts and, at the same time, rapid completion of operational preparations, with the determination to go to war whenever that should prove necessary.

Plan I envisaged an avoidance of armed conflict even in the event negotiations were ruptured. The reasoning was that the hardships which would result from such forbearance would be preferable to the risks involved in taking on the United States and Great Britain at a time when four years of fighting in China had still not brought that "Incident" to a close. Those who argued against this plan had the problem of oil foremost in their minds. They said that Japan's liquid fuel stocks would soon be exhausted and that Japanese military forces would be brought to a standstill within two years. To adopt Plan I, therefore, would be equivalent to deciding upon national suicide. Rather than do that, it would be better to attempt to break through the encirclement which was threatening the future of the nation. Thus, Plan I was quickly discarded.

Plan II was the brainchild and favorite of the supreme command but was opposed by Tojo, perhaps because it so obviously ran counter to the imperial injunction to restudy the entire situation, beginning with "a clean slate." The plan stemmed from the view that Japan could not achieve what she wanted through negotiations. A continuation of diplomatic efforts would work only to the advantage of the United States.

From the standpoint of operational considerations, the sooner Japan went to war the better. The supreme command therefore insisted that the decision to fight should be made at once, for only thus could the necessary preparations be pushed with maximum efficiency.

Plan III represented the inevitable compromise between Plans I and II. In essence, it differed from the imperial conference decision of September 6 only in the greater stress placed upon Japan's determination to resort to war in the near future. A new deadline was to be established. If Japan failed to achieve a diplomatic victory in the time set, a decision for war would be made at once.

The liaison conference at which the die was finally cast in favor of Plan III convened at 9:00 a.m., November 1, 1941, and did not adjourn until 1:30 a.m., November 2.[13] At that long session, both the civilian and military leaders of Japan were still so imbued with the idea that war was preferable to any compromise which failed to confirm the aggressive efforts of a decade that they closed their eyes to the enormous danger which their policy entailed. They did not deny that war was a gamble; they simply treated it as a gamble that had to be faced. If Japan took the chance, she might be defeated, but if she did not, she would be defeated anyway; therefore Japan should take the chance.

The supreme command could not say with certainty what the ultimate outcome might be, yet Japan *must* go to war.

Why?

Because war was seen as a now-or-never proposition.

If Japan went to war soon, final victory could not be regarded as absolutely certain, but if Japan hesitated she would never have another opportunity. Combined with this was a favorite general staff threat—if the cabinet let December pass without a decision for war, the supreme command would not hold itself responsible for the defense of the state.

The frame of mind of Japan's leaders was rather like the attitude of Shakespeare's Brutus:

> Our legions are brim-full, our cause is ripe:
> The enemy increaseth every day;
> We, at the height, are ready to decline,
> There is a tide in the affairs of men,
> Which, taken at the flood, leads on to fortune;
> Omitted, all the voyage of their life
> Is bound in shallows and in miseries.

[13] See the sources cited in footnote 9 above.

> On such a full sea are we now afloat;
> And we must take the current when it serves,
> Or lose our ventures.[14]

Clausewitz stated the matter in more prosaic terms: " 'A small State which is involved in a contest with a very superior Power, and foresees that each year its position will become worse' should 'make use of the time when the situation is farthest from the worse' if it considers war to be inevitable. The small State in this position is advised to attack."[15]

The naval general staff—always the more accommodating of the two branches of the supreme command—was willing to allow a continuation of diplomatic negotiations until November 20, but the army general staff (speaking largely through the vice-chief of staff) was considerably less obliging. It was prepared to give the diplomats only two more weeks, or until November 13. This led to an argument between Vice-Chief Tsukada and the foreign minister in which Tojo joined Togo in demanding that the supreme command promise to abandon the idea of going to war in the event that diplomacy succeeded. The controversy over the deadline for diplomacy finally became so intense that a twenty-minute recess was called to allow tempers to cool and to permit consultation between the chiefs of staff and their respective operations bureaus. The result was that the leaders of the supreme command finally gave their consent to a continuation of negotiations until November 30. Tojo then asked if it would not be possible to have another twenty-four hours, making December 1 the deadline instead. When Tsukada responded that such an extension would be absolutely out of the question, Navy Minister Shimada smoothed the way by indirectly suggesting that December 1 be accepted on the understanding that it be regarded as the equivalent of midnight, November 30. This meaningless compromise marked the actual acceptance of Plan III.[16]

The conferees then took up the problem of the negotiating position Japan would assume. They had before them two proposals, "A" and "B." The first, which contained a so-called concession envisaging the reten-

---

[14] *Julius Caesar*, Act IV, Scene III.

[15] As quoted in Kennedy, *Some Aspects of Japan and Her Defence Forces*, 137.

[16] As a result of this decision, Tōgō informed Nomura that an agreement with the United States had to be concluded by November 25 at the latest. This deadline, however, was subsequently extended to November 29. See the "Magic" intercepts of Cables Nos. 736, 763, 1140, 812, and 865 in *PHA*, Part 12, 100, 116, 159, 165, and 208. Tōjō testified that Tōgō's choice of November 25 had nothing to do with the fact that an order had been previously issued to the Pearl Harbor task force to sail on November 26. The foreign minister, Tōjō said, could not have known about that order. S 349:3, T 36825-27.

tion of Japanese troops in strategic areas of China until 1966, had already been approved. The army had argued against the imposition of any time limit, but the foreign minister, realizing the uselessness of attempting negotiations on such a basis, had gradually "prevailed" against the military view. He had suggested five years, then eight, then ten, and had finally accepted twenty-five as a compromise between the periods of from fifty to ninety-nine years being proposed by some of his still reluctant colleagues. The areas were North China, Inner Mongolia, and Hainan Island (from which the reinvasion of all of China, in force and at any moment, would have been a matter of no great difficulty).

Proposal B represented an alternative, stopgap approach. It was conceived on the principle that if a Japanese-American agreement could not be reached in any other way, a *modus vivendi* could perhaps be achieved by removing from immediate consideration practically all of the major issues of contention, especially those relating to China. The two countries were mutually to undertake not to advance by force into Southeast Asia or the South Pacific (French Indo-China was specifically excepted, since Japan had already occupied that area). The two countries were also to cooperate to ensure acquisition of the raw materials each might require from the Netherlands Indies. (Stated more bluntly, the United States would have to help Japan obtain all of the resources she wanted from the East Indies.) The United States was to agree to supply Japan annually with 1,000,000 tons of aviation fuel. In return, Tokyo would transfer Japanese troops in southern French Indo-China *to the northern part of that country*. If the principle of nondiscrimination in commercial relations were adopted throughout the world, Japan would be willing to agree, *if necessary*, to apply that principle to the Pacific, including China.

In short, Proposal B was an extraordinary diplomatic document. Its purpose was to permit Japan to concentrate on a new military offensive aimed at finally conquering and subjugating the long-suffering people of China. An American willingness to accept that proposal would have meant even more than a betrayal of China. It would have signified, in the opinion of Secretary Hull, "condonement by the United States of Japan's past aggressions, assent by . . . the United States to unlimited courses of conquest by Japan in the future, abandonment by the United States of its whole past position in regard to the most essential principles of its foreign policy in general . . . and acceptance by the United States of a position as a silent partner aiding and abetting Japan in her effort to create a Japanese hegemony in and over the western Pacific and Eastern

Asia." An American submission to Proposal B "would have placed Japan in a commanding position in her movement to acquire control of the entire western Pacific"; it would have destroyed American chances of asserting and maintaining the legitimate rights and interests of the United States in the Pacific; and, in the final analysis, it would have meant "a most serious threat" to American national security.[17]

This was the proposition favored by Shigenori Togo, the new foreign minister, who was afraid that Proposal A would stimulate the United States into raising once again the issue of Japan's violation of the Nine-Power Pact. The army general staff thought otherwise. Both Sugiyama and Tsukada argued that Proposal B would lead to nothing but a further delay in solving the China problem—a delay which would prove disastrous for Japan. So strong were Togo's views, however, that some of his colleagues believed he might resign rather than agree to shelve Proposal B. Since a resignation by Togo at that juncture would presumably have meant the end of the Tojo Cabinet, and consequently a new political crisis, the atmosphere at the conference became very strained. General Muto, who was present in his capacity as chief of the military affairs bureau, finally suggested a ten-minute recess. During that brief time, both he and Tojo managed to persuade the army general staff to adopt a more "conciliatory" attitude.

In the end, Proposal B was revised in such a way as to place the United States in the position of having to guarantee Japan a virtually unlimited supply of oil through a restoration of the conditions which had existed prior to the freezing of Japanese assets. A new item was added in the form of a demand that the United States agree not to obstruct the restoration of peace between Japan and China—i.e., the United States was to consent to a hands-off policy regarding China so that, deprived of the assistance which had kept it going for so long, that country would finally surrender to Japan. The original willingness to shift Japan's occupation forces from southern to northern French Indo-China was noticeably qualified. An addendum to the proposal noted that this offer would be made to Washington only "if necessary." Complete withdrawal from French territory was not to take place until the China Incident had been "settled" or a "just peace" had been established in the Pacific Ocean area.

Such was the price paid for supreme-command consent to the inclusion of Proposal B as part of Japan's "new" diplomatic offensive.

[17] Hull testimony, *PHA*, Part 11, 5370-71 (see also Part 2, 430-32). For a contrary view, see Schroeder, *The Axis Alliance and Japanese-American Relations, 1941*, 76-81.

When these issues had been settled, the liaison conference at last adjourned. Both Foreign Minister Togo and Finance Minister Kaya asked for a few more hours to think matters over before joining their colleagues in unanimously endorsing the November 2 decision. After the war Kaya wrote of the choices which he had felt were open to him at that critical moment in 1941. His first thought had concerned the *jūshin*— the group of ex-premiers politely called the "senior statesmen." He wondered if they might be able to prevent Japan from becoming involved in war, but he decided that they could not—they lacked the power and influence of their more famous predecessors, the elder statesmen (*genrō*) of the Meiji period. Kaya's second thought was resignation, but he discarded that idea also. Resignation would be unpatriotic and useless, since he would be replaced by someone else who would readily consent to the cabinet's policy. Kaya's third thought was to continue in his post so as to bore from within. But that would not work either, since sabotage would simply force a cabinet resignation. The younger officers would become active and a new and more war-minded cabinet would emerge. Thus Kaya came to the conclusion that he literally could do nothing but accept the existing situation in the hope that diplomacy would provide a solution to Japan's problems within the time limit set by the supreme command.[18]

The net effect of such rationalization was that late in the afternoon of November 2 Premier Tojo and the two chiefs of staff were able to report to the throne, allegedly with tears rolling down their cheeks, that the government had unanimously come to a decision regarding the course to be followed in the immediate future. The expression which appeared on the Emperor's face, as the new policy was unfolded to him, suggested to Tojo that His Majesty was distressed at the prospect of undertaking a war against the United States and Great Britain. This impression was confirmed when the Emperor asked the three men to redouble their efforts in behalf of a peaceful solution.[19]

Because the Emperor was obviously worried about the way matters were developing, Tojo decided to seek the advice and opinions of the

---

[18] See Kaya, 194-96. For Tōgō's postwar explanations of why he also subsequently decided against resignation (*c.* December 1), see Tōgō aff., S 337:8, T 35708-10; and Tōgō, 249-50. The views expressed in IMTFE, "Roling Opinion," 243-49 are also pertinent.

[19] Tōjō aff., S 343:17, T 36327-28; Kido SKD and corresp.; and Hattori, I, 215. In the course of the audience, the Emperor asked how Japan would justify an invasion of Thailand if such a move proved necessary. He also wanted to know whether it was absolutely certain that Japan would be able to acquire and transport the oil of the Indies even in the face of counterattacks by enemy aircraft and submarines.

army and navy councilors to the throne so as "to leave no stone unturned" with respect to the question at issue. A meeting was called two days later; it was convened in the presence of the Emperor, with Imperial Prince Kan'in presiding. The councilors were briefed by the army and navy chiefs of staff, who repeated in detail the views which each had expressed during the many liaison conferences held between October 23 and November 2. Again the "ifs" in Japan's position were duly noted, but the impression given to the councilors was more favorable than unfavorable. The result was that they, too, unanimously agreed that the course proposed by the supreme command was the correct one. As was the custom, His Majesty listened to the proceedings without uttering a single word.[20]

Formal confirmation of the new policy took place the very next day.[21] At the imperial conference of November 5, Tojo played the part of parliamentary chairman. Neither he nor anyone else threatened or cajoled. Indeed, Tojo went so far as to state that the negotiations must be carried on even at the cost of their interfering with operational preparations. The very fact that the United States had been willing to negotiate thus far, he declared, showed that she had her weak points. Once Washington clearly understood the extent of Japan's determination, the chances of a diplomatic success would be improved.

Tojo's words reflected a consensus. Everyone, including the chief civilians, Togo and Kaya, subscribed to the view that war would be inevitable unless the United States accepted Japan's demands. All were agreed that if diplomacy failed to produce a settlement by zero hours, December 1, Japan would make the final decision for war *regardless of*

[20] See Tōjō aff., S 343:17-18, T 36328-35; Tōjō interrog., Feb. 11, 2 and Mar. 13, 3-4; JRD Monograph No. 152, 2-3; and Hattori, I, 215-16.
In addition to those mentioned in the text, the two-hour meeting (2:00-4:00 p.m.) of the *Gunji-Sangiin*, on November 4, was attended by Imperial Prince Fushimi; Premier Tōjō; Navy Minister Shimada; army councilors: Imperial Prince Asaka, Imperial Prince Higashikuni, Terauchi, Nishio, Yamada, Doihara, Shinozuka; and navy councilors: Hyakutake, Katō, Oikawa, Shiozawa, Yoshida, and Hibino.
[21] On the imperial conference of November 5, which began at 10:30 a.m. and adjourned at 3:10 p.m., after an hour's recess for lunch, see Tōjō aff., S 343:18-20, T 36335-46; Tōjō-Webb exchange, S 348:13, T 36808-9; Tōjō interrog., Mar. 12, 4-5 and Mar. 15, 4-10 (which contains some garbled references); Kido aff., S 293:22, T 31030-31; Kido SKD; Suzuki aff., S 333:12, T 35221-22; Prosecution Exh. No. 1168, S 110:9-10, T 10331-38 (the English translation of the "Teikoku Kokusaku Suikō Yōryō" is so poor that the Tribunal's indulgence is inexplicable); IMTFE, Doc. No. 0004, 18-22; Hattori, I, 216-22; JRD Monograph No. 150, 24-33 and No. 152, 3-6; JRD, "Statements," I:50135 (Takushirō Hattori), 341; JRD, "Interrogations," I:49157 (Seizo Arisue), 49-50, and II:35901 (Shinichi Tanaka), 444; and CF 20, IV, 358.
The Emperor was briefed on the respective operational plans of the army and navy on November 3 and 5.

the state of the negotiations at that time. The same old jargon was brought into play, as if parrot-like utterances could conjure up a reality which did not in fact exist: No one understood Japan's true intentions; everyone was unjustly hostile; military force had been employed in the past out of Japan's love and desire for peace and security; the Japanese nation was sincere, all others were insincere.

And in the background there was the ever-recurring thought which left no room for less drastic measures: ". . . On such a full sea are we now afloat; And we must take the current when it serves, Or lose our ventures."[22]

But hand in hand with this, despite the deepening deterioration in Japanese-American relations, the leaders in Tokyo remained optimistic—believing, for one reason or another, that the gulf between the two countries was not yet so wide that it could not be bridged, if only the United States would do the bridging. Some members of the government—Tojo included—still clung to Matsuoka's view that Japan should act in a determined manner and thus convince the Americans that she meant business. Among the more positive-minded, the line between taking a firm stand and resorting to threatening measures was not clearly drawn.[23]

[22] Following the imperial conference, Admiral Yamamoto, acting on instructions from the chief of the naval general staff, issued an order to the combined fleet authorizing the carrying out of all necessary operational preparations for a war against the United States, Britain, and the Netherlands. Similar orders were issued by the army the following day. See J, B/VII, 946-66; and Hattori, I, 225-26 and 232: "Jūichigatsu itsuka no gozen kaigi kettei ni yoreba, jūnigatsu tsuitachi reiji made ni kōshō ga seiritsu shinai baai ni wa, *sono toki no kōshō keii ikan ni kakawarazu,* sensō wo kaishi suru koto ni sadamerarete wa aru" (italics mine).

On November 5, in Washington, General Marshall and Admiral Stark advised the President that at that time ". . . an unlimited offensive war should not be undertaken against Japan. . . ." War should be avoided, they declared, while the United States strengthened its defensive forces in the Far East, unless Japan attacked or directly threatened "territories whose security to the United States" was "of very great importance." Included in this category were the British Commonwealth and the Netherlands East Indies (as quoted by Feis, 302, citing *PHA*, Part 14, 1061-62). The members of the cabinet believed the American people would support the Administration if it struck back at Japan in the event the latter attacked British or Dutch territory in the Pacific (Feis, 303-4).

[23] For a time, early in November, the air of optimism in Tōkyō derived from reports sent earlier by the Japanese embassy in Washington, encouraging the view that two of the three major items in the negotiations (Japan's role in the Tripartite Alliance and the question of nondiscriminatory treatment regarding trade in China) had more or less been settled—at least that they were no longer seriously at issue, and that consequently the only remaining problem was Japan's involvement in war with China and Japan's intention to retain troops there even following a "settlement." Upon reading back over the record, however, the new foreign minister, Mr. Tōgō, had begun to question whether there was, in fact, any real basis for such optimism. The more he read, the more the suspicion grew in his mind that perhaps those two items had not actually been settled

The official brainwashing policy which had been directed at the Japanese people for more than a decade had by now taken full effect upon the leaders as well. The civil and military officials in Tokyo could not understand why Washington kept insisting on general principles which ran counter to the observed realities of the situation: the *fait accompli* in Manchuria, the war in China, the occupation of French Indo-China.

Japan's leaders saw the American position in terms of a rigid demand that Japan repudiate the policies of the past—thus forgoing the still ungarnered fruits of aggression in Asia—and they were in no temper to do that. Operational preparations were in full swing. There was a breathless emphasis upon intensifying those preparations and rushing them to completion. The fever for war among all who were participating grew proportionately. The closer their efforts carried them toward operational readiness, the more confident did the military become that success would attend a resort to arms. Those members of the ruling elite like Marquis Kido, who had especially vivid memories of the turbulent 1930's, believed that violence could easily break out anew in the tense atmosphere which then prevailed. The police guard around Kido's residence was increased from ten to fifteen. At night an additional squad was added, bringing the total to twenty-five. In traveling to and from his palace office by automobile, the lord privy seal took the precaution of using a different route every day.[24]

While the Japanese government waited for an American response to its proposals, much attention was given to matters relating to war. A basic economic program was drafted, and policies to be implemented vis-à-vis Germany, Italy, and Thailand were spelled out in detail. Included among them was a decision to the effect that Japan would not join Germany in fighting Russia—at least for the time being—even at the cost of a German delay on entering the war against the United States. The approach to Thailand was to follow standard procedure. The Thai government would be asked to allow Japanese troops to pass through its territory. If it did not accede to Japan's request, the imperial army would invade Thailand. Since the Thai premier was a friend of Japan, difficulties were not anticipated. Care had to be taken, however,

---

at all. So concerned did he become that he cabled Nomura asking specifically about the matter. In reply, the ambassador advised Tōgō that the earlier reports from the embassy, on which Tōkyō had naturally relied, had been *incorrect*.

[24] The text draws on material in Kido SKD and Kido aff., S 293:22, T 30132-33; Tōgō aff., S 337:5-6 and 7, T 35688-89 and 35699-700; and Hattori, I, 222-26.

to guard against tipping Japan's hand to the Anglo-American enemy.[25]

As further cover and concealment, negotiations for the acquisition of raw materials were to be resumed with the Netherlands East Indies. Talks would also be conducted with Moscow for the purpose of camouflaging Japan's forthcoming drive southward. What Japan would ultimately demand from the Soviet Union would depend on how the war situation developed.

On Tojo's orders, consideration was also given to drafting a plan for expediting the successful termination of the hostilities which were now so imminent. What emerged was a very general and, at points, rather quaint war-guidance scheme—the outgrowth of earlier staff thoughts on the subject.[26] Although Japan's relations with her Axis partners were not of the best, she nevertheless looked forward in this plan to the ways in which they could be of assistance, notwithstanding the fact that to date no steps had been taken to commit the Germans and Italians to a combined and coordinated strategy. Much emphasis was also given to the surrender of England. In fact, that beckoning mirage exercised such hypnotic effect that a decisive role was assigned to Britain's capitulation. Through an initial *Blitzkrieg* on a grand scale, Japan would assume "a strategically dominant position" in the Pacific. She would capture the vital resource-areas of the South and secure the main lines of communication, thereby creating a structure of long-term self-sufficiency and self-defense. By thus assuming the posture of invincibility, Japan would so impress the United States with the hopelessness of fighting that Washington would be willing to accept a Japanese-formulated peace.

To rob the United States of the will to fight, Germany and Italy were to be encouraged to conduct operations in the Near East, North Africa, and the Suez area aimed at weakening the Allied power of resistance. They were also to take "measures" against India; intensify

[25] For material relating to economic planning for wartime, see Hattori, I, 285-86; and JRD Monograph No. 150, 44-46. On Japan's approach to Germany, Italy, and Thailand, see Hattori, I, 288-96; and JRD Monograph No. 150, 52-57. All of these measures were discussed and approved at liaison conferences held between November 10 and 13.

[26] The text which follows presents the gist of a liaison conference decision of November 15, 1941 (not November 13), entitled "Tai Bei-Ei-Ran-Shō Sensō Shūmatsu Sokushin ni kan suru Fukuan." See Hattori, I, 281-85; S 110:10, T 10338-42 (possibly a preliminary draft; Americans of German ancestry are mentioned as a channel for spreading dissension although it is admitted that an effort to employ that group had proved impractical and ineffective during World War I); JRD, "Interrogations," I:49157 (Seizō Arisue), 50-51; and JRD Monograph No. 45, 26-28, and No. 150, 46-49. At another liaison conference on November 20, approval was given to a policy relating to the administration of occupied areas in the South ("Nanpō Senryō-chi Gyōsei Jisshi Yōryō"). See also Tōjō aff., S 344:4 and 5-6, T 36388-89 and 36393-404.

their destruction of American shipping in the Atlantic and Indian Oceans; strengthen their offensive in Central and South America militarily, economically, and politically; tighten the blockade against England; and—if the situation permitted—launch the cross-Channel invasion which had thus far been postponed. Japan, for her part, would do everything in her power to conduct the war in the Pacific and in China in such a way as to contribute to Britain's fall. Australia and India were to be cut off from communication with England and alienated from the mother country. Burma was to be granted independence as quickly as possible so that India would be stirred to demand her own freedom.

Japan planned to exert the utmost efforts to prevent other nations from joining in the war. Tokyo would endeavor to utilize third powers to advantage: the Soviet Union, because of her geographical position; South America, because Japan hoped to secure vital resources there (to be transported to the homeland by submarine); Portugal, because of her Asian possessions (Timor and Macao); and Norway and Sweden, because of their shipping in the Pacific. Japan would also work most scrupulously to prevent the outbreak of war with the Russians while she remained engaged in operations in the South. In fact, if Germany and the Soviet Union proved receptive, Japan would encourage them to make peace with each other and thereby add the Russian colossus to the side of the Axis. Following an adjustment of Soviet-Japanese relations, Japan would consider fostering a Soviet debouchment into the India-Iran area. She would also strive to contribute to antiwar sentiments among the American people by luring the main strength of the U.S. fleet to its destruction in the Far East and by emphasizing, through propaganda, the senselessness of a Japanese-American war.

In other words, the government's war guidance plan envisaged employing much the same approach toward the United States as had already been tried in China without success. Through initial military victories and the threat of further and more decisive action, Japan would seek a "reconsideration" of the situation by the American people. To encourage a sensible attitude on their part, Japan and her allies would refuse to conclude an immediate peace with England following that country's surrender, and would thus use England to induce the United States to give in. As a further means of hastening the restoration of peace with the United States, Japan would consider being "reasonable" about the disposition of the Philippines and about the postwar supply of rubber and tin.

As might have been expected, no thought was given to the policies to be adopted in the event that future developments did not correspond to current estimates. The leaders of Japan spoke only of victory. Only thus did they foresee a termination of the war. The conclusion of Japan's principal operations in the South, they felt, would create an opportunity for the restoration of peace. A similar victory in China (especially the surrender of Chiang Kai-shek) or a favorable development in the European war (especially the collapse of England, the end of German-Soviet hostilities, or the success of Japan's policy toward India) would serve that purpose equally well—or so they thought. Although such planning was natural enough in the circumstances, the effect upon those who were a party to it was much the same as if Japan, in mid-November 1941, had already fought and won the war.

From a Japanese point of view, the program which thus emerged also satisfied the requirements of "responsible" leadership. Before the Russo-Japanese conflict of 1904-1905, Marquis Ito and others had busied themselves with schemes relating to the termination of hostilities and their foresight had proved of value. Now that Japan once more had a war guidance program, everyone could proceed with confidence, knowing that appropriate measures had been devised to cope with developments in the future. And so the nominal leaders of Japan and their decision-making "subordinates" passed to other, more pressing matters.

In an address before the 77th extraordinary session of the Diet on November 17—the first such address ever to be broadcast in Japan—Tojo served notice that third powers were expected not to obstruct the successful conclusion of the China Incident which Tokyo had in mind.[27] In less oblique terms, this amounted to a demand that the United States step aside to permit Japan to land the knockout blow. According to Tojo, the Japanese government also wanted normal trade relations restored. In other words, the ABD powers were told to stop all defensive preparations and acts of retaliation, even though those preparations and acts were clearly the result of prior aggressive moves on the part of Japan. A Western willingness to oblige would have signified that Japan, having

[27] On the Tōjō, Tōgō, and Shimada speeches, which follow in the text, see Tōjō aff., S 343:20-21, T 36349-55; Hattori, I, 226-29; S 237:14-15, T 24375-78; the Tolischus dispatch in *NYT*, November 19, 1941, 10; Tolischus, 294-301; *Japan Year Book, 1943-44*, 181-82; Grew, *Ten Years in Japan*, 480; JRD Monograph No. 147, 72-73; and *Facts on File*, 1941, 437 L.

The 77th Extraordinary Diet (November 15-21, 1941) approved all thirteen of the government's bills, including a supplementary budget amounting to 4,315,000,000 yen (roughly $1,017,000,000), of which 3,800,000,000 yen ($874,000,000) was earmarked for the military.

been a "bad boy" in the Pacific and in Eastern Asia in general, was not to be chastised by the powers but was rather to be allowed to return to the family of nations with a friendly pat on the head, and in full possession of the ill-gotten gains of a decade.

Tojo also announced Japan's determination to prevent the expansion of the European war and its spread to the Far East. Precisely what was intended is not clear; certainly the ABD powers had no desire to see the hostilities then raging in Europe break out in the Pacific as well. One correspondent with entrée at the American embassy later wrote that Tojo's third point "presumably contained the promise that in case the first two demands were accepted, Japan would make 'utmost efforts' to sidetrack the Axis alliance."[28] But if the twisted language of that time is taken into account, Tojo's purpose may have been to warn the United States to stay out of the European war, regardless of the threat to American security posed by Hitler and Mussolini, or else be prepared to fight Japan in the Pacific.[29]

Tojo's speech was followed by the somewhat less challenging but hardly less pointed remarks of Foreign Minister Togo. The negotiations with the United States, he said, need not drag on for a long time. Although desirous of seeing the talks successfully concluded, Japan would reject any proposal that might impair her status as a major power. The deadline for signing an agreement was November 29 and could not be changed. After that date the situation would develop "automatically."

The two speeches together received the unanimous support of both houses of the Diet, but far surpassing either in terms of popular appeal and as a reflection of the spirit of the times was an address by a "veteran politician" named Toshio Shimada.[30] It was he—not Tojo—who pulled the sword from its scabbard and brandished it before the nation.

Japan had been fighting a "holy war" in China for well over four years, Shimada declared, but the end was still not in sight. The "dying Chiang Kai-shek regime" was "on the verge of destruction," and yet the war went on.

Why could China continue to resist? Because a group of hostile powers, with the United States as the nucleus, were treacherously giving assistance to the Chiang regime. Using Chiang as a "robot," they were

---

[28] Tolischus, 297.
[29] It should be noted that, for the most part, Tōjō did not write his own speeches. Addresses given in his capacity as premier were prepared for him by the cabinet secretariat (Hoshino intv.).
[30] See footnote 27 above.

purposely obstructing the completion of Japan's "holy war." They were interfering in the internal affairs of Thailand. They were applying powerful pressure to Burma—using that country as a foothold for activities directed against Japan. They were preventing the Netherlands East Indies from supplying the raw materials Japan needed. They were unjustly strengthening the defenses of Singapore, Guam, the Philippines, Hawaii, and other bases in the Pacific.

The Japanese people, Shimada insisted, were not a war-loving race. They had already been fighting for five years and consequently would not want to undertake hostilities against the United States and Great Britain. So long as room remained to negotiate, perhaps Japan should continue to do so. There was a saying, however, that even the Buddha could not be flouted more than three times and that twice was the limit of a saint. The cause of justice had been trampled underfoot, Japan's good-will had been ignored, her independence had been menaced, her course of advance had been cut off. The patriotism of the Japanese people—their sense of what was right and just—absolutely forbade that they tolerate such a state of affairs any longer or that they docilely await self-destruction, all the while submitting to insults and threats.

The government should not underestimate the attitude of the people. The entire nation was overwhelmed by a feeling of "being burned alive by a great fire"—of "being attacked by an unseen air raid." The people wanted the government to act. They wanted it "to stop grazing by the side of the road." Of what was the government afraid? Whatever Japan might fear, its opponents would fear also. Once the nation went to war, it would not be Japan alone that would incur casualties and suffer destruction.

According to Shimada, Prince Konoe had once used the phrase "the cancer of the Pacific." If there was such a cancer, Shimada asserted, it lay imbedded in the minds of the leaders of America. A surgical operation was required to remove that cancer. Performing such an operation was Japan's momentous responsibility—the grave and pressing duty of the Japanese people. *When would the government let the nation take up the scalpel?*

So spoke Representative Shimada to the thunderous cheers of his colleagues—including some who would later say that Japan had been driven to war against their own wishes by a group of defiant and reckless militarists. A far more accurate estimate of the situation, however, was cabled to the *New York Times* by its very perceptive Tokyo correspondent, Otto Tolischus: "In so far as Diet members speak at all, they are so belligerent that the government appears moderate by comparison."[31]

The same was true of members of extremist organizations. The nationalists had "backed the Tojo Cabinet almost to a man." Nineteen fervent societies had petitioned the premier to go to war with the United States. One group had even sent him an amulet and a teacup "to seal the bargain." The amulet represented a god who is believed to possess the power to ensnare devils.[32]

As time passed, the ultranationalists grew noticeably restless. Some two weeks after the Shimada oration, Seigo Nakano, a leading Fascist, revealed his impatience with the government's continued forbearance. He wanted an immediate seizure of military bases at strategic points in Greater East Asia. He "accused Tojo of failing to heed the real voice of Japan." The premier should get off his horse, Nakano said, doff his uniform, and listen to the demands for action being voiced in the streets and shops.[33]

Whether or not the masses wanted the government to *act*, as persons like Shimada and Nakano insisted, decisiveness proved to be the order of the day. Early in November the professional diplomat, Saburo Kurusu, had hurriedly departed for the American capital to aid Nomura in his difficult mission. Concurrently, Japan's admiral-ambassador had been ordered to submit Proposal A to the United States government. On November 10 he had read a "vague and uncertain" memorandum to the President in an effort to explain Japan's true intentions. On that same day, some ten thousand miles to the westward, Vice-Admiral Nagumo, who was to lead the attack against Pearl Harbor, had issued a secret order to the component parts of his task force designating Hitokappu Bay in the Kuriles as the place of rendezvous. Battle preparations were to be completed by November 20; for planning purposes, "X-Day" would be regarded as beginning at zero hours, December 8, Tokyo (December 7, Hawaii).[34]

By the time Kurusu had arrived on the scene, the United States

[31] Tolischus dispatch, *NYT*, November 19, 1941, 10.
[32] See "The Brocade Banner," 123.
[33] Tolischus, 314-15.
[34] See J, B/VII, 966-68 and 970; Nomura, "Kafu Kaisō," *Dai Nippon Teikoku Shimatsuki*, Dai-isshū (Saron Rinji Zōkangō), December 15, 1949, 27; Hattori, I, 222-26; Morton, 1332; "Magic" intercepts No. 1127, 1131 (Part 3), 1133 (Part 2), 1134, 798, and 1136 in *PHA*, Part 12, 146, 149, 151-52, 155-56, 158; and Feis, 304-8. See also Tōjō cross-examination, S 347:11, T 36706-7; and Kenryō Satō, "Dai-Tōa Sensō wo Maneita Shōwa no Dōran," 125.

government had rejected Proposal A. Notwithstanding Nomura's advice to Tokyo that the presentation of Proposal B would make it more difficult to reach an understanding, the ambassador was instructed to submit that proposal. The date was November 20—the very day on which Japanese military orders were issued projecting simultaneous attacks against Malaya and the Philippines.[35]

Two days later, on November 22, still another liaison conference was held to discuss the next step to be taken in the Japanese-American negotiations. Proposals A and B represented Tokyo's last stand diplomatically—Japan's "final proposals, in name as well as in fact" and hence an unspecified but no less real *ultimatum* directed against the United States.[36] The liaison conference therefore agreed that a rejection by the United States of Proposal B would be followed by a Japanese decision for war. If the United States moderated its stand, however, especially on the supply of oil to Japan, Tokyo would immediately make "a concrete demand" upon the American government designed to guarantee Japan six million tons of oil per year—more than enough to maintain the desired level of Japan's reserves, and consequently more than enough to keep the imperial army advancing against the enemy on the continent and the imperial navy prowling the high seas.

Nowhere is the Japanese intention clearer or the handwriting on the wall easier to read. An American refusal to capitulate to Japan's demands would mean war; a concession at any point would mean further and more specific demands. That was the program which

[35] See the references in the preceding footnote. At the time in question, Nomura and Kurusu thought it might be possible to secure a *modus vivendi* based on a return to the *status quo ante*—to the situation just prior to Japan's occupation of southern French Indo-China and America's freezing of Japanese assets. They cabled their views to Tōkyō but found their government unreceptive.

[36] See paragraph 2 of Foreign Minister Tōgō's Cable No. 725 sent to Admiral Nomura in Washington on November 4, 1941: ". . . hon-kōshō wa saigo no kokoromi ni shite waga tai-an wa meijitsu tomo ni saishū-an nari to go-shōchi aritaku . . ." (see S 251:10). The "Magic" intercept version of this phrase, as translated in Washington, was as follows: ". . . this is our last effort. Both in name and spirit this counterproposal of ours is, indeed, the last. I want you to know that" (see *PHA*, Part 12, 92). The defense translation at the Tōkyō trial was as follows: "The present negotiations are our final effort, and you must realize that these proposals are truly our last" (see T 25961-62). On the translation factor in the "Magic" intercepts, see footnote 38 below.

Both before and after presenting Proposal B to Secretary Hull, Nomura and Kurusu—despite Tōgō's instructions—"talked emphatically about the urgency of the situation and intimated vigorously that this was Japan's last word and if an agreement along those lines was not quickly concluded ensuing developments might be most unfortunate"—indeed, "that otherwise something awful would happen." See Cables No. 726 (paragraph 1) and 735 (paragraphs 4 and 5), S 251:10-11; Cable No. 812 as intercepted by "Magic"; and Hull testimony, *PHA*, Part 11, 5370, 5397-98.

the Tojo Cabinet and the supreme command jointly adopted on November 22.[37]

In Washington Secretary Hull was well abreast of the situation. Eight months of conversations with Nomura, of sending proposals to Tokyo and of receiving others in return, of consultations with experts in the Department and with colleagues in the Administration at large, of watching and waiting in vain for any evidence that Japan was ready to forsake her aggressive policy in Asia, had left the Secretary and his advisers with the overwhelming impression that a hand extended in friendship might be caught in the door which Japan seemed about to slam shut. Confirming that impression were the conditions stipulated in the official texts of Proposals A and B. As added proof, if any were needed, and as "corroboratory evidence" of what was generally known from other sources, there was the secret view seen through "Magic." Because of mistakes in translation or errors in decoding, this view was sometimes out of focus in terms of the original phrases used but rarely in terms of the basic policy behind them.[38]

Hull did not readily discard the hope that tension might be eased and new departures encouraged through the adoption of some kind of temporary arrangement, but careful study of the matter produced the conviction that a *modus vivendi* should not be attempted. The British, Chinese, Australians, and Dutch—who were all vitally concerned— were unenthusiastic. There was the very real fear that a move of that

[37] The decision of the November 22 liaison conference is noted in Tōjō aff., S 343:21, T 36356-57. Feis, 311, gives the amount of oil involved as five million tons (and notes that that quantity would have kept the reserves intact). As Tōjō remembered it, the figure was six million tons (to be demanded from the Americans and the Dutch). See also "Magic" intercept No. 833, *PHA*, Part 12, 177.

[38] The material previously presented supports this judgment. At the Tōkyō trial, Tōgō's defense counsel, Ben Bruce Blakeney, charged that ". . . the intercepted telegrams . . . were . . . so garbled, tendentiously phrased and so ineptly translated as to constitute very different documents from those dispatched by the Japanese Foreign Ministry" (see T 43607-21, S 393:2). In his memoirs, Tōgō wavered between concluding that the leaks through "Magic," during his tenure as foreign minister, did not do much harm (Tōgō, 151-52) and that they did a great deal of damage (pp. 219-21). Although mistakes were made in translation (compare, for instance, the original texts of messages No. 725, 726, and 735, S 251:10-11, with the intercepts, *PHA*, Part 12, 92-96 and 99), the point is that the American government was more concerned with basing its policies on Japanese actions than on Japanese words. Neither the one nor the other (including words spoken directly, or tendered in official Japanese translations) provided any basis for confidence in Japan or for optimism respecting the future. Such distortions as did occur through mistranslations are genuinely assailable as such, but the records of the liaison conferences which were held following Tōjō's assumption of the premiership, and the Japanese originals of the cables sent from Tōkyō to Washington, together reveal that the distortions did not essentially do violence to the reality of Japan's intentions. See also Ballantine cross-examination, T 10901-39.

type would give Japan an opportunity to gain her ends in China after all. It seemed inevitable that such an arrangement would put a stop to the continuing build-up of American defensive strength in the Pacific, and to do so would most likely hasten rather than postpone the outbreak of war. If it became evident, however, that Japan intended to adopt a new policy of peace and friendship toward her neighbors, commercial relations would be restored at once. It was up to the Japanese to take the initiative. Japan had been the one to adopt a program of force in Eastern Asia; Japan would have to be the one to abandon that program. Then, and only then, would Washington consider adjusting its own Far Eastern policy.

Privately Hull was far from optimistic. He judged that the end of the road was just around the corner, that matters were now out of his hands—in the sense that they were beyond diplomatic bounds—and that the army and navy must therefore assume the major share of responsibility for safeguarding the security of the United States, a task which he had earlier hoped could be achieved through diplomacy alone.[39] The President held similar views, which he discussed on November 25 with Hull, Stimson, Knox, Marshall, and Stark. Mr. Roosevelt thought a surprise attack might be delivered by Japan (against Southeast Asia) as early as December 1. Because of the traditional requirement that the United States await the onslaught of the enemy before engaging in military action, the President called attention to the fact that the problem facing the American government was how to exercise the required restraint without enhancing the normal risks inherent in such a policy. If the Japanese were determined to plunge the Pacific into war, they would have to be the ones to fire the first shot. The situation called for letting them launch whatever aggression they were planning (against Allied possessions in Southeast Asia), without permitting the danger to the United States to become too great.[40]

[39] See Hull, II, 1079-80, containing the Secretary's denial that he ever made a statement, later attributed to him, to the effect that he had washed his hands of the matter.

[40] The text refers to the famous Stimson diary entry of November 25, which states that at a meeting at the White House on that day the President "brought up the event that we were likely to be attacked perhaps (as soon as) next Monday [December 1], for the Japanese are notorious for making an attack without warning, and the question was what we should do. The question was how we should maneuver them into the position of firing the first shot without allowing too much danger to ourselves."

See *PHA*, Part 11, 5419, 5421-22, 5433-34; Feis, 314; Langer and Gleason, *The Undeclared War*, 730 (which quotes a Stimson diary entry of similar import, dated October 16); Beard, *President Roosevelt and the Coming of the War, 1941*, 517-23, 565-69; Current, "How Stimson Meant to 'Maneuver' the Japanese," *Mississippi Valley*

The next day, November 26, Secretary Hull handed Nomura and Kurusu the American reply to Proposal B. In so doing, he and the other key members of the Administration knew that the United States was confronted by "a most complicated and delicate and dangerous situation." The Secretary personally believed that Japan's leaders were "determined and desperate . . . likely to break out anywhere, at any time, at any place."[41] But from the point of view of national policy the only alternative to a Far Eastern Munich was to state the American position once again and to hope for the best while expecting the worst. And that is exactly what Hull did, in the form of an outline of a "Proposed Basis for Agreement" tendered to Japan as "Strictly Confidential, Tentative and Without Commitment."[42]

Knowing "from Japanese acts and utterances that the Japanese proposal of November 20 was their last word," Hull felt "it was obviously desirable that the record of the American Government's position throughout the conversations be made crystal clear." His November 26 communication was directed, in the first instance, toward that end and, in the second instance, "toward keeping the door open for further conversations notwithstanding the ultimative character of the Japanese proposal of November 20." The American note of November 26 "was offered for the consideration of the Japanese Government as one practical example of a program to be worked out. It did not rule out other practical examples which either Government was free to offer."[43] In handing over this note in Washington, together with an

---

Historical Review, Vol. XL, No. 1 (June 1953), 67-74; and Current, *Secretary Stimson: A Study in Statecraft*, 155-63.

It might be added that FDR's remarks, as *paraphrased* by Stimson, constituted an appreciation of the classic difficulty faced by the United States when confronted by an aggressor—a difficulty with which Secretary Dulles was later to become associated in terms of a concept which was implicit in the policy contemplated by Roosevelt—"massive retaliation."

[41] See *PHA*, Part 2, 430-40, 553-55, 608-9, and Feis, 307-19.

[42] See *Foreign Relations (Japan: 1931-1941)*, II, 764-72 (note especially the "Oral Statement" handed by Hull to Nomura in explanation of the November 26 proposal). Although Nomura's Cable No. 1189 (S 252:1-2), which was intercepted by "Magic" (*PHA*, Part 12, 181-82), contained only the gist of the American proposal (especially Section II, which is misleading if not read together with Section I and the "Oral Statement"), the full text was dispatched later in a separate cable (see Tōgō, 238). Note that Tōgō does not quote the "Oral Statement" (he simply dismisses it by saying that it went over old ground and contained nothing new) nor does he include the words "Strictly Confidential, Tentative and Without Commitment," which should appear at the head of the note (pp. 233-34). In this connection, see also Yoshida, *Kaisō Jūnen*, I, 48-52.

[43] Hull testimony, in *PHA*, Part 11, 5369 and 5391 (see also Part 2, 430-40). This was spelled out at the time in the "Oral Statement" handed by Hull to Nomura. *Foreign Relations (Japan: 1931-1941)*, II, 766-67.

explanatory oral statement, Mr. Hull told Japan's representatives that the agreement being proposed by the United States "would render possible practical measures of financial cooperation." These were not mentioned in the note because it was feared that they "might give rise to misunderstanding."

In his reactions to the Hull overture, Mr. Kurusu was "depreciatory" and pessimistic. He said that when Nomura and he reported to Tokyo, the Japanese government "would be likely to throw up its hands" and that he felt the American response "could be interpreted as tantamount to meaning the end." However, he did not suggest that Hull had come up with anything but a type of agreement which—*as it stood*—would most likely be unacceptable to his government. Since the proposal was tentative and without commitment, he speculated that it might be better to defer sending it to Tokyo, pending further discussion on an informal basis in Washington. Nomura asked whether they could see the President and Hull replied that he was sure Mr. Roosevelt would be glad to see them at any time.[44]

Although Nomura and Kurusu were disappointed at this turn of events, it is clear from what they said to Hull (and from their subsequent cables to Tokyo) that they were nevertheless thinking in terms of taking the November 26 proposal as a basis for further negotiations. The two envoys even went so far as to propose to Tokyo, on December 1, that steps be initiated to arrange a high-level conference at some midway point in the Pacific such as Honolulu. On the assumption that a meeting between Roosevelt and Tojo would be too difficult to arrange, Nomura and Kurusu suggested that the two sides be represented by persons enjoying the "complete confidence" of their governments: Vice-President Henry Wallace or White House adviser Harry Hopkins for the United States, and ex-Premier Konoe or Viscount Ishii of the privy council for Japan. The object would be to have these persons make a final effort to reach an agreement on the basis of the latest proposals

[44] As paraphrased in a Ballantine memorandum of November 26, 1941, *Foreign Relations (Japan: 1931-1941)*, II, 764-66. See also JRD Monograph No. 147, 75-77. The American desire to refrain from provoking Japan is also revealed by the fact that on November 27 Marshall and Stark advised the President that the United States should avoid precipitating military action as long as was consistent with national policy. "The most essential thing now . . . ," they said, "is to gain time." Concurrently, the President refused to give the British and Dutch any promise that the United States would go to war if their territory were attacked. Nor would he agree to the issuance of a joint warning to Japan that certain action on her part would result in war. See Feis, 322-24 and 334-35. Such discussion as did take place regarding the advisability or effectiveness of sending Japan "a virtual ultimatum" did not occur until *after* the delivery of the Hull note to Nomura and Kurusu.

submitted by the two countries—the Hull note of November 26 and
Japan's Proposal B of November 20. Thus, it is again clear that for
Japan's representatives in Washington the document handed to them
by the Secretary of State was in no sense an ultimatum. It was a very
difficult proposition but not an utterly impossible one, and certainly not
a threat to use force to coerce compliance. The door to a settlement,
Nomura and Kurusu felt, was still open.[45] It was only when the Hull
note reached Tokyo that the idea of further negotiations was finally and
adamantly rejected. The decision in that regard had actually been made
at the imperial conference of November 5; it had been reiterated at the
liaison conference on November 22. All that remained, therefore, were
certain formal procedures by which that decision would be recast more
specifically and irrevocably as the highest policy of the state, enjoying
the widest possible sanction.

Having previously decided that they would go to war if the United
States did not accept their last diplomatic effort by November 29 at the
latest, Japan's civil and military leaders found it convenient, both from
the point of view of conscience and as an instrument of propaganda, to
treat the Hull note *as if it were an ultimatum*—as if Washington had
linked a demand for an acceptance of its terms by a specified time and
date with a threat to resort to force if those terms were rejected.[46]

The unreality of myths is the very essence of their attraction. Some of
Japan's leaders were so hobbled in their thinking that they undoubtedly
believed this self-created nonsense. Others, less naïve and more percep-

[45] See especially Cables No. 1189 (original Japanese, S 251:1-2), 1191, 1227 (which is
quoted in the text), and 876 (Tōkyō's rejection of No. 1227). Except as noted, the
originals are not available. The "Magic" version can be found in *PHA*, Part 12, 181-85,
213-14, and 224. See also Kurusu, 160-61; JRD Monograph No. 147, 78; and JRD,
"Nomura Diary," entry for November 26, 1941. Note that Nomura places the blame for
such hard terms mainly on the recent actions of his government and its leaders, although
in passing he also criticizes Britain, the Netherlands, and China. Note also the very
reasonable and conciliatory remarks made by Secretary Hull, as quoted by Nomura in
Cable No. 1191. Cable No. 1180 (which is discussed in Chapter 12) cannot be applied to
the point being made in the text since it was apparently sent *prior* to the interview with
Hull on November 26.

[46] The continuing discussion in the text relating to the "ultimatum" question draws,
in part, on the following: *PHA*, Part 2, 430-40, 553-56, 558-60, 613-15, and Part 11,
5367-72 and 5398-99; *Foreign Relations (Japan: 1931-1941)*, II, 964-72; Ballantine cross-
examination, T 10944-55; Ballantine corresp.; J, B/VII, 968-74 and 977; Grew, *Turbulent
Era*, II, 1248, n. 4; *Facts on File: 1945*, 372 K; Tōjō cross-examination, S 347:10, T 36702,
and S 348:9-11, T 36781-97; Tōjō interrog., Feb. 19, 12-13; Kaya, 196; Hattori, I, 229-32;
and Feis, 320-25, 327-28, and 334-35. For a convenient statement of Japan's "case," see
Tōgō, 233-52. I am indebted to Mr. Ballantine for calling to my attention the emphasis
given by Mr. Tōgō to Section II, which cannot be properly understood unless read in the
context of Section I and the "Oral Statement."

tive, consciously pictured the United States as throwing down the gauntlet because they recognized the enormous value of confusing the issue in the minds of the Japanese people, just as the issue had been confused in 1931 in relation to Manchuria and in 1937 with regard to the remainder of China. Without any knowledge of the actual terms of the American proposal, many Japanese who might have been expected to act more rationally rushed to accept the government's view that Washington had challenged Japan to fight. When Ambassador Grew strove to correct that impression by telling some of his prominent Japanese friends what the Hull note offered, they assured Grew that the masses "would be definitely opposed to an intransigent attitude" on the part of the government if they knew what the note contained.[47]

In choosing to ignore the obvious, that the "ultimatum" value assigned to the American note of November 26 belonged instead to their own Proposal B of November 20, a number of Japan's leaders—the military men in particular—also managed to overlook the fact that the imperial task force which would attack Pearl Harbor on December 7 was already steaming toward Hawaii, having set sail from Hitokappu Bay at 1800 hours on the evening of November 26.[48] They completely disregarded, too, the reciprocal nature of the Hull proposals and the latitude contained therein to negotiate for better terms or more gradual procedures. In taking such a stand, the leaders of Japan made war inevitable.

The reluctance of the Japanese government to withdraw all military, naval, air, and police forces from China and Indo-China can easily be appreciated in terms of the implication inherent in such a withdrawal that Japan's past policies had been wrong and aggressive. The government's reluctance in that regard can also be understood in terms of the collapse of Japanese power on the continent which might have accompanied such a withdrawal. But certainly both those issues were negotiable.[49] A decision by Japan to renounce her decade-old program of

[47] See Grew testimony, PHA, Part 2, 569 and Grew, Ten Years in Japan, 482-83, 485-86. The text of the Hull note was not published in Japan until after Pearl Harbor, and then the newspaper that carried it was confiscated.

[48] Hattori, I, 226 and 361-62. Orders had been issued to provide for the return of the task force to Japan in the event a Japanese-American agreement was reached between November 26 and December 7. See JRD, "Translation," II:51903 (Item 18), Reference No. 6. Japan's civilian leaders seem to have been kept in the dark with regard to operational matters.

[49] Hull's willingness to be patient in that regard—his understanding that such a withdrawal could not be effected immediately, that the matter was subject to negotiation—was clearly reported to Tōkyō by Nomura in Cable No. 1191, in which the ambas-

aggression would have placed a grave responsibility on the shoulders of Japan's neighbors, China and the Soviet Union included, to cooperate with the United States and Great Britain in helping the Japanese government attain through peaceful arrangements what it had been unable to secure by military force. The United States fully intended to assist Japan in every way in that regard, just as soon as it became clear that Japan honestly meant to reverse a course which had by now carried her into dangerous and uncharted waters. Writing in his diary on November 29, Ambassador Grew clearly posed the alternatives still open to Japan:

If she wants a political and economic stranglehold on the countries of East Asia (euphemistically called the New Order in East Asia and the East Asia Co-Prosperity Sphere)—which most of her extremists do want—and if she pursues her southward advance by force, she will soon be at war with all of the ABCD powers and will unquestionably be defeated and reduced to the status of a third-rate power. But if she plays her cards wisely, she can obtain without further fighting all of the desiderata for which she allegedly started fighting—strategic, economic, financial, and social security.

Japanese public opinion can always be molded, in a comparatively short time, and the clever move of the Government now would be to persuade the public that the Government, in the Washington conversations, had won a great diplomatic victory by achieving, without further force of arms, the securities or "freedoms" for which she had been fighting.[50]

But it was not to be. The leaders in Tokyo adopted the view that acceptance of the Hull proposals—instead of opening a way to the future—would actually reduce Japan to a less than third-rate power, incapable of maintaining either order at home or political and economic independence abroad. Insofar as that attitude was candid at all, it approached absurdity. Neither Hull nor anyone else in Washington was proposing that Japan take unilateral action in a vacuum. In the note of November 26, the United States promised to reciprocate by working for the conclusion of a multilateral agreement providing for equality of economic opportunity in French Indo-China, by negotiating a new trade treaty with Japan based upon most-favored-nation treatment and the reduction of trade barriers, and by removing the freezing order affecting Japanese assets in the United States. These and related measures (including Hull's oral promise of "practical measures of finan-

---

sador briefly recapitulated his conversation with Hull on November 26 concerning the American proposal of that date. For the "Magic" version, see *PHA,* Part 12, 183-85.
[50] See Grew, *Ten Years in Japan,* 482-86.

cial cooperation") constituted a *quid pro quo* which could have been made far more attractive to the Japanese people than the alternative of a new and greater war, had they been fully informed of the nature and the value of such an arrangement.

Washington also intended to buttress new agreements with Tokyo by working together with Japan to secure the establishment of a multilateral, nonaggression pact structure in the Pacific, embracing the British Empire, China, Japan, the Netherlands, the Soviet Union, Thailand, and the United States. While denying Japan the opportunity to return in the future to a policy of military aggression against her neighbors, such a structure would enormously have enhanced Japan's security toward any of the participating members whom she might still have regarded, rightly or wrongly, as constituting a threat. But what was the Japanese reaction? When Kurusu heard about it, he objected at once, referring to Japan's "bitter experience" with international organizations. What he probably had in mind was the action of the League of Nations with respect to the aggression perpetrated by the Kwantung army in Manchuria in 1931, but what he actually cited as an example was a *1905 award against Japan* in the so-called Perpetual Leases case. He also referred to the Washington Conference of 1921-1922 and said that the treaties concluded there (e.g., the Nine-Power Pact guaranteeing China's sovereignty and independence and the maintenance of the open door) had given "a wrong idea" to the Chinese and that they had taken advantage of the treaties "to flaunt Japan's rights."[51] In Tokyo, Foreign Minister Togo also objected to the conclusion of a nonaggression pact. He portrayed the Hull suggestion in that regard as an effort to restrain Japan, on the one hand, while increasing her worries in the North, on the other.[52] That was certainly a novel interpretation—especially in view of the fact that only seven months earlier Japan herself had taken the initiative in concluding a neutrality pact with the Soviet Union. Did Mr. Togo also regard that pact as a menace to Japan's security in the North? Or did the absence of other powers, serving as a watch-dog committee, make the difference? Only a government whose plans for the future were in conflict with the requirements of a multilateral nonaggression pact could have objected to an arrangement which—

[51] As paraphrased in a November 26, 1941 memorandum by Joseph W. Ballantine, *Foreign Relations (Japan: 1931-1941)*, II, 764. On the "Perpetual Leases" matter, see *Foreign Relations: 1905*, 692.
[52] Tōgō, 241-42.

in any other circumstances—is generally regarded as diplomatically advantageous.[53]

The plans of the Japanese government *did* run counter to undertaking such commitments. The leaders of that government *were* unshakably determined to resort to war. And so, on November 27, 1941, the count-down on the peace of the Pacific was begun.

A liaison conference met at the palace in the morning and afternoon.[54] Between the two sessions, the gist of the American proposal of November 26 arrived in the form of separate cables from the Japanese military and naval attachés in Washington, who offered the opinion that negotiating further was now "completely hopeless." The fact that these officers were reporting independently of the ambassador, that their cables reached Tokyo before any word was received from Nomura and Kurusu, and that the members of the liaison conference initially discussed the latest American proposal, and formed impressions about it, solely on the basis of information supplied by the attachés is suggestive of the role played by Japan's military representatives abroad.

Everyone was "dumbfounded" at the "harshness" of the American proposal.[55] It was interpreted as an ultimatum to which Japan could not possibly bow. It was decided that the United States knew full well that such a proposal would be unacceptable. It was judged that the American government had apparently already made up its mind to go to war, that there was no telling when Japan might be attacked by the United States, and that consequently the utmost vigilance was required.

Thus did Tojo and his colleagues react to the Hull note of November 26.[56] If one recalls the Bering Straits psychology, the views of

[53] Tōgō's objections to the multilateral nonaggression pact suggested by Hull are especially interesting in the light of the fact that the "Tai Bei-Ei-Ran-Shō Sensō Shūmatsu Sokushin ni kan suru Fukuan" of November 15, 1941 (see pp. 328-30 above) envisaged a Japanese effort to restore peace between Germany and the Soviet Union, add Russia to the Axis, conclude a nonaggression pact with Moscow, and encourage a Soviet debouchment into the India-Iran area.

[54] Tōjō aff., S 343:21-22, T 36355-61; Tōjō cross-examination, S 348:9-11, T 36781-97; Tōgō aff., S 337:7-8, T 35703-11; Tōgō, 238, 239-40, 250-51; and Hattori, I, 232.

[55] Commenting on a similar reaction in Washington on the part of Nomura and Kurusu, Hull later declared, ". . . all their talk of being 'dumbfounded' . . . was a prelude to an attempt, by outrageously false statements uttered in the utmost of bad faith, to shift to this Government responsibility for what they were planning." *PHA*, Part 11, 5398-99. In this regard, see Nomura's Cable No. 1190, S 252:4-5. The language problem is well illustrated by the defense translation (T 26093-95) and the "Magic" version (*PHA*, Part 12, 182-83), both of which require substantial revision.

[56] See footnote 54 above. Tōjō is incorrect in stating that Hull demanded that Japan withdraw recognition from Manchukuo. Japanese leaders (including Foreign Minister Tōgō) seem to have assumed that all American references to "China" automatically

General Kojiro Sato, the recurring emphasis upon the supposedly "soft underbelly" of the United States in the form of some twenty million Americans of German ancestry, and the potent ABCD encirclement psychosis, the suggestion that Tojo and others in Tokyo might really have believed that the United States was preparing to attack Japan may not appear quite so fantastic as at first sight. Given the dominance of the two types of individuals most prevalent on the Japanese decision-making scene in 1941—the fanatic expansionists and the naïve ultra-nationalists—there was literally no hope for the nation. Such qualms as had once existed were forgotten or suppressed. No one spoiled the spontaneous unanimity with which it was agreed, on November 27, that the decision for war should be confirmed at an imperial conference already scheduled for December 1.[57]

Arrangements were quickly made to permit the Emperor to consult the senior statesmen on the crisis confronting the nation so that His Majesty would not later have any cause for regrets. On the morning of Saturday, November 29, the ex-premiers gathered at the palace to listen to explanations from the chief cabinet ministers regarding the situation and the manner in which it was to be overcome.[58] The proceed-

---

included Manchukuo. That subject had been discussed briefly in Washington on April 16, 1941. When Nomura remarked, at that time, that Hull's advocacy of a principle calling for nondisturbance of the *status quo* except by peaceful means would interfere with the Manchurian situation, the Secretary replied that "the question of non-recognition of Manchuria would be discussed in connection with the negotiations and dealt with at that stage, and that this *status quo* point would not, therefore, affect 'Manchukuo,' but was intended to apply to the future from the time of the adoption of a general settlement." *Foreign Relations (Japan: 1931-1941)*, II, 409.

It would seem, therefore, that Japanese statements asserting that the Hull note was all the more unacceptable because it demanded that Japan sever its ties with Manchukuo should not be taken seriously.

[57] An imperial conference was not held immediately because Premier Tōjō knew that the Emperor was greatly concerned over the situation and was desirous of seeking the views of the senior statesmen (*jūshin*). The scheduling of an imperial conference for December 1, prior to the receipt of the Hull proposal of November 26, probably stemmed from the decision of November 5 which had designated zero hours, December 1, as the deadline.

It should also be noted that the cabinet was given a detailed report on the Washington negotiations by Foreign Minister Tōgō on the morning of November 28. The conclusion reached at the liaison conference the day before was discussed. All present expressed their agreement. Tōjō aff., S 343:21, T 36359-60.

[58] Both Hara and Kido had earlier discussed the pros and cons of modifying the imperial conference procedure to permit the senior statesmen to attend. When the Emperor asked the premier about the matter during an audience on November 26, Tōjō expressed the view that such an innovation would not be proper because the *jūshin* were not constitutionally responsible for the opinions they might present. He did not think it would be right to have the senior statesmen participate in an imperial conference at which a matter of such grave importance would come before the responsible officials of state—the cabinet ministers and the leaders of the supreme command. The Emperor then

ings, which the government carefully refrained from terming a "conference," began at 9:30 a.m. and ran on until 1:00 p.m., when a break was taken for a luncheon attended by the Emperor.[59] During the morning session the cabinet was represented by Premier Tojo (concurrently war minister and home minister), Navy Minister Shimada, Foreign Minister Togo, Finance Minister Kaya, and President of the Cabinet Planning Board Suzuki. The former premiers present were Abe, Hayashi, Hiranuma, Hirota, Konoe, Okada, Wakatsuki, and Yonai. Privy Council President Hara also attended, although he had never held the premiership. *No one was present from the supreme command,* either because the government wished to emphasize that this was not really a full-fledged conference or because attendance by the chiefs of staff might have led to embarrassing questions concerning war strategy and tactics. Admiral Okada later testified that Tojo refused to discuss certain matters on the grounds that they involved "state secrets." Although Tojo denied this, he did admit that he refrained from answering questions which dealt with purely operational matters—the sole prerogative of the supreme command. As a result, the senior statesmen learned nothing at all about the projected naval strike against Pearl Harbor or about any other phase of Japan's war plans. Questions pertaining to the diplomatic negotiations or the national potential were answered in detail by whatever minister was most concerned with the issue raised. Tojo, as premier, assumed the responsibility of explaining why a war with the United States and Great Britain "could not be avoided."

During the morning session neither the Emperor nor anyone else from the Court was present, but following the luncheon His Majesty

suggested, as an alternative, that an informal discussion between the government and the *jūshin* be held in his presence. At the liaison conference which met on the 27th, Tōjō put the matter to his colleagues. Everyone agreed that the status and role of the so-called senior statesmen, a purely honorary title, did not entitle them to attend an imperial conference of the type scheduled for December 1. It was feared that the "location of responsibility" might become "ambiguous." The Saturday meeting at the palace, which is discussed in the text, was arranged as a consequence. See footnote 59.

[59] On the senior statesmen's gathering of November 29, see Tōjō aff., S 344:1-2, T 36364-70; Tōjō cross-examination, S 344:19, T 36508-9; Tōjō interrog., Mar. 12, 6-8; Suzuki aff., S 333:12, T 35223-24; Tōgō aff., S 337:8, T 35711-12, and cross-examination, S 337:20-21, T 35801-3; Tōgō, 253-54; Okada aff., S 278:17-18, T 29258-62; Kido aff., S 293:13, T 30958, and S 293:22-24, T 31032-44; Kido interrog., Mar. 11, 720; Kido corresp.; Prosecution Exh. 1196, T 10452-60 (a good example of the language problem which plagued the proceedings, and the Tribunal's view thereof); Kido SKD and corresp.; *PHA*, Part 20, 4012-13 (the views attributed to Suzuki may have been held by him earlier but not in late October or thereafter); Hattori, I, 233-34 and corresp.; JRD Monograph No. 150, 33-34; Wakatsuki, 418-21; and Okada, "Tōjō Seiken to Jūshin-tachi," 89-90. The imperial luncheon had been Tōjō's idea.

spent an hour in the imperial study listening to the views of the ex-premiers. Marquis Kido, who was in attendance upon the Emperor, later recorded the substance of what was said. The only remark attributed to His Majesty was a noncommittal statement about the crisis facing the nation ("Taihen muzukashii jidai ni natta ne"), which was meant as an invitation to the senior statesmen to speak their minds. Baron Waka-tsuki, the first to reply, testified to his faith in the "spiritual strength" of the Japanese people but expressed concern over Japan's ability to fight a protracted war from the point of view of matériel. The matter still worried him, he said, despite the explanations he had heard during the morning—a view which was seconded by Admiral Okada. Baron Hiranuma noted that careful attention would have to be paid to "stiffen-ing" popular sentiments in the face of the hardships which would accompany an extended war. Prince Konoe combined an apology for his personal failure to bring about an adjustment in Japanese-American relations with an expression of appreciation to the Tojo Cabinet for the "earnest efforts" it had made in that regard. On the basis of the government's explanations, he found it regrettably necessary to conclude that a continuation of the negotiations offered no prospect of success. But even if the talks were ruptured, was it necessary to resort to war immediately? Might it not be possible to find a solution by persevering for a while longer?

The spirit of Konoe's remarks was echoed to some extent by Admiral Yonai. Lacking data, he said, he could not offer concrete opinions, but if he could be permitted the use of a slang expression, he would like to urge that great care be taken to guard against "going broke in a single throw" while trying to avoid a gradual decline in the nation's fortunes—a reference to the naval general staff's earlier advocacy of a "surgical operation" as the one remaining means of escaping such a decline.[60]

Mr. Hirota, who was the only former premier present with practical diplomatic experience, spoke with the ambiguity of an oracle. The true intentions of parties engaged in diplomatic negotiations, he said, only became clear after two or three crises had occurred. What purpose would be served, therefore, by going to war immediately? Even if war were inevitable and fighting actually broke out, careful attention should

---

[60] ". . . jiri-hin wo saken to shite doka-hin ni naranai yō ni jūbun no go chūi wo negaitai to omoimasu." Although this remark has been attributed to Okada, Kido has affirmed that it came from Yonai. Kido corresp. It should be noted that the phrase *jiri-hin* seems to have been very much in vogue at the time to express the idea of "wasting away" (gradual decline or exhaustion).

always be paid to seizing an opportunity to terminate hostilities through diplomatic means.

The remaining two *jūshin*, Generals Hayashi and Abe, were equally cautious in their approach but somewhat more positive in their views. They credited the government with having thoroughly studied the matter and suggested that there was no alternative but to trust in its conclusions.

When everyone had spoken, Baron Wakatsuki felt moved to add a further thought. If Japan's existence and defense were at stake, he said, the nation would have to fight even if defeat could be predicted— even if it meant a country in ruins. But using the national power to implement such ideals as the stabilization of East Asia or the creation of a co-prosperity sphere would be dangerous indeed.

As each of these observations was presented, Tojo offered an explanation based upon the unanimous views of his colleagues in the cabinet and the supreme command. At times, his manner was brusque. He said that the government had so repeatedly restudied the question of not going to war, even if the negotiations were broken off, that it had practically gotten a headache as a result. Every angle had been considered. The conclusion reached was that to persevere under such circumstances would be to jeopardize Japan's defense and her existence as a nation. In going to war, the government naturally desired to win a quick victory, but Japan would have to contend with whatever action the enemy might take. Since the situation would not always develop as expected or desired, Japan must be prepared to fight a long war. This whole matter, he said, had been discussed at the liaison conferences held after the formation of his cabinet. Two questions, in particular, had been explored: (1) Would Japan be able to obtain needed supplies and to rely on the preservation of morale if the fighting dragged on for a long time? and (2) When and how could the war be terminated?

The answer to the first question, Tojo declared, would depend upon the results obtained at the beginning of hostilities. Because of the very nature of war, nothing positive could be said, but the supreme command seemed to be "rather confident" with regard to success at the outset. If Japan could obtain this success, she would be able to secure strategic bases in the Pacific and thus acquire important resources, especially oil. Both the army and the government would exert "their utmost efforts" in that regard. Thereafter, it would be a matter of maintaining sea communications—chiefly a task for the navy. Concerning the morale of the people, the government would take the necessary precautions, but in the final analysis it would trust in their feelings of loyalty.

The question of ending the war had been of primary concern. A proposal to negotiate peace at a favorable opportunity through the good offices of either the Soviet Union or the Vatican had been discussed, but a definite plan capable of inspiring confidence had not as yet been formulated. If anyone had any "brilliant ideas" (*myōan*), Tojo said, he would like to hear them.

If Japan's initial operations were successful, the government would immediately secure strategic points in the Pacific that would permit the imperial forces to hold out in the event of a long war. Once this defense perimeter was established, Japan would conduct active operations and develop the national potential to the maximum. She would employ political and military means to force Britain and the Chungking regime to leave the war and in that way would cause the United States to lose the will to fight on. The government intended to proceed on that basis. The question of how to bring the war to an end would have to be decided later.

Following these explanations by the premier, the senior statesmen retired from the imperial presence to spend another hour in consultation with Tojo and his cabinet colleagues before finally adjourning at 4:00 p.m. Although the desirability of exercising prudence had been the main burden of their advice, not one of the *jūshin* had taken a positive stand against the war which the government intended launching. No remarkable views were presented or practical suggestions offered. Kido, who had been a silent witness of the scene in the imperial study, decided that the trend of events was "beyond control." Whereas he had earlier believed that the influence of the throne might be used to secure support for a settlement favorable to Japan, Kido now felt that would no longer be possible. The government was unanimous in its interpretation that the Hull note left no further room for negotiations. War would be declared, and the rise or fall of Japan would be placed in the hands of the gods.[61]

Because the supreme command had wisely avoided putting in an appearance at the palace on November 29, the spotlight of attention at the senior statesmen's gathering focused directly on Premier Tojo and his principal ministers even though they deserved far less notice as initiators of policy than did the bureau and section chiefs, and their

[61] See footnote 59 above.

respective staffs, who formed the nucleus group within imperial headquarters. In Washington and elsewhere on this last weekend before
Pearl Harbor, the name and figure of Hideki Tojo also loomed suddenly
in men's minds, creating the first of what was to become a series of
sinister images. The *New York Times* for Sunday, November 30,
greeted its readers with a headline in bold-faced type spread across five
columns of its front page:

RUSSIANS ROUT NAZIS AT ROSTOV;
TOJO WOULD 'PURGE' ORIENT OF U.S.;
ROOSEVELT MAY CURTAIL VACATION

The middle line of this eye-catching display referred rather loosely to
a United Press dispatch from Tokyo, dated November 29, announcing
that Premier Tojo had declared that "American and British 'exploitation' of Asiatic peoples must be 'purged with vengeance.'" The remarks
attributed to Tojo were described as being occasioned by the first
anniversary of the Basic Treaty and Joint Declaration concluded by
Japan, Manchukuo, and Nanking China. The words of his statement,
as reported in the dispatch, were highly provocative:

Chiang Kai-shek is dancing to the tune of American and British communism because the United States and Britain desire to fish in troubled
waters, throwing the Asiatic peoples against each other.

This is the stock in trade of Britain and the United States and therefore we
must purge this sort of action with vengeance.

There are many countries engaged in actions hostile toward our co-prosperity
sphere and they are trying to throw obstacles in our path and exploit Asia at
the expense of the Asiatic peoples and thereby satisfy their greed for possessions.

Tojo was also quoted as reiterating his nation's determination to
coordinate an Asiatic front "so that a chorus of victory may go up in
the camp of justice as speedily as possible." "Nothing can be permitted
to interfere with this sphere," the premier was alleged to have said,
"because this sphere was decreed by Providence. You are witnessing
communism's cruelties and dastardly destruction. You are trying your
best to eliminate British and other Western exploitations."
Although the curious English in which these remarks were couched
should have served as a warning that the translation might not be an
accurate rendition of what Tojo had said, the U.P. story contained other
confirmative news which left no doubt as to what had been meant. The

Japanese government was authoritatively reported to have replied adversely to the American note of November 26. Japanese newspapers were frankly telling their readers that their government would be unable to continue the negotiations if Washington held fast to its present position and to the principles of the Nine-Power Pact. "The United States was charged with 'insincerity' in negotiations with Japan and with conducting military conversations against Japan." In this latter regard, the powerful newspaper *Asahi* was quoted as saying, in the grandiloquent manner of the day, that Japan was "vigilantly watching developments." The *Asahi* also let it be known that President Roosevelt's announcement that American merchant vessels in the Pacific would not be armed for the present was "a crafty bargaining statement." Taken together, these remarks hardly constituted a basis for optimism.[62]

At the American embassy in Tokyo, Ambassador Grew was depressed and chagrined. He regarded the Tojo speech, at such a critical moment, as completely nonsensical and as stemming from the prevailing Japanese belief that the United States could be intimidated "by a sufficient amount of saber rattling." If Japan really wanted to remain at peace with the United States, it seemed "the height of stupidity to continue to inflame domestic public opinion." "Once again I am impressed," Grew wrote, "with the truth of the remark of a Japanese friend that when dogs are frightened, they bark, and the more they are frightened, the louder they bark; and also that the Japanese are really children and should be treated as children. The Prime Minister's speech seems to me to be utterly childish. Where is the much-vaunted Japanese statesmanship of olden days?"[63]

Secretary Hull, who was apprised of the contents of the press dispatch on the evening of the 29th, took such a serious view of the Tojo statement that he put in a call to the President, who was having a belated Thanksgiving dinner with the patients of the infantile paralysis center at Warm Springs, Georgia. Later that same evening the presidential press secretary announced that Mr. Roosevelt had decided to cut short his stay and to leave for Washington the following morning, Sunday, November 30.

By the time the President had departed from Warm Springs, looking "grim and intent," Nomura and Kurusu had become aware of "the

[62] See *NYT*, November 30, 1941, 1, and the Tolischus dispatch on page 25.
[63] See Grew, *Ten Years in Japan*, 483-84.

rumble" caused by Tojo's words.[64] In the course of a late evening telephone conversation with the chief of the American bureau of the Japanese foreign office, Kurusu went straight to the point, unaware that "Magic" was listening in:

Kurusu: "The President is returning tomorrow. He is hurrying home."

Yamamoto: "Is there any special significance to this?"

Kurusu: "The newspapers have made much of the Premier's speech, and it is having strong repercussions here."

Yamamoto: "Is that so."

Kurusu: "Yes. It was a drastic statement he made. The newspapers carried large headlines over it; and the President seems to be returning because of it. There no doubt are other reasons, but this is the reason the newspapers are giving."

[After a pause:]

"Unless greater caution is exercised in speeches by the Premier and others, it puts us in a very difficult position. All of you over there must watch out about these ill-advised statements. Please tell Mr. Tani" [president of the board of information].

Yamamoto: "We *are* being careful."

Kurusu: "We here are doing our best, but these reports are seized upon by the correspondents and the worst features enlarged upon. Please caution the Premier, the Foreign Minister, and others. Tell the Foreign Minister that we had expected to hear something different, some good word, but instead we get this" [the Tojo statement].

[After another pause, Kurusu resumed speaking, employing voice code. He asked about the internal situation, but Yamamoto's reply was indistinct beyond the words, "No particular. . . ."]

Kurusu: "Are the Japanese-American negotiations to continue?"

Yamamoto: "Yes."

Kurusu: "You were very urgent about them before, weren't you; but now you want them to stretch out. We will need your help. Both the Premier and the Foreign Minister will need to change the tone of their speeches!!!! Do you understand? Please all use more discretion."[65]

[64] On the President's return to Washington, see the Kluckhohn dispatches in *NYT*, November 30, 1941, 1, and December 1, 1941, 1; and *PHA*, Part 2, 441, and Part 11, 5399-401. What was published in the *New York Times* as a United Press dispatch is referred to elsewhere as an Associated Press item. It may be that both wire services carried the news, or that one is being confused with the other.

[65] See *PHA*, Part 12, 206-7 (the punctuation is as given in the "Magic" transcript). Note that this is "a preliminary condensed version" of the full eight-minute conversation in "Telephone Code." Some allowance should be made for possible errors in recording, decoding, or translation.

In order to determine the facts and to warn against any further indiscretions, Nomura dispatched a secret cable (No. 1222) to Tōkyō on November 30 (also intercepted by

The next morning, December 1, Nomura and Kurusu drove to the State Department for a conference with Hull.[66] They found the scene there "highly dramatic," with the corridors crowded not only with newspapermen but even with members of the Department staff, who apparently thought that history was about to be made in the form of an immediate decision for war or peace. The scene in the Secretary's office was no less dramatic, though considerably more restrained and formal. The two envoys found Hull awaiting them with what they took to be "a deeply pained expression." According to the report they subsequently sent to Tokyo, Hull lost no time in bringing up the subject of the Tojo statement, which he described as one of the reasons why the President had suddenly returned to the capital. Nomura and Kurusu replied that they were certain the trouble arose from an erroneous and exaggerated account in the vernacular press. They suggested that what had appeared must be an excerpt taken out of context. They advised the Secretary that at that very moment they were awaiting the delivery of the full text of the disputed speech. In the course of these explanations, they noticed that "the Secretary showed visible signs of relief"—or so Tokyo was informed.

The American memorandum of this same conversation notes that Kurusu asked why the President was returning to Washington earlier than had previously been announced. In reply, Hull informed him that "one of the factors in the present situation was the loud talk of the Japanese Prime Minister," who "seemed to be in need of advice which would deter him from indulging in such talk" at a time when Japan's ambassador was speaking about restoring good relations between the two countries. Nomura and Kurusu then tried to convince Hull that the United States was taking "a more serious view" of the Tojo statement "than was warranted" under the circumstances. Kurusu said that "what the Prime Minister had done was nothing more than a ten-minute broadcast." When the Secretary retorted that "a broadcast was all the more effective," Kurusu replied that Tojo had been misquoted and asked whether the Department had received any information from

---

"Magic" but not translated until December 5) in which he asked for the Japanese and English texts of the Tōjō statement. See S 254:12 and *PHA*, Part 12, 207. See also pages 208 (Cable No. 865 from Tōkyō) and 212-14 (Nomura Cables No. 1226 and 1230).

Mr. Yamamoto was concurrently serving as chief of the East Asian bureau.

[66] The text, which follows, draws on the "Magic" intercept of Cable No. 1225, *PHA*, Part 12, 210-12; Kurusu, 154-56; and the Ballantine paraphrase of the December 1, 1941 conversation of Hull, Nomura, and Kurusu as given in its entirety in *Foreign Relations* (*Japan: 1931-1941*), II, 772-77. Cable No. 1225 reveals how little of what was said at great length by Mr. Hull was even reported to Tōkyō, let alone accurately.

Ambassador Grew. Hull answered in the negative but added that the Department considered "the Associated Press [United Press?]" to be "reliable" and felt that "credence" should be given to its reports. Kurusu then remarked that "Japanese news services did not always correctly translate statements into English."

Never had a truer word been spoken. The surprising thing is that so much trust was placed in such translations by foreign correspondents and diplomats. Generally, of course, the gist was there, despite the awkward expressions; the fine points were the ones that suffered mutilation. The official Domei News Agency translation of the Tojo statement, dispatched by Ambassador Grew on the afternoon of December 1, is a case in point:

It is certainly the most fortunate lot of the three powers [Japan, Nanking China, and Manchukuo] to have the privilege of collaborating together under this banner for cutting open the thorny way, and 1 year has already gone by since we started this honorable work together, and if it is not the greatest task of the present century what else can it be.

However if we look around we find that there are still many countries who are indulging in actions hostile to us. In fact they are trying to throw obstacles in the way of the construction of the East Asia co-prosperity sphere and are trying to enjoy the dream of exploitation of East Asia at the cost of the 1,000 million populace of the East Asiatic peoples to satisfy their greed of possession.

The fact that Chiang Kai-shek is dancing to the tune of Britain, America, and communism at the expense of able-bodied and promising young men in his futile resistance against Japan is only due to the desire of Britain and the United States to fish in the troubled waters of East Asia by putting [pitting?] the East Asiatic peoples against each other and to grasp the hegemony of East Asia. This is a stock in trade of Britain and the United States.

For the honor and pride of mankind we must purge this sort of practice from East Asia with a vengeance.[67]

Despite the obviously unsatisfactory nature of this translation, it is doubtful that very much thought was given in Washington or in Tokyo to checking the original Japanese. It was convenient to rely on what an official agency of the Japanese government provided by way of English-language handouts. Everyone knew what Japan's actions had been on the continent, and everyone could see what they currently were. The

[67] See Foreign Relations (Japan: 1931-1941), II, 148-49. The Grew cable (citing a "Domei report in Advertiser" as the source) was sent from Tōkyō (via Shanghai) at 3:00 p.m. on December 1. It was received in Washington at 5:03 a.m., December 5. In this connection, see also the "Magic" intercept of Cable No. 878 from Tōkyō (Part 1) in PHA, Part 12, 225.

Japanese press and radio were crowded to excess with ultranationalistic statements of various kinds—all of which added up to the same grim picture. A mistake here or there in translation was not going to alter the fact that Japan was implementing an aggressive policy in Asia. If a translation distributed by Domei put Japan's position in the most awkward of terms, the Japanese would have no one to blame but themselves. At least they could not charge that the Americans had purposely distorted the meaning of the original through mistranslation.

Had the Grew cable arrived immediately in Washington, it probably would have added considerable fuel to the fire, but it was sent via Shanghai and perhaps for that reason was not received at the State Department until December 5. By that time an official explanation of the Tojo statement had been tendered to the United States government, and Japanese and American attention had been diverted by other, more pressing developments. The explanation, which came in the form of a cable from the Japanese foreign office to Nomura and Kurusu, was received in Washington on December 1 and conveyed to the State Department the following day. This somewhat delicate mission was entrusted to Hidenari Terasaki, the first secretary, who called initially on Joseph W. Ballantine and then on another Departmental officer, Max W. Schmidt. In his conversation with the latter, Terasaki explained that as soon as he had seen the American press reaction to the remarks attributed to Tojo, he had cabled Tokyo, deprecating statements of that kind by the premier at a time when diplomatic conversations were in progress. ". . . Both he and his Government had been 'flabbergasted'" by what had occurred. He had therefore been very much relieved upon the receipt of the message from Tokyo which he had just delivered. Noting that what he was about to say was confidential and off the record, Terasaki added that when Kurusu had talked with Yamamoto over the trans-Pacific telephone on Sunday evening (November 30) and had referred to General Tojo's speech, "Mr. Yamamoto had been nonplused and had asked, 'What speech?'"[68]

The message from Tokyo delivered by Terasaki was essentially another of the "So sorry, mistake" kind with which Japan had frequently answered foreign protests in the early years of the China Incident.[69]

[68] See *PHA*, Part 12, 210-12 ("Magic" intercept of Cable No. 1225) and 223 (intercept of Cable No. 1234), and *Foreign Relations (Japan: 1931-1941)*, II, 777-78 (Max W. Schmidt paraphrase of a conversation with Hidenari Terasaki on December 2, 1941).

[69] See S 254:12 for the original Japanese text of Cable No. 866 (the foreign office explanation of the so-called Tōjō statement), and *Foreign Relations (Japan: 1931-1941)*, II, 778, for the text of the official explanation handed by Mr. Terasaki to Mr. Ballantine on December 2, 1941.

Persons not familiar with Japanese procedures would find much therein smacking of the implausible. Even if an explanation of that nature had subsequently appeared in the American press, it is doubtful that many readers would have paid much attention or been really convinced. According to the account tendered by Mr. Terasaki, the so-called Tojo speech had been drafted by members of the staff of the "Asia Development League"—of which Tojo was president—for delivery at a meeting to be held under League auspices on November 30, commemorating the first anniversary of the conclusion of the Sino-Japanese Basic Treaty. Since November 30 was a Sunday, however, and there would be no evening editions of the newspapers, the reporters assigned to cover the event had importuned the League staff to release in advance the draft of the remarks they had prepared. This had been done, on the evening of November 29, without the knowledge of Premier Tojo or of any other governmental official. Neither Tojo nor anyone else in the government had seen or inspected the contents of the statement. Despite the preview coverage in Japan's Saturday newspapers, Premier Tojo had not personally spoken at the League meeting, or anywhere else, on November 30. Neither the premier nor any other official had ever given his consent to the draft released to the press. As a consequence, appropriate measures were being taken against the League. The Japanese government wished to advise the United States that the sentence which had caused so much trouble, "For the honor and pride of mankind we must purge this sort of practice from East Asia with a vengeance," was a mistranslation of the original. The latter did not contain any such expression as "purge . . . with a vengeance." In fact, the sentence should actually read, "For the honor and pride of mankind, this sort of practice must be removed."[70]

Since Mr. Terasaki was highly regarded in Washington, his remarks were taken as "literally true"—as indeed they were.[71] News items in the Japanese and American press to the contrary notwithstanding, Tojo had

[70] The Japanese original, as recorded by "Magic" (but apparently not translated until after the war), reads as follows: "Jinrui no meiyo no tame ni jinrui no kyōji no tame ni danjite kore wo tettei-teki ni haigeki seneba naranu." A great deal depends on the value assigned to the character-compound haigeki (suru): "to reject," "to denounce," "to eliminate," or "to expel." In any case, it is quite clear that "purge . . . with a vengeance" was a very fanciful translation. It is also clear, in context, that the object of the verb haigeki seneba naranu was the practices ascribed to the powers, and not the powers themselves (as suggested by the New York Times headline quoted earlier: "Tojo Would 'Purge' Orient of U.S.").

[71] Ballantine corresp.: "I had no reason to doubt that Mr. Terasaki, who was a person of high character, told us what was literally true. The significant fact was, if I recall correctly, that no denial that the Prime Minister had made the speech attributed to him was given publicity in the Japanese press."

not spoken the words attributed to him. The *New York Times* correspondent on the scene reported from Tokyo that the anniversary in question was widely celebrated at mass meetings organized by the governments concerned in the principal cities of Japan, Nanking China, and Manchukuo. "The highlight of these meetings was the reading of a message from Premier Tojo. . . . However, though it had been announced that General Tojo would be the chief speaker at the main rally, held in Tokyo . . . he did not appear and no explanation was offered for his absence. His message was read, and the main speeches were made by General Kisaburo Ando, executive vice president of the Imperial Rule Assistance Association and [by] the 'Ambassadors' of the Nanking and Manchukuo regimes."[72]

Although this dispatch appeared on the front page of the December 1 edition of the *New York Times*, the pertinent remarks concerning Tojo were so far along in the text that only the dedicated reader who turned to page 8 would have found them. That same day, adding further to the confusion, Mr. Kurusu spoke briefly to the press as he and Nomura left the State Department, looking far more grim than when they had entered. Premier Tojo, he said, had been "badly misquoted" in the dispatches sent from Tokyo. "He only made a broadcast for ten minutes. . . ."[73]

And so, a week before Pearl Harbor, General Tojo became the man of the hour—a premier committed to purging America and Britain

[72] See the Tolischus and Kluckhohn dispatches in *NYT*, December 1, 1941, 1 and 8, and December 2, 1941, 1 and 4; Tolischus, 312-13, in which the author notes that ". . . the statement read in his [Tōjō's] name, instead of repeating his usual phrases, was in the special style of the *Nichi Nichi*, where it was probably written"; T 26372-78, S 254:12; Grew, *Turbulent Era*, II, 1249, n. 5; Grew, *Ten Years in Japan*, 483-86 (diary entry for December 6: "The address was read by proxy, as is often done in Japan, and it is pointed out that the substance and tone of the speech are different from all General Tōjō's previous addresses"); *Foreign Relations (Diplomatic Papers: 1941)*, IV, 726-28 (two Grew cables received in Washington on December 6 and 7, containing reports along the lines of the preceding diary entry); Tōjō interrog., Feb. 4, 1-2 (in which he "admits" to believing in 1941 that Japan, China, and Manchukuo were called upon to oppose at all costs the "ambitions" of the United States and Great Britain "to control" Asia and their effort to do so "by taking advantage of quarrels among nations in Greater East Asia"; Masanori Itō, *Gunbatsu Kōbōshi*, III, 372-74; and Millis, *This Is Pearl!*, 279-83 and 294.

In writing about the event in 1943, Mr. Tolischus (p. 313) noted that a subsequent check of the so-called Tōjō statement had revealed that, despite the government's attempt "to backwater," the translation proved to be "substantially correct" and that the tone of the other speeches given and of the resolutions passed left no doubt as to what was meant. "But Tojo's nonappearance at the rally, and other signs, raised a question. Were the extremists trying to rush even the Tojo Government off its feet? It was impossible to find a satisfactory answer."

[73] See the Tolischus and Kluckhohn dispatches in *NYT*, December 1, 1941, 1 and 8, and December 2, 1941, 1 and 4.

from the Orient with a vengeance—a threatening figure whose ominous shadow had suddenly been cast upon the scene by the illuminating power of words which he had never spoken in a speech which he had never made.

Despite the injustice done to Tojo personally by the staffs of the Asia Development League and the Domei News Agency, the aims of the Japanese government were actually clarified, rather than distorted, by the misguided efforts of both organizations. Their unauthorized remarks and mistranslations constituted a kind of retributive justice in view of the fact that so much of what Japan had been saying officially had to be stripped of the glib euphemisms in which it was couched before the hard core of meaning was revealed. The reality of Japan's belligerent posture and aggressive intentions was further confirmed by the continuing out-pourings of "Magic," from which it could be judged that something big was about to happen in "the South." The exact when, where, and how were unfortunately far more elusive. Even the Germans, who might have been expected to know the details, were as much in the dark—a fact which reflects one of the major failures in Japan's war planning.

As a consequence of a liaison conference decision made immediately following the meeting of the senior statesmen on November 29, the Japanese government had informed its ambassador in Berlin to advise Hitler and Ribbentrop that war might suddenly break out between "the Anglo-Saxon nations and Japan"—indeed, that it might come more quickly than anyone expected. A "no separate peace" agreement was suggested, but Tokyo did not divulge anything more substantial than the implication that Japan would soon precipitate hostilities. The same liaison session also approved the agenda for the imperial conference scheduled for Monday, December 1—a decision which was subsequently endorsed, as usual, by the full cabinet and by the appropriate organs of the supreme command. The members of the government—civilian and military—remained unanimous in their insistence that Japan had been "cast adrift" by the Hull note of November 26, that further negotiations were useless, and that consequently war was inevitable.[74]

[74] See PHA, Part 12, "Magic" intercepts of Cables No. 985 and 986 from Tōkyō to Berlin, dated November 30, 204-6; Tōjō aff., S 344:2, T 36370, S 344:3, T 36379, and S 344:5, T 36396; Hattori, I, 232 and 238; and Feis, 328-29 and 336, in which it is noted that the President, on December 1, "asked for a copy for his own private files on the intercept of the cable [No. 985] sent on November 30 by the Japanese Foreign Minister, Togo, to the Japanese Ambassador in Berlin, Oshima."
The cabinet's endorsement of the November 29 liaison conference decision regarding the agenda for the imperial conference took place at a special meeting held on the

And yet, despite this united front of "expert" opinion, the idea persisted, or was consciously fostered, that the imperial navy still had misgivings. The belief that the navy was "not entirely confident" was conveyed to the Emperor on Sunday, November 30, by his brother, Prince Takamatsu. His Majesty, who was surprised by this development, was encouraged by Kido to summon the chief of the naval general staff and the navy minister to inquire directly of them where matters stood. Exactly what Nagano and Shimada reported to the throne is not known. At the time, they were credited with assuring the Emperor that the navy was "reasonably confident" with respect to Japan's war outlook. The very phrase used to express this idea—*sōtō no kakushin*—although ambiguous as to the degree of assurance, nevertheless suggested considerably more, rather than less, confidence. Much later, however, when the war had been fought and lost and Shimada was standing trial, the erstwhile navy minister declared that the advice Nagano and he had given on November 30, 1941, concerned naval preparations for war and not the ultimate outcome of the war. If that is so, then it is obvious that either they misunderstood the Emperor or he misunderstood them. Because of the statements made by Prince Takamatsu, His Majesty had temporarily withheld the sanction which Tojo had earlier sought for the imperial conference at which the decision for war would be confirmed. As soon as Nagano and Shimada had departed, however, the Emperor instructed Kido to inform Tojo that the imperial conference could be held as originally planned.[75]

If the Emperor had entertained any hopes of seeing a policy of forbearance emerge at the last moment, those hopes must have vanished as soon as Nagano and Shimada revealed by their remarks that Prince Takamatsu's information was incorrect. The throne's permission to convoke an imperial conference meant either that the Emperor had found the Nagano-Shimada presentation convincing, or that for want of a nail a shoe would be lost. . . . In the absence of the only possible basis for imperial interference—lack of unanimity within the councils of the state—an Empire might be destroyed.

The final forging of the chain of circumstances by which the Japanese government irrevocably linked the fate of the nation to the use of force

morning of December 1, several hours prior to the convocation of the imperial conference itself.

[75] On the Takamatsu episode, see Kido aff., S 293:24, T 31045-47; Shimada aff., S 328:10, T 34666-67; Kido SKD and corresp.; and Tōjō aff., S 344:2, T 36370-71 (which incorrectly quotes Tōjō as telling the Emperor, "The high command is fully convinced of victory").

took place the following afternoon, in Room One, East, of the imperial palace in circumstances of solemn formality.[76] The two-hour session, which began at 2:00 p.m., was attended by all of the cabinet ministers—not just by those who had participated in the liaison conferences of late October. Also present were the chiefs and vice-chiefs of the army and navy general staffs, the heads of the military and naval affairs bureaus of the war and navy ministries, the chief cabinet secretary, and—as was customary—the president of the privy council. The meeting was devoted largely to long statements by Premier Tojo, Foreign Minister Togo, and Chief of the Naval General Staff Nagano, who contributed little that had not already been said before. Perhaps subconsciously there was an urge among these men toward self-hypnosis. Perhaps it was merely that standard operating procedure imparted a mechanical character to the conference, giving the detached observer a feeling that everything had been set in motion by the winding of a single spring, which was now slowly and automatically uncoiling.

Tojo reported that while the army and navy had been striving to complete operational preparations in accordance with the decision of the imperial conference of November 5, the government had repeatedly tried, in every way possible, to bring about an adjustment of relations with the United States. The American government, however, had not made a single concession with regard to its earlier demands. The United States, in fact, had added new conditions and had called for unilateral concessions on Japan's part. In league with the British, Dutch, and Chinese, the United States was now insisting that Japan totally and unconditionally withdraw her troops from China, repudiate her recognition of the

[76] On the imperial conference of December 1, 1941, see Tōjō aff., S 344:2-3, T 36371-83; IMTFE Exh. Nos. 2954 and 2955, S 252:2-4, T 26072-93; Tōjō cross-examination, S 347:4, T 36722; Tōjō interrog., Feb. 6, 4, Feb. 8, 1-5, Feb. 11, 2-3, and Mar. 1, 6-7; Kido aff., S 293:24, T 31047; Kido "Nikki," S 111:3, T 10523 (revised T 11144; the translation misrepresents the meaning of *tsui ni*, which is closer to "after all" or "in the end" than to "at last"); Kido SKD and corresp.; Tōgō, 240-43 and 254-55; Shimada aff., S 328:10, T 34664-67; Kaya aff., S 291:15, T 30655-58; Suzuki aff., S 333:12, T 35224-25; Hattori, I, 234-37; JRD Monograph No. 150, 34-42; IPS Doc. No. 0004, 23-24; J, B/VII, 976-78; CF 20, IV, 358; IMTFE, "Roling Opinion," 118-23; and Ohmae corresp.

In addition to the Emperor, the conference was attended by the following: Tōjō (prime minister, home minister, and war minister concurrently), Tōgō (foreign minister), Shimada (navy minister), Kaya (finance minister), Suzuki (president of the cabinet planning board), Iwamura (justice minister), Hashida (education minister), Ino (agriculture minister), Kishi (commerce minister), Terashima (communications minister), Koizumi (welfare minister), Sugiyama (chief of the army general staff), Nagano (chief of the naval general staff), Hoshino (chief secretary of the cabinet), Mutō (director of the military affairs bureau, war ministry), Oka (director of the naval affairs bureau, navy ministry), Tanabe (vice-chief of the army general staff), Itō (vice-chief of the naval general staff), and Hara (president of the privy council).

Nanking government of Wang Ching-wei, and reduce the Tripartite Pact to a scrap of paper. Submission to such demands would be equivalent to forfeiture of the Empire's power and authority; Japan would be prevented from settling the China Incident; and in the end the very existence of the state would be endangered. It had thus become clear that Japan could not possibly secure its own demands through diplomatic means. At the same time, the four powers had steadily been increasing their economic and military pressure. From the standpoint of national strength and strategic considerations, the Empire absolutely could not permit the current situation to continue any longer. Operational requirements, in particular, would not allow any further delay. Matters had now come to such a pass that the Empire, in order to overcome the current crisis and perfect the national defense, must undertake hostilities against the United States, Great Britain, and the Netherlands. It was truly regrettable that after more than four years of fighting in China it should be necessary to plunge further into war, thus causing great anxiety to His Majesty. However, the national power was now several times greater than it had been prior to the outbreak of the China Incident; the solidarity within Japan was firmer than ever before; the morale of the officers and men of the army and navy was without parallel. Mature reflection on these facts, Tojo said, convinced him that the nation, united to the very death, would break through the crisis with which it was confronted.

Foreign Minister Togo echoed Tojo's views, but spoke in far more specific terms and in greater detail. The foreign minister reiterated the familiar charge that from beginning to end the United States had held fast to its traditional principles and had ignored the realities of the situation in Eastern Asia. She had demanded that Japan adhere to and implement principles which she herself could not readily put into effect. Despite the many concessions made by Japan, the United States had not yielded one iota throughout the more than seven months of negotiations.[77] It was the consistent aim of the United States to attempt to obstruct the Empire's fixed and inalterable national policy: the establish-

[77] The Japanese were using the term "concession" in a very limited and special sense, as is indirectly revealed in the testimony of Kumaichi Yamamoto, concurrently chief of the American and East Asian bureaus of the foreign office in late 1941 (S 251:7-8, T 25941). By a "treaty" concluded with the Nanking (puppet) government of Wang Ching-wei (established by force of Japanese arms and maintained thereby), Japan had secured the "right" to station troops in certain parts of China, including areas around Shanghai and Amoy; thus, Proposal A, which envisaged a Japanese occupation of Hainan Island, and parts of North China and Inner Mongolia, but which said nothing about Shanghai and Amoy, represented a "concession" on Japan's part.

ment of the Greater East Asia co-prosperity sphere. If the government accepted the latest American proposal, the international status of the Empire would drop even below what it had been prior to the Manchurian Incident. Acceptance would endanger the existence of the state.

As Togo spoke on in this vein, his remarks tended to suggest, though never quite openly, that a negotiated settlement would mean forsaking the opportunity to conquer China, to dominate Eastern Asia, to secure the fruits of an Axis victory in Europe, to invade the Soviet Union, and to obtain raw materials at will and in unlimited quantities—regardless of the needs of other states. When he at length sat down, it was with the conclusion that even if negotiations were continued, it would be "practically impossible" to realize satisfactorily the Empire's demands. Only in the use of the qualifier "practically" did Togo depart at all, and then only minutely, from the official line.

Admiral Nagano, who followed the foreign minister, spoke on behalf of both branches of the supreme command—for the army as well as the navy—which was by no means the usual practice. It was thought that having Nagano represent the army would impress everyone with how closely both services were working together at a crucial moment in Japan's history. The army and navy, Nagano said, were ready for action; they awaited only the imperial command. The ABD powers had steadily been augmenting their military preparations, especially in the southern area. At present, however, their build-up was practically equivalent to what the supreme command had expected. The latter was therefore confident of being able to carry out military operations according to the prearranged plan. With regard to the Soviet Union, appropriate diplomatic measures were being taken and strict vigilance was being maintained. Under the current circumstances, the supreme command did not feel any great anxiety in that direction. The morale of the fighting forces was exceedingly high; the officers and men were "burning with a desire to give their lives for the state"; they were ready "to go forth in high spirits to accomplish their great mission" as soon as the imperial command was given. On this point there need be no concern whatsoever.

When Nagano had finished, Tojo again took the floor to discuss matters falling within his responsibility as home minister. Finance Minister Kaya and Agriculture Minister Ino also reported on problems under their respective jurisdictions. Then, as previously scheduled, Dr. Hara of the privy council posed a number of questions which were answered by whatever member of the government was most competent to do so. Included among Hara's requests for information was a question relating to the prospects of a Japanese naval victory in the light of the continuing build-up of American armaments. Admiral Nagano gave a characteristic answer. He admitted that such a build-up was in progress, but he declared that 40 per cent of American naval strength was in the Atlantic and that a sudden transfer to the Pacific would be difficult. The European war situation would similarly prevent the British from moving any major portion of their fleet to the Far East.

For those who might have been concerned about Anglo-American naval cooperation, Nagano also had an answer. An amalgamation of naval forces, he said, would work against the enemy rather than to his advantage. The real problem, however, was how Japan would fare if the war became a protracted one. There was no way of calculating definitely what the outcome would be, since a great deal would depend on various abstract as well as concrete factors, including the total national strength and developments in the world situation. (Not a word was said about the impending Pearl Harbor strike or about any other features of Japan's over-all operational plan.)

Hara also asked about the probability of air raids against the Japanese homeland and about countermeasures. The task of replying to this embarrassing inquiry fell to Chief of the Army General Staff Sugiyama, who borrowed a page from Nagano's book. The answer, he said, depended to a great extent upon the success or failure of Japanese operations in the early days of the war as well as thereafter. If Japan achieved victory in the initial months, there was little fear that the homeland would be subjected to air raids, but if a long war ensued it could not be said that there would be no danger of Japan being attacked. The United States might try to pressure the Soviet Union into providing air bases in Siberia. It was necessary to be on guard against such a development, for if that happened, greater precautions would have to be taken in the homeland. Emergency measures for air defense would be inaugurated immediately upon the outbreak of war. Adequate protection for Japan proper, however, would have to be postponed until the increased need for anti-air raid defense on the part of forces in the field had been met. Measures at home would gradually be improved as the war developed. When Hara asked what would be done to assist the victims of a widespread conflagration, if such a catastrophe occurred despite the government's plans for fighting fires caused by incendiary raids, he was told that some of the refugees would be evacuated from the affected areas while others would be given substitute housing of simple construction.

When Hara had finally exhausted his questions, he made a closing statement in which he gave his blessings and uttered what amounted to an oath of allegiance to the officially inspired view, the monolithic orthodoxy: Japan had made repeated concessions but to no avail.... The American attitude had not changed in the slightest from what it had been at the time of the Manchurian Incident.... Japan had gone as far as she could go.... To do more would mean abandoning the achievements of the past decade and nullifying the gains made since the Sino-Japanese and Russo-Japanese wars of the Meiji period.... Undertaking a new and greater war could not be helped.... Although prolonged hostilities seemed unavoidable, it would be better to have a short war.... The government should exert itself toward that end.... War being the only course remaining to Japan, he would put his faith and trust in the peerless loyalty of the officers and men of Japan's fighting forces.

Tojo immediately responded with a promise that the points raised by the privy council president would be given the utmost consideration and that every effort would be made to bring the war to an early conclusion.... Although Japan had decided to fight, the government was prepared to call a halt at any time before the blow was struck, should the United States indicate a willingness to accede to Japan's demands.... There was no responsibility greater than that which devolved upon the present leaders of Japan.... They were determined to set His Majesty's mind at rest by speedily accomplishing, in perfect unity and with confidence in certain victory, the objectives of the war which Japan must now undertake....

These words at length brought the imperial conference to a close. Everyone arose and bowed as His Majesty, ever the silent spectator of the scene, left the chamber.

The decision for war had been made.

$\mathcal{Y}$esterday, $\mathcal{D}$ecember 7

DURING the last days remaining before Pearl Harbor, the messages exchanged between Tokyo and Washington assumed an ominous tone. The impression conveyed by "Magic" to its small and select audience was that the situation was beyond repair and that a drastic development might occur at any moment.[1] As early as November 26, the day on which Secretary Hull had revealed his new proposals, the foreign office had suggested to Nomura and Kurusu that they occasionally communicate with Tokyo by telephone rather than by cable in order to save time. A special voice code was provided for their use and they were even given the residential phone numbers of several of the top personnel, including that of the foreign minister himself (*Ginza* 3614). Any reference to the Japanese-American negotiations was to be in terms of a "marriage proposal"; the President was to be "Miss Kimiko"; and the Japanese army, "Mr. Tokugawa." Mention of the birth of a child—an odd thought under the circumstances—was to signify a "critical turn" in the situation. "Yielding" or "not yielding" would be equivalent to selling or not selling a mountain—a rather unlikely activity at best.[2]

The day after this message was sent, Mr. Kurusu made a first and somewhat painful attempt to use this clumsy code in a conversation with the chief of the American bureau of the foreign ministry. The recording device at "Magic" was already in operation before the monitor in Tokyo flipped the switch on his own machine. In the course of a seven-minute conversation, the tenseness of the situation was several times revealed:

[1] The quotations which follow from the Japanese messages are taken from the "Magic" intercept versions which were distributed to top American leaders in Washington. They were naturally unaware of the translation errors contained in the intercepts (see footnote 38, p. 335 above). Whenever possible, references to the original Japanese cables will be included, together with whatever comment seems necessary in terms of the point being made in the text.

[2] *PHA*, Part 12, 178 ("Magic" intercept of Cable No. 836 of November 26, 1941), and Kurihara corresp. *Keisei kyūten suru* (the decode of *kodomo ga umareru*) literally means a "sudden" or "rapid" change, without indicating whether for better or for worse. The phrase was translated by "Magic" as "critical turn" presumably because such a rendition seemed to fit the context of the situation.

Literal Translation   *Decode of Voice Code*

. . . .

KURUSU: "How do things look there? Does it seem as if a child might be born?" "Does it seem as if a crisis is at hand?"

YAMAMOTO: (In a very definite tone): "Yes, the birth of the child seems imminent." "Yes, a crisis *does* appear imminent."

KURUSU: (In a somewhat surprised tone, repeating Yamamoto's statement): "It *does* seem as if the birth is going to take place?" (Pause.) "A crisis *does* appear imminent?"

KURUSU: "In which direction . . ." (Stopped himself very abruptly at this slip which went outside the character of the voice code. After a slight pause he quickly recovered, then to cover up the slip, continued:)

KURUSU: "Is it to be a boy or a girl?"

YAMAMOTO: (Hesitated, then laughing at his hesitation took up Kurusu's cue to reestablish the voice code character of the talk. The "boy, girl, healthy" byplay has no other significance):

YAMAMOTO: "It seems as if it will be a strong healthy boy."

KURUSU: "Oh, it's to be a strong healthy boy?" (Rather long pause.)

YAMAMOTO: "Yes."

. . . .

YAMAMOTO: "The matrimonial question, that is, the matter pertaining to arranging a marriage—don't break them off." "Regarding negotiations, don't break them off."

KURUSU: "Not break them? You mean talks." (Helplessly:)

KURUSU: "Oh, my." (Pause, and then with a resigned laugh:)

KURUSU: "Well, I'll do what I can." (Continuing after a pause:)

KURUSU: "Please read carefully what Miss Kimiko had to say as contained in today's telegram." "Please read carefully what the President had to say as contained in today's telegram."

. . . .

Literal Translation	*Decode of Voice Code*
KURUSU: "But without anything,—they want to keep carrying on the matrimonial question. They do. In the meantime we're faced with the excitement of having a child born. On top of that Tokugawa is really champing at the bit, isn't he? Tokugawa is, isn't he?"	"But without anything, —they want to keep on negotiating. In the meantime we have a crisis on hand and the army is champing at the bit. You know the army."
(Laughter and pause.)	
KURUSU: "That's why I doubt if anything can be done."	
YAMAMOTO: "I don't think it's as bad as that."	
YAMAMOTO: "Well,—we can't sell a mountain."	"Well,—we can't yield."
KURUSU: "Oh, sure, I know that. That isn't even a debatable question any more."	
YAMAMOTO: "Well, then, although we can't yield, we'll give you some kind of a reply to that telegram."	
KURUSU: "In any event, Miss Kimiko is leaving town tomorrow, and will remain in the country until Wednesday."	"In any event, the President is leaving town tomorrow, and will remain in the country until Wednesday."
YAMAMOTO: "Will you please continue to do your best."	
KURUSU: "Oh, yes. I'll do my best. And Nomura's doing everything too."	
YAMAMOTO: "Oh, all right. In today's talks, there wasn't anything of special interest then?"	
KURUSU: "No, nothing of particular interest, except that it is quite clear now that southward—ah—the south, the south matter is having considerable effect."	
YAMAMOTO: "I see. Well, then, good bye."	
KURUSU: "Good bye."[3]	

[3] See *PHA*, Part 12, 188-91 (some allowance is necessary for possible translation errors made at the time). The conversation took place between 2327 and 2334 hours, EST, November 27, 1941. The telegram mentioned by Kurusu was No. 1206 (*ibid.*, 192-95); the telegram mentioned by Yamamoto was probably No. 1189 (*ibid.*, 181-82), in which the gist of the Hull note of November 26 was reported. "The south matter" was in regard to American intelligence that a Japanese troop build-up was taking place in French Indo-China and that the Japanese government was increasing its pressure against Thailand.

The next day, November 28, the foreign minister advised Japan's representatives in Washington that the negotiations would soon be ruptured—in fact, if not in name. But he wanted Nomura and Kurusu to avoid giving the impression that the talks were being suspended. The two envoys were to inform the American government that they were still awaiting instructions and that consequently the opinions of Tokyo were as yet unknown to them. They were then to offer their own personal view that Japan's position had always been "just" and her attitude conciliatory, even to the extent of enduring "great sacrifices"—all "for the sake of the peace of the Pacific." The United States, however, had remained "unbending," thus "making it impossible for Japan to establish negotiations."[4]

But just twenty-four hours later a completely opposite tack was suggested—or so it seemed from a reading of "Magic":

We wish you would make one more attempt verbally along the following lines:

The United States government has (always?) taken a fair and judicial position and has formulated its policies after full consideration of the claims of both sides.

However, the Imperial Government is at a loss to understand why it has now taken the attitude that the new proposals we have made cannot be made the basis of discussion, but instead has made new proposals which ignore actual conditions in East Asia and would greatly injure the prestige of the Imperial Government.

With such a change of front in their attitude toward the China problem, what has become of the basic objectives that the U.S. government has made the basis of our negotiations during these seven months? On these points we would request careful self-reflection on the part of the United States government.

(In carrying out this instruction, please be careful that this does not lead to anything like a breaking off of negotiations.)[5]

[4] *Ibid.*, 195, "Magic" intercept of Cable No. 844 of November 28, 1941, sent by the American bureau chief (Yamamoto) on orders from Foreign Minister Tōgō. Both the "Magic" version and the IMTFE translation (T 10441-43) require revision in terms of the original Japanese, S 111:3. Cable No. 844 also rejected a proposal made by Nomura and Kurusu, two days earlier, in the hope of easing the crisis that was building up. For the details, see footnotes 66 and 68 below and the corresponding text.
Since all cables leaving the foreign ministry (or coming into it) bore the designation "the foreign minister" as addressor or addressee, care must be exercised in deciding which telegrams were actually seen by the minister or in any way approved by him. Yamamoto aff., S 252:6, T 26106-7; Kameyama aff., S 253:4, T 26202-4; and Tōgō aff., S 337:11, T 35732-34.
[5] *PHA*, Part 12, 199, "Magic" intercept of Cable No. 857 of November 29, 1941

Finally on December 1—the day of the imperial conference—Tokyo sent a further warning to the effect that care was being taken in Japan to give the impression that all was not at an end. The November 29 deadline had "come and gone," but "to prevent the United States from becoming unduly suspicious" the press and others were being advised that despite "some wide differences" between the two sides, the negotiations were continuing.[6] This cable was followed by yet another, which starkly emphasized the widening gap between appearances and reality: the embassy was to burn immediately certain telegraphic codes and to destroy one of the two "B" machines with which it was equipped for cryptographic purposes.[7]

All of these cables were intercepted by "Magic," decoded, translated, and distributed to the appropriate authorities at the highest decision-making level within the American government. As soon as the code-destruction message had been processed, a military intelligence officer was dispatched to reconnoiter the Japanese embassy. He found that papers were being burned in the back yard. The date was December 3; the army's conclusion: "at the least a break in diplomatic relations and probably war" in the very near future. The navy's assistant chief of operations was even more positive in his reaction. "If you rupture diplomatic negotiations you do not necessarily have to burn your codes. The

(possibly a mistake for November 30). This "Magic" version is a strange hodgepodge of the correct and the incorrect (see S 111:4 for the original). The sentence, "The United States government has (always?) taken a fair and judicial position . . . ," is particularly far off-base—the *Japanese* government and not the American being the intended subject.

No explanation is given for the parentheses around the concluding sentence in the "Magic" version quoted in the text above, but the following statement was made by the prosecution: "Strangely, the last line . . . is missing from the Japanese text, but the Japanese document shows that there was some additional writing at one time at the end of that document, and that an attempt has been made to cross out and cover up that particular writing." See T 10444-51, S 111:3-4.

For Tōgō's denial that there was any deceitful purpose behind these final messages, see his affidavit, S 337:8-9, T 35712-14.

[6] *PHA*, Part 12, 208 ("Magic" intercept of Cable No. 865 of December 1, 1941), and Kurihara corresp. The original read: "Ōden dai 812 gō no kijitsu wo keika shi jōsei wa masu masu shinten shi tsutsu aru mo waga hō wa kono sai fu-hitsuyō ni Bei-gawa no giwaku wo masazaru yō keikai suru kenchi yori shinbun sono ta ni tai shite wa hi-ga no shuchō wa kyori dai naru mono aru mo kōshō wa keizoku-chū nari to no shushi wo motte shidō shi oreri (ijō ki-shi kagiri no fukumi made)." In this connection, see also the Tōjō-Kubota exchange on the morning of December 8, 1941: S 113:7, T 10691-92; and J, B/VII, 989-90.

[7] *PHA*, Part 12, 215 ("Magic" intercept of Cable No. 867 of December 2, 1941). In this connection, see also the second paragraph of footnote 33 below.

Cable No. 896 of December 5 (*ibid.*, 234) ordered First Secretary Terasaki and certain other members of the embassy staff to "leave by plane within the next couple of days."

diplomats . . . can pack up their codes with their dolls and take them home."[8]

While Washington sifted these intercepted messages for whatever clues they might contain, Japan's civil and military leaders anxiously awaited the launching of the attack, with which the Japanese nation—in their phrase—was to contribute toward the stabilization of East Asia and the peace of the world. At imperial headquarters, there was a conscious determination to maintain an outward calm, despite an inward feeling which combined "unending worry" with fatalistic "resignation."[9] On the night of December 1, however, a cable arrived that sent an involuntary shiver down many spines. A transport plane belonging to Japan's expeditionary army in China had crashed in Chinese-held territory in Kwangtung province. Among its passengers had been a Major Sugisaka who was carrying a very secret order addressed to the commander of the 23rd Army stationed at Canton. The nature of this document was such that Japan's determination to go to war could be inferred from its contents. Imperial headquarters was plunged into gloom. It was feared that the major had probably not had time to destroy the order prior to the accident, which presumably had occurred without the slightest warning. The order could have been burned in the crash, but it could also have been thrown clear. If so, it would be lying on the ground somewhere and would soon be picked up by the local inhabitants.

Air reconnaissance the next morning deepened the pessimism and chagrin of the night before. The plane had met its end in mountainous terrain too difficult of access and too far from Japanese lines to permit sending out a search party to retrieve whatever remained. The scene of the crash was already surrounded by the Chinese, who were swarming there "like ants." If the order were found, Chungking would be informed immediately. The Generalissimo would alert Washington and London. With this foreknowledge of Japan's intentions, American and British forces might launch a full-scale attack before Japan could make

[8] The "army" in this case means Brig. Gen. Sherman Miles (chief of military intelligence), Colonel Leonard T. Gerow (chief of the war plans division), and Lt. Col. Rufus S. Bratton (chief of the Far Eastern section, military intelligence division)—all of the War Department general staff. The assistant chief of naval operations was Rear Admiral Royal E. Ingersoll. The remark quoted in the text was made during testimony at an inquiry into the Pearl Harbor attack. See Bratton aff. and related submissions, T 26245-46, S 253:11, and T 26261-63, S 253:13.

[9] See Hattori, I, 349.

a move. The feeling prevailed in Tokyo that the only thing left to do was "to close one's eyes and pray to the gods."[10]

It was thus with justifiable anxiety about their carefully laid plans that the army and navy chiefs of staff reported jointly to the throne on December 2. Speaking for General Sugiyama as well as for himself, Admiral Nagano explained to the Emperor that the day of the week and the phase of the moon had both entered into the selection of an appropriate time to attack. An approximately 20-day-old moon spanning the hours "from midnight to about sunrise" was considered best for the purposes at hand. A day of rest, such as Sunday, when the number of warships in Pearl Harbor would be comparatively great, had also recommended itself. December 8 had been chosen because it would be a Sunday in Hawaii (December 7) with a moon-age of 19.

Nagano also advised the Emperor that Britain and the United States might attack Japan prior to December 8, but in view of the operational difficulties and general confusion that would arise from any last-minute changes, the supreme command respectfully requested imperial sanction for the issuance of "imperial orders" confirming December 8 (Tokyo) as "X-Day." The Emperor naturally complied. In the late afternoon an encoded order was flashed to the advancing task force: "Ascend Mt. Niitaka! 1208." In clear text, "December 8 has been fixed as the day hostilities will commence. Attack as planned!"[11]

Although he was both premier and war minister, General Tojo did not personally have any connection with operations, which were solely the prerogative of the supreme command. During the last week before Pearl Harbor, Tojo was received by the Emperor on several occasions, but operational matters, including the projected naval strike against Hawaii, were never discussed.[12] Whatever the Emperor learned of Japan's plan of attack came either from the supreme command directly or from His Majesty's chief aide-de-camp.[13] The division of responsibility

[10] *Ibid.*

[11] *Ibid.*, 345-49 and 362, and Hattori corresp. In Japanese: "Niitaka-yama nobore 1208" and "Kaisen-bi wa jūnigatsu yōka to kettei seraru. Yotei-dōri kōgeki wo kekkō seyo." Niitaka-yama, a Formosan peak, was apparently chosen for this historic signal because it was the highest mountain in the Japanese Empire.

[12] At least, so Tōjō testified: S 348:4, T 36749-50 (cross-examination).

[13] Japanese records seem to be rather silent on the question of exactly how much the Emperor personally knew of Japan's over-all plan of attack. A comment by Mr. Keenan, recalling an audience with the Emperor following the conclusion of the Tōkyō trial, is not without interest in the light of Nagano's report to the throne on December 2. According to the chief prosecutor, the Emperor remarked that ". . . he knew that war steps were to be taken, but he didn't know the objective. He was not told. He didn't know that Pearl Harbor was going to be bombed. He said that he had issued instruc-

and of functions was carefully maintained. Just as the supreme command had long been in the habit of formulating national policies to the practical exclusion of everyone else, so now did it exert a similarly rigid control over the details relating to the implementation of the December 1 decision for war. Only where there was clearly a constitutional overlapping of authority did the supreme command deign to consult any of His Majesty's cabinet ministers.

One such matter was the nature of the final communication to be sent to the United States and the time of its delivery to responsible American officials in Washington.[14] In this regard the postwar assertions of the foreign minister must be weighed against the denials or the silence of the other principals. The point at issue is whether the naval general staff ever suggested launching hostilities without prior indication to the United States that Japan was terminating the negotiations.[15] Except for this question, the testimony is generally in agreement. The conclusions to be drawn therefrom, however, remain largely a matter of individual interpretation.[16]

---

tions—and this was verified in the trial—for due notice to be given before any belligerent act was made." See "Joseph Keenan Meets the Press," *American Mercury*, Vol. LXX, No. 316 (April 1950), 460.

[14] Kennedy, in *Some Aspects of Japan and Her Defence Forces*, 137 n., states that while he was attached to the Japanese army in 1919-1920, he "heard the opinion expressed that the sooner Japan fought America the better, as otherwise America might join the League of Nations, in which case three months' notice would have to be given before hostilities could be opened, and this would be fatal to Japan, whose only chance of success lay in a sudden, rapid blow."

[15] An affirmative statement in that regard was made by Mr. Yamamoto (the 1941 chief of the American bureau of the foreign ministry) during his testimony for the defense, and was subsequently pursued by Mr. Tōgō, who stated that two of his co-defendants (Nagano and Shimada) had tried to dissuade him from testifying about the matter (he was told it would not be in his interest to do so). Nagano and Itō (chief and vice-chief of the naval general staff) were both dead when the issue finally came up in open court. Other defendants who had been present at the liaison conference in question either remained silent or denied any knowledge or memory of a naval general staff proposal in favor of launching hostilities without terminating the negotiations. Even Tōgō has stated that the navy subsequently agreed with his own opinion in favor of following diplomatic procedures. Tōgō also testified that it was Nagano who later advocated handing over Japan's final note to Hull personally.

When this subject came up during a pre-trial interrogation (Mar. 18, 5) at Sugamo prison, General Tōjō declared: "You asked me that before and I answered it. I don't remember any such thing. . . . The Emperor had made it very plain that he was opposed to any attack before the delivery of the final note. I dare say that the Navy General Staff would like to have done so [from a purely operational standpoint], but, since the Emperor's position was very plain [and 'diplomatic procedures' required notification] no one would have advocated such a thing."

[16] The text which follows draws on material in Yamamoto aff., S 252:4-5, T 26093-97; Yamamoto cross-examination, S 252:10, T 26134-36, S 252:13-14, T 26156-62, and S 253:16-19, T 26285-304; Tōgō aff., S 337:9-10, T 35714-24; Tōgō cross-examination,

The idea of sending a final notification to the United States was first discussed at a liaison conference preceding the December 1 decision for war.[17] The American bureau of the foreign ministry subsequently prepared a draft of such a notification, using as a guide the various points of view expressed at the liaison conference, and incorporating as well suggestions made by the chiefs of the military and naval affairs bureaus of the war and navy ministries (Muto and Oka). At a liaison conference on December 4, Foreign Minister Togo submitted this draft note for approval. Although it was in no sense a declaration of war, Togo argued that it satisfied the requirements of international law— especially in view of the fact that Japan had been "challenged" with an "ultimatum" and therefore possessed the "right" to resort to a "war of self-defense" without a declaration of her intent to do so.

According to Article 1 of Hague Convention III, to which Japan was pledged to adhere, ". . . hostilities . . . must not commence without previous and explicit warning, in the form either of a reasoned declaration of war or of an ultimatum with conditional declaration of war."[18] That the note presented by the foreign minister failed to comply with this obligation is revealed by its contents.[19] In many respects it seems to

---

S 338:5-10, T 35834-57 and 35861-62; Tōgō interrog., S 111:11-12, T 10505-12; questions to Tōgō by the president of the Tribunal, S 342:8 and 9, T 36131-33 and 36141-42; Tōjō aff., S 344:4-5, 6 and 7, T 36388-93, 36408, and 36410; Tōjō cross-examination, S 345:3, T 36528-33, S 348:4-5, T 36750-51, and S 348:12, T 36779-803; Tōjō interrog., Feb. 15, 5-6, Feb. 18, 1-5, Feb. 19, 1-13, Feb. 20, 1-7, Feb. 21, 1-3, Feb. 23, 3, Mar. 12, 8-9, Mar. 18, 1-6, Mar. 25, 4-5, and Mar. 26, 3-4; CF 20, III, 254; Shimada aff., S 328:11, T 34673-74; Oka aff., S 316:10, T 33400-3; Shiba aff. and cross-examination, S 315:13-316:1, T 33321-35; Hattori, I, 238-39; J, B/VII, 978-1000; JRD Monograph No. 150, 42-44; IPS Doc. No. 0004, 52-56, 58-61, and 226-29; Blakeney intv.; and the Keenan statement cited in footnote 13 above.

[17] The records do not agree on the date of this particular conference (November 29 being an "educated guess"), but despite some contradictory testimony it seems fairly certain that the initial discussion with regard to a final note preceded the imperial conference of December 1.

[18] T 420-21. See also Tōjō interrog., Mar. 26, 3-4. Mr. Tōgō's assertions to the contrary notwithstanding (S 332:9, T 35719), the Hull note of November 26, containing a proposed basis for agreement with Japan, was *not* an ultimatum demanding that Japan choose between "humiliating surrender or war." See Chapter 11 above.

In this regard, see the arguments of Ben Bruce Blakeney, Tōgō's counsel, T 26233-44, S 253:9-10, and related submissions, T 26244-84, S 253:10-16. It should be noted that the Americans cited came to the conclusion that Japan intended to go to war on the basis of (1) intercepted cables relating to the destruction of codes and coding apparatus, and (2) an instruction specifying a 1:00 p.m. delivery of the note in question on Sunday, December 7 ("a very unusual request"). Only in the light of these revelations did the final note, as intercepted by "Magic," convey the impression of an "ultimatum" or bespeak the imminence of war.

[19] Some postwar Japanese opinion admits as much. See, for instance, Hattori, I, 240, in which the key words in the concluding portion of the note are described as follows:

have been written more for propaganda effect than for any pertinence to the international legal requirements of the situation. The note reviewed at great length the positions taken by the two sides.[20] It assigned to Japan "the utmost sincerity" as compared with the United States, which was described as "holding fast to theories in disregard of realities, and refusing to yield an inch on its impractical principles. . . ."

The jargon of the decade was present in profusion: "It is the immutable policy of the Japanese Government to insure the stability of East Asia and to promote world peace and thereby to enable all nations to find each its proper place in the world." The "China Affair" had broken out "owing to the failure on the part of China to comprehend Japan's true intentions." Despite Japan's "best efforts"—including the Axis alliance—"to prevent the extention [*sic*] of war-like disturbances," America and Britain had "resorted to every possible measure to assist the Chungking regime so as to obstruct the establishment of a general peace between Japan and China. . . ." The negotiations had not made any progress because the American government, "adhering steadfastly to its original assertions, failed to display in the slightest degree a spirit of conciliation. . . . Finally on November 26th, in an attitude to impose upon the Japanese Government those principles it has persistently maintained, the American Government made a proposal totally ignoring Japanese claims . . ."—an approach which Japan viewed as "a source of profound regret."[21]

The Japanese government had "always maintained an attitude of fairness and moderation" and had made "all possible concessions often in spite of great difficulties" in order to reach a settlement. But the American government, "obsessed with its own views and opinions," was "scheming for the extension of the war" in Europe and was "preparing to attack in the name of self-defense, Germany and Italy," two powers that were "striving to establish a new order in Europe."[22]

"Migi ketsugo ni wa, waga hō no jiyū kōdō wo ryūho suru mune ga meiki serarete orazu, keishiki-teki ni wa kokusaihō-jō no sensō tsūkoku to minashi-gatai mono de atta."

[20] See *Foreign Relations (Japan: 1931-1941)*, II, 786-93 (the official text of the note) and *PHA*, Part 12, 239-45 (the "Magic" intercept of Cable No. 902, Japan's final note, dispatched from Tōkyō in English). A facsimile copy of the note, in the form in which Nomura handed it to Hull, is in the author's possession.

[21] Note the absence of any charge that the American proposal was an ultimatum.

[22] In postwar testimony unencumbered by diplomatic niceties, Mr. Hull castigated this 1941 presentation of the Japanese case as "a false and fraudulent statement in the worst of bad faith . . . and a monstrous misrepresentation of our position in what turned out to be a brazen attempt to shift from themselves to us responsibility for their attack upon us." *PHA*, Part 11, 5386.

Despite its great length and its peculiar slant on world affairs, the note submitted by Mr. Togo to the liaison conference contained nothing more explicit than a concluding statement which indicated that a prolongation of the Hull-Nomura conversations would be useless: ". . . the earnest hope of the Japanese Government to adjust Japanese-American relations and to preserve and promote the peace of the Pacific through cooperation with the American Government has finally been lost. The Japanese Government regrets to have to notify hereby the American Government that in view of the attitude of the American Government it cannot but consider that it is impossible to reach an agreement through further negotiations."

This was the note which Foreign Minister Togo described as "equivalent to a declaration of war"—a document giving Japan complete freedom of action with regard to the commencement of hostilities. He felt the assertion that the Japanese government had lost the "earnest hope" it had originally entertained with respect to adjusting relations "clearly signified a cessation of peace; that is to say, a resort to war." To include a specific declaration of war or even a phrase about reserving freedom of action would have been "merely to reiterate the obvious." So far as the foreign minister was concerned, Japan's final note was "stronger than the 'ultimatum' stipulated in the Hague Convention." Consequently, "there were no grounds for the insertion" of anything more explicit.[23]

When Mr. Togo spoke in this manner, he did so with the full weight of his position as foreign minister. There can be no question but that his colleagues in the liaison conference found his arguments convincing and reassuring. The foreign minister was their authority on the subject. If he said that Japan's final note was in accordance with international law and Japan's treaty obligations, nothing more need be done. In fact, the matter was closed, and entirely put out of mind.

The time of delivery of this note in Washington, however, presented a special problem that required an adjustment between "the strategic and diplomatic necessities" of the situation. Handing over the note was not to be allowed to interfere with the success of the surprise attack, but at the same time it was felt that the presentation should precede the

[23] Tōgō testified that he had never seen (or heard any mention of) a proposal allegedly made by Rear Admiral Oka to the effect that Japan's final note should contain a phrase explicitly stating that the Empire was reserving to itself freedom of action (see the Tōgō material cited in footnote 16 above). For an American view, see Ballantine aff., T 10830-49, S 114:5-7, and Ballantine cross-examination, T 10969-86, S 115:15-17 and S 116:2.

outbreak of hostilities. The Emperor had cautioned the premier repeatedly on that point and had also spoken in the same vein to the foreign minister and the two chiefs of staff. As a consequence, Premier Tojo insisted on December 4, and his colleagues agreed, that the foreign minister's note be presented, *without fail*, to the government of the United States *prior to the launching of military operations*. The exact time of its delivery in Washington was to be decided by the foreign minister in consultation with the chiefs of the army and navy general staffs. The three men were also to confer together and agree upon the time at which the note would be dispatched from Japan. The next day, Friday, December 5, the action taken by the liaison conference, together with the wording of the note, received the approval of the full cabinet. At no point did the supreme command reveal the plan to strike Pearl Harbor or the exact time at which military operations would begin. Even the attack date itself was known only to those few cabinet ministers who regularly attended liaison conferences: Tojo, Togo, Kaya, Shimada, Suzuki, and Hoshino.[24]

Although the members of the December 4 conference had envisaged further consultation between the foreign minister and the two chiefs of staff with regard to the delivery of Japan's note, Admiral Nagano and General Sugiyama never actually conferred with Mr. Togo in person. Instead, they either delegated that task to their subordinates or permitted them to take the initiative on their own responsibility. Thus it came to pass, on the afternoon of December 5, that the foreign minister received a visit from Vice-Admiral Seiichi Ito, the vice-chief of the naval general staff, accompanied by Lt. Gen. Shinichi Tanaka, the chief of the

[24] With the exception of the war and navy ministers, the others might not even have known the date had it not been for a specific question in that regard put by Foreign Minister Tōgō. He testified that the response was "about Sunday." According to Colonel Hattori, however, Admiral Nagano replied, in a whisper, "December 8."

The evidence suggests that the navy was even reluctant to inform the army of the details of its "Operation Z" (Z *sakusen*: Pearl Harbor attack plan). The fact that such an operation was being studied was first reported by the operations section of the naval general staff to its army counterpart in August 1941 as "top secret" information. Some war ministry leaders also learned of the matter at that time. It would appear that Tōjō did not learn of the navy's decision to adopt the plan until a day or two before the imperial conference of December 1, such was the care with which operational (supreme-command) matters were kept secret. In this regard, see Hattori, I, 312 and 355; Tōjō aff., S 344:5, T 36396-97 and S 344:6-7, T 36407-9; Tōjō cross-examination, S 347:11, T 36707, and S 348:3-5, T 36740-51; Tōjō interrog., Feb. 8, 1-2, Feb. 21, 4-5, and Mar. 1, 7-8; JRD, "Statements," IV:50461 (Sadatoshi Tomioka), 344; JRD, "Interrogations," II:35901 (Shinichi Tanaka), 417-18 and 434-36; JRD, "Translation," V (Item 19, Sadatoshi Tomioka), (Item 24, Akira Mutō), and (Item 34, Shinichi Tanaka); JRD Monograph No. 152, 44; and Ward, "The Inside Story of the Pearl Harbor Plan," *U.S. Naval Institute Proceedings*, Vol. LXXVII, No. 12 (December 1951), 1279.

operations bureau of the army general staff.[25] It was these supreme-command officers, Ito and Tanaka, imbued with the views of the nucleus group (*chūken shōkō*) which they represented, who arranged with the foreign minister the all-important *when* of Japan's final note.

What occurred that Friday afternoon in Tokyo was essentially a game of blindman's buff, with Mr. Togo in the role of the blindman and the supreme command very successfully avoiding the buff. At that moment, the attack against Pearl Harbor was only some sixty hours away. Certainly Ito was well aware of that fact, and presumably so was Tanaka, but Togo was not informed.

The admiral began the consultation by declaring that the time of delivery in Washington, which had previously been set for 12:30 p.m. Sunday, December 7, would now have to be postponed a half-hour, to one o'clock in the afternoon. When Togo inquired why, Ito replied that the change was necessary only because he had earlier made a "mistake" in his calculations. When Togo wanted to know "how much time" was needed between the notification and the attack, Ito said that was an "operational secret" and could not be divulged. In response to still another question from the foreign minister, Ito declared that the delivery of the note at 1:00 p.m. in Washington, on Sunday, would leave a *sufficient* margin of time before the attack. Togo thereupon made a decision which he was later to have cause to regret. Without ever determining the precise hour at which hostilities would begin, he nevertheless gave his consent to the delivery time specified by the supreme command.[26]

The next evening, Saturday, December 6, Togo dispatched the first of several cables designed to inform the embassy in Washington of the procedures it was to follow and of the text of the note it was to deliver. In what can conveniently be called a "pilot message," the foreign minister advised Nomura and Kurusu that he was about to transmit

[25] Tanaka appeared on behalf of his immediate superior, Vice-Chief of Staff Lt. Gen. Moritake Tanabe, who was on his way to the Kansai district to offer prayers for victory. I am here following Hattori (who says Tanaka called on Tōgō) rather than Tōgō (who says Tanabe). Hattori was chief of the second section (operations) of Tanaka's first bureau (operations) at the time in question.

[26] International law requires notice in advance but does not specify how long in advance. At the Tōkyō trial, the prosecution charged that the foreign minister had conspired with the supreme command to give the appearance of compliance with the requirements of international law while intending to violate those requirements by a carefully engineered delay in the delivery of the final note. The defense argued that Mr. Tōgō had done all that was humanly possible to ensure delivery of the note before the outbreak of war and that he could not be held responsible for the fact that the navy had cut the time between delivery and attack so fine that a delay at any point would mean an attack without prior warning.

separately, in English, the answer of the Japanese government to the American proposal of November 26—an answer which he had already told them, a week earlier, would constitute a *de facto* rupturing of the negotiations. Since this answer was very long, Togo informed the two envoys that the entire text, which would be cabled in fourteen separate parts, might not arrive until the next day. The current situation being "extremely delicate," he cautioned them to keep the receipt of the note "strictly secret for the time being." He would wire them later, he said, as to when they were to present it to the United States government. In the meantime they were to complete in advance all necessary arrangements (decoding, preparation of suitable copies, etc.) so that they would be in a position "to hand over" the note "at any time" following the receipt of his instructions in that regard.[27]

Although Japan's final communication was originally to have been sent at 4:00 a.m., Sunday, December 7, Tokyo time, its dispatch was subsequently advanced seven and a half hours. Thus, the first part of the fourteen-part message actually left the foreign ministry at 8:30 p.m. on Saturday, December 6. By 1:50 a.m. the following morning, all but the fourteenth part had been transmitted by the Tokyo central telegraph office. That last and key segment, however, was not sent from Japan until fifteen hours and ten minutes later: at 5:00 p.m., Sunday, December 7, in Tokyo (3:00 a.m., Sunday, December 7, Washington). One hour and twenty-eight minutes after that, at 6:28 p.m., Tokyo (4:28 a.m., December 7, Washington), Togo's critical instruction was on its way: Japan's final note was to be delivered to the United States government— "if possible, to the Secretary of State" personally—at 1:00 p.m., Sunday, December 7, Washington time.[28]

---

[27] Cable No. 901 (S 111:15, T 10534-36), dated December 6, 1941, dispatched from the foreign office at 8:30 p.m. and from the Tōkyō central telegraph office at 9:10 p.m. (7:10 a.m. December 6, Washington). Although addressed to Nomura, this cable, as well as all others, was obviously meant for Kurusu as well. See Kameyama aff., S 253:2-3, T 26190-91 and 26193. See also "Magic" intercept of Cable No. 901 in *PHA*, Part 12, 238-39. Neither the "Magic" nor the prosecution translation is entirely satisfactory.

On the *de facto* rupturing of the negotiations, see "Magic" intercept of Cable No. 844, dated November 28, 1941, *ibid.*, 195.

[28] The time in Washington, in December 1941, was fourteen hours earlier than that in Tōkyō. Japan's final note was sent in English, but in code, as Cable No. 902. The first thirteen parts left the foreign office between 8:30 p.m., December 6, and 12:20 a.m., December 7, Tōkyō. These same parts were transmitted from the central telegraph office between 10:10 p.m., December 6, and 1:50 a.m., December 7. The fourteenth part left the foreign office at 4:00 p.m., December 7, Tōkyō. It was transmitted by the central telegraph office via Mackay at 5:00 p.m. and via RCA at 6:00 p.m. Tōgō's instruction concerning the delivery time (which had been approved at a liaison conference on December 6), Cable No. 907, left the foreign office at 5:30 p.m., December 7, Tōkyō. It was transmitted by the central telegraph office via RCA at 6:28 p.m. and via Mackay at

In order to assure "speedy and accurate arrival" in the American capital, the foreign ministry ordered the central telegraph office to send the fourteenth part, and the instruction concerning the time of delivery, via RCA *and* Mackay, both American companies. Thus, except for the long delay of fifteen hours between the transmission of parts 13 and 14, it would appear that the foreign office took every precaution to ensure that the final note could be delivered at the time specified. Even the fifteen-hour delay indicated nothing more than a hypersensitivity to security. Insofar as the note said anything that might be regarded as revealing Japan's next move, it did so only in part 14. The fifteen-hour delay was tied to that single fact, and not to any clandestine intention to cause a late delivery by postponing 'the transmission of the concluding part of the note. The necessity of maintaining secrecy had been stressed in a supplementary instruction which cautioned Nomura against using "typists" or other persons who might be security risks.[29] This naturally put the burden of typing and processing Japan's final note on top-clearance personnel, who would generally be poorly qualified for the job. But whatever delay this might have entailed could have been minimized by strict adherence, on the part of the embassy, to the foreign minister's "pilot message." That pertinent cable had warned that the transmission of the component parts of the final note might be spaced over at least twelve hours. It had also ordered the ambassador in Washington to make all necessary arrangements, beforehand, so that he would be able to present the note *at any time* following the arrival of instructions from the foreign minister. Why, then, did the delivery of Japan's final note take place a full hour after the attack on Pearl Harbor?

The answer lies partly in Tokyo and partly in Washington. There can be no doubt that the supreme command, especially the naval general staff, was determined to cut to the minimum the time between the delivery and the attack. This intention was facilitated by the absence of any accepted international standard or requirement in that regard, and

---

6:30 p.m. See Kameyama aff., S 253:2-4, T 26189-204; Tōgō aff., S 337:10, T 35721-23 and 35725-27; Hattori, I, 239-40; and *PHA*, Part 12, "Magic" intercepts of Cables No. 902 and 907, 239-45 and 248; and Prosecution Exh. No. 1218, S 111:15 (the Japanese text of Cable No. 907), T 10537. Two technical errors, made during the transmission of Cable No. 902, were subsequently corrected.

"Magic" intercept records actually show somewhat earlier times throughout. See Defense Exh. No. 2968, T 26229-30, S 253:8.

[29] Cable No. 904, dispatched from the foreign office at 11:00 p.m., December 6, Tōkyō: S 111:15, T 10536-37, and *PHA*, Part 12, "Magic" intercept of same, 245. Evidence to be cited hereinafter suggests that this message arrived in Washington *at least* twenty-four hours in advance of the 1:00 p.m. delivery time specified in the late afternoon of the next day.

by the foreign minister's willingness to consent to the proposals of the supreme command without a full exploration of the facts upon which the giving or withholding of his consent should have hinged. Togo's blind acceptance of Admiral Ito's December 5 correction of an earlier miscalculation of the "appropriate" time of delivery simply meant, in practical terms, that the handing over of the note at 1:00 p.m. would precede the strike against Pearl Harbor by about twenty minutes— twenty-five at the most.[30] If a mishap occurred at any point in the line of communication which began in the first section of the American bureau of the foreign ministry in Tokyo and ended in Secretary Hull's office in Washington, the result could very easily be a note delivered *after* the attack was under way. That such a mishap did indeed occur, without premeditation, and that it took place within the Japanese embassy in Washington, is now almost beyond question. At least, the circumstantial evidence is such that a reasonable basis exists for a judgment against the cloak-and-dagger interpretation presented by the prosecution at the Tokyo trial: that the late delivery was the outcome of a conspiracy formed by Japan's top leaders for that very purpose.

What actually happened can best be described by the word "snafu"— American army slang for any situation "snarled or stalled in confusion." A "snafu" in the Japanese embassy in Washington during the twenty-four hours from noon of December 6 through noon of December 7 logically explains one of the costliest mistakes ever committed by the Japanese government or its agents.[31]

The foreign minister's pilot message, announcing that Japan's reply to the Hull note of November 26 would soon be dispatched and or-

---

[30] It will be helpful to remember that, *in December 1941*, the time situation was as follows: when the attack on Pearl Harbor began on Sunday, December 7, at approximately 7:50 a.m., it was 1:20 p.m. in Washington D.C. (5½ hours later than Hawaii) and 3:20 a.m., *December 8*, in Tōkyō (14 hours later than Washington; 19½ hours later than Hawaii). See Prosecution Exh. 1222, T 10543-51, S 111:16-18, and Morison, 92, n. 19.

The order to attack was given at 7:49 a.m., Hawaii time. Most accounts use 7:50 a.m. to designate the beginning of the strike. As nearly as can be determined, the first bomb hit at 7:55.

[31] Except as separately noted, the reconstruction which follows in the text is based on Yūki aff. and related material, S 253:5-9, T 26207-32; Yamamoto aff., S 252:7, T 26117, and S 252:8-11, T 26124-44; Tōgō aff., S 337:10, T 35725-27; Kameyama aff., S 253:3-4, T 26195-201; Kurusu, 184-85; JRD, "Nomura Diary," entry for December 7, 1941; Nomura, 29; JRD Monograph No. 150, Appendix 6; and Murata, "'Treachery' of Pearl Harbor," *U. S. Naval Institute Proceedings*, LXXXII, No. 8 (August 1956), 904-6.

The confusion over the signal to attack Pearl Harbor, as described by Walter Lord in his *Day of Infamy*, 50-51, the reporting of success two minutes *before* the first bomb fell (p. 67), and the misadventures of Ensign Sakamaki (as indexed in Lord) invite comparison with the present account of what went on inside the Japanese embassy in Washington on December 6 and 7.

dering that all preparations be made to carry out prompt delivery on receipt of instructions in that regard, was delivered to the embassy during the morning of Saturday, December 6. Immediate processing produced a deciphered text by noon. By early evening the first eight or nine parts of the final note itself (Cable No. 902), which had been dispatched *in English,* had been received and deciphered.[32] But then the decoding process was gratuitously interrupted while the entire staff of the embassy's cable section attended a farewell dinner-party given for a friend who had received orders transferring him to another post.

The records are silent on the amount of *sake* required to launch the departing member on his way in proper style. Knowing that there was still work to be done on the in-coming note, the cryptographers concerned may have exercised appropriate restraint. At least their story later was that they returned to the embassy on Massachusetts Avenue about 9:30 Saturday evening, and at once resumed their decoding work, finishing the first thirteen parts of Cable No. 902 before midnight. While they awaited the arrival of the concluding segment, they busied themselves in disposing of the remnants of the coding machine which they had destroyed on December 5 (more than forty-eight hours after they had received instructions from Tokyo ordering the *immediate and complete* demolition of the apparatus). The night wore on and still part 14 of Cable No. 902 did not arrive. Finally, about dawn on Sunday, December 7, acting on the advice of the counselor of embassy, all the members of the cable section, except for a single duty-officer, left the premises to return to their respective lodgings. At approximately the time they were comfortably settled in bed (between 7:00 and 8:00 a.m.), a batch of several cables suddenly arrived at the embassy. Among them was the missing portion of Cable No. 902—part 14—purposely delayed by Tokyo so as to maintain maximum security as long as possible. In the forwarding instructions to the Mackay and RCA organizations, which had handled this message, appeared the plain, unencoded English phrase, "VERY IMPORTANT."

The duty-officer who had been left behind in the cable section quickly got on the telephone to summon his colleagues back to work, but it was not until sometime between 9:30 and 10:00 a.m. that the cable section was again fully staffed.

[32] The fact that Japan's final note was sent in English rather demolishes a charge made outside the courtroom by General Ryūkichi Tanaka (a leading witness for the prosecution) to the effect that General Mutō, the chief of the military affairs bureau, engineered the late delivery by the simple means of ordering the military attaché in Washington to cause delays in the *translation* of the note (Tanaka, "I Know Everything About Them," 9). The role of Tanaka is discussed in Chapter 15.

By that late hour on Sunday morning, December 7, the import of the situation had finally begun to make an impression. Despite the foreign minister's pilot message, which had been received some twenty-four hours earlier, apparently not a single word of Japan's final note had been typed the night before. This extraordinary fact will perhaps always remain something of a conundrum. The usual procedure was for the cable section to handle the deciphering and for the typing pool to produce clean copies. For security reasons, however, the foreign ministry had specified that no regular typists (low-clearance personnel) were to be used in the preparation of the Japanese note. In the light of the earlier pilot message, this instruction, which had arrived in Washington on Saturday, should have resulted in the immediate typing of clean copies of the various parts of the fourteen-part message *as each was received and decoded*. That was clearly the only way to offset the disadvantage of using maximum-clearance personnel who were not familiar with the operation of an English-language typewriter. But nothing of the kind was done—perhaps because the elimination of regular typists, being an unusual departure from routine, created an extraordinary malfunctioning within the embassy that was not set right until it was practically too late. Thus, it was Sunday morning before anyone began copying the verbose note with which Japan proposed (in eleven double-spaced, typewritten pages) to twist and turn, in the language of diplomacy, toward the denouement of war.

The man who took on the task of preparing a clean copy of the note for subsequent delivery to the State Department was fated to endure a miserable five hours. His name was Okumura, and his rank was "secretary"—diplomatic, not stenographic. He was the only embassy officer with adequate security clearance who was more or less capable of operating a typewriter. Even before the cable section personnel returned to the scene Sunday morning, Okumura was earnestly hunched over an embassy machine in an all-out, do-or-die effort to type up the thirteen accumulated parts of the note. While he pecked along as best he could, proofreading was begun in an adjoining room. Concern gradually mounted as the decoding of the other cables that had arrived at the embassy earlier that morning clarified the nature of the activity in which all were by then desperately engaged. Aside from part 14 of No. 902, the most significant cable was one bearing the number "907" and the designation "Extremely Urgent, Very Important" (*Dai-shikyū, Goku-jūyō*): the instruction to deliver Japan's final note to the United States government, preferably to Secretary of State Hull personally, at one o'clock that afternoon. Also received were two "Urgent" messages and another marked "Extremely Urgent." The former were in the nature of "greetings"—in this case from the foreign minister and the chief of the American bureau to Ambassadors Nomura and Kurusu and their respective staffs—a kind of signing-off with an appreciative telegraphic pat on the back for the now vain efforts which the embassy had made to secure a diplomatic settlement. The "Extremely Urgent" cable provided the final, fitting touch by ordering the immediate destruction of the only remaining cipher machine, all machine codes, and all secret documents.[33]

As of mid-morning on December 7, when the processing of these cables was in progress, Ambassador Nomura had not as yet read the entire text of the note he was to deliver at one o'clock. When the deciphered instruction in that regard was handed to him sometime between 10:30 and 11:00 a.m., he took immediate steps to secure an appointment with the Secretary of State at the specified hour. This was a "very unusual request" for an ambassador to make, as was duly noted by the chief of intelligence of the U.S. Army, who was among those kept fully informed by "Magic" of the contents of the cables being decoded at the Japanese embassy. Such was the efficiency of this World War II version of the earlier "Black Chamber" that the President and other top-level personnel in the Administration were actually able to read these cables before Ambassador Nomura ever saw them, and in some cases before they had even been deciphered by the cable section in the Japanese embassy—an outstanding cryptographic-intelligence achievement.[34]

Despite Secretary Okumura's best efforts, it was not until approximately 11:00 a.m. that he finally managed to produce a typewritten copy of the first thirteen parts of the note from Tokyo. The fourteenth part, although received at least three hours earlier, had either not been

---

[33] The original Japanese text of Cable No. 907 is given in S 111:15, T 10536-37. The "Magic" intercept versions of Cables No. 907-10 (described above) can be found in *PHA*, Part 12, 248-49.

The embassy apparently only narrowly escaped an even more embarrassing and incriminating position during the last twenty-four hours before Pearl Harbor than that being described in the text. Had Nomura's staff acted upon their original understanding of the first code-destruction message (December 2), they would have destroyed their entire complement of two cipher machines. The embassy would thus have been without any mechanical means of decoding Japan's final note. Fortunately, the matter was set straight by Tōkyō's urgent reply of clarification to a cable of inquiry sent by the embassy. See Cables No. 867, 1268, and 897 as intercepted by "Magic," *PHA*, Part 12, 215 and 236-37.

[34] For information relating to American knowledge of the contents of these cables, see Defense Exh. Nos. 2968 and 2969, T 26229-32, S 253:8-9, and Bratton aff. and related submissions, T 26233-67, S 253:9-14, and T 26274-84, S 253:15-16. See also Feis, 336-41.

decoded or was still lying around in the cable section awaiting delivery to the "typist." At any rate, it had not reached Okumura by the time he had completed the thirteenth part. As he looked at his handiwork, he decided that it was much too poorly done to serve as an official document to be handed to the Secretary of State. Saying that he had only intended the sheets as a rough draft, and that there was still enough time to redo the whole thing, Okumura turned back to his typewriter and started all over again from the very beginning, being assisted now by a junior interpreter.

Despite the efforts these two men made, nothing could alter the fact that neither of them was a professional typist. As the minutes ticked by, the strain and pressure increased. The result was that they became even slower at their work than they might otherwise have been, and their typing errors grew in number. Then, to make matters worse, the cable section passed along two messages ordering corrections in the text of the note. The first necessitated the retyping of a page only recently completed with much trouble; the second required that two additional pages be redone, one because a sentence had been dropped in transmission and the other because the insertion of that sentence threw the remainder out of kilter. The "typists" thus found it necessary to recopy the succeeding page in order to come out even. What had seemed entirely possible at eleven that morning became more and more unlikely as the hands of the clock glided toward the deadline. It was approximately 12:30 p.m. when the fourteenth part of the note was finally delivered to Okumura and his helper, but it might as well have been a half hour or even an hour later. They were nowhere near finishing the first thirteen parts.[35]

Ambassador Nomura, who could no longer contain himself, kept poking his head in at the door to urge the two men on and to inquire after their progress. When it became apparent that the ambassador and Mr. Kurusu would be unable to keep their appointment with Hull, the State Department was informed that the work on the document

[35] The day, and perhaps the honor of Japan, might yet have been saved if only someone had grabbed Okumura's first draft, no matter how messy its appearance, and had ordered the harassed gentleman and his assistant to start on part 14 immediately. Hull later wrote (II, 1097): "Nomura's last meeting with me was in keeping with the ineptitude that had marked his handling of the discussions from the beginning. His government's intention, in instructing him to ask for the meeting at one o'clock, had been to give us their note a few minutes in advance of the attack at Pearl Harbor. Nomura's Embassy had bungled this by its delay in decoding. Nevertheless, knowing the importance of a deadline set for a specific hour, Nomura should have come to see me precisely at one o'clock, even though he had in his hand only the first few lines of his note, leaving instructions with the Embassy to bring him the remainder as it became ready."

the envoys wished to deliver was not yet completed and that, as a consequence, they might be delayed. The embassy was told in reply that the Secretary of State would receive Ambassador Nomura and Mr. Kurusu whenever they were ready. More than an hour later, at approximately 1:50 p.m., Okumura and his assistant finally reached the end of their typing marathon. The text of the note was immediately handed to Nomura and Kurusu who were poised for departure in the foyer of the embassy. They reached the State Department at two o'clock but were kept waiting by Mr. Hull. Thus, it was 2:20 p.m. before they were finally ushered into the Secretary's office. At that very moment the attack upon Pearl Harbor was already an hour old, the toll of dead and wounded was mounting, and the American navy—stunned and shocked, but also intensely angry and combative in its collective reaction—was beginning to turn its thoughts to the long road back.

Had Nomura and Kurusu arrived as originally scheduled, they would have been able to deliver their message some twenty minutes before the first bomb was dropped on Pearl Harbor. It would have taken Secretary Hull at least half that time to read through the fourteen-part note.[36] He would then have had five or ten minutes in which to act upon what he had read—in sum, upon the last two sentences, the only passage providing a basis for a predictive judgment:

. . . the earnest hope of the Japanese Government to adjust Japanese-American relations and to preserve and promote the peace of the Pacific through cooperation with the American Government has finally been lost.

The Japanese Government regrets to have to notify hereby the American Government that in view of the attitude of the American Government it cannot but consider that it is impossible to reach an agreement through further negotiations.[37]

Even if Hull had concluded that those two sentences implied an imminent resort to force on Japan's part, he would not have had time to translate that conclusion into meaningful action. Thus, even without the embassy's mismanagement, Japan's final note would have

[36] A slow or thoughtful reader might have required a full twenty minutes (as estimated by Feis, 332). Feis also notes (p. 341) that 2:20 p.m. was "about two and a half hours after the [Japanese] landing at Kota Bharu (British Malaya). . . ." In other words, even a prompt one o'clock delivery would have meant handing over the note more than one hour after the commencement of a surprise attack against Great Britain, without either an ultimatum or a declaration of war. Since the United States was representing Britain in the Hull-Nomura conversations, Japan thus violated Hague Convention III in relation to Britain even before the commencement of hostilities against the United States. For Tōgō's views, see his affidavit, S 337:11, T 35731-32.

[37] See footnote 20 above.

preceded the attack by so small a margin of time as to render it in-
conceivable that any warning could have reached American or Allied outposts in the Pacific until well after the fact. That was precisely what the supreme command had intended. When Admiral Ito
was later asked by Foreign Minister Togo why the naval general
staff had originally been opposed to a final note if the navy meant
all along to attack so soon after its delivery, the vice-chief avoided
giving a clear-cut reply. He would only say that he was sorry that matters had worked out as they had, owing to an "excess of caution" on the
part of the service he represented![38]

When Togo subsequently also discussed the issue with Premier
Tojo, the latter was inclined to suspect that American authorities
had held up the delivery in order to put Japan in a bad light.[39] By
the time the war had ended, however, the reports obtained from
repatriated embassy personnel and other evidence had disabused the
premier of that convenient supposition. The prosecution, on the
other hand, was not so easily dissuaded from its belief that the entire
event had been planned in Tokyo with malice aforethought. During
its pre-trial interrogations of Tojo at Sugamo Prison, the prosecution
returned repeatedly to the subject. Tojo's answers were as revealing
as they were typical:

Q. What information had the Emperor been given about the time of the
delivery of Nomura's final note?
A. I presume the Foreign Minister told him. I did not inform him. I can't
say definitely about that matter. It was the Foreign Minister's responsibility. If you ask him, he will be able to tell you. . . . The responsibility
was delegated. . . . The person who could say whether the Emperor was
informed or not is the Foreign Minister. I cannot say. I would like to
explain a little about the situation at that time. There was a tremendous
lot to be done and it was necessary to rely upon people who had been
charged with responsibility. . . .
Q. Didn't all the information you received [after the outbreak of the war]
indicate that the final note was delivered late?
A. I did get the impression from the majority of the reports that the notification had been late.
Q. Did you then inform or discuss that matter with the Emperor?
A. No, for this reason. The reports that came in were all uncertain. I should
regard the report of an Ambassador, for example, as certain, but this

---

[38] Tōgō aff., S 337:10. ". . . Itō jichō wa meitō wo sake, amari ni nen wo ire-sugita no
de dōmo mōshiwake arimasen to itte [ʔayamatta]."
[39] See Tōgō aff., S 337:10, T 35726-27.

information was not of that character and, since it was uncertain, and particularly since the Emperor also received similar intelligence, I did not report it to him. The basis of a report to the Emperor must be something definite and factual. . . .

. . . .

Q. You and the cabinet realized, did you not, that the shorter the notice given the United States, the more probability there was of a mishap?

A. It can be said so theoretically.

Q. Did you and the cabinet not recognize that as a practical possibility?

A. Yes, from the practical point of view, it is also true that the shorter the time allowed, the more chance of a hitch, but it is not enough to leave it at that. Ambassador Nomura was a very responsible official and we relied upon his carrying out so grave a responsibility perfectly. Also, the the Foreign Office had time to study and perfect all phases of the procedure in the light of its great responsibility. . . .

. . . .

Q. Togo states that a few days after the attack on Pearl Harbor he informed the Emperor that the attack had taken place before the delivery of the final note, that the Emperor stated that he had heard the same thing and was very angry about it. Togo states that he informed you of these facts. Is that not true?

A. I don't remember whether he informed me of this or not, but I believe it is true that the Emperor was angry. It would be very like the Emperor.

Q. What investigation did you make or facts did you learn as to why the Emperor's wishes had not been respected?

A. We respected the Emperor's wishes. The Japanese people did and I, as Prime Minister, certainly did. I can make no excuse for the fact that the results were just the opposite.

Q. Did you learn from Togo, Nomura or Kurusu, or anyone else, why it was that the note was not delivered prior to the attack?

A. I have heard that there were technical reasons that delayed the delivery of the note, including garbles in the coded text. I am deeply conscious of my responsibility for the delay in the message. Nevertheless, for the Foreign Office, at a time like this and on a matter of this moment, to be unable to carry out an order of the government, shows an extreme degree of irresponsibility.

Q. Is it not possible that the Chiefs of Staff are at fault in this matter for having planned the attack too close to the time of delivery of the note and thus making it possible that the Emperor's wishes would not be followed?

A. No, it is my fault, not theirs, because I was the senior member of the Liaison Conference.

Q. Who was it suggested that this matter be delegated to the Chiefs of Staff and Togo?

A. It was my judgment, which was also the judgment of everyone, and the responsibility for it is mine also. We had absolutely no idea of not respecting the Emperor's wishes and truly I feel deeply my sense of responsibility at the turn things took. . . .

. . . .

Q. Do you not agree that the attack made under such circumstances was nothing but murder and not warfare?

A. No, I don't agree. I think it was legal defense in the face of challenge.

Q. Do you, as a Japanese, feel proud of the fact that several thousand Americans were killed at Pearl Harbor in this manner?

A. No, I am not proud of it. . . . I sympathize with those who died, but Japan had been challenged . . . and so she took justifiable self-defense. . . .[40]

For Tojo personally, and later for many other Japanese, this thought became the ultimate rationale—the only possible means of justifying the timing of their attack on Pearl Harbor. If the late delivery of Japan's final note had been the only evidence of apparent connivance and duplicity on the part of her leaders, the American government might more readily have believed—despite a record which did not inspire confidence—that only an honest mistake had been committed after all. But if the Nomura-Kurusu failure to arrive at the State Department at the appointed hour on December 7 produced a charge of bad faith and trickery, what occurred in Tokyo that same day sealed the judgment against Japan in most minds.

As the clouds of war had slowly gathered on the horizons of the Pacific, various individuals—Japanese and American—had independently sought some means of clearing the atmosphere of the storm with which their nations were threatened. Among the thoughts which had come to mind, at least as early as mid-October, had been the beneficial effect that might result from an exchange of messages between the President and the Emperor. For one reason or another which seemed valid at the time, nothing was done until the crisis of early December caused a reconsideration of this idea. The result was a sudden decision within the American government to take the initiative, despite the fact that there was little hope in Washington that such a move would stay Japan's hand.[41] A draft letter which had been under study at the State

[40] A selection from pertinent material in the following (in the order quoted): Tōjō interrog., Feb. 20, 4-7, Feb. 21, 2-3, Mar. 18, 1-6 (as corrected, S 344:4, T 36391), and Feb. 19, 6-9. See also Mar. 26, 3-4.

[41] For information relating to the origin of the idea of having the President communicate directly with the Emperor (a move which it was feared, at one time, might be interpreted as interference in Japan's internal affairs), and the final decision in that

Department was superseded by one prepared at the White House. Presidential approval was given in a short memorandum personally written by Mr. Roosevelt: "Dear Cordell [,] Shoot this to Grew—I think can go in gray code—saves time—I don't mind if it gets picked up [.] FDR."[42] Since the gray code was the least secret of those employed at the time, the President's instruction was clearly based on the belief that speed in processing was more important than security in transmission. The object was to get the letter to the Emperor as quickly as possible. It was a case of "grabbing at straws to save the peace" at a time when the known fact that a Japanese armada was sailing westward across the South China Sea implied that the *status quo* of the Far East might collapse at any moment.[43] Because of a feeling that time was running out, and in order to enhance the chances of the message reaching its destination without being sidetracked by officious or hostile elements in Tokyo, the State Department announced to the press, on the evening of Saturday, December 6, that a presidential message was being sent to the Emperor of Japan.[44] At 8:00 p.m., within twenty minutes after that announcement, a triple-priority cable was hurriedly dispatched by

---

regard, see *PHA*, Part 2, 553, Part 11, 5372-74, 5384-86, and Part 20, 4016; Terasaki, *Bridge to the Sun*, 65-69; Kurusu, 157-60, 175-76; Konoe, 141-42; Moore, 269-70; *Foreign Relations (Diplomatic Papers: 1941)*, IV, 671; Feis, 323 and 334-37; and Langer and Gleason, *The Undeclared War*, 730-31.

In cabling a copy of the presidential message to the Emperor to the American ambassador in China for communication to Chiang Kai-shek, Hull instructed the ambassador to inform the Generalissimo that "this message, as the situation now stands, would seem to represent very nearly the last diplomatic move that this Government can make toward causing Japan to desist from its present course; that if the slender chance of acceptance by Japan should materialize, a very effective measure would have been taken toward safeguarding the Burma Road; and that it is very much hoped that Chiang Kai-shek will not make or allow to be spread in Chinese Government circles adverse comment." *Foreign Relations (Diplomatic Papers: 1941)*, IV, 727 (Cable No. 286, dispatched December 6, 1941, 9:00 p.m., Washington).

[42] As copied from a photostat of the original in the President's handwriting. Also, *Foreign Relations (Japan: 1931-1941)*, II, 784, and *Foreign Relations (Diplomatic Papers: 1941)*, IV, 723, n. 71 (note the variations); Grew testimony in *PHA*, Part 2, 692; Ballantine aff., T 10824, S 114:4; and Parks intv.

[43] The phrase in quotes is from Secretary Hull's testimony in *PHA*, Part 11, 5374. On the reports Washington received regarding the Japanese armada, which consisted of two large fleets of cruisers, destroyers, and transports rounding the southern tip of French Indo-China, see Feis, 337, especially footnote 10.

[44] See *NYT*, December 7, 1941, 1. The announcement ". . . gave no details as to the character of the message." For the text of the President's message (including the preliminary and the final drafts), see *Foreign Relations (Japan: 1931-1941)*, II, 784-86, and *Foreign Relations (Diplomatic Papers: 1941)*, IV, 721-26. (Note especially the deletion on p. 724 with respect to Japan's occupation of southern French Indo-China. This helps explain why Tōjō and other Japanese later argued that the President had admitted, in his message to the Emperor, that the Japanese were entirely justified in being in French Indo-China. See, for example, Tōjō aff., S 343:1-2, T 36197-205, and cross-examination, S 347:12, T 36712-13.)

Secretary Hull to alert Ambassador Grew: "An important telegram is now being encoded to you containing for communication by you at earliest possible moment text of message from the President to the Emperor."[45] Since Tokyo was fourteen hours later than Washington, Hull's cable left the State Department at a time equivalent to 10:00 a.m., Sunday, December 7, in the Japanese capital.

At almost exactly that hour the chief of the first section of the American bureau of the foreign office received word from the Domei News agency that a presidential message, addressed to the Emperor, was reported to be on its way to Japan. The section chief, Mr. Kase, promptly conveyed this information to his superiors, including Foreign Minister Togo. Kase also telephoned the news to the lord privy seal's chief aide and requested him to advise the foreign office immediately in the event that the President's message arrived at the palace. Mr. Kase did this, he later said, because he and others at the foreign office remembered that at the time of the *Panay* incident in December 1937, Mr. Roosevelt's message to His Majesty had been sent directly rather than through the usual diplomatic channels.[46]

In order to determine the facts pertaining to what was clearly an unexpected development, as yet unconfirmed by any reliable source, the authorities at the foreign office quickly dispatched an urgent cable to the embassy in Washington requesting an immediate report. This cable crossed en route a brief dispatch sent on Ambassador Nomura's own initiative. Nomura revealed that his embassy did not know the contents of the President's message. The assumption was that it concerned the

[45] Cable No. 817 (sent in "confidential code"), *Foreign Relations* (*Diplomatic Papers: 1941*), IV, 727.

[46] American records do not contain any mention of a presidential message to the Emperor at the time of the *Panay* incident (Parks corresp. citing pertinent State Department publications). Kase, Nomura, and other Japanese, however, seem to have been under the impression that the Emperor was the intended recipient of the American protest at the time in question. Terasaki, 67-69, reports, for example, that the Reverend Dr. E. Stanley Jones, representing certain members of the Japanese embassy, advised Mr. Roosevelt on December 3, 1941, against following the same procedure as in 1937: " 'The Japanese tell me,' Jones said, 'that you must not send the cable as you sent the other cable to the Emperor over the sinking of the *Panay*. They tell me that the reason you got no reply from the Emperor was that it never got to him, but was held up in their Foreign Office. This time, they tell me, you must not send it through the Foreign Office, but direct to the Emperor himself. I don't know the mechanics of it, but that's what they suggest.'

"Mr. Roosevelt said, 'Well, I'm just thinking out loud. I can't go down to the cable office and say I want to send a cable from the President of the United States to the Emperor of Japan, but I could send it to Grew, for Grew as an ambassador has the right of audience to the head of a state and he can give it to the Emperor direct, and if I do not hear within twenty-four hours—I have learned to do some things—I'll give it to the newspapers and force a reply!' "

reinforcement of Japanese troops in French Indo-China and a Japanese advance against Thailand, matters to which reference had been made in separate State Department releases. According to Nomura, the sending of the presidential message directly rather than via diplomatic channels—i.e., through the Japanese embassy in Washington—might be construed as having resulted from the way in which the Japanese government had handled a similar personal message at the time of the *Panay* affair.[47] This interpretation by the ambassador, which ignored the possibility that the President's message might be sent through Ambassador Grew, served to confirm the foreign ministry's earlier and equally limited supposition that within a few hours, at the most, Japan's equivalent of Western Union would be bicycling up to the palace gates to deliver F.D.R.'s cable at the imperial household ministry.

Thanks to Nomura's confirmation that such a cable had been sent, however, Kase ordered all the members of his section to stand by for the important work of translation and processing which he expected would descend upon them once the message arrived. But the day passed, and nothing happened. Apparently no effort was made to get in touch with the central telegraph office, the ministry of communications, or the American embassy—any one of which might conceivably have been able to shed some light on the matter. The minds of all concerned at the foreign office were riveted to the idea that the cable, when it finally appeared, would bear some such forwarding address as "His Imperial Majesty, The Emperor of Japan; The Palace; Tokyo." At any rate, that is the impression created by Japanese accounts.

About 8:00 or 8:30 Sunday evening, after some ten hours of fruitless waiting, Section Chief Kase decided to get in touch once again with the lord privy seal's aide to make sure that there had not been a slip-up. A phone call to the private residence of the official in question netted a still negative reply—the board of chamberlains and the duty officer at the imperial household ministry reported that no message had as yet arrived at the palace.[48]

Meanwhile, at the nearby American embassy, Ambassador Grew was

---

[47] See the preceding footnote.

[48] See Kase aff. and related submissions, S 252:14-15, T 26166-70; Kase cross-examination, S 252:15-16, T 26175-79; and Yasumasa Matsudaira aff., S 252:16, T 26179-81. The foreign office cable of inquiry to Nomura was No. 905; the dispatch he sent on his own initiative was No. 1275, which arrived in Tōkyō Sunday afternoon. It is interesting to note that even a personal message delivered directly to the palace would not have reached the Emperor until after processing within the foreign office.

Marquis Yasumasa Matsudaira, private secretary and aide to the lord privy seal, should not be confused with Mr. Tsuneo Matsudaira, the imperial household minister.

tuning in on a daily news broadcast beamed to the Far East by a radio station in San Francisco. He was surprised to hear the announcer report that a presidential message had been sent to the Emperor. Nothing was said about the contents of the message or "the channel of transmission." Since he could only surmise that he might become personally involved, Mr. Grew also decided to wait and see. He had found that "as a rule, the Japanese were expeditious in getting the telegrams through." About 9:00 p.m., Secretary Hull's alert duly arrived at the embassy, followed an hour and a half later by the President's message. It was only then that a sinister picture of foul play began taking shape in the mind of the ambassador.[49]

The President's triple-priority message, which had required roughly an hour of processing within the State Department, had left Washington at 9:00 p.m., Saturday, December 6, which was 11:00 a.m., Sunday, December 7, in Tokyo. It bore on its face a Japanese stamp reading "12 noon," indicating that it had arrived in Tokyo in very good time, but that it had since been gathering dust, somewhere or other, for *ten and one-half hours.* Mr. Grew's subsequent guess was that the contents of the message had been deciphered by Japanese cryptographers and that the "military authorities" had intervened in order to keep the message from reaching the Emperor until they gave the word.

On the evening in question, however, there was little time for such speculation. As the decoding of the President's message got under way, the counselor of embassy phoned the foreign minister's secretary to arrange for a midnight appointment. The secretary asked whether the ambassador's visit could not be deferred until the following morning. In view of the late hour, the foreign minister desired to retire for the night as soon as possible. When it was explained that the request for an interview was prompted by a matter of "extreme importance and urgency," the secretary readily consented to make the necessary arrangements. As a consequence, Ambassador Grew later drove to the foreign minister's official residence and there presented the President's message. It was then approximately 12:15 a.m., Monday, December 8. Grew first read the document aloud to Togo and afterwards handed him the English text. The ambassador also requested an audience with the Emperor. He did so partly to impress upon the foreign minister the importance of the matter in hand and partly to ensure, thereby, that the message would reach its intended recipient even if an audience proved impossible. The Emperor did not often have occasion to consort

[49] See the Grew references in footnote 58 below.

with ambassadors and a middle-of-the-night tête-à-tête would have been unprecedented. The foreign minister was thus reluctant to commit himself, but upon being pressed Togo promised to present the ambassador's request to the throne. Mr. Grew then departed, feeling that even if he were not received in audience, the communication he had brought would at least reach the Emperor that night. Hull's instructions had left the precise method of communication to Grew's discretion. The ambassador was to act "at the earliest possible moment" and in such a manner as he deemed "most appropriate."[50]

As soon as Grew had gone, Togo handed the President's message to Section Chief Kase, who had been present as interpreter, and instructed him to have it translated into Japanese immediately. Togo then telephoned the imperial household minister to consult him concerning Grew's request for an audience at such a late hour. Upon being informed that the ambassador wished to present a letter from the President, the household minister advised Togo to get in touch with the lord privy seal—the matter being political in nature, and not ceremonial. When Marquis Kido was briefed over the telephone, he in turn suggested that the Emperor would receive the foreign minister, despite the hour, but that Togo should first confer with Premier Tojo.

The time required for these phone calls was unimportant in comparison with that needed to prepare a Japanese translation of the President's message. Although there is some confusion on the point, it would appear that at least an hour was spent at that task. It was thus close to 2:00 a.m. before Togo finally called on Tojo to apprise him of the contents of the message and to confer on its significance. The premier immediately asked whether the communication contained any concessions with respect to the position taken by the United States to date. When Togo replied in the negative, Tojo said, "Well, then, nothing can be done, can it?"[51] Although he approved having the foreign minister report immediately to the throne, Tojo apparently also

[50] Cable No. 818 (sent in "confidential code"): "Please communicate at the earliest possible moment in such manner as you deem most appropriate a message to the Emperor from the President reading as follows. . . ." The text can be found in *Foreign Relations (Japan: 1931-1941)*, II, 784-86, and *Foreign Relations (Diplomatic Papers: 1941)*, IV, 723-25.

[51] As told by Tōgō (S 339:1): "Soko de Tōjō wa sore ja shikatta ga nai ja nai ka . . . to yū koto wo mōshimashita." A somewhat tantalizing question is raised by a draft message prepared within the State Department by the division of Far Eastern affairs. If that message had been sent, instead of being superseded by one drafted in the White House, would Tōgō have replied negatively to Tōjō's question . . . ? For the texts of the two messages, see *Foreign Relations (Diplomatic Papers: 1941)*, IV, 721-26.

remarked that the planes from the navy's task force had probably already taken off from their carriers.[52]

The scene which followed at the palace remains somewhat obscure, owing to the claims and counterclaims of the principals—Togo and Kido—both of whom arrived somewhat prior to 3:00 a.m. The two men conferred briefly before Togo was received alone by the Emperor, but how much the foreign minister told the lord privy seal about the President's message remains at issue between them. They did not meet again after the audience, nor was Kido called into the Emperor's presence.[53] The one certainty is that Foreign Minister Togo saw the Emperor at approximately 3:00 a.m., Monday, December 8—the very hour, by Washington time, at which Nomura and Kurusu were supposed to hand over Japan's final note. The planes of the navy's task force were indeed streaking toward their target, for it was then 7:30 a.m., Sunday, in Hawaii. Some twenty minutes later, as Togo was leaving the palace to return to his official residence, the planes received a prearranged telegraphic signal, "*To, to, to . . . ,*" and the attack began.[54] In retrospect it seems appropriate to note, although perhaps it was only coincidental, that the Emperor appeared before the foreign minister in naval uniform.[55]

The final act of this diplomatic drama of December 1941 was soon played out behind closed doors at the foreign minister's residence. About 4:00 o'clock in the morning, Mr. Togo was informed that the imperial navy had successfully attacked the United States territory of Hawaii. The channel of communication was a direct telephone line from the office of the chief of the naval affairs bureau.[56] As a conse-

[52] Since Tōgō has denied having any prior knowledge of the navy's plans to attack Pearl Harbor (a denial supported by Tōjō in other testimony), the premier's remark presumably could only have alerted the foreign minister to the fact that hostilities would soon be launched by planes from a naval task force—the place(s) of attack still remaining a secret.

[53] Kido testified that he was in his office, but when Tōgō did not come by after the audience, he went home. Tōgō testified that when he did not see Kido in the waiting room after the audience, he asked a chamberlain about the lord privy seal's whereabouts; when the chamberlain replied that Kido did not appear to be in his room, Tōgō decided to return to his official residence.

[54] The signal, which came from Vice-Admiral Nagumo, stood for "Zengun totsugeki seyo!" ("All forces, strike!"). Hattori, I, 362-63.

[55] At the time in question the Emperor generally wore a uniform (army or navy), because Japan was on a war footing as a result of the China Incident.

[56] There was also a direct line between the foreign office and the military affairs bureau. When asked about the matter, one officer explained that the need for such lines had arisen following the Manchurian Incident of 1931: "Without constant consultation with the military, the foreign office could not conduct diplomacy." Ordinary lines were always busy; they also presented a "security" problem.

quence, the foreign minister gave instructions to Mr. Kase to summon the American and British ambassadors for separate interviews. Because Kase had trouble getting through to the American embassy on the telephone, it was close to 7:30 a.m. before Ambassador Grew arrived at Togo's residence. The foreign minister "entered the reception room almost immediately." He was wearing formal dress and "his manner was equally formal and grim." Since Grew had previously found Togo "habitually somewhat sphinx-like," the ambassador "received no impression of unusual developments." But then Togo "slapped a document on the table, clearly a gesture of finality," and began delivering an oral statement in Japanese which was immediately interpreted into English by Mr. Kase (and later sent to the ambassador in writing):

His Majesty has expressed his gratefulness and appreciation for the cordial message of the President. He has graciously let known his wishes to the Foreign Minister to convey the following to the President as a reply to the latter's message.

"Some days ago, the President made inquiries regarding the circumstances of the augmentation of Japanese forces in French Indochina to which His Majesty has directed the Government to reply. Withdrawal of Japanese forces from French Indochina constitutes one of the subject matters of the Japanese-American negotiations. His Majesty has commanded the Government to state its views to the American Government also on this question. It is, therefore, desired that the President will kindly refer to this reply.

"Establishment of peace in the Pacific and consequently of the world has been the cherished desire of His Majesty for the realization of which He has hitherto made the Government to continue its earnest endeavors. His Majesty trusts that the President is fully aware of this fact."

Although Mr. Grew did not know it at the time, this reply—or words to a similar effect—had been discussed by Togo and Tojo prior to the foreign minister's audience with the Emperor. Others may also have contributed a phrase here or a thought there. When Togo gave the Emperor the President's message, he also recommended the above reply. Since the matter came before the throne on the government's responsibility and with its recommendation, His Majesty—as usual—posed no objections.

As soon as Kase had finished interpreting the oral statement, Togo handed Ambassador Grew a long memorandum in English which the foreign minister described as having been communicated to Secretary Hull by Ambassador Nomura, breaking off the negotiations. It was Grew's understanding, on the basis of Kase's rendition of Togo's remarks, that this memorandum was the real imperial reply to the presidential message.[57] Grew knew nothing of the Pearl Harbor attack nor did Togo reveal by any word or gesture that Japan and the United States were now at war. The foreign minister may have assumed that the ambassador already knew, because of an early-morning radio announcement in Japanese. He may simply have preferred to avoid the issue, since it would inevitably have placed both men in a most awkward position.

Before taking his leave, Grew asked whether his request for an audience had been denied; simultaneously, he offered several arguments in support of his right to be received by the Emperor. In reply, Togo merely said that he had no desire or intention to stand between the ambassador and the throne. The foreign minister then thanked Mr. Grew for his cooperation during the Hull-Nomura conversations and for his efforts in behalf of friendly relations between Japan and the United States. As was his custom, Togo accompanied the ambassador downstairs and saw him off at the door. It was not until roughly an hour later that Mr. Grew finally learned of the attack on Hawaii from the bold headlines of a Japanese extra which, by then, was being wildly hawked upon the streets.[58]

As in the case of the late delivery of Japan's final note in Washington, there was enough of a suspicious nature in this extraordinary affair to produce questions, doubts, and charges. At the postwar Tokyo trial, the prosecution addressed itself to a full measure of each—but

[57] Both Kase and Tōgō later testified that Grew was in error and that he had apparently misunderstood what was said. The point is basically insignificant but did not appear so to the prosecution at the time of the Tōkyō trial. The prosecution also made much of the fact that the American and British ambassadors were not informed until hours after the commencement of hostilities. There could have been no argument about that, if Japan's final note had been delivered to Secretary Hull *prior* to the attack.

[58] The reconstruction of what happened in Tōkyō from the evening of December 7 through the morning of December 8 is based on material in the following: Kase aff. and related submissions, S 252:14-15, T 26166-74; Kase cross-examination, S 252:15-16, T 26175-79; Tōgō aff., S 337:10-11, T 35727-31; Tōgō cross-examination, S 337:19-20, T 35792-801, S 338:3-4, T 35825-29, S 338:10-13 and S 339:1-8, T 35869-935, S 339:9-10, T 35942-49; Yasumasa Matsudaira aff., S 252:16, T 26179-81; Kameyama aff., S 253:1-2, T 26184-89; Kameyama direct examination, S 253:4, T 26204-6; Prosecution Exh. Nos. 1220-23, S 111:16-18, T 10541-51; Ballantine aff., T 10824-30, S 114:4-5; Ballantine cross-examination, T 10967-79, S 115:14-16, and T 10986-89, S 116:2-3; Grew aff., T 10551-55, S 111:18; Grew, *Ten Years in Japan*, 486-93; Grew, *The Turbulent Era*, II, 1249-53; Grew testimony, *PHA*, Part 2, 569-71, 692-94; Grew corresp.; *Foreign Relations (Diplomatic Papers: 1941)*, IV, 731-32; U. S. Dept. of State, *Peace and War*, 838-39; Parks corresp.; Tōjō aff., S 344:7, T 36410-11; Tōjō interrog., Feb. 19, 13-15, Feb. 23, 1-3, and Mar. 8, 5; Kido "Nikki" for December 8, 1941, S 113:6, T 10683; Kido aff., S 293:25, T 31048-50; Kido cross-examination, S 299:8-10, T 31604-12; Kido SKD and corresp.; Hattori, I, 240; JRD Monograph No. 150, 66-67; and CF 20, III, 254.

not with much success. It was easier to allege deception and dissimulation than to prove it. And yet innuendo and purely speculative explanations added momentum to the idea that a high-level conspiracy had existed. Were it not for an obscure bit of testimony offered by the defense, the matter might still remain in doubt. But one day, nearly five years after the event, a government employee named Shirao appeared in the courtroom and testified to his personal knowledge of circumstances which fit the pattern of the times so well, and are so logical, that no one in search of the truth can ignore what this otherwise unknown man had to say.[59]

In late 1941 Mr. Shirao was in charge of the censorship office, which was a part of the ministry of communications. On Saturday, November 29, a friend of his, Lt. Col. Tomura, who was then on duty in the communications section of the army general staff, telephoned him in the evening at his home. Tomura explained that it had been decided thenceforth, "as a precaution" (*keikai no tame*), to hold up the delivery of all foreign telegrams by five hours. Without giving the matter a second thought, Shirao immediately got in touch with the central telegraph office and issued orders that all incoming and outgoing cables, except those of the Japanese government, should be so delayed. The following Thursday, December 4, Shirao confirmed his oral order with written instructions which he disseminated to those immediately concerned, even though he had not received similar confirmation from his friend, Tomura, or from anyone else in the army general staff. Two days later, on Saturday, December 6, the lieutenant colonel again got in touch with Shirao to advise him that the delaying of foreign cables should thereafter be varied according to an alternating schedule of five hours one day, ten hours the next. Since the central telegraph office was then operating on the original instructions, the effect of this change was to make Sunday, December 7, a day on which all foreign cables, of whatever nature, would automatically be held up *ten hours*. That is presumably what happened to the President's message, despite an earlier assertion by Tojo, during a pre-trial interrogation, that it was ". . . unthinkable in Japan that anyone would stop such a message." It would be "irreverent." Japanese "would not do such a thing."[60]

In all probability, the delay of ten and one-half hours in the delivery

[59] What follows is based on Shirao aff., S 111:20-21, T 10566-72, and Shirao cross-examination (note the confusion in terms, etc.), S 111:21-22, T 10573-77, S 112:3-5, 6-7, T 10581-95, 10600-7. See also Kameyama aff., S 253:1-2, T 26184-89; Kameyama direct examination, S 253:4, T 26204-6; Tōgō aff., S 344:7, T 36411; and Tōjō interrog., Feb. 23, 2.

[60] Tōjō interrog., Feb. 23, 2.

to Ambassador Grew of the presidential message took place without Premier Tojo or Foreign Minister Togo ever being the wiser. It was just another case of supreme-command dabbling in affairs of state—of a staff officer who belonged to the nucleus group promoting a policy which may not have had any top-level sanction even within the army general staff. If the policy actually derived from higher authority, that source saw fit to keep the matter a closely guarded secret within the circle of the supreme command. At no point in his conversations with Shirao did Lt. Col. Tomura ever indicate that he was acting on instructions from above. He personally had no right to tell Shirao to do one thing or another with respect to foreign communications, and he apparently never actually *ordered* Shirao to do anything. Tomura, however, was a friend of Shirao's and an army general staff officer. What he said was thus interpreted by Shirao as equivalent to a request emanating from Tomura's superiors. It was on that basis that Shirao acted. From a narrow legalistic point of view there were no grounds for his action, but in terms of practical realities in 1941, and Japanese bureaucratic methods in general, Shirao's compliance with a vague request from a friend in the army general staff was by no means unusual. Government censorship of foreign telephone calls and cables had begun in July 1941. Not only the foreign ministry but also the supreme command regularly sent messengers to the communications ministry to obtain copies of cables in code which might be of interest to them. Since everyone knew that Japan was then confronted by an unprecedented crisis, Shirao did not find Tomura's instructions at all strange. Shirao did his job and minded his own business, both of which required that he cooperate with the proper authorities. Of these, the supreme command was the most powerful, and hence the most proper.

What apparently no one in the Japanese foreign office knew on the afternoon of Sunday, December 7, was well known to Mr. Shirao. He not only was aware that the President's message had arrived but was also cognizant, in a general way, of its contents. He had heard all about it over the telephone in the late afternoon—sometime between 4:00 and 6:00 p.m. He could not later recall exactly from whom he received the information, but he tended to think that it came from his friend, Lt. Col. Tomura. He did remember that the latter had got in touch with him to request that all cables be delayed thereafter for *fifteen hours*. Shirao later felt that Tomura had probably mentioned the President's message at that time. Shirao personally did nothing about the presidential message because it was beyond the scope of his responsibility. Presumably he did not appreciate the significance of the message or the possible meaning of the delay. The orders in that regard applied to all incoming and outgoing messages. Any decision as to exceptions would have to emanate from the organ responsible for the policy in the first place—the army general staff.[61]

Ever since that fateful day in early December 1941, those concerned with the issue of war or peace between Japan and the United States have speculated on the significance of the delayed delivery of the President's message to the Emperor. A popular view is that earlier recourse to such a direct appeal might have prevented the outbreak of hostilities. Tojo later declared that the die had already been cast by the time the cable arrived, but that Japan would not have been able to begin the war had the President's message come "a few days earlier" and had the Hull note of November 26 been "a little more conciliatory."[62] Even the Emperor is said to have remarked, after the war, that he would have stopped the attack if the cable had reached him a day sooner.[63] Such opinions should not be taken too seriously. They are *ato no matsuri*—"the doctor after death."

The nature of the Japanese decision-making process in 1941 was such that the Emperor could have intervened at the last moment only if he had been prompted to do so by the government. Presumably the influence of the throne would have been necessary to control the reaction of the fanatics to a *volte-face* in national policy. The government itself would have reconsidered its decision to use force only if the President's communication had indicated an American readiness to capitulate to Japan's demands. In such an eventuality, even the supreme command would have been willing to forgo the risks and hardships of the battlefield for the enticements of the diplomatic chamber. The prestige of the throne could then have been employed against various fringe elements which might otherwise have been slow to grasp the advantages of a

[61] Apparently the delaying of important messages was not without precedent, as is revealed by the following excerpt from Pooley (ed.), *The Secret Memoirs of Count Tadasu Hayashi*, 49, with reference to the outbreak of the Sino-Japanese war of 1894-1895: ". . . on the 19th [July 1894] the Japanese Minister in London informed Lord Kimberley that Japan would insist even by force on a satisfactory solution of the situation. As a result Lord Kimberley telegraphed to Rome, Berlin, Paris, and St. Petersburg, asking the Governments of the Powers to instruct their representatives at Pekin and Tokio to use all their efforts for the maintenance of peace. At the same time Mr. Gresham, the American Secretary of State, telegraphed to Mr. Dunn and Mr. Foster, the United States representatives at Tokio and Pekin, offering the services of the United States as mediator. These dispatches were held up by the Japanese authorities."

[62] Kurusu, *Nichi-Bei Gaikō Hiwa*, 160, paraphrasing Tōjō, and Tōjō interrog., Feb., 19, 15.

[63] Terasaki, 215-16.

change in direction. Only when backed by the power and responsibility of the men to whom the imperial prerogatives were constitutionally delegated did appeals to the throne ever assume any meaning.

If Tojo's alleged estimate of "a few days" is changed to "several months," the arguments in behalf of the beneficial results which might have attended a presidential message to the Emperor grow in strength. Had such an approach been adopted at any time in October, either while Konoe was still premier or just after Tojo's assumption of the office, the Japanese government might have felt encouraged to explore the matter further. Without a fundamental change in that government's attitude, however, it is difficult to believe that the course of events would even then have been more than temporarily diverted. Once the imperial conference decision of September 6 had been reinforced by the national policy review of late October, which in turn culminated in the new and more positive decision of November 5, the prospects for peace faded rapidly. To suggest, as the prosecution subsequently did, that the ten and one-half hour delay in the delivery of the President's message made the difference between war and peace is to adopt an untenable position. Even Tojo's estimate of the situation stipulated not only an earlier arrival of the message but, significantly, "a little more conciliatory attitude" on the part of the United States than that expressed in the Hull note of November 26. Japanese records reveal that the view attributed to Tojo would accurately reflect the realities of the time only if the phrase were amended to read: "a *far more* conciliatory attitude." The then chief of the operations section of the operations bureau of the army general staff has since written that not only was it too late for something like the President's message to make any difference but that the contents of Mr. Roosevelt's cable were not especially compelling.[64]

Perhaps, as the Japanese saying goes, it is useless to continue reckoning the age of a dead child.[65] The fact of the matter, however, is simply this: on November 26, 1941, *ten full days* before Pearl Harbor, Admiral Nomura and Mr. Kurusu sent an urgent and top-secret cable to Tokyo in which they recommended an exchange of messages between the President and the Emperor as the only means of "breaking the impasse" and of "changing the atmosphere."[66] The two envoys hoped

[64] Hattori, I, 240: "Shikashi toki sude ni osoku katsu shinden no naiyō mo toku ni toriageru hodo no mono de wa nakatta."

[65] A paraphrase of a Japanese proverb quoted by Mr. Kurusu in a letter to Bernard M. Baruch (Kurusu, 176).

[66] Cable No. 1180 of November 26, 1941, S 159:13-14. Both the IMTFE translation

that if that were done, their government would rise to the occasion by advocating the neutralization of French Indo-China, Thailand, and the Netherlands East Indies. They even pointed out that a similar proposal had been made by Mr. Roosevelt some months before, thereby implying the possibility of a favorable American response if only Japan would act.[67]

On November 28, the chief of the American bureau, on instructions from the foreign minister, briefly and pointedly informed Nomura and Kurusu that the measures they had suggested were regarded as "inappropriate" at that time—a conclusion which had been reached at the highest level as a result of the impression made by the "unreasonable" American counterproposal of November 26, which had meanwhile arrived in Tokyo.[68] Since the Japanese government had already decided to go to war unless the United States accepted the "Proposal B" ultimatum of November 20, the leaders in Tokyo were in no mood to be

---

(T 16195-98) and the "Magic" intercept version (*PHA*, Part 12, 180-81, and T 10418-20, S 110:19-20) require revision. Those in the American government who saw the "Magic" version were under the impression, because of mistranslation, that Nomura and Kurusu were suggesting an exchange of messages between the President and Foreign Minister Tōgō. In this regard, see also Hull testimony, *PHA*, Part 11, 5373-74. The intercept also mistakenly suggested to its readers that Nomura and Kurusu wanted Tōgō to show their cable "to the Minister of the Navy, if only to him." Actually, the envoys requested the foreign minister to carry the proposals they were making "at least as far as Lord Keeper of the Privy Seal Kido" ("Hon-den aruiwa hon-shi to shite saigo no iken gushin taru beki ni tsuki sukunakutomo Kido Naidaijin made o shimeshi no ue shikyū orikaeshi nanibun no go kaiden setsubō su").

[67] According to the Nomura and Kurusu cable, the President had suggested the neutralization of French Indo-China and Thailand in September. Actually, the Roosevelt proposal concerning French Indo-China was made on July 24, 1941. It was broadened to include Thailand on August 1, but the Japanese government remained uninterested (see Feis, 238 and 249, n. 14). In late November Nomura and Kurusu feared the United States and Great Britain might carry out a protective occupation of the Netherlands East Indies. They thought Japan might be able to forestall this by seizing the initiative in the form of a neutralization proposal embracing French Indo-China, Thailand, and the Indies. See the cable cited in the preceding footnote.

[68] See Cable No. 844 of November 28, 1941: S 111:3. Both the IMTFE translation (T 10441-43) and the "Magic" intercept version (*PHA*, Part 12, 195) require revision (e.g., "Please acknowledge the above-mentioned situation" [T 10443], and "From now on do the best you can" ["Magic," p. 195] for ". . . migi ni go ryōshō aritashi"—literally: "I want you to understand the foregoing"; i.e., "Please bear the foregoing in mind").

The Hull note was described as a *rijujin naru tai-an.* The effect in English depends on the value assigned to *rijujin naru*: "unreasonable," "unjust," "unfair," "outrageous," "absurd."

Because of the mistranslation of Cable No. 1180 noted in footnote 66 above, American officials who read the intercept of Cable No. 844, in conjunction with No. 1180, would have been under the impression that an exchange of messages between Roosevelt and Tōgō (rather than between Roosevelt and the Emperor) was being rejected. See also Hull testimony, *PHA*, Part 11, 5373-74.

distracted by a scheme of the type proposed by Japan's representatives in Washington. Among those who were hurriedly consulted, the view prevailed that the Nomura-Kurusu plan would not work. As a consequence it was not even reported to the throne.[69]

In the week that followed this negative response, nothing happened to change the minds of those in whose hands lay the destiny of the Japanese nation. Thus, even if the President's message of December 6 had reached the Emperor during the afternoon of December 7 (Tokyo), rather than at three o'clock in the morning of December 8, the reply of His Majesty's government would not have differed substantially from that which was presented to Mr. Grew, some four and one-half hours later, as the returning planes of the imperial task force were eagerly being flagged to safe and triumphant landings—their mission accomplished.

In Washington the reception given by Secretary Hull to Ambassador Nomura and Mr. Kurusu, when they paid their final visit to his office, was stiff and unfriendly.[70] At almost the exact moment that they arrived at the State Department (2:00-2:05 p.m.), the President personally telephoned from the White House to relay an unconfirmed report that the Japanese had attacked Pearl Harbor. Hull briefly toyed with the thought of breaking the appointment, but he decided to abide by the

[69] The matter was discussed privately by Tōgō, Tōjō, and Shimada. Tōgō testified that he also talked with Kido, as the two envoys in Washington had requested him to do in their cable, and that the privy seal agreed with the consensus that such a plan would not work. Kido testified that Tōgō either never discussed the matter with him or did so only in a very cursory way, and that he did not see the Nomura-Kurusu dispatch or Tōgō's answer. The Emperor was not informed, according to Tōgō, because there was no place to lodge responsibility for such a proposal, since those in official positions who were consulted were unanimous in feeling that the proposal did not offer a practical solution.

In addition to the pertinent cables already cited, see JRD, "Nomura Diary," entry for November 26, 1941; Nomura, 27-28; Kurusu, 158-60, 175-76; Tōjō aff., S 343:21-22, T 36360; Tōgō interrog., T 10506-8, S 111:11; Tōgō aff., S 337:7 and 8, T 35704-5 and 35706-8; Tōgō cross-examination, S 338:2-3, T 35818-25; Kido aff., S 293:23, T 31036-37; Yamamoto aff., S 252:1-2, T 26064-68.

[70] See Hull, II, 1095-1100; Kurusu, 185-86; Nomura, 29; and JRD Monograph No. 150, Appendix 6.

Nomura has stated that he was mainly worried about what might happen in the southwestern Pacific area (Southeast Asia) but that he never even imagined that an attack might be made on Hawaii. He and Kurusu did not learn of that until they had returned to the embassy from their interview with Hull (with whom Nomura remembered shaking hands upon leaving). Hull has written (p. 1099): ". . . I did not feel that they [Nomura and Kurusu] were aware, when they came to my office, that an attack had been made at Pearl Harbor. In fact, I am satisfied that they did not learn of the attack until they returned to their Embassy."

book, feeling that "there was one chance out of a hundred" that the report might not be true.

When Nomura and Kurusu entered, Hull greeted them coldly, not even asking them to sit down. As Nomura handed over the final note, he "diffidently" explained that decoding difficulties had prevented him from keeping the one o'clock appointment specified by his government. When Hull asked why that particular hour had been chosen, the ambassador replied that "he did not know, but that was his instruction." Hull took the note and "made a pretense of glancing through" it. The "Magic" version had already reached him that morning. After several pages, he purposely asked whether Nomura was presenting the document under instructions from his government. Nomura replied affirmatively, and Hull at last admitted to himself that the one-in-a-hundred chance was gone. When he finished skimming the eleven pages, he fixed his eye upon the uncomfortable ambassador and lashed him with these words: "I must say that in all my conversations with you during the last nine months I have never uttered one word of untruth. This is borne out absolutely by the record. In all my fifty years of public service I have never seen a document that was more crowded with infamous falsehoods and distortions—infamous falsehoods and distortions on a scale so huge that I never imagined until today that any Government on this planet was capable of uttering them."

Nomura's face remained "impassive," but Hull sensed that he was "under great emotional strain." The ambassador seemed on the point of saying something, but before he could begin, Hull nodded toward the door. Nomura and Kurusu "turned without a word and walked out, their heads down."

The next day, Mr. Roosevelt publicly added his own vibrant denunciation to that already privately uttered by Secretary Hull. The President addressed himself not only to what had happened throughout the Pacific but also to the grave and enormous task which lay ahead.[71] The scene was the Congress of the United States; the audience—the American people, and ultimately the world:

Yesterday, December 7, 1941—a date which will live in infamy—the United States of America was suddenly and deliberately attacked by naval and air forces of the Empire of Japan. . . .

The facts of yesterday speak for themselves. The people of the United

[71] The President's message to the Congress (on Monday, December 8, 1941), which is quoted in part in the text which follows, is given in full in *Foreign Relations (Japan: 1931-1941)*, II, 793-94.

States have already formed their opinions and well understand the implications to the very life and safety of our Nation. . . .

Always will we remember the character of the onslaught against us.

No matter how long it may take us to overcome this premeditated invasion, the American people in their righteous might will win through to absolute victory. . . .

With confidence in our armed forces—with the unbounded determination of our people—we will gain the inevitable triumph—so help us God.

III · THE WILL OF HEAVEN

Yoshi naki yū wo konomite, mōi wo furuitaraba, hate wa yo no hito mo imikiraite sairō nado no gotoku omoinamu. Kokoro subeki koto ni koso.

If you delight in senseless valor and make a display of violence, the world will in the end detest you and will look upon you as wild beasts. Of this you should take heed.

> The Emperor Meiji, to the soldiers and sailors of Japan, January 4, 1882.

CHAPTER 13

The Fate of the Nation

AND SO war came to Japan. The "Tiger" signal from the task force, denoting success at Pearl Harbor, was relayed by the naval authorities in Tokyo to the premier's official residence sometime between 4:00 and 5:00 a.m., Monday, December 8. General Tojo was asleep when the call was received, but from that moment all thought of further rest was forsaken. As other messages added bits and pieces of information to the gradually emerging picture, Tojo "rejoiced over the miraculous success" achieved at Hawaii and humbly "gave thanks to Heaven" for this auspicious beginning.[1]

At six o'clock in the morning imperial headquarters issued the first bulletin: "Today, December 8, before dawn, the imperial army and navy entered into a state of war with American and British forces in the western Pacific."

One hour later, at 7:00 a.m., this cryptic announcement was broadcast throughout Japan. Almost incessantly thereafter the air was filled with the stirring strains of patriotic songs, including such favorites from the Meiji period as *Gunkan-māchi* and *Battō-tai*: "The Man-of-War March" and "The Drawn-Sword Brigade." Soon the streets were resounding to the ringing of the bells used by newspaper vendors to call attention to the extras which Japan's fourth estate was already pouring into the news breach made by the imperial headquarters release.[2]

On his way to the palace that morning, much earlier than usual, Marquis Kido became conscious of the fact that it was an exceptionally fine day. As his automobile proceeded from the top of the hill of Akasaka-mitsuke toward Miyake-zaka, he saw a splendid sunrise. He had known about the decision to resort to force but not about the operational plans with which that decision would be implemented. He had consequently been "astonished" when the office of the imperial aide-de-camp had telephoned, an hour or so before, to advise him of the assault on Pearl Harbor. Since then, his mind had been filled with thoughts about the coming of the war and about the attacks which were then

[1] Tōjō aff., S 344:7, T 36409, and Tōjō interrog., Feb. 20, 4.
[2] See Hattori, I, 26 and 352-54. The Japanese original of the IGHQ announcement quoted in the text reads as follows: "Teikoku rikukai-gun wa hon-yōka mimei nishi-Taiheiyō ni oite Bei-Ei gun to sentō jōtai ni ireri."

in progress. Closing his eyes, he instinctively bowed toward the rising sun and silently offered a prayer to the gods.

A short time later, Kido learned directly from the premier and the two chiefs of staff that the strike against Hawaii had been a great success. Along with Tojo, and countless other Japanese throughout the land, the lord privy seal felt profoundly grateful for the divine assistance which had seemingly attended the opening of this new and desperate effort to make the impossible possible.[3]

As the morning waned, the excitement which already gripped the nation grew in intensity as men in all walks of life eagerly absorbed the latest reports and quickly spread the newest rumors. At 11:40 a.m. an imperial rescript which had only that morning been approved at a rather belated but otherwise routine session of the privy council was promulgated to the nation.[4] Basically, it was just another formality—the means by which the Emperor advised his "loyal and brave subjects" that "He" was thereby declaring war upon the United States and Great Britain.[5] The content of the rescript clearly reflected the thinking of the leaders of His Majesty's government who were responsible for the drafting of all such imperial utterances.[6]

[3] Kido SKD; Kido aff., S 293:25, T 31049-50; and Kido "Nikki" for December 8, 1941, S 113:6. The translations offered at the trial (see T 10683-85 and 16192-95) require revision. Kido's position is that he was against a war with America and Britain but that once hostilities began it was only natural for him, as a patriotic Japanese, to pray for a favorable outcome.

[4] See Prosecution Exh. 1241, S 113:7-8, T 10690-700, and Tōjō aff., S 344:6, T 36404-7. The fact that the privy council had not been consulted on the decision for war (except insofar as the inclusion of its president in imperial conferences and at meetings of the senior statesmen may be regarded as a kind of indirect representation of the whole group by its chief member) indicated the extent to which the influence of that once powerful body had deteriorated. Whether or not the privy council would be consulted was entirely dependent upon the advice tendered to the throne by His Majesty's responsible official of state. There was no Constitutional requirement that the privy council be consulted (Article LVI of the Meiji Constitution reads: "The Privy Councillors shall . . . deliberate upon important matters of State, when they have been consulted by the Emperor"). See also Tōjō interrog., Mar. 13, 3.

[5] The prosecution made much of the fact that this rescript declaring war was not issued until more than eight hours after the Pearl Harbor attack. The Japanese defense is that the rescript was meant only for home consumption and had nothing to do with any declaratory requirements under international law, which were to have been met by Japan's final note (scheduled for delivery before the attack). The point is perhaps debatable, but the Japanese position seems more reasonable than the stand taken by the prosecution.

[6] The liaison conference played a primary role in deciding the content of the rescript. Deliberations in that regard can be traced back to the middle of November. As noted in Chapter 10 above, the Emperor first spoke with Kido about such a rescript on October 13, 1941. There was also postwar testimony to the effect that an entirely different rescript was drafted, toward the end of November, for use in the event Japan did not go to war. Copies of that draft rescript, however, were subsequently destroyed. In both cases,

Again the mobilization of the total strength of a united nation was demanded. Again the stabilization of East Asia and the peace of the world were signalized as Japan's aims. Again China was charged with having failed to understand Japan's true intentions and with having forced her to take up arms. Again America and Britain were denounced for aiding Nationalist China in its struggle against Japan, for possessing an inordinate ambition to dominate the Far East, and for pursuing policies which threatened the very existence of the Empire. Again Japan's patience and forbearance were extolled, while America and Britain were blamed for manifesting not the slightest spirit of conciliation.

This trend of affairs would, if left unchecked, not only nullify Our Empire's efforts of many years for the sake of the stabilization of East Asia, but also endanger the very existence of Our nation. The situation being such as it is, Our Empire for its existence and self-defense has no other recourse but to appeal to arms and to crush every obstacle in its path.

The hallowed spirits of Our Imperial Ancestors guarding Us from above, We rely upon the loyalty and courage of Our subjects in Our confident expectation that the task bequeathed by Our Forefathers will be carried forward, and that the source of evil will be speedily eradicated and an enduring peace immutably established in East Asia, preserving thereby the glory of Our Empire.[7]

Kido, who saw the Emperor immediately after the promulgation of this rescript, found that His Majesty was calm and collected even though Japan was now engaged in a struggle which would determine the rise or fall of the nation. Later, the Emperor told his chief adviser that the declaration of war against the United States and Great Britain had been a very heart-rending decision for him. It was especially unbearable, he said, to make an enemy of the royal family of Britain, with whom such close friendship had been enjoyed in normal times. Kido felt that there was really nothing he could say in reply.[8]

---

the actual work was done in the cabinet secretariat. See Hattori, I, 237-38 and 282; Inada aff., S 278:8-9, T 29199-201; Kido aff., S 293:24-25, T 31047-50 (requires correction); Kido SKD and corresp.; Tōjō aff., S 344:6, T 36404-7; Tōjō cross-examination, S 348:9, T 36779-81; and Tōjō interrog., Feb. 7, 1-2.

[7] Prosecution Exh. 1240, S 113:6-7, T 10685-89 (an official Japanese government translation). The concluding phrase, ". . . preserving thereby the glory of Our Empire" (". . . Teikoku no kōei wo hozen semu koto wo kisu") represents a revision made at the suggestion of the lord privy seal. The original had read, ". . . promoting thereby, at home and abroad, the just and righteous cause of the imperial way" (". . . kōdō no taigi wo chūgai ni sen'yō sen koto wo kisu").

[8] Kido SKD.

It was because His Majesty entertained such feelings, however, that a special sentence had been inserted in the rescript at the Emperor's own request: "It has been truly unavoidable and far from Our Wishes that Our Empire has now been brought to cross swords with America and Britain."[9]

As soon as the imperial rescript had been promulgated, General Tojo broadcast a brief message to the nation in his capacity as premier. His delivery, although not especially noteworthy, was in comparatively measured tones. Despite circumstances of which an Araki or a Matsuoka would have taken full advantage, there was nothing rabid or fanatical in what Tojo said or in his manner of saying it. His remarks carefully followed the standard pattern—emphasizing that Japan had been challenged, that despite Japanese efforts for peace all had been lost owing to the intractable attitude of the United States, and that as a result Japan had no other choice but to draw the sword of battle in her own defense. . . . The "key to success," Tojo declared, lay in "firmly believing in the certainty of victory." Japan had never been defeated in her 2,600-year history. That alone inspired faith in her ability to crush any enemy, no matter how strong he might be. The task before each and every Japanese was to vow not only to preserve untarnished the brilliant history of the fatherland but also to construct "a glorious tomorrow" for the Empire. . . . The enemy, boasting of his richness in resources, was seeking by their means to dominate the world. "To annihilate this enemy and to establish a stable new order in East Asia, the nation must necessarily anticipate a long war. . . ." Firmly believing that final victory would be theirs, the people of Japan must march forward to the very end, overcoming whatever difficulties and obstacles they found in their path. A Heaven-sent test had been imposed upon them. Only when they had met that test successfully could they expect to be honored by posterity as "the builders of Greater East Asia. . . ." The fate of the Empire—the destiny of East Asia—truly depended upon the outcome of the struggle ahead. Now was the time, Tojo said, for

[9] "Imaya fukō ni shite Bei-Ei ryōkoku to kintan wo hiraku ni itaru makoto ni yamu wo ezaru mono ari ani chin ga kokorozashi naramuya." The official Japanese government translation is quoted in the text, but the phrase, "*has now been brought* to cross swords" contains an implication not present in *kintan wo hiraku ni itaru*, which might be revised to read, "*has now come*. . . ." *Fukō ni shite* should also be included: "has now unfortunately come. . . ."

Although the insertion was requested by the Emperor, it was made "on the government's responsibility." An underlying purpose may have been the desire of the lord privy seal and others at the Court to emphasize publicly that the responsibility for war lay with the government and not with the throne.

the one hundred million people of Japan to devote their entire energies
—indeed, offer their very lives, if need be—to the service of the state.
. . . As for himself, confidently believing that victory was always to be
found in "the august virtues of His Imperial Majesty," he wished to
join with his fellow-countrymen in pledging faithful assistance to the
throne in the "monumental task" which was now beginning.[10]

So ended an unparalleled moment in Japanese history. But in a
larger sense, as the people themselves were soon to learn, the moment
did not really end. It lived on in their memories and in all that they
said and did through four years of a back-breaking war. Regularly
throughout those years, on the eighth day of every month, right to the
very end in August 1945, the imperial rescript of December 8, announcing the declaration of war with America and Britain, appeared boldly
at the top of the front page of every newspaper throughout Japan.
And to commemorate further the beginning of that "momentous task"
in which His Majesty's subjects became more desperately engaged as
time passed, every male member of the body politic was "encouraged"
to wear the so-called national uniform—a khaki affair with wrap-
around leggings and a peaked cap of an unflattering cut, which made
every civilian look more or less like a soldier. The women of Japan,
already long-suffering, were forced to endure the further indignity of
monpe, a baggy and unattractive bloomer-type garment which was
warm and practical, and supposedly "good" for the war effort.[11] As
the months passed, the national uniform was seen more and more frequently, thus adding considerably to the wartime drabness which slowly settled upon the land, until even the government showed its aware-
ness of the spreading down-in-the-mouth aspect of the one hundred
million by sponsoring a national "Smile Week" in March 1943. That,
of course, was when Japan was no longer riding the crest of the wave.

In the early days of the war, however, and for some months thereafter, the actual successes achieved—and the more nebulous ones produced by a formidable phalanx of propagandists—inspired great national confidence in the future. Victory was in the air and there were
few who were not caught up in a spirit of buoyant optimism. Some
strategically placed individuals, like the editor of the officially backed

[10] Shunichirō Itō, 1-3, and a recording of the Tōjō broadcast replayed for the author
at Radio Tōkyō, some fifteen years after the event.
[11] Terasaki, 113, notes that women not appearing in *monpe* on mandatory occasions
were publicly scolded by station attendants and even barred from riding the trams
(*shōsen*).

TAKING IT THE HARD WAY

From the *Japan Times & Advertiser*, December 10, 1941. (Courtesy of the *Japan Times*.)

Japan Times & Advertiser, were inclined to gloat publicly—as much for foreign as for home consumption. Two weeks after Pearl Harbor, the editor informed his readers:

ROOSEVELT HAS COOKED AMERICA'S GOOSE

The Hawaiian debacle and the sweeping victories being scored by the Imperial Japanese Army and Navy forces on all fronts have swept away a good deal of the braggadocio spirit of the American people. Only a few weeks ago they were boasting that the United States could finish off Japan in three months. Today these same Americans are trembling in their shoes and they have every reason for doing so.

WHO'S GOING TO RESCUE THEM?

From the *Japan Times & Advertiser*, December 16, 1941. (Courtesy of the *Japan Times*)

The ultimate course the present war will take may be judged fairly accurately by comparing the situation now with that when the United States entered the first World War.

In 1917 the British, French, Italian and Russian armies were pressing the Germans. Japan was on the side of the allies. So the Americans had every reason to be optimistic.

Today the situation is reversed. The British haven't a single soldier on European soil and are not likely to have any for the duration. They are the

"CAN WE GET HOME?"

From the *Japan Times & Advertiser*, December 20, 1941. (Courtesy of the *Japan Times*)

ones who are being pressed. The French are out of the picture while the Italians are fighting on the German side. The Russians have been pressed back as far as Moscow. Japan has just crushed the United States Pacific fleet.

We said the other day, that the British will soon be cursing Roosevelt as "that blasted idiot." We hate to think what his own people will be calling the Would-be Lord High Protector of the Universe when they awaken to the full realization of what he got them into.

A penny for your thoughts, F.D.R.[12]

This scornful gibe was followed the next day by more of the same, as if the editor had found it impossible to do justice to the subject at one sitting. The Anglo-American partnership, he predicted, would not withstand the pressure of events. By joining forces with the British, the United States was heading for a fall. No country that Britain had "acclaimed as partner" had so far escaped destruction. "Czechoslovakia, Poland, Holland, Belgium, France, Greece, Russia, and now the United States!" Each had been "hailed as friend and ally" while being used "to deflect the war from England's shores." But when that had been done, each in turn had been "cast aside . . . broken and maimed. . . . To receive England's embrace is to receive the sentence of death. The fetid breath of the dying British Empire poisons all who come in contact with it. Those who would arrest the inevitable decay of the moribund old monster are themselves contaminated and rushed to an untimely grave. . . ."

The Pacific fleet, the editor said, was a good example. Once "the boast of America and the envy of decrepit Britannia," it had now vanished from the seas. "Only a few battered hulks" remained. With "her battle fleet annihilated in the most humiliating disaster in all history," the United States had been "reduced at one stroke to a third-rate naval Power."

Between America and destruction there now remains only the United States army. While the Americans were once proud of their navy, they have always admitted the inferiority of their army. In view of the revelation of the navy's weakness, how much more pitiful must the army be! Composed of unwieldy masses of raw conscripts, armed only with paper weapons still "on order" in uncompleted factories, officered by college boy amateurs fresh from short summer training courses, the United States army can hardly be of much comfort to the frightened American populace. . . .

What confidence can Americans have in the wisdom of their politicians who have led them into such a predicament? What confidence can Americans have in the ability of their admirals and generals who have already failed so miserably in their first test? What more does Japan have in store for the Americans who heretofore have so blindly mis-gauged Japan and who today are too bewildered to solve the mystery of Japan's strength?

All this might have been avoided if the United States had only confined

[12] Editorial in *Japan Times & Advertiser*, December 22, 1941, 2.

herself to her own affairs. All this might have been prevented if the United States had not succumbed to Britain's wiles. But Roosevelt chose otherwise. Not content to stay within one hemisphere, he went forth to receive Churchill's kiss of death.[13]

Exactly what might be expected in the future from the *Japan Times & Advertiser* was revealed a week later at a Shinto ceremony of purification held before a small shrine in the paper's Tokyo headquarters. On behalf of the assembled employees, the editor solemnly read a New Year's resolution: "We pledge to fulfil our duties as Japanese subjects; to develop the spirit of volunteering to fall as martyrs in a national crisis, to rid ourselves of liberal and egoistic ideas and to fully cooperate in carrying out the national policy, to do our utmost to further the observance of discipline, and to be high and exact in our principles."[14] Such was the offering rendered to the god of war at a time when duty and patriotism required that special public obeisances be made for the good of the state.

With all news media equally accommodating, perhaps it was unnecessary for Premier Tojo to insert invective in his public speeches. Perhaps it was simply out of character for him to do so. Whatever the reason, Tojo did not himself indulge in the sputterings of a Hitler or a Mussolini, nor did he echo any of the innumerable made-in-Japan types whose fulminations had helped to create the unhealthy attitude of which the war was now a logical culmination. Tojo remained adamant toward the American and British enemy, but he did not treat Japan's foes with contempt or subject them to fanatical abuse. Even during the first months, when all was going enormously well, he kept cautioning against the intoxication of victory and emphasizing the need and wisdom of preparing for a long and hard effort.[15]

But in the atmosphere of 1942, such warnings seem to have made little impression. As Tojo himself publicly boasted, Hong Kong fell in eighteen days, Manila in twenty-six, and Singapore in seventy.

The Japanese success at Singapore served as the occasion for a "First Victory Day," followed soon thereafter by a "Second," with which Japan celebrated the capture of Rangoon and the "unconditional surrender" of the Netherlands East Indies.[16] During that period of phe-

---

[13] Editorial in *ibid.*, December 23, 1941, 6.

[14] *Ibid.*, January 1, 1942 (morning edition), 4.

[15] See *Facts on File: 1941*, 470 B, 487 H; *Facts on File: 1942*, 61 E, 134 G; CF 20, I, 50; and Tolischus, 401.

[16] February 18 and March 12, 1942, respectively. See *Japan Year Book: 1943-44*, 186, and *Japan Times & Advertiser*, March 12, 1942 (evening edition), 1.

Japan did not attack or declare war upon the Netherlands East Indies until January

nomenal military achievement, it was only natural that the impending doom of America and Britain should be a favorite topic of discussion. Japanese seemed especially gratified when they could cite the enemy to support their prophecies. On one occasion, facts and figures allegedly emanating from Senator Harry F. Byrd of Virginia produced the desired authority: as of September 1, 1940, the United States possessed only 56 four-engined heavy bombers suitable for combat; by late 1941, less than two hundred more had been produced, despite Roosevelt's announced goal of five hundred per month; "America's total annual production of combat planes of all types" was "less than the number reported destroyed in the Russian-German war in a single month. . . ."[17]

Some time later, *Life* magazine was triumphantly quoted to the effect that the United States was no better off on land than on sea: a third-rate power, relying upon an army composed of "untrained and undisciplined" troops notoriously lacking in morale. "Last year [1941]," the Japanese account stated, "the magazine Life sent a reporter to investigate morale in a typical division of the United States army. Fifty per cent of the privates said they would 'go over the hill' when their original year of service was over. In other words, that they would desert. He found the letters OHIO chalked on artillery pieces and latrine walls. It meant 'over the hill in October.' . . ."[18]

Although members of the Japanese government had access to somewhat better sources of information than the press, cabinet ministers and supreme-command officers seem generally to have been far more optimistic about the future than the total picture warranted. The reexamination of national policy conducted at the end of October 1941 by the new Tojo Cabinet had made it clear that Japan would be in serious trouble if she became involved in a war lasting more than two years. It was that fact which haunted Tojo and caused him repeatedly to emphasize the need to prepare for a protracted war. The initial victories made the task more difficult because they led to false expectations of an early collapse of the enemy's will to fight. The successes of the first months also sanctioned an uncritical faith in Japan's ability to hold an extended perimeter, enclosing a national defense zone containing the

---

11-12, 1942, even though the Dutch had joined the United States and Britain from the outset. See Hattori, I, 296-97; Tōjō aff., S 344:5, T 36400; Tōjō cross-examination, S 347:13-14, T 36721-27; and van Mook, *The Netherlands Indies and Japan*, 130.

[17] JRD, "Translation," V (Item 24), quoting *Japan Times & Advertiser*, December 10, 1941.

[18] JRD, "Translation," V (Item 24), citing an editorial in *Japan Times & Advertiser*, January 9, 1942.

vital resources which would make a protracted war possible. Japan's leaders never came up with any precise thoughts on how to terminate such a war. They simply believed that at some future date some opportunity or other would somehow present itself.

The army made a major miscalculation in assuming that Japan's Axis partners in Europe would be victorious; the navy made a major miscalculation in relying on the old concept of great warships and big guns vying for command of the sea (thus overlooking the potentialities of the submarine); the two services together failed to appreciate the role that would be played by air power, and they proved totally unprepared for an island-hopping strategy of amphibious assault on a grand scale.

If such mistakes were made in the field of their professional competence, the wishful thinking with regard to the unfamiliar area of American psychology and morale can more easily be understood. Whenever a disadvantage on the practical, material plane could not be explained away, the tipping of the scales to favor Japan was generally accomplished, without much difficulty, by a "but also" argument in the realm of the spiritual. In a situation in which admitted contradictions and deficiencies argued against the wisdom of pursuing a policy of calculated risk, the day was saved for the advocates of action by the emphasis given to the *decisive* influence expected from Japan's allegedly superior fighting morale, military training, and general *esprit de corps*. It was not until after the commencement of hostilities that battle experience gradually corrected the distorted picture of an American enemy hampered at every turn by conflicts of selfish personal interest and by an absence of patriotic fervor.[19]

In fairness it must be said that the mind-over-matter factor had demonstrated its value again and again throughout Japanese history—the most recent example, and the one most often cited in the Japan of the 1930's, being the Russo-Japanese war of 1904-1905. An imperial Japanese army lieutenant, writing soon after that event, had proudly noted a salient point that was to be reiterated frequently in the years ahead: the initial failure to take Port Arthur and the mounting casualties which had accompanied each new attempt had not discouraged his brothers-

[19] On the war outlook of Japan's leaders, see (in addition to the material presented in Chapter 11 above) Hattori, I, 276-80, and III, 32; JRD, "Interrogations," I:49157 (Seizō Arisue), 24-26, II:48366 (Sadamu Shimomura), 241, and II:n.n. (Shinichi Tanaka), 423; JRD, "Statements," I:50612, (Takushirō Hattori and Sadatoshi Tomioka), 380-81; JRD, "Translation," V (Items 18-22 and 24); and Ōi intv.

in-arms; ". . . on the contrary, the repeated failures only added to their keen determination and abundant resourcefulness."[20]

As General Kojiro Sato had remarked some years later, in explaining how ten thousand Japanese could defeat fifteen thousand Russians: "To divide 4 by 2 and obtain 2 is an ordinary material judgment. But if we should obtain 3, an invisible coefficient [the Japanese spirit] must have been multiplied by the visible quotient."[21]

The tendency to divide 4 by 2 and come up with 3 proved Japan's undoing in the Greater East Asia War. For once, the exercise of self-discipline and will power failed to produce the miraculous.[22] And yet, despite the evidence which accumulated as the months passed, an old stalwart like Admiral Suetsugu still found it possible, as late as the summer of 1944, to tell a session of active and retired colleagues, ". . . determination takes precedence over strength in an operation."[23]

It is understandable that the civil and military leaders of Japan in 1941 should have thought of the use of force as a possible answer to the problems confronting them, but it is inexcusable that they should have resorted to force as the solution. This judgment is not based on any "day of infamy" at Pearl Harbor but rather on the irresponsibility of Japan's leaders toward their own people. The decision for war was not fantastic in terms of the Japanese view of the world at that time; it was fantastic in terms of the means at Japan's disposal to secure victory through a further reliance upon arms. As Kido had earlier told Konoe, Japan simply did not have what was needed to implement successfully the action her leaders desired to take.[24]

Japan's fateful choice contained flaws so apparent that it was fully realized that serious structural weaknesses might develop with the passage of time. In a postwar interrogation, Tojo admitted as much: ". . . Japan had been fighting with China for more than four years and her strength was not sufficient to warrant taking on powerful new enemies."

Why then did he and his colleagues gamble the future of Japan on what appeared to be such poor odds?

"It was considered that, although Japan was not prepared, she had

---

[20] Sakurai, *Human Bullets*, 254.
[21] Kōjirō Satō, 82.
[22] See Reischauer, 172-75.
[23] JRD Doc. No. 55773 ("Takagi Notes," June 30, 1944).
[24] See pp. 236-38 above. In addition to the material already presented on this aspect, see Tōjō aff., S 343:12-13, T 36283-89; Hattori, I, 266 and 269-76; JRD Monograph No. 150, Appendix 1; JRD, "Translation," II:51021 (Item 21, Kikusaburō Okada), 1-34; and JRD, "Statements," III:50418, 126-27, and III:61688, 133-36 (both Kikusaburō Okada).

been challenged and had to fight, no matter what the state of her pre-paredness was."[25]

Such was the approach of the leaders of Japan, on whom must rest the ultimate responsibility for the Greater East Asia War.[26]

Some day the full story will be told of how that war was fought and lost within the same councils of state that brought it into being. This is neither the time nor place, and yet some points deserve at least passing mention, for it is clear that the very inadequacies of the system that had hampered Tojo in his short tenure as premier, before the war began, were to cause him grave trouble to the end and account ultimately for his fall.

The rivalry which had existed for years between the army and the navy was not stifled by the obvious need for thoroughgoing service co-operation and coordination created by the outbreak of hostilities in the Pacific. If anything, the rivalry increased, for at stake now was not simply the army or navy share of the current year's budget, and how that would influence the expansion plans of one service or the other, but, rather, the honor of each service as reflected in victory or defeat on the field of battle. In practice, this meant frequent disagreements between the two on matters of strategy and tactics.[27]

The dichotomy in the approach of the imperial army and navy helps explain the recurrence of the ambiguous and the vacuous in policy-decisions made at liaison conferences. It was sometimes only through largely empty phrases that agreement could be achieved: "To cause Britain to surrender and to deprive the United States of its will to fight, we shall continue building up a political and military structure of long-term invincibility by successively expanding the war results we have achieved to date. At an opportune time we shall adopt positive measures."[28]

[25] Tōjō interrog., Feb. 26, 1. See also Tōjō aff., S 343:12, T 36282-83, S 344:16, T 36485-88, and JRD, "Interrogations," I:48484 (Naruhiko Higashikuni), 134-37.

[26] Some of the evidence which has since come to light regarding miscalculations and unpreparedness is startling in its revelations. See, for example, JRD, "Statements," IV:50731 (Sadatoshi Tomioka and Hidemi Yoshida), 349-50; JRD Monograph No. 152, 8-11; JRD, "Interrogations," II:35901 (Shinichi Tanaka), 460; Hattori, II, 126-29; and Sansom, "Japan's Fatal Blunder," *International Affairs*, Vol. XXIV, No. 4 (October 1948), 549.

[27] The extent of the territory to be occupied in the opening phases of the war and the order of occupation produced one of the first clashes. Another and related argument occurred over a divergence of views on the strategic role to be played in a vast arc of probable confrontation extending from the North Pacific to the Indian Ocean. See Hattori, I, 261-63, and II, 129-36, 138-39; JRD, "Interrogations," II:35901 (Shinichi Tanaka), 418-19, 422, 445-59; JRD, "Translation," V (Item 34, Shinichi Tanaka interro-gation); and JRD, "Interrogations," I:49157 (Seizō Arisue), 54.

[28] The sentence quoted in the text is the opening statement of a liaison conference

When strategic thinking became that vague, even the imperial army and navy found that they could agree. But it was a poor way, and a disastrous way, for Japan's civil and military leaders to approach the enormous responsibilities with which they were entrusted.

The basic deficiency was that the men who made the decision to launch hostilities against the United States and Britain failed to provide a war-guidance structure in keeping with the concept of modern and total war—a concept that was new and foreign to their thinking. On one side of the throne stood the cabinet, responsible for state affairs exclusive of military operations; on the other side stood the supreme command, responsible for the national defense *and anything related thereto*. In practical terms, this meant a continuous invasion by the army and navy general staffs of what was nominally the cabinet's sphere of authority. The traditional position of the Emperor was such that he could not provide the unity and the coordination which were lacking. The liaison conference procedure, which had earlier been established for that very purpose, inevitably failed to solve the problem, since it perpetuated the divisive aspects of the existing structure. Presumably nothing short of constitutional amendment could have produced the needed revisions and reforms.[29]

The independence of the supreme command was the all-encircling reef upon which the ship of state eventually foundered. As war minister, Tojo had already been aware of the problems arising from this independence, but it was not until he became premier that the matter assumed personal significance for him. After having been a soldier all his life, he suddenly learned what it was like to be a politician, with the whole broad picture constituting his responsibility and with a supreme command, including the general staff of his own service, setting his position as premier at naught. During postwar interrogations Tojo declared: "This matter of the relation of the cabinet authority to that of the Supreme Command is very basic. If it is not understood, nothing will be understood." And later he added: "I am not saying that the independence of the Supreme Command is a bad thing. There are some good points about it too, for example, being able to conduct operations without political interference. It was a good thing in 1890, when the Constitution was established, for the High Command to be untram-

---

decision in early March 1942 entitled "Kongo Toru-beki Sensō Shidō no Taikō" (Hattori, II, 132-33). The phrase "positive measures" was later defined, in a report to the Emperor, as signifying "for example, the invasion of India, Australia, etc."

[29] For a fuller discussion of the "fatal flaws" in Japan's war guidance structure, see Hattori, IV, 118-19.

meled, but in these days where the influence of a single action is felt around the world, a certain amount of control by the political authority is necessary. However, under the Japanese system it was impossible."[30]

When Tojo was asked whether he did not realize that Japan's defeat was due, in large part, to the independence of the supreme command, he revealingly replied: "To speak plainly, it was a big cause. Actually, it was, but in the trials, I don't want to emphasize that too much. What I do want to plead is that we, as subjects, I and the Chiefs of Staff, did not discharge our responsibilities to the Emperor. It is not the Emperor's responsibility. The civil ministers ought to have understood the problems of command and the Chiefs of Staff ought to have understood the civil problems. All ought to have cooperated in discharging their responsibilities to the Emperor. . . . Men use systems; men should not be used by systems [*Hito ga seido wo tsukau seido ni hito ga tsukawareru ni arazu*]. . . . If I and the other men had fully understood this, the Supreme Command should have taken account of the political aspect of things and adjusted military operations accordingly. We should have risen above the system in which we found ourselves, but we did not. It was the men who were at fault." By "the men" he meant himself and the army and navy chiefs of staff, but—as he put it—"especially myself."

When had he first realized the truth of the situation he was describing?

"From the time I became Prime Minister I . . . felt it poignantly, and I imagine that not only I but all Prime Ministers . . . felt the same."[31]

Among the many illustrations that Tojo might have cited in support of his remarks was a dispute which developed within the government regarding policy toward the island of Timor—a dispute which pitted the premier against the chief of the naval general staff. After much haggling, adamancy at last gave way to a so-called compromise that was in reality a victory for the supreme command.[32]

That Tojo would lose an argument over policy is hardly surprising. For years the trend had been toward an expansion of supreme-command power at the expense of the authority and influence of the cabinet

[30] See Tōjō interrog., Mar. 20, 1, Mar. 13, 4-5 and Mar. 19, 1-4.

[31] *Ibid*. See also Tōjō aff., S 344:3-4, T 36383-88, and S 344:14-15, T 36473-80; Tōjō interrog., Feb. 7, 3-5; *PHA*, Part 20, 4015-16; Maxon, 217-19; and Shigemitsu, *Sugamo Nikki*, 426.

[32] The question was whether Japanese troops should evacuate Portuguese Timor once they had expelled the Dutch and Australians. It was eventually decided that if Portugal remained neutral toward Japan, the troops would be withdrawn once the enemy forces had been driven out, but if Portugal's attitude were not favorable, *or if the over-all strategic situation made it necessary*, Japan's troops would be retained and Portuguese Timor would be used as a base of operations. See Hattori, II, 119-20.

ministers, including even the service ministers. The fact that Premier Tojo was a general, and concurrently war minister, made him more acceptable to the supreme command, but it did not endow him with any special privileges.

In matters of army administration, including the disposition of personnel, Tojo—as war minister—exercised considerable power. He was a disciplinarian who would not tolerate dissident elements. Whether he used his power legitimately to prevent a recurrence of assassinations and attempted *coups d'état* of the type which had marred the 1930's, or used it abusively to sidetrack competitors who might otherwise have displaced him, remains largely unanswerable because of the unknown element of primary motive. Tojo was also "a great plugger."[33] Ability and hard work produced impressive results. Even after the war, his decisions and guidance in army administrative matters were described as having been "good and perfectly timed."[34] But running the war ministry and serving as premier were two entirely different problems. It was in the political sphere of action that Tojo, general and war minister though he was, nevertheless failed in precisely the same manner as had his civilian and naval predecessors.

In an age of totalitarianism in Germany and Italy, it was perhaps inevitable that Tojo should have been regarded abroad, especially in the United States, as the Japanese equivalent of Hitler or Mussolini. Much was made of what appeared to be a great concentration of power in his hands. He began the war not only as premier and war minister but also as home minister. It was overlooked that he soon relinquished the latter post, which he had taken only as a temporary expedient. He subsequently held, at various times, a number of other portfolios, but only very briefly, until a suitable person could be appointed. Tojo was not without a certain interest in personal glory and advancement (the jingle of medals on his chest may have betokened his pride), but if he possessed a lust for power, as was sometimes said, the desire remained unfulfilled. Although the Japan of his day was certainly a military dictatorship, Tojo was not the dictator. It was the supreme command which held the power of decision.[35]

By the end of 1942, it was clear to Japan's civil and military leaders that the Allied counteroffensive had begun, that it would gradually

[33] JRD, "Interrogations," I:49157 (Seizō Arisue), 29-30.
[34] *Ibid*.
[35] The text draws, in part, on interviews with Kido, Hoshino, and Umezu.

increase in intensity, and that it would accelerate more and more after late 1943.[36] The people of Japan still thought in terms of the victories that had been won; the announcements of imperial headquarters continued to hide actual failures with fictitious successes; and the *Japan Times* remained editorially triumphant: "From the icy rocks of the Aleutians, across the vast expanse of the Pacific and among its countless islands, down the littoral of the Asiatic continent, through the fabled lands of the Indies to the very gates of the Antipodes, and then around into the Indian Ocean, the undisputed power of Japan has been established. The sting of Japan's lash has been felt as far afield as the mainland of America, in the harbors of Australia and off the coast of Africa, and even in the Atlantic. Over tens of thousands of miles, from the Arctics to the Tropics, over the seven seas and in five continents, the land has rumbled to the tread of Japan's legions or the skies have thundered to the roar of Japan's winged knights of the air."[37]

But the decision-makers in Tokyo were not permitted such luxuries of the imagination. No matter how regretfully, they were forced to see 1942 in a rather different light. It had been the year of the Doolittle raid (an omen for the future), of Japan's defeat at Midway (which broke the magic spell), and of the intensification of the Allied counteroffensive in the South Pacific as heralded by the landing on Guadalcanal (the first stepping-stone to Tokyo). It was thus with considerable point that Tojo warned at the end of the year that the "real war" was just beginning.[38]

Despite his words, even Tojo did not fully appreciate what was in store. Within the government, there was still optimism and a belief that the element of "if" offered a reasonable prospect of success: *if* an invincible political and strategic structure could be established, and *if* closer offensive coordination could be achieved with Germany and Italy, and *if* future Allied counteroffensives could be parried, and *if* enemy strength could be destroyed, it would still be possible to deprive the Americans and British of their fighting spirit and to achieve Japan's war aims.[39]

On the American side of the Pacific, however, the President of the United States had rather different plans for Japan. In his first address of

[36] See Hattori, II, 217.

[37] *Japan Times Advertiser*, War Anniversary Number, December 8, 1942, 8 (editorial: "One Year of Victories"). Also quoted by Buss, "Inside Wartime Japan," *Life*, January 24, 1944, 86. The name of this newspaper changed from *Japan Times & Advertiser* to *Japan Times Advertiser* on October 5, 1942, and to *Nippon Times* on January 1, 1943.

[38] *Facts on File: 1942*, 416 C.

[39] See, for example, Hattori, II, 224.

the new year, Mr. Roosevelt declared: "The period of our defensive attrition in the Pacific is drawing to a close. Now our aim is to force the Japanese to fight. Last year, we stopped them. This year, we intend to advance."[40]

And that is precisely what happened. The Americans, with the help of their Allies, did advance despite strenuous Japanese efforts at home and abroad to consolidate and augment their fighting strength. For Japan, 1943 became a year of accelerating deterioration, and hence of greater and greater hardship. In these circumstances, the ever-obedient masses were called upon to face the future with a faith in ultimate victory that was supposed to grow stronger as the national crisis deepened.[41]

Concurrently, the *Japan Times*, which had by then changed its name to the *Nippon Times*, was daily decorating the top of its front page with boxed "inspirational" captions designed to show the outside world that Japan was by no means daunted: "Smite Until Our Foes Bend on Their Knees" . . . "Through Unity and Determination to Anglo-Saxon Surrender" . . . "Fight Onward Till Asia is Asia's Own" . . . "America and Britain Dig Their Graves, Greater East Asia Builds a Paradise" . . . "The Die Is Cast, Let's Fight to the Last."[42]

As the year progressed, it began to look as if fighting to the last might be the prospect facing the Japanese nation. Despite the exertions of the propagandists and the censors, a hint of Japan's declining fortunes appeared from time to time in various public pronouncements. After the middle of 1943, Tojo's speeches tended to stress the increasing seriousness of the situation confronting Japan. He warned that air raids could be expected, that "a time of emergency" was at hand, and that the United States was beginning to overcome the difficulties which had harassed her at the outset. In referring to the construction of invincible fortifications against an invasion, Tojo was revealing that an Allied drive at the Japanese heartland was a distinct possibility.

On the second anniversary of the Pearl Harbor attack, Tojo predicted that 1944 would be Japan's year to win, but he also declared that victory would not be achieved easily. Later in the month, reports from Japan indicated that Radio Tokyo was warning the nation that the war was turning "from one of self-existence to one of self-defense" and that American counterattacks in the South Pacific were being pushed for-

[40] Rosenman, *Working with Roosevelt*, 366-67.
[41] From Tōjō's speech to the 82nd extraordinary session of the Diet, June 16, 1943. On efforts to strengthen the domestic structure for the conduct of the war, see Hattori, III, 59-63.
[42] See the *Nippon Times* for the period January 1943-April 1944.

ward "in dead seriousness." The mobilization of women to aid in the war effort had already taken place; now Radio Tokyo began appealing to children to substitute for adults wherever possible. By the end of the month, the people of Japan were being told that the fighting in the Pacific had reached "the decisive stage" in which "the rise or fall" of the nation would be determined.[43]

This grim picture was not relieved in the new year. Toward the latter part of January 1944 Tojo admitted to the imperial Diet the seriousness of enemy attacks upon Japan's sea lanes. But he also spoke of the logistical problems being encountered by the Allies as a result of their lengthening lines of communication. In a war of attrition, he said, the spirit of the Japanese people would enable them to endure far greater hardships than the enemy. The spirit of the people would soar as difficulties became more intense.

Tojo also mentioned the material ingredients of victory. He declared that air power would be decisive and that consequently aircraft production, which had doubled during the past year, would have to be increased further.[44]

Whether Tojo realized it or not, this was easier said than done. The problem once again was inter- as well as intra-service rivalry. A munitions ministry had been established several months earlier to take over important activities which previously had been dominated by the two services. As a practical matter, however, this innovation had affected only the form and not the essence. The munitions ministry very soon found its efficiency being impaired by virtue of the fact that the supreme command, which placed orders for aircraft, was still composed of separate army and navy divisions.[45]

A certain amount of army-navy rivalry was perhaps to be expected. Equally disruptive, but less excusable, was the disharmony which continued to manifest itself within each service. If army-navy unification was a highly desirable but nevertheless utopian idea, there seemed at least a possibility that something might be done about eliminating conflicts between the service ministries and their respective general staffs. The deepening military crisis supplied the opportunity.

National policy called for a strengthening of Japan's "vital perimeter of defense" as a countermeasure against the American offensive which

---

[43] See *Facts on File: 1943*, 195 N, 307 M, 340 G, 348 A, 364 B, 395 J, 403 J, and 411 M.

[44] See Hansen, *Fighting for Freedom*, 342-46, and *Facts on File: 1944*, 25 N.

[45] Hattori, IV, 123. See also USSBS, *Interrogations of Japanese Leaders of World War II*, II, 390, for an interesting comment by Admiral Kichisaburō Nomura regarding interservice cooperation during the war.

was growing in strength and gaining in momentum. The procurement of the shipping needed to transport men and supplies, however, soon became entangled in the rivalries within and between the services. Tojo convoked a number of meetings with Navy Minister Shimada and the two chiefs of staff, Sugiyama and Nagano, but agreement was not readily obtainable. For the most part, the group failed to act "until it was too late."[46]

The knowledge that such obstructionism could exist at a time when operational needs made decisive action imperative apparently impressed Tojo deeply and led him to think along unprecedented lines. As he saw it, the only remaining way of breaking through the barriers preventing coordination was for one man to hold the separate administrative and operational reins in his own two hands. The manner in which Tojo acted in this matter might have produced greater repercussions had it not been for the specific circumstances which gave him a last chance to make good on his promise to lead the nation to victory.

In mid-February 1944 the largest carrier-launched air armada in history blasted Japan's strategic Caroline Islands base at Truk, sinking from 19 to 26 ships (imperial headquarters in Tokyo admitted to 18) and destroying an estimated 201 planes (IGHQ said 120, as if some censor had merely transposed the "1").

More revealing than either set of figures was the fact that *no aerial opposition* was encountered by the Americans on the second day of the attack. Admiral Nimitz's communiqué declared that the Pacific Fleet had repaid the Japanese visit to Pearl Harbor two years before and had "effected a partial settlement of the debt." As a result of the attack, the imperial navy was left without a single plane in the southeastern Pacific.[47]

The shock produced in Tokyo by the devastating American naval strike against Truk jolted Tojo into instantaneous action. On the night of February 19 he carried out a reorganization and consolidation of his cabinet. By the next evening he had obtained imperial sanction for his assumption of the post of chief of the army general staff, succeeding General Sugiyama. This appointment was announced officially on February 21, together with the designation of Navy Minister Shimada as chief of the naval general staff, succeeding Admiral Nagano. This constituted the first time since the inauguration of Japan's modern military

[46] See JRD, "Interrogations," I:49157 (Seizō Arisue), 31-32.
[47] See *NYT*, February 18, 1944, 1, and February 21, 1944, 1; *Facts on File: 1944,* 55 A and J; Hattori, III, 93-94; and *Japan Year Book, 1946-48,* 181-82.

establishment that any man had ever occupied both the administrative and command posts concurrently in either the army or the navy.[48]

One of the Emperor's brothers, Imperial Prince Chichibu, who was then convalescing near the slopes of Mt. Fuji, "issued a series of written protests" against the Tojo appointment. A few officers in the general staff and in the war ministry privately declared that Tojo was a "tyrant" or secretly referred to him as "Takauji," the name of a military usurper who had lived in the fourteenth century.[49] A less extreme opinion held that Tojo was a man who had always tried to do the best thing, but had always ended up doing the worst. "If he would only take things in their proper order . . . he would be more successful."[50]

Other officers, however, "welcomed" Tojo's stepping in as chief of staff. They regarded the move as a "timely measure" which might help provide the critically needed coordination between army administration and military command, short of an out-and-out merger of the two. Apparently the majority view was that this new move "would serve to dispel the growing defeatist attitude among members of the Court, the [senior] statesmen, and Navy personnel. Thus a ray of hope was cast over the future direction of the war."[51]

But it was a comparatively weak ray, as events were soon to prove. Only four days after Tojo and Shimada assumed their new supreme-command duties, Radio Tokyo reported that a special cabinet meeting had decided upon "a simplification of the national livelihood." A fifteen-point program was announced, calling for the further mobilization of students, the reorganization of the labor structure, the conversion of more businesses to war production, the consolidation of the anti-air raid network, the closing of *geisha* and other luxury establishments, a revision of rewards and punishments, more war work by women, a reduction of holidays, and similar measures.[52]

A week later, dispatches from Tokyo to Berlin and Moscow revealed that the Tojo Cabinet was tightening the nation's belt even more. New measures envisaged the mobilization of the teen-age youth of the country

---

[48] See JRD, "Interrogations," I:49157 (Seizō Arisue), 31-32; Tōjō interrog., Mar. 13, 5; Tōjō aff., S 344:15, T 36478-80; Hattori, III, 95; Kido corresp.; Shimada aff., S 329:11, T 34775; and *Japan Year Book, 1946-48,* 169. An additional (i.e., "second") vice-chief of staff was appointed in both the army and navy.

[49] See Hattori, III, 175-76; JRD, "Interrogations," I:49157 (Seizō Arisue), 32; and JRD Doc. No. 57597 ("Takagi Notes," May 23, 1944).

[50] Admiral Okada quoting an unnamed reserve general. JRD Doc. No. 58228 ("Takagi Notes," March 18, 1944).

[51] JRD, "Interrogations, I:49157 (Seizō Arisue), 32.

[52] See *Facts on File: 1944,* 65 N, and *Japan Year Book, 1946-48,* 169.

below the college level. School buildings were thenceforth to be used to store military goods; their yards were to be converted into vegetable gardens. Afternoon newspapers were proscribed as a means of saving paper, and approximately 10,000 places of amusement were ordered closed. The government also decreed the beginning of the so-called decentralization of urban concentrations—that is, the evacuation of metropolitan centers as a response to the intensification of enemy air raids.[53]

Toward the latter part of March 1944, Tojo told the Diet that Japan had reached "the most critical situation in the history of the Empire." He warned of new American attacks "of greater weight than any hitherto experienced." But he did not give up hope of victory for Japan. In essence, he apparently still believed that Japan could win, if—as he had once reportedly said—everyone got up earlier and worked harder. The key to victory lay in an expansion of war production.[54]

Privately, however, Tojo was not always able to maintain such a bold front. One of his military aides noted that as the war situation grew worse, Tojo showed signs of worry and strain. And yet he never remained dejected for long. That was one of his strong points. His thinking always tended toward the positive. His shoulders might sag at the end of the day from the physical and psychological burdens of his office, but the next morning he would reappear, ramrod straight, ready to tackle the problems of another day—and ready also, apparently, to believe that they could be tackled successfully.[55]

If Tojo personally was not troubled by more than passing moments of doubt, there were others who found it increasingly difficult to persuade themselves that all was still well. Activity behind the scenes had gradually been gaining momentum. Tojo's appointment as chief of staff was not universally accepted within the ruling elite as the best or wisest solution to Japan's burgeoning misfortunes. In some ways, Tojo's elevation to that post made it more difficult for those in opposition to force him out; in other respects, his assumption of command responsibility made it easier.

Changes at the top during a time of crisis could produce an unfortunate reaction in public morale and provide the enemy with a valuable propaganda advantage. On the other hand, Tojo's ability to see the matter through to the end would depend solely on the progress of military

[53] *Facts on File: 1944,* 74 B.
[54] See *ibid.,* 97 J.
[55] Based, in part, on an interview with Colonel Hattori.

operations in the Pacific. Any improvement would enhance his reputation as a man who had the answers; further deterioration in the fortunes of war would suggest that Tojo had nothing personally to offer and that the nation should consequently be given a blood transfusion in the form of new leadership.

As the winter of 1943-1944 turned to spring, consultations among the members of the ruling elite became more frequent and persistent. Much of what was said tended to suggest that Admiral Shimada, serving both as chief of the naval general staff and as navy minister, was the weakest link in Tojo's war organization—the point at which the outsiders should concentrate their attack.

In a long conversation on March 7, for example, ex-Premier Okada told Imperial Prince Fushimi, a highly respected naval elder, that "key personnel" in the army and navy had apparently "lost confidence in their leaders" and that "a wide gulf" was developing "between the front lines and central headquarters." Shimada had "gradually lost prestige"; he had been accused of "being obscure, of resembling a 'mild spring breeze.' " He seemed to be "enveloped in a haze"—unable to see "into the future." It was feared that he would compromise with Tojo to a greater extent than the navy as a whole was now willing to permit.

According to Okada, Admiral Shimada appeared to be "affable to his superiors, but harsh with his subordinates." People everywhere were saying that the Tojo Cabinet, as a whole, was lacking in "warmth." In an address at a conference of prefectural governors, Tojo had urged a policy of kindness to the people, but in actual fact officials were "oppressing the people" and public opinion was consequently being alienated. Okada felt that anything might happen, and that it would be good to have a man in charge who understood the situation in the navy. He specifically recommended that the former premier, Admiral Yonai, be recalled to active naval duty. Okada believed Yonai should be given a position from which he could advise and assist Shimada and, if necessary, step into the breach in case of trouble. Prince Fushimi was impressed with Okada's arguments but said that he wanted to give the matter more thought before personally urging such a course upon Shimada.[56]

The Okada-Fushimi tête-à-tête was only one of a number of similar exchanges taking place behind the scenes, but—like all of them—it was

[56] JRD Doc. No. 58228 ("Takagi Notes," March 7, 1944). See also the items for March 18 and May 24, and Doc. No. 57597 (especially Takagi's notations for April 1, May 23, June 5, and June 8, 1944). The general complaint against Shimada in naval circles was that he was too subservient in his relations with the army. He was regarded as Tōjō's *kaban-mochi*—literally, Tōjō's "brief-case carrier."

symptomatic of a growing dissatisfaction with the existing order. Okada's reference to "key personnel" signified that members of the nucleus group—especially at the section-chief level—were growing restive. With ultimate defeat beginning to hover over the nation, Shimada was accused not only of having monopolized the top posts but of having surrounded himself with "toadies and tea-makers." There was already the inkling of a suspicion, which later grew in strength, that Shimada might sacrifice the navy and even ignore the national welfare simply to serve Tojo. As one officer later pointed out, the problem confronting Japan was of enormous magnitude and significance. It was not in the nature of a military "map exercise" or an annual "grand maneuver." Unless something positive were done soon, it might be too late.[57]

For his part, Tojo found the drag of the system more than he could handle. Perhaps if he had taken over as chief of staff earlier, he might have enjoyed greater success, but by 1944 the problem posed by the independence of the supreme command—and by the growing power of the enemy—was largely beyond solution.[58]

The various pressures building up against Tojo came rapidly to a head as a result of the blows then being landed by American forces in the Pacific. Anxiety over the war effort and dissatisfaction with the cabinet went hand in hand. The months of May and June brought both to a climax. In the Southwest Pacific an Allied amphibious landing was made on the island of Biak. Positions on the northern coast of New Guinea were being consolidated in preparation for an advance westward. In the North Pacific, air and naval strikes were being stepped up from American bases in the Aleutians. Far to the south and west, cities in Honshu and Kyushu were receiving the first American air raids launched from China. And then, in mid-June, came Operation "Forager"—the American invasion of Saipan in the Marianas, a strategic area of great importance because of its position well within Japan's inner zone of defense. The American capture of Saipan, which soon became a foregone conclusion, meant the acquisition of a forward base "which would serve both for continuing operations against the enemy's sea communications and for direct long-range air attacks on the homeland of Japan."[59]

[57] See JRD Doc. No. 58228 ("Takagi Notes," June 25 [28?] and June 27, 1944) and Doc. No. 57597 ("Takagi Notes," June 8, 1944).
[58] See Tōjō aff., S 344:15, T 36478-80.
[59] See USSBS, *The Campaigns of the Pacific War*, 209-11; Hattori, III, 172-73; and Butow, *Japan's Decision to Surrender*, 27.

This major military threat, coming on top of the disintegration of Japan's front in Burma, and the multiplication of problems within the home islands, made remedial action at the highest level imperative. Tojo argued that a cabinet resignation at such a critical juncture would exert an adverse effect upon the people of Japan and would interfere with the conduct of the war. He therefore proposed to strengthen his cabinet through another reorganization. On July 13 he called on the lord privy seal, Marquis Kido, to discuss the situation. To the premier's surprise the privy seal posed three conditions which Tojo interpreted as reflecting the views of the senior statesmen, who had become more active in their opposition to the cabinet since the beginning of July. The conditions stipulated by Kido envisaged the separation, once again, of the two top army posts of war minister and chief of the army general staff, the replacement of the navy minister, and the formation of a "united-front cabinet" through the inclusion of members of the senior-statesmen group. In practical terms this meant that Tojo was being advised to step out as army chief of staff and to obtain Shimada's resignation as navy minister. Tojo was also being told, in effect, that he would have to take into his cabinet someone like Admiral Yonai who could speak for the ex-premiers.

Of these three conditions, the first was the easiest to resolve. Tojo simply decided to give up his newly acquired post as chief of staff. He inclined toward the appointment of his senior vice-chief as successor, but a consideration of various factors induced him to recommend, instead, the commander-in-chief of the Kwantung army.

The second condition was personally distasteful to Tojo. He was reluctant to ask for Shimada's resignation because the navy minister had always worked closely with him and had smoothed the way with respect to naval matters on more than one occasion. After some delay, however, Tojo became convinced that Shimada would have to relinquish the naval portfolio. It was Tojo's desire, nevertheless, to have Shimada remain as naval chief of staff.

The most difficult condition to meet was the third, for it involved obtaining the voluntary resignations of certain cabinet ministers as well as the acceptance of cabinet appointments by one or more of the ex-premiers. As a first step, Tojo asked Minister of State Nobusuke Kishi to resign, but he refused to do so. Several cabinet colleagues then began saying that a resignation en masse would be more appropriate than a cabinet reorganization, but despite these developments Tojo still believed that he could meet the third condition. He therefore asked the ex-premiers, Yonai, Hirota, and Abe, to join his cabinet as ministers without portfolio. Of the three, only General Abe was willing to oblige.

It was at this juncture that the anti-Tojo intrigue of the senior statesmen took a turn which made a continuation in office by Tojo practically impossible. On the evening of July 17, as Tojo was still trying to reorganize his cabinet, the ex-premiers assembled at the home of Baron Hiranuma and there adopted a resolution calling for the establishment of a "united-front cabinet." Since Yonai and Hirota were demurring on Tojo's request for their services, this amounted to a demand that Tojo resign. The resolution was conveyed to the lord privy seal that same night; the next morning Kido informed both the Emperor and Tojo of what had occurred. Confronted by this vote of no confidence by the very group which had sanctioned placing him in power in 1941, Tojo bowed to the inevitable. By mid-morning he had collected the resignations of his cabinet colleagues and had presented them to the throne. The date was July 18, 1944—two years and nine months since his elevation to the highest ministerial office in the land, and exactly four years, to the day, since he had entered the world of politics as war minister in the second Konoe Cabinet.[60]

The news of Tojo's fall produced a brief sensation throughout the world, but the event was quickly overshadowed by other developments, notably the nomination of Mr. Roosevelt for a fourth term and the attempted assassination of Hitler. The trend of official American thinking was satisfaction that Tojo was out, but disbelief that his successors would depart from the policies which had prevailed to date.[61] The speed with which Tojo disappeared from public view, even in Japan, was the

---

[60] On the fall of the Tōjō Cabinet: Hattori, III, 174-81 and 191; Kido "Nikki," S 120:5-6, T 11372-78; Butow, *Japan's Decision to Surrender*, 27-28; JRD, "Interrogations," I:49157 (Seizō Arisue), 32-33; JRD files: Takagi, "Memo on the Course of the War"; JRD Doc. No. 57597 ("Takagi Notes," June 8 and 17, 1944) and Doc. No. 58228 ("Takagi Notes," June 27 and July 16, 1944); Mitarai direct examination, S 173:6, T 17797-98; Kido corresp.; Shigemitsu, *Shōwa no Dōran*, II, 227-31; Shigemitsu, Hattori, and Mrs. Tōjō intv.; Tōjō aff., S 342:12, T 36172-73; and Kase, 78-82. See also Okada, "Tōjō Seiken to Jūshin-tachi," 86-88, 90-94; Okada, *Okada Keisuke Kaiko-roku*, 205-30; Okada Taishō Kiroku Hensan-kai, *Okada Keisuke*, 371-89; Wakatsuki, 424-25; and Kido corresp. The Emperor was kept fully informed of developments, but—despite some statements to the contrary—he did not personally play any part in the fall of Tōjō. The three conditions posed by Kido on July 13 originated with the lord privy seal.

The senior statesmen who met together on the evening of July 17 were Konoe, Okada, Yonai, Hiranuma, Hirota, Wakatsuki, and Abe. All except Abe were in entire agreement with the resolution. All except Konoe and Hiranuma had participated in the *jūshin* meeting of October 17, 1941, at which Tōjō's nomination to the premiership had been sanctioned.

[61] See, for example, *NYT*, July 20 and 21, 1944.

more surprising because of the role he had supposedly played as a twentieth-century shogun.

From the very beginning of the war, Tojo had been a focus of attention on both sides of the Pacific. In Japan, regardless of where power actually rested, Tojo was the titular leader of the nation at war. As such he was frequently endowed with the attributes of a paragon. He was pictured in Japanese propaganda as kindly, sincere, frank, honest, courageous, diligent, humane, steadfast, gentle, and decisive. . . .[62] This was a rather atypical development, since emphasis upon individual leadership had not been a prominent feature of Japanese political life. As the war turned against Japan, however, Tojo became one of the major casualties. The press still wrote glowingly on occasion, but the public—although silent—took to a kind of personal fault-finding that was to reach its apex following the surrender. Dissatisfaction stemmed from the fact that Tojo as war leader extraordinary did not really fit the accepted molds of the past. And perhaps more importantly, because he failed to lead the people to the promised land.

After the war, some Japanese would resentfully recall that Tojo's two eldest sons had escaped military service (on the basis of near-sightedness and essential employment in industry). Postwar critics would also ridicule the fact that Mrs. Tojo had become something of a public figure in her own right, thus breaking a hoary tradition: wives—even those of prominent generals and politicians—were to be seen and not heard. Mrs. Tojo had made public appearances, speeches, broadcasts, and in other ways had been both active and vocal in the war effort. She had thus incurred, behind her back, the carping designation, "Tō Bi-rei"—a play upon words which likened her to Madame Chiang Kai-shek (Soong Mei-ling), known in Japan as "Sō Bi-rei."

Censure of Tojo personally was later to include a variety of charges. It was rumored that he had blackmailed individuals with information collected while he was chief of the *kenpeitai* in Manchuria; that he had dismissed, or forced into retirement, all those who had disagreed with him; that he had even driven an opponent (Seigo Nakano) to commit suicide.

Tojo was also accused of misusing army funds for personal political gain and of buying influence in high places by bestowing gifts on the right people, including members of the imperial household ministry and the board of chamberlains. The senior statesmen and the privy

---

[62] See Bainbridge, 26ff., for an interesting profile constructed from Japanese domestic propaganda.

councilors were said to have received presents of Western clothing, tobacco, and whiskey purloined from the occupied areas of the South. It was also asserted that Tojo had given automobiles to the imperial brothers, Chichibu and Takamatsu. When this was reported to the throne, the Emperor had allegedly remarked that if there was enough empty space in the ships to transport automobiles, it would be better to bring back rice.

In short, by the time the cabinet had fallen, Tojo had largely lost the personal popularity his position as premier and war minister had given him during the victories of the early months of 1942. It was later reported that for days after the public revelation of Japan's defeat at Saipan, Tojo's telephone rang and anonymous voices asked his wife, "Hasn't Tojo committed hara-kiri yet?" If the truth were known, the very same people had probably shouted the loudest "Banzai!" upon "Banzai!" when all had been going well.[63]

In the United States and elsewhere in the Allied world, Tojo had understandably been unpopular from the very beginning. As the smoke had cleared from Oahu, the figure of Japan's military premier—impassively diabolic—had emerged in the public eye as the man responsible. Thereafter he had served as the convenient symbol of all that Americans hated in their Japanese enemy. "Tojo" was a name known to practically everyone; his was one of the few "faces" of the war that was widely recognized. Within the Allied camp he was pictured as "sinister, threatening, brutal, a Hitler with the added danger of Oriental mysticism."[64] Descriptions of him hewed to a cut of features and character equally forbidding. He was called "the tight-lipped little Hideki Tojo," "the grim little Minister of War," "the tough little general."[65] To others he was the "bullet-headed Tojo," "the beak-nosed, bald-pated Tojo," "this ugly little man" with "sharp, pointed features" and a "scarred bald head," whose "zeal as the Heinrich Himmler of the Army still clings to him like a malignant odour."[66]

The *New Yorker* magazine made him the subject of a profile: "He comes as close as a Japanese can to looking important. He is fairly tall, as his race grows, standing five feet six inches—two and a half inches

[63] The text draws on a variety of sources, some of which must remain of a privileged nature. See *ibid.*; Lee, *One Last Look Around*, 95-96; JRD Doc. No. 56008 ("Takagi Notes"); and an Associated Press dispatch ("Tojo Sees Time Vindicating Japan . . .") in *NYT*, September 11, 1945, 1-2.

[64] Lee, 96.

[65] Millis, 140, 176, 177.

[66] Wheeler, *Dragon in the Dust*, 213; Kelley and Ryan, *Star-Spangled Mikado*, 44 and 49; Lee, 113; and Lory, 129.

taller than the average of his male countrymen. He weighs about a hundred and fifty-five pounds and is compactly built and healthy. His small, egg-shaped head, practically bald, is splotched with a stubble of bristly hairs. He has no eyelashes, you can count the hairs in his eyebrows, his mustache is scrawny and his whole face has a parched look, as though he had caught his head in an oven. Thin-lipped, his ears ironed in close to his head and his forehead angrily furrowed, Tojo peers at the world morosely through horn-rimmed spectacles. His movements are as brisk as a terrier's. During business hours he walks with the hurried, agitated step of a man pursued. He is an impatient listener and a fast talker. When he speaks, which is no oftener than he has to, he spatters his words like a burst of machine-gun bullets. He is humorless, hardboiled, and as subtle as a pile-driver. He speaks no foreign language and is not gifted in the use of his own. 'He cannot fire an audience,' a Chinese intelligence officer has said, 'but he can make his junior officers jump.' Tojo is a man with no time for a hobby, for the arts, or for any other wasteful foolishness. 'Endeavor and hard work,' he once explained to a group of Japanese adolescents called the Student Morals Discussion Committee, 'have been my friends throughout life, as I am just an ordinary man possessing no brilliant talents.' After making the usual discount for Japanese mock modesty, there is still something in what Tojo says."[67]

Other descriptions pictured the premier as "tortured by ambition," "envious of his father's record," a wise-guy type who strutted and swaggered.[68] But perhaps the most revealing portrait, in terms of the role Tojo played in American propaganda, appeared in early February 1944 as part of "The Guilty" series run by *Collier's*, a magazine which then had a circulation in excess of 2,800,000.[69] The admixture of information and misinformation makes the entire piece a caricature of a caricature:

"The real ruler of Japan is not Hirohito but chunky, granite-faced Hideki Tojo. As Premier, War Minister and Home Secretary, all power is in his hands, for he controls the courts and the police, as well as policies and military operations. The members of the Japanese Diet are his rubber stamps, for his assassins are quick to liquidate dissenters. More than any other, this walking venom sac embodies the fanaticisms

[67] Bainbridge, 28.
[68] Gayn, *Japan Diary*, 206-7, and Lory, 174-75.
[69] The Tōjō sketch, which is quoted in full in the text that follows, appeared in the February 5, 1944 issue of *Collier's*, page 60. The circulation figure is from N. W. Ayer & Son's *Directory: Newspapers and Periodicals, 1945*.

and ferocities of his race, for even as he forced war with China and the United States, so is he waging both wars with a barbarity unknown since man quit running about on all fours."

In point of fact, Tojo had relinquished the home affairs portfolio in February 1942, he never enjoyed the control attributed to him, nor was he the chief of a band of assassins. Tojo was not responsible for the outbreak of the China Incident.

"The horrors of Nanking, Hong Kong and Shanghai did not proceed from the sudden fury of wild beasts excited by the smell of blood. Japanese troops acted under the direct orders of Tojo himself, conveyed in these precise words: 'In pursuit, be thorough and *inexorable.*' The bayoneting of British and Canadian captured and wounded, the rape and murder of hospital nurses, the torture of prisoners, the beheading of Chinese noncombatants until the very gutters ran blood—all of these bestialities trace back to Hideki Tojo, insane with his hate of 'foreign devils' and infatuated with the German theory of *Schrecklichkeit.*"

The atrocities committed by Japanese military forces before and during the Greater East Asia War were judged by the International Military Tribunal for the Far East to have been committed "on a scale so vast, yet following so common a pattern in all theaters, that only one conclusion is possible—the atrocities were either secretly ordered or wilfully permitted by the Japanese Government or individual members thereof and by the leaders of the armed forces."[70] The words attributed to Tojo, however, "In pursuit, be thorough and inexorable" are from the Field Service Code (Senjin-kun), issued in his capacity as war minister on January 8, 1941, more than four years after the rape of Nanking, an event with which he had no connection whatsoever. The statement quoted might more accurately have been translated from the original as, "Pursuit should be carried out to the very end in a decisive and thorough manner."[71] The Field Service Code also advised the soldiers of Japan to deal with matters justly and to conduct themselves in such a way as not to be ashamed of their behavior either in the sight of heaven or in the eyes of man.

"The Death March from Bataan, that ghastly journey in the course of which hundreds of American soldiers died of starvation, beating and stabbing, is another crime that lies at Tojo's doorstep. His violation of every rule of civilized warfare was deliberate, and warfare in the

---

[70] J, B/VIII, 1001.

[71] "Tsuigeki wa dandanko to shite aku made mo tettei-teki naru beshi." The Japanese text of the *Senjin-kun* can be found in Shunichirō Itō, 139-50.

Pacific is marked by the same ordered animalism. Captives lashed to trees and bayoneted into pulp; others mutilated, daubed with honey and staked out on the ground for the ants to eat; still others blinded and broken and thrown into the jungle and its night creatures. For these and all other atrocities, Hideki Tojo, supreme war lord, is responsible."

No evidence was produced at the Tokyo trial to show that Tojo had ever personally ordered or committed any atrocities, but he was found guilty of having permitted *the commission of various war crimes. The Tribunal believed that "the barbarous treatment of prisoners and internees was well known to Tojo." His judges concluded that he had not taken "adequate steps to punish offenders" or to prevent the continued commission of war crimes.*[72]

"The whole life of the man is red with blood and black with treachery. He first rose to fame in 1932 when he and his assassins set out to still every voice that preached peace or liberalism. Prime Minister Inukai, Finance Minister Inouye and Baron Takuma Dan, head of the great House of Mitsui, were murdered in swift succession, and, two years later, Major General Nagata, chief of the Military Affairs Bureau, and Tojo's superior, was stabbed to death as he sat in his office."

Tojo had absolutely nothing to do with any of the assassinations mentioned here. Even his worst enemies in Japan would not suggest such a connection.

"The pace, however, was too fast even for a people accustomed to assassination, and an imperial order sent Tojo to the sticks. A forceful schemer and unresting, he soon reappeared as head of the Military Gendarmerie, a combination of Gestapo and Ogpu, and then bobbed up in command of the Kwantung army. He proceeded to aggravate the 'China Incident' by marching his men into the province of Chahar, starting the bloody business that was to lay China waste."

The bloody business that laid China waste was started in the vicinity of the Marco Polo Bridge near Peking. Tojo was nowhere near the scene. Not even the prosecution at the Tokyo trial attempted to link him directly with the event.

" 'Slaughter battles,' the massacre of unarmed civilians, was a Tojo invention, and it was Tojo who accelerated the opium traffic, even doping the candy given to little children. He also rounded up vast numbers of Chinese for deportation to Manchuria where they died by thousands under the lash of Japanese masters."

[72] J, C/X, 1208.

*The Japanese were engaged in an extensive drug traffic on the conti-
nent and they were known for their employment of forced labor, but
the charges against Tojo personally remain unsubstantiated.*

"There were still some sane men in the Tojo government and, in
1936, the indefatigable Tojo engineered another 'patriotic purge.' Officers of the army, forming a murder gang, shot down 80-year-old Taka-
yashi [*sic*], Minister of Finance, Admiral Saito, Lord Keeper of the
Seals, and Inspector General Watanabe. Prime Minister Okada was on
the list, but the assassins killed his brother-in-law by mistake. On the
heels of this purge, Tojo was made Vice-Minister of War, and lost no
time in declaring for the Greater East Asia Co-Prosperity Sphere, meaning an end to all white interference in the Orient."

*There was no "Tojo government" in 1936, and Tojo did not engineer
the February mutiny in which Takahashi, Saito, and Watanabe were
assassinated. Tojo, who was in Manchuria at the time, rounded up
Japanese in sympathy with the mutiny and put them all in jail. He was
not made vice-minister of war until March 1938, more than two years
after the mutiny.*

"Konoye, the Prime Minister, stood out against war with the United
States, and so did Baron Hiranuma, the Home Secretary, but when an
assassin's bullet put Hiranuma in a hospital bed, Konoye found it
expedient to resign, and deadly Hideki Tojo took his place. With the
army under his absolute control and Hirohito no more than a puppet,
the iron-willed gangster struck the match that was to set fire to his
powder train. Hurrying Kurusu to Washington to keep the United
States cajoled and befooled, he launched his attack on Pearl Harbor."

*The implication that there was a connection between Tojo and the
attempt on Hiranuma's life, or between the attack on Hiranuma and
Konoe's resignation as premier, is without foundation. Kurusu was not
sent to the United States as an emissary of deceit. Tojo did decide for
war, but the Pearl Harbor attack was not his contribution.*

"There will be no peace as long as 'Old Razor Blades' stays at the
head of Japan's government. As venomous as he is implacable, he has
ordered a war to the death and he means just that: No quarter. Kill,
burn, torture and hara-kiri—the samurai way—rather than capture.
That is the sad part of it. Hitler and Mussolini, in all likelihood, will
break and crawl at the last, but Hideki Tojo will never let himself live
to be tried by 'foreign barbarians.' The only thing to do is to hasten the
day when he will plunge a knife into his belly, draw it across and
turn it upward. . . ."

So spoke *Collier's* magazine to its readers in February 1944. Within six months, Hideki Tojo, "supreme war lord," had been relegated to the role of private citizen and, unofficially, "army elder"—a term used loosely ·to describe any prominent retired officer, especially one who had once held a key post at the center.

And yet the war did not end. It was not to end for another year, despite a rapidly accelerating rate of deterioration. As the months passed, each exacting a heavy toll, Tojo lived a quiet life compared with the busy days and nights of his premiership. His participation in affairs of state had come abruptly to an end, but not his interest in the outcome of events or his concern about the nation's future. As late as the end of February 1945 he still possessed what might be called the optimism of the damned.

By that time the situation had become so threatening that His Majesty, breaking with standard procedure, insisted upon listening personally to the views of the senior statesmen, even though it was feared by the lord privy seal that such a move would antagonize the army. To minimize that possibility, Marquis Kido made arrangements for the ex-premiers to be received individually over a period of nearly three weeks rather than together, as a group, on a single day.[73] Tojo's turn came on February 26. The underlying theme of his advice to the Emperor was that the Allies were preparing to step up their activities against Japan, but that all was not lost.[74]

Tojo began his presentation by noting that a conference would open in San Francisco on April 25 at which both Nationalist China and the Soviet Union would be present. The date was a significant one for Japan. Unless her neutrality pact with the Soviet Union were renewed by then, expiration would automatically occur a year later. The Allied aim, he said, was to dispose of Germany by April in order to demonstrate that Japan was in a helpless condition and unable to continue the war. The air attacks to which the homeland had recently been subjected were intended to further that aim. The enemy might strike next at various other points (Formosa, the Ryukyu chain, Shanghai) in order to show the world that Japan could not lift a finger in retaliation. At

---

[73] For additional material on these February audiences, see Butow, *Japan's Decision to Surrender*, 44-50.

[74] The gist of Tōjō's remarks to the throne was recorded at the time by the grand chamberlain. It forms part of an imperial household document entitled "Shōwa Nijūnen Nigatsu, Jikyoku ni kan suru Jūshin Hōtō-roku," a copy of which was lent to the author by the former lord privy seal, Kōichi Kido. Also, Kido corresp.

least, such action could be expected in view of the "adventurous character of the United States. . . ."

The air raids being experienced by Japan, however, were insignificant in comparison with those being launched against Germany. The situation would be comparable, Tojo declared, only if Tokyo were being raided, day after day, by several thousand planes based in Okayama or Shikoku (a distance equivalent to that separating German targets from Allied bases). Instead, Japan was merely faced with an attack about once a week by one hundred or so B-29's coming from bases well in excess of 2,000 kilometers away. From the standpoint of modern war, however, such attacks were only a prelude to what was to come. If the Japanese people were to feel discouraged over such a "small matter" as the current raids, it would be impossible to speak in terms of completing the Greater East Asia War or any other such major enterprise. . . .[75]

The "pressing requirement of the moment" was to make it manifestly clear that both political and military strategy were under His Majesty's direct administration and command. The army and navy must cooperate fully and flawlessly with each other and truly act as though they constituted a single organization. Such an organization was spoken of as if it existed, Tojo said, but in reality it did not. In a situation in which one had to think about coming face to face with the enemy at close quarters, it was essential that the army and navy be united and that they be of assistance to each other. . . .[76]

Even if the Soviets abrogated the neutrality pact with Japan, all would be well so long as the people of Japan believed that the war was based on justice and that the imperial land could not be destroyed. It might still be possible to grasp peace by watching developments in Europe, but if Japan became exhausted everything would be lost. . . .

When the Emperor asked whether there was no danger of a Soviet entry into the war against Japan, Tojo replied at length and in a manner which combined frankness with naiveté. He cited the reports of two Japanese who had been able to make personal observations abroad.

[75] Although there was evidence of anxiety among the people, Tōjō believed that they could bear up under difficulties. He admitted that there was concern about rationing and other matters of daily livelihood, but he informed the throne that complaints against the rationing system had really arisen from the fact that in former days the people had gorged themselves with food. To date, he declared, not a single one of His Majesty's subjects had died of starvation (!).

[76] Tōjō also told the Emperor that Japan should utilize North China, Korea, Manchuria, and the Japanese homeland as her base of operations. With the imperial navy in command of the Tsugaru and Korean Straits (at the northern and southern extremities of Honshū), and with the imperial army ready and prepared, there would be no cause for concern, even if the enemy attempted to trespass upon the homeland. . . .

One man believed that the Russian people did not desire war and that even if Germany were crushed, the Kremlin would be unable to divert Soviet military strength to the Far East.[77] The other thought that if a "big chance" to do Japan damage should occur, the Kremlin would deploy large military forces for that purpose. Tojo admitted to the Emperor that it was not difficult to reach either of these diametrically opposite conclusions. He personally felt that it was a fifty-fifty proposition whether or not the Soviets would join in the war against Japan in case of an Allied victory in Europe. . . .

If Japan lost Iwo Jima and Formosa, and if the Ryukyu chain and the China mainland also fell to the enemy, the Soviet Union would probably conclude that a "little push" would be sufficient to get rid of Japan. For the moment, however, he could not believe that Japan would be faced with such an ugly state of affairs by April 25. As matters stood, the situation was really a "tie."

In concluding his remarks to the throne, Tojo referred to the men of the special attack (*kamikaze*) corps, for whom he felt great admiration. He repeated to the Emperor a conversation he had had with a youth of twenty who was going from the Matsumoto regiment to Formosa. The young man had said that he regarded meeting death as a returning home, and that he would positively carry out a suicide attack within two months after arriving at his new post. His plane was one of the old types (so slow that it would very likely be shot down before it ever reached its target), but he was not worried. He had told Tojo: "I have become accustomed to flying in that airplane, so it is quite good enough. . . ."

Nearly two weeks before Tojo's historic audience, the Emperor had listened to an equally positive but far more pessimistic report on Japan's prospects by none other than Prince Fumimaro Konoe. The prince had bluntly said that he believed Japan had already lost the war and that unless hostilities were ended soon, defeat might be accompanied by a Communist revolution.[78]

As the event turned out, Konoe's predictions proved closer to reality

[77] Tōjō's source had explained that deep conflicts existing among the Americans, the British, and the Russians would become more intense, making it necessary for the Soviet Union to retain powerful armies in Europe. The truth was that the Soviets were suffering from fatigue and weariness and that reconstruction and reorganization were necessary. It would therefore be difficult for them to become engaged in the Soviet Far East on a major scale.

[78] See Butow, *Japan's Decision to Surrender*, 47.

than Tojo's. The war in the Pacific had already entered its final phase by late February 1945. The heavy casualties suffered at Iwo Jima did not prevent the throwing of an Easter Sunday invasion punch at Okinawa. The date was April 1—hardly more than a month after Tojo's call at the palace. The long-awaited German surrender on May 7/8 provided a brief but potentially decisive moment which the Japanese government might have utilized to advantage to terminate hostilities in the Pacific. But the government was not prepared psychologically, politically, or diplomatically to take the initiative. The new cabinet of Admiral Baron Kantaro Suzuki struggled a while longer with the insurmountable problems that beset a nation fighting a battle which has already been lost. It was thus not until mid-August 1945, after crisis had been piled upon crisis, that the hostilities which the Tojo Cabinet had begun in December 1941 finally came to a fearful end.

In a war that was the bloodiest in human memory, covering more of the world with greater misery than any previous conflict, the cost to the Japanese people of their own share of the enterprise was staggering. Defeat reduced by nearly half the territory over which Japan had claimed sovereignty when the war began. Yet in that restricted area it would be necessary to find room for some 7,000,000 Japanese nationals returning home from overseas, and to accommodate, as well, an annual population increase exceeding 1,000,000.

In terms of August 1945 prices, the losses incurred in the general national wealth amounted to 65,300,000,000 yen. The further loss of various military properties added another 40,400,000,000—for an astronomical total of 105,700,000,000 yen. The toll in terms of human lives, civilian and military, was in excess of 2,500,000 *dead and missing* (three-fifths of whom were members of the imperial Japanese army). Approximately 8,750,000 Japanese suffered personal property losses as a result of the extension of the air war to Japan proper.[79] There can be little wonder, then, that Okinori Kaya, who had been Tojo's finance minister, should eventually declare that the Greater East Asia War was "the greatest misfortune in Japan's history" and that the suffering endured by the Japanese people as a result of that war was beyond the power of words to express.[80]

A man less sure than Hideki Tojo that he had had no other choice—that there had been no other way—might have found it more difficult to live with the knowledge of the human and material cost of the decision for

[79] Hattori, IV, 455-58.
[80] Kaya, 190.

war which had been made in 1941. Whatever else history may say about General Tojo, there can be no heavier responsibility assigned to him, or greater censure, than that the ultimate effect of the policies adopted during his premiership was to bring the one hundred million people of Japan to the threshold of annihilation.

CHAPTER 14

When Honor's Lost

THE American Occupation of Japan was already into its second week before General MacArthur found time to order the arrest of Hideki Tojo and thirty-nine other war-criminal suspects, including the members of the Pearl Harbor cabinet.[1] This lack of dispatch prompted the conclusion among some newsmen that the Supreme Commander was "deliberately" giving Japan's war leaders "enough time to commit suicide."[2] Perhaps such a thought crossed a few minds in Tokyo or in Washington. There were those who later wished that it had, but the delay seems more likely to have been inadvertent than contrived: there were simply too many other matters of greater importance demanding immediate attention.

The center of American activity for the first ten days of the Occupation was the port of Yokohama, with Tokyo, the capital, falling largely into the category of the great unknown. The agents of the Counter Intelligence Corps were new to their task and were finding much that was unfamiliar in a land in which, even without the disruptions of defeat, foreigners had generally been mystified. The need to place Tojo in custody at once may not have appeared quite so pressing to the Supreme Commander as it later seemed to others with equally long memories of the Pacific war.

The formerly extensive Empire of Japan had been reduced to the status of a "tight little island." An individual of no prominence might have been able to lose himself in the masses, but a former wartime premier would have found it far more difficult to effect an escape from the due processes of law. Indeed, there was every likelihood of his being turned over to the authorities by his compatriots if he tried to do so.

The correspondents themselves were scarcely less slow in undertaking what might have been considered a worthwhile venture: tracking down General Tojo and recording for posterity whatever he had to say about

[1] See the Kluckhohn dispatch, *NYT*, September 12, 1945, 1 (the complete roster of those ordered arrested on Tuesday, September 11, is given on page 3), and *Nippon Times*, September 13, 1945, 1.
[2] Kelley and Ryan, 56, give this as their conclusion and further state that "it was clear to everybody" that that was SCAP's intention. The italics of the original have been dropped.

the "light from the East" which was now extinguished. The newsmen, however, were overwhelmed by the opportunity for reporting an infinite variety of scenes which attracted their attention in every quarter. It was thus not until September 10, the day before MacArthur acted, that a few enterprising members of the press got around to seeking out the Japanese "Hitler," alias the "would-be Napoleon of the Orient," "the shaven-headed one-time terror of Asia."

Among them was Clark Lee of the International News Service, who was guided in the general direction of Tojo's residence by a Japanese national whose only tangible reward was a package of American cigarettes, obtainable at GI establishments for five cents.[3] Lee and his party found their way without difficulty, thanks largely to the help given them during the last stage of their quest by an obliging Japanese policeman. The Tojo dwelling revealed itself as a very modest, single-story, Japanese-style house with a semi-Western exterior. The building stood on a rise of ground bordered on one side by homes of a more elaborate type, some of which had been burned out during the war, and on the other side by broad fields so intensively cultivated that they seemed about to encroach upon the few narrow roads and lanes which cut through them.

The premises were guarded by a number of Japanese policemen and soldiers who reacted to the Americans in a way that was soon to become standard—with curiosity, but without any apparent hostility. The Japanese security detail was there to protect the general from assassination, a fate which some fanatics had allegedly wanted to impose during the declining months of the war.[4]

On the way out to the house, Lee had said to Harry Brundidge, one of his companions, "Don't shake hands with him," and Brundidge had replied, "I wouldn't shake hands with the bastard for anything in the world." But when Tojo suddenly appeared around a corner of the house, Lee found himself grasping the firm hand which Tojo thrust out at him. The ex-premier was informally attired "in white shorts and

---

[3] The text which follows draws on Lee, 92-98 and 102; Brundidge, "Tojo Tried to Die," *American Mercury*, August 1953, 7; and an AP dispatch ("Tojo Sees Time Vindicating Japan. . . ."), *NYT*, September 11, 1945, 1. The text also relies in part, as elsewhere in this chapter, on material gathered during visits by the author to the scene of the events described, and on interviews with Mrs. Tōjō.

[4] Colonel Hattori (intv.) confirmed that a general staff major had contemplated killing Tōjō in 1944. He was arrested, dropped in rank to private first-class, and put in prison. Other wartime reports of attempts on Tōjō's life either proved false or unverifiable. The Japanese police at Tōjō's residence, on the day in question, told the American correspondents that their mission was to protect Tōjō from assassination.

shirt, gray socks that came up over his knees, and low black button shoes." He motioned the correspondents to some garden furniture and offered them Japanese cigarettes sold under the brand name of "Hope." Tojo struck Lee as being "nervous, not knowing what to expect next, although he was perfectly in control of himself. . . . He looked hard as nails. But there was something wrong in his demeanor. If you had interviewed him ten years before, say, in Manchuria, or if it had been possible to interview him just before he dispatched the carriers to attack Pearl Harbor and started the invasion fleets for the Philippines and Southeastern Asia, his replies would have been gruff and condescending. He would have used the prescribed means of a Japanese general dealing with an American—a superior air, deceiving half-truths, denial of knowledge of any embarrassing matter. All his adult life he had studied that manner, and now it was gone and without it he was only another little man. Outwardly hard as nails, but inwardly you sensed a softness—the hard something that had been his self-discipline, his beliefs, his power and authority, his life-and-death control over millions, wasn't there and the man was hollow inside."

Tojo said through an interpreter that he was completely out of politics and military affairs, that he could not discuss such matters "because it [was] not for a defeated general to talk," that he was now just a "farmer" tending his crops. But when he was asked whether he believed Japan's cause had been just, he responded quickly and with emphasis: "Hai, Hai! [Yes, Yes!] I do believe that Japan's fight was based on righteousness. I realize that America will not agree with that. However, I believe that it will take time and an impartial third party to make the final decision as to whether America's fight was just, or Japan's was."

"I was responsible for the war. I accept full and complete responsibility. But I do not believe that makes me a war criminal. There is a difference between leading a nation in a war which it believes right and just, and being a war criminal. . . . But again, that is for the victorious nation to decide."

When the issue of army-navy unity came up, Tojo suggested that the correspondents ask the American forces what they thought of Japanese service cooperation during the war. "His humorous observation seemed to cheer him up and suddenly his mood changed. He smiled, sat forward in his chair, and picked up Brundidge's field cap. Like a delighted kid he tried it on, turning it this way and that. It fitted his bullet-shaped head like a washtub. He mugged, smiled a solid-gold smile out from under the American eagle, and murmured, 'Oki, oki! (Too big.)' He might have been referring to American power, as much as to the size of the hat."

Soon thereafter the correspondents took their leave. Tojo accompanied them to the gate and even waved to them as they drove away to file their stories of an interview with "the most brilliant and successful Asiatic commander since Genghis Khan."[5]

An Associated Press team which also visited Tojo's home on September 10 had much the same experience. Tojo would not discuss his possible trial as a war criminal, "but was willing to talk of many things, in moods ranging from steely-eyed impassivity to hearty laughter."

"Real soldiers fight to the finish in the field," Tojo said. "War ends when peace is declared. Each respects an enemy who fights hard and cleanly, and so MacArthur has the respect of myself as well as the Japanese people."

When the ex-premier was asked who was responsible for starting the war, he replied: "You are the victors and you are able to name him now. But historians 500 or 1,000 years from now may judge differently."

"When Tojo was told that he was more widely known in America than any other Japanese except the Emperor, he shot back: 'For good or for bad?'"

During these exchanges, "American planes constantly droned overhead. Tojo explained that his house was in line with the regular run between Atsugi airfield [where MacArthur had landed on August 30] and Tokyo." It had also been on the B-29 circuit during the last months of the war and had only narrowly escaped the devastation of the fireraids. A small, detached building which Tojo had used as a study and reception room, and which had housed his personal papers, had been destroyed during a very severe incendiary attack on May 25, 1945. An air-raid shelter, which had saved the lives of his family on that occasion, was being filled in by a laborer while the correspondents were on the premises. "You burned my three best pine trees," Tojo said. "Now I have to replace them with bamboo."[6]

The next day, Tuesday, September 11, the rather ordinary and tranquil scene of these interviews became one of crassness and violence. When MacArthur's roundup order reached the ears of the American

---

[5] See the citations in footnote 3 above. "Oki, oki!" should of course be "Ōkii, ōkii!"

[6] AP dispatch ("Tojo Sees Time Vindicating Japan. . . ."), *NYT*, September 11, 1945, 1, and Mrs. Tōjō intv. See also the Murlin Spencer and Russell Brines dispatch, *NYHT*, September 11, 1945, 2 (late city edition). It would appear that Spencer and Brines interviewed Tōjō before Lee and Brundidge arrived on the scene (see Spencer's letter to the editor in the July 5, 1958, issue of *Editor & Publisher*).

press shortly after noon, correspondents, photographers, and assorted personnel (including the White Russian girl friend of one of the pressmen) made a mad dash for the Tamagawa quarter of the Setagaya ward where Tojo lived.

Tokyo, like many other Japanese cities, is a labyrinthine place, puzzling even to those who know it by long association. But the correspondents proved more adept at finding their way through its maze of streets than the CIC agents who had been given the mission of bringing Tojo in. One team reportedly got lost and never did reach the house; a second team accepted the help of one of the correspondents who had interviewed Tojo the day before. When this contingent at last arrived, it found the ex-premier's residence already under the surveillance of a group of restless, sweltering, and excited newsmen, some of whom had been there for several hours, harrying the Tojo household with requests for cold beer, or scotch and ice, and with offers to drive Tojo to MacArthur's headquarters so that he could give himself up, which would have been a scoop indeed.[7]

While the press milled around the garden, Tojo sat at his desk in the one Western-style room in the house, to the left of the front entry. His four daughters and his youngest son had recently been sent to Kyushu, the southernmost island of Japan. He had wanted his wife to accompany them but she had decided to stay with him until the last possible moment. If Tojo died, she wanted their children to hear from her own lips how he had died. She did not want them to read a questionable account in the newspapers.

As the activity outside the house increased, Tojo told his wife to take the maid and go to the home of some relatives who lived in the same section of the city. On leaving the room, Mrs. Tojo said simply, *Daiji wo o tori ni naru yō ni,* "Please don't do anything rash."

Some weeks before, soon after he had tearfully listened to the imperial broadcast announcing the surrender, Tojo had asked a doctor named Suzuki, who lived across the street, to mark the location of his heart on his chest with charcoal. Tojo seemed to be concerned about the fact that the heart is not always where one expects to find it. He told the doctor, "In case the need should arise, it wouldn't do to aim at the wrong spot. . . ." Later, when he was bathing, he had called out suddenly for charcoal because the mark had begun to disappear.

[7] See Lee, 99-104; Brundidge, 7-9; the George E. Jones dispatch, *NYT*, September 12, 1945, 1 and 2; and the Murlin Spencer letter to the editor in the July 5, 1958, issue of *Editor & Publisher*.

Although Mrs. Tojo knew that her husband might take his life, she also knew that he regarded suicide as the easiest way out, and that he was concerned about the need to explain Japan's actions and to assume the responsibility which might otherwise mistakenly be assigned by the Allied powers to the Emperor. She therefore fetched the maid and departed with her by a side door. The two women walked down the slope behind the house, and then doubled back along a road which skirts the Tojo compound to the left of the main entrance at a comparatively short distance from the house. As they drew abreast of the lane leading to the front gate, Mrs. Tojo saw a number of parked vehicles and a great deal of activity. She decided not to continue on immediately but to ask permission from the Suzukis to enter the portion of their property opposite her own home so she could observe what was happening there. She borrowed a round, broad-brimmed, gardening hat because she felt it would help hide her features. She also made a pretense of weeding the garden so that her presence would not attract undue attention. She was thus engaged when the CIC agents finally appeared and piled out of their jeeps.[8]

The arresting party, which arrived at 4:00 p.m., was headed by Major Paul Kraus, a Nisei captain, three lieutenants, and a special agent.[9] Two men, thought to be Tojo's secretaries but actually a former policeman and a member of the *kenpeitai*, finally came to the door in response to Kraus' efforts to gain entry. They were told to inform Tojo that officers of the Counter Intelligence Corps wanted to talk with him. Roughly six minutes passed before the two men returned to ask whether the officers had credentials. After an affirmative answer had been conveyed to Tojo, the general sent word that he would receive only those who were in charge. These exchanges all took place through the door, which remained closed and locked. Twelve minutes had already gone by since the arrival of the arresting party. Then, without further ado, Tojo unexpectedly appeared at an open window at the side of the house to the left of the front entry. "He could be seen only from the shoulders up." He "stated that he was 'Tojo Taisho' (General Tojo). He spoke to Major Kraus through a civilian interpreter . . . and repeatedly asked if this were an official arrest. Major Kraus answered that he was directed

[8] Mrs. Tōjō intv.
[9] The text which follows is based on the CIC report written by Major Paul Kraus (CF 20, I, 6), which is corroborated by the Dr. Johnson account to which full reference is made in footnote 13 below.

to bring Tojo to Yokohama and that he should get ready immediately for the trip. Tojo agreed and closed the window."[10]

Kraus and the other officers returned to the front door. It was then 4:17 p.m. Suddenly a shot rang out inside the house. Kraus and a lieutenant named Wilpers immediately broke the lock on the front door and pulled it open. The door to the room to the left of the entry was also locked. Wilpers kicked out the panels and scattered the furniture which had been piled against the door. Tojo "was sitting in an overstuffed chair with his left side towards the door, bleeding from a self-inflicted bullet wound just below the heart. He was still conscious and pointed the pistol which was still in his right hand." Major Kraus ordered him to drop it, and he did. Lieutenant Wilpers circled around to the other side of the chair and picked up the weapon. It was a .32 caliber Colt of the type supplied to American pilots for use in the event of their being forced to parachute from disabled aircraft.[11] Wilpers also retrieved a .25 caliber pistol and an unsheathed hara-kiri knife, covered with a white cloth, both of which were on a table within Tojo's reach. Somewhat later three swords were added to this collection. The two "secretaries" were immediately placed under guard, and the adjoining rooms were sealed with "CIC signs." Major Kraus ordered the Japanese police to remain on duty outside "and not to permit anyone to leave." Wilpers gathered together some documents which he found on Tojo's desk, and also a "last statement" which had been written the day before.

At 4:45 p.m. Major Kraus left the premises to advise headquarters of what had occurred and to obtain an American doctor, an ambulance, and a military police guard. Five minutes later, the remaining officers sent for a Japanese doctor and then moved Tojo "from the chair to a bed in the same room where he would be more comfortable." It was 5:15 p.m. before the Japanese physician arrived. "Tojo was conscious and refused treatment. Lt. Wilpers ordered the doctor to do everything he could to save Tojo's life." As a result, "two bandages were placed on the wound where the bullet had entered and come out." Another

[10] Other accounts indicate that Tōjō appeared at the window twice (e.g., see the George E. Jones dispatch, *NYT*, September 12, 1945, 1 and 2, and the Murlin Spencer letter to the editor in *Editor & Publisher*, July 5, 1958). Jones wrote that someone remarked, "This is beginning to look like a Romeo and Juliet balcony scene."

[11] Eichelberger corresp. The serial number of the weapon was 535330; Tōjō said that the war ministry had given it to him. It later developed that the pistol was the same one which Tōjō's son-in-law, Major Koga, had used to end his own life on August 15 (see p. 468 below).

sixty minutes passed before the American medical team which had been summoned by Major Kraus finally appeared in the room where Tojo had shot himself two hours before.[12]

In charge was James B. Johnson, Jr., of Newark, Ohio—a civilian surgeon turned army captain for the duration, and currently on duty with the 1st Medical Squadron of the 1st Cavalry Division, which had jurisdiction over the area in which the Tojo home was located. When the word had been passed to him that his services were wanted because Tojo had "shot himself in the heart," Johnson had thought someone was kidding him. He "wasn't much in the mood for jokes." He had just recovered from an illness, and he was irked by the fact that he had been in the Pacific for more than twenty-eight months "with no immediate prospect of replacement." Although the war had ended, he was still thinking in terms of combat medical procedure, which called for casualties to be brought to the clearing station, except in a very few instances. Johnson "couldn't exactly see much point either" in going to a patient who had shot himself through the heart more than an hour before. What could a doctor do in such a case except administer first aid or sign a death certificate?

But like all men in every military service in the world, Johnson knew by experience that it was not his to reason why. Once he was convinced the whole thing was not a practical joke, his only thought was to get to the patient as quickly as possible so as to determine whether anything could be done.

Some difficulty was encountered in finding an ambulance with a full tank of gas, but a medical administrative officer finally turned up in one. "He had heard the news and was quite enthused over the whole situation." According to regulations, however, an officer could not drive an ambulance. The two men therefore quickly picked up a sergeant and a medical technician and then joined a veritable "parade" of five jeeps and a weapons carrier of MP's.

Upon arrival at the scene, Johnson found Tojo lying on a bed "partially covered by a crazy quilt of brown, white and blue patches." The room was only dimly lit by a carbon-filament bulb and was so crowded with assorted personnel that it had to be partially cleared to

[12] Major Kraus' CIC report (CF 20, I, 6). See also the Robert Trumbull dispatch, *NYT*, September 13, 1945, 1 and 3; the AP dispatch ("American Doctors Trying to Save Tojo After He Shoots Self to Escape Arrest"), *NYHT*, September 12, 1945 (late city edition), 1; and the Frank Kelley dispatch, *NYHT*, September 12, 1945 (late city lift), 1.

give the doctor room to work. "Professional courtesy" prompted Johnson to consult the Japanese physician, who quickly informed him, through an interpreter, "that the General was shot through the heart—and would die—and nothing could be done for him." Johnson took a look at the patient and decided that "he wasn't dying very rapidly."

Upon pulling back the quilt, Johnson noted that Tojo's undershirt "had blood on it, but not as much as one would expect to see from a heart wound and the dressings underneath were not very bloody." Tojo's pulse, however, "was so weak that it was scarcely perceptible." It was then that Johnson realized that he had come without a stethoscope. Upon request, the Japanese doctor produced "an ancient diaphragm with two long pieces of rubber tubing." With the sergeant standing behind him and holding the tubes in his ears, Johnson was able to listen to Tojo's "weak but steady" heartbeat.

The dressings which had been applied earlier proved to be "perfectly round pieces of gauze," held in place "with several narrow strips of an opaque adhesive material, arranged neatly in a spoke-like radiation that gave the effect of an artistic sunburst." Upon removing the chest bandage, Johnson recognized immediately "what is known as a sucking wound." The lung was punctured. When Tojo breathed, "he sucked air in and blew it out through the hole in his chest."

Johnson placed his "bare thumb on the hole to plug the leak" and instructed his assistants to start administering plasma. "Tojo showed signs of pain and discomfort and made his first acknowledgement" of the presence of the American doctor. Tojo told the interpreter he did not want to get well. Johnson's reply was "direct and not very genteel." Johnson felt that he "had a job to do and the patient's condition, not the patient, was of prime importance."

The fact that he was treating Tojo "meant nothing" to Johnson. During the war, he had been required to give medical aid to Japanese prisoners of war and had invariably done his best to save their lives. "A living prisoner had always meant a source of information which might save Americans. . . . Tojo automatically fell into the category . . . of an enemy prisoner with a sucking wound of the chest, whose life" Johnson felt he "must make every effort to maintain."

When the plasma had been running about a minute, Tojo's pulse "began to pick up." Johnson then decided to get Tojo "in shape to stand the trip to a hospital." Although Johnson had no surgical instruments with him, he had long ago learned to improvise. On this occasion he simply grabbed what the Japanese doctor had on hand: an "antiquated" needle-holder, a pair of well-worn scissors, some white silk thread, and a dull curved needle.

Since there were no facilities for sterilization, Johnson "proceeded without asceptic technique. . . . With the first stitch, the patient flinched and again proclaimed his lack of desire to recover." In the absence of an anesthetic, Johnson "injected some morphine into a vein" and Tojo "readily relaxed." When the closures were completed in front and back, Johnson applied airtight bandages of adhesive plaster. When he reached for the scissors he had borrowed, he discovered that "the Japanese doctor, his nurse and all of his equipment, had disappeared."

It now seemed to Johnson that Tojo "would survive, barring accident and infection." At Major Kraus' request, Johnson submitted to ten or fifteen minutes of "rapid fire" quizzing by the press, "while Tojo tolerated and endured his American blood plasma and enjoyed his morphine. The crowd spontaneously thinned out as the newsmen took hurried leave. . . . The interest in Tojo . . . had died like interest in a defeated vice-president."

Johnson was anxious to get Tojo to the 1st Cavalry Division's clearing station as quickly as possible, but the desired escort was not yet ready to return. The Americans had heard about the extremist Black Dragon Society and "didn't know where Tojo stood with them." Johnson thought "a lone ambulance would be easily spotted on the torn up streets of Tokyo." When Major Kraus agreed to accompany him, however, the doctor decided to delay no longer. Even so, he set out "with a slightly uneasy feeling." As the ambulance picked its way through the gutted roads of the recently occupied capital, the two men discussed the attempted suicide as though Tojo were not present at all. The patient remained quiet the entire time. Once his pulse began to weaken and become irregular, but he was still alive when they reached the clearing station, and he "responded very favorably" to the plasma which was quickly administered. "One correspondent who had been around all evening and who apparently hadn't written a line, turned up again and for at least the tenth time said, 'Oh boy, what a story! What a story!'"[13]

A GI movie just outside the surgery tent was drawing to a close to the strains of "Auld Lang Syne" as Tojo was once again loaded into the ambulance. General Eichelberger, the 8th Army commander, had

[13] The text is based on "Tojo's First Trial," an absorbing account written by Dr. James B. Johnson, Jr., on April 28, 1946, from notes made by him at the time of the experience. The author is greatly indebted to Dr. Johnson for permission to quote from his unpublished account. Also Johnson corresp.

ordered the ex-premier transferred to the 98th Evacuation Hospital in Yokohama, the only U.S. military hospital as yet established by the Occupation forces. This further trip, which began at 7:20 p.m. and ended at 9:40, also proved "uneventful." The patient opened his eyes once but did not speak. At the hospital, which was located in what had formerly been an elementary school, Tojo was taken directly to the operating room, where he was given still another transfusion—his fourth in less than four hours. After a diagnosis by a staff surgeon, he was transferred to the comparative luxury of a bed which had been especially procured for him. The establishment was so new that the other patients, 321 Americans, all had to lie on camp cots.[14]

General Eichelberger, who had come to the hospital from his headquarters, found Tojo "very low and losing great quantities of blood." His eyes were closed and he seemed to be nearing the end. But when he was told that Eichelberger was present, Tojo opened his eyes and tried to bow from the neck. "I am dying," he told the interpreter. "I am sorry to have given General Eichelberger so much trouble." Eichelberger replied, "Do you mean tonight or for the last few years?"[15]

The members of the press who had stayed with the story were not allowed into the room. They had to content themselves with standing in the hallway, separated from the scene by a partition consisting largely of glass windows and doors.[16] That slight impediment was apparently overcome by some means not revealed. In one of their accounts, later published as part of a book, Tojo was quoted as having said: "Please don't go to any trouble over me. I am going to die anyway." To which "gruff, beloved Eichelberger" reportedly responded: "You are going to get better if I have to pump blood into you myself."[17]

In their catch-it-on-the-rebound treatment of the events of September 11, the editors of *Newsweek* gave their readers still another version: At the hospital Tojo "groaned" to the American attendants, "Don't

[14] CF 20, I, 6 (Major Kraus' CIC report); Johnson, "Tojo's First Trial"; and the Robert Trumbull dispatch in *NYT*, September 13, 1945, 1 and 3.

[15] Tōjō answered, "Tonight." Eichelberger, *Our Jungle Road to Tokyo*, 266-67, and Eichelberger corresp. Tōjō also told the interpreter that he would like General Eichelberger to have his "new sword"—a blade some three hundred years old with a beautiful hilt and guard which Eichelberger subsequently presented to his home town, Urbana, Ohio.

See also the Trumbull dispatch, *NYT*, September 13, 1945, 1 and 3, and the Frank Kelley dispatch, *NYHT*, September 13, 1945 (late city edition), 3 (in which the offer of the sword is described as having been made to Eichelberger on the morning of September 12 rather than on the previous night, as the general remembers it).

[16] Eichelberger corresp.

[17] Kelley and Ryan, 55.

go to any trouble over me. I am to die anyway." But General Eichelberger told the medical staff, "Give him the best attention you can. I want an alibi if he dies."[18]

For Major Kraus, who had brought Tojo in, a singular experience was drawing to a close. As his final act, the major stationed a Nisei interpreter at Tojo's bedside to record whatever the patient might say during the night.[19] It was then 10:30 p.m. Orders were issued to forestall any further attempt by Tojo to take his own life.

It had been a grueling day for everyone, including the correspondents. They had been present at a great news story. The dispatches they filed to their home offices and their later reminiscences reflected that fact. At times their fast-moving accounts diverged on various details and in some instances read more like fictionalized re-creations than like the sober and factual reports historians prefer. But the newsmen's knack for snatches of conversation and vivid word pictures serves a purpose. If their material is read more for what it reveals about the reactions of those present than for what it tells concerning the suicide episode, much can be learned about the place Tojo held in the minds of Americans who had traveled the long road from the South Pacific to the heart of the Empire which had attacked Pearl Harbor on a peaceful Sunday in December 1941. The correspondents had "lived" the war for millions of Americans at home. In a sense, Tojo at bay was the last war story to come out of the Pacific, and the newsmen made the most of it.

Time magazine, commenting in retrospect on the events of September 11, 1945, described the scene at Tojo's house that afternoon as revealing the "harum-scarum behavior of the press under stress." Cornelius Ryan, then of the *London Telegraph*, wrote: "The whole thing was a cross between a Marx Brothers movie, *Hellzapoppin* and an Irish wake."[20]

Indeed it was, as the accounts written by the men who were there amply demonstrate. Clark Lee, who had interviewed Tojo in the garden the day before, was among the first to push into the room. In comparison with the staid CIC report submitted by Major Kraus, with its emphasis upon the exact time of every occurrence (as if one of the agents had clocked each development), Lee's description has an impetuous air:

---

[18] *Newsweek*, September 24, 1945, 56. See also the Trumbull dispatch, *NYT*, September 13, 1945, 1 and 3.

[19] Kraus' CIC report, CF 20, I, 6.

[20] *Time*, June 16, 1947, 65. See also Kelley and Ryan, 46.

Tojo lay back in a small armchair, his eyes closed and sweat standing out on his forehead. His open shirt outlined a V of hairless brown chest and flat belly. Blood oozed slowly from a wound just above his heart.

"The bastard has killed himself," an excited voice panted in my ear.

"No. The son of a bitch is still breathing. Look at his belly going up and down."

It was a small room, about fourteen feet long and ten wide, and Tojo's chair was just a foot or two inside the door. A small wooden table was beside him, and a cluttered desk opposite. There was a sofa behind him, and above it a very large oil painting in somber colors, depicting this now bleeding soldier of Japan in one of his moments of triumph.

Into this room now crowded a dozen people, all but two or three of them Americans. . . . The reporters pushed past Tojo, brushing his knees, talking loudly and excitedly. . . .

"The yellow bastard didn't have nerve enough to use a knife," a reporter said. "He knew he wouldn't kill himself with that small bullet."

"Don't be a jackass," another snapped. "You can't put a shot through yourself where he did and expect to live."[21]

Other eyewitnesses added their own distinctive touches:

For a moment everybody was too stunned to do anything. Tojo leaned back and a long squirt of blood shot out from his chest like water coming out under pressure from a hole in a burst pipe. Then a fly which had been making an aerial reconnaissance of his sweating brow landed to make a closer inspection.

Tojo was wearing a white shirt open nearly to the waist, gray military riding breeches and brown riding boots. Behind him was a divan. Above it hung a painting, eight feet by six, depicting the ex-warlord on horseback, standing on a bluff, and behind him, members of his staff, also mounted, reviewing a stream of armored cars and tanks moving along a road. In the foreground of the picture lay a crumpled and dirty Chinese flag still on its short staff. The artist had painted on it the tire marks of vehicles which had passed over it. . . .

In one corner of the room stood a tall hatrack, in another a cedarwood cupboard. This cupboard was a veritable arsenal. It contained several Japanese, German and American-type automatic revolvers and hundreds of rounds of ammunition to fit. Hanging from the wall near the door was a red, white and purple tapestry showing a dragon with blood dripping from its fangs.[22]

The newspaperman plying his trade stops, looks, and listens. He also fires questions at whoever is in a position to answer them. Then he

[21] Lee, 105.
[22] Kelley and Ryan, 46.

breaks for a telephone to flash the news to his home office. This compulsion to report soon gripped those who had crowded into Tojo's "study." The only phone in the house was down a passageway, a short distance from the room. There was the inevitable scramble and then disgruntled curses while the long-winded victor relayed his story. The non-agency and "afternoon" men helped those who represented the wire services and the big morning papers. While one correspondent dictated over the line, which was none too good, another kept him posted on the latest developments by shouting down the hall from the door of the room in which Tojo still lay, oozing blood. A typical conversation ran roughly as follows:

"The joint is swimming in blood . . . no, he's not dead . . . hold on for a minute until I find out. . . . Is the old boy dead yet?"

"No, but he's getting weaker."

"He's getting weaker . . . did you get that? . . . Yeah, he's getting weaker . . . better get a flash ready. . . . The fly is still there . . . yeah, sitting on his forehead . . . hold on. . . . Is the fly still there?"

"Yeah, it's still there . . . seems to be using the old boy's dome for a skating rink."

"Yeah, the fly's still there . . . no, he hasn't made a statement yet . . . hold on."

"He's unconscious, and he's getting cold . . . he won't last much longer. . . ."

"Get this quick . . . at four-thirty Tojo lapsed into unconsciousness . . . his body is going cold . . . no he isn't dead . . . for God's sake hold that 'dead' flash. . . . Look, chum, I wish he would die too. . . ."[23]

Within the room where Tojo lay, there was constant commotion. Bets were being made "on how soon Tojo's small chest would stop heaving"; cigarettes were being lit, puffed, and ground out; wisecracks were being exchanged ("Tojo has earned himself a Purple Heart"); arguments of various kinds were in progress; and that peculiar species—the souvenir-hunters—were busily at work. "Some one had clipped a neat triangle out of Tojo's blood-sodden riding breeches." Others, equally ghoulish, "were soaking their handkerchiefs in the gore."[24]

A photographer for *Yank* magazine snaked an arm through a window from the garden and "liberated" one of Tojo's swords. He was hobbling off with it inside the right leg of his trousers when a CIC officer made him put it back.[25]

[23] *Ibid.*, 47.

[24] See *ibid.*, 53; Lee, 106; the George E. Jones dispatch, *NYT*, September 12, 1945, 1 and 2; and *Newsweek*, September 24, 1945, 56.

[25] Brundidge, 10, and Lee, 106.

Harry Brundidge, "an old hand at police reporting," had surreptitiously retrieved the bullet from the bloody back of Tojo's chair. He showed it to Clark Lee for identification purposes. "Best souvenir of the day," Brundidge whispered, "there can't be two of these."[26]

There was little pity among the correspondents for Tojo. "They had seen hundreds of American and British troops die on the sweltering islands of the Pacific, and they had seen the living skeletons of men and women, ravaged by tuberculosis and beri-beri, released from Japanese prison camps. Only one man showed real emotion—Tojo's secretary. Pushing his way through the crowd, he reached his master and with his hands joined began crying bitterly. He placed his arms around Tojo's head and held it lovingly, moving it gently back and forth to the accompaniment of a strange wailing."[27]

More people were arriving every minute. The room was now full of correspondents, officers and G.I.'s. The air was thick with tobacco smoke. Everybody was waiting for Tojo to die, but he would not oblige.

The photographers arrived. Press photographers are a special race of people. They are happy and good-humored, but nothing is sacred to them, and here was one of the biggest photographic stories of the year.

"Move Tojo's head a little to the right. . . . Hold it . . . swell. . . . I want a shot of Tojo holding the revolver . . . do you mind pressing the gun into his hand? . . . Here comes the fly again . . . I must get one of that. . . ."

Flash bulbs exploded one after another. The photographers crawled all over the room. They stood on chairs. They lay full length on the floor. They crossed and uncrossed Tojo's legs. They photographed the house, his secretary and his servant. Never before had a suicide been so fully recorded.

An Army photographer, who seemed to have stepped straight from the pages of Damon Runyon, came into the room. A dead cigar hung from one side of his mouth. He walked up to the body and looked it over. Raising his camera, he took a photograph.

"Say, bud," he asked, "who is the character?"

A correspondent, busily making notes, answered off-handedly, "Tojo."

The photographer, moving his cigar to the other side of his face, took another picture.

"Who did you say it was?" he asked again.

"Tojo! Tojo!" snapped the correspondent.

The photographer turned to another correspondent. "Say, who is this guy Tojo?"

[26] Lee, 110.
[27] Kelley and Ryan, 48. See also the George E. Jones dispatch, *NYT*, September 12, 1945, 1 and 2.

"Tojo, General Tojo, the Japanese dictator, prime minister at the time of Pearl Harbor," he was told.

The photographer's mouth opened in astonishment. Then he hurled his cigar out of the window.

"D'ya mean to say," he yelled, "that this character is the cause of it all? Only for him I'd be back home? Why, the old son of a bitch! I've a good mind to smack him a fast one with this camera!"

That about summed up the average G.I.'s pity for the bleeding Tojo.[28]

The din grew louder and louder, and the air heavier with smoke as the death watch continued. "An American and an Australian reporter, seeing each other for the first time in months, embraced over Tojo's head and exchanged loud memories of Guadalcanal." A newly-arrived photographer "found a stepladder somewhere, squeezed it into the corner at the foot of the bed [to which Tojo had been transferred], climbed up, and focused. . . . the bulb exploded with a vigorous pop. Reporters who were facing the other way didn't know what had happened. Somebody shouted, 'Booby trap!' The knights of the typewriter made a line plunge for the door and then, discovering it was a false alarm, trooped shamefacedly back into the room, their heavy boots scuffing the polished floor."[29]

Earlier in the afternoon, when he had briefly looked out on the assembled crowd, Tojo had angrily slammed the window shut when a flash bulb had gone off in his face. Now he was at the mercy of the photographers. Through the long period of waiting, Tojo lay mostly with his eyes closed. He occasionally grimaced with pain; at other times his face was a mask. He groaned and twitched and bled, but did not die. He tried to resist the attentions of the Japanese doctor by declaring that his body was his own. When a correspondent asked him why he had not shot himself in the head, he replied, "I wanted to be recognized." He was also quoted later as having said, "Let MacArthur have my corpse. . . . For my corpse I do not care. . . . I have told my family all about it [Tojo had written his personal will and had given his wife hair and nail clippings for the family tomb] . . . but tell MacArthur that I am not to be shown in public."[30]

---

[28] Kelley and Ryan, 49-50.

[29] Lee, 109; repeated, almost verbatim, in Brundidge, 11.

[30] Kelley and Ryan, 48 and 52-53. The parenthetical comment derives from an interview with Mrs. Tōjō. See also *Time*, September 24, 1945, 22, and the Jones dispatch, *NYT*, September 12, 1945, 1 and 2, in which the statement about wanting to be recognized is interpreted as apparently indicating Tōjō's "aversion to the anonymous death of Hitler."

"Down the hall a reporter was on the telephone laboriously spelling out *h* (for *Harry*), *e* (for *everybody*), *m* (for *Mary*), *r* (for *Robert*), *r* (for *Robert*), *h* (for *Harry*), *a* (for *Agnes*), *g* (for *George*), *e* (for *everybody*) . . . 'That's what I said, dammit . . . bleeding. . . .' "[31]

Between lapses into unconsciousness, Tojo made various statements presumably intended for the Japanese public. What he is reported to have said is open to question, and may reflect the greater or lesser skill of the several interpreters who were present. He was later quoted to the effect that he believed the Greater East Asia War was "a just and righteous one," that in the long run history would decide, that he did not want to be tried by the victors, that he now realized the war had been bad for the people (according to *Newsweek*, this was missing from the Japanese version given out by Domei, the official news agency), and that he wished to assume the entire responsibility.[32]

Among the documents appropriated by the CIC was a so-called final statement signed by Tojo in the formal manner (with his titles, court rank, and decorations). It bore the date of the previous day, September 10, 1945. Although the Japanese original has since disappeared, the English translation that was made by the Occupation authorities at the time perhaps comes closest—all things considered—to what Tojo meant to say to posterity.

The statement began with an expression by Tojo of his "deepest apologies to the boundless imperial benevolence" and his fervent hope for the safety of the imperial family and for national prosperity. The Greater East Asia War had come to "an inglorious conclusion." He had decided to take his life in expiation for having caused the Emperor "deep anxiety," for having brought death to a countless number of His Majesty's "faithful subjects," for having "dishonored" Japan's "glorious history by failing to attain the objectives of the war," and for having been "a bearer of public trust" at the outbreak of the conflict. In that way he might also pay his debt to the officers and men who had died on the battlefield, and to their families.

Having "received special favors from the Emperor," Tojo had written, he felt that he could "in no way atone for the injury" to the dignity of Japan resulting from "the disgrace of control by enemy

[31] Brundidge, 12 (the necessary *o* is omitted in the original).
[32] See Lee, 107-8; *Newsweek*, September 24, 1945, 56; Kelley and Ryan, 48, 50-51; the Jones dispatch, *NYT*, September 12, 1945, 1 and 2 (and the AP and UP items which follow it); *Nippon Times*, September 13, 1945, 1 ("Tojo's Condition Grave After Suicide Attempt"); and the Frank Kelley dispatch, *NYHT*, September 12, 1945 (late city lift), 1.

nations." This would have "a detrimental effect on the national soul." The future would determine "the right course for the Empire." He did not think it would be decided by the Allied victory. "Beyond the surrender demands, Japan must find her own way."

Although Japan had been defeated, he still believed—"in the light of all history"—that the concept of the Greater East Asia War had been right. The "spiritual vitality" of their "divine state" could never be taken from the Japanese. As long as the imperial house existed "in its solemn glory," it would be "nourished by the unflagging loyalty of the people." Imperial Japan would return to prosperity.

Although "numerous difficulties" were besetting "the future course of the Empire," the efforts of the whole people would "surely preserve" the national polity. Consequently, he was not abandoning his hope that "the eternal glory of the Empire" would be achieved. "Looking toward the Imperial Palace from afar," Tojo had concluded, "I pray for the health and long life of His Imperial Majesty. . . . I am determined to devote the life of my spirit to the protection of the welfare and prosperity of the nation."

After the date and his signature, Tojo had added a postscript expressing his "deep gratitude to the peoples of Greater East Asia" who had given "their fullest co-operation" in the task of "freeing" that region of the world. It was a matter of regret that the Japanese had been unable to attain their objectives. He would continue his prayers for the "lasting well-being" of the peoples of Asia. . . .[33]

Since Tojo's suicide attempt was unsuccessful, his so-called final statement became little more than a curiosity, greeted with laughter and scorn by the Japanese public and then quickly forgotten. It seems very doubtful, however, that Tojo would have survived had it not been for the American medical treatment he received during the critical period immediately following his abortive effort.

In the first twelve to fourteen hours alone, Tojo lost one-half his normal blood supply and received a total of six or seven transfusions.[34]

[33] CF 20, I, 5. In the absence of the Japanese original, some allowances must be made for possible translation errors. In the above paraphrase, the word "policy" was replaced by "polity," which seemed to be the more likely choice in terms of the context.

[34] The Trumbull dispatch, *NYT*, September 13, 1945, 1 and 3. See also the chief surgeon's comment in an item rather misleadingly entitled "Tojo's Condition Good at U.S. Army Hospital," *Nippon Times*, September 14, 1945, 1. In the Frank Kelley dispatch, *NYHT*, September 13, 1945 (late city edition), 3, the surgeon was quoted as saying, ". . . he has a serious wound for a man his age. How he missed his heart, I don't know; the bullet just skinned it."

Some Americans could not understand the attention being showered on Tojo by the U.S. Army. People later asked Dr. Johnson, "Why didn't you let him die?" The doctor's father-in-law had already supplied an answer which seems to have occurred to a number of others at the time: "I hope Jimmie saves him so we can hang him right."[35]

An American mess sergeant at the hospital, in responding to a request for B-type blood to aid Tojo's recovery, explained: "I'd like to see him live so he gets his just due when he is tried. It would be too easy for him to come in here and pass out comfortably. Let him suffer a little bit for those seventeen months I spent in New Guinea."[36]

The temper of the times also emerges in an editorial in the *New York Herald Tribune*. The paper told its readers that the sergeant had "achieved a unique place in history so extraordinary and in a way so baffling that it makes one a trifle giddy to contemplate it. . . . If the sergeant is an imaginative man, as seems not impossible, and if, as one hopes, he is able to attend General Tojo's trial as a war criminal, he is sure to experience some peculiar emotions. To observe one's own heart's blood being tried, as it were, for high treason to the human race, to realize that one has saved this primitive and cruel life in order that it may be properly disposed of, to toy with the mystical idea that one has transfused vitality into this creature which, dedicated to a suicidal code, could not even make a success of suicide, will add up to a singular experience which may well leave [the] Sergeant . . . wondering where he leaves off and Tojo begins. It will afford revenge, but of a pretty baffling kind."

Having thus pictured the dilemma in which the presumably imaginative sergeant might find himself, the editorial offered a further thought of "a pretty baffling kind" in itself: "In volunteering his blood, the sergeant was a bold man. He was getting himself, through the curious intervention of modern science, pretty deep into those ancient mysteries of life and death, of blood and redemption which have been the central themes of so many great religions. And he was also making himself a symbol. The destructive and self-destructive impulses of ancient Japan can only be halted and turned to better expression in the modern world by a massive transfusion from the main intellectual and social blood stream of modern culture. . . . We find that in the act of destroying the savage and barbaric in Japan we must pour out [a]

[35] Johnson, "Tojo's First Trial."
[36] Sergeant John A. Archinal, as quoted in the Robert Trumbull dispatch, *NYT*, September 13, 1945, 1 and 3.

great transfusion of Western thought and institutions if our enemy is to be left neither a primitive danger nor a corrupting corpse in our own society. . . ."[37]

A day was to come, however, when other Americans would reason that it might have been better for all concerned if Tojo's reluctance to return to the world of the living had been respected. One of the correspondents who had been present in Tojo's "study" following the shooting later claimed that he had participated in an effort to speed Tojo's death by moving him from one position to another. The idea allegedly was to induce greater bleeding so that a "Tojo Is Dead" flash, which a noncompetitive colleague had sent prematurely, would not have to be "killed."[38] Dr. Johnson supposedly congratulated those responsible for having *saved* Tojo. "If that blood hadn't been drained out," the doctor was quoted as saying, "it would have gone to his lungs and drowned him. If you'd just left him alone the flash would have stood up. . . ."[39]

But Dr. Johnson himself made no reference to such an episode in his personal account of the several hours he spent ministering to Tojo. And when the doctor was questioned about the matter a decade later, he said in reply: "Nothing could be further from the truth than the news-papermen's accounts. . . . Apparently [Tojo] had not been moved very much or it would have increased the bleeding and produced suffocation. I made no such statement as has been attributed to me. . . . Apparently the correspondents thought that that was a good story."[40]

Sometimes history must contend with the apocryphal. Among the counterfeit stories which subsequently appeared concerning September 11, 1945, was a rather engaging although entirely spurious one to the effect that Tojo had not shot himself at all. When the arresting party arrived, according to this tale, Tojo decided to go quietly. As he strode out of his house, however, a nervous MP—seeing a sword in Tojo's hand—shot him down. The "trigger-happy" soldier was afraid that the general intended using the sword on the arresting party.[41]

Sometimes history must also contend with speculation. Various

---

[37] See "Archinal-Tojo," *NYHT*, September 13, 1945, 22.

[38] See Lee, 106-7, 109, 111, 113, and Brundidge, 11-12, for somewhat conflicting versions of this episode. Note also a passing reference in Kelley and Ryan, 52, and in *Time*, June 16, 1947, 66.

[39] *Ibid.*

[40] Johnson corresp.

[41] The author first heard this story in Tōkyō in 1951-1952; it was repeated to him in Princeton, N.J., in 1955, with slight variation in detail, by a Japanese visitor.

persons have wondered why Tojo did not attempt suicide earlier and in the traditional manner, or why he chose to aim at his heart, thus increasing the chances of a non-fatal wound. There are no simple answers to these questions. There are explanations to suit every point of view, including one to the effect that Tojo had postponed his suicide because he could not decide whether to accept the proffered leadership of a group of *kamikaze* pilots who wished to upset the surrender by attacking the Americans as they landed in Japan.[42]

Two days after his suicide attempt, Tojo said in a hospital interview "that he had planned for a long time to kill himself and that when he saw United States officers standing outside his house, he 'knew the time had come.'" When asked why he had not committed hara-kiri, he replied: "While hara-kiri is the traditional manner of ending your life, I feared I might miss." The act was always performed in the presence of a second who would ensure success by a sweep of the long sword if the principal faltered. There had been no one to perform that service for Tojo.[43]

Another interpretation is that Tojo was afraid to die and therefore clung to life until the last possible moment, shooting himself when he realized that the alternative was death at the hands of the Americans. One former official, wearing a Western-style suit, thought a moment when asked about the suicide attempt, then cocked the fingers of his right hand in imitation of a pistol, pulled the left side of his coat away from his body with his other hand and "shot" through the fabric—his way of saying that Tojo had aimed to miss. In other words, as an army general responsible for the deaths of so many thousands of servicemen, Tojo knew that he was expected to take his own life; but he did not want to die, and so he merely went through the motions.[44]

How Tojo (even assuming the presence of Dr. Suzuki's charcoal mark) could aim so expertly as to achieve a near-miss at the heart was not explained. The medical evidence was against this theory, for the wound was "at the level of the fifth interspace in the mid-clavicular line"—normally "the exact area for striking the apex of the heart." The bullet missed the apex only because Tojo's heart was elongated and narrow.[45] Was Dr. Suzuki aware of that when he marked Tojo's chest,

[42] Stunkard intv.
[43] *NYT*, September 14, 1945, 8 ("Tojo Feels Better; He Talks of Plight"), and *NYHT*, September 14, 1945 (late city edition), 7 ("Tojo Is Better; Planned to Kill Self Long Ago").
[44] The author personally witnessed this "explanation" in Tōkyō in 1946.
[45] Johnson corresp.

as he is said to have done? Did Tojo aim wide of the mark so as to miss the apex, or was his aim imprecise either because no mark was present or because it did not accurately define Tojo's "somewhat anomalous" heart?[46] Or would the bullet have hit the apex had it not been for the rather unfamiliar "kick" of the American Colt?[47]

No less bizarre are the explanations as to why Tojo aimed at his heart. There is the statement reportedly made by Tojo himself that he wanted to be recognized—that he wanted MacArthur to know, upon seeing the body, that it belonged to Tojo, that it was not a *nisemono*—the corpse of someone else.[48] There is also the contention of a correspondent to the effect that Tojo had unnatural reasons for not wanting to die with his face "mussed up."[49] Between these two extremes lies a composite explanation formed from many bits and pieces of information regarding Tojo's attempt to take his own life.

Toward the end of the war a change of thinking occurred among Japanese officers of a rational frame of mind. They felt that committing suicide would serve no useful purpose. In Tojo's case, however, there were two problems. From a traditional point of view, he would normally have been expected to take his life as an admission of the failure of the policies his cabinet had endorsed in 1941 and as the only means by which he could acknowledge and thus absolve his personal responsibility. But times had changed since the feudal past. Japan was to be occupied by a victor who had made it plain that "the authority and influence of those" who had "deceived and misled the people of Japan into embarking on world conquest" would "be eliminated for all time" and that "stern justice" would "be meted out to all war criminals."[50]

Although Tojo presumably had no feelings of personal guilt, he feared that the Allied powers might endeavor to implicate the Emperor and make him personally responsible for the acts and decisions of the cabinet and the supreme command. To prevent this from happening, it was necessary that Tojo (and others prominent in the Pearl Harbor

[46] Mrs. Tōjō has noted that her husband, although a right-handed writer, generally used his left hand whenever he did something requiring strength. She believes that he may have held the gun with his left hand (and perhaps that affected his aim). Major Kraus' CIC report, however, states that the gun was found in Tōjō's right hand.

[47] Blewett intv.

[48] This amplification of the "recognition" remark reported in Kelley and Ryan, 53, was obtained during an interview with Mrs. Tōjō.

[49] See Lee, 108.

[50] Paragraphs 6 and 10 of "The Potsdam Proclamation" (Butow, *Japan's Decision to Surrender*, 243).

period) accept the responsibility that was theirs.[51] It was even said later that War Minister Shimomura had called on Tojo on the evening of September 10 to urge him, for the above reasons, not to take his own life.

On the other hand, Tojo was confronted with the obligation to abide by the code of the battlefield insofar as it became applicable in the special circumstances of post-surrender Japan. This so-called *Senjin-kun* had been issued in January 1941 while Tojo held the war portfolio. The code had reemphasized that death, even when self-inflicted, was to be preferred to capture on the field of battle. Tojo is said to have expected arrest and trial by his fellow-Japanese for having lost the war, but not seizure by the Americans. He was anxious to absolve the throne of all responsibility, but he did not want to violate the code all servicemen had held in esteem, nor did he intend to allow himself to be handled like a Mussolini. He therefore composed a final statement assuming the blame for what had occurred so that he would be able to commit suicide, if necessary, and still perform his duty toward the Emperor. When he looked out the window on the afternoon of September 11, he saw a virtual mob of Japanese and Americans (even the correspondents still wore GI clothing). He decided then, on the spur of the moment, that submission could only bring dishonor, and so he grabbed a pistol and shot himself through the heart. It is thought that Tojo might even have surrendered himself at MacArthur's headquarters, had he been requested to do so by a specified time, and had he been assured that his status would be prisoner of state and not prisoner of war.[52]

There is no doubt that in the short run Tojo's reputation suffered greatly from his failure to succeed in his suicide attempt. This was partly due to the fact that a number of his compatriots did take their own lives. Among them were two members of Tojo's war cabinet, the 1941 chief of the army general staff (followed by his wife), the general who had been in command of the Kwantung army at the time of the Manchurian Incident, the vice-admiral who had instituted the first organized *kamikaze* attacks, the minister of war in the surrender cabi-

[51] The then foreign minister (Mamoru Shigemitsu) had been informed by Tōjō, prior to his attempt at suicide, that he would assume responsibility for the war and that he was determined not to cause the Emperor any trouble. See Shigemitsu, *Sugamo Nikki*, 103.

[52] The text is based on information obtained from a variety of sources: Mrs. Tōjō, Kiyose, Blewett, and Umezu intv.; Maxon corresp.; Johnson, "Tojo's First Trial"; Shigemitsu, *Sugamo Nikki*, 58; Hanayama, *Heiwa no Hakken*, 251; Lee, 104; and *Nippon Times*, September 13, 1945, 1 ("Tojo's Condition Grave After Suicide Attempt").

net, the ultranationalistic judo instructor who had once practiced character assassination against professors of higher learning who advocated the so-called organic theory of the constitution, and Tojo's own son-in-law—a major with the imperial guards division who had shot himself on August 15, after listening to the imperial broadcast announcing the surrender.[53] The pistol he had used was the one Tojo chose for himself on September 11.[54]

Despite these and other suicides, however, "the number of cases of seppuku [hara-kiri] was surprisingly small. There was very little violence. The vows of the nationalists to die for the Emperor were lost in the confusion of surrender, and militarism seemed to have vanished suddenly from the land like mist on an August morning."[55]

The Japanese people nevertheless were looking for—and needed—a scapegoat, and Tojo was the most convenient and likely candidate. The fact that he had been Japan's premier at the time of Pearl Harbor made him an obvious choice; the suicide fiasco helped confirm it. "From all over the country a sadistic chorus went up: 'Tojo is to blame for everything. He got us into war. He is a miserable bungler. He should have killed himself months ago. He should have used a knife.'"[56]

The resentment of the people was also expressed in such sayings as "Going to be another Tojo, not even able to kill yourself?"[57] Many letters were sent to the Tojo home. They were not all critical, but some years later Tojo's youngest daughter, who was only thirteen years old in 1945, recalled that one angry writer had asked for the location of the Tojo burial plot so that he could turn up the family graves.[58]

When it subsequently became known in Japan that Tojo would be tried as a war criminal, a new flood of letters and postcards appeared, many of them addressed to General MacArthur personally. One individual respectfully requested that Tojo and his family be executed. The charge was collusion with the *zaibatsu* (financial clique) and promo-

---

[53] In the order mentioned: ex-Education Minister Kunihiko Hashida, ex-Welfare Minister (Surgeon Lt. Gen.) Chikahiko Koizumi, Field Marshal Gen Sugiyama, General Shigeru Honjō, Vice-Admiral Takijirō Ōnishi, General Korechika Anami, "Professor" Muneyoshi Minoda, and Major Hidemasa Koga, who was the husband of Tōjō's second daughter, Makie.

[54] Hanayama, 251.

[55] "The Brocade Banner," 130.

[56] Lee, 108-9. See also the Trumbull dispatch, *NYT*, September 13, 1945, 1 and 3, in which it is noted that "Tojo" had become "a base name of obloquy" and also "a laughing stock."

[57] Terasaki, 234.

[58] Kimie Tōjō in a WRCA-TV interview by Cecil Brown, telecast in the United States on September 7, 1958.

tion of aggression. The communication bore neither a signature nor a return address—only the words: "The voice of one who is starving to death."[59]

The gist of another denunciation, also addressed to MacArthur, was that Tojo had demolished the peace of the world and that even a death sentence would not be sufficient punishment. Again Tojo was accused of having profited enormously by working hand in glove with the *zaibatsu*. He was also charged with having pocketed donations made by the Japanese people to the war effort. The writer of this particular card, perhaps uncertain about MacArthur's ability to read Japanese, added a line in English: "I hope your stay in order to Japanese and please do it national of the commonplace."[60]

Another card not only advocated a death penalty for Tojo and other war criminals but also called for the immediate trial and judgment of the military clique as a whole. This should be done, the writer urged, without the benefit of defense counsel. Such assistance to the accused, he declared, would be entirely unnecessary.[61]

Still others with complaints of various kinds suggested that Tojo be executed without a trial, that he be publicly hanged in Hibiya Park in central Tokyo, that his head be exhibited there, and that Mrs. Tojo be given a life sentence.[62]

Such was the reaction, in the short run, of many of the people of Japan toward the man on whom they chose to lay the shame and misery of defeat. It would thus seem that Tojo had but little choice except suicide in the special circumstances of September 11, 1945. It must have been quite plain to him even then that the people for whom he had once acted as premier would now consider themselves betrayed. Since so many had died in a war that had brought suffering and destruction in place of glory and dominion, Tojo felt the need to conform to the code of the warrior as he knew it.

> When Honour's lost, 'tis a Relief to die;
> Death's but a sure Retreat from Infamy....[63]

[59] CF 20, III, 147.
[60] See CF 20, IV, 394.
[61] *Ibid.*
[62] See CF 20, I, 37 and 42.
[63] These lines, which are quoted in Nitobe, *Bushido*, 114, are from Sir Samuel Garth (1661-1719), *The Dispensary*, Canto V, q.v.

CHAPTER 15

Closing the Gates

WITH the progress of time the passions of the people cooled. Those Japanese who had once fixed their attention on Hideki Tojo—and in some cases their hatred—did not tarry long over the past. The difficulties of current life provided a far more logical focus of concern. While the Japanese press attempted to keep abreast of the unorthodox news being made by the Occupation, Tojo was carefully nursed back to health and then quietly transferred from the 98th Evacuation Hospital to the XI Corps Stockade (No. 2).[1]

The stockade had formerly been the Omori Prisoner of War Camp. It was located between Yokohama and Tokyo on land reclaimed from the waters of the bay—a place fouled by the hunger, dirt, humiliation, and death which had been the constant companions of the Allied prisoners who had only recently been released from its precincts.[2] In their place, Tojo and other Japanese leaders lived for a time as transients—their first stop on a journey in the general direction of a goal called justice. They were taken off an earlier diet of such American "delicacies" as beef, bacon, eggs, and peaches and were given instead the rice, dried fish, and whalemeat which had been found on the premises when the XI Corps took over. To these were added American coffee, sugar, and rock candy. The "same thin blankets" the Allied prisoners had once used were deloused and reissued to the Japanese inmates. The buildings were repaired and whitewashed, new bathing and toilet facilities were installed, and bugs were sprayed with DDT. The prisoners "were expected to clean, launder and pick up for themselves." Except for that and frequent roll calls, they were left alone.[3]

Tojo had once paid an unannounced visit to Omori in October 1943. A Japanese-speaking British officer who was then "registered" there later recalled the scene vividly. He and some of his comrades were on

[1] *Nippon Times*, September 13, 1945, 3, September 14, 1945, 1, and September 15, 1945, 1 (on Tōjō's condition in the hospital); Tōjō's Sugamo Prison "201" file (containing the authority for his transfer to XI Corps Stockade No. 2 on October 7, 1945); CF 20, I, 4, in which Tōjō's detention is explained in terms of his having permitted an attack on Pearl Harbor and the Philippines prior to a declaration of war; and Hardy corresp.
[2] Bush, *Clutch of Circumstance*, 150ff.
[3] *Life*, November 12, 1945, 29, and Eichelberger corresp.

the point of taking the one and only bath they were allowed each week. Suddenly a prison officer—"a strict but just man" known to the inmates as "Puss in Boots"—came charging into their midst shouting "*Kiotsuke!*"—"Attention!" The POW's snapped to, "some in the bath, some outside and all stark naked. And just behind 'Puss in Boots' came a sturdy-looking gentleman attired in a grey tweed suit, a grey felt hat, and carrying a walking stick with an ivory handle which seemed to be shaped in the form of a dog or horse's head." Puss in Boots shouted, "*Keirei!*"—"Salute!" and the prisoners dutifully bowed from the waist in the Japanese manner. "Tojo raised his hat . . . , smiled, and proceeded to ply" his "almost petrified" guide with questions.

The premier subsequently visited all of the huts and in one of them "apparently expressed much sympathy" for "the camp idiot" whom he found "sitting in a corner gnawing a bone." Tojo took special pains to look into the food situation. In fact, his visit to Omori had been prompted by reports reaching him of a high death rate from malnutrition among POW's but on the day in question he found that "they were having pork and everything seemed all right." At the cookhouse his manner so impressed one British prisoner that the man later described Tojo as "not a bad old bugger"—a "fatherly sort of old cove."[4]

The scene in 1945 was rather different. Tojo was no longer sturdy at ninety-four pounds (although he soon gained weight), and for a time he was shunned by most of his fellow prisoners. A current issue of *Life* reported the change in Tojo's circumstances with the words: "War Lord Tojo Is Treated with Silent Contempt by Camp's Other Prisoners." The former premier willingly posed for a staff photographer, saying, "I want to be a good loser." But unlike some of his colleagues, he drew the line at a suggested shot of him sitting in the communal bath. Among the rather imaginative captions provided by *Life* was one which read: "Only companion to talk to Tojo is Black Dragon Member Hashimoto, suggesting Tojo was secret leader of the Black Dragon."[5]

It soon became apparent that Omori had limited possibilities as a detention camp. Larger quarters were needed—something of a more permanent nature in a better location. The answer was found in Sugamo Prison in the northwestern quarter of Tokyo, an area which derived its name from the fact that in earlier times wild ducks had

---

[4] Bush, 173-74, supplemented by Tōjō interrog., Mar. 26, 2-3, Mar. 27, 6, and Mar. 29, 6-8.
[5] *Life*, November 12, 1945, 32. See also Kelley and Ryan, 55; Lee, 109; and Hardy corresp.

nested there. An MP officer of the 7th Cavalry Division had discovered the prison just as the Japanese were evacuating it for conversion into much-needed office space. Since at least fifteen hundred persons were expected to be in custody in the near future, the Occupation authorities decided that Sugamo should remain a prison, under their jurisdiction. The U.S. Army moved in as the Japanese moved out. The Americans repaired and renovated the buildings and dusted everything with generous doses of the ubiquitous DDT. "Cursed with a kind heart," General Eichelberger ordered additional heating facilities installed; the food served to the prisoners was "quite good."[6]

When these facts became known, criticism arose in both Japanese and American circles. It was generally felt that Sugamo inmates were living a life of luxury, while the people of Japan, who had already paid a heavy price, were suffering through another cold winter—often without shelter, occasionally without food, and practically always without heat, except for the negligible amount generated by a few pieces of charcoal. Unfavorable comparisons were also made between life at "Hotel Sugamo" and the miserable conditions typical of the prisoner-of-war camps which had been under the jurisdiction of some of the very men who were now being "pampered" by the Occupation. There were a few individuals, however, who questioned the educational value of treating Japanese prisoners in the same manner as the Japanese had frequently treated Allied captives. Eventually, public attention shifted elsewhere. Sugamo generally remained a good place to live, except for the uncertainty facing each prisoner regarding the disposition of his case.

For a brief time following his arrival at Sugamo, Tojo experienced certain petty annoyances of a type which reflected the psychology of the times. Had his jailers been Japanese rather than American, he might not have fared any better. Admission procedure called for a complete physical examination, to be followed by a "delousing" treatment (not because the prisoners were unclean, but because conditions then prevailing in defeated Japan were conducive to the spread of vermin). The GI's in charge of the dusting "were a little enthusiastic with Tojo so that both he and his clothes were thoroughly blanketed with gray DDT powder." The prison commandant, who happened to see him shuffling away down a corridor immediately afterwards, felt that Tojo looked "rather 'down in the mouth.'"

[6] Hardy and Eichelberger corresp. By December 7, 1945, General MacArthur's headquarters had ordered the arrest of 363 persons as war criminal suspects (*Facts on File: 1945*, 385 M and 387 E).

A few days later the commandant also noticed that Tojo had temporarily been assigned to Cell No. 44. Someone had learned that "four" is regarded as an unlucky number because its basic pronunciation in Japanese is the same as the reading given to the character for "death." Apparently Tojo was once again "on the receiving end of some G.I. humor." If "4" was unlucky, "44" presumably was even more so.[7]

Another feature of the admission procedure was the fingerprinting of all incoming prisoners. Tojo was processed on December 8, 1945—the fourth anniversary of Pearl Harbor, in terms of Japanese datelines. It is impossible to tell whether this was by design or coincidence, but strangely enough the time noted on Tojo's "Basic Personnel Record" was "14:20"—the exact hour, to the very minute, that Nomura and Kurusu were ushered into Hull's office in Washington in December 1941 to deliver Japan's final note.

The B.P.R. description of Tojo adhered to the usual bald pattern:

Height	5	ft.	4	in.
Weight	130			
Eyes	Brown			
Skin	Ruddy			
Hair	Black			
Age	63			

Above the words, "Grade and arm or service," appeared the notation, "Gen (Ex-premier)." Tojo's "Occupation" was described as "Official"; "Religious preference" as "Shinto"; and "Knowledge of languages" as "None." The "Inventory of Personal Effects Taken from Internee" amounted to 970 yen.[8]

Newspapermen were allowed to visit Sugamo but were not permitted to photograph or interview the prisoners. Most visitors came equipped with a standard inquiry: "Where are Tojo and Tokyo Rose?" Occasionally the ex-premier would be found scrubbing the floor or

[7] Hardy corresp. Although there were frequent changes in block, tier, and cell assignments, the records (which seem to be incomplete) do not show an assignment to Cell No. 44.

[8] From Tōjō's Sugamo Prison "201" file. The prison commandant, Colonel Robert M. Hardy, Jr., believes that Tōjō was transferred to Sugamo on or about November 4 (corresp.), but the material in the "201" file supports the December 8 date.

Another document in the file gives Tōjō's religion as "Shinto-Buddhist." Like many Japanese, Tōjō respected and followed both religions. It was chiefly to Buddhism, however, that he turned his thoughts during the last years of his life.

performing some other menial task expected of all inmates, regardless of their former rank or station in life.[9]

Meals were delivered to each cellblock in large containers. The prisoners would queue up with their bowls and cups and file past the dispensers. "Tojo would always just fall in line with the others and . . . then take his food back to his cell and eat." Each prisoner washed his own dishes.[10] Later, when procedures were changed somewhat, Tojo and others of the "VIP" group (the so-called "Class A's") performed KP on a cooperative basis by organizing themselves into "companies," such as the Tōjō-gumi. A former foreign minister wrote that it was quite a sight to see Tojo or Hirota (also an ex-premier) going from table to table to ask whether anyone wanted another cup of GI coffee.[11]

Such comradeship was not in evidence at first, however, especially insofar as Tojo was concerned. The men with whom he had once sat at cabinet or imperial conference sessions seemed to prefer to stay out of his way. In the exercise area, which was under constant MP surveillance and was surrounded by high walls and wire entanglements, Tojo was frequently seen, during the early months of his confinement, "walking slowly, quietly and alone around the yard," continually puffing on a cigarette.[12]

As time passed, Tojo's fellow-prisoners relented in their attitude toward him, possibly because they learned that he was determined personally to accept the major responsibility for the events of his premiership—possibly because the circumstances of their confinement stimulated a live-and-let-live attitude and a we-are-in-this-together relationship toward each other. Tojo was nicknamed tera-kozō, "the Buddhist priestling," because of the interest he exhibited in the words of Dr. Shinsho Hanayama, a Buddhist priest who was engaged by the American authorities to serve as one of the prison chaplains.

In warm weather Tojo would appear in the exercise yard in a shirt, pair of drawers, felt hat, and prison-issue geta (clogs); during the cold months he generally wore baggy trousers of a type favored by farmers and a jin-baori, a short kimono-like coat, originally designed to be worn over a suit of armor and so cut as to give a samurai maximum freedom to employ his sword.[13] On one occasion "a brawny second lieutenant"

[9] Hardy corresp.

[10] Hayden corresp., and Newsweek, January 28, 1946, 39.

[11] Shigemitsu, Sugamo Nikki, 197.

[12] Hayden, Hardy, and Profita corresp. See also Shigemitsu, Sugamo Nikki, 20. Tōjō was a heavy smoker, consuming from 25 to 60 cigarettes a day.

[13] Shigemitsu, Sugamo Nikki, 58, 316, and Hanayama, 88.

stopped Tojo and searched his pockets to see whether he was carrying more than the single cigarette each prisoner was allowed to have in his possession at any one time. Tojo became angry and said that he would prefer being hanged to being insulted.[14]

Frequent cell inspections were routine and were consequently taken in stride by the prisoners, including Tojo. Among his personal effects the prison adjutant once found a "complete photo layout of the Pearl Harbor attack done in color by *Life* magazine." Tojo, who was standing at attention against one wall of the cell, smiled when the officer looked up at him. He had been saving "everything he could get his hands on regarding the attack," for possible use in his defense.[15]

Throughout his confinement, Tojo remained the prey of souvenir hunters. At the 98th Evacuation Hospital, attendants had made off with the buttons from his army trousers. At Sugamo, others raided his personal belongings, taking such items as handkerchiefs, pipes, and even a Buddhist rosary.[16] Tojo also continued to serve as a source of inspiration for inveterate storytellers. Among the tales which emanated from Sugamo from time to time were several variations on the same theme. One of these was to the effect that Tojo was somewhat confused by the strange language of the prison guards. Informed that "Hubba, hubba" stood for "Hurry up," he allegedly replied: "I always thought it meant 'Remember Pearl Harbor!'"[17]

All prisoners were closely restricted with respect to the number of personal belongings allowed in their cells, which were only sparsely furnished. The main concern of the prison authorities was to guard against the entry of implements of self-destruction, but there may also have been some desire to keep life in Sugamo from becoming too home-like.

In order to pass time (the wealth of prisoners since the dawn of history) and to compensate for the lack of certain conveniences, a number of inmates took to making various things for themselves. Tojo fashioned small paper and cardboard boxes to hold his coveted cigarettes and also cone-shaped paper holders in which to smoke them. Admiral Oka, the former chief of the naval affairs bureau, who was adept at doing things with his hands, made a number of miniature

[14] Shigemitsu, *Sugamo Nikki*, 394-95.

[15] Hayden corresp. The interpretation that Tōjō was saving such material for possible use at his trial is my own. It seems to be borne out by the evidence as a whole.

[16] Robert Trumbull dispatch, *NYT*, September 13, 1945, 1 and 3, and Shigemitsu, *Sugamo Nikki*, 264.

[17] This story was attributed to special prosecutor John W. Fihelly (see *Facts on File: 1946*, 110 H).

chests of drawers which he gave to his fellow prisoners. Since wood, nails, and tools were proscribed, Oka used cardboard, paper, and paste. Some of the paper came from the bountiful pages of American magazines. Tojo's chest featured on each end an advertising spread showing a nude woman, seen from behind, sitting on her bed in the early morning and stretching. Underneath, the caption began: "FAIR MORNING . . . To wake up gorgeously rested. . . ."[18]

Letters and other communications from the outside were generally not delivered to Tojo in the form in which they were received. He was given photostatic copies, instead, because the prison authorities feared that the originals might be impregnated with poison.[19]

As the time approached for Tojo to reappear in public to stand trial, he asked a prison officer to obtain a necktie for him to wear when he went to court. He "found it quite humorous" when the officer indicated that security regulations prohibited supplying such an item. Tojo revealed that he already had several articles that could be used if he wanted to hang himself, including two short pieces of rope (one of which was serving as a belt) and his prison blanket. When the officer remained firm, Tojo said he would submit a written request for a necktie to the prison commandant.[20]

Until preparations for the trial were begun, the inmates of Sugamo were sometimes assailed by boredom. Family visits were very restricted. The normal procedure was to admit only one close relative per month, for a stay of about thirty minutes. Mrs. Tojo went to Sugamo for the first time in February 1946. Nearly a half-year had passed since the day in September when she had taken leave of her husband and had circled around to the Suzukis' garden, whence she could observe the activity outside her own home without being seen. When the shot had rung out, she had knelt and prayed to the Buddha. She had felt then that Tojo was facing his most difficult moment. Two days later she had left for Kyushu to join her children. After her reunion with her husband at Sugamo, Mrs. Tojo returned to the southern island and remained there until November, when she again took up permanent residence in the capital.[21]

Tojo impressed the prison commandant as being "quick and efficient in every task assigned him." He seemed "to welcome work as a relief" from the tedium of long hours in his cell, where he spent most of his

---

[18] The chest is now in Mrs. Tōjō's possession.
[19] Mrs. Tōjō and Hanayama intv.   [20] Brosious corresp.
[21] Mrs. Tōjō intv., and Tōjō's Sugamo Prison "201" file.

time preparing for the defense which he knew he would soon have an opportunity to offer.[22] Other prison personnel found him "a conventional, model" inmate, "a well-disciplined man," "an excellent prisoner."[23] But he was also remembered as the only one of the Class A group who "griped." He complained about the very complete physical examinations for concealment of poison—sometimes conducted in the middle of the night—which, by their very nature, tended to be humiliating. He also objected to the treatment accorded Class B and C prisoners, who comprised the majority of those being detained. Tojo seemed to ignore the fact that they were being held on suspicion of having committed atrocities; he insisted that they deserved more consideration than they were receiving.[24]

The tempo of life in Sugamo slowly picked up as members of the International Prosecution Section began the enormous task of preparing their case for court. For a period of several months in early 1946, this involved practically daily sessions in the interrogation rooms at the prison. Inmates like Tojo, who had been key figures in 1941 and who consequently were the most likely to be named in the indictment, received the most attention. Between mid-January and the end of March 1946 Tojo was interrogated fifty-one times by a special prosecution team, whose members spent with him alone a total of nearly 124 hours: the equivalent of four hours of interrogation per day, seven days a week, for a solid month. Most of this took place in the afternoon; the longest session was five hours and fifty minutes—the shortest, an hour and a half. The transcript of the thousands of questions asked and answered amounted to 337 single-spaced typewritten pages. Of this, the prosecution later introduced about one-seventh (roughly 49 pages) in court.[25]

The investigation team assigned to Tojo consisted of an interrogator, an interpreter, and a stenographer. The interrogator was "a great big Irishman" named John W. Fihelly, on loan from the Justice Department as a special prosecutor.[26] Fihelly would ask questions; these would be rephrased by the interpreter (Commander Yale Maxon, USNR) in "less florid English" which the stenographer could get down on paper

[22] Hardy corresp.

[23] Stunkard intv.; Oberlin and Brosious corresp.

[24] Stunkard intv.

[25] Based on calculations made from a copy of the transcript of the interrogations in the author's possession. See also CF 20, III, 148. The discrepancy (59 interrogations and 329 pages) arises, in part, from the omission of the March 25 interrogation (when Maxon's place was taken by Mr. Denis Kildoyle). Omitted from both reckonings is a Chemical Warfare Section interrogation conducted on April 2, 1946.

[26] McEwen and Hardin corresp.; Fihelly intv.

and which could be more easily rendered into Japanese. The interpreter would then listen to Tojo's reply and, if necessary, would clarify any doubtful points before dictating the answer, in English, to the stenographer. Except for an occasional word or phrase, no Japanese discourse was recorded as part of the interrogation transcript prepared from the stenographer's shorthand notes, although Commander Maxon personally kept some "rough scribble sheets" as he went along. Despite the complexity of the process, the results proved quite satisfactory to all concerned. Months later, after the prosecution's case had been lodged in court, Maxon received word from Tojo to the effect that "he appreciated the care which had been taken in quoting him accurately" and acknowledging that he had indeed said everything attributed to him.[27]

Throughout the interrogation period, Tojo proved most cooperative. He seemed to enjoy the sessions and "to look forward to them from day to day."[28] He was clearly bent upon accepting personal responsibility (in a noncriminal sense) for developments which occurred during the period when he had held one or more official positions in the Japanese government. In that respect, Tojo sowed a case against himself which the prosecution was later to harvest to its own advantage in court. Only when the interrogator endeavored to link Tojo to earlier events which the trial subsequently proved were not of his doing would he register an objection.

Tojo never admitted that either he or Japan had committed any wrong. It was always someone else who was to blame—the Chinese at first, and then later the Americans and the British. Japan had been forced to look out for herself. . . . She had gradually been encircled and strangled. . . . She had acted in self-defense. . . .

Tojo's memory for details was not good, and he frequently complained about the lack of reference materials with which to refresh his memory. He had a small notebook of the diary type which contained a chronology and brief description of major events, and he would sometimes refer to this to clarify a date or another minor point. His occasional vagueness, however, was not motivated by a desire to obstruct. He simply could not remember exactly all of the specific things the prosecution wanted to know. The interrogators might have been greatly aided in their inquiry if they had supplied Tojo with the various documents which later occupied a central place in the prosecution's case. One difficulty in that respect, which also hampered the defense, was the ever-present security-consciousness of the prison authorities, whose responsi-

[27] Maxon corresp.   [28] Hardy corresp.

bilities encouraged them to regard practically everything, including paper products, as potential instruments of self-destruction.[29]

The general atmosphere which prevailed during the interrogations is revealed in a smattering of excerpts:

Q. This will be enough for today. It has been rather slow, but we want to take as much time as possible so you may express yourself freely. Under the American concept of justice a defendant is presumed to be innocent until he is shown to be guilty. You are to have time to explain things fully and may make a supplemental statement after the questioning is over if you desire.

A. Thank you. These are important matters for Japan and for world peace. What happens to me is of slight importance but the matters themselves are important.[30]

. . . .

Q. You said that at the beginning of the war, you knew nothing about the Navy war plan. Do you mean that you knew nothing about the attack on Pearl Harbor?

A. Well, I knew the date. That was a matter of importance from the standpoint of foreign relations, for example, and as Prime Minister, I knew that, but as for the details of the Navy's campaign throughout the war, I did not know them. Since the war has come to an end, I have read in the newspapers for the first time about Japanese fleet movements and the like. I am not trying by this explanation to avoid political responsibility but am only explaining these things in order to make clear the Japanese system of government organization.

Q. By the fleet movements that you read of in the press to which you referred a moment ago, do you mean movements relating to the Pearl Harbor attack or movements that took place during the course of the war?

A. I am referring to the dispositions of naval forces previous to the attack. I learned about these things for the first time by reading about them in the newspapers since the end of the war. You need not put that in the record if you don't want to.[31]

. . . .

Q. You realize, do you not, that you and . . . other responsible officials will probably be charged and tried as war criminals as being the parties responsible for . . . attacks on American and British possessions?

---

[29] For a defense complaint in that regard, see T 10596-99: "It is our understanding that all of the documents of the accused, with the exception of six books, booklets or pamphlets, have been taken from them and put in a box away from their cell so that they do not have free access to them. When they desire a document, it is necessary to call one of the jailers to secure the document, and they have difficulty in describing it, and in some instances they are unable to obtain the document they require."

[30] Tōjō interrog., Jan. 15, 6.

[31] Tōjō interrog., Feb. 7, 3.

A. I have not yet received the indictment so I do not know for what reasons I am to be tried. You are the representatives of the victorious nation and I am the representative of the defeated nation, and I know that I am suspected of being a war criminal. However, I have not yet received the indictment.

Q. Actually, no one has been indicted yet in connection with the matters on which we have been interrogating you. It is true that some people have been charged by military courts martial in connection with atrocities.

A. I realize that at the present time I am a war crimes suspect, but I understand that you are investigating the facts. I do not know for sure that I will be charged until I receive an indictment. Regardless of whether the present investigation results in the finding of my guilt or innocence as a war criminal, I am the person bearing chief political responsibility.

Q. During the various interrogations to date, you have received fair treatment from us, have you not?

A. Yes. I appreciate very fully that I have.[32]

. . . .

Q. Your answers to questions which we have asked you have assisted and will assist us in our investigation. We are only too glad to let you make such explanations as you desire. As you realize, not only will these assist us in our investigation but, should you be tried in connection with these matters, the answers made to these questions could be used against you, so we wish and have wished to give you the opportunity to make full answers in this investigation. We are sure that you have realized from the beginning this situation.

A. Yes. I am very thankful for the way this investigation has been conducted and I am thankful for the efforts you have made to interpret just what I have said. I realize that this trial will, of course, be a trial of me as an individual, but it is not only such—it is also a trial through me of the actions taken by the Empire. It is also a trial of the righteousness or unrighteousness of these actions. In this connection, my responsibility is very great since I had important relations with these matters. I also hope that the feelings and thoughts and outcries of the Asiatics will be heard at the trial for this will have an important relationship to the maintenance of peace in the future. I feel that these matters are important and not just an excuse. That is the way I feel.[33]

Tojo was only one of many Sugamo inmates who were daily being interrogated, by other prosecution teams, with reference to past activities and associations. Still other staff members combed Japanese government agencies, private dwellings, newspaper offices, and even public libraries

[32] *Ibid.*, 5-6.
[33] Tōjō interrog., Feb. 26, 4-5. See also Feb. 7, 5-6.

for documents and records which would aid the prosecution in the preparation of its case. These were scanned for pertinent material and, if judged important enough, were then translated in all or in part. Few of the lawyers associated with the prosecution "had any knowledge about Japan, the Japanese, or the principal figures involved—or any real appreciation of the magnitude of the venture they were undertaking." Nevertheless, the work progressed. Dossiers were prepared on each leading suspect and from these the final selection of defendants was made. Various "tests of inclusion or exclusion" were employed. One criterion ruled out listing anyone as a defendant "unless the evidence against him was so strong," in the view of those making the selection, "as to render negligible the chances for acquittal."[34]

By the end of April 1946 preparations for the trial were by no means complete, but an indictment naming twenty-eight defendants and covering an eighteen-year period was duly presented to an especially convened International Military Tribunal for the Far East, composed of eleven judges representing the nations which had been at war with Japan. The indictment, which was "largely a British document" prepared by the associate counsel representing the United Kingdom, consisted of fifty-five counts arranged into three groups: "Crimes Against Peace," "Murder," and "Other Conventional War Crimes and Crimes Against Humanity."[35]

Count 1, which covered "the entire scope of Japanese aggression," charged that between January 1, 1928, and September 2, 1945, "all the accused together with other persons" had "participated as leaders, organizers, instigators, or accomplices in the formulation or execution of a common plan or conspiracy" and that they were consequently "responsible for all acts performed by any person in execution of such plan. . . . The object of such plan or conspiracy was that Japan should secure the military, naval, political and economic domination of East Asia and of the Pacific and Indian Oceans, and of all countries bordering thereon and islands therein, and for that purpose they conspired that Japan

[34] Horwitz, "The Tokyo Trial," *International Conciliation*, No. 465 (November 1950), 494-96. Mr. Horwitz was a prosecution lawyer. It should be added that only a few of the non-Japanese lawyers associated with the defense had any knowledge of Japan or the Japanese.

The failure to name any member of the *zaibatsu* (financial clique) resulted largely from the fact that pretrial investigation convinced the prosecution that there was "no evidence . . . that any industrialist [had] occupied the position of a principal formulator of policy" (Horwitz, 498).

[35] Horwitz, 498. The indictment was the work primarily of Mr. Arthur S. Comyns-Carr.

should alone or in combination with other countries having similar objects, or who could be induced or coerced to join therein, wage declared or undeclared war or wars of aggression, and war or wars in violation of international law, treaties, agreements and assurances, against any country or countries which might oppose that purpose."[36]

This "overall conspiracy was broken down into its constituent smaller conspiracies," which were delineated in counts 2 through 5 of the indictment. "The substantive crimes against peace" were spelled out in counts 6 through 36. Counts 37-52 dealt with "murder"—including "murder as a crime against peace." The remaining counts "charged the defendants with the commission of conventional war crimes and crimes against humanity." Included therein was the assertion that the accused had "ordered, authorized and permitted conduct in violation of the Laws and Customs of War" and had "recklessly" disregarded "their legal duty to take adequate steps to secure observance" of those Laws and Customs "and to prevent their breach."[37] In short, the prosecution's indictment was a masterpiece of all-inclusiveness.

The Tribunal met, for its first public session, on Friday, May 3, 1946. The proceedings were held in a building which had once housed the assembly hall of the military academy and which had subsequently been requisitioned for the war ministry. The Occupation authorities had picked this hall, where Tojo and his fellow officers had once lectured to young cadets, as the most appropriate place in which to construct an impressive courtroom for the trial of Japan's Class A war criminals.

Into this historic setting there now filed, under heavy guard, a group of defendants the majority of whom had held some of the highest civil and military offices in the land: Araki—the army orator, who had once fired the zeal of the younger officers of the 1930's; Hiranuma and Hirota—both ex-premiers who had worked well with the military; Kaya—who had joined the new Tojo Cabinet in October 1941 as finance minister; Kido—the lord privy seal who had served from mid-1940 onward as the eyes and ears of the throne; Matsuoka—the garrulous foreign minister who had helped link Japan not only to Fascist Germany and Italy but also to Communist Russia; Nagano—the chief of the naval general staff who had once likened war to a surgical operation;

[36] See U.S. Dept. of State, "Trial of Japanese War Criminals," 47, and Horwitz, 499.
[37] Horwitz, 498-501. For the text of the indictment, see the State Department publication in the preceding footnote, 45-104; T 26-73 (does not include the appendices); or "Judgment," Annex A-6, 29-130.

Shimada—also of the navy, who had cooperated closely with Tojo, to the chagrin of many naval officers; Suzuki—of the cabinet planning board whose 1941 studies had helped to "clarify" the issue of war or peace in many minds; Togo—the civilian diplomat who had held the cabinet portfolio for foreign affairs not only on December 7, 1941, but also—somewhat ironically—on August 15, 1945; and Tojo—the so-called "cause of it all," who more than any other individual symbolized the war and personified the defeat. There were many others as well: Doihara and Itagaki; Hashimoto and Okawa; Hoshino, Muto, Oka, and Sato; Hata, Koiso, and Minami; Kimura and Matsui; Oshima and Shiratori; Shigemitsu and Umezu.[38]

Among those who did not appear in the prisoners' dock but who had been mentioned in various quarters as possible defendants were the Emperor and Prince Konoe. During the first few months of the Occupation it had looked as if the man who had been premier at the time of the China Incident, on the occasion of the signing of the Tripartite Pact, and during Japan's absorption of French Indo-China, might actually avoid the taint of personal responsibility. In early December 1945, however, Konoe's name had suddenly appeared on a list of persons who were to present themselves at Sugamo Prison by a specified date. The night before the deadline, the prince entertained a small group of friends and relatives at his Ogikubo residence, a place of many memories in the recent history of Japan. Early the next morning he was found dead in his bedroom. Beside him lay an empty vial of poison.[39]

In the case of the Emperor, the chief prosecutor later revealed that he believed His Majesty should have been "interrogated" prior to the trial but that there had been no way of telling what the repercussions might be if the Emperor were called as a witness. General MacArthur had once said that if the prosecution wanted to try the Emperor, a million soldiers would have to be added to the Occupation forces.[40] The Russians, the Chinese, the Australians, and the New Zealanders all thought that "Hirohito" should be named a defendant, but MacArthur and others successfully blocked such a move. The decision not to try the Emperor was made more on political than on judicial grounds, but subsequently "thorough investigation convinced the prosecution that no evidence was available to support" war-guilt charges against the figure-

[38] Brief biographical sketches of each of the defendants appear in Horwitz, 578-83. A more detailed presentation of their careers can be found in T 684-805, S 11:8-S 12:9.

[39] *Nippon Times*, December 17, 1945, 1. See also Kase, 190-91, and *Facts on File: 1945*, 387 E and 401 L. Konoe's arrest had been ordered on December 6.

[40] "Joseph Keenan Meets the Press," 458.

head who occupied the throne.[41] In fact, after it was all over, the chief prosecutor personally ventured the view that there would have been more reason to try Stalin than Hirohito. When asked under what indictment, he replied, "... planning and initiating wars of aggression—the same indictment that was brought against the Japanese war criminals at Tokyo. . . ."[42] This was a strange but interesting remark in the light of the fact that among the eleven justices who took their places opposite the defendants on May 3, 1946, and who were to sit in judgment upon them, was a duly authorized representative of the Union of Soviet Socialist Republics.[43] And assisting in the prosecution was a Soviet lawyer especially dispatched from Moscow to act as an associate counsel.[44]

As reported by *Time* magazine, the opening of the Tokyo trial compared rather unfavorably with the Nuremberg "show." The courtroom was fitted ". . . with dark walnut-tone paneling, imposing daises, convenient perches for the press and motion picture cameramen. The klieg lights suggested a Hollywood premiere." But whereas Nuremberg had had a Wagnerian touch, the production being staged in Tokyo reminded *Time* of Gilbert and Sullivan: "The 28 Japanese war criminals, clutching ribboned copies of their indictment, shuffled into court like schoolboys carrying their primers to class. In the shadow of reckoning and doom, they giggled and gossiped. In the role created by Robert Jackson, U.S. Chief Prosecutor Joseph B. Keenan ... (who looks like W. C. Fields) had to deal with the *opéra bouffe* element which the West so often finds in the Japanese character. The chief Jap defendant, Hideki Tojo, picked his nose unconcernedly and flirted with an American stenographer. Hiroshi Oshima, wartime ambassador to Germany, affected the dandy, with white pocket handerchief, smart bow tie and black-ribboned pince-nez."[45]

What *Time* described as "comic indifference" was soon transformed into "broad buffoonery." The dignity of the court was shattered briefly

[41] *Ibid.*, 456; Horwitz, 497. See also *Facts on File: 1945*, 358 G, *Facts on File: 1946*, 21 G, *Facts on File: 1947*, 306 B, and U.S. Dept. of State, *Bulletin*, Vol. XXII, No. 554 (February 13, 1950), 244.

[42] "Joseph Keenan Meets the Press," 456.

[43] Major General of Justice I. M. Zaryanov of the Military Collegium of the Supreme Court of the Soviet Union. For a roster of judges, see U. S. Dept. of State, "Trial of Japanese War Criminals," iv.

[44] S. A. Golunsky, then head of the Legal and Treaty Department and a member of the Board of the Soviet Ministry of Foreign Affairs (T 24).

[45] *Time*, May 20, 1946, 24. See also *Life*, May 27, 1946, 47.

by the mad antics of Dr. Shumei Okawa, who had served as propagandist and mentor for many "brainless patriots" during the early 1930's. The marshal of the court was reading the indictment. Some of the defendants were taking notes. "Okawa alone was restless. He kept unbuttoning his shirt [actually a pajama-top] and scratching his bare, sunken chest." When the garment began slipping off, Sir William Webb—the Australian president of the Tribunal—ordered the MP guards to make the defendant presentable. As soon as the American colonel stationed behind Okawa buttoned him up, Okawa would start undressing again. "Gradually the eyes of the audience became focused on this act of comedy, and the indictment was forgotten. After the second or third time, the colonel put his hands on Okawa's shoulders, and whenever he felt motion, he pressed Okawa's arms down. Eventually Okawa turned back and smiled reassuringly at the colonel. Everything was still again, and the reading of the indictment went on."[46]

Then, without warning, Okawa leaned forward and with the palm of his hand slapped Tojo's bald head. "The smack resounded through the room." The court was thrown into an uproar.[47] News photographers vied with one another to record the scene. Tojo smiled at his assailant, who was immediately hustled out by the colonel and his MP's.[48] During the recess which followed, the correspondents rushed to interview the prisoner. Was he as mentally unbalanced as he appeared, or was he cleverly acting the part of a madman so as to escape trial as a war criminal? The newsmen found Okawa in a cooperative mood and competent in English: "Tojo is a fool. . . . I must kill him. I'm for democracy. . . . America is not democracy. . . . I don't want to go to America, because she is democrazy. . . . You know what I mean? Demo crazy. . . ."[49]

"I am a Doctor of Law and Medicine. I haven't eaten in 70 days. You see, I eat air. . . . I am the next emperor of Japan. . . . I killed Tojo. I did it to save him. That's Japanese friendship. I killed him to save the reputation of his respectable family. This is the saddest day of my life."[50]

[46] Gayn, 208. See also Time, May 28, 1946, 24; Newsweek, May 13, 1946, 50; and Life, May 27, 1946, 47.

[47] See Life, May 27, 1946, 47-48, 50, and Gayn, 208. Gayn states that Ōkawa slapped Tōjō with "a rolled copy of the indictment" but the photographs in Life and motion picture footage in the author's possession show that Ōkawa used his bare hand.

[48] Gayn, 208; Shigemitsu, Sugamo Nikki, 9; Time, May 20, 1946, 24; and Newsweek, May 13, 1946, 50.

[49] As recorded by Mark Gayn, 209. Also, Time, May 20, 1946, 24, and Life, May 27, 1946, 46ff.

[50] As recorded in Newsweek, May 13, 1946, 50.

At the American hospital to which he was taken, Okawa professed to believe that the nurse attending him was Mrs. MacArthur's "daughter." "American girl has good constitution," he said. "Japanese girls are too thin."[51]

While speculation on the true state of his mind continued, Okawa underwent psychiatric tests. They revealed that he was suffering, among other things, from "psychosis with syphilitic meningo-encephalitis (general paresis)." Sir William ordered Okawa transferred to the psychiatric ward of the Tokyo Imperial University Hospital. Following malaria-fever therapy at that institution, the patient was placed in a hospital for the insane, where treatment gradually resulted in an improvement in his condition. After some months had passed, the question of his ability to stand trial was raised. Okawa was examined by both Japanese and American psychiatrists. They generally agreed in their diagnoses, but their recommendations proved contradictory. The Japanese doctor found that Okawa was "still lacking in the various faculties needed in standing trial, such as the power to discriminate between right and wrong." The American psychiatrists, on the other hand, concluded that the patient now possessed "the ability to understand the nature of the proceedings against him" and "to differentiate between right and wrong."

In the end, Okawa was not brought to trial, and perhaps it was just as well. He spent his time in the asylum completing a manuscript of more than 400 pages entitled "Introduction to Religion." He also talked with his doctors about the visits he had enjoyed during the early months of his confinement. "The souls of a great many people came to me," he said, "such as King Edward VII, President Wilson, Prince Connaught, etc. That's why my English improved very fast."

Gradually the delusions of grandeur which had possessed Okawa at the height of his illness faded away, but the visitations continued. According to him, they were really more in the nature of command performances. "When I concentrate my attention," he explained, "by sitting after the Zen fashion as quiet reigns around, I can make anyone I like come to my side and freely exchange thoughts with me." Among those whom Okawa claimed to have summoned were the samurai leader, Saigo of Satsuma, and the Emperor Meiji—both long dead.

By Okawa's own report, one of his most frequent visitors was the prophet Mohammed, who would appear dressed in a green mantle and white turban, with eyes glowing brilliantly. The spiritual communion

[51] *Ibid.*

he achieved with Mohammed, Okawa declared, helped him to understand more completely the content of the Koran, which he had been studying for some time.[52]

While Okawa was communing with his many visitors from the other world, the International Military Tribunal for the Far East was concentrating its attention on more mundane matters. At the very outset of the trial, the right of Sir William Webb to sit in judgment was questioned by the defense. He had earlier served as war crimes commissioner acting in the interests of Australia—a post in which he presumably could have developed feelings prejudicial to the Japanese. The members of the bench, with Sir William abstaining from participation, "declined to entertain the challenge, holding that they were without authority to review the appointments of the Supreme Commander or to pass on the qualifications of his appointees." Despite this ruling, the Tribunal did accept, for review and decision, several defense motions attacking the legality and jurisdiction of the court. Thus were raised, at the very beginning, "the most fundamental issues of the trial—whether aggressive war was a crime in international law; whether killing in the course of an aggressive war constituted murder; whether there was individual responsibility for international crimes." After the arguments for and against had been tendered, the motions which had been offered by the defense were denied by the Tribunal.[53]

It then devolved upon the prosecution to present its case against the defendants, who had all pleaded not guilty to the charges.[54] It took Mr. Keenan the better part of a day to deliver his opening address. It was the prosecution's contention that between the years 1928 and 1945 the defendants, among others, had entered into a common conspiracy to invade, subjugate, and exploit the northeastern provinces of China known as Manchuria. The invasion and subsequent acts of the Japanese forces were to take place under the pretext of an incident especially created for that purpose. Once Manchuria was firmly in hand, it would be used as a base for securing the complete domination of Eastern Asia

[52] The text is based on the following unnumbered IMTFE documents: "Medical Certificate" and "Report of a Psychiatric Examination of Ōkawa, Shūmei" (dated 23 February 1947) addressed to Sir William Webb by the head of the Tōkyō Municipal Hospital at Matsuzawa, and "Psychiatric Examination of Japanese Prisoner of War" (Ōkawa), dated 13 March 1947 and addressed, by the examining American doctors, to the Commanding Officer of the 361st Station Hospital.
See also T 376-77; *Facts on File: 1947*, 114 C; and Brosious corresp.
[53] See Horwitz, 502-3.
[54] Since Ōkawa had been removed from the courtroom, his plea was deferred. *Ibid.*, 502.

and the Pacific and Indian Oceans. To bring this about, the conspirators would attempt to seize control of the Japanese government either by a *coup d'état* or by gradual infiltration into all of the key positions in the government. The plan was also to be implemented by waging wars of aggression against any nation or people which might stand in the way of the conspiracy.

Thus, the Manchurian Incident had served as the curtain raiser for all that was to follow. According to the prosecution, the Japanese government was initially reluctant to comply with the wishes of the conspirators, but as time passed it was gradually forced to acquiesce in, and cooperate with, their purposes. By 1936, the Japanese government had lost its power to control the conspirators. In that year, the prosecution contended, the entire plan was adopted as national policy. Once they had gained the ascendancy, the conspirators "accelerated their program of preparing Japan militarily, politically and economically for war." In the years that followed, Japan launched and waged wars of aggression against China, against all of the other prosecuting powers, and against Thailand and the Mongolian People's Republic. In the course of those wars, the Japanese government either ordered or permitted the commission of "innumerable atrocities against prisoners of war and civilian internees and against civilian populations in occupied areas."[55]

As Mr. Keenan saw it, the Tokyo trial was "no ordinary trial" but rather "a part of the determined battle of civilization to preserve the entire world from destruction." The accused had ". . . decided to take the law into their own hands and to force their will upon mankind. They declared war upon civilization. They made the rules and defined the issues. . . . They willingly dealt with human beings as chattels and pawns. That it meant murder and the subjugation and enslavement of millions was of no moment to them. That it encompassed a plan or design for the murder in all parts of the world of children and aged, that it envisaged the entire obliteration of whole communities, was to them a matter of complete indifference. That it should cause the premature end of the very flower of the youth of the world—their own included—was entirely beside the point. . . . Their purpose was that force should be unloosed upon the world. . . . In this enterprise millions could die; the resources of nations could be destroyed. All of this was of no import in their mad scheme for domination and control of East

[55] The text follows the summary in Horwitz, 503-4. For Keenan's detailing of the "conspiracy," see T 436-52.

Asia, and as they advanced, ultimately the entire world. This was the purport of their conspiracy."[56]

Was civilization to stand idly by and permit the commission of such outrages without any attempt on its part to discourage, through judicial procedure and the imposition of punishment, the occurrence of similar crimes in the future? The prosecution's purpose, Mr. Keenan said, was one of "prevention or deterrence." There was no thought whatsoever of "the small, meaner purpose of vengeance or retaliation."[57] If the punishment of individuals who had "already . . . brought civilization to the brink of disaster" could not be vindicated, justice itself would become "a mockery."[58]

In the closing sections of his address, the chief prosecutor returned to this theme: ". . . individuals are being brought to the bar of justice for the first time in history to answer personally for offenses that they have committed while acting in official capacities as chiefs of state. We freely concede that these trials are in that sense without precedent. . . . However, it is essential to realize that if we waited for precedent and held ourselves in a straitjacket by reason of lack thereof, grave consequences could ensue without warrant or justification. . . . It is no longer a theory but a fact, as has been so well demonstrated by recent scientific developments, that another war will mean the end of civilization. . . . Today we must realize that no sound, reasonable step to bring about world peace can be avoided. The development of the art of destruction has proceeded to such a state that the world cannot wait upon the debating of legal trivialities. The plain reason is that the world itself may be destroyed while these niceties are being debated, developed and decided upon. . . . We have no particular interest in any individual or his punishment. They are representative in a certain sense of a class and a group. They are being prosecuted because they were converts to the rule of the tooth and claw. We can not be concerned with their individual concepts, their alleged justification on the ground of achievement of national ambitions, or their alleged patriotic endeavors. We need only . . . take a few steps to the top of this building to see what they have brought upon their own people. These events speak more eloquently than any human . . . could achieve by way of description."[59]

With the conclusion of Mr. Keenan's address, the prosecution immediately launched into the presentation of its "case-in-chief," which was

[56] T 384-86.   [57] T 386-88.   [58] T 391.
[59] See T 459-61 and 463-64. For the entire text of Mr. Keenan's opening address, see T 383-475.

divided into fourteen phases.[60] No one knew—and apparently least of all the prosecution—how long the court would be engaged in the pursuit of justice. Developments at Nuremberg seemed to suggest that the proceedings in Tokyo might end before the year was out. When the trial had been in progress only a few weeks, Sir William Webb was described as complaining that both sides were "too exhaustive" in their handling of the case: "If we are going to have every 'i' dotted and every 't' crossed, this case will never finish." The defense was said to be upset over what it regarded as a scanty allotment of time for preparation, "inadequate transportation, insufficient clerical help, and poor translation facilities." Some defense lawyers were reportedly dissatisfied because they "had expected sumptuous quarters, good publicity, and the admiration of the Japanese." Six had already resigned.[61]

Four months later, in September 1946, the trial was described as entering upon "another dreary day." By that time the defendants had somehow transformed themselves from "a dejected crew" wearing "ragged oddments of clothing" into one of "Tokyo's best-dressed groups." Observers were then of the opinion that the trial might be over by March 1947.[62] But when the new year came, the proceedings were clearly far from being over. The prosecution, which had begun its presentation of evidence in mid-June 1946, did not close its case-in-chief until nearly the end of January 1947.[63] Each of the defendants then immediately filed motions to dismiss on the grounds that the prosecution had failed to establish the charges contained in the indictment. After arguments by both sides had been tendered, the Tribunal ruled against the motions. A three weeks' recess was granted to the defense to give the lawyers for the accused more time to prepare for their own presentation in court. This began toward the end of February 1947.[64] A *Newsweek* correspondent reported from Tokyo that the Japa-

[60] See Horwitz, 504-25. A recess intervened between Mr. Keenan's opening address delivered on June 4, 1946, and the beginning of the case-in-chief on June 13.

"The court ignored, for the moment at least, a petition by four defendants [Hiranuma, Kaya, Shigemitsu, and Umezu] asking that the world be their judge and that their cases be submitted to an international panel of religious and intellectual leaders, including Pope Pius XII, Mahatma Gandhi, and H. G. Wells." *NYT*, June 13, 1946, 8 ("War Trial of Tojo and 25 Others Opens; Allies to Stress International Law Violation").

[61] *Newsweek*, July 1, 1946, 38.

[62] *Newsweek*, September 30, 1946, 43.

[63] The prosecution's case-in-chief covers pages 492 through 16259 of the "Transcript of Proceedings" (cited throughout this work as "T").

[64] Horwitz, 525. With respect to the motions to dismiss, see T 16262-990, 16992-93, and 16997. With respect to Tōjō, see T 16628-35 and 16950-58 (the "Okawa" of p. 16956 should be "Oikawa").

The accused were represented by both Japanese and American lawyers. Among the

nese people, who had taken quite an interest in the trial at first, were now refusing free tickets to the daily sessions and were exhibiting "a supreme indifference to the fate of the defendants." Everyone seemed certain that the men in the dock would eventually be convicted and executed.

In order "to avoid repetition of the same evidence on behalf of two or more defendants" and yet "preserve the individual interests of each," the Japanese and American lawyers representing the accused "adopted a joint plan of presentation. Under this plan all evidence supporting defenses common to most or all of the accused was first introduced." Subsequently, individual defendants offered supplementary or new evidence pertaining to their respective cases. During these presentations, defendants who were in disagreement with aspects of the joint defense "introduced contradictory evidence."[65]

The defense presentation was primarily concerned with denying the existence of any conspiracy and with showing that the defendants and the government of Japan had been provoked into acting in self-defense by the activities of other nations which had sought to interfere with Japan's legitimate rights and interests in Asia and to threaten Japan's existence as a nation. These themes ran through the joint presentation which was offered by the defense in the form of "a modified phase plan" consisting of five divisions. Upon the completion of this presentation, sixteen defendants, including Tojo, took the witness stand to refute the charges lodged by the prosecution. The nine defendants who did not take the stand relied on the introduction of witnesses and documentary evidence.[66]

All of the defendants argued that they had had the responsibility, as the leaders of Japan, to maintain the defense and welfare of the nation. They had tried to accomplish this through peaceful means; when their efforts had failed, there had been no other choice but to go to war. The defendants denied the existence of any criminal intent on their part or of any knowledge of the alleged illegality of what they had done. They denied that they had ever violated the provisions of international law. On this they all agreed. But on the question of individual responsibility,

---

former were a number of men who had gained prominence, more than a decade earlier, in the defense of the perpetrators of the May 15 incident (1932). See "The Brocade Banner," 47, n.2.

[65] Horwitz, 525.

[66] The different total, 25 defendants instead of the original 28, stems from the fact that the proceedings against Ōkawa had by then been dropped, and the presentations with respect to Matsuoka and Nagano had been suspended following their deaths during the course of the trial.

a difference of approach developed. "Only Tojo placed his entire reliance upon the pleas of self-defense and lack of criminal intent. He assumed full responsibility for all acts committed by him and did not seek in any way to minimize the importance of the decisions and acts to which he had been a party. He believed at the time and still believed that the acts were necessary and unavoidable. He had hoped to obtain his ends by peaceful means; but when that could not be accomplished he had acted according to his conviction that they must be obtained through war."

The other defendants tried either to deny their personal responsibility or to minimize their roles: the civilians blamed the military for leading the nation to ruin; the war ministry and army general staff said the armies in the field were responsible for prisoners of war; the field commanders claimed they had followed the orders sent to them from Tokyo.

Despite the fact that the charter of the Tribunal had "expressly denied the validity of superior orders as a defense," a number of the accused pleaded innocent on that ground. Many charged the prosecution with "attempting to hold them liable on a theory of vicarious responsibility for acts committed not by them but by their subordinates." Some defendants asserted that they were answerable only to their own sovereign. Oshima and Shiratori, who had held the ambassadorial posts in Berlin and Rome, claimed diplomatic immunity "even though they were not charged with crimes against the nations to which they had been accredited but with crimes against other nations and the international community."[67]

In presenting their case before the Tribunal, the accused and their American and Japanese lawyers spent a total of 187 days in court, or—in terms of the calendar—from February 24, 1947, until January 12, 1948.[68] By then it had become abundantly clear that while the prosecution's purpose was to show that the defendants were guilty of starting the war, the defense hoped to demonstrate that the accused were merely guilty of losing it. Each side regarded the other (and with considerable justification) as acting on the questionable premise that to contend was to prove. The prosecution and defense also found themselves in disagreement over the role of General Ryukichi Tanaka, a giant of a man with an "elephant-like body" and a memory to match.[69] Tanaka,

---

[67] See Horwitz, 525-34.

[68] *Ibid.*, 534. The defense presentation covers pages 17004-37175 of the "Transcript of Proceedings."

[69] Tanaka, "I Know Everything About Them," 1, and Umezu intv.

who was known behind his back as "The Monster" (because of his size) and as "Stinky" (because of his irascible temper), played a unique role as ". . . a witness whom both prosecution and defense adduced from time to time, as occasion demanded, and whom both prosecution and defense cross-examined as a witness of no credit, again as occasion demanded."[70]

Although the prosecution believed that Tanaka had once been "closely allied to the conspiratorial coterie until his break in 1941 with Tojo," it nevertheless found him extremely helpful in the preparation and presentation of its case.[71] Tanaka nursed an abiding hatred for a number of the defendants, especially for Tojo. The ex-premier had allegedly once placed him under house arrest and threatened him with confinement in an insane asylum. "Look at me!" Tanaka would say to members of the prosecution staff. "Do *I* look crazy?"[72]

Called by *Life* magazine "a sybaritic and unsavory character," and described by one irate defense counsel as a "professional witness" with a "slight regard . . . for the truth," Tanaka saw himself as "a hero of war and apostle of peace" who expected to be assassinated for his efforts on behalf of justice.[73]

Although he seemed to be mentally competent during the trial, Tanaka was recognized as being "out to get" his old rivals.[74] One member of the defense came to the conclusion that an uncontrollable desire for notoriety led Tanaka to perjure himself during the course of his testimony.[75] Another defense lawyer remembered Tanaka as a very clever and effective witness for the prosecution. Whenever the defense tried to expose him, it usually got the worst of the bargain.[76]

Like Dr. Okawa, General Tanaka eventually suffered a breakdown in his health, but not until after the trial had ended. Nonprofessional diagnoses of his condition ranged from *kodai-mōsōkyō* (megalomania) to *shinkei-suijaku* (nervous prostration or neurasthenia). Tanaka was said to have experienced bitter disappointment when the chief prose-

[70] J, B/V, 653. On Tanaka's nicknames: *Time*, January 5, 1948, 24-25, and Fleisher, Steiner, and Umezu intv.

[71] See Horwitz, 509.

[72] Fleisher intv.

[73] The text draws on *Life*, January 26, 1948, 89; Fleisher and Furness intv.; and T 34378.

[74] *Life*, January 26, 1948, 89, and *Time*, January 5, 1948, 24-25. In addition to Tōjō, Tanaka hated General Akira Mutō. Tanaka had apparently expected to be named chief of the military affairs bureau. He never forgave the fact that the post went to Mutō.

[75] The source is privileged.

[76] Tanaka gave damaging testimony against practically all of the defendants. Notable exceptions were Hata, Shigemitsu, and Umezu. Furness and Umezu intv., and *Life*, January 28, 1948, 89.

cutor failed to take him to the United States after the trial, as had allegedly been promised. To a Japanese newspaperman who tried to interview him, Tanaka kept repeating, "Keenan is a liar."[77]

If General Tanaka's testimony provided a measure of relief from the boredom which the prosecution's presentation occasionally produced, a corresponding service was performed with respect to the sometimes tedious submissions of the defense when Tojo at length gained his day in court. Following a comparatively brief opening statement by Dr. Ichiro Kiyose (Tojo's Japanese lawyer), George Francis Blewett of Philadelphia (Kiyose's American colleague) began reading an affidavit of more than 60,000 words which ran to 318 double-spaced transcript pages. According to a *Newsweek* report, Tojo sat in a faded khaki uniform, with hands clasped in his lap, looking like a "wizened owl" as he listened to Mr. Blewett.[78] The reading, which had begun on a Friday, was continued on the following Monday and completed the next day. The prosecution subsequently spent four days in cross-examination. The courtroom was crowded to the bursting point. The judges' bench was full, the lawyers' seats were all taken, and the galleries reserved for visitors presented the solid front of a capacity audience. Everyone wanted to hear what Tojo would have to say.[79]

Thus did this smallish man, who had been the premier of Japan at the time of Pearl Harbor, again draw the world's attention. Press and radio reported the event; the camera's magic recorded it on film. No one could have asked for a better stage from which to speak his lines to history.

There is absolutely no doubt that Tojo made the most of the opportunity. Rather than remain on the defensive, he chose to counterattack by challenging the prosecution's contentions on a wide front. The views that he had held at the time of the events were now expounded to the best of his and his lawyers' ability, and to the limit of the skill possessed by those who had to deal with the constantly vexatious problem of Japanese-to-English and English-to-Japanese translation and interpretation.

[77] The sources are privileged. The author visited General Tanaka at his home in Tōkyō in August 1956. He was then in poor health, but his memory of events in the past was still good.

[78] *Newsweek*, January 5, 1948, 39. See also *Time*, January 5, 1948, 25, and *Life*, January 26, 1948, 87-88.

The affidavit was originally written in Japanese by Kiyose on the basis of information supplied by Tōjō. When it was completed, Tōjō checked it for errors and omissions. It was then translated into English and given to Blewett, who made some revisions and corrections. Kiyose intv.

[79] Shigemitsu, *Sugamo Nikki*, 323, and *Facts on File: 1948*, 9 H.

Tojo vigorously accepted the administrative responsibility for the decision for war, but he no less vigorously denied that he had been prompted by any considerations other than those arising out of the needs of national defense. He took pains to protect the imperial position and to present his arguments in such a way as not to compromise the person of the Emperor.[80] Tojo also refrained from pointing a finger at others who might reasonably have been charged with sharing the responsibility which he kept imputing to himself. He stood by his former subordinates and cabinet colleagues. He implicated others only when he felt the necessity of thereby clarifying the case for Japan.[81]

It was during cross-examination, rather than through his affidavit, that Tojo commanded the most attention. It had been expected that Mr. Fihelly would match wits with the defendant on behalf of the prosecution. It was he who had interrogated Tojo at Sugamo Prison and who had familiarized himself thoroughly with the facts that might be adduced from the interrogations. But at the last moment, and perhaps because Tojo was the central figure of the trial, the chief prosecutor decided to begin the cross-examination himself. If it became prolonged, he would turn it over to Fihelly. There were "many duties," Keenan told the court, "required of the Chief of Counsel."

The Tribunal had a standing rule that only one member of the prosecuting team would be permitted to cross-examine a defendant. Thus whoever began would normally be expected to complete the task. For this reason Keenan's suggestion posed a problem. Despite the fact that neither Tojo nor his lawyers had any objection to more than one cross-examiner, a majority of the members of the Tribunal ruled against the chief of counsel. Keenan had therefore to decide whether to take on Tojo or to turn him over to Fihelly at once. Keenan elected to proceed on his own.[82]

During the next few days, it frequently seemed as if Mr. Keenan

---

[80] This approach, which was common to the other defendants also, has apparently led some students of the period to suspect that perhaps the Emperor was in greater need of "protection" than has generally been believed. This is a challenging view, but it is by no means the only explanation of the zealousness Tōjō and other defendants displayed in their courtroom treatment of the role of the Emperor.

[81] The numerous references to Tōjō's affidavit and cross-examination, which have appeared throughout this book (especially in Part II), bear out the above. In addition, the following are applicable: Katsuko Tōjō, "Saigo wa Kōfuku," *Daiyamondo*, Vol. XL, No. 17 (May 15, 1952), 151; Shigemitsu, *Sugamo Nikki*, 103, 322, 326; *Newsweek*, January 5, 1948, 39; and *Time*, January 5, 1948, 25.

[82] T 36533-35; Blewett, Blakeney, Furness, and Fihelly intv. Following this incident Mr. Fihelly severed his connection with the case and returned to the United States.

were being led in the direction in which General Tojo wanted to go.[83] The chief prosecutor was undoubtedly at a disadvantage because he had not personally prepared the case against Tojo. Another reason for Keenan's lack of success was clearly the language barrier, a difficulty which persisted throughout the trial. Still another was more personal. Among those who saw Mr. Keenan at close quarters, it was common knowledge that he was not always in a condition which would permit him to achieve the peak of performance. If a lawyer's ability is measured by the cases he has won, the chief prosecutor had much in his past to recommend him. Earlier in his career, he had gained fame as a gangbuster—he had convicted "Machine Gun" Kelly in the early 1930's of the kidnapping of a wealthy oil man. It was Mr. Keenan, also, who had written the so-called Lindbergh kidnapping law, and who had "played a major role in getting ten crime laws through Congress, extending the Federal war on gangsters, racketeers and kidnappers." This record, plus his political work over the years on behalf of the Administration in Washington, had led to his appointment in Tokyo. Unfortunately, however, there were times during the trial when Mr. Keenan's colleagues, and even his antagonists on the defense bench, felt that it would have been better if he had not appeared in court at all.[84]

Whatever the reason or reasons, the chief prosecutor got off to a bad start from which he never subsequently recovered:

MR. KEENAN: Accused Tojo, I shall not address you as General because, of course, you know there is no longer any Japanese Army.

I want to ask you if this affidavit or testimony or argument, as it may be called, that you have given from the witness stand or through your counsel at the lectern for the preceding three or four days has been intended for the purpose of convincing this Court of your innocence or has been intended to be a continuation of imperialistic, militaristic propaganda to the people of Japan.

MR. BLEWETT: Mr. President.

THE PRESIDENT: Mr. Blewett.

MR. BLEWETT: It is the purpose of the defense counsel and the wish of the accused not to put trivial objections, but I must object to this question as not being proper cross-examination.

[83] A reading of the cross-examination, T 36533-815, S 344:17-S 349:5, supports the opinion that the advantage lay with the witness and not with the prosecutor. This is also the view of many who were there: Blakeney, Blewett, Furness, Handleman, and Shigemitsu (*Sugamo Nikki*, 326).

[84] The text draws on an obituary in *NYT*, December 9, 1954, 33, and on material relating to the chief prosecutor's career and his conduct of the trial obtained during interviews with Blakeney, Blewett, Furness, Handleman, and Umezu.

MR. KEENAN: Mr. President, this question is put to this witness in all sincerity by the prosecution in view of the nature and contents of this affidavit, which is considered by the prosecution to be an insult to the intelligence of this Tribunal and to these proceedings.

THE PRESIDENT: The Tribunal may or may not take the view that the affidavit is of assistance to us, but I have not yet heard any Member suggest that the purpose of the witness is to insult the Tribunal.

The objection is sustained and the question disallowed.[85]

Among comments written at the time or recorded later are characterizations of Tojo on the witness stand as "argumentative," "disdainful," "vague," "clever," "biting," or "incisive."[86] *Life* magazine described him as testifying "with the cold assurance of a conquering samurai. . . ."[87] These judgments, while not necessarily incorrect, were based almost exclusively on the court interpreter's rendition of what Tojo said. A rather less critical view is obtained when the Japanese record is read in addition to the English transcript. It is then obvious that a breakdown in communication from one language to the other frequently occurred. When Keenan's questions reached Tojo in garbled or altered form, the replies—even if accurately rendered—could easily create the impression that the witness was attempting to respond to suit himself, or to answer questions which had not been asked rather than those which had. If Keenan's queries had been clearer, or if the interpreter had had more time to deal with the problem, the results might have been more satisfactory.[88]

The prosecution's language division once estimated that it required "at least eight hours of work to prepare a creditable translation of a single page of material." In court, experience had shown that simultaneous interpretation was impossible. Since the proceedings had to be interrupted at the end of each sentence whenever oral testimony was given, the speed of the trial at such times "was reduced to one-fifth of its normal pace." It was for that reason that the court had come to prefer written presentations which could be prepared in advance.[89] Even so, the language problem was responsible for a multiplication of

---

[85] T 36535-36. For the rendition into Japanese, including a statement by Keenan which does not appear in the English transcript ("Shōnin ni kikimasu": "I shall refer to you as 'witness.'"), see S 345:4.

[86] *Facts on File: 1948,* 9 H; Deverall, 51; Blakeney intv.

[87] *Life,* January 26, 1948, 87.

[88] In addition to the examples cited in earlier chapters, see T 36537, S 345:4; T 36586-91, S 346:6-7; T 36665-74, S 347:5-6; and T 36699-703, S 347:10.

[89] Horwitz, 539.

errors which sometimes escaped correction entirely, or which—when discovered—were not always immediately or adequately revised.[90]

In addition to his difficulties with Tojo and with the language barrier, Keenan also found himself occasionally in trouble with the court. There seemed to be a basic antagonism between Sir William Webb and the chief prosecutor, which had become so noticeable that their relationship was described as the Keenan-Webb feud. The president of the Tribunal could be rather sarcastic. When Keenan complained to the court that Tojo was "going to ridiculous limits" to answer "a simple question, the date when he first learned that Pearl Harbor was to be attacked," Sir William told Tojo: "Just state the date when you learned that, if you recollect it. If the learned counsel requires you to say how you came to know that you may tell him, but apparently he doesn't want to know that."[91]

On at least one occasion, Mr. Keenan was confounded at every turn. When the prosecutor asked Tojo whether he was "familiar with" the so-called Hull note of November 26, 1941, Tojo replied: "I shall never forget it no matter how long I live" (*Kore wa mō isshōgai wasuremasen*).

MR. KEENAN: . . . Since you have referred in this court to this document . . . in a manner which I will not characterize other than to say it was thrown in your face, I will ask you to examine it very carefully at this moment.

THE ACCUSED: I have looked through this document.

MR. KEENAN: Now, in the first place that document was handed by the Secretary of State of the United States himself to Ambassadors Nomura and Kurusu as far as you know in a very dignified fashion, is that not true?

[90] To cite but one example: On December 26, 1947, a number of corrections were read into the record (T 36164-70). They applied to errors made during the proceedings held on August 27 and 28, 1946 (T 4356-401). Thus, the mistakes made at that time were not corrected until a year and four months later. In the meantime, some 31,000 pages of testimony had been added to the transcript.
Another problem occurred, on the language level, whenever a witness such as Tōjō was shown a document and asked to verify it or comment upon it. In such cases, if the witness began quoting from the document (in Japanese), the interpreter would not translate what the witness was saying but would merely read to the court the pertinent parts of the basic translation of the said document prepared beforehand. Thus, if this basic translation was incorrect, as was frequently the case, the interpreter—in relying thereon—was putting words into the mouth of the witness which he was not, in fact, saying. See, for example, Tōjō cross-examination, T 36678-79, S 347:6 (the monitor's remarks were apparently not conveyed to the witness) and T 36684-88, S 347:7-8 (which suggests that Keenan missed Blewett's point entirely).

[91] See T 36743-47, S 348:3-4 and *passim*. Tōjō's answer was to the effect that he had first learned of the projected attack on or about December 1 or 2. Note the difficulty encountered by the interpreter and the language monitor in rendering into Japanese Keenan's statement: "I apologize to the Court, but from this witness I have found that I must be very exact to get the record straight."

THE ACCUSED: In form, yes.

MR. KEENAN: And it was—

THE ACCUSED: In contents there was no spirit of concession—there was no spirit of conciliation whatsoever.

MR. KEENAN: We will come to that in a moment. As a matter of fact it was handed to your ambassadors at a time when they were receiving the utmost courtesy in the Capital of the United States, being privileged to see the Secretary of State and even the President of the United States almost at their will. Do you not admit that?

THE ACCUSED: That is a fact, and it has nothing to do with the contents of this document.

MR. KEENAN: But I suppose you know that the President of the United States is the highest authority of that Republic?

THE ACCUSED: I know it in the same sense that I know that the Emperor of Japan is the highest authority in Japan.

MR. KEENAN: Well, there is this difference, the people of the United States choose their President every four years by direct voice. That is not true in Japan, or was not true in Japan at the time we are talking of. Was there that difference?

This was too much for Sir William, who interposed to ask the relevancy of the line of questioning being so doggedly pursued by the chief of counsel. Keenan replied that he was attempting to show that Tojo had been dealing with "direct responsible authorities" whereas the representatives of the United States had been dealing with "those of ambiguous responsibility."

THE PRESIDENT: But that, at all events, is your submission.

MR. KEENAN: But, Mr. President, if it is offensive in any way to take a few moments in this courtroom in this historic trial to let the people here know the authority of the President of the United States Government I shall not press the point, I shall go immediately to something else on a further indication from the Court.

THE PRESIDENT: Go immediately to something else.

MR. KEENAN: I believe the Court means that it would like to have me so do, it is not a command.

THE PRESIDENT: It is the acceptance of an invitation by you. We don't want to hear any more questions of that type.[92]

According to *Life* magazine, which reported the above incident in abbreviated form, Mr. Keenan had "snapped" at Sir William. The "red-faced" president of the Tribunal had then "leaned across the bench

[92] See T 36781-84 and S 348:9. See also the Keenan-Webb exchange in T 36569-72, S 346:3-4.

and shouted" at the chief of counsel. Tojo "sneered"; the rest of the defendants "smiled."[93]

A few minutes later the accused and the chief prosecutor were at loggerheads over Tojo's efforts to portray the Hull note as ignoring the realities of the situation—the alleged military, political, and economic encirclement of Japan by America and Britain. Keenan immediately took offense. "I am not interested," he told Tojo, ". . . in your insolent remarks about the honesty of the representatives of the United States of America." This thrust at the accused was largely lost in the interpretation from English into Japanese, which said nothing about insolence.[94]

Ultimately, Tojo admitted that the Nine-Power Pact (which Japan had violated) contained words to the same effect as those found in Hull's four principles, which had been recapitulated in the November 26 note. The differences between Japan and the United States, Tojo said, had arisen from an American failure to recognize the changes which had taken place since the conclusion of the Nine-Power Pact in 1922. When Keenan suggested that the proper procedure, in the event of such changes, was for the nations concerned to meet together so as to undertake whatever revisions "equity required," Tojo likened the effect of the treaty on Japan to a situation in which an 18-year-old found herself wearing the same clothes she had been given at the age of ten. Naturally the clothes would be coming apart at the seams. Although Japan had wanted to sew them back together again, and had tried to do so, she had found it impossible to mend the torn parts because she had grown so large in the meantime.

MR. KEENAN: Well, I suggest to you that there was a possibility of sticking a pin in now and then in the process of mending the dress. Would you accept that revision?

THE ACCUSED: That is perfectly true, but the body grew too quickly for that and the child's parents wouldn't mend those tears for her.

THE PRESIDENT: It is not necessary to resort to metaphors and similes to explain such simple things.

THE ACCUSED: Then I shall tell you of the facts.

MR. KEENAN: That will be very helpful.

[93] *Life*, January 26, 1948, 87-89. *Life* attributed the "feud" to Sir William's disagreement with the American decision "to absolve and 'use' " the Emperor. Be that as it may, *Life* was being unfair when it charged that "Webb's tribunal" had refused to let a War Department expert, Mr. Fihelly, assist Keenan in the cross-examination of Tōjō.

[94] See T 36783-86, S 348:9-10.

Among the "facts" which Tojo offered were the absence of the Soviet Union from among the signatories to the Nine-Power Pact, the outbreak of the China Incident, and the replacement of the concept of free trade by the bloc economy idea. A conference to rectify matters, he declared, had been impossible, because after the Manchurian and China Incidents, and especially in the period immediately preceding the Pacific War, the United States and Great Britain (the principal signatories) had been hostile to Japan.

This was a very poor excuse. If Japan had seen no point in a multilateral conference prior to 1941, because a "hostile" America and Britain would dominate such a conference and treat Japan "unfairly," what hope or purpose could there have been in Japan's negotiating with the United States alone, as she did in 1941, in circumstances in which other and possibly more friendly powers would find it rather difficult to be of assistance to Japan? Unfortunately for the record, Mr. Keenan did not inquire into the views of the accused in that regard. Tojo therefore completed his reply by stating that during the 1941 negotiations Japan had had the revision of the Nine-Power Pact in mind when she had asked the United States to recognize the new order—specifically the Konoe declaration, the basic treaty between Japan and Nanking (Puppet) China, and the so-called Sino-Japanese joint declaration. Mr. Keenan then asked Tojo whether he had considered Japan "bound" by the Nine-Power Pact between October and December 1941. Tojo replied that he had.[95]

The chief of counsel seemed at last to have gotten an admission, and so he turned to another matter. But what had he actually gotten? What had Tojo really said?

In putting Keenan's question into Japanese, the interpreter had used the character compound, *kōsoku*, to express the idea of "bound": ". . . Nihon wa Kyūkakoku jōyaku ni yotte kōsoku sarete oru to kangaete orimashita ka?" Tojo had replied: "Kōsoku sarete otta to kangaete orimashita."[96]

In the English transcript, everything appears to be in order. The accused is asked a simple question and he answers it. But in the Japanese, the matter is not quite so simple. The basic meaning of the verbal form of *kōsoku* is "to check," "to restrain," or "to fetter." It was in *that* sense that Tojo understood the question, and it was in that sense that he replied affirmatively—using the same word which the inter-

[95] See T 36786-97, S 348:10-11.
[96] S 348:11.

preter himself had employed in translating the question which Keenan had phrased with an entirely different idea in mind.

Despite such difficulties, some of which were not always apparent to the participants, the machinery of the trial ground on. In the total span of the proceedings, Tojo's appearance on the stand was very brief but, in its way, memorable. According to *Newsweek*, Tojo had three aims in mind. The first was to clear the Emperor of complicity in the events described by the prosecution as criminal; the second was to lay the blame for the war upon the Western powers; the third was to "rehabilitate his reputation" before he was hanged.[97] Although the degree of Tojo's success in any of these respects is a matter of opinion, the *Newsweek* correspondent and other observers felt that Tojo's stock rose, in Japan at least, following the presentation of his testimony. One critic later wrote that the trial had produced a metamorphosis from "Tojo the Idiot" to "Tojo the Teacher." At the one extreme he had been castigated for fumbling his suicide; at the other he was being pitied and admired as "an anti-democratic martyr."[98]

A Japanese newspaper declared that "the average man on the street" was expressing "more sympathy than hatred" for the ex-premier. Those who had been asked for their views had indicated that they thought Tojo had told the court the truth.[99] *Time* magazine reported in a similar vein. Said one Japanese: "I used to think that Tojo should be hanged. Now I don't know. If we had won, we would have tried the Americans." Another remarked, "When you people have left these islands, the Japanese will return to traditional worship of exalted human beings. First to be enshrined will be Hideki Tojo."[100]

There was even a faint flickering of uneasiness among the victorious Americans. When the trial had begun in the spring of 1946, no one had foreseen that it might still be in progress in 1948. In the intervening period much had happened.

There was the appearance and development of a Hiroshima-conscience. If the utilization of the atomic bomb could not be justified, what about the prosecution of the Japanese enemy for atrocities? If the bomb could be justified, how many other deeds of war might perhaps be explained away?

There was the knowledge that Japan had honored her surrender obligations and had shown an amazing aptitude for "democracy," in

[97] *Newsweek*, January 5, 1948, 39.
[98] Solow, "A Rather Startling Result," *Fortune*, Vol. XXXIX, No. 4 (April 1949), 158.
[99] As recorded in Deverall, 51.
[100] *Time*, January 5, 1948, 25.

one form or another. Thousands of Americans were living in Japan and were learning to like the Japanese people as much as they generally seemed to like the Americans. Despite some friction and even occasional incidents, the record showed nothing of the deeply rooted antipathy which might have been expected to bedevil the occupation of one nation by another.

There was the appearance of a new challenge to world peace in the form of Soviet ambitions and the spread of communism in the East as well as in the West. Mr. Keenan was among those who were troubled by the presence of a Soviet judge and prosecutor in the courtroom.

There was also some realization, in a few minds at least, that it might be misleading to compare the Japanese case too closely with the German example. Guilt by association could be as fallacious on the national as on the individual level. Japan and her leaders had engaged in a program of aggression and had joined the Berlin-Rome Axis, but were the order and magnitude of the crimes committed by all of these addicts of destruction really the same?

The prosecution thought so. It emphasized Japan's alliance with Germany and Italy, "whose disgraceful actions in respect to people of peaceful neighboring countries had already made them outlaws, and a stench in the nostrils of law-abiding nations." Tojo, the prosecution declared, had become in a "vague and irresponsible manner . . . a bedfellow of the German crowd of lawbreakers and murderers, thereby rejecting the friendship of the United States and Britain."[101]

Hitler's grimly determined rapacity, the naked evil of his calculated policy of exterminating millions of helpless and innocent people, his frighteningly effective employment of the Big Lie (to say nothing of countless little ones), and his repeatedly demonstrated allegiance to the double cross had long since set a mold of thought with regard to totalitarianism, its men and methods, that could perhaps all too readily be applied as a standard of measurement with respect to Hitler's Axis partner, Japan. If the Nazi dictator had ever tried a Tojo-like defense, the rank hypocrisy of it would have been apparent instantly.

Was Tojo the Far Eastern Hitler? He somehow failed to fit the pattern. Unlike the "Führer" and "Il Duce," Tojo was a reflector, not a creator, of national thought. His word was not law. It was not his to command or dictate. He was one among many and not even first among equals. He was a militarist—misguided, naïve, and narrow in

[101] T 41968 and 41982-83.

outlook; he regarded war as a legitimate instrument of national policy; he apparently believed what he had told the court and failed to recognize the patent contradictions between his contentions and the facts. This had been his undoing.

By the time Tojo had presented his personal defense, more than eighteen months had passed since the marshal of the court had first banged his gavel and declared, "The International Military Tribunal for the Far East is in session and is ready to hear any matter brought before it." And still the end was not in sight. With the conclusion of the presentation of individual defenses, the prosecution introduced evidence in rebuttal, consisting mainly of excerpts from the Saionji-Harada memoirs—a vast accumulation of material which had become available only after the defense had begun its case. This was followed by surrebuttal and other submissions, including evidence in mitigation and another unsuccessful defense motion to dismiss.[102] And then—at long last—the final arguments: the summations for the prosecution and the defense.[103]

The prosecution began what Mr. Keenan called "the closing of the gates" on February 11, 1948, a day which had once been celebrated as a national holiday commemorating the "founding" of the Empire of Japan in the year 660 B.C.—a holiday which was forbidden by order of General MacArthur.[104] The only important new element introduced by the prosecution was a vigorous attack upon the self-defense plea of the accused. The prosecution asserted that that "amounted to nothing more than a contention wholly unsupported by proof." "Unambiguous official documents" clearly showed that Japan had followed a program

[102] For the rebuttal and surrebuttal evidence, see T 37176-38585 and 38586-915. On the question of dismissal: T 38940-47.

The Charter contained no provision requiring the hearing of evidence in mitigation, but the Tribunal offered to listen to whatever the accused might wish to present in that regard. Normally, mitigating evidence is tendered only after a finding of guilt has been handed down, but the Tribunal ruled that such evidence was to be submitted in advance of the court's verdict. Only Marquis Kido "availed himself of the opportunity." The others opposed the procedure because "they felt that it placed them in an anomalous position, and that in all fairness such evidence should be offered only after the Tribunal had concluded that they were guilty of the offenses charged" (Horwitz, 535).

[103] The Charter called for the accused to address the Tribunal first and for the prosecution to follow. In the light of the length and complexity of the case, however, the Tribunal decided to reverse the order of presentation but to give the prosecution the opportunity to reply to the defense summation. No time limitations were imposed. Horwitz, 535-36.

[104] See T 38949-42075 for the prosecution's summation.

of aggression. The prosecution accused the defense of having "deliberately treated as nonexistent the most important evidence in the case." Within the councils of the state "the motivating concept" had always been "the aggrandizement of the Japanese Empire." Self-defense had merely been the pretext for that aggrandizement. The prosecution insisted that the extent to which Japan had used her armed forces had clearly revealed this to be true. "In each instance against, at the most, minor threats Japan had used unlimited force not commensurate with the danger involved and not necessary to protect against it."[105]

In the segment of its summation reserved for Tojo personally, the prosecution repeated its principal contentions, arguing from the very general to the very particular. Even at that late date and after so much trouble had already been caused by language difficulties, the prosecution managed to begin with a charge against the defendant that was purely mythical, because it stemmed from an error of fact and a mistranslation of terms. Tojo was described as having been, at the time of the Manchurian Incident, the chief of the very important operations bureau of the army general staff, when in fact he had merely headed a section (that is, a segment of a bureau), and not even a section of the operations bureau at all, but rather a section of the general affairs bureau—a post in which he had been concerned with troop education rather than with aiding and abetting military operations on the continent.[106]

In its final arguments, the prosecution also charged that Tojo "knew or should have known" of Japan's aggressive plans at various times and of the widespread atrocities committed by Japanese troops during the period when he served as war minister and premier.[107] The phrase, "knew or should have known," was an interesting if not altogether satisfactory way of arguing the guilt of the accused.

It was March 2, 1948, before the prosecution completed its presentation; the defense began its own summation the same day and continued on into the middle of April, spending a total of thirty-one days in court in its effort to have its interpretation of history, and of the role of the

---

[105] Horwitz, 536-37.

[106] For the details, see T 41954-55 and 47415-18. See also p. 43 above.

[107] T 41960, 41973, and 42025. The absence of any comment in Tōjō's affidavit, on unlawful aerial bombardment in China prompted the prosecution to declare (T 41964): "From this lack of showing it may be inferred that Tojo condoned the illegal actions of the Air Forces, and in doing so he became a party thereto by ratification, waiver, or consent." According to the prosecution, Tōjō also "must have known that prisoners of war were being treated illegally because complaints on such matters were under consideration at biweekly meetings of the Prisoners' Bureau [of the war ministry], as he admitted" (T 42017).

defendants, accepted by the Tribunal.[108] Whereas the prosecution had dealt with Tojo in 73 pages of summation out of a total of more than 3,000, the defense devoted 253 pages out of more than 6,000 to arguments in his behalf.[109] The prosecution's reply to the defense presentation as a whole added another 303 pages of transcript. It was therefore not until the afternoon of Friday, April 16, 1948, that the final word was delivered. In its closing paragraph, the prosecution achieved a certain eloquence:[110] "These defendants were not automatons; they were not replaceable cogs in a machine; they were not playthings of fate caught in a maelstrom of destiny from which there was no extrication. These men were the brains of an empire. . . . It was theirs to choose whether their nation would lead an honored life . . . or . . . would become a symbol of evil throughout the world. They made their choice. For this choice they must bear the guilt—a guilt which is perhaps greater than that of any group of men who have stood before the bar of justice in the entire history of the world. These men were not the hoodlums who were the powerful part of the group which stood before the Tribunal in Nuernberg, dregs of a criminal environment thoroughly schooled in the ways of crime and knowing no other methods but those of crime. These men were supposed to be the elite of the nation, the honest and trusted leaders to whom the fate of the nation had been confidently entrusted. Some of them were men who were held in high respect and esteem as men of peace and good will by the leaders and representatives of other nations."

Having thus opened up, at the very end of the trial, an avenue of thought which could have been enormously challenging had anyone chosen to explore it, the prosecution quickly sealed the approach with its own findings: "These men knew the difference between good and evil. They knew the obligations to which they had solemnly pledged their nation. With full knowledge they voluntarily made their choice for evil, to disregard the obligations and to betray the faith which their own people and others had in them! With full knowledge they voluntarily elected to follow the path of war bringing death and injury to millions of human beings and destruction and hate wherever their forces went. They gambled with the destiny of the people of their nation and like common felons everywhere brought only death and

[108] See T 42076-48110 for the defense summation.
[109] See T 41953-42025 and 47274-526 for the prosecution and defense summations concerning Tōjō.
[110] T 48410-12.

hurt and destruction and chaos to those whose care had been entrusted to them. For this choice these men now stand before this Tribunal awaiting judgment. They must be judged for what their acts were and for what they were intended to be. These acts were pursuant to their own choice. They made their choice for aggression and for war and they made it freely and voluntarily. For this choice they must bear the guilt."

CHAPTER 16

The Fate of the Man

IN THE TWO YEARS that had passed between the opening of the Tokyo trial in the spring of 1946 and the presentation of the prosecution's closing argument in mid-April 1948, court statistics had reached astronomical proportions. The Tribunal had been in session during that period for a total of 417 days. Nearly 1,200 persons had given either oral or written testimony. Close to 5,200 exhibits had been received in evidence from the prosecution and the defense. More than 800 other documents had been tendered for identification.[1] The daily transcript of the proceedings had grown to an enormous total of 48,412 double-spaced mimeographed pages—roughly the equivalent, in book form, of something like fifty-four volumes of at least five hundred pages each. Estimates on the cost of the trial were eventually to run as high as $10,000,000—roughly a dollar for every word spoken in the courtroom.[2]

It was inevitable that a trial of such length and scope should become the subject of controversy and criticism. Whatever view finally prevails, however, no one will charge that the trial was conducted in unseemly haste. Rather, the contrary will be said: that the proceedings were too long-drawn-out. Two years had been devoted to plowing up the facts of Far Eastern history for the period 1928 to 1945; another seven months were spent by the judges in reaching a verdict.

It was consequently not until November 4, 1948, that the court at length reconvened for the delivery of that verdict. At the beginning of the trial, the eleven judges had "signed a joint affirmation to administer justice according to law, without fear, favor or affection."[3] Now the time had come for their judgment. The scene was vividly described by *Newsweek* magazine: MP's "in shining white helmets" dotted the "bleak corridors" of the former war ministry building and "mounted guard" over the aisles of the chamber where the final act would take place. Attorneys "gossiped in the well of the court. Visitors jostled to have passes scrutinized. Women in quietly gorgeous kimonos climbed

[1] "Chronology and Statistical Summary of the Trial . . . Prepared by Paul M. Lynch, Court Clerk."
[2] See *Newsweek*, November 22, 1948, 36; *Time*, November 22, 1948, 32; and *Facts on File: 1948*, 362 D.
[3] T 21.

the stairs to the balcony reserved for Japanese." Tojo and the other defendants "lumbered to their usual seats and gazed self-consciously ahead." Sir William Webb began reading the majority opinion "in a husky monotone as though to himself. . . . Tojo soon relapsed into his customary wideawake doze."[4]

Those who had expected the courtroom drama to be concluded in one session were destined for disappointment. It took Sir William seven days in court to read the nearly 1,500-page "Judgment."[5] Much of what it contained seemed like a passing of history in review, with those privileged to see or hear its contents enjoying a closer association with the events of their time than is normally afforded a contemporary audience.

It was the majority view that the criminal conspiracy to wage wars of aggression, charged by the prosecution, had been proved. Speaking for the Tribunal, Sir William declared: "These far-reaching plans for waging wars of aggression, and the prolonged and intricate preparations for and waging of these wars of aggression were not the work of one man. They were the work of many leaders acting in pursuance of a common plan for the achievement of a common object. That common object, that they should secure Japan's domination by preparing and waging wars of aggression, was a criminal object. Indeed no more grave crimes can be conceived of than a conspiracy to wage a war of aggression, for the conspiracy threatens the security of the peoples of the world, and the waging disrupts it. The probable result of such a conspiracy, and the inevitable result of its execution is that death and suffering will be inflicted on countless human beings. . . . The conspiracy existed for and its execution occupied a period of many years. Not all of the conspirators were parties to it at the beginning, and some of those who were parties to it had ceased to be active in its execution

---

[4] *Newsweek*, November 15, 1948, 40.

[5] In the same format as used for the "Transcript of Proceedings," the "Judgment" runs from page 48413 to 49858. The "Judgment" cited in this book is a reduced format version with its own pagination running from page 1 through 1218, not counting the annexes.

The member for India (R. M. Pal) dissented from the majority and filed a statement of his reasons. The members for France and the Netherlands (Henri Bernard and Bernard V. A. Roling, respectively) dissented with regard to only part of the majority judgment. They also filed statements. The member for the Philippines (Delfin Jaranilla) filed a separate concurring opinion. The President (Sir William Webb of Australia) generally shared the view of the majority with respect to the facts, "but without recording any dissent" he filed a brief statement of his "reasons for upholding the Charter and the jurisdiction of the Tribunal and of some general considerations that influenced" him "in deciding on the sentences." J, B/X, 1212.

before the end. All of those who at any time were parties to the criminal conspiracy or who at any time with guilty knowledge played a part in its execution are guilty of the charge. . . ."[6]

The Tribunal's finding with reference to war crimes was no less positive.[7] The many revelations of the heinous misdeeds of Japan's military forces had come as a shock to the Japanese people and—it would seem—to a number of the defendants as well. The knowledge that crimes of sickening barbarity had been committed time and again, in many places, over many years, had already appalled the civil and military leaders of the Allied camp and had fired in them a determination to seek out the perpetrators of atrocities. The evidence which had been presented had convinced the Tribunal that "from the opening of the war in China until the surrender of Japan in August 1945 torture, murder, rape and other cruelties of the most inhumane and barbarous character" had been "freely practiced by the Japanese Army and Navy." Over a period of several months the Tribunal had listened to witnesses testifying "in detail to atrocities committed in all theaters of war on a scale so vast, yet following so common a pattern . . . that only one conclusion [was] possible—the atrocities [had been] either secretly ordered or wilfully permitted by the Japanese Government or individual members thereof and by the leaders of the armed forces. . . . Ruthless killing of prisoners by shooting, decapitation, drowning, and other methods; death marches in which prisoners including the sick were forced to march long distances under conditions which not even well-conditioned troops could stand, many of those dropping out being shot or bayonetted by the guards; forced labor in tropical heat without protection from the sun; complete lack of housing and medical supplies in many cases resulting in thousands of deaths from disease; beatings and torture of all kinds to extract information or confessions or for minor offences; killing without trial of recaptured prisoners after escape; killing without trial of captured aviators, and even cannibalism; these

[6] See J, C/IX, 1137-44. The Tribunal did "not find it necessary to consider whether there was a conspiracy to wage wars in violation of the treaties, agreements and assurances specified in the particulars annexed to Count 1" of the indictment. The Tribunal was of the opinion that "the conspiracy to wage wars of aggression was already criminal in the highest degree." For an alternative view, see IMTFE, "Roling Opinion," 63-69.

[7] For the full particulars, see J, B/VIII, 1001-136.

The Tribunal found that "formal and informal protests and warnings against violations of the laws of war lodged by the Allied Powers and the Protecting Power during the Pacific War were ignored; or when they were answered, the commission of the offenses was denied, or untruthful explanations were given." J, C/VIII, 1117.

[were] some of the atrocities of which proof was made before the Tribunal."[8]

In the European theater of operations 4 per cent of the prisoners of war taken from the forces of the United States and the United Kingdom died in captivity; in the Pacific 27 *per cent* paid with their lives.[9] Among them had been twenty-four Allied airmen executed without a trial in the city of Fukuoka in Kyushu: eight on June 20, 1945; eight on August 12; and eight on August 15—the day the war ended.[10]

Cruelty and death at the hands of the Japanese had not been meted out only to the white man. The peoples of Greater East Asia, where Japan had supposedly intended to build a paradise, had also had a grim experience. The construction of a railway between Burma and Thailand was a case in point.[11] "Prior to and during the work prisoners were constantly subjected to ill-treatment, torture and privation of all kinds, commencing with a forced march of 200 miles . . . under almost indescribable hardships." In eighteen months some 16,000 out of 46,000 prisoners of war succumbed. In addition, approximately 150,000 Asians were used in the work, of whom at least 60,000 died— Burmese, Tamils, Javanese, Malayans, and Chinese: the very peoples of Greater East Asia for whose benefit Japan was allegedly engaged in constructing a co-prosperity sphere. Each mile of that infamous railway cost not only the lives of 80 Allied prisoners of war but the lives of 300 Asians as well. It was a strange way in which to build an Asia for the Asiatics.

With the completion of the reading of the judgment against Japan, Sir William turned to the Tribunal's verdict against each of the accused. The findings concerning Tojo were rather less extensive than the prosecution's view of the defendant might have produced, but they were to prove no less of a condemnation. Tojo's association "with the conspirators as a principal in almost all of their activities" was dated from his assumption of the post of chief of staff of the Kwantung army in March 1937. He was described as having "planned and prepared for an attack" on the USSR; as having "recommended a further onset on China in order to free the Japanese Army from anxiety about its rear in the projected attack" on the Soviet Union; as having "helped

[8] J, C/VIII, 1001-2.   [9] *Ibid.*, 1002-3.   [10] *Ibid.*, 1028-29.
[11] For full particulars, see *ibid.*, 1049-57, 1082, 1123-25. Somewhat different but no less appalling figures are cited in Maung Maung's *Burma in the Family of Nations*, 104, n.17 (see also pages 95-97 for a brief but interesting statement of what the Japanese Occupation meant for Burma).

to organize Manchuria as a base for that attack"; and as having never abandoned "at any time thereafter" the intention of launching such an attack "if a favourable chance should occur." From May until December 1938 as vice-minister of war, and in various concurrent appointments, he was judged to have "played an important part in almost all aspects of the mobilisation of the Japanese people and economy for war." At that time, too, he had "opposed suggestions for a peace of compromise with China."

The Tribunal found that after his assumption of the war portfolio in July 1940, Tojo's history had been "largely the history of the successive steps by which the conspirators planned and waged wars of aggression against Japan's neighbours, for he was a principal in the making of the plans and in the waging of the wars." In the Tribunal's view, Tojo had "advocated and furthered the aims of the conspiracy with ability, resolution and persistency."

As war minister and premier, Tojo had "consistently supported the policy of conquering the National Government of China, of developing the resources of China in Japan's behalf, and of retaining Japanese troops in China to safeguard for Japan the results of the war against China."

Regarding Tojo's role in the negotiations preceding the attacks of December 7, 1941, the Tribunal was of the opinion that Tojo had maintained a "resolute attitude ... that Japan must secure terms which would preserve for her the fruits of her aggression against China and which would conduce to the establishment of Japan's domination of East Asia and the Southern Areas. All his great influence [had been] thrown into the support of that policy." "The importance of the leading part he played in securing the decision to go to war" could not be "overestimated." The Tribunal therefore ascribed to him "major responsibility for Japan's criminal attacks on her neighbours." Special note was made of the fact that in the course of the trial Tojo had "defended all these attacks with hardihood," alleging that they had been "legitimate measures of self-defense." The Tribunal treated this plea as "wholly unfounded." Tojo was therefore adjudged guilty of the conspiracy, as charged in the indictment, and guilty as well of having waged a war of aggression against the Republic of China, the United States of America, the British Commonwealth of Nations, the Kingdom of the Netherlands, and the Republic of France. Only with respect to the charge of waging aggressive warfare against the Mongolian People's Republic and the Soviet Union, in the summer of 1939, was Tojo declared "not guilty."[12]

The important question of Tojo's relationship to war crimes was accorded special attention in the verdict. In early 1946, at Sugamo Prison, five entire interrogations had been devoted to that subject alone. At that time Tojo freely admitted that as Japan's premier and war minister he had believed that the provisions of the Hague and Geneva Conventions with respect to the handling of prisoners of war had been applicable to Japan and should have been followed by her. He declared that atrocities had not been brought to his notice at all. At one point, he said: "I am astounded at the truth regarding atrocities that is now being revealed in the newspapers. If the Japanese had followed the Emperor's instructions [to treat POW's as "unfortunate individuals" deserving of "the utmost benevolence and kindness"], these atrocities would never have happened." When the interrogator responded, "But you, as Minister of War during the period when those atrocities were committed, are the responsible party for their commission, are you not?" Tojo replied, "Yes."

When he was asked what explanation he could give for the fact that he did not learn of atrocities "when they were so widespread and of such a serious nature," Tojo said, "I was always under the impression that army commanders in the field who were responsible for the treatment of prisoners understood what was required of them in this connection."

Tojo also admitted to having been aware, during the war, that the United States and Great Britain intended holding Japanese officials and the Japanese government responsible for maltreatment of prisoners and for violations of international agreements in that regard. "If these atrocities are true," he said, "treaties have been violated."

Complaints from the Allied powers, he explained, had been "routed" by the foreign ministry "to the Minister of War's office." From there they had been sent "to the various army commanders through the Prisoner of War Information Bureau," which had been established within the war ministry immediately after the outbreak of hostilities in

---

[12] The text quotes from the verdict against Tōjō, J, C/X, 1206-7. In the words of the "Judgment": "Wars of aggression having been proved, it is unnecessary to consider whether they were also wars otherwise in violation of international law or in violation of treaties, agreements and assurances" (as had been charged in the indictment). Despite the fact that there were 55 counts in all, the Tribunal considered the charges against individual defendants only in respect to Counts 1, 27, 29, 31, 32, 33, 35, 36, 54, and 55. See J, C/IX, 1143-44. The findings with respect to Tōjō on Counts 54 and 55 are discussed in the text which follows.

the Pacific. Once complaints had been passed along through the chain of command, the war minister heard no more about them. "The army commanders in the field were responsible for all matters relating to prisoners of war under their jurisdiction and no replies would be received by the War Ministry unless . . . in connection with something that required investigation."[13]

Under Japanese practice, the commander of an expeditionary army in the field was "not subject to specific orders from Tokyo." In the performance of his mission, he enjoyed "considerable autonomy." This was called "the heavy responsibility of an expeditionary force commander."[14]

Tojo admitted to having heard of mistreatment of prisoners of war in the construction of the Burma-Siam Railway and declared that he had ordered a court martial in that connection. He had also personally "heard rumors of mistreatment of prisoners of war at Bataan." These were to the effect that prisoners "had been made to walk long distances in the heat"; deaths had "usually" been described as resulting from "sickness." When he had visited the Philippines in May 1943, he had inquired about the matter of the then chief of staff of the Japanese army there. That officer (who had not held the post at the time of the alleged mistreatment) had informed Tojo that the "march" had resulted from "lack of transport facilities," that there had been "some suffering" and "deaths," but no atrocities.

When pressed by the interrogator as to whether the question of the Bataan death march had ever been taken up on any other occasion by anyone else, Tojo said that if a complaint had been received from the United States government, he felt "sure" it must have been forwarded by the prisoner of war information bureau. When asked if he knew personally whether that had actually been done, Tojo declared that as premier and war minister he had not been able to attend to such "details." Matters of that kind had been "left to the discretion" of the chiefs of the bureaus concerned. He admitted that he had never person-

---

[13] The text is based on Tōjō interrog., Mar. 25, 1-7. It should be noted that no organization had been set up prior to 1942 to deal with Chinese prisoners captured in the fighting on the continent between 1937 and 1941. In another interrogation (Mar. 27, 6 and "Attachment"), Tōjō produced a copy of the "Code of the Battlefield" (*Senjin-kun*) in which he had marked several passages which he regarded as specific injunctions against the commission of illegal or barbarous acts by Japanese troops. See also Tōjō aff., S 344:7-8, T 36412-18.

[14] See Tōjō interrog., Mar. 27, 1-7 and "Attachment." The Tribunal's view of this statement was as follows: "This can mean only that under the Japanese method of warfare such atrocities were expected to occur, or were at least permitted, and that the Government was not concerned to prevent them" (J, B/VIII, 1047).

ally discussed the question with Lt. Gen. Honma, who had been in command at the time.[15]

In a supplementary statement, Tojo argued, in effect, that the protest procedure he had described had been a reasonable one. Protests had been forwarded to the proper field commander. Tojo had "presumed that investigations were made, followed by courts martial or other suitable action." The Emperor had not been informed about Allied complaints, even though he was technically the commander-in-chief of Japan's military forces. In Tojo's own words: "I understood the Emperor's feelings very well. On my own responsibility, I sent these protests to the responsible field commanders for investigation as to the facts. The Emperor was busy and had a great deal of work so I did this on my own. Consequently, the Emperor is not responsible in connection with this matter. I am responsible."

Tojo also asserted that the "inhumane acts" of which he had been reading since the end of the war "were certainly not the intention of those in authority." The fact that atrocities had been perpetrated was "very much to be regretted." No one had even suspected their occurrence. The Emperor, in particular, "because of his benevolence," would have been opposed. And also the people of Japan, who believed that "neither Heaven nor Earth would permit such things." It would be "too bad" if the world were to think that "these inhumane acts" had resulted from the Japanese character.[16]

Tojo also reemphasized that the treatment of prisoners was "the responsibility of various army commanders," that he had "relied upon them to have regard for humane considerations and to follow the terms of international treaties and rules." But in this connection he also made a characteristic statement: "Of course, since I was the supervisor of military administration, I am completely responsible."

He had then gone on to suggest that the difference in the standard of living and in manners and customs in Japan, on the one hand, and in Europe and America, on the other, had "affected the treatment of prisoners." "Inhumane acts," of course, were "not permitted under Japanese manners or customs either," but the difference in living standards could explain why American and British prisoners had thought the rations they received "were very very unappetizing," even though they were the same as those issued to Japan's troops. That was also true, he said, of living quarters. The barracks at Omori, for example, which were of a primitive type used in bivouacs, would not have struck Japa-

[15] Tōjō interrog., Mar. 25, 8-14. See also Mar. 27, 1-2 and 5, and Mar. 28, 1-8. See also J, B/VIII, 1044-47.
[16] See Tōjō interrog., Mar. 26, 1-7.

nese troops as being bad, but European and American prisoners had considered them "very poor."

There was also the difference in views with respect to the status of POW's. Under Japanese law, anyone who became a prisoner "while still able to resist" was regarded as a criminal and subject to a maximum punishment of death. This was entirely unlike the Western view of honoring a prisoner because he had "discharged his duties."

Finally there was the matter of face-slapping. "In Japanese families where the educational standard is low," Tojo explained, "slapping is used as a means of training." In the Japanese army and navy, although it had been forbidden, the practice had continued "because of the influence of the customs of the people. This, of course . . . ought to be corrected; it ought to be stopped; but I don't think it is a crime. It is something that comes from custom."[17]

When the question of Japan's treatment of the Doolittle fliers was raised, Tojo readily assumed administrative responsibility for the orders and regulations issued in that regard. He claimed that the raid had been contrary to international law because it had been aimed not at Japan's military forces but "against non-combatants, primary school students, and so forth." It had been "homicide," and he had ordered trial by court martial: "You probably won't be able to understand this unless you understand something about Japanese feelings at this time. This was the first time Japan had been bombed, and it was a great shock. Public feeling ran very high. Now, of course, since the indiscriminate bombing of medium and small cities which were undefended and the use of the atom bomb, all things which are not permitted under international law, the tragic spectacle of this country today makes this first raid look like a very small thing, but it was a great shock to the people at the time." (The Japanese bombing of civilians in China springs immediately to mind, but the interrogator was apparently too absorbed in the fate of the Doolittle fliers to pursue that aspect of the question. Nor did he seek any facts or figures with reference to Tojo's charge that primary school children had been killed in the Doolittle raid.)

The chief of the army general staff, Sugiyama, had personally gone to Tojo and "demanded severe punishment" for the eight members of the Doolittle group who had been captured by the Japanese in China. The ordering of courts martial was a military administration function and was consequently part of the duties of the war minister. Tojo had complied with Sugiyama's demand.

Q. Was not this order, which was issued by you for the trial of these fliers, an ex post facto law?

A. Yes, it was.

[17] *Ibid.*

Q. Then the order of occurrences was as follows: the raid, the capture of the fliers, the order which you issued, the trial, and the executions?

A. Yes.

Q. And the order that you issued provided for the trial and punishment?

A. Yes, it was the basis. However, the order, in turn, was based on the fact of the raid. Of course the order was not an order to execute eight men, it was an order whereby trials could be held on the fact of the raid.

Q. So that, as the result of the raid, this order or law was promulgated by you and made retroactive to the date of the raid?

A. Yes.

When word had arrived from Shanghai that the eight fliers had been sentenced to death, the chief of staff, who was not in the habit of going directly to the war minister on army business, had again called on Tojo and had again "demanded" resolute action: the execution of the eight Americans. But Tojo, in turn, knowing of His Majesty's "benevolence" and out of respect for the Emperor's "feelings," had suggested limiting the number to be executed. "Therefore, it was decided that only the three who had killed primary school students would receive the death penalty. This was discussed with the Emperor, since the Emperor in Japan is the only one who can commute a sentence, and it was decided that way. That one point was the Emperor's only relation to the thing."

Q. So the Emperor reviewed all eight cases and commuted the death penalties from eight to three?

A. No, he didn't review them. In Japan, courts martial have only one hearing. That is because of their military character. Ordinary trials have three hearings.

Q. On what basis did the Emperor take this action? Did you propose it?

A. Yes, I did. It was on my responsibility as adviser to the Throne, but the commutation was the Emperor's because of the fact that the Emperor is invariably benevolent.[18]

With so many interesting and pertinent statements from Tojo in its possession, the prosecution had not failed to introduce appropriate selections in court during the presentation of its case. In the prosecution's

---

[18] See Tōjō interrog., Mar. 27, 1-7. The Doolittle raid took place on April 18, 1942—not October 18 as is stated in the interrogation. See also J, B/VIII, 1024-27 and 1063, in which the Tribunal finds that the Doolittle fliers were tortured by their Japanese captors in China and that the trial given them was "a mere mockery"; Tōjō aff., T 36419-20, S 344:8, in which it is revealed that the retroactive orders in question were issued in July and August 1942; and Tōjō direct examination, T 36490-91, S 344:17.

During interrogation, Tōjō denied that he had ever issued orders "to obtain intelligence from captured fliers by all possible means prior to their trial and execution." He also denied the existence of a policy to the effect that captured American airmen would not be regarded as prisoners of war, but he admitted that the maximum penalty meted out to the Doolittle raiders had been given as a deterrent to prevent future raids.

view, the evidence as a whole had shown that "throughout the government of Japan" there had been "a total disregard of all duty toward prisoners, internees, and civilian populations and a callous indifference to human life and human suffering."[19] "In one of [the] few instances directly linking top leaders with actual war atrocities," the prosecution's star witness, General Tanaka, had testified that Tojo (and his war ministry subordinates, Muto and Sato) had been in favor of brutal treatment of POW's.[20] Tojo himself had subsequently said comparatively little about war crimes in his affidavit, but what he did say was in line with the statements he had made during the interrogations.[21] He denied that he had ever ordered or even suggested that prisoners be made to work against their will or that they be subjected to severe labor. He called Tanaka's testimony in that connection "a gross error" (*hijō naru machigai*) and a purely "arbitrary interpretation" (*dokudan-teki kaishaku*). Tojo also drew attention to the manner in which the prosecution had translated the word *gunji* as "military affairs." Although literally correct, the context had made it appear as if there had been an illegal employment of POW's. Tojo declared that the word actually had a broad meaning, so that the use of prisoners "on work connected with military affairs" included employing them in the making of clothing for soldiers and civilians, in coal mining, in the cement industry, and in the processing of rice—all of which had significance for the prosecution of the war and hence fell into the category of *gunji*.[22]

What the members of the Tribunal thought of Tojo's explanation is not known, but in another regard the majority remained unimpressed by his remarks and apparently unaware that inexact translation was again providing the basis for a judgment which might not otherwise have been made. Tojo had said that he had considered the Hague and Geneva Conventions applicable to Japan and had consequently caused a prisoner of war information bureau to be established, following the outbreak of hostilities. "This statement," the judges declared, ". . . must be interpreted in the light of his statement made during a meeting of the Investigation Committee of the Privy Council on 18 August 1943. He then said: 'International Law should be interpreted from the view

[19] Horwitz, 523.

[20] *Life*, January 26, 1948, 89.

[21] See Tōjō aff., S 344:7-9, T 36412-26. Tōjō revised several incorrect interrogation statements which he attributed to his faulty memory. See also T 36161-63, S 342:11, and direct, cross, and redirect examination: S 344:18, T 36495; S 348:13-14, T 36804-11; and S 349:5, T 36837-39.

[22] Tōjō aff., S 344:8-9, T 36422-24. Note the unsatisfactory way in which *Furyo Shori Yōryō* is rendered into English as "Summary of the Disposal of the Prisoners of War." "Principal Points Concerning the Handling of Prisoners of War" would more accurately reflect both what was said and what was meant. See also Tōjō interrog., Mar. 28, 4.

point of executing the war according to our own opinions.' This idea was the basis upon which the policy of the Japanese Government for its treatment of prisoners of war and civilian internees was developed."[23]

In this particular instance, the Tribunal was relying upon an *excerpt* from a prosecution translation of a document recording the *gist* of what was said by a number of those present at the meeting in question. The matter under discussion was the transfer to Thailand, by a treaty between Japan and Thailand, of certain disputed territory on the frontiers of Burma and Malaya. Although the words attributed to Tojo had appeared only in paraphrase in both the Japanese original and the prosecution's English translation, they had somehow emerged as a direct quotation in the Tribunal's "Judgment."

What Tojo actually said is open to speculation. A member of the so-called Investigation Committee had asked whether the government interpreted the contemplated measures "as being not in contravention of international law." Tojo, in his capacity as premier, had then replied *to the effect* that Japan should abide by international law as long as the enemy adhered to its provisions, but that from the standpoint of carrying out the war, international law should be interpreted from Japan's own point of view.

Such an approach to law, although natural enough, contains an obvious danger, but the words themselves, in their correct order and as a paraphrase of the original, are rather less damning than the version cited in the "Judgment." The latter also failed to reveal that Tojo coupled the above statement with a remark to the effect that he believed that the measures under consideration were perfectly in accord with the requirements of international law.[24]

The majority of the members of the Tribunal were no less positive in their conclusions regarding Tojo's personal responsibility for war crimes. In their verdict, they noted that as war minister (July 1940-July 1944) Tojo had been "charged with the care of prisoners of war and of civilian internees in the theatre of war and with the supply of billets, food, medicines and hospital facilities to them." As home minister (October 1941-February 1942) he had been "charged with a similar duty towards civilian internees in Japan." As premier (October 1941-July 1944) Tojo had "above all" been "charged with continuing responsibility for the

---

[23] J, B/VIII, 1096-97.
[24] S 120:4, T 11364-67. As recorded in the Japanese original: "Hayashi iin yori, seifu wa hon-an no sochi wo kokusai-hō ni ihan sezaru mono to shite nasu mono naru ka to toi, Tōjō naikaku-sōridaijin yori, kokusai-hō wa tekikokugawa no junshu subeki kagiri kore ni shitagau wa mochiron naru mo kokusai-hō no kaishaku wa sensō suikō no kanten yori dokuji no kenkai wo motte subeku konkai no sochi wa kokusai-hō yori mite nanra sashi-tsukae nashi to shiryō suru mune tōben ari."

care of prisoners and civilian internees. . . . The barbarous treatment of prisoners and internees was well known to Tojo. He took no adequate steps to punish offenders and to prevent commission of similar offences in the future. His attitude towards the Bataan Death March gives the key to his conduct towards these captives. He knew in 1942 something of the conditions of that march and that many prisoners had died as a result of these conditions. He did not call for a report on the incident. When in the Philippines in 1943 he made perfunctory inquiries about the march but took no action. No one was punished. His explanation is that the commander of a Japanese Army in the field is given a mission in the performance of which he is not subject to specific orders from Tokyo. Thus the head of the Government of Japan knowingly and wilfully refused to perform the duty which lay upon that Government of enforcing performance of the Laws of War."

With respect to the Burma-Siam Railway, which the court described as "designed for strategic purposes," the Tribunal found that Tojo had "advised" that prisoners of war be used in its construction. "He made no proper arrangements for billeting and feeding the prisoners, or for caring for those who became sick in that trying climate. He learned of the poor conditions of the prisoners employed on the project, and sent an officer to investigate. We know the dreadful conditions that investigator must have found in the many camps along the railway. The only step taken as a result of that investigation was the trial of one company commander for ill-treatment of prisoners. Nothing was done to improve conditions. Deficiency diseases and starvation continued to kill off the prisoners until the end of the project."

The Tribunal also found that statistics relating to the high death rate in prison camps from malnutrition and other causes had been discussed at conferences over which Tojo had presided. In the view of the judges, "the shocking condition of the prisoners in 1944, when Tojo's Cabinet fell, and the enormous number of prisoners who had died from lack of food and medicines" were "conclusive proof that Tojo took no proper steps to care for them."

With respect to the China "Incident," the Tribunal noted that the defense had argued that the rules of war did not apply to hostilities in China and that consequently Chinese captives were not entitled to either the status or the rights of prisoners of war. The Tribunal found that Tojo "knew and did not disapprove of that shocking attitude."

Tojo was also adjudged responsible for an instruction to the effect that prisoners who did not work should not eat. The majority firmly believed that Tojo's "repeated insistence" on that instruction had "conduced in large measure to the sick and wounded being driven to work and to the suffering and deaths which resulted." Tojo was also declared responsible for the measures which had been taken to prevent knowledge of the ill-treatment of prisoners of war from reaching the outside world.

In the light of its verdict, the Tribunal found Tojo "guilty," under Count 54 of the indictment, of having "ordered, authorised and permitted" commanders-in-chief of Japanese military and naval forces, officials of the war ministry, persons in charge of camps and labor detachments for POW's and civilian internees, the civil and military police of Japan and their subordinates, "frequently and habitually to commit . . . breaches of the Laws and Customs of War . . . against the armed forces of the countries" with which Japan had been at war and "against many thousands of prisoners of war and civilians" who had then been "in the power of Japan."

With regard to Tojo's role in the treatment of the Doolittle fliers, the Tribunal said nothing at all. With respect to Count 55 of the indictment, in which Tojo had been charged with "deliberately and recklessly" disregarding his "legal duty to take adequate steps to secure the observance and prevent breaches" of the Laws and Customs of War, the Tribunal handed down a "no finding" judgment.[25]

The day of reckoning finally arrived. At 3:53 p.m. on Friday, November 12, 1948, the eleven justices filed into a hushed courtroom to take their seats at the bench for the last time. The dock opposite was completely empty. One minute later, General Sadao Araki, who had once been a vociferous advocate of Japan's "holy mission" to establish a new order in East Asia, was escorted into the courtroom to hear his sentence: life imprisonment. One after the other, each of the defendants in turn was admitted to the chamber—in alphabetical order. "None . . . quailed; one or two were so old and infirm that they hardly seemed to know what was happening."[26]

Tojo was the twenty-second and last to enter.[27] That morning he had penned a Japanese-style poem which appeared to express his long-held expectation of the worst:

[25] See J, B/X, 1207-9, and U. S. Dept. of State, "Trial of Japanese War Criminals," 60-62 (Counts 53, 54, and 55).

[26] The quoted sentence is from *Time*, November 22, 1948, 32. The description of the scene is based on *Newsweek*, November 22, 1948, 35-36. See also *NYT*, November 13, 1948, 1 and 3.

[27] "Twenty-second and last" by virtue of the fact that of the 28 men indicted in 1946, only 25 remained, of whom three (Kaya, Shiratori, and Umezu) were absent from the proceedings on November 12 because of illness. J, B/X, 1213 and 1218.

Hateshi-naku
Sumeru mi-sora ni
Ware wo yobu
Mi-koe wo takaku
Aogite-zo kiku.

Gazing upward,
I hear reverently
The voice of the Buddha,
Calling me
From the pure and boundless sky.[28]

The voice in the courtroom was that of Sir William Webb: "Accused Tojo, Hideki, on the Counts of the Indictment on which you have been convicted, the International Military Tribunal for the Far East sentences you to death by hanging."[29]

Upon entering the dock, Tojo had carefully adjusted the earphones through which he would hear the verdict. He had pressed his thumbs slightly against a wooden railing and had looked straight ahead, in the direction of the bench. As his sentence was repeated in Japanese, he nodded slightly, removed the earphones, bowed quickly to the court, and retired from the room.[30]

Commenting some ten days later on Tojo's final appearance in court, *Time* magazine observed: "Last week, in his faded army jacket and horn-rimmed spectacles, he did not look like the toothy, maniacal symbol of Japanese frightfulness that U.S. cartoonists had made of him after Pearl Harbor."[31]

---

[28] See Hanayama, 173. According to both *Time* (November 22, 1948, 32) and *Newsweek* (November 22, 1948, 36), Tōjō's reaction to his sentence was expressed in a poem which read, "Oh, look! See how the cherry blossoms fall mutely." This is a rather off hand rendition of "Ara tōto oto naku chirishi sakura ka na," in which Tōjō philosophically and reverently likens his fate to that of cherry blossoms which suddenly, in full flower, flutter to the ground in quiet acceptance of death—a time-honored symbol of the samurai.

[29] J, C/X, 1217. The rendering in Japanese was as follows, "Hikoku Tōjō Hideki: Hikoku ga yūzai no hantei wo uketa kisojō chū no soin ni motozuite, kyokutō kokusai gunji saibansho wa, hikoku wo kōshukei ni sho suru." *Kyokutō Kokusai Gunji Saiban Hanketsu Sokki-roku*, 223.

[30] This description of the scene derives from motion picture footage (sound) in the author's possession. An account in *Newsweek*, November 22, 1948, 35-36, is not borne out by the film record (e.g., Tōjō neither "held firmly to a table" nor "rubbed the palms of his hands on his trousers").

[31] *Time*, November 22, 1948, 31-32. Also, *Facts on File: 1948*, 361 D; *Life*, November 29, 1948, 40-41; Kiyose, "Ishi Ima Nao Ikin," *Daiyamondo*, Vol. XL, No. 17 (May 15, 1952), 141.

Tōjō had earlier instructed his defense counsel not to appeal against a death penalty.

Of the more than twoscore individuals originally indicted, two—Matsuoka and Nagano—had died, and a third—Okawa—had been found mentally incompetent to stand trial. Of the remaining defendants, seven—Doihara, Hirota, Itagaki, Kimura, Matsui, Muto, and Tojo—were sentenced to death by hanging. The ex-foreign ministers, Togo and Shigemitsu, were given twenty years and seven years, respectively. The rest, including the former lord privy seal, Koichi Kido, were remanded to Sugamo Prison for life.[32]

The Buddhist chaplain at Sugamo, Dr. Hanayama, felt that some of the Japanese newspaper accounts of the courtroom scene on November 12, 1948, gave an oversimplified interpretation of the way in which the defendants had bowed toward the judges following the sentencing. According to the Japanese press, bowing in such circumstances was a common practice. Hanayama, however, considered that too superficial. He had seen the defendants at close quarters at the prison and had watched the development or deepening of religious faith among them. Their bowing to the court, he believed, was not just the observance of a "custom." It represented a respectful acceptance of the verdict of the Tribunal and an expression of gratitude for the trouble taken by the judges during the long trial. "For those who are trying to grasp eternal life, bowing is the natural posture for invoking the sacred name of the Buddha. . . ."[33]

Immediately after the sentencing, Ben Bruce Blakeney, who had served as American counsel for Togo and Umezu, asked the colonel in charge of courtroom security for permission to talk with the defendants. This officer had grown so fond of his charges that he could barely speak through the tears that were streaming down his face. What

---

After the sentencing Tōjō was quoted as describing the long proceedings as a "victors' trial."

[32] When he was later asked about the procedure that had been followed in the determination of the individual penalties, Sir William Webb replied: ". . . I am sure that each member of the tribunal was aware of the principles of punishment recognized in his own country. But just how he came to decide on the facts of each convicted individual's case that the punishment should be death and not imprisonment for years I am unable to say and, if I did know, I would not be at liberty to tell you. In most instances the choice was between life imprisonment and death. In only two cases was imprisonment for years thought to be adequate." Webb corresp.

An IMTFE judge, who refused to permit his name to be used, was quoted in the press (Frank White article, *Nippon Times*, December 10, 1948, 1) as saying that the vote had been 6-5 in Hirota's case and 7-4 in all the other death sentences. The method of execution (by hanging or firing squad) was also reported as having been decided by a 6-5 vote.

With the passage of time, the Allied powers gave their consent to the release of members of the Class A group. The last to be freed (on March 30, 1956) was former Lt. Gen. Kenryō Satō.

[33] See Hanayama, 172-73.

Blakeney was asking was strictly forbidden, but the colonel gave his consent.

Upon entering the off-limits area, Blakeney found that the defendants, who were waiting to be returned to the prison, had already been divided into two groups: the seven who had been condemned to death in one room, the remainder in another. Blakeney went first to the condemned. To his surprise he found them sitting around, smoking and talking as if nothing at all had happened. He began addressing them in Japanese. He had been studying the language and this was his first "speech." Blakeney tried to convey the disappointment of the defense with respect to the verdict. He told the seven men that the defense had done its best and that they would have to entrust the court's decision to the judgment of history. As Blakeney spoke on, Tojo suddenly realized that this was a formal call. He immediately stood up and snapped to attention. The others followed suit. When Blakeney had finished, Tojo bowed deeply and expressed the sincere appreciation of the defendants for all that Blakeney and his colleagues had done in their behalf.[34]

The prison security precautions, which had previously been so strict as to cause some grumbling among the inmates, were now even more rigorously enforced. Goering's "cheating of the executioner" at Nuremberg stood as a warning to the prison authorities. As a consequence, from November 12 on, the seven condemned men were watched *at all times* by a squad of eight MP's under the direction of a corporal of the guard. A noncommissioned medical aid man and a guard officer were also on duty in the immediate vicinity. The prisoners were placed in seven adjoining cells in a cellblock which had been cleared of all other inmates. The individual cells were eight feet long, five and one-half feet wide, and ten feet high. Each contained a desk, wash basin (hot and cold running water), and sanitary facilities. A mattress, placed on the floor in the Japanese manner, served as a bed; each man was permitted as many blankets as he wished. The entire cellblock was heated, even though only seven cells, instead of the usual fifty, were being used. Double wire-mesh screens covered the windows on the

[34] Blakeney intv. Blakeney then went to the second room, where he repeated his speech. When he had finished, Mr. Tōgō came over and shook hands (also strictly forbidden). The officer to whom reference is made in the text was Lt. Col. Aubrey S. Kenworthy. Earlier in the year the defendants had given him a scroll of appreciation for his many kindnesses to them (see *Life*, January 26, 1948, 90).

inside. The doors, which were made of heavy bars, allowed an unobstructed view to and from the corridor.

While one guard sat in a position which permitted him to observe two cells at once, another walked back and forth, checking on first one prisoner and then the other. At fifteen-minute intervals, these guards changed posts. The medical aid man examined each prisoner every quarter-hour to check his respiration and to look for arterial bleeding. As an added precaution, this was done through the bars from outside the cell. The guard officer and the corporal of the guard also made their own separate inspections every fifteen minutes. Guard details were changed every six hours.

The condemned men were allowed to visit each other twice a day, from 1:30 to 3:00 p.m. and again from 7:00 to 9:00 p.m., "but only two could be together at any one time in any one cell." The prisoners passed the hours by reading, writing, and playing cards—mostly solitaire. Books and writing materials were supplied, and also Japanese cigarettes. But each man could have only one cigarette at a time, and it had to be lighted by a guard. The one visit per month with family members was continued. All of the condemned had their December visit on the very first day of that month, since no one knew how long they had to live.[35]

General MacArthur had given the defendants until November 19 to submit appeal petitions. On November 24 the Supreme Commander had upheld all of the verdicts of the Tribunal. In a public pronouncement on that occasion, MacArthur had declared: "No duty I have ever been called upon to perform in a long service replete with many bitter, lonely and forlorn assignments and responsibilities is so utterly repugnant to me as that of reviewing the sentences of the Japanese War Criminal defendants adjudged by the International Military Tribunal for the Far East. It is not my purpose, nor indeed would I have that transcendent wisdom which would be necessary, to assay the universal fundamentals involved in these epochal proceedings designed to formulate and codify standards of international morality by those charged with a nation's conduct. The problem indeed is basically one which man has struggled to solve since the beginning of time and which may well wait complete solution till the end of time. In so far as my own immediate obligation and limited authority extend in this case, suffice it that under the principles and procedures prescribed in full detail

[35] See GHQ, SCAP, Public Information Office "release" dated 23 December 1948. A shorter version can be found in *NYT*, December 23, 1948, 6.

by the Allied Powers concerned, I can find nothing of technical commission or omission in the incidents of the trial itself of sufficient import to warrant my intervention in the judgments which have been rendered. No human decision is infallible but I can conceive of no judicial process where greater safeguard was made to evolve justice. . . ."[36]

Six days later, on November 30, a stay of execution had been ordered pending action by the Supreme Court of the United States on requests for review by two of the condemned (Doihara and Hirota).[37] Thus the seventh anniversary of the attack upon Pearl Harbor came and passed.

On December 15 and 16, lawyers acting for the petitioners argued that the Supreme Court had jurisdiction over the International Military Tribunal for the Far East. The Tribunal, they said, had been created under American direction and was essentially a national court of the United States. On December 20 the appeals of the convicted men were rejected in a 6-1 *per curiam* opinion, which held that the Tribunal was not a court of the United States, that MacArthur had acted "as an agent of the Allied powers" in establishing it, and that therefore the Supreme Court had "no power to review, to affirm, set aside or annul" the convictions returned by that Tribunal.[38]

[36] See the *Nippon Times*, November 25, 1948, 1, and the Lindesay Parrott dispatch, *NYT*, November 24, 1948, 1.

[37] Appeals were subsequently filed on behalf of Kido, Kimura, Mutō, Oka, Satō, Shigemitsu, Shimada, Tōgō, and Umezu. See 335 U. S. 876-81; *Facts on File: 1948*, 362 D, 390 D, 398 N, and 410 L-N; and the Lindesay Parrott and Lewis Wood dispatches, in *NYT*, November 24, 1948, 1, and December 7, 1948, 1, respectively. The vote on the requests was 5-4, with Mr. Justice Jackson, who had disqualified himself from other war crimes cases because of his role as prosecutor at Nuremberg, breaking a tie between Black, Douglas, Murphy, and Rutledge *for* and Vinson, Reed, Frankfurter, and Burton *against*. In explaining his stand in favor of hearing the appeals, Jackson declared: "This public division of the court, equal if I do not participate, puts the United States before the world, and particularly before Oriental peoples, in this awkward position: Having major responsibility for the capture of these Japanese prisoners, it also has responsibility for their fate. If their plea ends in stalemate in this court the authorities have no course but to execute sentences which half of this court tells the world are on so doubtful a legal foundation that they favor some kind of provisional relief and fuller review. The fact that such a number of men so placed in the United States are of that opinion would for all time be capitalized in the Orient, if not elsewhere, to impeach the good faith and to discredit the justice of this country and to comfort its critics and enemies." *NYT*, December 7, 1948, 21.

Earlier appeals by General Yamashita and Honma, who had been tried in the Philippines, had been rejected by the Court in February 1946 by a vote of 6-2 (Murphy and Rutledge dissenting) on the grounds that the Court lacked jurisdiction (*Facts on File: 1946*, 53 J).

[38] See 338 U. S. 197-215, and *Facts on File: 1948*, 410 L-N. Vinson, Black, Reed, Frankfurter, Burton, and Douglas constituted the majority (the last-named issued a separate opinion in July 1949). Murphy dissented, Rutledge reserved decision, and Jackson abstained.

Three years earlier, in December 1945, it had been reported that MacArthur had

While these legal steps were in progress, Tojo had been preparing for his death. He would not permit his lawyers to enter an appeal on his behalf. He had never doubted what the verdict would be—or at least that was the impression he conveyed. That he would incur the severest penalty seems generally to have been a widely held view among the people of Japan and of the United States. Dr. Kiyose, Tojo's Japanese counsel, had warned Mrs. Tojo at the beginning of the trial not to hope for a favorable outcome.[39] An Occupation general who had come into possession of Tojo's horse had promised to give the animal to Kiyose's American colleague, Mr. Blewett, if the latter won an acquittal for his client. The general had told Blewett: "You'll *need* the horse, if you do."[40]

Despite the time and efforts devoted to the trial, Tojo thought of the proceedings as being "something like a monkey show" (". . . saru shibai mitai na mono nan da yo!") in which everything, including the end of the performance, is predetermined from the outset. He told Mrs. Tojo that the trial was bigger than any individual, that it was a matter of state. It was also a question, he said, of going through the formalities of democracy for the sake of appearances.[41]

When he heard of the stay-of-execution order, Tojo's only show of emotion was a kind of resigned annoyance. He was being interviewed by several lawyers who were working on the defense of the last chief of the naval general staff, then under indictment before a special court in Tokyo. The lawyers assumed that Tojo had probably not heard of the order and that the reprieve it offered would be welcome news. But his response surprised them. Although manacled to an MP, Tojo slapped the table with some papers he was holding and said: "For my part, I wish they'd hurry up and get it over with."[42]

Tojo utilized the gift of time bestowed by the stay of execution to prepare messages to the Japanese people, to compose more *haiku* and *waka* (Japanese-style poems), to communicate indirectly with his family, and to talk with Dr. Hanayama. The interest taken by Tojo in

---

placed the Tōkyō defendants under Allied jurisdiction so as to preclude appeals to the Supreme Court (*Facts on File: 1945*, 395 J).

[39] Mrs. Tōjō intv.

[40] Blewett intv.

[41] Katsuko Tōjō, 151; Mrs. Tōjō intv.

[42] Blakeney, Furness, and Umezu intv. Umezu, who acted as interpreter on this occasion, does not remember Tōjō's exact words but they were to the following effect: "Dōmo hayaku yatte kuren to komaru desu na."

As early as 1946, Shigemitsu noted in his prison diary (*Sugamo Nikki*, 59) that Tōjō would sometimes stroke the nape of his neck and say, "I wish they'd hurry up with it." See also Hanayama, 244, 254, and 255.

religious books had grown with the passing of the months. During his last days, he spent much of the time he was allowed with Hanayama in discussion of religious matters.[43] On one occasion Tojo expressed his admiration for the *Dai Muryōju Kyō* ("The Great Sutra of Everlasting Life")—especially for the "Forty-eight Vows" (*Yonjūhachi Gan*) which it contains. Japan's political leaders, he said, should read those vows and through them effect a rebirth of the life of the nation. The "Vows" dealt with the basic problems of human existence. Such things as the United Nations and world peace could not be achieved, Tojo declared, until the cravings of man had ceased. . . . The creation of states came from greed. Such "pretty words" as "self-existence and self-defense" merely arose out of the avarice of nations. In the end, war was the result. Man had turned his back on religion; degeneration had set in. That was why he felt the new leaders of Japan should read the "Vows." It was regrettable, he said, that he himself had only discovered them during his incarceration at Sugamo. Being in prison gave one an opportunity to come to an understanding of life.[44]

During his meetings with Hanayama, Tojo was generally handcuffed to two GI's, who flanked him on each side. Normally an officer was in attendance also. At first it had bothered Tojo to be manacled in that way, but he had soon grown philosophical about it. When he raised a hand (as he frequently did in offering prayers or in responding to messages conveyed by the chaplain), the guard had to raise his also. When Tojo moved or walked, the GI's had to do so, too. Tojo chose to interpret this as part of the providence of the Buddha.[45]

In his talks with Hanayama, Tojo described himself as "a common, ordinary man" (*bonjin*). The practice of Zen Buddhism (which had been very popular with the samurai of old because of its emphasis on intuitive understanding through self-reliant contemplation) was beyond him, he said. His was a simple and implicit faith in the power of the supplication, "Namu Amida Butsu," to open the way to enlightenment and peace.[46]

When unfavorable press comment developed over a posthumous name conferred in advance by a relative who was the chief priest of a temple in Kyushu, Tojo entrusted the matter to his wife. As a result, the original name, which certain newspapers had twisted into "Atonement in the other world for sins committed in this," was replaced by one which Dr. Hanayama had given to each of the twenty-seven Japa-

---

[43] See Hanayama, 241-66.
[45] *Ibid.*, 259.
[44] *Ibid.*, 257-58.
[46] *Ibid.*, 259-61.

nese who had already been executed at Sugamo Prison for war crimes. Basically, the new name signified the prospect of a life everlasting beyond the grave. Even this did not go unnoticed. *Newsweek* reported that Tojo had chosen a "death" name: "Little Brother Hideki."[47]

Perhaps because of his military training, or because of the strength he derived from the holy books he was reading, Tojo gave the impression of great composure, as though he were untroubled by his approaching death.[48] He was glad to learn that he would be executed on Japanese soil, for he had feared he might be taken abroad and disgraced.[49]

Tojo's calmness impressed Hanayama and others who saw him toward the end. On only one occasion did the chaplain think that the strain of waiting had taken effect. During a meeting with Hanayama on December 10, Tojo remarked that he had been honored by a visit from the Goddess of Mercy, Kannon. When Hanayama looked startled, Tojo hastened to explain that the appearance had come about in an unusual way. He pulled out a handkerchief and showed it to the chaplain. In one corner was the trademark, "Cannon." "In English," Tojo said, "that means a 'big gun,' but when pronounced in Japanese it is exactly the same as 'Kannon.' So you see, the Goddess of Mercy has come to me in altered form." Watching Tojo as he spoke, and listening to his words, Dr. Hanayama realized that Tojo's mind had not snapped; he had simply endowed a common object with a precious meaning.[50]

Of more significance were Tojo's views on the affairs of this world. At a meeting only a few days after the sentencing, Tojo had given Dr. Hanayama what amounted to a message to posterity. In it, Tojo expressed his relief at having been able to meet a measure of his responsibility through the medium of the trial. As far as he personally was concerned, the punishment was deserved. He was sorry that he alone had not been able to assume all of the responsibility himself, and that many friends and colleagues had incurred punishment as well. At least, the throne had not been put to any trouble as a result of the trial. His only regret was that his death could not atone for the defeat, or for the havoc of war which had been experienced by his compatriots.

Tojo indicated that he did not wish to say anything concerning the judgment handed down by the Tribunal. He believed the time might

---

[47] See *ibid.*, 242 and 246, and *Newsweek*, December 13, 1948, 41.

[48] Tōjō did have some difficulty sleeping, but that was because a 100-watt bulb was kept burning in his cell at all times. He was unable to convince the prison authorities that it should be turned off at night. See Hanayama, 270 and 293.

[49] Hanayama, 253.

[50] *Ibid.*, 265. The translation is necessarily rather free.

come when the true intentions of Japan would be understood. The maltreatment of prisoners of war and the crimes committed against humanity were extremely deplorable. He felt acutely that it was his responsibility that the humane feelings possessed by the Japanese people since ancient times and the benevolence of the Emperor had not been thoroughly inculcated. The atrocities had stemmed from a lack of virtue on the part of only one segment of the military. He fervently hoped that the peoples of the world would not go astray in their judgment—that they would not lay at the door of the Japanese nation, or even of the military as a whole, the crimes committed by that misguided segment.

Only three years had passed since the end of the war, Tojo said, but the world was still beset by strife. Looking at the situation in the Far East, he could not but entertain fears concerning the future of his country. And yet he firmly believed that the spirit of Japan (*Nihon seishin*), which had been cultivated through three thousand years, would not be lost in the space of a single day. Ultimately, through the efforts of the Japanese themselves and the sympathy of the world, the nation would effect a splendid recovery. He also believed that the peoples of East Asia could look to a glorious future.

For the benefit of those Japanese who had suffered as a result of the war, he desired to ask not only the Japanese government but also the Allied powers to extend measures of aid and succor. The people of Japan had given their all for the state. They bore not the slightest guilt. If anyone deserved blame, it was the leaders, and not the masses. Since the account against the leaders had already been settled, pity should be shown to the people. He also wished to request that sympathetic consideration be given to the families of war criminals in Sugamo and that prisoners of war held by the Soviet Union be returned to Japan as speedily as possible.[51]

Such were the thoughts which had occupied Tojo's mind even though he was soon to go to his own death. Paradoxically, his only personal worry seems to have been his health. He wanted to be robust at the end—not weak from a fever or suffering from a chill or other

[51] Dr. Hanayama very kindly sent the author a photograph of the original document, which was written by Tōjō at Sugamo on November 17, 1948. Tōjō used a hard pencil and both sides of a very thin piece of paper. The document bears his first name as a signature. See also Hanayama, "Shūkyō ni Urazukerareta Jinsei," *Chōtetsu Bunka*, No. 38 (November 1956), 4-7. Allowances must be made for a few minor errors in both sources. The version given in Hanayama, 242-44, is a paraphrase. In the latter work, see also pp. 258-59 and 263-64. Also, Hanayama intv. and corresp.

ailment. He had even requested extra bedding as a precaution against catching a cold.[52]

Something of what Tojo had in mind is revealed in a story about the members of a *kamikaze* unit who had been forced to take shelter when their airstrip was bombed and strafed by American planes. When the attack was over, they had emerged laughing from their impromptu cover. "Without saying it, each pilot seemed to be thinking, 'We are lucky. Until we hit the enemy, our lives are very dear. We can't afford to squander them by getting killed carelessly.'"[53] Similarly, Tojo did not want to die of a sudden illness. He wanted to be executed by the Americans; in fact, he was *glad* that was to be his fate. In his eyes, death on the gallows would mean that he could enter the ranks of Japan's lost warriors and could thus join those who had given their lives in battle during the Greater East Asia War.[54]

By the time the Supreme Court had handed down its decision, more than five weeks had passed since November 12, the day of sentencing. The holiday spirit was infecting the homes and billets of those Americans who were living in Japan as members of the Occupation forces, but the preparations being made at Sugamo were not of a festive sort. On Tuesday, December 21, 1948, the provost marshal of the Eighth Army and the commandant of the prison each received *twenty* copies of an order designating them to carry out the sentences of Hideki Tojo and the other six condemned men ". . . at Sugamo Prison, APO 181, at 0001 hours or as soon thereafter as practicable, 23 December 1948." Thus, in terse but punctilious military language were the day and the hour set.[55]

Official notification was given to the condemned men at 9:00 p.m. on the evening of December 21.[56] They were brought in relays to the chaplains' office for that purpose; Tojo was the last to enter. He was handcuffed to an officer, while another stood guard. As usual, he wore a string of prayer beads on his left wrist; the short tassel, which is

[52] This desire to be in perfect health at the time of execution was shared by others at Sugamo. See Hanayama, 259; Blakeney and Blewett intv.; and *Newsweek*, December 13, 1948, 41.

[53] Inoguchi, Nakajima, and Pineau, 108.

[54] Mrs. Tōjō intv.

[55] Letter Order No. 12-442, HQ, Eighth Army, Lt. Gen. Walton H. Walker, 21 December 1948. The two officers designated to execute the sentences were Colonel Victor W. Phelps (provost marshal) *or* Colonel Morris C. Handwerk (commandant of the prison). Tōjō's Sugamo Prison "201" file.

[56] Hanayama, 268-71; GHQ, SCAP, Public Information Office "release" dated 23 December 1948; *Time*, January 3, 1949, 18-19; and Mrs. Tōjō intv.

common to all Buddhist rosaries, had been removed—apparently another, rather farfetched, precaution against suicide.

Tojo nodded after each word of the notification. When the reading was completed, he raised the hand with the beads, bent his head in acknowledgment, and said "Okay, okay"—practically the only English he knew. Dr. Hanayama, who was present, felt that Tojo was trying to express not only his satisfaction but also his appreciation.

When he was asked if he had any requests, Tojo responded characteristically. He thanked the prison commandant for granting practically all of his recent petitions. He raised the same hand as before and again bowed. Then he remonstrated against the security measures, some of which he described as undignified. The authorities were too strict, he said. "We will never commit suicide or anything like that. We will show you how splendidly we can die. . . . If you were treated as we have been, you would understand our objections to the security precautions."[57]

Tojo also asked that the seven men be given at least one Japanese meal—any dish would be all right—and a cup of *sake*. He further requested that something be done for the families of those inmates of Sugamo who were living in straitened circumstances. He reminded the authorities that Japanese servicemen, unlike American GI's, were not rich. Wages were being paid for work done in the prison, but disbursement to the families of the men doing the work had not as yet been allowed. When Tojo finished speaking, the commandant replied that the security measures and pay procedures were out of his hands. He was only following orders from above.

Upon leaving the room, Tojo—like the others before him—was asked to step on a scale so that he could be weighed.

The weather had been "unseasonably warm" in Tokyo, but on December 22 it turned cold.[58] Dr. Hanayama visited each of the seven men twice, once between 9:00 a.m. and 5:00 p.m., and again during their last hours, between 7:30 and 11:30 p.m. He saw Tojo for the first time in the late afternoon, receiving from him then a number of

[57] Translated somewhat freely to provide the necessary context.

Tōjō seems to have had no intention of "cheating the hangman" and would probably not have tried to end his life even if he had been given an opportunity to do so. The circumstances of September 1945 and of December 1948 were entirely different. Following the executions, the authorities stated: "At no time during their incarceration did any of the condemned men commit any act of violence" (GHQ, SCAP, Public Information Office "release" dated 23 December 1948).

[58] *Time*, January 3, 1949, 18-19.

poems he had written—most of them expressing religious sentiments.[59] Tojo mentioned that his father had died on December 26 and his father-in-law on December 29. Now he was going on the 23rd: it was "a very strange destiny" (*mattaku kushiki en desu*).

When Tojo asked about the execution, Hanayama told him that he would die instantly. Tojo said that he was very thankful that he would become part of the soil of Japan. He also enumerated a number of other blessings: With his death, which could serve as a preparatory move for peace, he could render his apologies to the Japanese people and become a cornerstone in the rebuilding of Japan. He could leave the world without a care, knowing that the Emperor had not been caused any trouble. He was glad that he was to be hanged; death by suicide would have had no meaning. It was a good time to die. He had lived too long already. He had only a few teeth left, his eyes were not good, his memory was poor. Now, indeed, was the time to go. It was a relief to be able to die knowing that the charges that he had once received enormous sums of money from the Mitsubishi *zaibatsu* had been thoroughly investigated by the authorities and declared to be without foundation.[60] It was a far better thing to go in an instant than to linger on suffering from illness. It was easier to die than to be assailed by worldly passions while confined to prison for life. It was also a joy to leave the world knowing, through faith, that he would be reborn in Amida's paradise.

As Dr. Hanayama arose to leave, Tojo asked him to explain to the prison commandant, in greater detail than had been possible the previous evening, that the families of the many Japanese servicemen being held in Sugamo needed some kind of help.

Hanayama's second meeting with Tojo took place during the evening of December 22, from 9:30 to 10:30 p.m. Again Tojo talked of religious matters. He also produced several poems which he had dedicated to the man who had offered him the comfort of religion. Most of the hour, however, was spent by Tojo in reading aloud a long document which he had addressed to Kiyose, Blewett, and Hanayama. This was Tojo's final statement to the world. He had begun writing it on December 2 and had completed the task several days later. He had gone over it during the 22nd and had made some corrections. Since both men knew that the document would have to pass through the hands of American

[59] Hanayama was with Tōjō from 4:00 until 4:50 p.m. The text which follows draws on Hanayama, 293-95 (also 244, 251-52, and 264), and Mrs. Tōjō intv.

[60] See *Nippon Times*, April 8, 1946, 3 ("Investigations Fail to Discover Tojo Accepted Rumored Bribe from Zaibatsu").

censors, the purpose of the reading was to permit Dr. Hanayama to commit as much of it as possible to memory and to summarize the main points in his own notebook. This was apparently allowed by the authorities; at least, no one interfered on the evening in question even though the two men were under close observation the entire time.[61]

In this final "testament," Tojo repeated much of what he had already said, either in court or in the message he had given Hanayama shortly after the sentencing. To his expressions of regret to the Emperor and the people, and to his denial of having committed any crime, Tojo added the thought that the death penalty, although comforting personally, could not expiate his responsibility toward the nation. . . . Regarding the rightness or wrongness of the Tokyo trial, he was prepared to await "the verdict of history." But had eternal peace been the object, Tojo asked, would it not have been necessary to look at things with a little broader attitude? The trial had been political in nature; it had been conducted by the victors. . . .

The Americans, who were the real rulers of Japan, should not alienate the feelings of the Japanese or infect them with Communist ideas.[62] The United States should recognize the sincerity of the peoples of East Asia. The fact that Japan had been unable to obtain their cooperation had been a basic cause of her defeat. . . .[63]

The leaders of America and England had committed great blunders during the war. They had completely destroyed Japan, a bulwark against communism; they had turned Manchuria into a base for the communization of Asia; they had divided Korea, thus making it a source of disorder in the future. It was up to the men who had made

[61] The author believes that the original document, which was never released by the Occupation authorities, is now part of official files in Washington, D.C. Although he was able to secure the declassification of some material, in this particular case all efforts ended in failure.

During the evening of December 23, 1948 (that is, more than eighteen hours after the execution), Dr. Hanayama orally conveyed Tōjō's last words to members of his family and to some friends who had gathered at the Tōjō residence for a funeral service. The text of this "testament," which was later published in Japan, was written down by Dr. Kiyose and one of Tōjō's sons while Hanayama spoke from his notes and from memory. See Sugamo Isho Hensankai, *Seiki no Isho*, 683-85; and *Daiyamondo*, Vol. XL, No. 17 (May 15, 1952), 140-45. Also Hanayama and Mrs. Tōjō intv.

[62] For the moment, Tōjō said, the people of Japan were grateful to the United States for food supplies and other similar assistance. . . . And yet there were persons who were already spreading anti-American propaganda. He therefore hoped that the American army would not lose the hearts of the Japanese people. . . .

[63] Tōjō also said that the peoples of East Asia should forget recent events and should cooperate with each other in the years ahead. They should have the right to live in the world just as others did. . . . It would be fortunate indeed if the recent war resulted in an understanding that the peoples of East Asia had the right to survival.

these mistakes to remedy them. He was therefore glad, Tojo said, that President Truman had been re-elected. . . .

Three years had already passed since the termination of the war. The United States should consequently adopt an attitude of magnanimity. The purging of persons in public office and in the teaching profession should cease, as should the arrest of war crimes suspects. . . .

Careful attention should be paid to the youth of the country.[64] That was the great task for the future. The recent appearance of unreliable tendencies was often the result of influences coming from the Occupation forces. It was important to preserve the good in the customs of Japan. . . .

With the execution providing the occasion, he hoped a great memorial service would be held for all victims of the war. Everyone should be included—the belligerents and the neutrals—so that the service could constitute a spiritual cornerstone for world peace. . . .[65]

He wished to apologize with all his heart for the atrocities which had been committed.[66] However, the American military should also express their sympathy, compassion, and repentance with regard to the tragic results that had arisen from their indiscriminate air attacks upon Japan and from the dropping of the atomic bombs. . . .

The concept of the independence of the supreme command had definitely been a mistake. Because of that concept, the imperial army and navy had been unable to take united action. When it came to rebuilding Japan's military forces, the national character of the Japanese people should be borne in mind in deciding whether the new system should be based on conscription or on the employment of professionals.[67] "Spirit" (*seishin shugi*) should form the basis of the education of the new military units. Loyalty and patriotism must be inculcated as before, but also something that had been lacking in the past: a sense of responsi-

[64] In the future, Tōjō declared, Japan's school system should not rely solely on developing simplicity, fortitude, and health. Schools should turn out whole individuals. Religious education was important. The manners and customs of Europe and America should be taught.

[65] Tōjō also expressed his earnest hope that the battlefield graves of Japan's fallen warriors would be properly tended. If the families wished, the remains of those buried in foreign lands should be returned to the homeland and their souls enshrined at Yasukuni.

[66] Further study of the prisoner-of-war question was necessary, Tōjō said. A prisoner-of-war concept should be perfected among the nations of the world.

[67] Tōjō mentioned that Japan, under the leadership of the United States, had renounced the threat or use of force as a means of settling international disputes. That was wise, he said, but better still would be a complete elimination of armaments by all the nations of the world. . . . A third world war—with the United States and the Soviet Union as the protagonists—was inevitable. Japan, China, and Korea would become the battlefield. It was therefore the responsibility of the United States to devise a policy for defending Japan.

bility. In that respect, Japan should learn from the American army. . . .

Having thus elaborated his views at some length—largely in a rambling fashion—Tojo closed his final statement with two poems:

> *Ware yuku mo mata kono tochi ni kaeri kon*
> *Kuni ni mukuyuru koto no taraneba.*

Even though I now depart,
I shall return again to this land,
That I may repay in full
My debt to my country.

> *Saraba nari koke no shita nite ware matan*
> *Yamato Shimane ni hana kaoru toki.*

This is farewell.
I shall wait beneath the moss,
Until the flowers again are fragrant
In this island country of Japan.[68]

The end was now near. Twenty minutes before the time set for the hangings, four of the condemned—Doihara, Matsui, Tojo, and Muto—were led from their cells on the third floor of the cellblock to a small Buddhist chapel on the first floor. There were two guards per man. Each was manacled—with the handcuffs linked in turn to a band around the body, making arm movement impossible. All wore the U.S. army fatigues, stenciled with a large "P" on the back, with which they had long since become familiar.

Tojo had not wanted to die in such "rags." Dressing up for one's death was a time-honored custom. When a samurai went to the field of battle determined not to return, he always wore his finest garments and perfumed his helmet with incense. Tojo had petitioned the authorities for better clothing, but his wish had not been fulfilled.

As the four men arrived at the chapel, Dr. Hanayama was told that he had only seven minutes. He immediately handed around individual sticks of incense, which he lighted with the altar candles, so that each of the condemned could personally place an offering in the burner. He also obtained the signatures of all—written with the traditional brush

[68] See footnote 61 above. "Until the flowers again are fragrant" could mean "until the resurgence of Japan." The preceding January Tōjō had written in a similar vein: "Koke no shita/Mataruru kiku no/Hana zakari" (Mrs. Tōjō intv.).

and "India" ink on heavy Japanese paper. Then he served each man a final sip of wine; Tojo's request in that regard had been met, and he seemed quite pleased.[69]

Hanayama was informed that he had two more minutes. He therefore read, in a loud voice, the first three eulogies, and the last, of the *Sanseige*, a Buddhist holy text in verse known as "The Three Pledges." The four men bowed—listening in silence with their eyes closed. Then someone suggested a "banzai." Matsui, the eldest, was asked to lead. The building resounded to the national cheer: three for His Majesty and three for the Empire of Japan.

In accordance with a prevailing custom, the condemned had removed their dentures for transmittal later to their families, together with spectacles, prayer beads, hair and nail clippings, and other reminders of their earthly existence. For that reason, all except Matsui declined the cakes which Hanayama offered them. The four men exchanged goodbyes, somehow managing to shake hands with each other and with several American officers, including a chaplain. They also grasped Hanayama's hand and thanked him very warmly for his many labors on their behalf.

A steel door swung open to permit the party to leave the cellblock. The prison officer of the day led the way across a courtyard to the place of execution. Behind him walked the American chaplain and Dr. Hanayama. Then Doihara, Matsui, Tojo, and Muto—still guarded as before. Several American officers brought up the rear.

Perhaps two minutes passed in all. Throughout this walk to death the voices of the four men could be heard repeating the supplication, "Namu Amida Butsu."

At the entrance to the brightly lighted gallows, which were in a small, whitewashed building blocked from view by a concrete wall, Hanayama bid them all farewell.[70] He then hurried back to the chapel to minister to the three men who would follow: Itagaki, Hirota, and Kimura.

Within the death house, the sentences were carried out with the quiet

---

[69] Accounts which say the condemned drank "grape juice" are incorrect. They drank *Budōshu*—a wine made from grapes. The wine was followed by water, with Dr. Hanayama drinking a small amount before he handed the cup to each of the condemned in turn.

[70] See Hanayama, 308-11; GHQ, SCAP, Public Information Office "release" dated 23 December 1948; *NYT*, December 23, 1948, 1 (the Lindesay Parrott dispatch) and 6; *Time*, January 3, 1949, 19; *Newsweek*, January 28, 1946, 40, December 6, 1948, 43, and January 3, 1949, 49; *Facts on File: 1948*, 410 E-K; *Asahi* (*Shukusatsu-ban*), December 23, 1948, 51-52, and December 24, 1948, 55; and Mrs. Tōjō intv.

impersonality and cold efficiency common to such scenes. As Tojo and his companions entered from the courtyard, they were individually identified in front of witnesses. They then walked, unassisted, up the thirteen steps and turned to face the last persons they would see on earth. "No final messages were voiced on the gallows"; only the murmuring of Buddhist prayers.

When the death ropes and hoods had been adjusted, the chief executioner saluted the commander of the execution detail. Reporting that all was in readiness, he turned toward the condemned and gave his signal. The time was 00:01:30 hours.[71]

Later that same night, the bodies of the dead were conveyed by closely guarded U.S. Army vans to a Japanese crematorium in Yokohama. As the trucks sped through the floodlighted gates of the prison, "soldiers with fixed bayonets stood in a light drizzle, barring the way to newsmen." At the crematorium, every precaution was taken to ensure absolute security in the handling of the ashes. The American authorities seemed to be acting on the assumption that they could thus guard against the possibility of a subsequent enshrinement of Tojo and the other executed men. Whether the effort was in vain or not, no one can say. All such attempts at finality are destined to be undone by later claims that they did not succeed. Although the ashes were secretly scattered by the authorities, the belief that a token of them fell into Japanese hands will always remain current in some quarters.[72]

[71] In other words, one and one-half minutes past midnight—roughly sixty seconds from the time the condemned men had entered the chamber. GHQ, SCAP, Public Information Office "release" dated 23 December 1948; *NYT*, December 23, 1948, 1 (the Lindesay Parrott dispatch) and 6; Tōjō's Sugamo Prison "201" file (which contains a death certificate and fingerprints taken after death); and *Facts on File: 1948*, 410 K.

Among the official witnesses were the members of the Allied Council for Japan: William J. Sebald (U. S.; chairman), General Chen Shang (China); Patrick Shaw (British Commonwealth), and Lt. Gen. Kuzma N. Derevyanko (USSR). Their presence had been requested by General MacArthur.

Tōjō was officially declared dead at 00:10:30 hours.

[72] See GHQ, SCAP, Public Information Office "release" dated 23 December 1948; *NYT*, December 23, 1948, 1 and 6; and *Newsweek*, January 3, 1949, 26-27. Also Hanayama and Yano intv. The bodies were taken to the Kuboyama Kasōba (Yokohamashi, Nishi-ku).

The attitude of the American authorities with respect to the ashes is difficult to understand in view of the fact that such "relics" as hair and nail clippings were "cleared" for transfer to the families of the executed men (Tōjō's were placed in the family tomb at Zōshigaya in Tōkyō). Mrs. Tōjō endeavored to obtain her husband's ashes, but without success.

In this connection, the following item from *Newsweek* (May 12, 1958, 38) is of interest: "ASHES. . . . It was a gay party for the last ten major Japanese war criminals freed from life sentences and one of the guests had thrilling news. Everyone remembered how Japan's wartime Prime Minister Hideki Tojo . . . and six others had been hanged

Using a news technique which has repeatedly proved its worth in terms of public interest, *Time* magazine, among others, sent a roving correspondent into the streets of Tokyo on December 23 to cull the reactions of the common man. The predominant sentiment was expressed in the phrase, *Hotto shita ne!*—a sigh of relief coupled with the thought, "At last, it's over."

Many said, *Kinodoku, kinodoku*: "A pity, a pity." According to *Time*, that was what many other Japanese had said during the war when American prisoners had been led through the streets of Tokyo. "Tojo and friends, through their thought control police, had tried then to stop the expression of *kinodoku*. It persisted, even for them."

One uncommon man, a "prominent Japanese publisher," told an American: "We all went into war together and all suffered, but they died for us. What they did was wrong, but we all did it together...."[73]

The same thought came also from the mouth of a "ricksha boy," who said: "It wasn't the responsibility of those people alone."[74]

But perhaps the most interesting comment of all, in terms of its earlier reporting, was made by *Time* magazine itself: "Last week, at midnight after the winter solstice, the paths of Japan's top war leaders ended without glory, but with a dignity that seemed enhanced a little by the doubt and confusion among the victors."[75]

When he had earlier upheld the sentences pronounced by the Tribunal, General MacArthur had publicly declared: "I pray that an Omnipotent Providence may use this tragic expiation as a symbol to summon all persons of goodwill to a realization of the utter futility of war—that

---

and cremated ten years ago and their ashes scattered. But the ashes were saved, declared one of their attorneys, Shohei Sanmonji. His story: On the two nights after the execution, Dec. 24 and 25, Sanmonji and a Buddhist priest [not Dr. Hanayama] had sneaked into the Yokohama crematory and stolen the black boxes of ashes which they hid in a Buddhist temple. Later this year, he said, they would be placed in a new tomb dedicated to 'Seven samurai who died for the nation.' U. S. officials were unmoved. Tojo's ashes, they said were long gone with the wind."

Word of Mr. Sanmonji's "feat" first appeared in the Japanese press in April 1955 (see the *Asahi* for April 22, 1955). Another version of the above story is that only some scrapings from the crematorium were retrieved. It is said that these were later buried in the garden of General Iwane Matsui's residence in Atami, beneath a statue of Kannon made from the ashes of Chinese and Japanese soldiers killed in the China Incident.

There are also persons who claim that Tōjō's ashes are buried at the Gokokuji (literally: "Defense of the Fatherland Temple") in Bunkyō-ku, Tōkyō. Others believe that the ashes were brought to the United States or that they were committed to the sea off the coasts of Japan.

[73] *Time*, January 3, 1949, 19.
[74] *Newsweek*, January 3, 1949, 26-27.
[75] *Time*, January 3, 1949, 19.

most malignant scourge and greatest sin of mankind—and eventually to its renunciation by all nations."[76]

Doubt, confusion, and tragic expiation. These were strange words in the context in which they were used. The imbalance left by years of destruction, defeat, and foreign occupation, by the snuffing out of millions of lives but the survival of men who might have responded differently to the crises of their day, demanded rectification. Tojo himself had come to this view. He had even said that it would not be right for him to remain alive after so many had fallen in the service of the state. The supreme penalty imposed by the Tribunal had to be carried out if he was to meet, in some measure, his responsibility toward the Japanese people.[77]

Months before his death, Tojo had rationalized his role in a poem written at Sugamo Prison:

> *Juyō kyūtsū*
> *Ten no mei nari.*[78]

> Whether life is long or short,
> Whether we succeed or fail,
> Is in accordance with the will of Heaven.

Perhaps no other epitaph is needed. Time is the leveler of emotions. The greater the distance from the event, the harder it is for men to understand the shape and meaning of the past. And yet, if one reviews the period of power during which the fate of the nation and the fate of the man were closely linked, one must inevitably come to the stark and haunting judgment of an American contemporary, Henry L. Stimson.[79]

"The face of war," Stimson wrote, "is the face of death."

[76] See *Nippon Times*, November 25, 1948, 1, and the Lindesay Parrott dispatch in *NYT*, November 24, 1948, 1. Following the executions, the Japanese press pledged that a MacArthur suggestion for a national day of prayer would be observed.

[77] Mrs. Tōjō and Hanayama intv.

[78] The original, which was written in the late autumn of 1947, is in the author's possession.

[79] See Stimson and Bundy, *On Active Service*, 633.

Acknowledgments

The author's indebtedness to a number of individuals and institutions is very great. Grants in aid of research were received from the Rockefeller Foundation, the Social Science Research Council, the Center of International Studies at Princeton University, and the Princeton Faculty Research Committee. In this connection, the author wishes especially to thank Cyril E. Black, Hugh Borton, Wesley Frank Craven, Frederick S. Dunn, Charles B. Fahs, Klaus Knorr, William W. Lockwood, Elbridge Sibley, and Joseph R. Strayer.

For their valuable advice regarding various aspects of his work, the author desires to express his appreciation to Joseph W. Ballantine, Ben Bruce Blakeney, George Francis Blewett, Herbert Feis, Maritis B. Jansen, Ken Kurihara, Jean MacLachlan, Hideo Masutani, Atsushi Ōi, E. Taylor Parks, the late Bunshirō Satō, Kurt Steiner, Yoshikazu Umezu, Tomohiko Ushiba, and Professors Craven, Dunn, and Strayer.

The research connected with this book was greatly aided by the willingness of a number of individuals to answer letters or grant interviews in regard to matters on which they could speak with particular authority. Their names are given in Sections II and III of the Bibliography.

Many others have been helpful and in a variety of ways. It is a pleasure to be able to thank each in turn: Edward L. Beach, William Beidelman, George B. Bikle, Thomas E. Blades, John Braeman, R. Miriam Brokaw, Claude A. Buss, Alvin D. Coox, Percy E. Corbett, Gordon A. Craig, Elizabeth D'Arcy, Armand Derfner, Paul S. Dull, Naomi Fukuda, George A. Furness, Hugh H. Gardner, Charles C. Gillispie, Eric F. Goldman, Gladys Greenwood, John W. Hall, Noburu Hiraga, W. Stull Holt, Leon N. Hurvitz, James B. Johnson, Jr., George H. Kerr, Seiko Kodaira, Robert W. Krauskopf, Kinuko Kubota, Charles M. Kurashita, John M. Maki, Jean McDowall, Richard N. McKinnon, Franz Michael, Edith Mihalco, Louis Morton, Frederick W. Mote, Kiyoaki Murata, Ogden Nash, Yasumasa Oda, Toshikazu Ohmae, Ernst L. Presseisen, H. Anthony Reynolds, Henry Rosovsky, Alice C. Russell, Emi Sawada, Peggy Skinner, Thomas C. Smith, Kenzi Tamaru, George E. Taylor, Shih-kang Tung, Gordon B. Turner, Toshio Ueda, Jacob van Staaveren, Helen Vitous, James T. Watkins IV, Helen Weigel, Arthur F. Wright, and Muraji Yano.

The following organizations deserve special mention for their cooperation: Department of the Army (Office of the Chief of Military History; Office of the Adjutant General; and Office of the Chief of Information); Department of State (Historical Division); Gaimushō (Bunsho-shitsu); Headquarters, U.S. Army Forces, Far East (Japanese Research Division); Hoover Institution on War, Revolution, and Peace; Kokuritsu Kokkai-Toshokan; Kokusai Bunka Kaikan; Library of Congress; National Archives and Records Service (World War II Branch, War Records Division); and Princeton University Library.

Finally, the author must end on a personal note by expressing his gratitude to his wife Irene and daughter Stephanie, to his mother, Louise M. Butow, and to his parents-in-law, Julian and Elsa Elkeles. This book has been a long labor, and they no doubt have suffered from it more than he.

ABBREVIATIONS USED
IN THE FOOTNOTES

NOTE: *All Japanese names are given in the Western manner. Macrons have been employed in the footnotes, bibliography, and index but appear in the text only when Japanese phrases or sentences are quoted. Romanization follows the standard used in the 1954 edition of* Kenkyusha's New Japanese-English Dictionary.

aff.   affidavit

CF 20, III, 77   Case File 20 [the IPS case number assigned to General Tōjō], Vol. III, Doc. No. 77 (see under "International Military Tribunal for the Far East, International Prosecution Section" in Section I of the Bibliography)

corresp.   correspondence between the author and the person named (e.g., Kido corresp.; see Section III of the Bibliography for a complete list)

Def.   Defense

Doc.   Document

Exh.   Exhibit

Foreign Relations   Foreign Relations of the United States . . . (see under "United States Department of State" in Section I of the Bibliography)

IMTFE   International Military Tribunal for the Far East (commonly called "the Tokyo trial"; see Section I of the Bibliography)

interrog.   pretrial interrogations conducted by the IPS early in 1946 (e.g., "Tōjō interrog., March 14, 1-7" is a reference to pages 1-7 of the March 14, 1946 interrogation of General Hideki Tōjō; see under "International Military Tribunal for the Far East, International Prosecution Section" in Section I of the Bibliography)

intv.   interview(s) between the author and the person named (e.g., Mrs. Tōjō intv.; see Section II of the Bibliography for a complete list)

IPS   International Prosecution Section of the IMTFE

J, B/IV, 208-10   "Judgment" of the IMTFE, Part B, Chapter IV, pages 208-10

JRD   Japanese Research Division (see Section I of the Bibliography)

JRD, "Interrogations," I:49157 (Seizō Arisue), 49   Japanese Research Division, "Interrogations of Japanese Officials on World War II," Vol. I, Doc. No. 49157 (the interrogation of Seizō Arisue), page 49

No.   Number

NYHT   New York Herald Tribune

NYT   New York Times

PHA   Pearl Harbor Attack, Hearings Before the Joint Committee on the Investigation of the Pearl Harbor Attack . . . (see under "United States Congress" in Section I of the Bibliography)

S 344:4 *Kyokutō Kokusai Gunji Saiban Sokki-roku,* Section 344, page 4 (see Section I of the Bibliography)

SCAP Supreme Commander for the Allied Powers

SKD "Sensō Kaihi e no Doryoku" (see under "Kido" in Section I of the Bibliography)

T 36386-88 "Transcript of Proceedings" of the IMTFE, pages 36386-88

Bibliography

This bibliography is largely limited to sources cited in the footnotes. In some cases, however, material which proved helpful in a general way has also been included, even though the opportunity for specific citation did not arise. The breakdown is as follows:

I. DOCUMENTS, RECORDS, AND REPORTS

Dai-Tōa Shō. *Dai-Tōa Kaigi Giji Sokki-roku* (The Stenographic Record of the Proceedings of the Greater East Asia Conference). Tōkyō: Dai-Tōa Shō, 1943.

Documents on American Foreign Relations. (A continuing series, begun in 1938.) Boston: World Peace Foundation, 1939-1951; New York: Council on Foreign Relations, 1952-

Documents on British Foreign Policy, 1919-1939. London: His Majesty's Stationery Office, 1947-

Documents on German Foreign Policy, 1918-1945. Washington, D.C.: U.S. Government Printing Office, 1949-

Documents on International Affairs. London: Royal Institute of International Affairs, 1929-

Dull, Paul S., and Michael Takaaki Umemura. *The Tokyo Trials: A Functional Index to the Proceedings of the International Military Tribunal for the Far East.* Ann Arbor: University of Michigan Press, 1957.

Furness, George A. "Petition on Behalf of Shigemitsu, Mamoru for Review of Judgment, Verdict and Sentence of the International Military Tribunal for the Far East."

Gaimushō (hensan). *Nihon Gaikō Nenpyō narabi ni Shuyō Bunsho* (Chronological Tables and Major Documents Pertaining to Japan's Foreign Relations). 2 vols. Tōkyō: Nihon Kokusai Rengō Kyōkai, 1955.

International Military Tribunal for the Far East. "Analyses of Documentary Evidence."

———. "Chronology and Statistical Summary of the Trial from April 29, 1946 to April 16, 1948, prepared by Paul M. Lynch, Court Clerk."

International Military Tribunal for the Far East. "General Index of the Record of the Defense Case."

———. "General Index of the Record of the Prosecution's Case."

———. "Index of Exhibits (Nos. 1-3915)."

———. "Index of Language Corrections Affecting Documents Admitted into Evidence and the Court Records of the International Military Tribunal for the Far East."

———. "Index of Witnesses (Defense)."

———. "Index of Witnesses (Prosecution)."

———. "Judgment."

———. "Medical Certificate"; "Report of a Psychiatric Examination of Ōkawa, Shūmei"; and "Psychiatric Examination of Japanese Prisoner of War [Ōkawa]."

———. Miscellaneous Documents: Prosecution and Defense.

———. "Separate and Dissenting Opinions of Sir William Webb, *et al.*"

———. "Transcript of Proceedings" (48,412 pages).

International Military Tribunal for the Far East, International Prosecution Section. "Case File 20: General Hideki Tōjō, Evidential Facts Adduced from his Interrogations."

———. Case File 20: General Hideki Tōjō, Miscellaneous Documents. 4 vols. (Nos. 1-438).

———. Case File 20: Statements Concerning Hideki Tōjō Obtained During the Interrogation of War Criminal Suspects and Others.

———. "Chronological Summary" (Doc. No. 0001). 2 vols.

———. "Decisions of Imperial Conferences, Liaison Conferences, Privy Council Meetings, Cabinet Meetings, Four Ministers' Conferences, Five Ministers' Conferences, Senior Statesmen's Meetings, Supreme War Plans Council, Joint Conferences and Miscellaneous Conferences, as Found in the Prosecution's Evidence" (Doc. No. 0004).

———. Interrogations:

Araki, Sadao	Nagano, Osami
Hiranuma, Kiichirō	Oka, Takasumi
Hirota, Kōki	Satō, Kenryō
Hoshino, Naoki	Shigemitsu, Mamoru
Kaya, Okinori	Shimada, Shigetarō
Kido, Kōichi	Suzuki, Teiichi
Matsuoka, Yōsuke	Tōgō, Shigenori
Mutō, Akira	Tōjō, Hideki

———. Miscellaneous Documents Obtained from the Residences of Prince Fumimaro Konoe, December 1945.

———. "Summary of Errors and Mis-statements Made by the Defense."

———. "Summary of Events Leading to War" (prepared by Roy L. Morgan).

Japanese Research Division, Office of the Military History Officer, United States Army Forces, Far East and Eighth United States Army (Rear).

"Diary of Admiral Kichisaburō Nomura, 1 Jun-31 Dec 1941 (Ambassador to U.S.A.)."

———. "Interrogations of Japanese Officials on World War II." 2 vols.

———. Japanese Monograph 45: "Imperial General Headquarters Army High Command Record, mid-1941-August 1945."

———. Japanese Monograph No. 119: Outline of Operations Prior to Termination of War and Activities Connected with the Cessation of Hostilities."

———. Japanese Monograph Nos. 144, 146, 147, 150, and 152: "Political Strategy Prior to Outbreak of War" (Parts I-V).

———. "Memo on the Course of the War," by Sōkichi Takagi.

———. Miscellaneous Documents.

———. "Personal History Statements." 2 vols.

———. "Special Studies." 4 vols.

———. "Statements of Japanese Officials on World War II. 4 vols.

———. "Study of Japanese Intelligence Planning Against the USSR."

———. "Study of Japanese Operational Planning Against the USSR."

———. "Translation of Japanese Documents." 7 vols.

Kido, Kōichi. "Dai-sanji Konoe Naikaku Kōtetsu no Tenmatsu" (The Circumstances Relating to the Fall of the Third Konoe Cabinet).

———. "Dai-sanji Konoe Naikaku Sō-jishoku no Zengo no Jijō" (The Situation Before and After the Resignation en Masse of the Third Konoe Cabinet).

———. "Kido Kō Nikki Tekiroku" (Extracts from the Diary of Marquis Kido, covering the period 1942-1945).

———. "Nikki" (Diary).

———. "Sensō Kaihi e no Doryoku" (Efforts to Avoid War).

King, Fleet Admiral Ernest J. *United States Navy at War, 1941-1945, Official Reports to the Secretary of the Navy.* Washington, D.C.: U.S. Navy Department, U.S. Government Printing Office, 1946.

Konoe, Fumimaro. "Dai-sanji Naikaku Sō-jishoku no Tenmatsu" (The Facts Pertaining to the Resignation en Masse of My Third Cabinet).

Kunaishō. "Shōwa Nijūnen Nigatsu, Jikyoku ni kan suru Jūshin Hōtō-roku" (Remarks Made to the Throne by the Senior Statesmen in February 1945 Concerning the Situation Confronting Japan).

Kyokutō Kokusai Gunji Saiban Hanketsu Sokki-roku (The Stenographic Record of the "Judgment" of the International Military Tribunal for the Far East).

Kyokutō Kokusai Gunji Saiban Sokki-roku. (The Stenographic Record of the International Military Tribunal for the Far East). 416 gō.*

"Meiji Sanjūhachinen Sangatsu Shikan-gakkō Dai-jūshichi-ki Seitō Sotsugyō

---

* An especially valuable source, the existence of which is not generally known. The present study may represent the first use of this material.

Jinmei" (Roster of Graduates of the Seventeenth Class of the Military Academy, March 1904).

Morley, James W. "Check List of Seized Japanese Records in the National Archives," *Far Eastern Quarterly*, Vol. IX, No. 3 (May 1950), 306-33.

Nippon Hōsō Kyōkai, Hōsō Bunka Kenkyūjo. " 'Oto no Raiburarī' Shiryō Risuto" ("Sound Library" Holdings). Selected Recordings.

Office of Strategic Services. Miscellaneous Documents.

Survey of American Foreign Relations. 4 vols. New York: Council on Foreign Relations, 1928-1931.

Tanaka, Ryūkichi. "I Know Everything About Them" (as recorded by Yumi Goto).

United States Army, General Headquarters, Supreme Commander for the Allied Powers. Sugamo Prison "201" File for General Hideki Tōjō.

United States Army, General Headquarters, Supreme Commander for the Allied Powers, Counter Intelligence Section. "The Brocade Banner: The Story of Japanese Nationalism."

United States Army, General Headquarters, Supreme Commander for the Allied Powers, Public Information Office. Release dated 23 December 1948.

United States Congress, Joint Committee on the Investigation of the Pearl Harbor Attack. *Pearl Harbor Attack, Hearings Before the Joint Committee on the Investigation of the Pearl Harbor Attack, Congress of the United States, Seventy-Ninth Congress. . . .* 39 parts. Washington, D.C.: U.S. Government Printing Office, 1946.

United States Department of State. *Foreign Relations of the United States: Diplomatic Papers*. ("The Far East" volumes for the period 1931-1941 as noted hereunder.) Washington, D.C.: U.S. Government Printing Office, 1946-1956.

1931	Vol. III	1937	Vols. III and IV
1932	Vols. III and IV	1938	Vols. III and IV
1933	Vol. III	1939	Vols. III and IV
1934	Vol. III	1940	Vol. IV
1935	Vol. III	1941	Vols. IV and V
1936	Vol. IV		

——. *Foreign Relations of the United States: Diplomatic Papers, 1940* (Vol. I, General). Washington, D.C.: U.S. Government Printing Office, 1959.

——. *Papers Relating to the Foreign Relations of the United States: Japan, 1931-1941*. 2 vols. Washington, D.C.: U.S. Government Printing Office, 1943.

——. *Peace and War, United States Foreign Policy, 1931-1941*. (Publication 1983.) Washington, D.C.: U.S. Government Printing Office, 1943.

————. *Trial of Japanese War Criminals.* Washington, D.C.: U.S. Government Printing Office, 1946.

United States General Staff. *General Marshall's Report: The Winning of the War in Europe and the Pacific; Biennial Report of the Chief of Staff of the United States Army, July 1, 1943 to June 30, 1945, to the Secretary of War.* New York: Simon & Schuster, n.d.

The United States in World Affairs: An Account of American Foreign Relations. (A continuing series, begun in 1931.) New York: Council on Foreign Relations, 1932-

United States Library of Congress, Legislative Reference Service. *Events Leading up to World War II: Chronological History of Certain Major International Events Leading up to and During World War II with the Ostensible Reasons Advanced for Their Occurrence, 1931-1944.* Washington, D.C.: U.S. Government Printing Office, 1945.

United States Reports (Cases Adjudged in the Supreme Court). Vols. 291, 335, and 338. Washington, D.C.: U.S. Government Printing Office, 1934, 1949, and 1950.

United States Strategic Bombing Survey. Miscellaneous Records.

United States Strategic Bombing Survey (Pacific), Naval Analysis Division. *The Campaigns of the Pacific War.* Washington, D.C.: U.S. Government Printing Office, 1946.

————. *Interrogations of Japanese Officials.* 2 vols. Washington, D.C.: U.S. Government Printing Office, 1946.

Uyehara, Cecil H. (comp.). *Checklist of Archives in the Japanese Ministry of Foreign Affairs, Tokyo, Japan, 1868-1945; Microfilmed for the Library of Congress 1949-1951.* Washington, D.C.: Photoduplication Service, Library of Congress, 1954.

Young, John (comp.). *Checklist of Microfilm Reproductions of Selected Archives of the Japanese Army, Navy and Other Government Agencies, 1868-1945.* Washington, D.C.: Georgetown University Press, 1959.

II. INTERVIEWS

Blakeney, Ben Bruce

Blewett, George Francis

Bowles, Gordon T.

Coox, Alvin D.

Feis, Herbert

Fihelly, John W.

Fleisher, Eric W.

Furness, George A.

Gardner, Hugh H.

Hanayama, Shinshō

Handleman, Howard

Hattori, Takushirō

Hirano, Motokuni

Hoshino, Naoki

Iguchi, Sadao

Inagaki, Kazuyoshi

Inoue, Goro

Inoue, Tadao

Kanamori, Tokujirō

Kido, Kōichi

Kido, Takahiko
Kiyose, Ichirō
Komatsu, Takashi
Kubota, Kinuko
Kurashĭta, Charles M.
Kurihara, Ken
Masutani, Hideo
Matsudaira, Yasumasa
Matsukata, Saburō
Matsumoto, Shigeharu
Misawa, Shigeo
Morgan, Roy L.
Murata, Kiyoaki
Obayashi, Ryōichi
Oda, Yasumasa
Ōi, Atsushi
Osumi, Hideo
Ōyama, Azusa

Parks, E. Taylor
Presseisen, Ernst L.
Satō, Bunshirō
Shigemitsu, Mamoru
Steiner, Kurt
Stunkard, Albert
Suzuki, Jūzō
Takagi, Yasaka
Tanaka, Ryūkichi
Tōjō, Katsuko
Tomabechi, Toshiyuki
Tōyama, Takashi
Ueda, Toshio
Umezu, Yoshikazu
Ushiba, Tomohiko
van Staaveren, Jacob
Yamanashi, Katsunoshin
Yano, Muraji

III. Correspondence

Baba, Kyoko
Ballantine, Joseph W.
Berman, Sam
Blades, Thomas E.
Blakeney, Ben Bruce
Blewett, George Francis
Brosious, H. H.
Cason, F. H.
Daujat, John
De Martino, Richard
Dull, Paul S.
Eichelberger, Robert L.
Fields, Fred T.
Fihelly, John W.
Fukuda, Naomi
Furness, George A.
Gaine, James J.
Gardner, Hugh H.
Grew, Joseph C.
Hammack, Valentine C.
Hanayama, Shinshō
Handwerk, Morris C.
Hardin, G. C.

Hardy, Robert M., Jr.
Harrison, John A.
Hattori, Takushirō
Hauxhurst, H. Austin
Hayden, Hayden C.
Horwitz, Solis
Johnson, James B., Jr.
Jordan, John R.
Kaltenborn, H. V.
Kennedy, Malcolm D.
Kenworthy, Aubrey S.
Kido, Kōichi
Krauskopf, Robert W.
Kurashita, Charles M.
Kurihara, Ken
Kuroda, Yasumasa
McEwen, James M.
Maki, John M.
Masutani, Hideo
Maxon, Yale C.
Morgan, Roy L.
Mulvihill, Robert C.
Murata, Kiyoaki

Nash, Ogden

Oberlin, Ben G.

Ohmae, Toshikazu

Ōi, Atsushi

Parks, E. Taylor

Phelps, Calhoun W. J.

Profita, Vincent

Rosovsky, Henry

Satō, Kenryō

Sawada, Emi

Shaw, Patrick

Spencer, Murlin

Strauss, Lewis L.

Stunkard, Albert

Terasaki, Gwen

Tōjō, Katsuko

Ushiba, Tomohiko

van Meter, Donald S.

Waldorf, Douglas L.

Webb, William F.

IV. GENERAL WORKS

A. Books and Articles

Abel, Theodore. "The Element of Decision in the Pattern of War," *American Sociological Review*, Vol. VI, No. 6 (December 1941), 853-59.

Allen, Lafe F. "Japan's Militarists Face the Music," *American Foreign Service Journal*, Vol. XXIV, No. 8 (August 1947), 14ff.

Amau, Eiji. "Nichi-Bei Kōshō Tenmatsu-ki" (An Account of the Japanese-American Negotiations), *Dai Nippon Teikoku Shimatsu-ki*, Dai-isshū, Saron Rinji Zōkangō, Tsūkan 38 (December 15, 1949), 30-39.

Aoki, Tokuzō. *Taiheiyō Sensō Zenshi* (The Historical Background of the Pacific War). 3 vols. Tōkyō: Gakujutsu Bunken Fukyūkai, 1953.

Arima, Rainei. "Tōjō Hitori wo Semerarenu" (Tojo Alone Cannot Be Blamed), *Seikei Shishin*, Vol. II, No. 7 (July 1955), 33-34.

Asahi Shinbun Hōtei Kisha-dan. *Tōjō Jinmon-roku* (Tōjō: The Record of His Cross-examination in Court). Tōkyō: Niyūsusha, 1949.

———. *Tōkyō Saiban* (The Tōkyō Trial). 8 vols. Tōkyō: Niyūsusha, 1947-1949.

Ausubel, Nathan (ed.). *Voices of History, 1945-46; Speeches and Papers of Roosevelt, Truman, Churchill, Attlee, Stalin, De Gaulle, Chiang and Other Leaders Delivered During 1945.* New York: Gramercy, 1946.

Bailey, Thomas A. *Theodore Roosevelt and the Japanese-American Crises: An Account of the International Complications Arising from the Race Problem on the Pacific Coast.* Stanford: Stanford University Press, 1934.

Bainbridge, John. "Razor on Horseback," *New Yorker*, Vol. XIX, No. 9 (April 17, 1943), 26ff.

Ballantine, Joseph W. "American Policy in Eastern Asia," *Social Science*, Vol. XXVII, No. 4 (October 1952), 195-203.

———. "Mukden to Pearl Harbor: The Foreign Policies of Japan," *Foreign Affairs*, Vol. XXVII, No. 4 (July 1949), 651-64.

Baudouin, Paul. *The Private Diaries, March 1940 to January 1941.* Translated by Sir Charles Petrie. London: Eyre & Spottiswoode, 1948.

Beard, Charles A. *President Roosevelt and the Coming of the War, 1941: A Study in Appearances and Realities.* New Haven: Yale University Press, 1948.

Black, John R. *Young Japan: Yokohama and Yedo; A Narrative of the Settlement and the City from the Signing of the Treaties in 1858, to the Close of the Year 1879, with a Glance at the Progress of Japan During a Period of Twenty-one Years.* 2 vols. London: Trubner, 1881.

Blumenson, Martin. "The Soviet Power Play at Changkufeng," *World Politics*, Vol. XII, No. 2 (January 1960), 249-63.

Borton, Hugh. *Japan's Modern Century.* New York: Ronald, 1955.

Brines, Russell. *MacArthur's Japan.* Philadelphia: Lippincott, 1948.

———. *Until They Eat Stones.* Philadelphia: Lippincott, 1944.

Brown, Delmer M. *Nationalism in Japan: An Introductory Historical Analysis.* Berkeley: University of California Press, 1955.

———. "Recent Japanese Political and Historical Materials," *American Political Science Review*, Vol. XLIII, No. 5 (October 1949), 1010-17.

Brundidge, Harry T. "Tojo Tried to Die," *American Mercury*, August 1953, 7-12.

Bush, Lewis. *Clutch of Circumstance.* Tōkyō: Okuyama, n.d.

Buss, Claude A. "Inside Wartime Japan," *Life*, Vol. XVI, No. 4 (January 24, 1944), 84ff.

Butow, Robert J. C. "The Hull-Nomura Conversations: A Fundamental Misconception," *American Historical Review*, Vol. LXV, No. 4 (July 1960), 822-36.

———. *Japan's Decision to Surrender.* Stanford: Stanford University Press, 1954.

Byas, Hugh. *Government by Assassination.* New York: Knopf, 1942.

Byrnes, James F. *Speaking Frankly.* New York: Harper, 1947.

Causton, E. E. N. *Militarism and Foreign Policy in Japan.* London: Allen & Unwin, 1936.

Chiang Kai-shek. *Soviet Russia in China: A Summing-Up at Seventy.* New York: Farrar, Straus and Cudahy, 1957.

Churchill, Winston S. *The Second World War (The Gathering Storm; Their Finest Hour; The Grand Alliance; The Hinge of Fate; Closing the Ring; Triumph and Tragedy).* 6 vols. Boston: Houghton Mifflin, 1948-1953.

Cohen, Jerome B. *Japan's Economy in War and Reconstruction.* Minneapolis: University of Minnesota Press, 1949.

Colegrove, Kenneth W. *Militarism in Japan* (World Affairs Books No. 16). Boston: World Peace Foundation, 1936.

Collier's. "The Guilty: Hideki Tojo," Vol. CXIII, No. 6 (February 5, 1944), 60.

Collis, Maurice. *The Great Within.* London: Faber, 1941.

Conroy, F. Hilary. "Japanese Nationalism and Expansionism," *American Historical Review*, Vol. LX, No. 4 (July 1955), 818-29.

Corbett, P. E. *Law and Society in the Relations of States*. New York: Harcourt, Brace, 1951.

Craig, Gordon A., and Felix Gilbert (eds.). *The Diplomats, 1919-1939*. Princeton: Princeton University Press, 1953.

Craigie, Sir Robert. *Behind the Japanese Mask*. London: Hutchinson, 1945.

Current, Richard N. "How Stimson Meant to 'Maneuver' the Japanese," *Mississippi Valley Historical Review*, Vol. XL, No. 1 (June 1953), 67-74.

———. *Secretary Stimson: A Study in Statecraft*. New Brunswick, N.J.: Rutgers University Press, 1954.

Deane, John R. *The Strange Alliance: The Story of Our Efforts at Wartime Co-operation With Russia*. New York: Viking, 1950.

December 7, The First Thirty Hours (by the correspondents of *Time, Life,* and *Fortune*). New York: Knopf, 1942.

Dennett, Tyler. *Roosevelt and the Russo-Japanese War: A Critical Study of American Policy in Eastern Asia in 1902-5, Based Primarily upon the Private Papers of Theodore Roosevelt*. Garden City, N.Y.: Doubleday, Page, 1925.

Deverall, Richard L-G. *The Imperial Japanese Army: Hideki Tojo's Military Socialism*. Bangalore, India: Deccan Herald Press, 1951.

Dōmei Tsūshinsha, The Overseas Department. *Wartime Legislation in Japan: A Selection of Important Laws Enacted or Revised in 1941*. Tōkyō: Nippon Shōgyō Tsūshinsha, 1941.

Dull, Paul S. "The Assassination of Chang Tso-lin," *Far Eastern Quarterly*, Vol. XI, No. 4 (August 1952), 453-63.

Dulles, Foster Rhea. *The Imperial Years*. New York: Crowell, 1956.

Editor & Publisher: The Fourth Estate, Vol. XCI, No. 28 (July 5, 1958), Letter to the Editor from Murlin Spencer, Chief of Bureau, Associated Press, Seattle, Wash.

Eichelberger, Robert L. (in collaboration with Milton Mackaye). *Our Jungle Road to Tokyo*. New York: Viking, 1950.

Elsbree, Willard H. *Japan's Role in Southeast Asian Nationalist Movements, 1940 to 1945*. Cambridge, Mass.: Harvard University Press, 1953.

Feis, Herbert. *The Road to Pearl Harbor: The Coming of the War Between the United States and Japan*. Princeton: Princeton University Press, 1950.

Ferrell, Robert H. "The Mukden Incident, September 18-19, 1931," *Journal of Modern History*, Vol. XXVII, No. 1 (March 1955), 66-72.

Fleisher, Wilfrid. *Volcanic Isle*. Garden City, N.Y.: Doubleday, Doran, 1941.

Gaimushō (hensan). *Shūsen Shiroku* (The Historical Record of the Termination of the War). Tōkyō: Shinbun Gekkansha, 1952.

Gayn, Mark. *Japan Diary*. New York: Sloane, 1948.

Gilbert, G. M. *The Psychology of Dictatorship; Based on an Examination of the Leaders of Nazi Germany.* New York: Ronald, 1950.

Grew, Joseph C. *Ten Years in Japan: A Contemporary Record Drawn from the Diaries and Private and Official Papers of Joseph C. Grew, United States Ambassador to Japan, 1932-1942.* New York: Simon and Schuster, 1944.

————. (edited by Walter Johnson, assisted by Nancy Harvison Hooker). *Turbulent Era: A Diplomatic Record of Forty Years, 1904-1945.* 2 vols. Boston: Houghton Mifflin, 1952.

Griswold, A. Whitney. *The Far Eastern Policy of the United States.* New York: Harcourt, Brace, 1938.

Hanayama, Shinshō. "Dai Ōjō Datta" (His Was a Peaceful Death), *Daiyamondo*, Vol. XL, No. 17 (May 15, 1952, Rinji Zōkan: Nihon no Kokuhaku), 146-50.

————. *Heiwa no Hakken: Sugamo no Sei to Shi no Kiroku* (The Discovery of Peace: A Record of Life and Death at Sugamo Prison). Tōkyō: Asahi Shinbunsha, 1949.

————. "Last Days of Tojo," *Collier's*, Vol. CXXV, No. 18 (May 6, 1950), 28ff.

————. "Shūkyō ni Urazukerareta Jinsei" (A Life Supported by Religion), *Chōtetsu Bunka*, No. 38 (November 1956), 2-12.

Hansen, Harold A., John G. Herndon, and William B. Langsdorf. *Fighting for Freedom: Historic Documents Selected and Edited with Interpretive Comments.* Philadelphia: Winston, 1947.

Harada, Kumao (Jutsu). *Saionji Kō to Seikyoku* (Prince Saionji and the Political Situation). 9 vols. Tōkyō: Iwanami Shoten, 1950-1952, and 1956.

Hasegawa, Yukio. "Tōjō Harakiri Mokugeki-ki" (An Eyewitness Account of Tōjō's Suicide Attempt), *Bungei Shunjū*, Vol. XXXIV, No. 8 (August 1956, Tokubetsugō), 218-33.

Hashimoto, Mochitsura. *Sunk: The Story of the Japanese Submarine Fleet, 1941-1945.* New York: Holt, 1954.

Hattori, Shisō. *Tōjō Seiken no Rekishiteki Kōkei* (The Historical Background of Tōjō's Political Power). Tōkyō: Hakuyōsha, 1949.

Hattori, Takushirō. *Dai-Tōa Sensō Zenshi* (A Complete History of the Greater East Asia War). 4 vols. Tōkyō: Masu Shobō, 1953.

Hauser, Ernest O. "Tojo," *Life*, Vol. XII, No. 13 (March 30, 1942), 69ff.

Hayashi, Saburō (in collaboration with Alvin D. Coox). *Kōgun: The Japanese Army in the Pacific War.* Quantico, Va.: Marine Corps Association, 1959.

Higashikuni, Naruhiko. *Ichi Kōzoku no Sensō Nikki* (The War Diary of a Member of the Imperial Family). Tōkyō: Nihon Shūhōsha, 1957.

————. *Watakushi no Kiroku* (My Account). Tōkyō: Tōhō Shobō, 1947.

"Higeki no Hito, Tōjō Hideki wo Kataru Zadankai" (Hideki Tōjō—Man of Tragedy: A Symposium), *Seikei Shishin*, Vol. II, No. 7 (July 1955), 17-32.

Horwitz, Solis. "The Tokyo Trial," *International Conciliation*, No. 465 (November 1950), 473-584.

Hoshino, Naoki. "Kempei Shireikan Tōjō Hideki" (Hideki Tōjō, Commander of the Military Police), *Bungei Shunjū*, Vol. XXXIII, No. 12 (June 1955, Rinji Zōkan: Fūun Jinbutsu Tokuhon), 142-48.

Hull, Cordell. *The Memoirs of Cordell Hull*. 2 vols. New York: Macmillan, 1948.

Ike, Nobutaka. *Japanese Politics: An Introductory Survey*. New York: Knopf, 1957.

Ikeda, Sumihisa. "Tōsei-ha to Kōdō-ha" (The Imperial Way Clique and the Control Clique), *Bungei Shunjū*, Vol. XXXIV, No. 11 (November 1956, Tokubetsugō), 92-108.

Inoguchi, Captain Rikihei, and Commander Tadashi Nakajima, with Roger Pineau. *The Divine Wind*. Annapolis, Md.: United States Naval Institute, 1958.

Itō, Hirobumi. *Commentaries on the Constitution of the Empire of Japan*. Translated by Miyoji Itō. Tōkyō: Igirisu-Hōritsu Gakkō, 1889.

Itō, Jusshi. "Tōjō Taii to Yamashita Taii" (Captain Yamashita and Captain Tōjō), *Bungei Shunjū*, Vol. XXX, No. 6 (April 1952, Haru no Zōkan), 62-69.

Itō, Masanori. *Gunbatsu Kōbōshi* (A History of the Rise and Fall of the Military Clique). 3 vols. Tōkyō: Bungei Shunjū Shinsha, 1957-1958.

Itō, Shunichirō. *Shisei, Tetsu no Hito: Tōjō Hideki Den* (Hideki Tōjō: Man of Sincerity—Man of Iron). Tōkyō: Tenyū Shobō, 1942.

James, David H. *The Rise and Fall of the Japanese Empire*. London: Allen & Unwin, 1951.

Japan Times & Mail. *The National General Mobilization Law*. Tōkyō: Japan Times & Mail, 1940.

Johnson, James B., Jr. "Tojo's First Trial." *MS*.

Johnston, Reginald F. *Twilight in the Forbidden City*. London: Gollancz, 1934.

Jones, F. C. *Japan's New Order in East Asia: Its Rise and Fall, 1937-45*. London: Oxford University Press, 1954.

"Joseph Keenan Meets the Press," *American Mercury*, Vol. LXX, No. 316 (April 1950), 456-60.

Kaikōsha Kiji (Army Club News), Nos. 754-759 and 783.

Kase, Toshikazu. *Mizuri-gō e no Dōtei* (Journey to the *Missouri*). Tōkyō: Bungei Shunjū Shinsha, 1951.

Katō, Etsurō, Takeo Kishi, and Ryōichi Yasumoto. *Shin-Taisei Manga Tokuhon* (Cartoons of the New Order). Tōkyō: Dai Nippon Sekiseikai Shuppankyoku, 1940.

"Katsuko Fujin ga Kataru Tōjō Hideki" (Hideki Tōjō—As Told by Mrs. Tōjō), *Seikei Shishin*, Vol. II, No. 7 (July 1955), 35-36.

Kaya, Okinori. "Nippon no Unmei wa Kōshite Kakerareta" (Thus Was the Fate of Japan Put at Stake), *Kingu*, Vol. XXXII, No. 5 (May 1956), 190-98.

Keenan, Joseph Berry, and Brendan Francis Brown. *Crimes Against International Law*. Washington, D.C.: Public Affairs Press, 1950.

Kelley, Frank, and Cornelius Ryan. *Star-Spangled Mikado*. New York: McBride, 1947.

Kennedy, Captain M. D. *The Military Side of Japanese Life*. Boston: Houghton Mifflin, c. 1923.

——. *Some Aspects of Japan and Her Defence Forces*. London: Kegan Paul, 1928.

Kenwāji, S. (Lt. Col. Aubrey S. Kenworthy). "Bei Kenpeitaichō: Ichigaya no Kiroku" (The Reminiscences of the Commanding Officer of the American MP Detachment at the Tōkyō Trial), *Bungei Shunjū*, Vol. XXXI, No. 1 (January 1953, Shinnen Tokubetsugō), 128-37.

Kerlinger, Fred N. "Decision-making in Japan," *Social Forces*, Vol. XXX, No. 1 (October 1951), 36-41.

King, Ernest J., and Walter Muir Whitehall. *Fleet Admiral King: A Naval Record*. New York: Norton, 1952.

Kiyose, Ichirō. "Ishi Ima Nao Ikin" (His Dying Wishes Will Live on), *Daiyamondo*, Vol. XL, No. 17 (May 15, 1952, Rinji Zōkan: Nihon no Kokuhaku), 141.

Kodama, Yoshio. *I Was Defeated*. n.p. [Japan]: Booth and Fukuda, 1951.

Konoe, Fumimaro. *Ushinawareshi Seiji* (Lost Politics). Tōkyō: Asahi Shinbunsha, 1946.

Kurihara, Ken. *Tennō: Shōwa-shi Oboegaki* (The Emperor: Notes on Shōwa History). Tōkyō: Yūshindō, 1955.

Kurusu, Saburō. *Nichi-Bei Gaikō Hiwa: Waga Gaikō-shi* (The Secret Story of Japanese-American Relations: A History of Our Diplomacy). Tōkyō: Sōgensha, 1952.

Kyōiku Sōkanbu. *Gunjin Chokuyu Kinkai* (The Imperial Rescript to the Soldiers and Sailors of Japan: An Interpretation). Tōkyō: Gunjin Kaikan Shuppanbu, 1939.

Langer, William L. *The Diplomacy of Imperialism, 1890-1902*. New York: Knopf, 1951 (2nd ed.).

Langer, William L., and S. Everett Gleason. *The Challenge to Isolation, 1937-1940* (The World Crisis and American Foreign Policy). New York: Harper, 1952.

——. *The Undeclared War, 1940-1941* (The World Crisis and American Foreign Policy). New York: Harper, 1953.

Leahy, Fleet Admiral William D. *I Was There: The Personal Story of the*

Chief of Staff to Presidents Roosevelt and Truman, Based on His Notes and Diaries Made at the Time. New York: McGraw-Hill, 1950.

Lee, Clark. *One Last Look Around.* New York: Duell, Sloan & Pearce, 1947.

Liu, James T. C. "The Tokyo Trial: Source Materials," *Far Eastern Survey,* Vol. XVII, No. 14 (July 28, 1948), 168-70.

Lockwood, William W. *The Economic Development of Japan: Growth and Structural Change, 1868-1938.* Princeton: Princeton University Press, 1954.

Lord, Walter. *Day of Infamy.* New York: Holt, 1957.

Lory, Hillis. *Japan's Military Masters: The Army in Japanese Life.* New York: Viking, 1943.

MacNair, Harley Farnsworth. *Modern Chinese History, Selected Readings: A Collection of Extracts from Various Sources Chosen to Illustrate Some of the Chief Phases of China's International Relations During the Past Hundred Years.* Shanghai: Commercial Press, 1923.

Maki, John M. *Japanese Militarism: Its Cause and Cure.* New York: Knopf, 1945.

Masaoka, Naoichi (ed.) *Japan to America: A Symposium of Papers by Political Leaders and Representative Citizens of Japan on Conditions in Japan and on the Relations Between Japan and the United States.* New York: Putnam's, 1915.

Maung Maung. *Burma in the Family of Nations.* Amsterdam: Djambatan, 1956.

Maxon, Yale Candee. *Control of Japanese Foreign Policy: A Study of Civil-Military Rivalry, 1930-1945.* Berkeley: University of California Press, 1957.

Millis, Walter (ed., with the collaboration of E. S. Duffield). *The Forrestal Diaries.* New York: Viking, 1951.

Millis, Walter. *This Is Pearl! The United States and Japan—1941.* New York: Morrow, 1947.

Moore, Frederick. *With Japan's Leaders: An Intimate Record of Fourteen Years as Counsellor to the Japanese Government, Ending December 7, 1941.* New York: Scribner's, 1942.

Morison, Samuel Eliot. *The Rising Sun in the Pacific, 1931–April 1942* (History of United States Naval Operations in World War II, Vol. III). Boston: Little, Brown, 1948.

Morton, Louis. "The Japanese Decision for War," *United States Naval Institute Proceedings,* Vol. LXXX, No. 12 (December 1954), 1325-35.

Murata, Kiyoaki. " 'Treachery' of Pearl Harbor," *United States Naval Institute Proceedings,* Vol. LXXXII, No. 8 (August 1956), 904-6.

Nippon Times. *The Ideal and Spirit of Japan in the War: A Selection of Editorials from the Nippon Times, June 1942–May 1943.* Tōkyō: Nippon Times, c. 1943.

Nitobe, Inazo. *Bushido, The Soul of Japan: An Exposition of Japanese Thought.* New York: Putnam's, 1905 (10th rev. & enl. ed.).

Nomura, Kichisaburō. "Kafu Kaisō" (Reminiscences of Washington), *Dai Nippon Teikoku Shimatsu-ki,* Dai-isshū, Saron Rinji Zōkangō, Tsūkan 38 (December 15, 1949), 21-29.

——. "Stepping-Stones to War," *United States Naval Institute Proceedings,* Vol. LXXVII, No. 9 (September 1951), 927-31.

Oda, Shunyo. *Dengeki Saishō: Tōjō Hideki* (Hideki Tōjō: The Lightning Premier). Tōkyō: Sekai Kōronsha, 1942.

Ogata, Taketora. *Ichi Gunjin no Shōgai* (The Life of Mitsumasa Yonai). Tōkyō: Bungei Shunjū Shinsha, 1956.

Okada, Keisuke (Jutsu). *Okada Keisuke Kaiko-roku* (Memoirs). Tōkyō: Mainichi Shinbunsha, 1950.

Okada, Keisuke. "Tōjō Seiken to Jūshin-tachi" (The Senior Statesmen and the Tōjō Regime), *Dai Nippon Teikoku Shimatsu-ki,* Dai-isshū, Saron Rinji Zōkangō, Tsūkan 38 (December 15, 1949), 86-94.

Okada Taishō Kiroku Hensan-kai. *Okada Keisuke.* Tōkyō: Hosokawa Kappanjo, 1956.

Ōkuma, Shigenobu (comp.). *Fifty Years of New Japan.* 2 vols. London: Smith, Elder, 1909.

Piggott, Maj. Gen. F. S. G. *Broken Thread: An Autobiography.* Aldershot: Gale & Polden, 1950.

Pooley, A. M. (ed.). *The Secret Memoirs of Count Tadasu Hayashi, G. C. V. O.* New York: Putnam's 1915.

Presseisen, Ernst L. *Germany and Japan: A Study in Totalitarian Diplomacy, 1933-1941.* The Hague: Nijhoff, 1958.

Quigley, Harold S. *Far Eastern War, 1937-1941.* Boston: World Peace Foundation, 1942.

Redman, H. Vere. *Japan in Crisis: An Englishman's Impressions.* London: Allen & Unwin, 1935.

——. "Things I Have Learned in and from Japan," *Japan Society Forum,* Vol. VI, No. 5 (June 15, 1959), unpaged.

Reischauer, Edwin O. *The United States and Japan.* Cambridge, Mass.: Harvard University Press, 1957 (rev. ed.).

Rikugunshō, Shinbun-han. *Kokubō no Hongi to Sono Kyōka no Teishō* (The Basic Principles of National Defense and Proposals for the Strengthening Thereof). Tōkyō: Rikugunshō, 1934.

Roosevelt, Elliott. *As He Saw It.* New York: Duell, Sloan and Pearce, 1946.

Rosenman, Samuel I. *Working with Roosevelt.* New York: Harper, 1952.

Rōyama, Masamichi. *Foreign Policy of Japan, 1914-1939.* Tōkyō: Japanese Council, Institute of Pacific Relations, 1941.

Russell (Lord Russell of Liverpool). *The Knights of Bushidō: A Short History of Japanese War Crimes.* London: Cassell, 1958.

Sakurai, Tadayoshi. *Human Bullets: A Soldier's Story of Port Arthur.* Translated by Masujirō Honda. Boston: Houghton Mifflin, 1907.

Sansom, Sir George. "Japan's Fatal Blunder," *International Affairs,* Vol. XXIV, No. 4 (October 1948), 543-54.

————. *The Western World and Japan: A Study in the Interaction of European and Asiatic Cultures.* New York: Knopf, 1950.

Satō, Kenryō. "Dai-Tōa Sensō wo Maneita Shōwa no Dōran" (The Shōwa Upheavals Which Brought on the Greater East Asia War), *Kingu,* Vol. XXXII, No. 10 (October 1956), 88-125.

————. *Tōjō Hideki to Taiheiyō Sensō* (Hideki Tōjō and the Pacific War). Tōkyō: Bungei Shunjū Shinsha, 1960.

Satō, Kōjirō. *If Japan and America Fight.* Tōkyō: Meguro Bunten, c. 1921.

Scalapino, Robert A. *Democracy and the Party Movement in Prewar Japan: The Failure of the First Attempt.* Berkeley: University of California Press, 1953.

Schroeder, Paul W. *The Axis Alliance and Japanese-American Relations, 1941.* Ithaca, N.Y.: Cornell University Press, 1958.

Sherwood, Robert E. *Roosevelt and Hopkins: An Intimate History.* New York: Harper, 1948.

Shidehara Heiwa Zaidan. *Shidehara Kijūrō.* Tōkyō: Shidehara Heiwa Zaidan, 1955.

Shidehara, Kijūrō. *Gaikō Gojūnen* (Fifty Years of Diplomacy). Tōkyō: Yomiuri Shinbunsha, 1951.

Shigemitsu, Mamoru. *Shōwa no Dōran* (The Shōwa Upheavals). 2 vols. Tōkyō: Chūō Kōronsha, 1952.

————. *Sugamo Nikki* (Sugamo Diary). Tōkyō: Bungei Shunjūsha, 1953.

————. *Zoku Sugamo Nikki* (Sugamo Diary: Supplement). Tōkyō: Bungei Shunjūsha, 1953.

Shiobara, Tokisaburō. *Tōjō Memo: Kakute Tennō wa Sukuwareta* (Tōjō Memo: Thus Was the Emperor Saved). Tōkyō: Handobukku Sha, 1952.

Solow, Herbert. "A Rather Startling Result," *Fortune,* Vol. XXXIX, No. 4 (April 1949), 158ff.

Stettinius, Edward R., Jr. (edited by Walter Johnson). *Roosevelt and the Russians: The Yalta Conference.* Garden City, N.Y.: Doubleday, 1949.

Stimson, Henry L., and McGeorge Bundy. *On Active Service: In Peace and War.* New York: Harper, 1948.

Storry, Richard. *The Double Patriots: A Study of Japanese Nationalism.* Boston: Houghton Mifflin, 1957.

————. "Konoye Fumimaro, 'The Last of the Fujiwara,'" *Far Eastern Affairs: Number Two* (St. Antony's Papers, No. 7), 9-23.

————. "The Mukden Incident of September 18-19, 1931," *Far Eastern Affairs: Number One* (St. Antony's Papers, No. 2), 1-12.

Sugamo Isho Hensankai. *Seiki no Isho* (Testaments of the Century). Tōkyō: Sugamo Isho Hensankai Kankō Jimusho, 1953.

Sutton, David Nelson. "The Trial of Tojo: The Most Important Trial in All History?" *American Bar Association Journal,* Vol. XXXVI, No. 1 (January 1950), 93ff.

Takeuchi, Tatsuji. *War and Diplomacy in the Japanese Empire.* Chicago: University of Chicago Press, 1935.

Tanaka, Ryūkichi. *Hai-in wo Tsuku—Gunbatsu Sen-ō no Jissō* (Piercing the Causes of Defeat—The Facts Behind the Tyranny of the Military Clique). Tōkyō: Sansuisha, 1946.

———. *Sabakareru Rekishi: Haisen Hiwa* (History on Trial: The Secret Story of Japan's Defeat). Tōkyō: Shinpūsha, 1948.

Tanaka, Shinichi. *Taisen Totsunyū no Shinsō* (The Truth Behind the Plunge into War). Tōkyō: Gengensha, 1955.

Taylor, George E. *The Struggle for North China.* New York: Institute of Pacific Relations, 1940.

"Tennō no Daijin, Kokumin no Daijin" (Ministers of the Emperor, Ministers of the People), *Bungei Shunjū,* Vol. XXXVI, No. 10 (September 1958, Tokubetsugō), 158-67.

Terasaki, Gwen. *Bridge to the Sun.* Chapel Hill: University of North Carolina Press, 1957.

Theobald, Robert A. *The Final Secret of Pearl Harbor: The Washington Contribution to the Japanese Attack.* New York: Devin-Adair, 1954.

Tōgō, Shigenori. *Jidai no Ichimen* (An Aspect of the Times). Tōkyō: Kaizōsha, 1952.

Tōjō, Hideki. "Kyokutō no Shin-jōsei ni Tsuite" (On the New Situation in the Far East), *Gaikō Jihō,* December 15, 1933, 68-78.

———. "Yuigon" (Last Will and Testament), *Daiyamondo,* Vol. XL, No. 17 (May 15, 1952, Rinji Zōkan: Nihon no Kokuhaku), 142-45.

Tōjō, Katsuko. "Saigo wa Kōfuku" (He Was Happy at the End), *Daiyamondo,* Vol. XL, No. 17 (May 15, 1952, Rinji Zōkan: Nihon no Kokuhaku), 151.

Tōkyō Saiban Kenkyū-kai. *Tōjō Hideki Sensei Kyōjutsu-sho* (The Affidavit of Hideki Tōjō). Tōkyō: Yōyōsha, 1948.

Tolischus, Otto D. *Tokyo Record.* New York: Reynal & Hitchcock, 1943.

Ugaki, Kazushige. *Ugaki Nikki* (Ugaki Diary). Tōkyō: Asahi Shinbunsha, 1954.

U.S. Army, Office of the Chief of Military History (Kent Roberts Greenfield, gen. ed.). *Command Decisions.* New York: Harcourt, Brace, 1959.

U.S. President, 1933-1945 (Franklin D. Roosevelt). *The Public Papers and Addresses of Franklin D. Roosevelt, with a Special Introduction and Explanatory Notes by President Roosevelt.* (Volumes for 1939-1945.) New York. Macmillan, 1941; New York: Harper, 1950.

van Mook, Hubertus J. *The Netherlands Indies and Japan: Battle on Paper, 1940-1941.* New York: Norton, 1944.

von Dirksen, Herbert. *Moscow, Tokyo, London: Twenty Years of German Foreign Policy.* London: Hutchinson, 1951.

Wakatsuki, Reijirō. *Kofūan Kaiko-roku* (Memoirs). Tōkyō: Yomiuri Shinbunsha, 1950.

Walkinshaw, Robert B. "The Nuremberg and Tokyo Trials: Another Step Toward International Justice," *American Bar Association Journal,* Vol. XXXV, No. 4 (April 1949), 299ff.

Ward, Robert E. "The Inside Story of the Pearl Harbor Plan," *United States Naval Institute Proceedings,* Vol. LXXVII, No. 12 (December 1951), 1271-83.

Watanabe, Shigeo. *Ugaki Kazushige no Ayunda Michi* (The Road Traveled by Kazushige Ugaki). Tōkyō: Shin-Taiyōsha, 1948.

Wheeler, Post. *Dragon in the Dust.* Hollywood: Marcel, 1946.

Willoughby, Westel W. *The Sino-Japanese Controversy and the League of Nations.* Baltimore: Johns Hopkins Press, 1935.

Yabe, Teiji (henchosha). *Konoe Fumimaro* (Fumimaro Konoe). 2 vols. Tōkyō: Kōbundō, 1952.

Yanaga, Chitoshi. *Japan Since Perry.* New York: McGraw-Hill, 1949.

Yoshida, Shigeru. *Kaisō Jūnen* (Reminiscences). 4 vols. Tōkyō: Shinchōsha, 1957-1958.

Young, A. Morgan. *Imperial Japan, 1926-1938.* London: Allen & Unwin, 1938.

————. *Japan in Recent Times, 1912-1926* [Published in England as *Japan Under Taishō Tennō, 1912-1926*]. New York: Morrow, 1929.

B. Miscellaneous

Asahi Nenkan.

Asahi Shinbun.

Asahi Shinbun, Chōsabu. Miscellaneous Newspaper Clippings.

Current Biography.

Dai Jinmei Jiten.

Dōmei Jiji Nenkan.

Eugene Register-Guard.

Facts on File Yearbook.

Japan Chronicle.

Japan Times & Advertiser (Japan Times Advertiser; Nippon Times; Japan Times).

Japan Times & Mail.

Japan Weekly Mail.

Japan Year Book.

Kokuritsu Kokkai Toshokan, Shūgiin Chōsabu. Miscellaneous Newspaper Clippings.

Life Magazine.

Mainichi Nenkan.

Newsweek Magazine.

New York Herald Tribune.

New York Times.

Nihon Rekishi Dai-jiten.

Nippon Today and Tomorrow.

Old Oregon.

Oregon Daily Emerald.

Time Magazine.

U.S. Army, Audio-Visual Branch, Public Information Division. U.S. Signal Corps Still Photo and Motion Picture Holdings.

U.S. Department of State *Bulletin.*

Who's Who in Japan.

Index